# American Mosaic

As part of Houghton Mifflin's ongoing
commitment to the environment, this text
has been printed on recycled paper.

# American Mosaic

## MULTICULTURAL READINGS IN CONTEXT

### THIRD EDITION

**Barbara Roche Rico**
*Loyola Marymount University*

**Sandra Mano**
*University of California, Los Angeles*

HOUGHTON MIFFLIN COMPANY  BOSTON  NEW YORK

*For Our Students*

*Senior Sponsoring Editor*  Suzanne Phelps Weir
*Development Editor*  Janet Young
*Senior Project Editor*  Rosemary R. Jaffe
*Editorial Assistant*  Kate Hartke
*Senior Production/Design Coordinator*  Carol Merrigan
*Manufacturing Manager*  Florence Cadran
*Senior Marketing Manager*  Nancy Lyman

Cover design by Len Massiglia/LMA Communications
Cover image by Javier Arevalo (Mexican, b. 1937), "Los Encuentros," 1991.
Watercolor on paper, $43^1/4 \times 51^1/2$ inches. Private Collection, Los Angeles, CA.
Courtesy of Iturralde Gallery, Los Angeles, CA.

*(Since this page cannot legibly accommodate all the copyright notices, pages 709–713 constitute an extension of the copyright page.)*

*Printed in the U.S.A.*

Library of Congress Catalog Card Number: 00-133856

ISBN:  0-395-88661-9

1 2 3 4 5 6 7 8 9-QF-04 03 02 01 00

# CONTENTS

## 8 CHICANOS
### *Negotiating Political and Cultural Boundaries*    *553*

## 9   THE NEW IMMIGRANTS
### *Reviving, Challenging, and Refashioning the American Dream*    *643*

# PREFACE

## Purpose of the Text

Using a chronological framework, *American Mosaic: Multicultural Readings in Context* celebrates diversity by presenting the writings of many ethnic groups at a particularly generative period in their histories. We believe that all students will be enriched by hearing these voices and by understanding the period in which the authors were writing. Moreover, students will come to appreciate the contributions these writers have made to American culture.

Each chapter reflects what we consider to be an important period in the development of a particular ethnic group, by using readings that are representative of the attitudes and concerns of that time. Our intention is to let the authors speak for themselves about issues important to them. Our desire is not to provide a comprehensive coverage of American ethnic literature and history, but instead to suggest the richness of the American experience. *American Mosaic* is designed to allow students to develop historical awareness and critical thinking skills while they study the development of literary, political, and cultural voices within our country.

We have begun our historical examination during the late nineteenth century. Clearly American culture did not begin at that point. American Indian groups had developed many forms of expressive cultural production—what some critics call oral literature—long before the coming of the Europeans. One can also find earlier examples of immigrant writings and the writings of the "forced immigrants," Africans brought here as slaves. The late 1800s is an important period to examine, however, because it marked three important developments: the large influx of immigrants primarily from Europe and Asia who came for religious and economic reasons; the altering of the parameters of American society through nativist groups, exclusionary laws, and the establishment of reservations; and the change in the national character brought about by the growth of cities and the migrations north of African Americans. Throughout the text we have tried to reflect not only the changes experienced by the ethnic groups, but also the interaction of given ethnic groups with the majority culture.

As importantly, the readings selected illustrate how each group participated in the development and transformation of American culture.

To help students perceive the mosaic, we have presented in each chapter a combination of literary and historical material. The excerpt from the legal document included in each section suggests ways in which the dominant culture responded to each ethnic group. (These documents are, however, only a sampling; we urge students to explore further the legal context that can only be outlined in the chapter.) The readings themselves illustrate the emergence of multicultural voices. In addition to essays, we have included first person narratives, journalistic pieces, oratory, fiction, and poetic works, because we believe that expository essays alone do not reflect the richness of the literature that was produced. By concluding each chapter with an essay by a scholar who has extensively studied the culture of the group, we hope to illustrate how issues of culture can be explored across the disciplines.

The text's apparatus is designed to inform students and to encourage them to respond to and challenge what they read. Every chapter includes an introductory essay intended to be a starting point for discussion. Headnotes to the selections provide further background information. Pre-reading and post-reading questions foster critical thinking and allow students to respond creatively to the texts, both in class discussion and in writing. Each set of responding questions begins with a journal or in-class writing assignment, followed by a question inviting students to work collaboratively in small groups. The next two questions present essay topics that involve close re-reading of the text and ask students to incorporate their personal experience and outside information into their responses. Connecting questions at the end of each chapter relate selections within a chapter, then make connections to other chapters. Finally, suggestions for library research as well as lists of supplemental materials give students an opportunity to explore issues further.

## New to the Third Edition

The third edition of *American Mosaic* retains the strengths of the first two editions, while at the same time adding twenty-nine new selections and new features that will make the text more timely and pedagogically effective.

One of the most visible changes is an entirely new first chapter. Entitled "Points of Entry, Points of Departure," chapter 1 is designed to introduce students to multiethnic studies and the debates surrounding multicultural studies through a collection of essays that introduce and challenge the meanings of several important terms. The chapter will allow students to discover how the meanings of such terms as "melting pot," "cultural pluralism," "acculturation," "manifest destiny," and "multiculturalism" have changed over time. The reading selections and the apparatus invite students to consider not only the terms themselves, but the nature of the debates that have often surrounded them, both in the writer's own time and in our own.

In this edition, the first ethnic group to be addressed is that of the indigenous peoples, typically referred to as "American Indians" or "Native Americans." While it is impossible to cover or even highlight all the significant concerns, we have chosen as our focus for chapter 2 the formation of Native American identity—more specifically, the relationship between one's individual and collective identities and one's sense of place. To explore these relationships, we have added several selections, including works by Chief Joseph, D'arcy McNickle, and Linda Hogan. The two final essays examine the Makah whaling controversy, in which cultural values and environmental values appear to conflict. In these pieces, two journalists from outside the Indian culture assess not only the controversy itself but the ways in which the media's approach to it can often disclose assumptions about indigenous and "mainstream" cultures.

Our third chapter, entitled "Early Immigrants: In Search of the Land of Milk and Honey," makes use of several of the more evocative selections from the other two editions, while inviting students to consider both the use and the limitations of the "Ellis Island" or "nation of immigrants" metaphor. The essay by Jacob Riis and the study by Davidson and Lytle, which reconsiders Riis's methods and his cultural agenda, help to widen the perspectives for discussion here, we believe. The last work, "Shirt" by Robert Pinsky, poet laureate of the United States, invites us to consider from an intercultural perspective both the hardships and the innate dignity of the worker.

Chapter 4, on Chinese American experience, subtitled "The Lure of the Gold Mountain," has several new pieces, including a selection from Shawn Wong's *Homebase*, which presents through fiction a reflection on the Angel Island experience from the perspective of a newcomer. Both Wong's text and that of Amy Tan invite readers to consider the ways in which intergenerational relationships and tensions inform one's sense of place, one's sense of self. Finally, the essay by the late Amy Ling, studying the work of Sui Sin Far and her sister, raises interesting questions about the ways in which an author's persona can be shaped in response to the expectations and pressures of more than one cultural group.

Chapter 5 explores two issues considered central to the chronicling of African American identity: the migration north and the journey toward civil rights. We are pleased to be able to include in this section a selection from Ernest Gaines's *A Lesson Before Dying*, which dramatically reveals some of the inequities and assumptions that can be traced to a value system in which "separate but equal" is considered "good enough." Discussions of race can never be undertaken without a consideration of other intersecting factors such as gender and class. An essay by Mary Helen Washington, with which the chapter ends, considers this intersection with regard to the reception of several important writers.

Chapter 6, entitled "Puerto Ricans: The View from the Mainland," examines the ways in which images of migration, "outmigration" (or reverse migration), and exile inform the writing of Puerto Rican writers on the United States mainland. "The English Lesson," by prolific writer Nicholasa Mohr, invites readers to consider whether the slogans and metaphors of earlier generations of immigrants—upward mobility, assimilation, and the American Dream—are still operative, and how the images of opportunity relate to structures of power within the classroom. The final two essays address an issue that has been debated both within the Puerto Rican community and outside of it: Puerto Rican statehood. Here two authors—Rosario Ferre, who was born in Puerto Rico, and Linda Chavez, who is not Puerto Rican but considers herself "Hispanic"—present differing attitudes toward the controversy.

Chapter 7, "Japanese Americans: In Camp, in Community," has as its central metaphor the experience of the Internment. The new material that has been added, including the apology from then–attorney general Richard Thornburgh on behalf of the United States government, invites students to consider the ways in which issues of national security and of human rights have been re-examined. We also invite students to research the majority opinion, in the *Endo* decision written by Supreme Court Justice William O. Douglas (but not included here), to trace the principles that led the Supreme Court to have the camps closed. As both the essay by Ronald Takaki and the new article by Bob Pool suggest, the camp experience will remain a subject for not only archival research but also for historical, literary, and philosophical reflection.

Chapter 8 invites students to consider the relationships among geographical, political, and cultural borders in the writings of several prominent Chicanas and Chicanos. The excerpt from Ruben Salazar puts the term "Chicano" into a historical framework. The new selection by Graciela Limón prompts a consideration of the ways in which gender as well as ethnic boundaries inform or impair a young woman's expectations for her culture and herself. The essays with which the chapter ends explore the ways in which the image of the border is itself defined by assumptions about identity, entitlement, and a sense of place.

The final chapter, "The New Immigrants," takes an intercultural perspective on how the American Dream has been revived, challenged, and refashioned by several groups that have arrived in the United States since the 1940s. We invite readers to view this chapter comparatively, discussing the ways in which some of the concepts and issues outlined in earlier chapters are repeated or reassessed in the works of newer immigrants. Useful discussions would also emerge from comparative discussions about borders, quotas, and entitlement as represented in readings from earlier chapters, and in the legal analysis offered in the Peter Schuck essay "Border Crossing" included here.

From these lines of inquiry, we hope that students will discover that many controversial questions have many points of entry and many points of departure. From these encounters, we hope that students will come to see American culture not as a single, monologic entity, but as an ongoing conversation involving many ethnic and cultural groups. And we trust that they will find in the interplay of historical, literary, and cultural discourses an opportunity to assert their own voices.

## Acknowledgments

We would like to thank the Research Program in Ethnic Studies administered by UCLA's Institute for American Cultures, Norris Hundley, Chair, and the Chicano Studies Research Center Faculty Advisory Committee, David Hayes-Bautista, Chair, for the two-year grant that enabled both of us to undertake our research. We would also like to acknowledge a grant from the Rains Foundation administered through Loyola Marymount University, which provided additional support for this project. In addition, we thank the Loyola Marymount University Department of English, Linda Bannister, Chair, and the College of Liberal Arts, Kenyon Chan, Dean, for their continued encouragement.

In the preparation of this text, we have received the help and encouragement of many colleagues and friends. Mike Rose has acted from the outset as a mentor, commenting on and encouraging us in our work. We also appreciate the support of Anne Marie Albertazzi, Felipe Andalón, Héctor Calderón, Lee Carroll, Sandra Cisneros, Maria Cuevas, Robert Cullen, Michael Fried, Lucy Garza, Julie Krekeler, Russell Leong, Graciela Limón, Kenneth Lincoln, Bonnie Lisle, Sharon Locy, Cathy Machado, Regina Mandanici, Berenice Mirenda, Geraldine Moyle, Steven Osborn, Louise Phelps, Patricia Pierson, Sandra Ramirez, Manuel Rezende, Henrietta Rico, Mona Rivera, Alice Roy, A. LaVonne Brown Ruoff, Melissa Ryan, Santiago Sia, Ted Simpson, Robin Strayhorn, Betty Takahashi, Tracey Thompson, Lucy Wilson, W. Ross Winterowd, Gail Wronsky, Fatima Wu, and Kelly Younger.

In addition, we would like to thank our reviewers. For the first edition: Poonam Arora, University of Michigan, Dearborn; Betty Bamberg, University of Southern California; John Bodnar, Indiana University, Bloomington; Ron Estes, St. Louis Community College at Forest Park; Donald Fixico, Western Michigan University; Eugene Howard, Bucks County Community College, PA; Jacquelyn Jackson, Middle Tennessee State University; Yolette Jones, Volunteer State Community College, TN; Malcolm Kiniry, Rutgers University, Newark, NJ; Rhonda Levine, University of California, Santa Barbara; Shirley Lim, University of California, Santa Barbara; Lois Marchino, University of Texas, El Paso; Beverly Moss, Ohio State University; Dottie Perry, Norfolk State University, VA; Georgia Rhoades, University of Louisville; Vicki Ruiz, University of California, Davis; Melita Schaum, University of Michigan, Dearborn; Lacreta Scott, Cerritos College; Joseph Skerrett, University of Massachusetts, Amherst; Bruce Southerd, East Carolina University, Greenville; Antonio Stevens-Arroyo, Brooklyn College, City University of New York; Franklin O. Sutton, Community College of Allegheny County, PA; Michael Vivion, University of Missouri, Kansas City; Linda Woodson, University of Texas, San Antonio; and Maria Elena Yepes, East Los Angeles College.

For the second edition: Jeanne Anderson, University of Louisville; SDiane Bogus, DeAnza College; Diane Cogan, San Diego Mesa College; Lenore Navarro Dowling, Rio Hondo Community College; Ulrike Z. Jaeckel, University of Illinois at Chicago; Beatrice Kingston-Cataldo, College of Saint Elizabeth; Geraldine R. Lash, SUNY Technical College at Alfred; Edward Marx, City College of New York; Jim Murphy, Boston College; John T. Reilly, Loyola Marymount University; Jerry Shaw, The Wichita State University; Katharine Reid Stone, Georgia State University; Daphne Swabey, University of Michigan, Ann Arbor; Linda Woodson, University of Texas, San Antonio; and Kerry Candaele, Columbia University.

For the third edition: Lysbeth Em Benkert, Northern State University, SD; Sharon Delmendo, St. John Fisher College, NY; Ellen Shull, Palo Alto College; Elizabeth G. Westgard, Saint-Mary-of-the-Woods College, IN. We also thank Lesley Kawaguchi of Santa Monica College for historical accuracy reviewing.

We owe special thanks to several people at Houghton Mifflin: Suzanne Phelps Weir, senior sponsoring editor; Janet Young, Jennifer Roderick, and Ellen Darion, development editors; Rosemary Jaffe, senior project editor; and Kate Hartke, editorial assistant.

We would like to add a special note of appreciation to our husbands, Richard Rico and Morris Mano, and our families, who have contributed so much to this book.

We dedicate this book to our children, Richard James, Susie, and Robin; to our students; and to the memory of those who have walked before us and helped us to shape our ideas.

B.R.R.

S.M.

# American Mosaic

# 1

## POINTS OF ENTRY,
## POINTS OF DEPARTURE

*Above:* New York City, The Grand Demonstration on "Liberty Day."
(*Zan-2513 Frank Leslie's Illustrated Newspaper, November 6th, 1886,*
*"Liberty Day Parade"*)
*Opposite:* Statue of Liberty. (© *John Veltri, photographer*)

Aɴʏ ᴅɪsᴄɪᴘʟɪɴᴇ needs a kind of shared language, a set of terms to be used and a general understanding about their meanings, the contexts in which they appear, and the ways in which their significance has been modified over time. Often in debates about culture and values, terms are tossed about without much or any context. In this first chapter, we explore a few of these terms, trace their evolution, as well as the ways in which their original usage has been retained, refashioned, or overlooked. Let's begin with the observation that like other parts of our language, such words must be explored in a way that both acknowledges the cultural assumptions and limitations of a given period.

## The Nation of Immigrants

We begin with "the nation of immigrants." It is difficult to find a Fourth of July essay or an article about immigrants that does not make at least a passing reference to this expression, this myth that informs American cultural life. We can trace the popularization of this idea to the 1883 poem of Emma Lazarus, herself the daughter of immigrants. In the florid language of the time, Emma Lazarus's poem ascribes to Europe masculine images of control ("brazen giant") and empire ("conquering limbs astride from land to land"), which she contrasts with the more nurturing image of Liberty as "the Mother of Exiles" holding a "lamp" of "welcome." Rejecting the "storied pomp" of the so-called Old World, the mighty woman embodies the promise of America for all its newcomers inviting from near and far: "your tired, your poor, your huddled masses yearning to breathe free." Lazarus, who herself worked for immigrant rights, seems in the poem to memorialize the ideals of refuge, welcome, and opportunity, though in a language that might seem patronizing today.

It is generally remembered that "The New Colossus" was engraved at the foot of the Statue of Liberty. What is less well known is the rather lukewarm reception the work received at the monument's dedication ceremony—which the historian Alan Kraut has described as "merely polite applause." In the century that has followed, however, the "land of immigrants" and the image of "tired poor huddled masses" have become significant parts of the nation's collective memory, parts of a potent cultural myth. They have, moreover, contributed to an incomplete and overly sentimental understanding of the period: As Kraut explains in *Huddled Masses*, "Immigrants are romanticized as heroes and heroines bravely overcoming all obstacles . . . or they are pitied as bedraggled wayfarers, expelled from their homelands by vast social forces beyond their comprehension or control" (3). It is one of the ironies of history that the publication of the poem and the dedication of the monument coincided with the introduction in the United States Congress of several laws designed to impose greater restrictions on marginalized groups.

Joseph Bruchac's poem "Ellis Island" might be interpreted as what cultural critics have termed a "writing back"—providing a new response to the "nation of immigrants" myth given voice in Lazarus's sonnet. Initially, the poem seems strangely to echo Lazarus in its rejection of Old World values and class distinctions:

> after leaving the sickness,
> the old Empires of Europe,
> a Circle Line ship slips easily
> on its way to the island
> of the tall woman, green
> as dreams of forests and meadows
> waiting for those who'd worked
> a thousand years
> yet never owned their own.

As the poem progresses, however, what might be viewed by some as the promise of America becomes a story of "Lands invaded when the earth became owned." The two perspectives coexist, but the poet confesses that only "one part of my blood" loves the memory of the promise. Like Bruchac's poem, Greg Sarris's essay included in this chapter not only warns against a single monologic perspective, but also shows how cultural myths can be revivified and reinterpreted. Rather than "sculpting his experience" to fit the myth or completely rejecting the cultural myth, the author, by "writing back," can both expose its fragmentation and take part in its refashioning.

Greg Sarris's essay "Battling Illegitimacy" further develops this concept. While Bruchac's "Ellis Island" proposes "another voice," another attitude toward an icon of American culture, Greg Sarris's essay also argues for an acknowledgment of the importance of American cultural myths, rather than a suppression of them: "Where some Indian people once denied, or at least kept quiet their Indian heritage, they suddenly began denying that part which is white, Spanish, or whatever. . . . [I]n the name of ethnic pride we begin to make illegitimate so much of what we are, and have been, about." The individual must exercise *agency:* in Sarris's words, rather than "shaping experience to fit the books," the writer must participate in the process of naming and interpretation, "to examine our own framing devices . . . [and] to make visible the heretofore illegitimate so that we might consider human experience in the broadest sense possible."

## The Melting Pot and Models of Assimilation

Another key term, often applied casually and out of context, is "the melting pot." Dating from 1545, the first documented use of the word was utilitarian, defining "a vessel in which metals or other substances were melted" (*Oxford English Dictionary* [OED]). The first documented use of the term in a political context occurred in an 1887 address to the British Parliament by Member of Parliament Morley, which was quoted in the Pall Mall Gazette. Commenting in terms of British law, on what he called the "Irish question," Morley asserted, "I think it will be best for the Constitution of this country [Britain] not to send it to the melting pot" (OED). As David M. Fine explains in "Attitudes Toward Acculturation," the term has been used to represent several attitudes toward assimilation since it first appeared in Israel Zangwill's play by the same name in the first decade of the twentieth century. Although "the melting pot" could be interpreted as "the blending of the best of Old and New World cultures," it was more often associated with assimilation. This process involved replacing the attitudes, mores, and customs of one's country of origin with those of the new country. While some essayists such as Horace Kallen and Jane Addams at Hull House advocated a two-way process of exchange, as Fine suggests, the assimilationist view predominated.

### Acculturation, Manifest Destiny, and the View of the Frontier

Several of the terms used to describe territorial expansion and cultural exchange betray an *ethnocentricism*—a tendency to privilege the norms of one culture over those of another. Just as newer immigrants were advised to assimilate, American Indians were often expected to acculturate their ways to those of the Euro Americans. Early uses of *acculturation* in the nineteenth century implied the cultural superiority of one group over another. When assessing the effect of the English language on those of the native peoples, for example, J. W. Powell, who was then director of the Smithsonian Institution, discloses an ethnocentric bias: "The force of acculturation under the overwhelming presence of millions has wrought great changes. Primitive Indian society has either been modified or supplanted, primitive religions have been changed, primitive arts lost and . . . primitive languages have not remained unmodified. The period of European association has been one of rapid growth and development, especially in the accumulation of new words" (OED). Indian tribes were evaluated and assessed by the degree to which they had "acculturated" European ways. Several of the poems in chapter 2, among them "A Plea to Those Who Matter" and "Pocahontas," show the consequences of the pressure to acculturate.

Similarly, the term *manifest destiny*—which was extremely significant in determining American policy toward Indian tribes and other nations including Mexico, the Philippines, and several Caribbean countries—also reveals such an ethnocentrism. The phrase, which was used in Congress and adopted by presidents up to the early twentieth century to defend foreign-policy decisions, first appeared in an editorial by John L. O'Sullivan—himself an immigrant—in *The Democratic Magazine*, a rather obscure journal. In a tone that mixes aggressive rhetoric with religious fervor, O'Sullivan's editorial chides those who would object to the annexation of Texas, an objection that the writer referred to "as a hostile interference against us, for the avowed object of thwarting our policy and hampering our power, limiting our greatness and checking the fulfillment of our Manifest Destiny to overspread the Continent allotted by Providence for the free development of our yearly multiplying millions" (5). As historian Julius Pratt points out, O'Sullivan's rhetoric was appropriated almost verbatim during the congressional debate on the annexation of Oregon by Robert Winthrop, who further asserted that manifest destiny would "not be admitted to exist in any other nation." Manifest destiny, which provided some with an apology for territorial expansionism, also had disastrous effects for the environment and native peoples. Nature was seen as being at the service of humans; if nature impeded progress, it was to be managed even if natural resources were depleted in the process. The doctrine also forced a view of the cultural superiority of the Euro Americans over the indigenous peoples. As Ronald Takaki suggests, the decrease in the American Indian population was explained in a congressional report as "the irrepressible conflict between a superior and an inferior race when brought in the presence of the other." While such language is widely considered objectionable today, it is also worth noting that the doctrine of manifest destiny was criticized as early as 1867 "as the incarnation of recklessness as to right or wrong" (OED).

## *The American Dream*

Perhaps no term seems so "all-American" as "the American dream," an expression routinely invoked by politicians and public officials and often without review, what the OED has called "a catch-phrase for American values in general." The term might conjure up images of an "Ozzie and Harriet" or "Brady Bunch" existence—the proverbial suburban house with the white picket fence. But what are American values? Who defines them?

The term "American Dream" was introduced in 1931, in the midst of the Great Depression. James Truslow Adams, a merchant and self-educated historian, introduced the term in his book *The Epic of America*. Adams first celebrates what he calls the transition "from a continent which scarce sufficed to maintain a half million savages" to one that "now supports nearly two hundred and fifty times that number of as active and industrious people as there are in the world." Adams's vision privileges what he calls "the practical and the adaptive" talents that he perceives in the American spirit. In Adams's work, the so-called American Dream has less to do with expansion of the frontier or even material prosperity, than with an affirmation of the worth of the individual: "That dream of a land in which life should be better and richer and fuller for every man, with opportunity for each according to his ability or achievement" (404). Adams's perspective is not unlike those used to support early definitions of "acculturation" and "manifest destiny," in that they all depend on an ethnocentric bias. As Arnold Krupat suggests in his essay included in this chapter, "Americans [have] tended to define their own particular brand of civilization in direct opposition to a fantasized or ideologi-

cally constructed Indian 'savagery. ' . . . [T]o be an American was no longer
to be a European without yet becoming an Indian" (236). Such views, Krupat
contends, are informed by "the dichotomized paradigms of the us/them,
West/Rest type," all models that must be undone (237).

Even as Adams's text establishes or presents the dream, his ethnocentric
assumptions exclude many from it. Consider the question Langston Hughes
introduces in the poem "Harlem"—"What happens to a dream deferred?"—
or Martin Luther King's assertion in the "I Have a Dream" speech that the
American dream is for some "a bad check." It is a role for which some "need
not apply." The writings of Bruchac, Sarris, and Gates call attention to the
exclusionary practices that are performed on behalf of the mainstream, sometimes consciously, sometimes not. In Bruchac's poem the "immigration" celebrated by one is the "invasion" mourned by others. Sarris's work comments
that he "never knew a way to tamper with how others categorized him."
Gates's essay, which also merges the theoretical and the experiential, reveals
the irony and the consequences of the "I got mine parochialism." Hoffman's
work *Lost in Translation* further *problematizes* the situation of the insider and
the outsider, by showing just how provisional each role can be.

### *Multiculturalism and Family Values*

The essay by Arnold Krupat provides a context for beginning a discussion
about multiculturalism, a term that gained currency in the 1980s. One might
trace the beginnings of the multicultural movement to the work of the soci-
ologist and theorist Horace Kallen, who, as David M. Fine points out, wrote
about a kind of cultural pluralism, what he termed "cosmopolitanism" in the
early 1900s. Kallen returned to the concept in 1956, attributing to "cultural
pluralism" the following characteristics:

> This pluralism . . . postulates individuality . . . But it neither deprives the human
> person of his dynamic relations with his neighbors, nor converts the ever-
> ongoing communications between them to a preordained ineluctable harmony
> . . . It signalizes them as the ways that people who are different from one
> another do in fact come together and move apart, forming and dissolving the
> groups wherewith they secure to one another their diverse safety and happi-
> ness. (51)

The pattern of exchange suggested here and worked out in the curriculum of Jane Addams's Hull House is seen by many as instrumental in the formation of what would later be called a "multicultural approach."

Other critics, however, distinguish between cultural pluralism and multiculturalism. As Susan D. Greenbaum notes in the *Encyclopedia of Multiculturalism*, "Unlike the idea of cultural pluralism, which was conceived by white so-

ciologists as a response to massive immigration, multiculturalism in the 1980s and 1990s has been developed by activist members of cultural minorities to redress what is seen as a continuing pattern of unjust exclusion" (1179). Since its inception in the 1980s multicultural education has been represented as a way to expand the curriculum to reflect more fully the diverse nature of the American people. As Ronald Takaki points out in *A Different Mirror: A Multicultural History of America*, ". . . America has been racially diverse since our very beginning on the Virginia shore, and this reality is becoming visible and ubiquitous. Currently, one third of the American people do not trace their origins to Europe." In California as well as several urban areas such as Chicago, New York, and Atlanta "minorities are fast becoming a majority" (2). Arnold Krupat's essay reinforces this notion: "the multicultural 'future' is already here; nonetheless, inasmuch as monocultural supremacy is still promoted at the highest institutional levels, those of us who would speak for multiculturalism must continue to argue on its behalf" (236).

Part of what Takaki and Krupat are responding to are challenges to a multicultural curriculum advanced in such texts as Allan Bloom's *Closing of the American Mind* and E. D. Hirsch's *Cultural Literacy: What Every American Needs to Know*, which were written in the 1980s. These works propose a return to a core curriculum that reflects Euro American ideals and a shared sense of values. A more recent challenge to the multicultural approach has been advanced by Francis Fukuyama. In the essay "Immigrants and Family Values," included in this chapter, the author asserts the following:

> . . . the ideological assault on traditional family values—the sexual revolution; feminism and the delegitimization of the male-dominated household; the celebration of alternative life-styles; attempts ruthlessly to secularize all aspects of American public life . . . was not the creation of [new immigrants]. Rather [t]hey originated right in the heart of America's well-established white, Anglo-Saxon community.

Fukuyama further contends that what he calls "trendy multicultural programs" in actuality do a disservice to current immigrants by not allowing them to experience the processes of assimilation that enabled earlier generations of immigrants to learn English and prosper in this country.

Krupat's essay "For Multiculturalism" might be read as a response to Fukuyama's charges because it stresses that a truly multicultural approach does more than merely expand a given canon in the interest of diversity; it also prompts an interrogation of systems of thought to examine the power structures at their base. In this respect, Krupat's essay, like those of Gates, Sarris, and Hoffman, invites the reader to think more critically about the processes of naming and categorizing, to inspect more carefully the cultural frames we all use to interpret and to assess our surroundings.

**BEGINNING: Pre-reading/Writing**

*Working individually or in a group, use the Internet to locate and expand on examples of some of the terms explained in the introduction. Find and bring to class a list of related terms, such as nativism, upward mobility, cultural literacy, canon, multiculturalism, diversity. Share the definitions of the terms and the context in which you found them with classmates. How important is it to understand these terms before exploring the issues discussed in this chapter?*

# Emma Lazarus

*Emma Lazarus was born in New York City in 1849. The daughter of immigrants, Lazarus participated in immigrant relief activities in the New York area. Her writing, which included fiction and drama as well as poetry, enjoyed some prominence during her lifetime. Lazarus's most famous work, "The New Colossus," was engraved at the base of the Statue of Liberty in 1886.*

*Using what might seem to present-day audiences somewhat florid language, Lazarus's sonnet advances an image of the United States as a "nation of immigrants" that made the poem evocative for generations to come.*

*Emma Lazarus died in 1887.*

❖

# THE NEW COLOSSUS

NOT LIKE THE BRAZEN GIANT of Greek fame,
With conquering limbs astride from land to land;
Here at our sea-washed, sunset gates shall stand
A mighty woman with a torch, whose flame
Is the imprisoned lightning, and her name
Mother of Exiles. From her beacon-hand
Glows world-wide welcome; her mild eyes command
The air-bridged harbor that twin cities frame.
"Keep, ancient lands, your storied pomp!" cries she
With silent lips. "Give me your tired, your poor,
Your huddled masses yearning to breathe free,
The wretched refuse of your teeming shore.
Send these, the homeless, tempest-tost to me,
I lift my lamp beside the golden door!" ❖

## RESPONDING

1. In a journal entry, freewrite memories of and any associations you can make with the Statue of Liberty. Share your writing with the class. Has the Statue of Liberty become so commonplace a symbol that most Americans have forgotten its meaning? Consider the many ways the image has been used by commercial and other interests.

2. Working individually or in a group, research the history of the Statue of Liberty and the history of the poem. Use the Internet to find out when and why the poem was commissioned.

3. In an essay, discuss the contrasting images in the poem. What is the *old* Colossus, and to what classical image does the poem refer? Why is the new Colossus a "mighty woman"? How does the new land differ from the old?

4. Is America still the land of refuge for the "huddled masses yearning to breathe free" (line 11)? Write an essay arguing your point. Before writing the essay, you might want to research the history of immigration laws in the United States. What was U.S. immigration policy like when the poem was written? How has it changed since? Has new state or federal legislation reflected a change in attitude toward immigrants? Use the Internet to help you locate this information.

# JOSEPH BRUCHAC

*Poet, essayist, and fiction writer Joseph Bruchac was born in New York in 1942. After earning his bachelor's degree at Cornell University in 1965 and his doctorate at Union Graduate School in 1975, Bruchac worked and studied in Ghana. Upon returning to the United States, he taught courses in literature and creative writing at Skidmore College and the Greenfield Institute. He has published works of poetry, fiction, and nonfiction for adults and young people, as well as editing several anthologies including* Smoke Rising: A North American Indian Literary Companion *(1995). He is the founding editor of Greenfield Review Press, a leading publisher of Native American works.*

*The poem "Ellis Island," included here, isolates the ways in which a quintessentially American icon can elicit a variety of responses, based on the sociohistorical position of the interpreter.*

✚

# ELLIS ISLAND

BEYOND THE RED BRICK of Ellis Island
where the two Slovak children
who became my grandparents
waited the long days of quarantine,
5     after leaving the sickness,
the old Empires of Europe,
a Circle Line ship slips easily
on its way to the island
of the tall woman, green
10    as dreams of forests and meadows
waiting for those who'd worked
a thousand years
yet never owned their own.

Like millions of others,
15    I too come to this island,
nine decades the answerer
of dreams.

Yet only one part of my blood loves that memory.
Another voice speaks
20    of native lands
within this nation.
Lands invaded
when the earth became owned.
Lands of those who followed
25    the changing Moon,
knowledge of the seasons
in their veins.  ✚

---

RESPONDING

1.  Write a journal entry or a poem about returning to a place that has special
meaning for you. Compare what it means now to what it meant in the past.

2.  Poetry paints word pictures for the reader through figurative language such
as metaphors and similes. Working individually or in a group, find and

discuss the figurative language used to evoke images in this poem. Why did Bruchac choose the images he did? What associations is he trying to help the reader make? How do you respond to these word pictures?

3. Identify the two voices in the poem. In an essay, discuss whether the voices coexist or if one drowns out the other.

4. Write an essay on the theme of ownership as explored by Bruchac. Can people own parts of the earth? What gives people the rights of ownership? On what do they base their claims: tradition, work, entitlement?

# JAMES TRUSLOW ADAMS

*James Truslow Adams was born in New York in 1878. He studied at Brooklyn Polytechnic and received a bachelor's degree in 1898. After retiring from a career in business in 1912, he devoted himself to the study of history. During his life, he wrote and edited nearly two dozen books, including* The Epic of America *(1931),* The March of Democracy *(1932–1933), as well as studies of New England Puritanism, Jeffersonian Democracy, and the British Empire. He died in 1949.*

*In* The Epic of America, *written during the Great Depression, Adams is credited with introducing the phrase "the American dream," which has since assumed a prominent place in the popular rhetoric of the nation.*

## *From* THE EPIC OF AMERICA

### *Epilogue*

WE HAVE NOW TRACED, in very meagre outline but let us hope with a reasonable 1
emphasis on essentials for our purpose, the course of our story from that dateless period when savages roamed over our continent, coming from we know not where. We reached time and dates with the records of the rich but cruel civilization of Mexico and Central America. We have seen the surprise with

which the first white men were greeted when they landed on our islands and coasts, coming thereafter with increasing frequency and in larger numbers. We have seen the strivings and conflicts of French and English and Spanish. We have seen the rise of our own nation from a handful of starving Englishmen in Virginia to a people of 120,000,000 made up of all the races of the world. Beginning with a guard scarce sufficient to defend the stockade at Jamestown against a few naked Indians, we grew until we were able to select from nearly 25,000,000 men of military age such millions as we would to hurl back at our enemies across the sea, only nine generations later. A continent which scarce sufficed to maintain a half million savages now supports nearly two hundred and fifty times that number of as active and industrious people as there are in the world. The huge and empty land has been filled with homes, roads, railways, schools, colleges, hospitals, and all the comforts of the most advanced material civilization. The mere physical tasks have been stupendous and unparalleled. Supplied at each important stage of advance with new implements of science which hastened our pace; lured by such rewards for haste and industry as were never offered to man before; keyed to activity by a climate that makes expenditure of nervous energy almost a bodily necessity, we threw ourselves into the task of physical domination of our environment with an abandonment that perforce led us to discard much that we had started to build up in our earliest days.

2      Even so, the frontier was always retreating before us, and sending its influence back among us in refluent waves until almost yesterday. In the eighteenth century we had an established civilization, with stability of material and spiritual values. Then we began our scramble for the untold wealth which lay at the foot of the rainbow. As we have gone ever westward, stability gave place to the constant flux in which we have lived since. Recently a distinguished English man of letters complained to me at dinner that we made too much of the frontier as an excuse for everything. It is not an excuse, but it is assuredly an explanation. We let ourselves be too much deflected by it from the building of the civilization of which our forefathers laid the foundations, and the frontier has stretched from our doors until almost yesterday. When my great-grandmother, an old lady with whom I frequently talked as a young man, was born, the United States extended only to the Mississippi, without including even Florida and the Gulf Coast. Both my grandfathers were children when Thomas Jefferson, who carried our bounds out to the Rockies, died. When my father was a baby, the entire country south of Oklahoma and from the Rockies westward was still Spanish territory. When I was born, the Sioux and the Nez Percés were still on the warpath. I was five when the Southwest was first spanned by the Southern Pacific, and twelve when the frontier was officially declared closed.

3      While thus occupied with material conquest and upbuilding, we did not wholly lose the vision of something nobler. If we hastened after the pot of gold,

we also saw the rainbow itself, and felt that it promised, as of old, a hope for mankind. In the realm of thought we have been practical and adaptive rather than original and theoretical, although it may be noted that to-day we stand preëminent in astronomy. In medicine we have conferred discoveries of inestimable value on the world, which we have also led along the road of many humanitarian reforms, such as the treatment of debtors and the insane. Until the reaction after the World War, we had struggled for a juster law of nations and for the extension of arbitration as a substitute for war in international disputes. If in arts and letters we have produced no men who may be claimed to rank with the masters of all time, we have produced a body of work without which the world would be poorer and which ranks high by contemporary world standards. In literature and the drama, to-day, there is no work being done better anywhere than in the United States. In the intangible realm of character, there is no other country that can show in the past century or more two men of greater nobility than Washington and Lincoln.

But, after all, many of these things are not new, and if they were all the   4 contribution which America had had to make, she would have meant only a place for more people, a spawning ground for more millions of the human species. In many respects, as I have not hesitated to say elsewhere, there are other lands in which life is easier, more stimulating, more charming than in raw America, for America *is* still raw, and unnecessarily so. The barbarian carelessness of the motoring millions, the littered roadsides, the use of our most beautiful scenery for the advertising of products which should be boycotted for that very reason, are but symptoms of our slipping down from civilized standards of life, as are also our lawlessness and corruption, with the cynical disregard of them by the public. Many of these matters I have discussed elsewhere, and may again. Some are also European problems as well as American. Some are urban, without regard to international boundaries. The mob mentality of the city crowd everywhere is coming to be one of the menaces to modern civilization. The ideal of democracy and the reality of the crowd are the two sides of the shield of modern government. "I think our governments will remain virtuous . . . as long as they are chiefly agricultural; and this will be as long as there shall be vacant lands in any part of America. When they get piled upon one another in large cities, as in Europe, they will become corrupt as in Europe," wrote Jefferson in the days of the Bourbons.

If, as I have said, the things already listed were all we had had to contribute,   5 America would have made no distinctive and unique gift to mankind. But there has been also the *American dream*, that dream of a land in which life should be better and richer and fuller for every man, with opportunity for each according to his ability or achievement. It is a difficult dream for the European upper classes to interpret adequately, and too many of us ourselves have grown weary and mistrustful of it. It is not a dream of motor cars and high wages merely, but a dream of a social order in which each man and each woman shall be able to attain to the fullest stature of which they are innately capable, and be recognized by others for what they are, regardless of the fortuitous circumstances of birth or position. I once had an intelligent young Frenchman as guest in New York, and after a few days I asked him what struck him most among his new impressions. Without hesitation he replied, "The way that everyone of every sort looks you right in the eye, without a thought of inequality." Some time ago a foreigner who used to do some work for me, and who had picked up a very fair education, used occasionally to sit and chat with me in my study after he had finished his work. One day he said that such a relationship was the great difference between America and his homeland. There, he said, "I would do my work and might get a pleasant word, but I could never sit and talk like this. There is a difference there between social grades which cannot be got over. I would not talk to you there as man to man, but as my employer."

6    No, the American dream that has lured tens of millions of all nations to our shores in the past century has not been a dream of merely material plenty, though that has doubtless counted heavily. It has been much more than that. It has been a dream of being able to grow to fullest development as man and woman, unhampered by the barriers which had slowly been erected in older civilizations, unrepressed by social orders which had developed for the benefit of classes rather than for the simple human being of any and every class. And that dream has been realized more fully in actual life here than anywhere else, though very imperfectly even among ourselves.

7    It has been a great epic and a great dream. What, now, of the future? . . .

8    We have already tried to show how some of the scars were obtained; how it was that we came to insist upon business and money-making and material improvements as good in themselves; how they took on the aspects of moral virtues; how we came to consider an unthinking optimism essential; how we refused to look on the seamy and sordid realities of any situation in which we found ourselves; how we regarded criticism as obstructive and dangerous for our new communities; how we came to think manners undemocratic, and a cultivated mind a hindrance to success, a sign of inefficient effeminacy; how size and statistics of material development came to be more important in our eyes than quality and spiritual values; how in the ever-shifting advance of the frontier we came to lose sight of the past in hopes for the future; how we forgot to *live*, in the struggle to "make a living"; how our education tended to become utilitarian or aimless; and how other unfortunate traits only too notable to-day were developed.

9    While we have been absorbed in our tasks, the world has also been changing. We Americans are not alone in having to search for a new scale and basis for values, but for several reasons the task is more essential for us. On the one hand, our transplantation to the New World and our constant advance over its empty expanse unsettled the old values for us to a far greater extent than in Europe; and, on the other, the mere fact that there were no old things to be swept away here made us feel the full impact of the Industrial Revolution and

the effect of machinery, when we turned to industrial life, to a far greater extent than in Europe, where the revolution originated.

It would seem as though the time had come when this question of values   10 was of prime and pressing importance for us. For long we have been tempted and able to ignore it. Engaged in the work of building cities and developing the continent, values for many tended to be materialized and simplified. When a man staked out a clearing, and saw his wife and children without shelter, there was no need to discuss what were the real values in a humane and satisfying life. The trees had to be chopped, the log hut built, the stumps burned, and the corn planted. Simplification became a habit of mind and was carried into our lives long after the clearing had become a prosperous city. But such a habit of mind does not ignore values. It merely accepts certain ones implicitly, as does our most characteristic philosophy, the Pragmatism of William James. It will not do to say that we shall have no *a priori* standards and that the proof of the value of a thing or idea shall be whether it will "work." What do we mean by its "working"? Must we not mean that it will produce or conduce to some re-sult that strikes us as desirable—that is, something that we have already set up in our minds as something worth while? In other words, a standard or value?

We no longer have the frontier to divert us or to absorb our energies. We   11 shall steadily become a more densely populated country in which our social ideals will have to be such as to give us civilized contentment. To clear the muddle in which our education is at present, we shall obviously have to define our values. Unless we can agree on what the values in life are, we clearly can have no goal in education, and if we have no goal, the discussion of methods is merely futile. Once the frontier stage is passed,—the acquisition of a bare living, and the setting up of a fair economic base,—the American dream itself opens all sorts of questions as to values. It is easy to say a better and richer life for all men, but what *is* better and what *is* richer?

In this respect, as in many others, the great business leaders are likely to   12 lead us astray rather than to guide us. For example, as promulgated by them, there is danger in the present popular theory of the high-wage scale. The danger lies in the fact that the theory is advanced not for the purpose of creating a better type of man by increasing his leisure and the opportunity for making a wise use of it, but for the sole and avowed purpose of increasing his powers as a "consumer." He is, therefore, goaded by every possible method of pressure or cajolery to spend his wages in consuming goods. He is warned that if he does not consume to the limit, instead of indulging in pleasures which do not cost money, he may be deprived not only of his high wages but of any at all. He, like the rest of us, thus appears to be getting into a treadmill in which he earns, not that he may enjoy, but that he may spend, in order that the owners of the factories may grow richer. . . .

Just as in education we have got to have some aims based on values before   13 we can reform our system intelligently or learn in what direction to go, so with business and the American dream. Our democracy cannot attempt to curb, guide, or control the great business interests and powers unless we have clear notions as to the purpose in mind when we try to do so. If we are to regard man merely as a producer and consumer, then the more ruthlessly efficient big business is, the better. Many of the goods consumed doubtless make man healthier, happier, and better even on the basis of a high scale of human values. But if we think of him as a human being primarily, and only incidentally as a consumer, then we have to consider what values are best or most satisfying for him as a human being. We can attempt to regulate business for him not as a consumer but as a man, with many needs and desires with which he has nothing to do as a consumer. Our point of view will shift from efficiency and statistics to human nature. We shall not create a high-wage scale in order that the receiver will consume more, but that he may, in one way or another, live more abundantly, whether by enjoying those things which are factory-produced or those which are not. The points of view are entirely different, socially and economically.

14      In one important respect America has changed fundamentally from the time of the frontier. The old life was lonely and hard, but it bred a strong individualism. The farmer of Jefferson's day was independent and could hold opinions equally so. Steadily we are tending toward becoming a nation of employees— whether a man gets five dollars a day or a hundred thousand a year. The "yes-men" are as new to our national life as to our vocabulary, but they are real. It is no longer merely the laborer or factory hand who is dependent on the whim of his employer, but men all the way up the economic and social scales. In the ante-bellum South the black slave knew better than to express his views as to the rights of man. To-day the appalling growth of uniformity and timorousness of views as to the perfection of the present economic system held by most men "comfortably off" as corporation clerks or officials is not unrelated to the possible loss of a job. . . .

15      If the American dream is to come true and to abide with us, it will, at bottom, depend on the people themselves. If we are to achieve a richer and fuller life for all, they have got to know what such an achievement implies. In a modern industrial State, an economic base is essential for all. We point with pride to our "national income," but the nation is only an aggregate of individual men and women, and when we turn from the single figure of total income to the incomes of individuals, we find a very marked injustice in its distribution. There is no reason why wealth, which is a social product, should not be more equitably controlled and distributed in the interests of society. But, unless we settle on the values of life, we are likely to attack in a wrong direction and burn the barn to find our penny in the hay.

16      Above and beyond the mere economic base, the need for a scale of values becomes yet greater. If we are entering on a period in which, not only in industry but in other departments of life, the mass is going to count for more and the individual less, and if each and all are to enjoy a richer and fuller life, the level

of the mass has got to rise appreciably above what it is at present. It must either rise to a higher level of communal life or drag that life down to its own, in political leadership, and in the arts and letters. . . .

The point is that if we are to have a rich and full life in which all are to share and play their parts, if the American dream is to be a reality, our communal spiritual and intellectual life must be distinctly higher than elsewhere, where classes and groups have their separate interests, habits, markets, arts, and lives. If the dream is not to prove possible of fulfillment, we might as well become stark realists, become once more class-conscious, and struggle as individuals or classes against one another. If it is to come true, those on top, financially, intellectually, or otherwise, have got to devote themselves to the "Great Society," and those who are below in the scale have got to strive to rise, not merely economically, but culturally. We cannot become a great democracy by giving ourselves up as individuals to selfishness, physical comfort, and cheap amusements. The very foundation of the American dream of a better and richer life for all is that all, in varying degrees, shall be capable of wanting to share in it. It can never be wrought into a reality by cheap people or by "keeping up with the Joneses." There is nothing whatever in a fortune merely in itself or in a man merely in himself. It all depends on what is made of each. Lincoln was not great because he was born in a log cabin, but because he got out of it—that is, because he rose above the poverty, ignorance, lack of ambition, shiftlessness of character, contentment with mean things and low aims which kept so many thousands in the huts where they were born.

If we are to make the dream come true we must all work together, no longer to build bigger, but to build better. There is a time for quantity and a time for quality. There is a time when quantity may become a menace and the law of diminishing returns begins to operate, but not so with quality. By working together I do not mean another organization, of which the land is as full as was Kansas of grasshoppers. I mean a genuine individual search and striving for the abiding values of life. In a country as big as America it is as impossible to prophesy as it is to generalize, without being tripped up, but it seems to me that there is room for hope as well as mistrust. The epic loses all its glory without the dream. The statistics of size, population, and wealth would mean nothing to me unless I could still believe in the dream.  ✙

## RESPONDING

1.  In a journal entry, discuss what the term "the American dream" means to you. Is your definition of the American dream similar to or different from that of Adams? Is his dream a possibility for everyone, or do some people feel excluded from it? As you consider these questions, notice the language of the essay. Does it give you any clues about Adams's perspective?

2.  Working individually or in a group, list and explain the values that Adams talks about in the essay. What values does he consider to be important? Do you agree or disagree? Share your conclusions with the class.

3.  Adams despairs that Americans have lost sight of the important values that make the United States unique (see paragraph 5). He says we "forgot to *live*, in the struggle to 'make a living'" (paragraph 8). In an essay, present his position and discuss his reasons for believing that Americans are losing the "American dream." Do you share his concerns?

4.  Choose one of the topics Adams explores, such as individualism, materialism, education, the American dream, or the frontier. In an essay, discuss Adams's perspective and then present your own.

# HENRY LOUIS GATES JR.

*The critic and literary theorist Henry Louis Gates Jr. was born in 1950 in Keyser, West Virginia. He earned his bachelor's degree in history from Yale University in 1973 and his master's and doctoral degrees from Clare College, University of Cambridge, in 1975 and 1979. He has held professorships at Yale University, Cornell University, Duke University, and Harvard University. Among his publications are* Figures in Black: Words, Signs, and the Racial Self *(1987),* The Signifying Monkey: Toward a Theory of Afro-American Literary Criticism *(1987),* Loose Canons: Notes on the Culture Wars *(1992),* Colored People *(1994), and* The Future of the Race *(1996), with Cornell West. Gates has also edited several volumes, including* Black Literature and Literary Theory *(1984),* "Race," Writing and Difference *(1986), and* The Classic Slave Narratives *(1987). His research and writing have earned him awards from the Ford Foundation, the MacArthur Foundation, and the National Endowment for the Humanities, among others.*

*In the following essay, from* Loose Canons, *Gates explores some of the personal and theoretical assumptions connected with the process of naming. More specifically, he invites readers to consider the relationships between specific names or modes of classification and the value systems associated with them.*

⌗

# "WHAT'S IN A NAME?"
# SOME MEANINGS OF BLACKNESS

*The question of color takes up much space in these*
*pages, but the question of color, especially in this*
*country, operates to hide the graver questions of the*
*self.*

—James Baldwin, 1961

*. . . blood, darky, Tar Baby, Kaffir, shine . . .*
*moor, blackamoor, Jim Crow, spook . . . quadroon,*
*meriney, red bone, high yellow . . . Mammy,*
*porch monkey, home, homeboy, George . . . spear-*
*chucker, schwarze, Leroy, Smokey . . . mouli,*
*buck, Ethiopian, brother, sistah. . . .*

—Trey Ellis, 1989

I HAD FORGOTTEN THE INCIDENT COMPLETELY, until I read Trey Ellis's essay, "Remember My Name," in a recent issue of the *Village Voice* (June 13, 1989). But there, in the middle of an extended italicized list of the bynames of "the race" ("the race" or "our people" being the terms my parents used in polite or reverential discourse, "jigaboo" or "nigger" more commonly used in anger, jest, or pure disgust) it was: "George." Now the events of that very brief exchange return to mind so vividly that I wonder why I had forgotten it.

My father and I were walking home at dusk from his second job. He "moonlighted" as a janitor in the evenings for the telephone company. Every day but Saturday, he would come home at 3:30 from his regular job at the paper mill, wash up, eat supper, then at 4:30 head downtown to his second job. He used to make jokes frequently about a union official who moonlighted. I never got the joke, but he and his friends thought it was hilarious. All I knew was that my family always ate well, that my brother and I had new clothes to wear, and that all of the white people in Piedmont, West Virginia, treated my parents with an odd mixture of resentment and respect that even we understood at the time had something directly to do with a small but certain measure of financial security.

He had left a little early that evening because I was with him and I had to be in bed early. I could not have been more than five or six, and we had stopped off at the Cut-Rate Drug Store (where no black person in town but my father could sit down to eat, and eat off real plates with real silverware) so that I could buy some caramel ice cream, two scoops in a wafer cone, please, which I was busy licking when Mr. Wilson walked by.

4    Mr. Wilson was a very quiet white man, whose stony, brooding, silent manner seemed designed to scare off any overtures of friendship, even from white people. He was Irish, as was one third of our village (another third being Italian), the more affluent among whom sent their children to "Catholic School" across the bridge in Maryland. He had white straight hair, like my Uncle Joe, whom he uncannily resembled, and he carried a black worn metal lunch pail, the kind that Riley carried on the television show. My father always spoke to him, and for reasons that we never did understand, he always spoke to my father.

5    "Hello, Mr. Wilson," I heard my father say.

6    "Hello, George."

7    I stopped licking my ice cream cone and asked my Dad in a loud voice why Mr. Wilson had called him "George."

8    "Doesn't he know your name, Daddy? Why don't you tell him your name? Your name isn't George."

9    For a moment I tried to think of who Mr. Wilson was mixing Pop up with. But we didn't have any Georges among the colored people in Piedmont; nor were there colored Georges living in the neighboring towns and working at the mill.

10    "Tell him your name, Daddy."

11    "He knows my name, boy," my father said after a long pause. "He calls all colored people George."

12    A long silence ensued. It was "one of those things," as my mom would put it. Even then, that early, I knew when I was in the presence of "one of those things," one of those things that provided a glimpse, through a rent curtain, at another world that we could not affect but that affected us. There would be a painful moment of silence, and you would wait for it to give way to a discussion of a black superstar such as Sugar Ray or Jackie Robinson.

13    "Nobody hits better in a clutch than Jackie Robinson."

14    "That's right. Nobody."

15    I never again looked Mr. Wilson in the eye.

16    But I loved the names that we gave ourselves when no white people were around. And I have to confess that I have never really cared too much about what we called ourselves publicly, except when my generation was fighting the elders for the legitimacy of the word black as our common, public name. "I'd rather they called me 'nigger,'" my Uncle Raymond would say again and again. "I can't *stand* the way they say the word *black*. And, by the way," he would conclude, his dark brown eyes flashing as he looked with utter disgust at my tentative Afro, "when are you going to get that nappy shit *cut*?"

17    There was enough in our public name to make a whole generation of Negroes rail against our efforts to legitimize, to naturalize, the word *black*. Once we were black, I thought, we would be free, inside at least, and maybe from inside we would project a freedom outside of ourselves. "Free your mind," the slogan went, "and your behind will follow." Still, I value those all-too-rare,

precious moments when someone "slips" in the warmth and comfort of intimacy, and says the dreaded words: "Was he colored?"

I knew that there was power in our name, enough power so that the prospect 18 frightened my maternal uncles. To open the "Personal Statement" for my Yale admission application in 1968, I had settled upon the following: "My grandfather was colored, my father is Negro, and I am black." (If that doesn't grab them, I thought, then nothing will.) I wonder if my daughters, nine years hence, will adapt the line, identifying themselves as "I am an African-American." Perhaps they'll be Africans by then, or even feisty rapper-dappers. Perhaps by that time, the most radical act of naming will be a return to "colored."

I began to learn about the meanings of blackness—or at least how to give 19 voice to what I had experienced—when I went off to Yale. The class of 1973 was the first at Yale to include a "large" contingent of "Afro-Americans," the name we quickly and comfortably seized upon at New Haven. Like many of us in those years, I gravitated to courses in Afro-American studies, at least one per semester, despite the fact that I was pre-med, like almost all the other black kids at Yale—that is, until the ranks were devastated by organic chemistry. (Pre-law was the most common substitute.) The college campus, then, was a refuge from explicit racism, freeing us to read and write about our "racial" selves, to organize for recruitment of minority students and faculty, and to demand the constitutional rights of the Black Panther Party for Self-Defense—an action that led, at New Haven at least, to a full-fledged strike in April of 1970, two weeks before Nixon and Kissinger invaded Cambodia. The campus was our sanctuary, where we could be as black as the ace of spades and nobody seemed to mind.

Today the white college campus is a rather different place. Black studies, 20 where it has survived—and it has survived only at those campuses where *someone* believed enough in its academic integrity to insist upon a sound academic foundation—is entering its third decade. More black faculty members are tenured than ever before, despite the fact that only eight hundred or so Afro-Americans took the doctorate in 1989, and fully half of these were in education. Yet for all the gains that have been made, racial tensions on college campuses appear to be on the rise. The dream of the university as a haven of racial equity, as an ultimate realm beyond the veil, has not been realized. Racism on our college campuses has become a palpable, ugly thing.

Even I—despite a highly visible presence as a faculty member at Cornell— 21 have found it necessary to cross the street, hum a tune, or smile when confronting a lone white woman in a campus building or on the Commons late at night. (Once a white coed even felt it necessary to spring from an elevator that I was about to enter, in the very building where my department is housed.) Nor can I help but feel some humiliation as I try to put a white person at ease in a dark place on campus at night, coming from nowhere, confronting that certain look of panic in his or her eyes, trying to think grand thoughts like Du Bois but—for the life of me—looking to him or her like Willie Horton. Grinning, singing, scratching my head, I have felt like Steppin Fetchit with a Ph.D. So much for Yale; so much for Cambridge.

22 The meanings of blackness are vastly more complex, I suspect, than they ever have been before in our American past. But how to explain? I have often imagined encountering the ghost of the great Du Bois, riding on the shoulders of the Spirit of Blackness.

23 "Young man," he'd say, "what has happened in my absence? Have things changed?"

24 "Well, sir," I'd respond, "your alma mater, Fair Harvard, has a black studies department, a Du Bois Research Center, and even a Du Bois Professor of History. Your old friend Thurgood Marshall sits like a minotaur as an associate justice on the Supreme Court. Martin Luther King's birthday is a *federal* holiday, and a black man you did not know won several Democratic presidential primaries last year. Black women novelists adorn the *New York Times* best-seller lists, and the number one television show in the country is a situation comedy concerning the lives and times of a refined Afro-African obstetrician and his lovely wife, who is a senior partner in a Wall Street law firm. Sammy Davis, Jr.'s second autobiography has been widely—"

25 "Young man, I have come a long way. Do not trifle with the Weary Traveler."

26 "I would not think of it, sir. I revere you, sir, why, I even—"

27 "How many of them had to die? How many of our own? Did Nkrumah and Azikwe send troops? Did a nuclear holocaust bring them to their senses? When Shirley Graham and I set sail for Ghana, I pronounced all hope for our patient people doomed."

28 "No, sir," I would respond. "The gates of segregation fell rather quickly after 1965. A new middle class defined itself, a talented tenth, the cultured few, who, somehow, slipped through the cracks."

29 "Then the preservation of the material base proved to be more important then the primal xenophobia that we had posited?"

30 "That's about it, Doctor. But regular Negroes still catch hell. In fact, the ranks of the black underclass have never been larger."

31 I imagine the great man would heave a sigh, as the Spirit of Blackness galloped away.

32 From 1831, if not before, to 1965, an ideology of desegregation, of "civil rights," prevailed among our thinkers. Abolitionists, Reconstructors, neoabolitionists, all shared one common belief: If we could only use the legislature and the judiciary to create and interpret the laws of desegregation and access, all else would follow. As it turns out, it was vastly easier to dismantle the petty forms of apartheid in this country (housing, marriage, hotels, and restaurants) that anyone could have possibly believed it would be, *without* affecting the larger patterns of inequality. In fact, the economic structure has not changed one jot, in any fundamental sense, except that black adult and teenage unemployment are much higher now than they have been in my lifetime. Considering the

out-of-wedlock birthrate, the high school dropout rate, and the unemployment figures, the "two nations" predicted by the Kerner Commission in 1968 may be upon us. And the conscious manipulation of our public image, by writers, filmmakers, and artists, which many of us *still* seem to think will bring freedom, has had very little impact in palliating our structural social problems. What's the most popular television program in South Africa? The "Cosby Show." Why not?

Ideology, paradoxically, was impoverished when we needed it most, during the civil rights movement of the early 1960s. Unable to theorize what Cornel West calls "the racial problematic," unwilling (with very few exceptions) to theorize class, and scarcely able even to contemplate the theorizing of the curious compound effect of class-cum-race, we have—since the day after the signing of the Civil Rights Act of 1965—utterly lacked any instrumentality of ideological analysis, beyond the attempts of the Black Power and Black Aesthetic movements, to *invert* the signification of "blackness" itself. Recognizing that what had passed for "the human," or "the universal" was in fact white essentialism, we substituted one sort of essentialism (that of "blackness") for another. That, we learned quickly enough, was just not enough. But it led the way to a gestural politics captivated by fetishes and feel-bad rhetoric. The ultimate sign of our sheer powerlessness is all of the attention that we have given, in the past few months, to declaring the birth of the African-American and pronouncing the Black Self dead. Don't we have anything better to do?

Now, I myself happen to like African-American, especially because I am, as a scholar, an Africanist as well as an African-Americanist. Certainly the cultural continuities among African, Caribbean, and black American cultures cannot be denied. (The irony is that we often thought of ourselves as "African" until late into the nineteenth century. The death of the African was declared by the Park school of sociology in the first quarter of this century, which thought that the hyphenated ethnicity of the Negro American would prove to be ultimately liberating.) But so tame and unthreatening is a politics centered on onomastics that even the *New York Times*, in a major editorial, declared its support of this movement:

> If Mr. Jackson is right and blacks now prefer to be called African-Americans, it is a sign not just of their maturity but of the nation's success. . . . Blacks may now feel comfortable enough in their standing as citizens to adopt the family surname: American. And their first name, African, conveys a pride in cultural heritage that all Americans cherish. The late James Baldwin once lamented, "Nobody knows my name." Now everyone does. (December 22, 1988)

To which one young black writer, Trey Ellis, responded recently: "When somebody tries to tell me what to call myself in all uses just because they come to some decision at a cocktail party to which I wasn't even invited, my mama raised me to tell them to kiss my ass" (*Village Voice*, June 13, 1989). As he says, sometimes African-American jut won't do.

35    Ellis's amused rejoinder speaks of a very different set of concerns and makes me think of James Baldwin's prediction of the coming of a new generation that would give voice to blackness:

> While the tale of how we suffer, and how we are delighted, and how we may triumph is never new, it always must be heard. There isn't any other to tell, it's the only light we've got in all this darkness. . . . And this tale, according to that face, that body, those strong hands on those strings, has another aspect in every country, and a new depth in every generation. (*The Price of the Ticket*)

In this spirit, Ellis has declared the birth of a "New Black Aesthetic" movement, comprising artists and writers who are middle-class, self-confident, and secure with black culture, and not looking over their shoulders at white people, wondering whether or not the Mr. Wilsons of their world will call them George. Ellis sees creative artists such as Spike Lee, Wynton Marsalis, Anthony Davis, August Wilson, Warrington Hudlin, Joan Armatrading, and Lisa and Kelly Jones as representatives of a new generation who, commencing with the publication in 1978 of Toni Morrison's *Song of Solomon* (for Ellis, a founding gesture) "no longer need to deny or suppress any part of our complicated and sometimes contradictory cultural baggage to please either white people or black. The culturally mulatto *Cosby* girls are equally as black as a black teenage welfare mother" ("The New Black Aesthetic," *Before Columbus Review*, May 14, 1989). And Ellis is right: something quite new is afoot in African-American letters.

36    In a recent *New York Times Book Review* of Maxine Hong Kingston's new novel, Le Anne Schreiber remarks, "Wittman Ah Singh can't be Chinese even if he wants to be. . . . He is American, as American as Jack Kerouac or James Baldwin or Allen Ginsberg." I remember a time, not so very long ago, when almost no one would have thought of James Baldwin as typifying the "American." I think that even James Baldwin would have been surprised. Certainly since 1950, the meanings of blackness, as manifested in the literary tradition, have come full circle.

37    Consider the holy male trinity of the black tradition: Wright, Ellison, and Baldwin. For Richard Wright, "the color curtain"—as he titled a book on the Bandung Conference in 1955 when the "Third World" was born—was something to be rent asunder by something he vaguely called the "Enlightenment." (It never occurred to Wright, apparently, that the sublime gains in intellection in the Enlightenment took place simultaneously with the slave trade in African human beings, which generated an unprecedented degree of wealth and an unprecedentedly large leisure and intellectual class.) Wright was hardly senti-

mental about black Africa and the Third World: he actually told the first Conference of Negro-African Writers and Artists in Paris in 1956 that colonialism had been "liberating, since it smashed old traditions and destroyed old gods, freeing Africans from the 'rot' of their past," their "irrational past" (James Baldwin, *Nobody Knows My Name*). Despite the audacity of this claim, however, Wright saw himself as chosen "in some way to inject into the American consciousness" a cognizance of "other people's mores or national habits" ("I Choose Exile," unpublished essay). Wright claimed that he was "split": "I'm black. I'm a man of the West. . . . I see and understand the non- or anti-Western point of view." But, Wright confessed, "when I look out upon the vast stretches of this earth inhabited by brown, black and yellow men . . . my reactions and attitudes are those of the West" (*White Man, Listen!*). Wright never had clearer insight into himself, although his unrelentingly critical view of Third World cultures may make him a problematic figure among those of us bent upon decentering the canon.

James Baldwin, who in *Nobody Knows My Name*, parodied Wright's 1956 speech, concluded that "this was, perhaps, a tactless way of phrasing a debatable idea." Blackness, for Baldwin, was a sign, a sign that signified through the salvation of the "gospel impulse," as Craig Werner characterizes it, seen in his refusal "to create demons, to simplify the other in a way that would inevitably force him to simplify himself. . . . The gospel impulse—its refusal to accept oppositional thought; its complex sense of presence; its belief in salvation—sounds in Baldwin's voice no matter what his particular vocabulary at a particular moment" (Craig Werner, "James Baldwin: Politics and the Gospel Impulse," *New Politics* [Winter 1989]). Blackness, if it would be anything, stood as the saving grace of both white *and* black America.

Ralph Ellison, ever the trickster, felt it incumbent upon him to show that blackness was a metaphor of the human condition, and yet to do so through a faithful adherence to its particularity. Nowhere is this idea rendered more brilliantly than in his sermon "The Blackness of Blackness," the tradition's classic critique of blackness as an essence:

"Brothers and sisters, my text this morning is the 'Blackness of Blackness.'"
And a congregation of voices answered: "That blackness is most black, brother, most black . . ."
"In the beginning . . ."
"At the very start," they cried.
". . . there was blackness . . ."
"Preach it . . ."
"and the sun . . ."
"The sun, Lawd . . ."
". . . was bloody red . . ."
"Red . . ."

"Now black is . . ." the preacher shouted.

"Bloody . . ."

"I said black is . . ."

"Preach it, brother . . ."

". . . an' black ain't . . ."

"Red, Lawd, red: He said it's red!"

"Amen, brother . . ."

"Black will git you . . ."

"Yes, it will . . ."

". . . an' black won't . . ."

"Naw, it won't!"

"It do . . ."

"It do, Lawd . . ."

". . . an' it don't."

"Hallelujah . . ."

"It'll put you, glory, glory, Oh my Lawd, in the WHALE'S BELLY."

"Preach it, dear brother . . ."

". . . an' make you tempt . . ."

"Good God a-mighty!"

"Old aunt Nelly!"

"Black will make you . . ."

"Black . . ."

". . . or black will un-make you."

"Ain't it the truth, Lawd?"

*(Invisible Man)*

Ellison parodies the idea that blackness can underwrite a metaphysics or even a negative theology, that it can exist outside and independent of its representation.

40 And it is out of this discursive melee that so much contemporary African-American literature has developed.

41 The range of representation of the meanings of blackness among the post–*Song of Solomon* (1978) era of black writing can be characterized—for the sake of convenience—by the works of C. Eric Lincoln (*The Avenue, Clayton City*); Trey Ellis's manifesto, "The New Black Aesthetic"; and Toni Morrison's *Beloved*, in many ways the Ur-text of the African-American experience.

42 Each of these writers epitomizes the points of a post–Black Aesthetic triangle, made up of the realistic representation of black vernacular culture: the attempt to preserve it for a younger generation (Lincoln), the critique through parody of the essentialism of the Black Aesthetic (Ellis), and the transcendence of the ultimate horror of the black past—slavery—through myth and the supernatural (Morrison).

The first chapter of Eric Lincoln's first novel, *The Avenue, Clayton City*   43
(1988), contains an extended recreation of the African-American ritual of signifying, which is also known as "talking that talk," "the dozens," "nasty talk," and
so on. To render the dozens in such wonderful detail, of course, is a crucial
manner of preserving it in the written cultural memory of African-Americans.
This important impulse to preserve (by recording) the vernacular links Lincoln's
work directly to that of Zora Neale Hurston. Following the depiction of the
ritual exchange, the narrator of the novel analyzes its import in the following
way:

> But it was playing the dozens that perplexed and worried Dr. Tait the most of
> all when he first tuned in on what went on under the streetlight. Surely it
> required the grossest level of depravity to indulge in such willful vulgarity. He
> had thought at first that Guts Gallimore's appraisal of talking that talk as "nasty"
> was too generous to be useful. . . . But the truth of the matter was that in spite
> of his disgust, the twin insights of agony and intellection had eventually paid
> off, for suddenly not only the language but the logic of the whole streetlight
> ritual finally became clear to him. What he was observing from the safety and
> the anonymity of his cloistered front porch was nothing less than a teenage rite
> of passage. A very critical *black* rite of passage! How could he not have recog-
> nized it for so long? The public deprecation of black men and women was, of
> course, taken for granted in Clayton City, and everywhere else within the
> experience of the Flame Gang. But when those black men and women were
> one's fathers, mothers, and sisters, how could one approaching manhood accept
> that deprecation and live with it? To be a *man* implied responsibilities no colored
> man in Clayton City could meet, so the best way to deal with the contradiction
> was to deny it. Talkin' that talk—that is, disparaging one's loved ones within
> the in-group—was an obvious expression of self-hatred, but it also undercut the
> white man's style of black denigration by presupposing it, and to some degree
> narcotizing the black boys who were on the way to manhood from the pain of
> their impotence. After all, *they had said it first!* Playing the dozens, Tait reasoned,
> was an effort to prepare one to be able to "take it." Anyone who refused to play
> the dozens was unrealistic, for the dozens were a fact of life for every black man.
> They were implicit in the very structure of black-white relations, and if one
> didn't "play," he could "pat his foot" while the play went on, over and around
> him. No one could exempt himself from the cultural vulgarity of black debase-
> ment, no matter how offensive it might be.

Trey Ellis, whose first novel, *Platitudes*, is a satire on contemporary black   44
cultural politics, is an heir of Ishmael Reed, the tradition's great satirist. Ellis
describes the relation of what he calls "The New Black Aesthetic" (NBA) to the

black nationalism of the sixties, engaged as it is in the necessary task of critique
and revision:

> Yet ironically, a telltale sign of the work of the NBA is our parodying of the
> black nationalist movement: Eddie Murphy, 26, and his old *Saturday Night Live*
> character, prison poet Tyrone Green, with his hilariously awful angry black
> poem, "Cill [*sic*] My Landlord," ("See his dog Do he bite?"); fellow Black Packer
> Keenan Wayans' upcoming blaxploitation parody *I'ma Get You Sucka!;* play-
> wright George Wolfe, and his parodies of both "A Raisin in the Sun" and "For
> Colored girls . . ." in his hit play "The Colored Museum" ("Enter Walter-Lee-
> Beau-Willie-Jones. . . . His brow is heavy from 300 years of oppression.");
> filmmaker Reginald Hudlin, 25, and his sacrilegious *Reggie's World of Soul* with
> its fake commercial for a back scratcher, spatula and toilet bowl brush all with
> black clenched fists for their handle ends; and Lisa Jones' character Clean Mama
> King who is available for both sit-ins and film walk-ons. There is now such a
> strong and vast body of great black work that the corny or mediocre doesn't
> need to be coddled. NBA artists aren't afraid to publicly flout the official,
> positivist black party line.

This generation, Ellis continues, cares less about what white people think than
any other in the history of Africans in this country: "The New Black Aesthetic
says you just have to *be* natural, you don't necessarily have to *wear* one."

45     Ellis dates the beginning of this cultural movement to the publication of
*Song of Solomon* in 1978. Morrison's blend of magical realism and African-
American mythology proved compelling: this brilliantly rendered book was an
overnight bestseller. Her greatest artistic achievement, however, and most controversial, is her most recent novel, *Beloved*, which won the 1988 Pulitzer Prize
for Fiction.

46     In *Beloved*, Morrison has found a language that gives voice to the unspeakable horror and terror of the black past, our enslavement in the New World.
Indeed, the novel is an allegorical representation of this very unspeakability. It
is one of the few treatments of slavery that escapes the pitfalls of *kitsch*. Toni
Morrison's genius is that she has found a language by which to thematize this
very unspeakability of slavery:

> Everybody knew what she was called, but nobody knew her name. Disremem-
> bered and unaccounted for, she cannot be lost because no one is looking for
> her, and even if they were, how can they call her if they don't know her name?
> Although she has claim, she is not claimed. In the place where long grass opens,
> the girl who waited to be loved and cry shame erupts into her separate parts,
> to make it easy for the chewing laughter to swallow her all away.
>
>     It was not a story to pass on.

They forgot her like a bad dream. After they made up their tales, shaped and decorated them, those that saw her that day on the porch quickly and deliberately forgot her. It took longer for those who had spoken to her, lived with her, fallen in love with her, to forget, until they realized they couldn't remember or repeat a single thing she said, and began to believe that, other than what they themselves were thinking, she hadn't said anything at all. So, in the end, they forgot her too. Remembering seemed unwise. They never knew where or why she crouched, or whose was the underwater face she needed like that. Where the memory of the smile under her chin might have been and was not, a latch latched and lichen attached its apple-green bloom to the metal. What made her think her fingernails could open locks the rain rained on?

It was not a story to pass on.

Only by stepping outside the limitations of realism and entering a realm of myth could Morrison, a century after its abolition, give a voice to the silence of enslavement.

For these writers, in their various ways, the challenge of the black creative intelligence is no longer to *posit* blackness, as it was in the Black Arts movement of the sixties, but to render it. Their goal seems to be to create a fiction *beyond* the color line, one that takes the blackness of the culture for granted, as a springboard to write about those human emotions that we share with everyone else, and that we have always shared with each other, when no white people are around. They seem intent, paradoxically on escaping the very banality of blackness that we encountered in so much Black Arts poetry, by *assuming* it as a legitimate grounds for the creation of art.

To declare that race is a trope, however, is not to deny its palpable force in the life of every African-American who tries to function every day in a still very racist America. In the fact of Anthony Appiah's and my own critique of what we might think of as "black essentialism," Houston Baker demands that we remember what we might characterize as the "taxi fallacy."

Houston, Anthony, and I emerge from the splendid isolation of the Schomburg Library and stand together on the corner of 135th Street and Malcolm X Boulevard attempting to hail a taxi to return to the Yale Club. With the taxis shooting by us as if we did not exist, Anthony and I cry out in perplexity, "But sir, it's only a trope."

If only that's *all* it was.

My father, who recently enjoyed his seventh-sixth birthday, and I attended a basketball game at Duke this past winter. It wasn't just any game; it was "the" game with North Carolina, the ultimate rivalry in American basketball competition. At a crucial juncture of the game, one of the overly avid Duke fans bellowing in our section of the auditorium called J. R. Reid, the Carolina center, "rubber lips."

52    "Did you hear what he said?" I asked my father, who wears *two* hearing aids.

53    "I heard it. Ignore it, boy."

54    "I can't, Pop," I replied. Then, loud-talking all the way, I informed the crowd, while ostensibly talking only to my father, that we'd come too far to put up with shit like this, that Martin Luther King didn't die in vain, and we won't tolerate this kind of racism again, etc., etc., etc. Then I stood up and told the guy not to say those words ever again.

55    You could have cut the silence in our section of that auditorium with a knife. After a long silence, my Dad leaned over and whispered to me, "Nigger, is you *crazy*? We am in de Souf." We both burst into laughter.

56    Even in the South, though, the intrusion of race into our lives usually takes more benign forms. One day my wife and my father came to lunch at the National Humanities Center in Research Triangle Park, North Carolina. The following day, the only black member of the staff cornered me and said that the kitchen staff had a bet, and that I was the only person who could resolve it. Shoot, I said. "Okay," he said. "The bet is that your Daddy is Mediterranean— Greek or Eyetalian, and your wife is High Yellow." "No," I said, "it's the other way around: my dad is black; my wife is white."

57    "Oh, yeah," he said, after a long pause, looking at me through the eyes of the race when one of us is being "sadiddy," or telling some kind of racial lie. "You, know, *brother*," he said to me in a low but pointed whisper, "we black people got ways to *tell* these things, you know." Then he looked at me to see if I was ready to confess the truth. Indeterminacy had come home to greet me.

58    What, finally, is the meaning of blackness for my generation of African-American scholars? I think many of us are trying to work, rather self-consciously, within the tradition. It has taken white administrators far too long to realize that the recruitment of black faculty members is vastly easier at those institutions with the strongest black studies departments, or at least with the strongest representation of other black faculty. Why? I think the reason for this is that many of us wish to be a part of a community, of something "larger" than ourselves, escaping the splendid isolation of our studies. What can be lonelier than research, except perhaps the terror of the blank page (or computer screen)? Few of us—and I mean *very few*—wish to be the "only one" in town. I want my own children to grow up in the home of intellectuals, but with black middle-class values as common to them as the air they breathe. This I cannot achieve alone. I seek out, eagerly, the company of other African-American academics who have paid their dues; who understand the costs, and the pleasures, of achievement; who care about "the race"; and who are determined to leave a legacy of self-defense against racism in all of its pernicious forms.

59    Part of this effort to achieve a sense of community is understanding that our generation of scholars is just an extension of other generations, of "many thousands gone." We are no smarter than they; we are just a bit more fortunate, in some ways, the accident of birth enabling us to teach at "white" research institutions, when two generations before we would have been teaching at black

schools, overworked and underfunded. Most of us define ourselves as extensions of the tradition of scholarship and academic excellence epitomized by figures such as J. Saunders Redding, John Hope Franklin, and St. Clair Drake, merely to list a few names. But how are we *different* from them?

A few months ago I heard Cornel West deliver a memorial lecture in honor of James Snead, a brilliant literary critic who died of cancer this past spring at the age of thirty-five. Snead graduated valedictorian of his class at Exeter, then summa cum laude at Yale. Fluent in German, he wrote his Scholar of the House "essay" on the uses of repetition in Thomas Mann and William Faulkner. (Actually, this "essay" amounted to some six hundred pages, and the appendices were written in German.) He was also a jazz pianist and composer and worked as an investment banker in West Germany, after he took the Ph.D. in English literature at the University of Cambridge. Snead was a remarkable man.

West, near the end of his memorial lecture, told his audience that he had been discussing Snead's life and times with St. Clair Drake, as Drake lay in bed in a hospital recovering from a mild stroke that he had experienced on a flight from San Francisco to Princeton, where Drake was to lecture. When West met the plane at the airport, he rushed Drake to the hospital, and sat with him through much of the weekend.

West told Drake how Snead was, yes, a solid race man, how he loved the tradition and wrote about it, but that his real goal was to redefine *American Studies* from the vantage point of African-American concepts and principles. For Snead, taking the black mountaintop was not enough; he wanted the entire mountain range. "There is much about Dr. Snead that I can understand," Drake told West. "But then again," he concluded, "there is something about his enterprise that is quite unlike ours." Our next move within the academy, our next gesture, is to redefine the whole, simultaneously institutionalizing African-American studies. The idea that African-American culture is exclusively a thing apart, separate from the whole, having no influence on the shape and shaping of American culture, is a racialist fiction. There can be no doubt that the successful attempts to "decenter" the canon stem in part from the impact that black studies programs have had upon traditional notions of the "teachable," upon what, properly, constitutes the universe of knowledge that the well-educated should know. For us, and for the students that we train, the complex meaning of blackness is a vision of America, a refracted image in the American looking-glass.

Snead's project, and Ellis's—the project of a new generation of writers and scholars—is about transcending the I-got-mine parochialism of a desperate era. It looks beyond that overworked master plot of victims and victimizers so carefully scripted in the cultural dominant, beyond the paranoid dream of cultural autarky, and beyond the seductive ensolacements of nationalism. Their story—and it is a new story—is about elective affinities, unburdened by an ideology of descent; it speaks of blackness without blood. And this *is* a story to pass on. ✥

RESPONDING

1.  In a journal entry, tell about a time you or someone you know spoke out against injustice or insensitivity as Gates speaks out at the basketball game at Duke. Or speculate about how you would have reacted if someone insulted a group to which you belong.

2.  Working individually or in a group, list and try to define the following terms in the essay: black essentialism, canon, rite of passage, signifying onomastics. Compare your definitions with your classmates' and check them with outside sources.

3.  In an essay, explain what Gates means when he says that "certainly since 1950, the meanings of blackness, as manifested in the literary tradition, have come full circle" (paragraph 36).

4.  Gates states that "The dream of the university as a haven of racial equity, as an ultimate realm beyond the veil, has not been realized. Racism on our college campuses has become a palpable, ugly thing" (paragraph 20). Write an essay agreeing or disagreeing; use evidence from outside sources and your own experience.

# Greg Sarris

*Greg Sarris, born in Santa Rosa, California, received his bachelor's degree from the University of California, Los Angeles (UCLA), in 1978 and his master's and doctoral degrees from Stanford University. He has taught at several institutions, including Stanford, the University of California, Santa Cruz, and UCLA, where he is currently associate professor of English and associate director of the American Indian Studies Center. He has won grants from the Institute for American Cultures and the Irvine Foundation, among others. His publications include* Keeping the Slug Woman Alive: A Holistic Approach to American Indian Literature *(1993),* Mabel McKay: Weaving the Dream *(1994), and* Grand Avenue *(1994), as well as essays in many academic journals.*

*The essay that follows, first published in* Sequoia, *examines the issues of legitimacy, authority, and oppression as they relate to personal and collective identities.*

✠

# BATTLING ILLEGITIMACY: SOME WORDS AGAINST THE DARKNESS

I HAVE HEARD THAT SOMEONE SAID to American Indian writer Louise Erdrich, 1
"You don't look Indian." It was at a reading she gave, or perhaps when she
received an award of some kind for her writing. Undoubtedly, whoever said this
noted Erdrich's very white skin, her green eyes and her red hair. She retorted,
"Gee, you don't look rude."

You don't look Indian. 2

How often I too have heard that. But unlike Erdrich, I never returned the 3
insult, or challenged my interlocutors. Not with words anyway. I arranged the
facts of my life to fit others' conceptions of what it is to be Indian. I used others'
words, others' definitions. That way, if I didn't look Indian, I might still be
Indian.

Well, I don't know if I am Indian, I said, or if I am, how much. I was 4
adopted. I know my mother was white—Jewish, German, Irish. I was illegitimate. Father unknown. It was back in the fifties when having a baby without
being married was shameful. My mother uttered something on the delivery table
about the father being Spanish. Mexican maybe. Anyway, I was given up and
adopted, which is how I got a name. For awhile things went well. Then they
didn't. I found myself with other families, mostly on small ranches where I
milked cows and worked with horses. I met a lot of Indians—Pomo Indians—and
was taken in by one of the families. I learned bits and pieces of two Pomo
languages. So if you ask, I call myself Pomo. But I don't know . . . My mother
isn't around to ask. After she had me, she needed blood. The hospital gave her
the wrong type and it killed her.

The story always went something like that. It is true, all of it, but arranged 5
so that people might see how I fit. The last lines—about my mother—awe
people and cause them to forget, or to be momentarily distracted, from their
original concern about my not looking Indian. And I am illegitimate. That
explains any crossing of borders, anything beyond the confines of definition.
That is how I fit.

Last year I found my father. Well, I found out his name—Emilio. My mother's 6
younger brother, my uncle, who I met recently, remembered taking notes from
his sister to a "big Hawaiian type" on the football field. "I would go after school
while the team was practicing," my uncle said. "The dude was big, dark. They
called him Meatloaf. I think his name though was Emilio. Try Emilio."

To have a name, even a nickname, seemed unfathomable. To be thirty-six 7 years old and for the first time to have a lead about a father somehow frightened me. You imagine all your life; you find ways to account for that which is missing, you tell stories, and now all that is leveled by a name.

8     In Laguna Beach I contacted the high school librarian and made arrangements to look through old yearbooks. It was just after a conference there in Southern California, where I had finished delivering a paper on American Indian education. I found my mother immediately, and while I was staring for the first time at an adult picture of my mother, a friend who was with me scanned other yearbooks for an Emilio. Already we knew by looking at the rows and rows of white faces, there wouldn't be too many Emilios. I was still gazing at the picture of my mother when my friend jumped. "Look," she said. She was tilting the book, pointing to a name. But already, even as I looked, a dark face caught my attention, and it was a face I saw myself in. Without a doubt. Darker, yes. But me nonetheless.

9     I interviewed several of my mother's and father's classmates. It was my mother's friends who verified what I suspected. Emilio Hilario was my father. They also told me that he had died, that I had missed him by about five years.

10     I had to find out from others what he couldn't tell me. I wanted to know about his life. Did he have a family? What was his ethnicity? Luckily I obtained the names of several relatives, including a half-brother and a grandmother. People were quick about that, much more so than about the ethnicity question. They often circumvented the question by telling stories about my father's athletic prowess and about how popular he was. A few, however, were more candid. His father, my grandfather, is Filipino. "A short Filipino man," they said. "Your father got his height from his mother. She was fairer." Some people said my grandmother was Spanish, others said she was Mexican or Indian. Even within the family, there is discrepancy about her ethnicity. Her mother was definitely Indian, however. Coast Miwok from Tomales Bay just north of San Francisco, and just South of Santa Rosa, where I grew up. Her name was Rienette.

11     During the time my grandmother was growing up, probably when her mother—Rienette—was growing up too, even until quite recently, when it became popular to be Indian, Indians in California sometimes claimed they were Spanish. And for good reason. The prejudice against Indians was intolerable, and often only remnants of tribes, or even families, remained to face the hatred and discrimination. My grandmother spoke Spanish. Her sister, Juanita, married a Mexican and her children's children are proud *Chicanos* living in East Los Angeles. Rienette's first husband, my grandmother and her sister's father, was probably part Mexican or Portuguese—I'm not sure.

12     The story is far from complete. But how much Indian I am by blood is not the question whose answer concerns me now. Oh, I qualify for certain grants, and that is important. But knowing about my blood heritage will not change my complexion any more than it will my experience.

In school I was called the white beaner. This was not because some of my
friends happened to be Mexican, but because the white population had little
sense of the local Indians. Anyone with dark hair and skin was thought to be
Mexican. A counselor once called me in and asked if my family knew I went
around with Mexicans. "Yes," I said. "They're used to it." At the time, I was
staying with an Indian family—the McKays—and Mrs. McKay was a mother to
me. But I said nothing more then. I never informed the counselor that most of
my friends, the people she was referring to, were Indian—Pomo Indian. Kashaya
Pomo Indian. Sulfur Bank Pomo Indian. Coyote Valley Pomo Indian. Yokaya
Pomo Indian. Point Arena Pomo Indian. Bodega Bay Miwok Indian. Tomales
Bay Miwok Indian. And never mind that names such as Smith and Pinola are
not Spanish (or Mexican) names.

As I think back, I said nothing more to the counselor not because I didn't
want to cause trouble (I did plenty of that), but because, like most other kids, I
never really knew a way to tamper with how the authorities—counselors, teachers, social workers, police—categorized us. We talked about our ethnicity
amongst ourselves, often speculating who was more or less this or that. So many
of us are mixed with other groups—white, Mexican, Spanish, Portuguese, Filipino. I know of an Indian family who is half Mexican and they identify themselves as Mexicans. In another family of the same admixture just the opposite is
true. Yet for most of the larger white community, we were Mexican, or something.

And here I am with blue eyes and fair skin. If I was a white beaner, I was,
more generally, a kid from the wrong side of the tracks. Hood. Greaser. Low
Brow. Santa Rosa was a much smaller town then, the lines more clearly drawn
between the haves and the have-nots, the non-colored and the colored. Suburban sprawl was just beginning; there was still the old downtown with its stone
library and old Roman-columned courthouse. On the fringes of town lived the
poorer folk. The civil rights movement had not yet engendered the ethnic pride
typical of the late sixties and early seventies.

I remember the two guys who taught me to box, Manual and Robert. They
said they were Portuguese, Robert part Indian. People whispered that they were
black. I didn't care. They picked me out, taught me to box. That was when I
was fourteen. By the time I was sixteen, I beat heads everywhere and every time
I could. I looked for fights and felt free somehow in the fight. I say I looked for
fights, but really, as I think about it, fights seemed to find me. People said things,
they didn't like me, they invaded my space. I had reason. So I fought. And
afterwards I was somebody. Manny said I had a chip on my shoulder, which is
an asset for a good fighter. "Hate in your eyes, brother," he told me. "You got
hate in your eyes."

I heard a lot of "Indian" stories too. We used to call them old-time stories,
those about Coyote and the creation. Then there were the spook stories about
spook men and women and evil doings. I knew of a spook man, an old guy who

would be sitting on his family's front porch one minute and then five minutes later, just as you were driving uptown, there he'd be sitting on the old courthouse steps. The woman whose son I spent so much time with was an Indian doctor. She healed the sick with songs and prayer; she sucked pains from people's bodies. These are the things my professors and colleagues wanted to hear about.

18      I was different here too. I read books, which had something to do with my getting into college. But when I started reading seriously—about the middle of my junior year in high school—I used what I read to explain the world; I never engaged my experience to inform what I was reading. Again, I was editing my experience, and, not so ironically, I found meaning that way. And, not so ironically, the more I read the more I became separated from the world of my friends and what I had lived. So in college when I found people interested in my Indian experience as it related to issues of ecology, personal empowerment, and other world-views, I complied and told them what I "knew" of these things. In essence I shaped what I knew to fit the books and read the books to shape what I knew. The woman who was a mother to me came off as Castaneda's Don Juan. Think of the "separate reality" of her dream world, never mind what I remember about her—the long hours in the apple cannery, her tired face, her clothes smelling of rotten apples.

19      Now, as I sort through things, I am beginning to understand why I hated myself and those people at the university; how by sculpting my experience and their interests, I denied so much of my life, including the anger and self-hatred that seeps up from such denial. I wanted to strike back, beat the hell out of them; I imagined them angering me in some way I could recognize—maybe an insult, a push or shove—so that I could hurt them. Other times I just wanted them to be somewhere, perhaps outside the classroom, on a street, in a bar, where they came suddenly upon me and saw me fighting, pummelling somebody. Anger is like a cork in water. Push it down, push it down, and still it keeps coming to the surface.

20      Describing her life experience in a short autobiographical piece entitled "The Autobiography of a Confluence," Paula Gunn Allen says, "Fences would have been hard to place without leaving something out . . . Essentially, my life, like my work, is a journey-in-between, a road." Poet Wendy Rose writes about how she went to the Highland Games in Fresno to search for her Scottish roots: "It may have looked funny to all those Scots to see an Indian [Rose] looking for a booth with her clan's name on it." She adds: "The colonizer and the colonized meet in my blood. It is so much more complex than just white and Indian. I will pray about this, too." These American Indian writers, just as so many other ethnic minority American writers, are attempting to mediate the cultural variables that constitute their experience as Americans. They are attempting to redefine their experience based on the experience itself and not in terms of others' notions of that experience.

21      During the late sixties and early seventies, an odd reversal of affairs took

place. Where some Indian people once denied, or at least kept quiet their Indian heritage, they suddenly began denying that part which is white, Spanish, or whatever. The point here is that in the name of ethnic pride we begin to make illegitimate so much of what we are, and have been, about. We deny aspects of our history and experience that could enrich any understanding of what it means to be an American Indian in time, in history, and not just as some relic from a prelapserian past, as the dominant culture so often likes to see us. We in fact become oppressor-like; we internalize the oppression we have felt, and, ironically, using others' definitions, or even those created by ourselves, decide who is Indian and who is not. We perpetuate illegitimacy in our ranks.

But the danger isn't just for ourselves here. Ultimately, by accepting or  22 creating certain definitions by which we judge our own experiences, we allow others a definition by which we can be judged by them. Criteria that render certain kinds of experience illegitimate enable people to escape the broader, human issues in life as it is lived. They allow the phonies a way to dress up, showing how they are Indian, and they cheat the rest of us of a true and fully human and historical cultural identity. What we need are words—stories, poems, histories, biographies—that qualify and challenge given definitions, that allow all of us as students and teachers, Indians and non-Indians, the opportunity to examine our own framing devices in order that we might be able to see and consider the possibility of seeing beyond those frames. We need to make visible the heretofore illegitimate so that we might consider human experience in the broadest sense possible.

My father was a local hero, they say. He excelled in all sports, was voted junior  23 class president, and served as president of the local Hi-Y. He was charming, outgoing, women loved him. But there was the other side, the black-out drinking and violence. Like a Jekyll and Hyde, people told me. He would turn on a dime, get nasty and mean. He'd rip into people. Kick ass. You could see it coming in his eyes.

When my grandfather brought his family from East Los Angeles to Laguna  24 Beach, there was only one other minority family in town—a black family. Grandpa worked as a cook at Victor Hugo's, a glamorous waterfront restaurant. He settled his family in a small house in "the canyon," where the black family and season migrant families lived at the time, and where Grandpa still lives today. While my father was exalted locally as an athlete, he was constantly reminded of his color and class. Behind his back, people referred to him as a "nigger." To his face, the fathers of girls he dated told him: "Go away. We aren't hiring any gardeners."

I don't need to probe far here to get the picture. Illegitimacy in any form  25 cuts a wide swath. Those of us affected by it react in a number of ways. Our histories, if they are presented and examined honestly, tell the stories. For my father and me it was, among other things, violence. Unable to tell his story, unable to fill in those chasms between his acceptance and rejection by the world around him, my father fought, each blow a strike against the vast and imposing darkness. He became a professional boxer; in the Navy he was undefeated, and after he sparred with Floyd Patterson. He died at 52, three weeks before his fifty-third birthday, just five years before his first son would find his picture in a yearbook. He died of a massive heart attack, precipitated by years of chronic alcoholism.

26    Now sometimes I wonder at my being Filipino, for I am as much Filipino by one definition, that is by blood, as I am anything by that same definition. Grandpa came from a small village on the island of Panay in the South Central Philippines. He tells me I have second cousins who have never worn shoes and speak only the Bisian dialect of that island. Yet, if I am Filipino, I am a Filipino separated from my culture and to backtrack, or go back, to that culture, I must carry my life with me, as it has been lived—in Santa Rosa with Pomo Indians and all others, and in the various cities and universities where I have lived and worked.

27    "You have quite a legacy in that man," a friend of my father's said to me. "He was one hell of a guy."

28    Yes, I thought to myself, a legacy. Fitting in by not fitting in. Repression. Violence. Walls of oppressive darkness. The urge now, the struggle, the very need to talk about the spaces, to word the darkness. ⊞

---

## RESPONDING

1.  Sarris uses storytelling to define who he is. In a journal entry, tell a story that defines who you are.

2.  Working individually or in a group, trace Sarris's family tree. Discuss what defines our ethnicity—is it blood?—or culture—or upbringing?

3.  In an essay, explain how Sarris felt he was shaping and changing his experience to fit others' expectations. According to Sarris, what are some of the problems with that strategy?

4.  Sarris says, "We in fact become oppressor-like; we internalize the oppression we have felt, and, ironically, using others' definitions, or even those created by ourselves, decide who is Indian and who is not" (paragraph 21). Explain his position and write an essay agreeing or disagreeing with his conclusions.

# EVA HOFFMAN

*The critic and essayist Eva Hoffman was born in Krakow, Poland, in 1945.
She immigrated first to Canada, then to the United States in 1963. After
earning her bachelor's degree from Rice University (1967), she pursued
graduate study at Yale University before earning her doctorate from Harvard
University in 1974. Hoffman has held teaching positions at several institutions, including the University of New Hampshire and Tufts University. She
has been on the staff of* The New York Times *since 1980; she is currently
an editor of* The New York Times Book Review. *Her publications include*
Lost in Translation *(1989);* Exit into History *(1993), and* Shtetl: The
Life and Death of a Small Town and the World of Polish Jews *(1997).*

*The selection that follows, from Hoffman's* Lost in Translation, *explores
the ways in which a cultural context can inform what one says and what one
chooses to keep silent.*

⊞

# *From* LOST IN TRANSLATION

MY FRIENDS ASSURE ME that, having come to the republic's eastern shore, I've      1
landed in the real America at last. "Being American means that you feel like
you're the norm," one of my friends tells me, "and the Northeast is the norm
that sets the norm." An ironically timed statement, since we've entered a period
during which these very friends of mine will try to unwrap, unravel, and
demolish every norm passed on to them from their parents and the culture at
large; for a while, they will use their inheritance and their sense of entitlement
for that most luxurious of rights, the right to turn down one's privileges; for a
while at least, they will refuse to inherit the earth.

As for me, I want to figure out, more urgently than before, where I belong      2
in this America that's made up of so many sub-Americas. I want, somehow, to
give up the condition of being a foreigner. I no longer want to tell people quaint
stories from the Old Country, I don't want to be told that "exotic is erotic," or
that I have Eastern European intensity, or brooding Galician eyes. I no longer
want to be propelled by immigrant chutzpah or desperado energy or usurper's
ambition. I no longer want to have the prickly, unrelenting consciousness that
I'm living in the medium of a specific culture. It's time to roll down the scrim
and see the world directly, as the world. I want to reenter, through whatever
Looking Glass will take me there, a state of ordinary reality.

And that's when I begin fighting with my friends.      3

Although I've always thought of myself as a pliable, all-too-accommodating      4 sort of person, I now get into fights all the time. Sitting with a friend over an afternoon coffee at the Pamplona, or walking with another along one of the more bucolic Cambridge streets, I suddenly find myself in the middle of an argument whose ferocity surprises us both. Anything can start it, any conversational route can suddenly take a swerve that'll lead us down a warpath. We fight about the most standard and the most unlikely subjects: the value of exercise and the proper diet, the implications of China's Cultural Revolution, whether photography is a form of violence, and whether all families are intrinsically repressive. In the conversation of my friends, I sniff out cultural clichés like a hound on the scent of hostile quarry. An innocent remark like "Well, I don't know what to tell you, it really depends on how you feel" provokes in me the most bitter reflections on American individualism, and how a laissez-faire tolerance can mask a callous indifference. Behind the phrase "You've got to stay in control," thrown in as a conversational filler, I vengefully detect an ironical repression on the part of those who hate repression most. In the counternorms my peers profess, I perceive the structure of the norms they ostensibly reject, inverted like an underwater reflection, but still recognizable.

5      Much of the time, I'm in a rage: Immigrant rage, I call it, and it can erupt at any moment, and at seemingly minuscule provocation. It's directed with equal force at "the Culture"—that weird artifice I'm imprisoned in—and at my closest friends. Or rather, it's directed at the culture-in-my-friends. My misfortune is to see the grid of general assumptions drawn all over particular personalities, to notice the subjection to collective ideology where I should only see the free play of subjectivity. In the most ordinary, interstitial gestures—secretiveness about money, or a reluctance to let sadness show—I sense the tyranny of subliminal conventions. Where my friends suppose they're voicing their deepest beliefs, I whiff the dogma of intellectual fashion; in the midst of a discussion, I cease seeing the face of one person, and start throwing myself against the wall of an invisible, impregnable, collective force.

6      In Peter Schneider's novel, *The Wall Jumper*, the West German narrator has an East German girlfriend named Lena. Lena has chosen to live on the Western side of the Berlin Wall, but she's severe about what she sees there. When her boyfriend happens to glance at a cover of *Playboy*, she accuses him of decadence, and when he cracks jokes with friends in a bar, she scowls at their triviality. She thinks the West Germans' politics are frivolous, and their pleasures vapid. Her boyfriend sees how much she suffers from this hypersensitivity; for a while, he admires her severity; but finally, it drives him away.

7      I know what I'm supposed to think of Lena, but I identify with her. I think she's in the right. I want more severe standards of seriousness to obtain. In other words, I'm a scourge.

8      I think I also know the cause of Lena's defensiveness and seeming arrogance: It's that her version of things is automatically under suspicion and at a discount. That's the real subtext of my fights, the piercing provocation behind the trivial ones. My sense of reality, powerful and vulnerable, is in danger of coming under native domination. My interlocutors in these collisions stare at me with incre-

dulity or dismay; what am I getting so worked up about? They, after all, are only having a conversation. They don't want to question every sentence they speak, and they don't need to; the mass of shared conviction is so thick as to constitute an absoluteness, a reality of a kind. They explain politely and firmly where I'm wrong. Or they become goaded to anger themselves. At parties, my demurrals are often greeted with plain silence, as if they didn't need to be entertained. This increases my frustration, my ire, still more. Censorship in the living room, I mutter to myself bitterly, and after a while begin to censor myself.

"If you've never eaten a real tomato, you'll think that the plastic tomato is    9 the real thing, and moreover, you'll be perfectly satisfied with it," I tell my friends. "It's only when you've tasted them both that you know there's a difference, even though it's almost impossible to describe." This turns out to be the most persuasive argument I have. My friends are moved by the parable of the plastic tomato. But when I try to apply it, by analogy, to the internal realm, they balk. Surely, inside our heads and souls things are more universal, the ocean of reality one and indivisible. No, I shout in every one of our arguments, no! There's a world out there; there are worlds. There are shapes of sensibility incommensurate with each other, topographies of experience one cannot guess from within one's own limited experience.

I think my friends often suspect me of a perverse refusal to play along, an   10 unaccountable desire to provoke and disturb their comfortable consensus. I suspect that the consensus is trying to colonize me and rob me of my distinctive shape and flavor. Still, I have to come to terms with it somehow. Now that I'm no longer a visitor, I can no longer ignore the terms of reality prevailing here, or sit on the margins observing the curious habits of the natives. I have to learn how to live with them, find a common ground. It is my fear that I have to yield too much of my own ground that fills me with such a passionate energy of rage.

**My American Friend:** What did you think about that Hungarian movie last week?

**I:** I thought it was quite powerful.

**M.A.F.:** Me too. It was a very smart comment on how all of us can get co-opted by institutions.

**I:** But it wasn't about all of us. It was about the Communist party in Hungary circa 1948.

**M.A.F.:** Collaboration isn't the monopoly of the Communist party, you know. You can be bought and co-opted by Time, Inc., quite successfully.

**I:** I think there may be just the tiniest difference between those two organizations.

**M.A.F.:** You with your liberal quibbles. I don't think your eyes have been opened about this country.

**I:** For heaven's sake, don't you understand what went on over there? That people got imprisoned, tortured, hanged?

**M.A.F.:** Don't get so upset, this was a Hungarian movie. You don't have to be loyal to all of Eastern Europe.

**I:** I'm loyal to some notion of accuracy, which is more than I can say for you! The world isn't just a protection screen for your ideas, highly correct though they may be.

**M.A.F.:** I'm allowed to have my interpretation of the world. That's called theory, for your information.

**I:** That's called not thinking, as far as I can see. You're not allowed to let theory blind you to all distinctions.

**M.A.F.:** Spare me your sarcasm. Just because awful things happened over there doesn't mean that awful things don't happen here. You like to exaggerate these distinctions, as if you wanted to keep yourself apart.

**I:** This is not a psychological issue!

**M.A.F.:** On some level, everything is.

**I:** This makes me want to emigrate.

**M.A.F.:** Feel free.


**I:** How are things going with Doug?

**M.A.F.:** Terrible. We fuck each other blind, and then he won't tell his wife that we're involved.

**I:** I imagine that'd be hard to do.

**M.A.F.:** Why?

**I:** Why! Haven't you ever heard of possessiveness? Jealousy?

**M.A.F.:** Yes, I've heard about them. I just don't think they're natural instincts that we're supposed to accept as sacred. They may have served some purpose in the Paleozoic era, but we aren't running around being hunters and gatherers anymore, if you've noticed.

**I:** Yes, I've noticed. I've also noticed that we continue to be possessive and jealous.

**M.A.F.:** You know, you're becoming a perfect bourgeois.

**I:** And you're turning into a Stalinist of everyday life. You're not supposed to be jealous, you're not supposed to be guilty, you're supposed to get in touch with your anger. . . . What is this, some kind of internal morality squad?

**M.A.F.:** I'm beginning to suspect that you're threatened because I fuck a lot.

**I:** As far as I'm concerned, you're welcome to have as many affairs as you like.

**M.A.F.:** You see, you can't even say fuck.

**I:** I can say fuck very well, thank you.

**M.A.F.:** Why are you getting so hostile?

**I:** Because I believe you're attacking me.

**M.A.F.:** *I'm* attacking *you?*

**I:** I don't like being on trial for my vocabulary.

**M.A.F.:** You've been dripping disdain during this whole conversation. You've got me pegged as some naïve American country bumpkin.

**I:** I think you pretend to innocence. Some things are perfectly self-explanatory, you know.

**M.A.F.:** Nothing is, unless you're a reactionary.

**I:** I can't stand this!

**M.A.F.:** Believe me, the feeling is mutual.

The dialogues don't end, though, with our going off in a huff, or with whatever   11
tentative resolutions we're willing to settle for. Afterward, as I walk down the
street hardly conscious of my surroundings, or at night as I toss on my bed, the
furious conflicts continue to rage within my own head. The opposing voices
become mine, and each of them is ready to lacerate the other. In one of them,
I'm ready to dismiss all of American Culture as a misconceived experiment.
Scornfully, I think there's too much reinventing of the wheel going on around
here. The wheel has already been invented, why bother again? There's too much
surprise at the fact that the earth is round, and too much insistence the sun may
be moving around us after all. My American Friends think privileged thoughts,
I think bitterly, thoughts that cost nothing and that weren't produced by the
labor of their own experience. Surplus thoughts that do not have to be paid for
in consequences either. Do they, in their own private triangulations, in their
night accountings with themselves, believe that a marital squabble has causes
too deep for analysis, or that jealousy can be eliminated by ideological fiat, or
that the revolution is just around the corner? It is in my incapacity to imagine
my friends' private thoughts that the gap between us continues to exist. I can't
enter sufficiently into their souls to know where conviction stops and self-
presentation begins. Certainly, my American Friends do not deliberately say
things they believe to be untrue in order to make themselves look better or
somebody else look worse. Hypocrisy, that old-fashioned and un-American vice,
requires a public ideal of virtue to pretend to; it also needs the certainty of ego
to do the pretending effectively. For all their many certainties, my friends don't
seem to have that toughness, or hiddenness, which would enable them to pay
lip service to the proper pieties while keeping their true opinions to themselves.
The dance of personality happens differently here, and the ideal of personal
sincerity—supplanting common virtues, perhaps—is deeply ingrained. My
friends want, sincerely, to believe what they would like to believe. But I wonder
how much leeway that leaves for a willful self-deception—that subtle falseness
that the self only half-knows. "We French lie to others. Americans lie to
themselves," a Frenchman I know once remarks, and sometimes I think that my
friends' desire to possess only the best ideas prevents them from knowing which
ideas are really theirs.

12    But when the full force of my disapproval is spent, the dialogue with myself takes a U-turn, and I remember that my rage is an immigrant's rage, my suspiciousness the undignified, blinding suspiciousness of an outsider. Then I try, fairly, to think from the other point of view, to stand on the other end of the triangle's base. What's going on here, I think, is a new version of the grand Emersonian experiment, the perennial American experiment, which consists precisely of reinventing the wheel, of taking nothing for granted and beholding human nature with a primeval curiosity, as though nothing has ever been observed or thought before. This is the spirit that invented the cotton gin and Whitman's free verse, and the open marriage. My American Friends are just running a few theoretical experiments on themselves—but why should they do otherwise, since so little in their condition is given, and so little is forbidden either? They live in a culture which is still young, and in which the codes and conventions are still up for grabs. Since there are no rules for how to be a lover, they need to figure out the dynamics of an affair as if it were a complicated problem in physics, and their minds grow new muscles in the process. My American Friends have gained insights about the human mechanism they may never have come by if they had not needed to ask the most rudimentary questions about love and anger and sex. Their explorations are a road to a new, instead of an ancestral, wisdom—a wisdom that may be awkward and ungainly, as youthful wisdom is, but that is required in a world whose social, if not physical, frontiers are still fluid and open and incompletely charted.

13    Theodor Adorno, that most vitriolic of America's foreign critics, once warned his fellow refugees that if they lost their alienation, they'd lose their souls. A bracingly uncompromising idea of integrity: but I doubt that Adorno could have maintained it over a lifetime without the hope of returning home— without having a friendly audience back there for his dialectical satires. The soul can shrivel from an excess of crucial distance, and if I don't want to remain in arid internal exile for the rest of my life, I have to find a way to lose my alienation without losing my self. But how does one bend toward another culture without falling over, how does one strike an elastic balance between rigidity and self-effacement? How does one stop reading the exterior signs of a foreign tribe and step into the inwardness, the viscera of their meanings? Every anthropologist understands the difficulty of such a feat; and so does every immigrant.

14    It is no wonder—in our time of mass migrations and culture collisions and easy jet travel, when the whole world lies below us every time we rise into the skies, when whole countries move by like bits of checkerboard, ours to play on—it's no wonder that in this time we've developed whole philosophies of cultural relativity, and learned to look at whole literatures, histories, and cultural formations as if they were toy blocks, ours to construct and deconstruct. It's no wonder, also, that we have devised a whole metaphysics for the subjects of difference and otherness. But for all our sophisticated deftness at cross-cultural encounters, fundamental difference, when it's staring at you across the table from within the close-up face of a fellow human being, always contains an

element of violation. My American Friends and I find it an offense to our respective identities to touch within each other something alien, unfamiliar, in the very woof and warp of our inner lives. I suppose we could—following one kind of philosophy—adopt an attitude of benevolent openness to each other, and declare our differences interesting and beautiful; but such mellow tolerance is easier to maintain with, say, an Indian swami, who remains safely exotic, and doesn't intend to become our personal friend. Or, adhering to a later, and more skeptical philosophical fashion, we could accept each other's irreducible otherness and give up on our nettlesome and painful back and forth. We could declare each other products of different cultures—as we, of course, are—and leave it, respectfully, at that. But that would leave us separate and impermeable—something that is easier to accept with impersonal entities like class, or gender, or country than with a fellow human being clamoring to be understood.

My American Friends and I are forced to engage in an experiment that is 15 relatively rare; we want to enter into the very textures, the motions and flavors of each other's vastly different subjectivities—and that requires feats of sympathy and even imagination in excess of either benign indifference or a remote respect.

Of course, in these entanglements, our positions are not exactly symmetri- 16 cal. In the politics of daily perception, I'm at a distinct disadvantage. My American Friends are so many, and they share so many assumptions that are quite invisible to them, precisely because they're shared. These are assumptions about the most fundamental human transactions, subcutaneous beliefs, which lie just below the stratum of political opinion or overt ideology: about how much "space," physical or psychological, we need to give each other, about how much "control" is desirable, about what is private and what public, about how much interest in another person's affairs is sympathy and how much interference, about what's a pretty face or a handsome body, about what we're allowed to poke fun at and what we have to revere, about how much we need to hide in order to reveal ourselves. To remain outside such common agreements is to remain outside reality itself—and if I'm not to risk a mild cultural schizophrenia, I have to make a shift in the innermost ways. I have to translate myself. But if I'm to achieve this without becoming assimilated—that is, absorbed—by my new world, the translation has to be careful, the turns of the psyche unforced. To mouth foreign terms without incorporating their meanings is to risk becoming bowdlerized. A true translation proceeds by the motions of understanding and sympathy; it happens by slow increments, sentence by sentence, phrase by phrase.

Does it still matter, in these triangulations, that my version of reality was formed 17 in Eastern Europe? It is well known that the System over there, by specializing in deceit, has bred in its citizens an avid hunger for what they still quaintly call the truth. Of course, the truth is easier to identify when it's simply the opposite of a lie. So much Eastern European thinking moves along the axis of bipolar ideas, still untouched by the peculiar edginess and fluidity created by a more decentered world. Perhaps I'm not quite equal to the challenge of postmodern uncertainty. But as I wrestle with the American Friend in my head, I am haunted not by a longing for certainty but by the idea, almost palpable, of the normal. The normal, in my mental ideogram, is associated with a face: Pani Ruta's face, perhaps, or Piotr Ostropov's. It's not an innocent, or a particularly cheerful face; it bespeaks, instead, both a quick perspicacity and an unforced seriousness. *"C'est normale,"* the expression on this face says. *"N'exagères pas."* It's a face that has seen a lot, and is not easily astonished. It knows, in its cultural memory, the limits of human ideals, and the limitations of human passions. Foibles, in its steady gaze, are just that: foibles. It's not apt to work itself up into moral heat or analytic anguish. It has a stored knowledge, passed on through generations, of the devious traceries of the human heart, and it has learned where the mean lies in the soul, and what's excess. The normal is derived not from a conventional norm but from this knowledge of proportion. The face expresses a skepticism that is a hair's breadth away from cynicism, but is also adjacent to an acceptance of things as they are, and not as they should be or might be in a more ideal, a nonhuman world.

18    I think if I could enter the subjectivity of that face, then I could encompass both myself and my American Friend within it. I could then see our polarities within some larger, more capacious terms, and resolve our antitheses within a wiser synthesis. I could see that we're both—as the phrase echoes from my childhood—just human. It's that face that I keep as a beacon in my furious mono-dialogues and my triangulations. I want a language that will express what that face knows, a calm and simple language that will subsume the clangor of specialized jargons and of partial visions, a language old enough to plow under the superficial differences between signs, to the deeper strata of significance.

19    My Japanese friend gets angry at different things than I; it's bank clerks and salespeople in department stores who ignite his rage. They are so rude, he says, they mumble and ignore you, and since he is very polite and doesn't like to put himself forward, he just stands there, waiting to be noticed. Inside, though, he's seething.

20    My Japanese friend loves America. He came here because he felt innately mismatched with the Japanese weltanschauung. "You know how the Japanese control their emotions," he says. "Well, I was always very good at expressing myself. I think that much control is weird." But then, he finds himself getting angry at salespeople and bank clerks, and particularly, when they violate one of his rules of decorum, at his friends. "And then I hate myself," he tells me with a kind of perplexity.

21    I don't understand why it's rude salespeople who set my Japanese friend off. Most people around here seem quite polite to me. What's he getting so worked up about? I try to triangulate in an entirely different direction, somewhere to the far east of my usual points of reference. I know that to him, I'm often a puzzle, and that in his mind, all of Eastern Europe is a small abstract cluster

somewhere to the west of his imagination. Suddenly, I see us both as figures in a burlesque, running about and waving our hands on a stage grown too circumscribed and crowded for anyone on it to take himself very seriously. The drama of intercultural clash, repeated often enough, becomes a farce. Perhaps a computer species would be more appropriate to our overpopulated world. Computer people wouldn't have so much ego, which might have been suitable to a midsized country but loses all persuasiveness in a global village. In our new situation, they would comport themselves with less fuss and more innate dignity.

How far this is from Cracow, from the time when shadows moving across the    22
ceiling sufficed for the world, because I was without question its absolute center. We're called upon to travel so far beyond our borders, but neither my Japanese friend nor I can divest ourselves of those irrational, instinctive reactions that we take to be our personalities, our selves. To do so would be to jump outside the borders of our skin. How, with this bifocal vision, does one keep one's center? And what center should one try to keep? The cherishing of our particularity seems as outmoded as the wearing of many skirts. And yet, so long as we are not computer species, we cannot give up on our subjectivity, our ability to experience. Sometimes I see what I need: an objective subjectivity, a laser beam that concentrates my energy, and uses the collected light to illuminate and reflect the world.  ✠

---

## RESPONDING

1.  Hoffman discusses some assumptions about fundamental human transactions and beliefs (see paragraph 16). In a journal entry, describe your attitude toward personal space, control, beauty, humor, and so forth.

2.  Share your journal entries with the class or with a small group. Is there an "American" way of behaving? Do different cultures have different ways of responding in social situations? If there is an "American" culture, is it uniform, or are there subcultures within American culture that have different perspectives than the mainstream?

3.  Hoffman calls herself a "mild cultural schizophrenic" (paragraph 16) who has to translate herself without becoming assimilated. In an essay, discuss the conflicts she faces in trying to reconcile her old and new cultures.

4.  During the past century, circumstances have changed for immigrants to the United States. Unlike immigrants who arrived in the late 1800s or early 1900s, recent immigrants to the United States can maintain ties with their home countries. These connections enable them to keep their native identity and reject assimilation. Write an essay discussing the benefits and

disadvantages of keeping a native language and culture while living in a new country. Support your statements with examples from the readings and from your own knowledge and experience as well as that of your friends.

# Francis Fukuyama

*Francis Fukuyama was born in Chicago in 1952; he received his bachelor's degree from Cornell University in 1974 and a doctorate in political science from Harvard University in 1981. After holding research positions at the RAND Corporation and in government, Fukuyama taught at the University of California, Los Angeles, before becoming the Omer L. and Nancy Hirst Professor of Public Policy at George Mason University. His publications include* The End of History and the Last Man *(1992),* Trust: Social Values and the Creation of Prosperity *(1995), and* The Great Disruption: Human Nature and the Reconstitution of Social Order *(1999), as well as articles in a number of journals.*

*Fukuyama's essay, "Immigrants and Family Values," first published in* The Nation, *compares what the author considers the value systems of our nation's newest immigrants to the value systems of those who purport to speak for their concerns. In so doing, Fukuyama also challenges "multicultural approaches" to education, which he believes are detrimental to newcomers' chances for success.*

❖

# IMMIGRANTS AND FAMILY VALUES

1   AT THE REPUBLICAN CONVENTION in Houston last August [1992], Patrick J. Buchanan announced the coming of a block-by-block war to "take back our culture." Buchanan is right that a cultural war is upon us, and that this fight will be a central American preoccupation now that the cold war is over. What he understands less well, however, is that the vast majority of the non-European immigrants who have come into this country in the past couple of decades are not the enemy. Indeed, many of them are potentially on his side.

2   Conservatives have for long been sharply divided on the question of immigration. Many employers and proponents of free-market economics, like Julian Simon or the editorial page of the *Wall Street Journal*, are strongly pro-immigration; they argue for open borders because immigrants are a source of cheap labor and ultimately create more wealth than they consume. Buchanan and other traditional right-wing Republicans, by contrast, represent an older nativist po-

sition. They dispute the economic benefits of immigration, but more importantly look upon immigrants as bearers of foreign and less desirable cultural values. It is this group of conservatives who forced the inclusion of a plank in the Republican platform last August calling for the creation of "structures" to maintain the integrity of America's southern border.

Indeed, hostility to immigration has made for peculiar bedfellows. The [3] Clinton administration's difficulties in finding an attorney general who had not at some point hired an illegal-immigrant babysitter is testimony to the objective dependence of liberal yuppies on immigration to maintain their life-styles, and they by and large would support the *Wall Street Journal*'s open-borders position.

On the other hand, several parts of the liberal coalition—blacks and envi- [4] ronmentalists—have been increasingly vocal in recent years in opposition to further immigration, particularly from Latin America. The Black Leadership Forum, headed by Coretta Scott King and Congressman Walter Fauntroy, has lobbied to maintain sanctions against employers hiring illegal immigrant labor on the ground that this takes away jobs from blacks and "legal" browns. Jack Miles, a former *Los Angeles Times* book-review editor with impeccable liberal credentials, has in a recent article in the *Atlantic* lined up with the Federation for American Immigration Reform (FAIR) in calling for a rethinking of open borders, while liberal activist groups like the Southern California Interfaith Task Force on Central America have supported Senator Orrin Hatch's legislation strengthening employer sanctions. Environmental groups like the Sierra Club, for their part, oppose immigration because it necessitates economic growth, use of natural resources, and therefore environmental degradation.

But if much of the liberal opposition to immigration has focused on eco- [5] nomic issues, the conservative opposition has concentrated on the deeper cultural question; and here the arguments made by the Right are very confused. The symptoms of cultural decay are all around us, but the last people in the world we should be blaming are recent immigrants.

## II

The most articulate and reasoned recent conservative attack on immigration [6] came last summer in an article in *National Review* by Peter Brimelow. Brimelow, a senior editor at *Forbes* and himself a naturalized American of British and Canadian background, argues that immigration worked in the past in America only because earlier waves of nativist backlash succeeded in limiting it to a level that could be successfully assimilated into the dominant Anglo-Saxon American culture. Brimelow criticizes pro-immigration free-marketeers like Julian Simon for ignoring the issue of the skill levels of the immigrant labor force, and their likely impact on blacks and others at the bottom end of the economic ladder. But his basic complaint is a cultural one. Attacking the *Wall Street Journal*'s Paul Gigot for remarking that a million Zulus would probably work harder than a million Englishmen today, Brimelow notes:

This comment reveals an utter innocence about the reality of ethnic and cultural differences, let alone little things like tradition and history—in short, the greater part of the conservative vision. Even in its own purblind terms, it is totally false. All the empirical evidence is that immigrants from developed countries assimilate better than those from underdeveloped countries. It is developed countries that teach the skills required for success in the United States . . . it should not be necessary to explain that the legacy of [the Zulu kings] Shaka and Cetewayo—overthrown just over a century ago—is not that of Alfred the Great, let alone Elizabeth II or any civilized society.

7    Elsewhere, Brimelow suggests that culture is a key determinant of economic performance, and that people from certain cultures are therefore likely to do less well economically than others. He implies, furthermore, that some immigrants are more prone to random street crime because of their "impulsiveness and present-orientation," while others are responsible for organized crime which is, by his account, ethnically based. Finally, Brimelow argues that the arrival of diverse non-European cultures fosters the present atmosphere of multiculturalism, and is, to boot, bad for the electoral prospects of the Republican party.

8    A similar line of thought runs through Buchanan's writings and speeches, and leads to a similar anti-immigrant posture. Buchanan has explicitly attacked the notion that democracy represents a particularly positive form of government, and hence would deny that belief in universal democratic principles ought to be at the core of the American national identity.[1] But if one subtracts democracy from American nationality, what is left? Apparently, though Buchanan is somewhat less explicit on this point, a concept of America as a Christian, ethnically European nation with certain core cultural values that are threatened by those coming from other cultures and civilizations.

9    There is an easy, Civics 101–type answer to the Brimelow-Buchanan argument. In contrast to other West European democracies, or Japan, the American national identity has never been directly linked to ethnicity or religion. Nationality has been based instead on universal concepts like freedom and equality that are in theory open to all people. Our Constitution forbids the establishment of religion, and the legal system has traditionally held ethnicity at arm's length. To be an American has meant to be committed to a certain set of ideas, and not to be descended from an original tribe of ur-Americans. Those elements of a common American culture visible today—belief in the Constitution and the individualist-egalitarian principles underlying it, plus modern American pop and consumer culture—are universally accessible and appealing, making the United States, in Ben Wattenberg's phrase, the first "universal nation."

---

1. See, for example, his article, "America First—and Second, and Third," *The National Interest*, Spring 1990.

This argument is correct as far as it goes, but there is a serious counterar-  10
gument that reaches to the core of last year's debate over "family values." It
runs as follows: America began living up to its universalist principles only in the
last half of this century. For most of the period from its revolutionary founding
to its rise as a great, modern, industrial power, the nation's elites conceived of
the country not just as a democracy based on universal principles, but also as a
Christian, Anglo-Saxon nation.

American democracy—the counterargument continues—is, of course, em-  11
bodied in the laws and institutions of the country, and will be imbibed by anyone
who learns to play by its rules. But virtually every serious theorist of American
democracy has noted that its success depended heavily on the presence of certain
pre-democratic values or cultural characteristics that were neither officially
sanctioned nor embodied in law. If the Declaration of Independence and the
Constitution were the basis of America's *Gesellschaft* (society), Christian Anglo-
Saxon culture constituted its *Gemeinschaft* (community).

Indeed—the counterargument goes on—the civic institutions that Toc-  12
queville observed in the 1830's, whose strength and vitality he saw as a critical
manifestation of the Americans' "art of associating," were more often than not
of a religious (i.e., Christian) nature, devoted to temperance, moral education
of the young, or the abolition of slavery. There is nothing in the Constitution
which states that parents should make large sacrifices for their children, that
workers should rise early in the morning and labor long hours in order to get
ahead, that people should emulate rather than undermine their neighbors'
success, that they should be innovative, entrepreneurial, or open to technological
change. Yet Americans, formed by a Christian culture, possessed these traits in
abundance for much of their history, and the country's economic prosperity and
social cohesion arguably rested on them.

It is this sort of consideration that underlay the family-values controversy  13
during last year's election. Basic to this line of thought is that, all other things
being equal, children are better off when raised in stable, two-parent, heterosexual families. Such family structures and the web of moral obligations they
entail are the foundation of educational achievement, economic success, good
citizenship, personal character, and a host of other social virtues.

The issue of family values was badly mishandled by the Republicans and  14
deliberately misconstrued by the press and the Democrats (often not distinguishable), such that mere mention of the phrase provoked derisive charges of
narrow-minded gay-bashing and hostility to single mothers. Yet while many
Americans did not sign on to last year's family-values theme, few would deny
that the family and community are in deep crisis today. The breakdown of the
black family in inner-city neighborhoods around America in the past couple of
generations shows in particularly stark form the societal consequences of a loss
of certain cultural values. And what has happened among blacks is only an
extreme extension of a process that has been proceeding apace among whites as
well.

15    The issue, then, is not whether the questions of culture and cultural values are important, or whether it is legitimate to raise them, but whether immigration really threatens those values. For while the values one might deem central either to economic success or to social cohesion may have arisen out of a Christian, Anglo-Saxon culture, it is clear that they are not bound to that particular social group: some groups, like Jews and Asians, might come to possess those values in abundance, while WASPs [White Anglo-Saxon Protestants] themselves might lose them and decay. The question thus becomes: which ethnic groups in today's America are threatening, and which groups are promoting, these core cultural values?

### III

16    The notion that non-European immigrants are a threat to family values and other core American cultural characteristics is, in a way, quite puzzling. After all, the breakdown of traditional family structures, from extended to nuclear, has long been understood to be a disease of advanced industrial countries and not of nations just emerging from their agricultural pasts.

17    Some conservatives tend to see the Third World as a vast, global underclass, teeming with the same social pathologies as Compton in Los Angeles or Bedford-Stuyvesant in Brooklyn. But the sad fact is that the decay of basic social relationships evident in American inner cities, stretching to the most intimate moral bonds linking parents and children, may well be something with few precedents in human history. Economic conditions in most Third World countries simply would not permit a social group suffering so total a collapse of family structure to survive: with absent fathers and no source of income, or mothers addicted to drugs, children would not live to adulthood.

18    But it would also seem a priori likely that Third-World immigrants should have stronger family values than white, middle-class, suburban Americans, while their work ethic and willingness to defer to traditional sources of authority should be greater as well. Few of the factors that have led to family breakdown in the American middle class over the past couple of generations—rapidly changing economic conditions, with their attendant social disruptions; the rise of feminism and the refusal of women to play traditional social roles; or the legitimization of alternative life-styles and consequent proliferation of rights and entitlements on a retail level—apply in Third-World situations. Immigrants coming from traditional developing societies are likely to be poorer, less educated, and in possession of fewer skills than those from Europe, but they are also likely to have stronger family structures and moral inhibitions. Moreover, despite the greater ease of moving to America today than in the last century, immigrants are likely to be a self-selecting group with a much greater than average degree of energy, ambition, toughness, and adaptability.

19    These intuitions are largely borne out by the available empirical data, particularly if one disaggregates the different parts of the immigrant community.

The strength of traditional family values is most evident among immigrants from East and South Asia, where mutually supportive family structures have long been credited as the basis for their economic success. According to Census Bureau statistics, 78% of Asian and Pacific Islander households in the United States were family households, as opposed to 70% for white Americans. The size of these family households is likely to be larger: 74% consist of three or more persons, compared to 57% for white families. While Asians are equally likely to be married as whites, they are only half as likely to be divorced.[2] Though dropping off substantially in the second and third generations, concern for elderly parents is high in Chinese, Japanese, and Vietnamese households; for many, the thought of sticking a mother or father out of sight and out of mind in a nursing home continues to be anathema. More importantly, most of the major Asian immigrant groups are intent on rapid assimilation into the American mainstream, and have not been particularly vocal in pressing for particularistic cultural entitlements.

While most white Americans are ready to recognize and celebrate the social strengths of Asians, the real fears of cultural invasion surround Latinos. Despite their fast growth, Asians still constitute less than 3% of the U.S. population, while the number of Hispanics increased from 14.6 to over 22 million between 1980 and 1990, or 9% of the population. But here as well, the evidence suggests that most Latin American immigrants may be a source of strength with regard to family values, and not a liability.

Latinos today constitute an extremely diverse group. It is certainly the case that a segment of the Latino community has experienced many of the same social problems as blacks. This is particularly true of the first large Latino community in the U.S.: Puerto Ricans who came to the mainland in the early postwar period and settled predominantly in New York and other cities of the Northeast. Forty percent of Puerto Rican families are headed by women, compared to 16% for the non-Hispanic population; only 57% of Puerto Rican households consist of families, while their rate of out-of-wedlock births is almost double the rate for non-Hispanics. In New York, Puerto Ricans have re-exported social pathologies like crack-cocaine use to Puerto Rico over the past generation.

Other Latino groups have also brought social problems with them: the Mariel boat lift from Cuba, during which Castro emptied his country's jails and insane asylums, had a measurable impact on crime in the U.S. Many war-hardened immigrants from El Salvador and other unstable Central American countries have contributed to crime in the U.S., and Chicano gangs in Los Angeles and other Southwestern cities have achieved their own notoriety beside the black Bloods and Crips. Half of those arrested in the Los Angeles riot last year were Latinos.

Such facts are highly visible and contribute to the impression among white

2. Census Bureau Press Release CB92-89, "Profile of Asians and Pacific Islanders."

Americans that Latinos as a whole have joined inner-city blacks to form one vast, threatening underclass. But there are very significant differences among Latino groups. Latinos of Cuban and Mexican origin, for example, who together constitute 65% of the Hispanic community, have a 50% lower rate of female-headed households than do Puerto Ricans—18.9% and 19.6% versus 38.9%. While the rate of Puerto Rican out-of-wedlock births approaches that of blacks (53.0% vs. 63.1% of live births), the rates for Cuban and Mexican-origin Latinos are much lower, 16.1 and 28.9%, respectively, though they are still above the white rate of 13.9%.[3]

25      When looked at in the aggregate, Latino family structure stands somewhere between that of whites and blacks. For example, the rates of female-headed families with no husband present as a proportion of total families is 13.5% for whites, 46.4% for blacks, and 24.4% for Hispanics. If we adjust these figures for income level, however, Hispanics turn out to be much closer to the white norm.

26      Poverty is hard on families regardless of race; part of the reason for the higher percentage of Latino female-headed households is simply that there are more poor Latino families. If we compare families below the poverty level, the Hispanic rate of female-headed families is very close to that of whites (45.7% vs. 43.6%), while the comparable rate for blacks is much higher than either (78.3%). Considering the substantially higher rate of family breakdown within the sizable Puerto Rican community, this suggests that the rate of single-parent families for Cuban- and Mexican-origin Latinos is actually lower than that for whites at a comparable income level.

27      Moreover, Latinos as a group are somewhat more likely to be members of families than either whites or blacks.[4] Another study indicates that Mexican-Americans have better family demographics than do whites, with higher birthweight babies even among low-income mothers due to taboos on smoking, drinking, and drug use during pregnancy. Many Latinos remain devout Catholics, and the rate of church attendance is higher in the Mexican community than for the U.S. as a whole as well. But even if one does not believe that the United States is a "Christian country," the fact that so many immigrants are from Catholic Latin America should make them far easier to assimilate than, say, Muslims in Europe.

28      These statistics are broadly in accord with the observations of anyone who has lived in Los Angeles, San Diego, or any other community in the American Southwest. Virtually every early-morning commuter in Los Angeles knows the street-corners on which Chicano day-laborers gather at 7:00 A.M., looking for work as gardeners, busboys, or on construction sites. Many of them are illegal

---

3. Data taken from Linda Chavez, *Out of the Barrio* (Basic Books, 1991), p. 103.
4. Figures taken from *Poverty in the United States: 1991*, Bureau of the Census, Series P-60, no. 181, pp. 7–9; the percentage of people in families for whites, blacks, and Hispanics is 84.5, 84.8, and 89.0, respectively (pp. 2–3).

immigrants with families back in Mexico to whom they send their earnings. While they are poor and unskilled, they have a work ethic and devotion to family comparable to those of the South and East European immigrants who came to the U.S. at the turn of the century. It is much less common to see African-Americans doing this sort of thing.

Those who fear Third-World immigration as a threat to Anglo-American cultural values do not seem to have noticed what the real sources of cultural breakdown have been. To some extent, they can be traced to broad socioeco-nomic factors over which none of us has control: the fluid, socially disruptive nature of capitalism; technological change; economic pressures of the contem-porary workplace and urban life; and so on. But the ideological assault on traditional family values—the sexual revolution; feminism and the delegitimiza-tion of the male-dominated household; the celebration of alternative life-styles; attempts ruthlessly to secularize all aspects of American public life; the accep-tance of no-fault divorce and the consequent rise of single-parent households— was not the creation of recently-arrived Chicano agricultural workers or Haitian boat people, much less of Chinese or Korean immigrants. They originated right in the heart of America's well-established white, Anglo-Saxon community. The "Hollywood elite" that created the now celebrated *Murphy Brown*, much like the establishment "media elite" that Republicans enjoy attacking, does not represent either the values or the interests of most recent Third-World immi-grants.

In short, though the old, traditional culture continues to exist in the United States, it is over-laid today with an elite culture that espouses very different values. The real danger is not that these elites will become corrupted by the habits and practices of Third-World immigrants, but rather that the immigrants will become corrupted by them. And that is in fact what tends to happen.

While the first generation of immigrants to the United States tends to be deferential to established authority and preoccupied with the economic prob-lems of "making it," their children and grandchildren become aware of their own entitlements and rights, more politicized, and able to exploit the political system to defend and expand those entitlements. While the first generation is willing to work quietly at minimum- or subminimum-wage jobs, the second and third generations have higher expectations as to what their labor is worth. The extension of welfare and other social benefits to noncitizens through a series of court decisions has had the perverse effect of hastening the spread of welfare dependency. Part of the reason that Puerto Ricans do less well than other Latino groups may be that they were never really immigrants at all, but U.S. citizens, and therefore eligible for social benefits at a very early stage.[5]

As Julian Simon has shown, neither the absolute nor the relative levels of

29

30

31

32

---

5. Spain ceded Puerto Rico to the U.S. at the conclusion of the Spanish-American War (1898), at which point the island became a U.S. territory; its residents were granted U.S. citizenship in 1917; in 1952, the Commonwealth of Puerto Rico was proclaimed.

immigration over the past decade have been inordinately high by historical standards. What is different and very troubling about immigration in the present period is that the ideology that existed at the turn of the century and promoted assimilation into the dominant Anglo-Saxon culture has been replaced by a multicultural one that legitimates and even promotes continuing cultural differentness.

33     The intellectual and social origins of multiculturalism are complex, but one thing is clear: it is both a Western and an American invention. The American Founding was based on certain Enlightenment notions of the universality of human equality and freedom, but such ideas have been under attack within the Western tradition itself for much of the past two centuries. The second half of the late Allan Bloom's *The Closing of the American Mind* (the part that most buyers of the book skipped over) chronicles the way in which the relativist ideas of Nietzsche and Heidegger were transported to American shores at mid-century. Combined with an easygoing American egalitarianism, they led not just to a belief in the need for cultural tolerance, but to a positive assertion of the equal moral validity of all cultures. Today the writings of Michel Foucault, a French epigone of Nietzsche, have become the highbrow source of academic multiculturalism.

34     France may have produced Foucault, but France has not implemented a multicultural educational curriculum to anything like the degree the U.S. has. The origins of multiculturalism here must therefore be traced to the specific circumstances of American social life. Contrary to the arguments of multiculturalism's promoters, it was not a necessary adjustment to the reality of our pluralistic society. The New York City public-school system in the year 1910 was as diverse as it is today, and yet it never occurred to anyone to celebrate and preserve the native cultures of the city's Italians, Greeks, Poles, Jews, or Chinese.

35     The shift in attitudes toward cultural diversity can be traced to the aftermath of the civil-rights movement, when it became clear that integration was not working for blacks. The failure to assimilate was interpreted as an indictment of the old, traditional mainstream Anglo-Saxon culture: "WASP" took on a pejorative connotation, and African-Americans began to take pride in the separateness of their own traditions. Ironically, the experience of African-Americans became the model for subsequent immigrant groups like Latinos who could have integrated themselves into mainstream society as easily as the Italians or Poles before them.

36     It is true that Hispanic organizations now constitute part of the multiculturalist coalition and have been very vocal in pushing for bilingual/bicultural education. There is increasing evidence, however, that rank-and-file immigrants are much more traditionally assimilationist than some of their more vocal leaders. For example, most Chinese and Russian immigrant parents in New York City deliberately avoid sending their children to the bilingual-education classes offered to them by the public-school system, believing that a cold plunge into

English will be a much more effective means of learning to function in American society.

Hispanics generally show more support for bilingual education, but even here a revealing recent study indicates that an overwhelming number of Hispanic parents see bilingualism primarily as a means of learning English, and not of preserving Hispanic culture.[6] This same study indicates that most Hispanics identify strongly with the United States, and show a relatively low level of Spanish maintenance in the home. By contrast, multiculturalism is more strongly supported by many other groups—blacks, feminists, gays, Native Americans, etc.—whose ancestors have been in the country from the start.

Brimelow's *National Review* piece suggests that even if immigrants are not responsible for our anti-assimilationist multiculturalism, we need not pour oil on burning waters by letting in more immigrants from non-Western cultures. But this argument can be reversed: even if the rate of new immigration fell to zero tomorrow, and the most recent five million immigrants were sent home, we would still have an enormous problem in this country with the breakdown of a core culture and the infatuation of the school system with trendy multiculturalist educational policies.

The real fight, the central fight, then, should not be over keeping newcomers out: this will be a waste of time and energy. The real fight ought to be over the question of assimilation itself: whether we believe that there is enough to our Western, rational, egalitarian, democratic civilization to force those coming to the country to absorb its language and rules, or whether we carry respect for other cultures to the point that Americans no longer have a common voice with which to speak to one another.

Apart from the humble habits of work and family values, opponents of immigration ought to consider culture at the high end of the scale. As anyone who has walked around an elite American university recently would know, immigration from Asia is transforming the nature of American education. For a country that has long prided itself on technological superiority, and whose economic future rests in large part on a continuing technical edge, a depressingly small number of white Americans from long-established families choose to go into engineering and science programs in preference to business and, above all, law school. (This is particularly true of the most dynamic and vocal part of the white population, upwardly mobile middle-class women.) The one bright spot in an otherwise uniform horizon of decline in educational test scores has been in math, where large numbers of new Asian test-takers have bumped up the numbers.[7] In Silicon Valley alone, there are some 12,000 engineers of Chinese

37

38

39

40

---

6. See Rodolfo O. de la Garza, Louis DeSipio, et al., *Latino Voices: Mexican, Puerto Rican, and Cuban Perspectives on American Politics* (Westview Press, 1992).

7. This same group of Asians appears also to have lowered verbal scores, though this is something that will presumably be corrected over time.

descent, while Chinese account for two out of every five engineering and science graduates in the University of California system.

41      Indeed, if one were to opt for "designer immigration" that would open the gates to peoples with the best cultural values, it is not at all clear that certain European countries would end up on top.

42      In the past decade, England's per-capita GNP has fallen behind Italy's, and threatens to displace Portugal and Greece at the bottom of the European Community heap by the end of the decade.[8] Only a fifth of English young people receive any form of higher education, and despite Margaret Thatcher's best efforts, little progress has been made over the past generation in breaking down the stifling social rigidities of the British class system. The English working class is among the least well-educated, most state- and welfare-dependent and immobile of any in the developed world. While the British intelligentsia and upper classes continue to intimidate middle-class Americans, they can do so only on the basis of snobbery and inherited but rapidly dwindling intellectual capital. Paul Gigot may or may not be right that a million Zulus would work harder than a million English, but a million Taiwanese certainly would, and would bring with them much stronger family structures and entrepreneurship to boot.

## *IV*

43   This is not to say that immigration will not be the source of major economic and social problems for the United States in the future. There are at least three areas of particular concern.

44      The first has to do with the effects of immigration on income distribution, particularly at the low end of the scale. The growing inequality of American income distribution over the past decade is not, as the Democrats asserted during the election campaign, the result of Reagan-Bush tax policies or the failure of "trickle-down" economics. Rather, it proceeds from the globalization of the American economy: low-skill labor increasingly has to compete with low-skill labor in Malaysia, Brazil, Mexico, and elsewhere. But it has also had to compete with low-skill immigrant labor coming into the country from the Third World, which explains why Hispanics themselves tend to oppose further Hispanic immigration. The country as a whole may be better off economically as a result of this immigration, but those against whom immigrants directly compete have been hurt, just as they will be hurt by the North American Free Trade Agreement (NAFTA), the General Agreement on Tariffs and Trade (GATT), and other trade-liberalizing measures that are good for the country as a whole. In a city like Los Angeles, Hispanics with their stronger social ties have displaced

---

8. Residual patriotism toward my home country prompts me to point out that the United Kingdom has enjoyed a booming economy these last few years, one of the strongest in Europe.

blacks out of a variety of menial jobs, adding to the woes of an already troubled black community.

The second problem area has to do with the regional concentration of recent Hispanic immigration. As everyone knows, the 25 million Hispanics in the United States are not evenly distributed throughout the country, but are concentrated in the Southwest portion of it, where the problems normally accompanying the assimilation of immigrant communities tend to be magnified. The L.A. public-school system is currently in a state of breakdown, as it tries to educate burgeoning numbers of recent immigrants on a recession-starved budget.

The third problem concerns bilingualism and the elite Hispanic groups which promote and exist off of it. As noted earlier, the rank-and-file of the Hispanic community seems reasonably committed to assimilation; the same cannot be said for its leadership. Bilingualism, which initially began as a well-intentioned if misguided bridge toward learning English, has become in the eyes of many of its proponents a means of keeping alive a separate Spanish language and culture. Numerous studies have indicated that students in bilingual programs learn English less well than those without access to them, and that their enrollments are swelled by a large number of Hispanics who can already speak English perfectly well.[9] In cities with large Hispanic populations like New York and Los Angeles, the bilingual bureaucracy has become something of a monster rigidly tracking students despite the wishes of parents and students. The *New York Times* recently reported the case of a Hispanic-surnamed child, born in the United States and speaking only English, who was forced by New York City officials to enroll in an English as a Second Language Class. Bilingualism is but one symptom of a much broader crisis in American public education, and admittedly makes the problems of assimilation much greater.

These problems can be tackled with specific changes in public policy. But the central issue raised by the immigration question is indeed a cultural one, and as such less susceptible of policy manipulation. The problem here is not the foreign culture that immigrants bring with them from the Third World, but the contemporary elite culture of Americans—Americans like Kevin Costner, who believes that America began going downhill when the white man set foot here, or another American, Ice-T, whose family has probably been in the country longer than Costner's and who believes that women are bitches and that the chief enemy of his generation is the police. In the upcoming block-by-block cultural war, the enemy will not speak Spanish or have a brown skin. In Pogo's words, "He is us." ✣

45

46

47

---

9. On this point, see Linda Chavez's *Out of the Barrio*, pp. 9–38.

## RESPONDING

1.  In a journal entry, explore your feelings about immigration and recent immigrants. What do you know about recent immigrants to the United States? How do you feel about issues of assimilation? Should immigrants be encouraged to keep or abandon their native cultures?

2.  Working individually or in pairs, find the main idea of each paragraph in the essay. Then discuss Fukuyama's main argument and supporting points, in a small group or with the entire class.

3.  Fukuyama states that "The real fight ought to be over the question of assimilation itself: whether we believe that there is enough to our Western, rational, egalitarian, democratic civilization to force those coming to the country to absorb its language and rules. . . ." Review the rest of paragraph 39. In an essay, explain his position on this issue and your response to it.

4.  Fukuyama cites cultural breakdown and loss of cultural values as a major problem in American society today. He identifies several sources for this breakdown. In an essay, choose one of these topics, such as the effect of capitalism, technology, the sexual revolution, feminism, or alternative life-styles, and identify and explore its role in contemporary American society. You may need to do additional research as well as drawing from your own knowledge and experience.

# ARNOLD KRUPAT

*The critic and literary historian Arnold Krupat was born in New York in 1941. After graduating from New York University in 1962, he earned a master's degree and a doctorate from Columbia University. Among his publications are* For Those Who Came After: A Study of Native American Biography *(1985),* The Voice in the Margins: Native American Literature and the Canon *(1989), and* Ethnocriticism: Ethnography, History, Literature *(1992). He holds a professorship at Sarah Lawrence College, where he is also director of American Studies.*

*Krupat's essay, "Conclusion: For Multiculturalism," from* Ethnocriticism, *provides a historical context for examining what the author considers the current realities of a multicultural environment and the educational programs that such a world demands.*

⁜

# *From* Conclusion: For Multiculturalism

IN A LATE VOLUME OF VERSE called *May-Day and Other Pieces* (1867), Ralph Waldo Emerson published a long poem titled "The Adirondacs." The poem details a hiking trip to New York that Emerson had made in 1858 with a group of Boston friends. As they tramp through the wilderness, Emerson and his friends, as Gay Wilson Allen, his biographer, writes, "meet a traveler with a newspaper announcing that the [trans]Atlantic cable has been completed and is operating" (636). "Emerson exults," says Wilson Allen, who quotes, as illustrative of Emersonian exultation, a few lines from "The Adirondacs."[1] Emerson writes:

> Thought's new-found path
> Shall supplement henceforth all trodden ways,
> Match God's equator with a zone of art.

Emerson goes on in this inflationary vein with some lines from "The Adirondacs" that Wilson Allen does not quote, lines that are particularly interesting to me. For Emerson continues:

> It is not Iroquois or cannibals,
> But ever the free race with front sublime,
> And these instructed by their wisest too,
> Who do the feat, and lift humanity.
>             . . .
> 
>   We flee away from cities, but we bring
> The best of cities with us, these learned classifiers,
> Men knowing what they seek, armed eyes of experts.
> We praise the guide, we praise the forest life:
> But will we sacrifice our dear-bought lore
> Of books and arts and trained experiment,
> Or count the Sioux a match for Agassiz?
> O no, not we! (193)

Louis Agassiz, Professor of Natural History at Harvard, Emerson's alma mater, was, whatever his other achievements, a convert to the so-called "American School" of ethnology, which taught the theory of polygenesis—multiple creations—as an explanation of what were, in the nineteenth century, usually taken to be innate racial differences. And, in 1850, Agassiz had pronounced himself on the biologically determined characteristics of African Americans and

---

1. I want to thank Willard Gingerich for bringing these lines of Emerson to my attention.

Native Americans, distinguishing between "the submissive, obsequious negro" and the "indomitable, courageous, proud Indian" (in Dippie 92). Proud, but obviously no match, culturally, for the white "learned classifier" and his armed vision. Another of the hikers on Emerson's tramp through the Adirondacs was the famed jurist Oliver Wendell Holmes, Sr., who, in what must surely be an *ex cathedra* opinion, according to Brian Dippie, "likened the Indian to a red crayon sketch" (84), only the roughest version of the white man, who, no doubt, represented the highest form of Man in full oil portrait.

3    "[C]ount the Sioux a match for Agassiz?" No, Emerson proclaims, "no, not we." Emerson's "no" to the Sioux, the Iroquois, and any other presumptive "cannibals" or "savages" has been reiterated recently in regard to non-Western cultural production generally by the National Endowment for the Humanities report of October, 1989, called "50 Hours: A Core Curriculum for College Students." In it, Lynne Cheney, head of the Endowment, reaffirms the Western supremicism of the Endowment's former head, the egregious William Bennett, and thus offers official government support for the positions of such champions of the West's "dear-bought lore/ Of books and arts and trained experiment" as Allan Bloom, Walter Jackson Bate, and others.

4    Emerson's worry that anyone *might* think to "count the Sioux a match for Agassiz" finds a minor contemporary equivalent in such things as a 1988 column in the New York *Tribune* in which I am specifically chided (among others more notable than I) for "starting [my] American literature students with parallel readings in the Book of Genesis and Iroquois Indian creation stories. The list," writes the *Tribune* columnist with apparent disgust, "goes on and on." On and on to the point where Christopher Clausen, in a piece in *The Chronicle of Higher Education*, "bets" that Alice Walker's *"The Color Purple* is taught in more English courses today than all of Shakespeare's plays combined" (6).

5    But Clausen, like Emerson before him, is overreacting. I have no statistics for college English courses, but the *New York Times* for June 23, 1989, under the headline "School Reading Lists Shun Women and Black Authors," affirms that

> Required reading lists in the nation's high schools continue to emphasize the works of Shakespeare but largely ignore the literary contributions of women and members of minorities, a new survey says. (21)

And Arthur Applebee's monograph, *A Study of Book-length Works Taught in High School English Courses*, published the same year as the *Times* article appeared, finds that not Alice Walker, but, rather, John Steinbeck, Charles Dickens, and Mark Twain are, in fact, the most generally assigned American novelists. This is the case, as Henry Louis Gates, Jr., points out, "even in public schools with the highest proportion of minority students" (1990 13). No doubt there may be some study I have missed, but my guess is that the teaching of Sioux or

Iroquois—Native American—literatures in American high school and college courses generally occurs so infrequently and irregularly that the statistics are hardly even worth compiling.

So Professor Clausen is safe, at least for the moment—for all that one *could*, of course, make the case that high school students might actually learn more from a careful reading of Walker's novel (not my favorite book by an African American writer) than from *Romeo and Juliet*—which, according to the survey reported in the *Times*, tops the list of Shakespeare plays assigned. And, so far as American literature is concerned, one could also make the case that any number of African American, Native American, and Latino/a writers might be studied with at least as much pleasure and profit as Cooper, Longfellow, Whittier, William Cullen Bryant, or some of the other elite, WASP males who have traditionally been offered as among the best and brightest of American literary production.[2]

Given the social and political demands of American women and minorities of late, given the demands of colonized peoples from Africa to Armenia, to be heard, I can understand why Cheney and Bennett and Clausen feel threatened on the cultural front. I don't, however, know any particular reason why Emerson's pride in the achievement of transcontinental communication should need to affirm itself by means of a direct contrast to the presumed absence of artistic and scientific achievement among the Iroquois or D/Lakota (the Sioux). The obvious general reason for calumniating the Indians in order to praise Euramericans is, of course, the one Roy Harvey Pearce documented more than thirty-five years ago in his seminal *Savagism and Civilization*. There, Pearce showed how, from the first days of settlement, Americans regularly tended to define their own particular brand of "civilization" in direct opposition to a fantasized, or ideologically constructed Indian "savagery." In a simplified formulation, to be an American was no longer to be a European without yet becoming an Indian.

What is curious to note is that by 1860 or so, when Emerson wrote these lines, the need to praise white "civilization" by opposing it to red "savagism" was—in Emerson's Massachusetts, at least, if not in the Dakotas or New Mexico—already an anachronism. It is even more of an anachronism today—if, that is, one agrees, as I do, with James Clifford, that the "future is not (only) monoculture" (1988 16). Indeed, I believe the multicultural "future" is already here; nonetheless, inasmuch as monocultural supremacy is still promoted at the highest institutional levels, those of us who would speak for multiculturalism must continue to argue on its behalf. . . .

I understand the term multiculturalism to refer to that conceptualization and organization of cultural studies in the university which engages the other

---

2. This little list obviously does not include the major canonical figures whose canonical status seems, for now, justifiably secure.

in such a way as to provoke an interrogation of and a challenge to what we take as ours. In a certain sense, indeed, the term multiculturalism is redundant if, as I have suggested, culture is best conceived in a manner analogous to Bakhtin's conception of language as a socially plural construct in which our own speech is never entirely and exclusively our own, but always heteroglossic and polyvocal, formed always in relation to the speech of others. As Bakhtin says, "language lies on the borderline between oneself and the other. The word in language is half someone else's" (in Clifford 1988 41)—as culture is always, if not "half someone else's," at least never all one's own. No more than language as a medium of actual communication could culture *in historical time* ever be pure; only as the projection of an idealized logic could one posit either a strictly pure speech or culture.

10    A multicultural approach to the teaching of literature thus is consistent with the project of anti-imperialist translation, as I have tried to outline it, . . . appropriat[ing] Benjamin's citation of Pannwitz's remarks as an encouragement to permit one's "own" language or culture to be powerfully affected by the language or culture of the foreigner, by values and attitudes "we" had defined as Other and sought to engage only by means of domestication: by translation in the imperial sense. The intention is to dialogize dominant monologues, indeed, to show that dialogue is not an abstract ideal, nor is it only realized in—to refer specifically to Bakhtin's work—the "novel" in literature or "carnival" in society, but that it is everywhere. A multicultural commitment, then, does not particularly encourage one to urge additions to the curriculum or the canon in the name of (as I shall try to show) "diversity" or "tolerance" (important as these are), but, rather, to urge the deconstruction of all dichotomized paradigms of the us/them, West/Rest type, and so to undo manichean allegories at every level. It should be fairly obvious that to proceed in this way has strong implications for a variety of possible reorganizations of the institutionalized pedagogical curriculum, and, too, for the reorganization of the social order. Sociopolitically, as I have said, the multicultural perspective finds expression in a commitment to cosmopolitan values as these do not only propose an ideal vision of what might be, nor an option strictly for a privileged class of intellectuals (this is another point to which I shall return), but, rather, as they claim to be implicit, in varying degrees, in all social interaction.

11    In an essay called "Representations Are Social Facts: Modernity and Postmodernity in Anthropology," Rabinow proposes what he calls a "critical cosmopolitanism," one which would, in a variety of contexts, have a force "oppositional" (258) to the determinations of monoculturalists foremost, but also to those of liberal cosmopolitans. Rabinow's "critical cosmopolitanism" is

> suspicious of sovereign powers, universal truths, overly relativized preciousness, local authenticity, moralisms high and low. Understanding is its second value ["The ethical is the guiding value"], but an understanding suspicious of its own imperial tendencies. It attempts to be highly attentive to (and respectful of) difference, but it is also wary of the tendency to essentialize difference. (258)

As cosmopolitans,

> We live in between . . . insider's outsiders of a particular historical and cultural world; not members of a projected universal regime (under God, the imperium, or the laws of reason). (258)

Rabinow's ethical and epistemological cosmopolitanism has a wider—a global—frame of reference than that of the tolerance, diversity, or "cosmopolitanism" of the "liberal intelligentsia." For all that Rabinow says little about any politics his cosmopolitanism might found beyond the academy, its model of cultural mapping has implications not only for understanding but also, I believe, for changing the world.

In this regard, I should note that Hollinger has remarked with considerable realistic acumen that "Full-blown cosmopolitanism"—and, I would assume this might, on the face of it, hold both for "liberal" or more radical versions of cosmopolitanism—from the twenties to the fifties "was understood to be a realistic ideal primarily for intellectuals" (57). Liberal cosmopolitanism, and, surely, any other cosmopolitanism, represents a conscious *choice* of values on the part of those who have experienced, or, at least read widely. To the extent that this is so, cosmopolitan values are not, therefore, likely to appeal to many outside the "intelligentsia." In a period like our own, when most people's experience of anything very much beyond their immediate surroundings is experience presented by television—which, of course, has replaced reading as the primary source of other than immediately personal experience, and of information—it certainly is not easy to have wider hopes for cosmopolitan values than those Hollinger historically describes. About the only populist hope a radical cosmopolitanism (as I have tried to define it in relation to Bakhtin, progressive translation, multiculturalism, and ethnocriticism) might have beyond that of a liberal cosmopolitanism resides in the fact that it doesn't quite ask people simply to discard ethnic and local attachments for more global ones, but, rather—to appropriate a recent catchphrase—to try to see how the local is *already* global, the ethnic and regional *already* shot through with other and distant perspectives.[3] Nonetheless, as I think of the major news stories during the time I have worked on this book—the election of Violeta Chamorro in Nicaragua, the unification

3. For all this, it is necessary to take into account Fredrik Barth's insistence that "ethnic distinctions do not depend on an absence of social interaction and acceptance" (10) and that what is important is "the ethnic *boundary* that defines the group, not the cultural stuff that it encloses" (15). Barth traces the tendencies of peoples, however easily they move back and forth across boundaries, to persist in their identification as "A's" not "B's," declaring "their allegiance to the shared culture of A's" (15) on the basis of "criteria of origin and commitment" (28). Barth is most interested in regional diversities not necessarily influenced by colonialism; these he takes as culturally and historically the more usual case (36), for all that studies of the subject, in his view, have been dominated by attention to the colonial context. My own sense is that perhaps not colonialism but most certainly imperialism of a cultural, if not overtly political, sort reaches almost everywhere. Barth knows more about these matters than I do: but, as I think any reader may note, he also seems to *like* the idea of maintaining boundaries more than I do.

of the two Germanies, and a war in the Persian Gulf determined to produce and sustain the illusion of victory no matter the cost in Arab lives—it is indeed difficult to be optimistic in regard to any form of cosmopolitan social order. But this is not to say that nothing can be done.

13      Without overestimating the potential of curricular multiculturalism or ethnocritical discourse as politically functional in any direct or immediate manner—indeed one must remember in a cautionary fashion the example of those deconstructionists or postmodernists who affirmed or continue to affirm each of their readings as radical, subversive, transgressive, revolutionary, while the walls of Jericho showed no sign of tumbling down—still, one must not underestimate the possibilities of cultural work either. Yet, as Rabinow writes, and as James Clifford agrees, we are all already cosmopolitans: the problem is that many in power have yet to accede to that fact—a fact which, obviously enough, threatens their power.

14      Moreover—and this to me is more important even than the opinion of "those in power"—many marginalized people wish to maintain the ethnic "boundary" in the interest of, in Werner Sollors's phrase, "generating feelings of *dissociative belonging*" (1990 299 my emphasis), feelings which, however "dissociative," nonetheless serve to promote positive constructions of "minority" identity and worth. Inasmuch as ethnic and minority groups regularly suffer the representational and material disdain of the dominant society, it is not casually that one would recommend to them cosmopolitan values that may well seem a luxury beyond their current means. Nonetheless, . . . for the long term I believe exclusionary or "dissociative" strategies are inherently limited. Indeed, I find it of considerable interest (and admirable, too) that, although Werner Sollors's reputation as a critic rests on his assertion of the importance of ethnicity as a category, he nonetheless concludes the recent essay from which I have just quoted as follows:

> Although ethnicity remains potentially one of the most interesting aspects of modern literature around the world and opens many new possibilities for examining great [!] texts on a comparative basis, it is hardly an exaggeration to state that it may also bring out the worst in readers of literature. (1990 304)

Thus it seems to me that culture workers have more than merely abstract incentive to encourage multiculturalism and to practice ethnocriticism in the interest of promoting those cosmopolitan values that socially may found what I have elsewhere called the polyvocal polity:[4] the materialization of dialogic values in institutions other than *carnival*.

15      To say these things is, admittedly and unfortunately, to be no more than generally hortatory, and I confess to being unable to describe more specifically

---

4. See *The Voice in the Margin: Native American Literature and the Canon*, in particular chapter 5, "Local, National, Cosmopolitan Literature." I knew very little, when I wrote that chapter, about the history of the subject in the twenties.

the shape those institutions might take. But it would be a mistake to assume that my own limitations are exactly those of ethnocriticism, multiculturalism, cosmopolitanism, and polyvocal politics: these name possibilities yet to be realized, neither fantasies nor daydreams, but, rather, plans for the future.

I began this conclusion by quoting Emerson at—on? against?—the Indians. [16] I will end it by quoting the Indians at—on? against?—Emerson: by closing, that is, with some lines from no Sioux or Iroquois or cannibal, but from two contemporary Native American poets, Wendy Rose, of Hopi-Miwok background, and Jimmie Durham, a Cherokee. Wendy Rose writes:

> It's not that your songs
> are so much stronger
> or your feet more deeply
> rooted, but that
> there are
> so many of you
>     shouting in a single voice
>     like a giant child. (38)

And Jimmie Durham:

> In school I learned of heroic discoveries
> Made by liars and crooks. The courage
> of millions of sweet and true people
> Was not commemorated.
>
> Let us then declare a holiday
> For ourselves, and make a parade that begins
> With Columbus' victims and continues
> Even to our grandchildren who will be named
> In their honor. (11)  ✤

## Works Cited

Allen, Gay Wilson. *Waldo Emerson: A Biography.* New York: Viking Press, 1981.

Barth, Fredrik, ed. *Ethnic Groups and Boundaries: The Social Organization of Culture Difference.* Boston: Little, Brown, 1969.

Clifford, James. "On Ethnographic Authority." *Representations* 2(1983): 132–43.

Dippie, Brian. *The Vanishing American: White Attitudes and United States Relations.* Middletown, Conn.: Wesleyan University Press, 1982.

Durham, Jimmie. *Columbus Day.* Minneapolis: West End Press, 1983, 10–11.

Emerson, Ralph Waldo. "The Adirondacs." *Poems by Ralph Waldo Emerson,* vol. IX. New York: William H. Wise and Co., 1929 [1867], 182–95.

Gates, Henry Louis, Jr. "Editor's Introduction: Writing, 'Race' and the Difference It Makes." *Critical Inquiry* 12(1985): 1–20.

————. "Introduction: Tell Me, Sir . . . What *Is* 'Black' Literature?" *PMLA* 105(1990): 11–22.

Hollinger, David. "Ethnic Diversity, Cosmopolitanism, and the Emergence of the American Liberal Intelligentsia." *In the American Province: Studies in the History and Historiography of Ideas.* Bloomington: Indiana University Press, 1985, 56–73.

Krupat, Arnold. *The Voice in the Margin: Native American Literature and the Canon.* Berkeley: University of California Press, 1989.

Pearce, Roy Harvey. *Savagism and Civilization: A Study of the Indian and the American Mind.* Baltimore: Johns Hopkins University Press, 1967.

Rabinow, Paul. "Representations Are Social Facts: Modernity and Post-modernity in Anthropology." Clifford and Marcus, 234–61.

Rose, Wendy. "Backlash." *The Halfbreed Chronicles.* Minneapolis: West End Press, 1985, 38.

"School Reading Lists Shun Women and Black Writers." *New York Times,* June 25, 1989, 21.

Sollors, Werner. "Ethnicity." *Critical Terms for Literary Study,* ed. Frank Lentricchia and Thomas McLaughlin. Chicago: University of Chicago Press, 1990, 288–305.

## RESPONDING

1. In a journal entry, discuss the type of literature you read in high school. Did you feel that you could relate to the authors and the material? If so, in what way? If not, why not and what would you have preferred to read?

2. Working individually or in a group, list the pros and cons of maintaining an ethnic boundary "to promote positive constructions of 'minority' identity and worth" (paragraph 14). Share your findings with the class.

3. Review the excerpted poetry by Emerson, Rose, and Durham. Write an essay comparing the different perspectives of these authors.

4. Krupat argues for a multicultural curriculum. Imagine that you are designing a curriculum for a university literature class. What works would you include? Write Krupat a letter explaining your choices, and either support his position or try to persuade him to agree with yours.

✣

# CONNECTING

## *Critical Thinking and Writing*

1.   Write an essay discussing the role that the early settlers and recent immigrants have played in forming the United States. Use information from the readings as well as from your own experience.

2.   How completely should immigrants be asked to assimilate? Should they have to learn the language and culture of their new country? Should they retain their own native language and culture? Should they change their value system? Write an essay discussing this topic from a historical perspective. How have the attitudes of immigrants and the attitudes of others toward them changed over the years? (See Hoffman.)

3.   Adams reflects the attitude of the United States in the 1930s, with its desire to isolate itself from the rest of the world. Compare Adams's views with those of Krupat.

4.   *Civilized* and *savage* are terms that appear in the readings in this chapter. Define the terms and write an essay discussing the connotations of each. Have the definitions of these words changed over the years? From a present-day perspective, are we able to assign positive and negative connotations to each?

5.   Interview an immigrant and write an essay discussing her experience. Would she, or would you, characterize that experience as an example of assimilation or of accommodation? In your essay, be sure to define your terms and support your discussion with material from this chapter.

6.   Write a dialogue between Fukuyama and Krupat on the subject of multiculturalism. Alternatively, compose a letter from one man to the other, explaining the writer's position.

7.   How much of individual identity is shaped by language and culture? What characteristics are we born with and what characteristics develop as a result of our upbringing and the way society treats us? Review the selections by Hoffman, Gates, and Sarris to find support for your answer. You may also draw from your own knowledge and experience.

8.   Both Lazarus and Bruchac memorialize different aspects of American history. In an essay, compare their poems. How do the poems reflect the period in which they were written as well as the author's personal perspective?

9.   Krupat suggests that "many marginalized people wish to maintain the ethnic 'boundary'" in the interest of promoting "positive constructions of 'minority' identity and worth" (paragraph 14). Imagine that you are Gates or Sarris, and write a letter to Krupat agreeing or disagreeing that such a stance helps marginalized people maintain a good self-image.

10.   Gates, Sarris, and Hoffman make use of personal experience to support their theoretical positions. Sarris even calls attention to that fact in his essay (see paragraph 18). In an essay of your own, use personal experience to support a position you are taking about race, class, gender, or the immigrant experience.

11.   Write an essay discussing why we should or should not have a multicultural curriculum and, by extension, why we should or should not use a book like *American Mosaic*.

### *For Further Research*

1.   Use the Internet and other sources to research the academic debate about the place of canonical and noncanonical texts in literature courses. Then study the required reading in English courses on your campus. Write an essay theorizing about where your college or university and its faculty members stand on this issue.

2.   Choose one ethnic group that immigrated to the United States and, using the Internet and other sources, trace their experience in America. Write an essay explaining why, as a group, they did or did not realize the "American Dream." In general, would they have been better off staying at home?

## REFERENCES AND ADDITIONAL SOURCES

Adams, James Truslow. *The Epic of America*. New York: Blue Ribbon Books, 1931.

Addams, Jane. *Twenty Years at Hull House: With Autobiographical Notes*. New York: Macmillan, 1910, 1967.

———. *Forty Years at Hull House*. New York: Macmillan, 1935.

Bloom, Allan. *The Closing of the American Mind*. New York: Simon and Schuster, 1987.

Fine, David M. *The City, the Immigrant and American Fiction, 1880–1920*. Metuchen, N.J.: Scarecrow, 1977.

———. "Attitudes Toward Acculturation in the English Fiction of the Jewish Immigrant, 1900–1917." American Jewish Historical Society, Waltham, Mass.

Greenbaum, Susan D. "Multiculturalism." *The Encyclopedia of Multiculturalism*. Susan Auerbach, ed. Vol. 4. New York, London, Toronto: Marshall Cavendish, 1994, pp. 1179–87.

Hebst, Philip H. *The Color of Words: An Encyclopedia of Ethnic Bias in the United States.* Yarmouth, Me.: Intercultural Press, 1997.

Hirsch, E. D. *Cultural Literacy.* Princeton, N.J.: Films for the Humanities, Inc., 1988.

Kallen, Horace. "Concerning Varieties of Pluralism" in *Cultural Pluralism and the American Idea: An Essay in Social Philosophy.* Philadelphia: University of Pennsylvania Press: 1956, 46–55.

Kraut, Alan M. *The Huddled Masses: The Immigrant in American Society, 1880–1921.* Arlington Heights, Ill.: Harlan Davidson, 1982.

O'Sullivan, John. "Annexation" in *The United States Magazine and Democratic Review.* New Series. Vol xvii, 1845 (July–Aug.): 5–10.

*Oxford English Dictionary.* 2nd ed. Oxford: Clarendon Press; New York: Oxford University Press, 1989.

Powell, J. W. *Study of Indian Language.* 2nd ed. Washington: Government, 1880, p. 46 (as quoted in the *OED* "acculturation").

Pratt, Julius W. "The Origin of 'Manifest Destiny.'" *American Historical Review.* Vol 32 (1927), 795–98.

Takaki, Ronald. *A Different Mirror: A History of Multicultural America.* Boston: Little, Brown, 1993.

Weinberg, Albert K. *Manifest Destiny: A Study of Nationalist Expansion in American History.* Baltimore: Johns Hopkins University Press, 1935.

ESKIMO

INGALIK
TANAINA
KUTCHIN
ALEUT

DOGRIB
ESKIMO

Uninhabited
lands

PACIFIC
OCEAN

KASKA
SLAVEY
CHIPPEWYAN

TLINGIT
TSIMSHIAN
BEAVER

HAIDA
SARSI
CREE

ESKIMO

NASKAPI

CREE

BEOTHUK

MONTAGNAIS
MICMAC

KWAKIUTL
NOOTKA    SHUSWAP  BLACKFOOT
SALISH  THOMPSON
SANPOIL
GROS
CHINOOK   YAKIMA    VENTRE  ASSINIBOIN    OJIBWA      OTTAWA    IROQUOIS  ABENAKIS
NEZ PERCÉ                                            HURON

FLATHEAD    CROW    MANDAN    SIOUX   MENOMINI                MOHAWK              MASSACHUSETT
                    ARIKARA           SAC                     ONEIDA              WAMPANOAG
YUROK              CHEYENNE           FOX                     ONONDAGA            NARRAGANSETT
                                            POTAWATOMIS       CAYUGA              PEQUOT
POMO     SHOSHONE         PAWNEE                              SENECA
WASHO                                      MIAMI    ERIE  SUSQUEHANNOCK  DELAWARE
                          ARAPAHO          ILLINOIS  SHAWNEE
YOKUT   PAIUTE    UTE                                        POWHATAN
CHUMASH                              OSAGE                  TUSCARORA
                                     WICHITA
          WALAPAI  HOPI                        CHEROKEE
          MOHAVE  NAVAJO    KIOWA              CATAWBA
LUISEÑO   YUMA   ZUÑI                  CHICKASAW  CREEK
          PAPAGO  RIO GRANDE                          GUALE
          PIMA   PUEBLO                CHOCTAW       (YAMASEE)
                 APACHE    CADDO              MOBILE
                           NATCHEZ                              CALUSA

COAHUILTEC    Gulf of Mexico

ATLANTIC
OCEAN

WINNEBAGO

500 Miles
500 Kilometers

# 2

## AMERICAN INDIANS

*Reclaiming Cultural Heritage*

⊹

*Above:* Anasazi petroglyphs, Arizona. *(© Jonathan A. Meyers)*
*Opposite:* American Indian Tribes in North America.

# SETTING THE HISTORICAL AND CULTURAL CONTEXT

In James Welch's poem, "Plea to Those Who Matter," the speaker dramatizes the pressure to assimilate:

> Don't ignore me. I'll build my face a different way,
> a way to make you know that I am no longer
> proud, my name not strong enough to stand alone.
> If I lie and say you took me for a friend,
> patched together in my thin bones,
> will you help me be cunning and noisy as the wind?

The poem uses irony to identify ways in which American Indians have been asked to substitute dominant culture stereotypes for their traditional systems and beliefs. To obtain property and mineral rights belonging to American Indians, Euro Americans have often coerced tribes into signing treaties that were not in the tribes' best interests and then refused to honor any beneficial terms in these agreements. With the goal of acculturation, the majority culture has penalized those native people who have attempted to retain their cultural identity. In recent years, however, American Indians have become somewhat more successful in their struggles to regain their rights.

American Indian cultures had well-established, highly structured systems long before the coming of the Europeans. There is a record of several hundred languages spoken by native peoples engaged in hunting, gathering, or agrarian ways of life. Indians often participated in trade with other tribes, and often they lived communally. This communal approach toward the land contrasted markedly with the notion of individual property rights accepted by most Euro Americans.

To trace the history of the relationships between American Indian peoples and European settlers is a very complex task. Even the designation of each group as a "tribe" or as a separate "nation" is an issue that was subject to much legal interpretation and debate. (In the 1830s, for example, Supreme Court Justice John Marshall referred to Indians in one opinion as being "domestic, dependent nations," while he stressed their capacity for self-government in another opinion.) Further complicating matters, many native communities signed treaties with and received recognition from both state and federal governments. Although we cannot recount the intricacies of each of these relationships in this chapter, we will describe some crucial events from the period of the United States's rapid western expansion in the nineteenth century to the emergence of an American Indian rights movement in the twentieth century.

In her study of American Indian literature, A. LaVonne Ruoff comments on the history of relations between American Indians and Euro Americans: "Whites' settlement in Indian territory was inevitably followed by attempts to expand their land holdings and Indians' determined efforts to retain their ancestral land." The desire for land often caused the Euro Americans to ignore the terms of earlier treaties. Some of the earliest groups of European settlers negotiated with many Indian groups as separate nations, giving the nations some payment or remuneration for lands ceded; this practice became less common by the end of the eighteenth century. After the United States had defeated the British in the War of 1812, expanding agrarian and commercial interests attempted to force the American Indians from rich farmland in the South and East, and from western territories not yet settled or extensively explored. Although Indian nations had earlier been able to exercise some influence over the Euro Americans because of their past alliances with the British, they found themselves in a strategically weaker position after the British defeat. Andrew Jackson made expansion a central platform in his campaign for the presidency. In addition, other government officials increased pressure at both state and federal levels to have Indians removed from lands the whites viewed as desirable. Indian communities that had already ceded land to Euro Americans found themselves being coerced to give up even more land—land that had been guaranteed them in earlier treaties with the U.S. government and the states.

The Indian Removal Act of 1830 is one example of how the federal government overturned earlier treaties, denying American Indians what had been promised them. The Removal Act gave the federal government power to force those native peoples living east of the Mississippi River to move to a designated "Indian territory" in the West. Although the language of the act provides for "an exchange of lands," the process is more often regarded as a forced removal, by which most of the Indians were made to move westward against their wills.

The "Trail of Tears"—the forced migration of the so-called Five Civilized Tribes—dramatizes the dehumanizing nature of the removal process. A confederation composed of the Cherokee, Chickasaw, Choctaw, Creek, and Seminole of the southeast, the Five Civilized Tribes were designated as such by Euro Americans. When the rich land these tribes occupied was earmarked as desirable for the cultivation of cotton and other crops, these Indians— even the Cherokee who had already begun to adapt to Euro American ways— were instantly considered obstacles to the expansion of agriculture in the southeast. Through coercion and bribery, and often despite the protests of their leaders, Indian communities were forced from the lands of their ancestors and made to travel long distances to the newly designated "Indian territory" in the West. Although a few groups, such as the Eastern Band of the Cherokee, were able to hide in North Carolina and later return secretly to their native lands, many other tribes were permanently forced out. As they

made their way west, often in the winter months, the native people were exposed to cold weather, contaminated provisions, and disease. Many starved to
death or perished from infectious diseases to which they had no immunity. In
the Cherokee nation, for example, 4,000 Indians were reported to have died;
the Chocktaw were said to have lost 5,000 members; half of the Creek were
said to have died along the way. Midwest American Indian nations and tribes
were also forced from their lands to territories farther west: The Potawatomi
had to resettle in Kansas, and the Kickapoo were moved to Missouri. Once
they were settled in Indian territory, tribes attempted to reestablish themselves culturally—by forming schools, governmental systems, and the like. After a few decades, however, many tribes found that the assurances expressed
in the Indian Removal Act could easily be disregarded. Despite its promise
that it "[would] forever secure and guaranty [the land] to them, and their
heirs," the federal government continued to encroach on Indian territories
and their ways of life.

The next fifty years witnessed further assaults by Euro Americans on Indian territorial rights and cultural identity. The westward migration of settlers during the 1840s and 1850s increased the competition for land and for
resources. Not only was grazing land destroyed, but the buffalo herds upon
which the Indians had become even more dependent for their food came to
be depleted. Railroad companies, eager to encourage western expansion, extended their lines across Indian territories.

The Nez Percé was one of many tribes to experience forced displacement. Heinmot Tooyalakekt (also known as Chief Joseph), leader of the Nez
Percé, gives an account of their forced migration from the Oregon territory
in *An Indian's View of Indian Affairs*, which was first published in 1879. Chief
Joseph explores how the increase in the number of Euro American settlements and the settlers' desire to be separated from the Indians greatly affected relations between the two groups. After describing his tribe's first encounters with Euro Americans—its first meeting with French trappers and
later with Lewis and Clark—Chief Joseph recounts the tactics used by Euro
Americans to force native peoples from their land:

> A white officer . . . invited all the Nez Percé to a treaty council. After the
> council was opened, he made known his heart. He said there were a great many
> white people in the country, and many more would come; that he wanted the
> land marked out so that Indians and white men could be separated. If they were
> to live in peace, it was necessary, he said, that the Indians should have a country
> set apart for them . . .

Echoed in the demands is the Euro American belief in their "manifest destiny," their right to settle the territory, a position that is continually rebutted
in Chief Joseph's account through legal and moral arguments, as well as the

disclosure of the devastating effects that such policies had on his own tribe. Refusing to sign a treaty but forced to surrender to the U.S. Army by 1877, Chief Joseph first appeals to the Commissioner of Indian Affairs and then, in 1879, travels to Washington, D.C. to appeal to both Congress and the president for the return of Nez Percé territory:

> If the white man wants to live in peace . . . [t]reat all men alike. Give them all the same law. Give them all an even chance to live and grow. . . . The earth is the mother of all people, and all people should have equal rights upon it. You might as well expect the rivers to run backward as that any man who was born a free man should be contented when penned up and denied liberty to go where he pleases.

Despite Chief Joseph's appeals, the Nez Percé were not allowed to return to their land. He died on a reservation in 1904.

In addition to forced displacement, many native peoples experienced the consequences of governmental attempts to alter tribal customs and values through such legislation as the Dawes Act of 1887 and the Curtis Act of 1898. Under the Dawes Act of 1887, for example, native peoples were allotted single plots of land—160 acres—in exchange for giving up Indian ways. The act implicitly required that Indians reject their communal attitude toward land and accept a more individualistic, Euro American one. They were also forced to abandon their traditional nomadic way of life and to adopt an agrarian culture on the much smaller parcels of land allotted them. Whereas Indians considered themselves attached to the land of their ancestors, the act served to weaken those ties. Provisions in the law also allowed Indians to be exploited by unscrupulous agents who could cheat them or their heirs of their property. Initially, some tribes were exempted from the Dawes Act because of previous treaties they had signed with the federal government; the Curtis Act of 1898, however, eliminated all such exemptions. It also dissolved all tribal governments.

Government "acculturation" programs prevented many American Indians from practicing tribal customs and religion. Children were often taken from their parents and sent to foster parents and boarding schools in distant states, where they were required to speak English and adopt the customs of Euro Americans. Several of the works included in this chapter address elements of the acculturation process. In "Train Time," D'arcy McNickle, who spent three years as a student in an Indian boarding school, uses contrasting point-of-view narration to represent the different motivations of the boarding school director and his future charge; as his narrative isolates and expands a few moments in time, it discloses the preconceptions of each character's view of the other. Leslie Marmon Silko's short story "Lullaby," written several generations later, explores the relationships between language and power, silence and suffering, that can emerge when individuals confront institutional authority.

Other works in this chapter address in comparative ways a variety of power relationships between Euro American culture and indigenous peoples. "Pocahontas to Her English husband, John Rolfe," by Paula Gunn Allen, and James Welch's "Plea to Those Who Matter" address such assaults on Indian culture; like the poem by Joseph Bruchac in chapter 1, Allen and Welch also dismantle received notions about what it means to be civilized. In their essay, Vine Deloria Jr. and Clifford M. Lytle explore the background of treaty negotiations between Indians and the federal government, observing that in these agreements there is "little mention of the complex of ideas that constitutes nationhood." The authors go on to explore the distinction between the physical ownership of land and the spiritual possession of it—a difference that helps to explain some of the differences between Indian and Euro American attitudes toward treaty negotiation. Other writings in the chapter reflect upon events and traditions of the past to suggest ways in which American Indian culture and traditions can blend with modern life. The excerpt from Louise Erdrich's novel *Love Medicine* takes a wry approach to the effort to integrate the American Indian traditions with those of mainstream culture. Simon J. Ortiz further explores the connections that exist between the strength that he finds in his native oral culture and "the urge to write."

Indians were not granted U.S. citizenship until 1924. Until the 1930s, American Indians had to ask permission if they wanted to leave their reservations. Those living in Arizona and New Mexico remained disfranchised—they were not allowed to vote—until the late 1940s. The period between 1930 and 1945, however, saw some improvement in the status of American Indians. The Bureau of Indian Affairs instituted reforms that would allow them greater autonomy. The Indian Reorganization Act (IRA) (1934), for example, gave tribes greater control over their property and funds as well as over the administration of social programs. There was a general movement away from coerced assimilation and toward what IRA Director John Mills called "cultural pluralism."

Many of the reforms of the IRA were undermined, however, by the termination policy that began in 1953 during the Eisenhower administration. This policy was designed to "get the government out of the Indian business," that is, to dissolve the reservations, relocate their residents, and allocate private property—all largely without the consent of the people affected. Administered by Dillon S. Myer, who had run the Japanese American internment camps during World War II, the termination policy caused an erosion of tribal authority and loss of control of land by American Indians. Much of their former reservation territory was, as a result, signed over to Euro Americans. This policy was resisted by such Indian activists as D'arcy

McNickle, who resigned his position with the Bureau of Indian Affairs in protest against it.

The termination policy was renounced by the Kennedy administration, which took office in 1961. During this period, relations between the federal government and American Indian groups changed to reflect a growing appreciation among the American people of the values of pluralism. The federal government promised to help American Indians preserve their cultural heritage; it also pledged to negotiate any changes in treaties or contracts directly with the native peoples involved. There was also growing awareness that federal governmental policies toward American Indians could not be imposed from without—as had been typically done in the past—but had to be based on the initiative and cooperation of the people affected.

In 1961, the American Indian Chicago Conference, a meeting of more than 420 delegates from 67 tribes, issued a formal Declaration of Indian Purpose, which reaffirmed the resolve of American Indians for self-determination. The conference also advocated the abandonment of the termination policy, the establishment of broad educational programs, and the reorganization of the federal government's Bureau of Indian Affairs to ensure more local control. At the same time, the Task Force on Indian Affairs, established by the Kennedy administration, recommended improvements in educational, employment, and industrial programs; the task force also advocated greater protection for the rights of off-reservation American Indians. A key objective was an attempt to address the extreme poverty found on many tribal reservations. The Economic Opportunity Act of 1964, part of the War on Poverty initiated by the Kennedy administration and continued by the administration of President Lyndon B. Johnson, helped to address this need. The act stressed local initiative by encouraging the poor to help plan and administer the programs. Tribal governments were quick to set up community action programs.

The Civil Rights Act of 1968 was extended to protect the rights of American Indians. Although this law limited the powers to tribal governments, it guaranteed that the freedom from discrimination accorded by the Constitution would be fully applied to American Indians. In 1965, President Johnson created the National Council on Indian Opportunity. Chaired by Vice President Hubert Humphrey, the council emphasized American Indian leadership and initiative in solving their own problems. Many American Indians considered these reforms inadequate. Many who feared termination policies distrusted the federal government. President Johnson appointed Robert L. Bennett the first American Indian commissioner of Indian affairs in a hundred years. But these acts alone did not counteract centuries of broken promises. The U.S. government, however, did not earn the complete confidence of the tribes.

While some American Indians waited for the government to enforce the

Civil Rights Act, others took more direct action. In 1969 a militant political group occupied Alcatraz Island in San Francisco Bay and attempted to convert it into an American Indian cultural and educational center. The occupation came to symbolize the struggle for American Indian unity. Other protests followed, among them the 1972 Trail of Broken Treaties (an occupation of the Bureau of Indian Affairs building in Washington, D.C.) and a 1972 March on Washington organized by the American Indian Movement (AIM). In 1973 AIM seized the village of Wounded Knee on the Pine Ridge Reservation in South Dakota to call attention to the continuing problems faced by American Indians. (In 1890, Pine Ridge had been the site of a large-scale massacre of American Indians by American military forces.) Although AIM's action was condemned by many American Indians, the occupation lasted for more than seventy days.

During the 1970s and 1980s the government continued to endorse a policy of American Indian self-determination without termination. Under President Richard Nixon, procedural changes were made to improve the tribes' relationships with the government. Nixon's team on Indian affairs renounced the termination policy and restored sacred lands. The Alaska Native Claims Settlement Act passed in the early 1970s granted Alaskan American Indians legal title to 40 million acres of land. During this period American Indians assumed control of some federal programs and began to manage their own public schools. Relations continued to improve during the Carter administration, with the elevation of the Commissioner of Indian Affairs to an assistant secretary position. Additional legislation was passed, further guaranteeing the rights of American Indians and other indigenous peoples.

Despite these improvements, the situations on the reservations themselves were still cause for concern during the 1970s and 1980s. Many American Indians felt that government schools inadequately addressed the varying educational and cultural needs of the tribes. There also arose a demand for an educational system to validate tribal culture and to keep native traditions alive. Many on the reservation called attention to the high rate of non–American Indian adoption of American Indian children. They pointed out that approximately one-fourth of all American Indian children had been taken from their families and placed in foster or adoptive homes on the advice of the Bureau of Indian Affairs or state social workers. In 1978, Congress passed the American Indian Child Welfare Act to protect the interests of these children and their families.

Since World War II, steady numbers of American Indians have migrated to the cities, where they have generally attained higher standards of living than those remaining on reservations. In so doing, however, they have too often lost the support of the tribe. One of the ways in which several writers have chosen to strengthen their cultural connections is to explore more fully their traditional connections with the natural world and the environment. In contrast to concepts prevalent in eighteenth- and nineteenth-century Euro American thought (emphasizing progress and expansionism), the oral and written literature of American Indian peoples has traditionally privileged stewardship of the land. The writing of Chief Joseph speaks of the tribe's responsibilities to the land. Linda Hogan's poem "Crossings," included in this chapter, reasserts connections between the environment and one's collective memory: "the longing in me / comes from when I remember/ the terrain of crossed beginnings."

Although American Indian and environmental concerns have been traditionally seen as connected, they occasionally conflict with one another. Tribal leaders and environmentalists have sometimes clashed on issues related to land use and the expansion of Indian gaming. The chapter's final two essays, which focus on the debate over Makah whaling, illustrate some of the ways in which varied perceptions of customs, rights, and responsibilities can problematize an issue.

After many years of eroding autonomy, American Indian tribes are working toward becoming economically self-sufficient, while maintaining sovereignty over their reservations and dealing more effectively with the U.S. government. They also want to find ways to make decision-making processes more inclusive. American Indians are working to retain the traditions that have defined them for centuries.

## BEGINNING: Pre-reading/Writing

*American Indians have often been stereotyped in films and television as vicious savages or as romanticized innocents. Working individually or in a group, list the characteristics attributed to American Indians in early westerns, specific television series, and commercials. Has the portrayal changed over time? If so, in what ways? As you read the chapter, compare these depictions with those by American Indian authors.*

*The Indian Removal Act of 1830, passed during Andrew Jackson's adminis-tration, gave the president authority to transfer to the western territories any Indian tribes living in the East. The law dissolved tribal governments but guaranteed that American Indians would hold the new territories "in perpe-tuity"—a promise soon forgotten. The passage of this bill led to the forced relocation of 1838. Because of the suffering it caused, the journey from the East to the so-called Indian Territories of the West is often called the "Trail of Tears."*

⁜

## *From* THE INDIAN REMOVAL ACT

1  CHAP. CXLVIII.—*An Act to provide for an exchange of lands with the Indians residing in any of the states or territories, and for their removal west of the river Mississippi.*

2  *Be it enacted by the Senate and House of Representatives of the United States of America, in Congress assembled,* That it shall and may be lawful for the President of the United States to cause so much of any territory belonging to the United States, west of the river Mississippi, not included in any state or organized territory, and to which the Indian title has been extinguished, as he may judge necessary, to be divided into a suitable number of districts, for the reception of such tribes or nations of Indians as may choose to exchange the lands where they now reside, and remove there; and to cause each of said districts to be so described by natural or artificial marks, as to be easily distinguished from every other.

3  SEC. 2. *And be it further enacted,* That it shall and may be lawful for the President to exchange any or all of such districts, so to be laid off and described, with any tribe or nation of Indians now residing within the limits of any of the states or territories, and with which the United States have existing treaties, for the whole or any part or portion of the territory claimed and occupied by such tribe or nation, within the bounds of any one or more of the states or territories, where the land claimed and occupied by the Indians, is owned by the United States, or the United States are bound to the state within which it lies to extinguish the Indian claim thereto.

4  SEC. 3. *And be it further enacted,* That in the making of any such exchange or exchanges, it shall and may be lawful for the President solemnly to assure the tribe or nation with which the exchange is made, that the United States will forever secure and guaranty to them, and their heirs or successors, the country so exchanged with them; and if they prefer it, that the United States will cause a patent or grant to be made and executed to them for the same: *Provided always,* That such lands shall revert to the United States, if the Indians become extinct, or abandon the same.

SEC. 4. *And be it further enacted,* That if, upon any of the lands now occupied by the Indians, and to be exchanged for, there should be such improvements as add value to the land claimed by any individual or individuals of such tribes or nations, it shall and may be lawful for the President to cause such value to be ascertained by appraisement or otherwise, and to cause such ascertained value to be paid to the person or persons rightfully claiming such improvements. And upon the payment of such valuation, the improvements so valued and paid for, shall pass to the United States, and possession shall not afterwards be permitted to any of the same tribe.

SEC. 5. *And be it further enacted,* That upon the making of any such exchange as is contemplated by this act, it shall and may be lawful for the President to cause such aid and assistance to be furnished to the emigrants as may be necessary and proper to enable them to remove to, and settle in, the country for which they may have exchanged; and also, to give them such aid and assistance as may be necessary for their support and subsistence for the first year after their removal.

SEC. 6. *And be it further enacted,* That it shall and may be lawful for the President to cause such tribe or nation to be protected, at their new residence, against all interruption or disturbance from any other tribe or nation of Indians, or from any other person or persons whatever.

SEC. 7. *And be it further enacted,* That it shall and may be lawful for the President to have the same superintendence and care over any tribe or nation in the country to which they may remove, as contemplated by this act, that he is now authorized to have over them at their present places of residence: *Provided,* That nothing in this act contained shall be construed as authorizing or directing the violation of any existing treaty between the United States and any of the Indian tribes.

SEC. 8. *And be it further enacted,* That for the purpose of giving effect to the provisions of this act, the sum of five hundred thousand dollars is hereby appropriated, to be paid out of any money in the treasury, not otherwise appropriated.

APPROVED, May 28, 1830. ✠

---

## RESPONDING

1. Imagine that you are an American Indian reading this act today. In a journal entry, explain how you would respond. What would your feeling be toward the United States?

2. Write an essay discussing the government's assumptions about the future of American Indians. Support your opinions with evidence from the act.

3. Research the myth of the "vanishing American." Using evidence from the act, argue in an essay that the framers of the act did or did not give credence to this myth.

# CHIEF JOSEPH

*Heinmot Tooyalakekt, later known as Chief Joseph, was born into the Nez Percé tribe of Washington State in about 1840. Although several other tribes and one group of the Nez Percé had agreed to cede land to the federal government, Chief Joseph resisted the pressure and refused to surrender the land. The western expansion of the railroad intensified federal efforts to relocate tribal reservations to less desirable areas. When negotiations between General Howard and the Nez Percé failed to result in a treaty, the general gave the tribe thirty days to retreat. After an outlaw band of Joseph's tribe had killed four settlers and attacked some cavalry officers, the army began pursuit of the tribe. With his brother Ollokot, Chief Joseph led a group of seven hundred Nez Percé men and women across Idaho and Montana, close to the Canadian border, evading capture for several weeks. Chief Joseph's speech of surrender to the U.S. Army in 1877 is now famous. He spent his later years campaigning for the return of the tribe's land, even making a speech in Washington, D.C., in 1879. His efforts were unsuccessful. Chief Joseph died on a reservation in 1904.*

*The following selection is excerpted from Chief Joseph's* An Indian's View of Indian Affairs, *which was published in 1879, with an introduction by William Hare, a missionary bishop. In it, Chief Joseph recounts some of the events surrounding Euro American settlement of his native land, including the military skirmishes and the forced retreat. The selection concludes with Chief Joseph's appeal for a new relationship of mutual respect between the federal government and native peoples.*

❖

# *From* AN INDIAN'S VIEW OF INDIAN AFFAIRS

1   ON THE FOLLOWING MORNING I returned to my camp by agreement, meeting the officer who had been held a prisoner in my camp at the flag of truce. My people were divided about surrendering. We could have escaped from Bear Paw Mountain if we had left our wounded, old women, and children behind. We were unwilling to do this. We had never heard of a wounded Indian recovering while in the hands of white men.

On the evening of the fourth day General Howard came in with a small     2
escort, together with my friend Chapman. We could now talk understandingly.
General Miles said to me in plain words, "If you will come out and give up your
arms, I will spare your lives and send you to your reservation." I do not know
what passed between General Miles and General Howard.

I could not bear to see my wounded men and women suffer any longer; we     3
had lost enough already. General Miles had promised that we might return to
our own country with what stock we had left. I thought we could start again. I
believed General Miles, or *I never would have surrendered.* I have heard that he
has been censured for making the promise to return us to Lapwai. He could
not have made any other terms with me at that time. I would have held him in
check until my friends came to my assistance, and then neither of the generals
nor their soldiers would have ever left Bear Paw Mountain alive.

On the fifth day I went to General Miles and gave up my gun, and said,     4
"From where the sun now stands I will fight no more." My people needed
rest—we wanted peace. . . .

General Miles turned my people over to another soldier, and we were taken     5
to Bismarck. Captain Johnson, who now had charge of us, received an order to
take us to Fort Leavenworth. At Leavenworth we were placed on a low river
bottom, with no water except river-water to drink and cook with. We had always
lived in a healthy country, where the mountains were high and the water was
cold and clear. Many of my people sickened and died, and we buried them in
this strange land. I can not tell how much my heart suffered for my people while
at Leavenworth. The Great Spirit Chief who rules above seemed to be looking
some other way, and did not see what was being done to my people.

During the hot days (July, 1878) we received notice that we were to be     6
moved farther away from our own country. We were not asked if we were willing
to go. We were ordered to get into the railroad-cars. Three of my people died
on the way to Baxter Springs. It was worse to die there than to die fighting in
the mountains.

We were moved from Baxter Springs (Kansas) to the Indian Territory, and     7
set down without our lodges. We had but little medicine, and we were nearly
all sick. Seventy of my people have died since we moved there.

We have had a great many visitors who have talked many ways. Some of     8
the chiefs (General Fish and Colonel Stickney) from Washington came to see
us, and selected land for us to live upon. We have not moved to that land, for
it is not a good place to live.

The Commissioner Chief (E. A. Hayt) came to see us. I told him, as I told     9
every one, that I expected General Miles's word would be carried out. He said
it "could not be done; that white men now lived in my country and all the land
was taken up; that if I returned to Wallowa, I could not live in peace; that
law-papers were out against my young men who began the war, and that the
Government could not protect my people." This talk fell like a heavy stone
upon my heart. I saw that I could not gain anything by talking to him. Other
law chiefs (Congressional Committee) came to see me and said they would help

me to get a healthy country. I did not know who to believe. The white people have too many chiefs. They do not understand each other. They do not all talk alike.

10     The Commissioner Chief (Mr. Hayt) invited me to go with him and hunt for a better home than we have now. I like the land we found (west of the Osage reservation) better than any place I have seen in that country; but it is not a healthy land. There are no mountains and rivers. The water is warm. It is not a good country for stock. I do not believe my people can live there. I am afraid they will all die. The Indians who occupy that country are dying off. I promised Chief Hayt to go there, and do the best I could until the Government got ready to make good General Miles's word. I was not satisfied, but I could not help myself.

11     Then the Inspector Chief (General McNiel) came to my camp and we had a long talk. He said I ought to have a home in the mountain country north, and that he would write a letter to the Great Chief at Washington. Again the hope of seeing the mountains of Idaho and Oregon grew up in my heart.

12     At last I was granted permission to come to Washington and bring my friend Yellow Bull and our interpreter with me. I am glad we came. I have shaken hands with a great many friends, but there are some things I want to know which no one seems able to explain. I can not understand how the Government sends a man out to fight us, as it did General Miles, and then breaks his word. Such a Government has something wrong about it. I can not understand why so many chiefs are allowed to talk so many different ways, and promise so many different things. I have seen the Great Father Chief (the President), the next Great Chief (Secretary of the Interior), the Commissioner Chief (Hayt), the Law Chief (General Butler), and many other law chiefs (Congressmen), and they all say they are my friends, and that I shall have justice, but while their mouths all talk right I do not understand why nothing is done for my people. I have heard talk and talk, but nothing is done. Good words do not last long unless they amount to something. Words do not pay for my dead people. They do not pay for my country, now overrun by white men. They do not protect my father's grave. They do not pay for all my horses and cattle. Good words will not give me back my children. Good words will not make good the promise of your War Chief General Miles. Good words will not give my people good health and stop them from dying. Good words will not get my people a home where they can live in peace and take care of themselves. I am tired of talk that comes to nothing. It makes my heart sick when I remember all the good words and all the broken promises. There has been too much talking by men who had no right to talk. Too many misrepresentations have been made, too many misunderstandings have come up between the white men about the Indians. If the white man wants to live in peace with the Indian he can live in peace. There need be no trouble. Treat all men alike. Give them all the same law. Give them all an even chance to live and grow. All men were made by the same Great Spirit Chief. They are all brothers. The earth is the mother of all people, and all people should have

equal rights upon it. You might as well expect the rivers to run backward as that any man who was born a free man should be contented when penned up and denied liberty to go where he pleases. If you tie a horse to a stake, do you expect he will grow fat? If you pen an Indian up on a small spot of earth, and compel him to stay there, he will not be contented, nor will he grow and prosper. I have asked some of the great white chiefs where they get their authority to say to the Indian that he shall stay in one place, while he sees white men going where they please. They can not tell me.

I only ask of the Government to be treated as all other men are treated. If I can not go to my own home, let me have a home in some country where my people will not die so fast. I would like to go to Bitter Root Valley. There my people would be healthy; where they are now they are dying. Three have died since I left my camp to come to Washington.  13

When I think of our condition my heart is heavy. I see men of my race treated as outlaws and driven from country to country, or shot down like animals.  14

I know that my race must change. We can not hold our own with the white men as we are. We only ask an even chance to live as other men live. We ask to be recognized as men. We ask that the same law shall work alike on all men. If the Indian breaks the law, punish him by the law. If the white man breaks the law, punish him also.  15

Let me be a free man—free to travel, free to stop, free to work, free to trade where I choose, free to choose my own teachers, free to follow the religion of my fathers, free to think and talk and act for myself—and I will obey every law, or submit to the penalty.  16

Whenever the white man treats the Indian as they treat each other, then we will have no more wars. We shall all be alike—brothers of one father and one mother, with one sky above us and one country around us, and one government for all. Then the Great Spirit Chief who rules above will smile upon this land, and send rain to wash out the bloody spots made by brothers' hands from the face of the earth. For this time the Indian race are waiting and praying. I hope that no more groans of wounded men and women will ever go to the ear of the Great Spirit Chief above, and that all people may be one people.  17

In-mut-too-yah-lat-lat has spoken for his people.  18

YOUNG JOSEPH.

WASHINGTON CITY, D.C. ✠

---

## RESPONDING

1. In a journal entry, recount what you have learned throughout your schooling about the westward migration of settlers during the 1800s. From whose perspective was the migration presented?

2.   Working individually or in a group, use the reading and other resources to construct the American Indian perspective on the settlers' movement westward.

3.   Chief Joseph tries to convince his listeners that they should treat the Indians fairly. In an essay, present his arguments and examine why they may or may not persuade his audience. As you work, consider how Chief Joseph constructs his argument. What rhetorical strategies does he use to reach out to his audience? How effective are they in convincing you? How effective might the strategies have been in 1879? What interests might prevent Chief Joseph from winning over his listeners?

4.   Chief Joseph's speech reveals a great deal about his values. Write an essay discussing the values he believes in and comparing them to the values on which we base our democracy. You might choose to compare Chief Joseph's values with those expressed in the Bill of Rights (see chapter 3). In the United States's treatment of the Indians, were the values reflected in the Bill of Rights upheld?

# D'ARCY MCNICKLE

*The writer and activist William D'arcy McNickle was born in Montana in 1904. Of both Euro American and American Indian heritage, he and his family were adopted by the Flathead tribe. After his parents' divorce, he was sent to an Indian boarding school, which he later criticized in his writing. McNickle was one of the first American Indians to obtain a college education. After earning a bachelor's degree from the University of Montana, he later pursued graduate studies at Oxford and in Paris. From 1936 to 1952, he was employed by the Bureau of Indian Affairs (BIA) during the tenure of reformer John Collier. In this capacity, McNickle helped to design the first National Conference of American Indians, which was held in Denver in 1944. After resigning from the BIA over the government's "termination policy," which was designed to restructure reservations and to relocate their residents, McNickle became Director of American Indian Development, Inc. He later held executive positions at the Smithsonian Institution and the Newberry Library in Chicago. He died in New Mexico in 1977.*

*Throughout his career, McNickle published both fictional works and nonfiction studies of American Indian life. Perhaps his most famous work is his novel* The Surrounded, *published in 1936. His other works include the book-length studies* They Came First: The Epic of the American Indian *(1949; rev.*

*1975), Indians and Other Americans (1959; rev. 1970), and The Indian Tribes of the United States: Ethnic and Cultural Survival (1962; rev. 1973), and the novel Wind from the Enemy Sky (1978).*

*"Train Time," which McNickle wrote in 1936, makes use of complex strategies of point of view to represent the meeting of two cultures.*

⚏

# TRAIN TIME (1936)

ON THE DEPOT PLATFORM everybody stood waiting, listening. The train has just whistled, somebody said. They stood listening and gazing eastward, where railroad tracks and creek emerged together from a tree-choked canyon. 1

Twenty-five boys, five girls, Major Miles—all stood waiting and gazing eastward. Was it true that the train had whistled? 2

"That was no train!" a boy's voice explained. 3

"It was a steer bellowing." 4

"It was the train!" 5

Girls crowded backward against the station building, heads hanging, tears starting; boys pushed forward to the edge of the platform. An older boy with a voice already turning heavy stepped off the weather-shredded boardwalk and stood wide-legged in the middle of the track. He was the doubter. He had heard no train. 6

Major Miles boomed, "You! What's your name? Get back here! Want to get killed! All of you, stand back!" 7

The Major strode about, soldierlike, and waved commands. He was exasperated. He was tired. A man driving cattle through timber had it easy, he was thinking. An animal trainer had no idea of trouble. Let anyone try corraling twenty to thirty Indian kids, dragging them out of hiding places, getting them away from relatives and together in one place, then holding them, without tying them, until train time! Even now, at the last moment, when his worries were almost over, they were trying to get themselves killed! 8

Major Miles was a man of conscience. Whatever he did, he did earnestly. On this hot end-of-summer day he perspired and frowned and wore his soldier bearing. He removed his hat from his wet brow and thoughtfully passed his hand from the hair line backward. Words tumbled about in his mind. Somehow, he realized, he had to vivify the moment. These children were about to go out from the Reservation and get a new start. Life would change. They ought to realize it, somehow— 9

"Boys—and girls—" there were five girls he remembered. He had got them all lined up against the building, safely away from the edge of the platform. The air was stifling with end-of-summer heat. It was time to say something, never mind the heat. Yes, he would have to make the moment real. He stood soldier-like and thought that. 10

11    "Boys and girls—" The train whistled, dully, but unmistakably. Then it repeated more clearly. The rails came to life, something was running through them and making them sing.

12    Just then the Major's eye fell upon little Eneas and his sure voice faltered. He knew about little Eneas. Most of the boys and girls were mere names; he had seen them around the Agency with their parents, or had caught sight of them scurrying behind tipis and barns when he visited their homes. But little Eneas he knew. With him before his eyes, he paused.

13    He remembered so clearly the winter day, six months ago, when he first saw Eneas. It was the boy's grandfather, Michel Lamartine, he had gone to see. Michel had contracted to cut wood for the Agency but had not started work. The Major had gone to discover why not.

14    It was the coldest day of the winter, late in February, and the cabin, sheltered as it was among the pine and cottonwood of a creek bottom, was shot through by frosty drafts. There was wood all about them. Lamartine was a woodcutter besides, yet there was no wood in the house. The fire in the flat-topped cast-iron stove burned weakly. The reason was apparent. The Major had but to look at the bed where Lamartine lay, twisted and shrunken by rheumatism. Only his black eyes burned with life. He tried to wave a hand as the Major entered.

15    "You see how I am!" the gesture indicated. Then a nerve-strung voice faltered. "We have it bad here. My old woman, she's not much good."

16    Clearly she wasn't, not for wood-chopping. She sat close by the fire, trying with a good-natured grin to lift her ponderous body from a low seated rocking chair. The Major had to motion her back to her ease. She breathed with an asthmatic roar. Wood-chopping was not within her range. With only a squaw's hatchet to work with, she could scarcely have come within striking distance of a stick of wood. Two blows, if she had struck them, might have put a stop to her laboring heart.

17    "You see how it is," Lamartine's eyes flashed.

18    The Major saw clearly. Sitting there in the frosty cabin, he pondered their plight and at the same time wondered if he would get away without coming down with pneumonia. A stream of wind seemed to be hitting him in the back of the neck. Of course, there was nothing to do. One saw too many such situations. If one undertook to provide sustenance out of one's own pocket there would be no end to the demands. Government salaries were small, resources were limited. He could do no more than shake his head sadly, offer some vague hope, some small sympathy. He would have to get away at once.

19    Then a hand fumbled at the door; it opened. After a moment's struggle, little Eneas appeared, staggering under a full armload of pine limbs hacked into short lengths. The boy was no taller than an ax handle, his nose was running, and he had a croupy cough. He dropped the wood into the empty box near the old woman's chair, then straightened himself.

20    A soft chuckling came from the bed. Lamartine was full of pride. "A good boy, that. He keeps the old folks warm."

Something about the boy made the Major forget his determination to 21
depart. Perhaps it was his wordlessness, his uncomplaining wordlessness. Or
possibly it was his loyalty to the old people. Something drew his eyes to the boy
and set him to thinking. Eneas was handing sticks of wood to the old woman
and she was feeding them into the stove. When the firebox was full a good part
of the boy's armload was gone. He would have to cut more, and more, to keep
the old people warm.

The Major heard himself saying suddenly: "Sonny, show me your woodpile. 22
Let's cut a lot of wood for the old folks."

It happened just like that, inexplicably. He went even farther. Not only did 23
he cut enough wood to last through several days, but when he had finished he
put the boy in the Agency car and drove him to town, five miles there and back.
Against his own principles, he bought a week's store of groceries, and excused
himself by telling the boy, as they drove homeward, "Your grandfather won't
be able to get to town for a few days yet. Tell him to come see me when he
gets well."

That was the beginning of the Major's interest in Eneas. He had decided 24
that day that he would help the boy in any way possible, because he was a boy
of quality. You would be shirking your duty if you failed to recognize and to
help a boy of his sort. The only question was, how to help?

When he saw the boy again, some weeks later, his mind saw the problem 25
clearly. "Eneas," he said, "I'm going to help you. I'll see that the old folks are
taken care of, so you won't have to think about them. Maybe the old man won't
have rheumatism next year, anyhow. If he does, I'll find a family where he and
the old lady can move in and be looked after. Don't worry about them. Just
think about yourself and what I'm going to do for you. Eneas, when it comes
school time, I'm going to send you away. How do you like that?" The Major
smiled at his own happy idea.

There was silence. No shy smiling, no look of gratitude, only silence. 26
Probably he had not understood.

"You understand, Eneas? Your grandparents will be taken care of. You'll go 27
away and learn things. You'll go on a train."

The boy looked here and there and scratched at the ground with his foot. 28
"Why do I have to go away?"

"You don't have to, Eneas. Nobody will make you. I thought you'd like to. 29
I thought—" The Major paused, confused.

"You won't make me go away, will you?" There was fear in the voice, tears 30
threatened.

"Why, no Eneas. If you don't want to go. I thought—" 31

The Major dropped the subject. He didn't see the boy again through spring 32
and summer, but he thought of him. In fact, he couldn't forget the picture he
had of him that first day. He couldn't forget either that he wanted to help him.
Whether the boy understood what was good for him or not, he meant to see
to it that the right thing was done. And that was why, when he made up a quota

of children to be sent to the school in Oregon, the name of Eneas Lamartine was included. The Major did not discuss it with him again but he set the wheels in motion. The boy would go with the others. In time to come, he would understand. Possibly he would be grateful.

33     Thirty children were included in the quota, and of them all Eneas was the only one the Major had actual knowledge of, the only one in whom he was personally interested. With each of them, it was true, he had had difficulties. None had wanted to go. They said they "liked it at home," or they were "afraid" to go away, or they would "get sick" in a strange country; and the parents were no help. They, too, were frightened and uneasy. It was a tiresome, hard kind of duty, but the Major knew what was required of him and never hesitated. The difference was, that in the cases of all these others, the problem was routine. He met it, and passed over it. But in the case of Eneas, he was bothered. He wanted to make clear what this moment of going away meant. It was a breaking away from fear and doubt and ignorance. Here began the new. Mark it, remember it.

34     His eyes lingered on Eneas. There he stood, drooping, his nose running as on that first day, his stockings coming down, his jacket in need of buttons. But under that shabbiness, the Major knew, was real quality. There was a boy who, with the right help, would blossom and grow strong. It was important that he should not go away hurt and resentful.

35     The Major called back his straying thoughts and cleared his throat. The moment was important.

36     "Boys and girls—"

37     The train was pounding near. Already it had emerged from the canyon, and momentarily the headlong flying locomotive loomed blacker and larger. A white plume flew upward—*Whoo-oo, whoo-oo.*

38     The Major realized in sudden sharp remorse that he had waited too long. The vital moment had come, and he had paused, looked for words, and lost it. The roar of rolling steel was upon them.

39     Lifting his voice in desperate haste, his eyes fastened on Eneas, he bellowed: "Boys and girls—be good—"

40     That was all anyone heard. ✚

---

## RESPONDING

1.  Write a journal entry about a conflict you have experienced, perhaps concerning something you wanted to do and what someone in authority decided it would be *better* for you to do. The conflict might have involved which college you would attend, who your friends should be, or whether you should smoke. What arguments did you use to support your position? What arguments did the authority figure use? How was the conflict resolved?

2. Working individually or in a group, list all of the reasons why Major Miles wanted to send Eneas to boarding school. Next, list the reasons why Eneas resisted going. Discuss the consequences of the final decision.

3. Much of the story is presented from Major Miles's perspective. In an essay, describe what he is thinking and feeling when he encounters Eneas and his family. Why does he feel that what he is doing is in Eneas's best interest? Do you agree or disagree?

4. Consider the benefits and drawbacks of having to adapt to another culture. In an essay, discuss the immediate and long-term effects of the government's policy of sending Indian children to boarding school, away from their families and their culture. You may need to do additional research to write this essay.

# LESLIE MARMON SILKO

*The poet, novelist, and short-story writer Leslie Marmon Silko was born in New Mexico in 1948 of Laguna, Plains Indian, Mexican, and white ancestry. After earning her bachelor's degree from the University of New Mexico and attending law school, she devoted herself to writing, focusing primarily on American Indian themes. Silko's publications include* Laguna Woman: Poems *(1974), the novels* Ceremony *(1977) and* Almanac of the Dead *(1991), a poetry and short-story collection,* Storyteller *(1981), and* Yellow Woman and a Beauty of the Spirit: Essays on Native American Life Today *(1996). She was honored with grants from the National Endowment for the Arts in 1974 and from the MacArthur Foundation in 1983, among others.*

*"Lullaby," from* Storyteller, *describes an American Indian woman as she confronts government authorities whose language she cannot understand. At the same time, the story asks us to consider the ways in which language and power can be interconnected.*

# LULLABY

THE SUN HAD GONE DOWN but the snow in the wind gave off its own light. It came in thick tufts like new wool—washed before the weaver spins it. Ayah reached out for it like her own babies had, and she smiled when she remembered how she had laughed at them. She was an old woman now, and her life had become memories. She sat down with her back against the wide cottonwood tree, feeling the rough bark on her back bones; she faced east and listened to the wind and snow sing a high-pitched Yeibechei song. Out of the wind she felt warmer, and she could watch the wide fluffy snow fill in her tracks, steadily, until the direction she had come from was gone. By the light of the snow she could see the dark outline of the big arroyo a few feet away. She was sitting on the edge of Cebellota Creek, where in the springtime the thin cows would graze on grass already chewed flat to the ground. In the wide deep creek bed where only a trickle of water flowed in the summer, the skinny cows would wander, looking for new grass along winding paths splashed with manure.

2       Ayah pulled the old Army blanket over her head like a shawl. Jimmie's blanket—the one he had sent to her. That was a long time ago and the green wool was faded, and it was unraveling on the edges. She did not want to think about Jimmie. So she thought about the weaving and the way her mother had done it. On the tall wooden loom set into the sand under a tamarack tree for shade. She could see it clearly. She had been only a little girl when her grandma gave her the wooden combs to pull the twigs and burrs from the raw, freshly washed wool. And while she combed the wool, her grandma sat beside her, spinning a silvery strand of yarn around the smooth cedar spindle. Her mother worked at the loom with yarns dyed bright yellow and red and gold. She watched them dye the yarn in boiling black pots full of beeweed petals, juniper berries, and sage. The blankets her mother made were soft and woven so tight that rain rolled off them like birds' feathers. Ayah remembered sleeping warm on cold windy nights, wrapped in her mother's blankets on the hogan's sandy floor.

3       The snow drifted now, with the northwest wind hurling it in gusts. It drifted up around her black overshoes—old ones with little metal buckles. She smiled at the snow which was trying to cover her little by little. She could remember when they had no black rubber overshoes; only the high buckskin leggings that they wrapped over their elkhide moccasins. If the snow was dry or frozen, a person could walk all day and not get wet; and in the evenings the beams of the ceiling would hang with lengths of pale buckskin leggings, drying out slowly.

4       She felt peaceful remembering. She didn't feel cold any more. Jimmie's blanket seemed warmer than it had ever been. And she could remember the morning he was born. She could remember whispering to her mother, who was sleeping on the other side of the hogan, to tell her it was time now. She did not want to wake the others. The second time she called to her, her mother stood up and pulled on her shoes; she knew. They walked to the old stone hogan together, Ayah walking a step behind her mother. She waited alone, learning the rhythms of the pains while her mother went to call the old woman to help them. The morning was already warm even before dawn and Ayah smelled the bee flowers blooming and the young willow growing at the springs. She could remember that so clearly, but his birth merged into the births of the other children and to her it became all the same birth. They named him for the summer morning and in English they called him Jimmie.

It wasn't like Jimmie died. He just never came back, and one day a dark    5
blue sedan with white writing on its doors pulled up in front of the boxcar shack
where the rancher let the Indians live. A man in a khaki uniform trimmed in
gold gave them a yellow piece of paper and told them that Jimmie was dead.
He said the Army would try to get the body back and then it would be shipped
to them; but it wasn't likely because the helicopter had burned after it crashed.
All of this was told to Chato because he could understand English. She stood
inside the doorway holding the baby while Chato listened. Chato spoke English
like a white man and he spoke Spanish too. He was taller than the white man
and he stood straighter too. Chato didn't explain why; he just told the military
man they could keep the body if they found it. The white man looked bewildered; he nodded his head and he left. Then Chato looked at her and shook his
head, and then he told her, "Jimmie isn't coming home anymore," and when he
spoke, he used the words to speak of the dead. She didn't cry then, but she hurt
inside with anger. And she mourned him as the years passed, when a horse fell
with Chato and broke his leg, and the white rancher told them he wouldn't pay
Chato until he could work again. She mourned Jimmie because he would have
worked for his father then; he would have saddled the big bay horse and ridden
the fence lines each day, with wire cutters and heavy gloves, fixing the breaks
in the barbed wire and putting the stray cattle back inside again.

She mourned him after the white doctors came to take Danny and Ella    6
away. She was at the shack alone that day they came. It was back in the days
before they hired Navajo women to go with them as interpreters. She recognized
one of the doctors. She had seen him at the children's clinic at Cañoncito about
a month ago. They were wearing khaki uniforms and they waved papers at her
and a black ball-point pen, trying to make her understand their English words.
She was frightened by the way they looked at the children, like the lizard watches
the fly. Danny was swinging on the tire swing on the elm tree behind the
rancher's house, and Ella was toddling around the front door, dragging the
broomstick horse Chato made for her. Ayah could see they wanted her to sign
the papers, and Chato had taught her to sign her name. It was something she
was proud of. She only wanted them to go, and to take their eyes away from
her children.

She took the pen from the man without looking at his face and she signed    7
the papers in three different places he pointed to. She stared at the ground by
their feet and waited for them to leave. But they stood there and began to point
and gesture at the children. Danny stopped swinging. Ayah could see his fear.
She moved suddenly and grabbed Ella into her arms; the child squirmed, trying
to get back to her toys. Ayah ran with the baby toward Danny; she screamed
for him to run and then she grabbed him around his chest and carried him too.
She ran south into the foothills of juniper trees and black lava rock. Behind her
she heard the doctors running, but they had been taken by surprise, and as the
hills became steeper and the cholla cactus were thicker, they stopped. When she
reached the top of the hill, she stopped to listen in case they were circling around

her. But in a few minutes she heard a car engine start and they drove away. The children had been too surprised to cry while she ran with them. Danny was shaking and Ella's little fingers were gripping Ayah's blouse.

8     She stayed up in the hills for the rest of the day, sitting on a black lava boulder in the sunshine where she could see for miles all around her. The sky was light blue and cloudless, and it was warm for late April. The sun warmth relaxed her and took the fear and anger away. She lay back on the rock and watched the sky. It seemed to her that she could walk into the sky, stepping through clouds endlessly. Danny played with little pebbles and stones, pretending they were birds' eggs and then little rabbits. Ella sat at her feet and dropped fistfuls of dirt into the breeze, watching the dust and particles of sand intently. Ayah watched a hawk soar high above them, dark wings gliding; hunting or only watching, she did not know. The hawk was patient and he circled all afternoon before he disappeared around the high volcanic peak the Mexicans called Guadalupe.

9     Late in the afternoon, Ayah looked down at the gray boxcar shack with the paint all peeled from the wood; the stove pipe on the roof was rusted and crooked. The fire she had built that morning in the oil drum stove had burned out. Ella was asleep in her lap now and Danny sat close to her, complaining that he was hungry; he asked when they would go to the house. "We will stay up here until your father comes," she told him, "because those white men were chasing us." The boy remembered then and he nodded at her silently.

10     If Jimmie had been there he could have read those papers and explained to her what they said. Ayah would have known then, never to sign them. The doctors came back the next day and they brought a BIA policeman with them. They told Chato they had her signature and that was all they needed. Except for the kids. She listened to Chato sullenly; she hated him when he told her it was the old woman who died in the winter, spitting blood; it was her old grandma who had given the children this disease. "They don't spit blood" she said coldly. "The whites lie." She held Ella and Danny close to her, ready to run to the hills again. "I want a medicine man first," she said to Chato, not looking at him. He shook his head. "It's too late now. The policeman is with them. You signed the paper." His voice was gentle.

11     It was worse than if they had died: to lose the children and to know that somewhere, in a place called Colorado, in a place full of sick and dying strangers, her children were without her. There had been babies that died soon after they were born, and one that died before he could walk. She had carried them herself, up to the boulders and great pieces of the cliff that long ago crashed down from Long Mesa; she laid them in the crevices of sandstone and buried them in fine brown sand with round quartz pebbles that washed down the hills in the rain. She had endured it because they had been with her. But she could not bear this pain. She did not sleep for a long time after they took her children. She stayed on the hill where they had fled the first time, and she slept rolled up in the blanket Jimmie had sent her. She carried the pain in her belly and it was fed by

everything she saw: the blue sky of their last day together and the dust and pebbles they played with; the swing in the elm tree and the broomstick horse choked life from her. The pain filled her stomach and there was no room for food or for her lungs to fill with air. The air and the food would have been theirs.

She hated Chato, not because he let the policeman and doctors put the screaming children in the government car, but because he had taught her to sign her name. Because it was like the old ones always told her about learning their language or any of their ways: it endangered you. She slept alone on the hill until the middle of November when the first snows came. Then she made a bed for herself where the children had slept. She did not lie down beside Chato again until many years later, when he was sick and shivering and only her body could keep him warm. The illness came after the white rancher told Chato he was too old to work for him anymore, and Chato and his old woman should be out of the shack by the next afternoon because the rancher had hired new people to work there. That had satisfied her. To see how the white man repaid Chato's years of loyalty and work. All of Chato's fine-sounding English talk didn't change things. 12

It snowed steadily and the luminous light from the snow gradually diminished into the darkness. Somewhere in Cebolleta a dog barked and other village dogs joined with it. Ayah looked in the direction she had come, from the bar where Chato was buying the wine. Sometimes he told her to go on ahead and wait; and then he never came. And when she finally went back looking for him, she would find him passed out at the bottom of the wooden steps to Azzie's Bar. All the wine would be gone and most of the money too, from the pale blue check that came to them once a month in a government envelope. It was then that she would look at his face and his hands, scarred by ropes and the barbed wire of all those years, and she would think, this man is a stranger; for forty years she had smiled at him and cooked his food, but he remained a stranger. She stood up again, with the snow almost to her knees, and she walked back to find Chato. 13

It was hard to walk in the deep snow and she felt the air burn in her lungs. She stopped a short distance from the bar to rest and readjust the blanket. But this time he wasn't waiting for her on the bottom step with his old Stetson hat pulled down and his shoulders hunched up in his long wool overcoat. 14

She was careful not to slip on the wooden steps. When she pushed the door open, warm air and cigarette smoke hit her face. She looked around slowly and deliberately, in every corner, in every dark place that the old man might find to sleep. The bar owner didn't like Indians in there, especially Navajos, but he let Chato come in because he could talk Spanish like he was one of them. The men at the bar stared at her, and the bartender saw that she left the door open wide. Snowflakes were flying inside like moths and melting into a puddle on the oiled wood floor. He motioned to her to close the door, but she did not see him. She 15 held herself straight and walked across the room slowly, searching the room with every step. The snow in her hair melted and she could feel it on her forehead. At the far corner of the room, she saw red flames at the mica window of the old stove door; she looked behind the stove just to make sure. The bar got quiet except for the Spanish polka music playing on the jukebox. She stood by the stove and shook the snow from her blanket and held it near the stove to dry. The wet wool smell reminded her of new-born goats in early March, brought inside to warm near the fire. She felt calm.

16    In past years they would have told her to get out. But her hair was white now and her face was wrinkled. They looked at her like she was a spider crawling slowly across the room. They were afraid; she could feel the fear. She looked at their faces steadily. They reminded her of the first time the white people brought her children back to her that winter. Danny had been shy and hid behind the thin white woman who brought them. And the baby had not known her until Ayah took her into her arms, and then Ella had nuzzled close to her as she had when she was nursing. The blonde woman was nervous and kept looking at a dainty gold watch on her wrist. She sat on the bench near the small window and watched the dark snow clouds gather around the mountains; she was worrying about the unpaved road. She was frightened by what she saw inside too: the strips of venison drying on a rope across the ceiling and the children jabbering excitedly in a language she did not know. So they stayed for only a few hours. Ayah watched the government car disappear down the road and she knew they were already being weaned from these lava hills and from this sky. The last time they came was in early June, and Ella stared at her the way the men in the bar were now staring. Ayah did not try to pick her up; she smiled at her instead and spoke cheerfully to Danny. When he tried to answer her, he could not seem to remember and he spoke English words with the Navajo. But he gave her a scrap of paper that he had found somewhere and carried in his pocket; it was folded in half, and he shyly looked up at her and said it was a bird. She asked Chato if they were home for good this time. He spoke to the white woman and she shook her head. "How much longer?" he asked, and she said she didn't know; but Chato saw how she stared at the boxcar shack. Ayah turned away then. She did not say good-bye.

17    She felt satisfied that the men in the bar feared her. Maybe it was her face and the way she held her mouth with teeth clenched tight, like there was nothing anyone could do to her now. She walked north down the road, searching for the old man. She did this because she had the blanket, and there would be no place for him except with her and the blanket in the old adobe barn near the arroyo. They always slept there when they came to Cebolleta. If the money and the wine were gone, she would be relieved because then they could go home again; back to the old hogan with a dirt roof and rock walls where she herself had been born. And the next day the old man could go back to the few sheep they still had, to follow along behind them, guiding them, into dry sandy arroyos

where sparse grass grew. She knew he did not like walking behind old ewes when for so many years he rode big quarter-horses and worked with cattle. But she wasn't sorry for him; he should have known all along what would happen.

There had not been enough rain for their garden in five years; and that was 18 when Chato finally hitched a ride into the town and brought back brown boxes of rice and sugar and big tin cans of welfare peaches. After that, at the first of the month they went to Cebolleta to ask the postmaster for the check; and then Chato would go to the bar and cash it. They did this as they planted the garden every May, not because anything would survive the summer dust, but because it was time to do this. The journey passed the days that smelled silent and dry like the caves above the canyon with yellow painted buffaloes on their walls.

He was walking along the pavement when she found him. He did not stop or 19 turn around when he heard her behind him. She walked beside him and she noticed how slowly he moved now. He smelled strong of woodsmoke and urine. Lately he had been forgetting. Sometimes he called her by his sister's name and she had been gone for a long time. Once she had found him wandering on the road to the white man's ranch, and she asked him why he was going that way; he laughed at her and said, "You know they can't run that ranch without me," and he walked on determined, limping on the leg that had been crushed many years before. Now he looked at her curiously, as if for the first time, but he kept shuffling along, moving slowly along the side of the highway. His gray hair had grown long and spread out on the shoulders of the long overcoat. He wore the old felt hat pulled down over his ears. His boots were worn out at the toes and he had stuffed pieces of an old red shirt in the holes. The rags made his feet look like little animals up to their ears in snow. She laughed at his feet; the snow muffled the sound of her laugh. He stopped and looked at her again. The wind had quit blowing and the snow was falling straight down; the southeast sky was beginning to clear and Ayah could see a star.

"Let's rest awhile," she said to him. They walked away from the road and 20 up the slope to the giant boulders that had tumbled down from the red sandrock mesa throughout the centuries of rainstorms and earth tremors. In a place where the boulders shut out the wind, they sat down with their backs against the rock. She offered half of the blanket to him and they sat wrapped together.

The storm passed swiftly. The clouds moved east. They were massive and 21 full, crowding together across the sky. She watched them with the feeling of horses—steely blue-gray horses startled across the sky. The powerful haunches pushed into the distances and the tail hairs streamed white mist behind them. The sky cleared. Ayah saw that there was nothing between her and the stars. The light was crystalline. There was no shimmer, no distortion through earth haze. She breathed the clarity of the night sky; she smelled the purity of the half moon and the stars. He was lying on his side with his knees pulled up near his belly for warmth. His eyes were closed now, and in the light from the stars and the moon, he looked young again.

22    She could see it descend out of the night sky: an icy stillness from the edge
of the thin moon. She recognized the freezing. It came gradually, sinking
snowflake by snowflake until the crust was heavy and deep. It had the strength
of the stars in Orion, and its journey was endless. Ayah knew that with the wine
he would sleep. He would not feel it. She tucked the blanket around him,
remembering how it was when Ella had been with her; and she felt the rush so
big inside her heart for the babies. And she sang the only song she knew to sing
for babies. She could not remember if she had ever sung it to her children, but
she knew that her grandmother had sung it and her mother had sung it:

> The earth is your mother,
> she holds you.
> The sky is your father,
> he protects you.
> Sleep,
> sleep,
> Rainbow is your sister,
>     she loves you.
> The winds are your brothers,
>     they sing to you.
> Sleep,
> sleep.
> We are together always
> We are together always
> There never was a time
> when this
> was not so. ✤

---

RESPONDING

1.  The story takes place "back in the days before they hired Navajo women
    to go with them as interpreters" (paragraph 6). Ayah loses her children
    because she doesn't speak English and can't read the paper she is given to
    sign. In a journal entry, describe your reactions to the story's events. Or tell
    about a time when you or someone you know was in a situation where lack
    of understanding of language or customs created great difficulties.

2.  Working with a partner, write a dialogue between Ayah and the doctors
    who come to take away her children. If they spoke her language, what
    argument might they give her to convince her to allow the children to be
    taken away for treatment? How might she respond?

3. Chato ends his life in rags, spending his government checks on alcohol. Discuss the causes of his difficulties in an essay. In your opinion, who is responsible for his problems?

4. Write an essay explaining Ayah's attitude toward life and death, illustrating your explanation with examples from the text.

# JAMES WELCH

*A poet of Blackfeet and Gros Ventre heritage, James Welch was born in Browning, Montana, in 1940. After growing up on Montana's Blackfeet and Fort Belknap reservations and in Minneapolis, he earned a bachelor's degree from the University of Montana. Welch's writing includes the fictional works* Winter in the Blood *(1974),* The Death of Jim Loney *(1979),* Fools Crow *(1986), and* The Indian Lawyer *(1990); the nonfiction work (with Paul Stekler)* Killing Custer: The Battle of the Little Bighorn and the Fate of the Plains Indians *(1994); and the poetry collection* Riding the Earthboy 40 *(1971). He has received several awards, including a grant from the National Endowment for the Arts (NEA); in 1970 he was named to the NEA's literature panel.*

*The poem that follows, from* Riding the Earthboy 40, *examines the issues of tradition and identity, and the social pressures that threaten them.*

⊞

# PLEA TO THOSE WHO MATTER

You don't know I pretend my dumb.
My songs often wise, my bells could chase
the snow across these whistle-black plains.
Celebrate. The days are grim. Call your winds
to blast these bundled streets and patronize          5
my past of poverty and 4-day feasts.

Don't ignore me. I'll build my face a different way,
a way to make you know that I am no longer
proud, my name not strong enough to stand alone.
If I lie and say you took me for a friend,          10

patched together in my thin bones,
will you help me be cunning and noisy as the wind?

I have plans to burn my drum, move out
and civilize this hair. See my nose? I smash it
15    straight for you. These teeth? I scrub my teeth
away with stones. I know you help me now I matter.
And I—I come to you, head down, bleeding from my smile,
happy for the snow clean hands of you, my friends. ✤

---

## RESPONDING

1. Have you or someone you know ever felt you had to change your appearance or behavior to please someone in authority? Write a journal entry about that experience or about your reaction to that solution to being different.

2. Individually or with a partner, write a dialogue between the speaker and an Indian rights activist.

3. In an essay, identify and describe the speaker in the poem. According to the poem, who are "those who matter," and how is the speaker willing to change to please them?

4. Write an essay explaining the attitude of the poet toward the speaker. Does he approve or disapprove of the speaker's behavior? Support your opinion by citing examples from the poem.

---

# LOUISE ERDRICH

*Louise Erdrich, who is of Turtle Mountain Chippewa and German ancestry, inherits a mixture of Ojibwa, Cree, French, and Plains traditions. She was born in Little Falls, Minnesota, in 1954 and grew up in Wahpeton, North Dakota. Erdrich received a bachelor's degree from Dartmouth College in 1976 and a master's degree from Johns Hopkins University in 1977. In addition to contributing to* Atlantic Monthly, Chicago, The Kenyon Review, *and* North American Review, *Erdrich has published the poetry collection* Jacklight *(1984) as well as the novels* Love Medicine *(1984),* The Beet Queen *(1986), and* Tracks *(1988). Her later works include the novels* Bingo Palace *(1994) and* Tales of Burning Love *(1996), and the poetry collection* Last

Report on the Miracles at Little No Horse *(1998). Her work has earned her the National Book Critics' Circle Award (1984) and the O. Henry Award (1985).*

*In the following selection from* Love Medicine, *the young narrator, Lipsha Morrissey, describes his attitudes toward his extended family and the healing touch that he believes he has been given. The narrative provides a commentary not only on the Chippewa culture but on the culture beyond the Chippewa community.*

╬

# *From* LOVE MEDICINE

## *LIPSHA MORRISSEY*

I NEVER REALLY DONE MUCH with my life, I suppose. I never had a television. 1 Grandma Kashpaw had one inside her apartment at the Senior Citizens, so I used to go there and watch my favorite shows. For a while she used to call me the biggest waste on the reservation and hark back to how she saved me from my own mother, who wanted to tie me in a potato sack and throw me in a slough. Sure, I was grateful to Grandma Kashpaw for saving me like that, for raising me, but gratitude gets old. After a while, stale. I had to stop thanking her. One day I told her I had paid her back in full by staying at her beck and call. I'd do anything for Grandma. She knew that. Besides, I took care of Grandpa like nobody else could, on account of what a handful he'd gotten to be.

But that was nothing, I know the tricks of mind and body inside out without 2 ever having trained for it, because I got the touch. It's a thing you got to be born with. I got secrets in my hands that nobody ever knew to ask. Take Grandma Kashpaw with her tired veins all knotted up in her legs like clumps of blue snails. I take my fingers and I snap them on the knots. The medicine flows out of me. The touch. I run my fingers up the maps of those rivers of veins or I knock very gentle above their hearts or I make a circling motion on their stomachs, and it helps them. They feel much better. Some women pay me five dollars.

I couldn't do the touch for Grandpa, though. He was a hard nut. You know, 3 some people fall right through the hole in their lives. It's invisible, but they come to it after time, never knowing where. There is this woman here, Lulu Lamartine, who always had a thing for Grandpa. She loved him since she was a girl and always said he was a genius. Now she says that his mind got so full it exploded.

How can I doubt that? I know the feeling when your mental power builds 4 up too far. I always used to say that's why the Indians got drunk. Even statistically we're the smartest people on the earth. Anyhow with Grandpa I couldn't hardly believe it, because all my youth he stood out as a hero to me. When he started getting toward second childhood he went through different moods. He would stand in the woods and cry at the top of his shirt. It scared me, scared everyone, Grandma worst of all.

5    Yet he was so smart—do you believe it?—that he *knew* he was getting foolish.

6    He said so. He told me that December I failed school and come back on the train to Hoopdance. I didn't have nowhere else to go. He picked me up there and he said it straight out: "I'm getting into my second childhood." And then he said something else I still remember: "I been chosen for it. I couldn't say no." So I figure that a man so smart all his life—tribal chairman and the star of movies and even pictured in the statehouse and on cans of snuff—would know what he's doing by saying yes. I think he was called to second childhood like anybody else gets a call for the priesthood or the army or whatever. So I really did not listen too hard when the doctor said this was some kind of disease old people got eating too much sugar. You just can't tell me that a man who went to Washington and gave them bureaucrats what for could lose his mind from eating too much Milky Way. No, he put second childhood on himself.

7    Behind those songs he sings out in the middle of Mass, and back of those stories that everybody knows by heart, Grandpa is thinking hard about life. I know the feeling. Sometimes I'll throw up a smokescreen to think behind. I'll hitch up to Winnipeg and play the Space Invaders for six hours, but all the time there and back I will be thinking some fairly deep thoughts that surprise even me, and I'm used to it. As for him, if it was just the thoughts there wouldn't be no problem. Smokescreen is what irritates the social structure, see, and Grandpa has done things that just distract people to the point they want to throw him in the cookie jar where they keep the mentally insane. He's far from that, I know for sure, but even Grandma had trouble keeping her patience once he started sneaking off to Lamartine's place. He's not supposed to have his candy, and Lulu feeds it to him. That's *one* of the reasons why he goes.

8    Grandma tried to get me to put the touch on Grandpa soon after he began stepping out. I didn't want to, but before Grandma started telling me again what a bad state my bare behind was in when she first took me home, I thought I should at least pretend.

9    I put my hands on either side of Grandpa's head. You wouldn't look at him and say he was crazy. He's a fine figure of a man, as Lamartine would say, with all his hair and half his teeth, a beak like a hawk, and cheeks like the blades of a hatchet. They put his picture on all the tourist guides to North Dakota and even copied his face for artistic paintings. I guess you could call him a monument all of himself. He started grinning when I put my hands on his templates, and I knew right then he knew how come I touched him. I knew the smokescreen was going to fall.

10   And I was right: just for a moment it fell.

"Let's pitch whoopee," he said across my shoulder to Grandma.                    11

They don't use that expression much around here anymore, but for damn    12
sure it must have meant something. It got her goat right quick.

She threw my hands off his head herself and stood in front of him, over-    13
matching him pound for pound, and taller too, for she had a growth spurt in
middle age while he had shrunk, so now the length and breadth of her surpassed
him. She glared and spoke her piece into his face about how he was off at all
hours tomcatting and chasing Lamartine again and making a damn old fool of
himself.

"And you got no more whoopee to pitch anymore anyhow!" she yelled at    14
last, surprising me so my jaw just dropped, for us kids all had pretended for so
long that those rustling sounds we heard from their side of the room at night
never happened. She sure had pretended it, up till now, anyway. I saw that tears
were in her eyes. And that's when I saw how much grief and love she felt for
him. And it gave me a real shock to the system. You see I thought love got
easier over the years so it didn't hurt so bad when it hurt, or feel so good when
it felt good. I thought it smoothed out and old people hardly noticed it. I thought
it curled up and died, I guess. Now I saw it rear up like a whip and lash.

She loved him. She was jealous. She mourned him like the dead.                    15

And he just smiled into the air, trapped in the seams of his mind.                16

So I didn't know what to do. I was in a laundry then. They was like parents    17
to me, the way they had took me home and reared me. I could see her point
for wanting to get him back the way he was so at least she could argue with
him, sleep with him, not be shamed out by Lamartine. She'd always love him.
That hit me like a ton of bricks. For one whole day I felt this odd feeling that
cramped my hands. When you have the touch, that's where longing gets you.
I never loved like that. It made me feel all inspired to see them fight, and I
wanted to go out and find a woman who I would love until one of us died or
went crazy. But I'm not like that really. From time to time I heal a person all
up good inside, however when it comes to the long shot I doubt that I got
staying power.

And you need that, staying power, going out to love somebody. I know this    18
quality was not going to jump on me with no effort. So I turned my thoughts
back to Grandma and Grandpa. I felt her side of it with my hands and my
tangled guts, and I felt his side of it within the stretch of my mentality. He had
gone out to lunch one day and never came back. He was fishing in the middle
of Matchimanito. And there was big thoughts on his line, and he kept throwing
them back for even bigger ones that would explain to him, say, the meaning of
how we got here and why we have to leave so soon. All in all, I could not see
myself treating Grandpa with the touch, bringing him back, when the real part
of him had chose to be off thinking somewhere. It was only the rest of him that
stayed around causing trouble, after all, and we could handle most of it without
any problem.

Besides, it was hard to argue with his reasons for doing some things. Take    19

Holy Mass. I used to go there just every so often, when I got frustrated mostly, because even though I know the Higher Power dwells everyplace, there's something very calming about the cool greenish inside of our mission. Or so I thought, anyway. Grandpa was the one who stripped off my delusions in this matter, for it was he who busted right through what Father calls the sacred serenity of the place.

20    We filed in that time. Me and Grandpa. We sat down on our pews. Then the rosary got started up pre-Mass and that's when Grandpa filled up his chest and opened his mouth and belted out them words.

21    HAIL MARIE FULL OF GRACE.

22    He had a powerful set of lungs.

23    And he kept on like that. He did not let up. He hollered and he yelled them prayers, and I guess people was used to him by now, because they only muttered theirs and did not quit and gawk like I did. I was getting red-faced, I admit. I give him the elbow once or twice, but that wasn't nothing to him. He kept on. He shrieked to heaven and he pleaded like a movie actor and he pounded his chest like Tarzan in the Lord I Am Not Worthies. I thought he might hurt himself. Then after a while I guess I got used to it, and that's when I wondered: how come?

24    So afterwards I out and asked him, "How come? How come you yelled?"

25    "God don't hear me otherwise," said Grandpa Kashpaw.

26    I sweat. I broke right into a little cold sweat at my hairline because I knew this was perfectly right and for years not one damn other person had noticed it. God's been going deaf. Since the Old Testament, God's been deafening up on us. I read, see. Besides the dictionary, which I'm constantly in use of, I had this Bible once. I read it. I found there was discrepancies between then and now. It struck me. Here God used to raineth bread from clouds, smite the Phillipines, sling fire down on red-light districts where people got stabbed. He even appeared in person every once in a while. God used to pay attention, is what I'm saying.

27    Now there's your God in the Old Testament and there is Chippewa Gods as well. Indian Gods, good and bad, like tricky Nanabozho or the water monster, Missepeshu, who lives over in Matchimanito. That water monster was the last God I ever heard to appear. It had a weakness for young girls and grabbed one of the Pillagers off her rowboat. She got to shore all right, but only after this monster had its way with her. She's an old lady now. Old Lady Pillager. She still doesn't like to see her family fish that lake.

28    Our Gods aren't perfect, is what I'm saying, but at least they come around. They'll do a favor if you ask them right. You don't have to yell. But you do have to know, like I said, how to ask in the right way. That makes problems, because to ask proper was an art that was lost to the Chippewas once the Catholics gained ground. Even now, I have to wonder if Higher Power turned it back, if we got to yell, or if we just don't speak its language.

29    I looked around me. How else could I explain what all I had seen in my

short life—King smashing his fist in things, Gordie drinking himself down to the Bismarck hospitals, or Aunt June left by a white man to wander off in the snow. How else to explain the times my touch don't work, and farther back, to the old-time Indians who was swept away in the outright germ warfare and dirty-dog killing of the whites. In those times, us Indians was so much kindlier than now.

We took them in.                                                           30

Oh yes, I'm bitter as an old cutworm just thinking of how they done to us   31
and doing still.

So Grandpa Kashpaw just opened my eyes a little there. Was there any        32
sense relying on a God whose ears was stopped? Just like the government? I says then, right off, maybe we got nothing but ourselves. And that's not much, just personally speaking. I know I don't got the cold hard potatoes it takes to understand everything. Still, there's things I'd like to do. For instance, I'd like to help some people like my Grandpa and Grandma Kashpaw get back some happiness within the tail ends of their lives.

I told you once before I couldn't see my way clear to putting the direct    33
touch on Grandpa's mind, and I kept my moral there, but something soon happened to make me think a little bit of mental adjustment wouldn't do him and the rest of us no harm.

It was after we saw him one afternoon in the sunshine courtyard of the      34
Senior Citizens with Lulu Lamartine. Grandpa used to like to dig there. He had his little dandelion fork out, and he was prying up them dandelions right and left while Lamartine watched him.

"He's scratching up the dirt, all right," said Grandma, watching Lamartine  35
watch Grandpa out the window.

Now Lamartine was about half the considerable size of Grandma, but you      36
would never think of sizes anyway. They were different in an even more noticeable way. It was the difference between a house fixed up with paint and picky fence, and a house left to weather away into the soft earth, is what I'm saying. Lamartine was jacked up, latticed, shuttered, and vinyl sided, while Grandma sagged and bulged on her slipped foundations and let her hair go the silver gray of rain-dried lumber. Right now, she eyed the Lamartine's pert flowery dress with such a look it despaired me. I knew what this could lead to with Grandma. Alterating tongue storms and rock-hard silences was hard on a man, even one who didn't notice, like Grandpa. So I went fetching him.

But he was gone when I popped through the little screen door that led out    37
on the courtyard. There was nobody out there either, to point which way they went. Just the dandelion fork quibbling upright in the ground. That gave me an idea. I snookered over to the Lamartine's door and I listened in first, then knocked. But nobody. So I went walking through the lounges and around the card tables. Still nobody. Finally it was my touch that led me to the laundry room. I cracked the door. I went in. There they were. And he was really loving her up good, boy, and she was going hell for leather. Sheets was flapping on the

lines above, and washcloths, pillowcases, shirts was also flying through the air, for they was trying to clear out a place for themselves in a high-heaped but shallow laundry cart. The washers and dryers was all on, chock-full of quarters, shaking and moaning. I couldn't hear what Grandpa and the Lamartine was billing and cooing, and they couldn't hear me.

38     I didn't know what to do, so I went inside and shut the door.

39     The Lamartine wore a big curly light-brown wig. Looked like one of them squeaky little white-people dogs. Poodles they call them. Anyway, that wig is what saved us from the worse. For I could hardly shout and tell them I was in there, no more could I try and grab him. I was trapped where I was. There was nothing I could really do but hold the door shut. I was scared of somebody else upsetting in and really getting an eyeful. Turned out though, in the heat of the clinch, as I was trying to avert my eyes you see, the Lamartine's curly wig jumped off her head. And if you ever been in the midst of something and had a big change like that occur in the someone, you can't help know how it devastates your basic urges. Not only that, but her wig was almost with a life of its own. Grandpa's eyes were bugging at the change already, and swear to God if the thing didn't rear up and pop him in the face like it was going to start something. He scrambled up, Grandpa did, and the Lamartine jumped up after him all addled looking. They just stared at each other, huffing and puffing, with quizzical expression. The surprise seemed to drive all sense completely out of Grandpa's mind.

40     "The letter was what started the fire," he said. "I never would have done it."

41     "What letter?" said the Lamartine. She was stiff-necked now, and elegant, even bald, like some alien queen. I gave her back the wig. The Lamartine replaced it on her head, and whenever I saw her after that, I couldn't help thinking of her bald, with special powers, as if from another planet.

42     "That was a close call," I said to Grandpa after she had left.

43     But I think he had already forgot the incident. He just stood there all quiet and thoughtful. You really wouldn't think he was crazy. He looked like he was just about to say something important, explaining himself. He said something, all right, but it didn't have nothing to do with anything that made sense.

44     He wondered where the heck he put his dandelion fork. That's when I decided about the mental adjustment.

45     Now what was mostly our problem was not so much that he was not all there, but that what was there of him often hankered after Lamartine. If we could put a stop to that, I thought, we might be getting someplace. But here, see, my touch was of no use. For what could I snap my fingers at to make him faithful to Grandma? Like the quality of staying power, this faithfulness was invisible. I know it's something that you got to acquire, but I never known where from. Maybe there's no rhyme or reason to it, like my getting the touch, and then again maybe it's a kind of magic.

And here is what I did that made the medicine backfire. I took an evil shortcut. I looked at birds that was dead and froze.

All right. So now I guess you will say, "Slap a malpractice suit on Lipsha Morrissey."

I heard of those suits. I used to think it was a color clothing quack doctors had to wear so you could tell them from the good ones. Now I know better that it's law.

As I walked back from the Red Owl with the rock-hard, heavy turkeys, I argued to myself about malpractice. I thought of faith. I thought to myself that faith could be called belief against the odds and whether or not there's any proof. How does that sound? I thought how we might have to yell to be heard by Higher Power, but that's not saying it's not *there*. And that is faith for you. It's belief even when the goods don't deliver. Higher Power makes promises we all know they can't back up, but anybody ever go and slap an old malpractice suit on God? Or the U.S. government? No they don't. Faith might be stupid, but it gets us through. So what I'm heading at is this. I finally convinced myself that the real actual power to the love medicine was not the goose heart itself but the faith in the cure.

73    I didn't believe it, I knew it was wrong, but by then I had waded so far into my lie I was stuck there. And then I went one step further.

74    The next day, I cleaned the hearts away from the paper packages of gizzards inside the turkeys. Then I wrapped them hearts with a clean hankie and brung them both to get blessed up at the mission. I wanted to get official blessings from the priest, but when Father answered the door to the rectory, wiping his hands on a little towel, I could tell he was a busy man.

75    "Booshoo, Father," I said. "I got a slight request to make of you this afternoon."

76    "What is it?" he said.

77    "Would you bless this package?" I held out the hankie with the hearts tied inside it.

78    He looked at the package, questioning it.

79    "It's turkey hearts," I honestly had to reply.

80    A look of annoyance crossed his face.

81    "Why don't you bring this matter over to Sister Martin," he said. "I have duties."

82    And so, although the blessing wouldn't be as powerful, I went over to the Sisters with the package.

83    I rung the bell, and they brought Sister Martin to the door. I had her as a music teacher, but I was always so shy then. I never talked out loud. Now, I had grown taller than Sister Martin. Looking down, I saw that she was not feeling up to snuff. Brown circles hung under her eyes.

84    "What's the matter?" she said, not noticing who I was.

85    "Remember me, Sister?"

46    It was Grandma Kashpaw who thought of it in the end. She knows things. Although she will not admit she has a scrap of Indian blood in her, there's no doubt in my mind she's got some Chippewa. How else would you explain the way she'll be sitting there, in front of her TV story, rocking in her armchair and suddenly she turns on me, her brown eyes hard as lake-bed flint.

47    "Lipsha Morrissey," she'll say, "you went out last night and got drunk."

48    How did she know that? I'll hardly remember it myself. Then she'll say she just had a feeling or ache in the scar of her hand or a creak in her shoulder. She is constantly being told things by little aggravations in her joints or by her household appliances. One time she told Gordie never to ride with a crazy Lamartine boy. She had seen something in the polished-up tin of her bread toaster. So he didn't. Sure enough, the time came we heard how Lyman and Henry went out of control in their car, ending up in the river. Lyman swam to the top, but Henry never made it.

49    Thanks to Grandma's toaster, Gordie was probably spared.

50    Someplace in the blood Grandma Kashpaw knows things. She also remembers things, I found. She keeps things filed away. She's got a memory like them video games that don't forget your score. One reason she remembers so many details about the trouble I gave her in early life is so she can flash back her total when she needs to.

51    Like now. Take the love medicine. I don't know where she remembered that from. It came tumbling from her mind like an asteroid off the corner of the screen.

52    Of course she starts out by mentioning the time I had this accident in church and did she leave me there with wet overhalls? No she didn't. And ain't I glad? Yes I am. Now what you want now, Grandma?

53    But when she mentions them love medicines, I feel my back prickle at the danger. These love medicines is something of an old Chippewa specialty. No other tribe has got them down so well. But love medicines is not for the layman to handle. You don't just go out and get one without paying for it. Before you get one, even, you should go through one hell of a lot of mental condensation. You got to think it over. Choose the right one. You could really mess up your life grinding up the wrong little thing.

54    So anyhow, I said to Grandma I'd give this love medicine some thought. I knew the best thing was to go ask a specialist like Old Lady Pillager, who lives up in a tangle of bush and never shows herself. But the truth is I was afraid of her, like everyone else. She was known for putting the twisted mouth on people, seizing up their hearts. Old Lady Pillager was serious business, and I have always thought it best to steer clear of that whenever I could. That's why I took the powers in my own hands. That's why I did what I could.

55    I put my whole mentality to it, nothing held back. After a while I started to remember things I'd heard gossiped over.

56    I heard of this person once who carried a charm of seeds that looked like baby pearls. They was attracted to a metal knife, which made them powerful.

But I didn't know where them seeds grew. Another love charm I heard about I couldn't go along with, because how was I suppose to catch frogs in the act, which it required. Them little creatures is slippery and fast. And then the powerfullest of all, the most extreme, involved nail clips and such. I wasn't anywhere near asking Grandma to provide me all the little body bits that this last love recipe called for. I went walking around for days just trying to think up something that would work.

57     Well I got it. If it hadn't been the early fall of the year, I never would have got it. But I was sitting underneath a tree one day down near the school just watching people's feet go by when something tells me, look up! Look up! So I look up, and I see two honkers, Canada geese, the kind with little masks on their faces, a bird what mates for life. I see them flying right over my head naturally preparing to land in some slough on the reservation, which they certainly won't get off of alive.

58     It hits me, anyway. Them geese, they mate for life. And I think to myself, just what if I went out and got a pair? And just what if I fed some part—say the goose heart—of the female to Grandma and Grandpa ate the other heart? Wouldn't that work? Maybe it's all invisible, and then maybe again it's magic. Love is a stony road. We know that for sure. If it's true that the higher feelings of devotion get lodged in the heart like people say, then we'd be home free. If not, eating goose heart couldn't harm nobody anyway. I thought it was worth my effort, and Grandma Kashpaw thought so, too. She had always known a good idea when she heard one. She borrowed me Grandpa's gun.

59     So I went out to this particular slough, maybe the exact same slough I never got thrown in by my mother, thanks to Grandma Kashpaw, and I hunched down in a good comfortable pile of rushes. I got my gun loaded up. I ate a few of these soft baloney sandwiches Grandma made me for lunch. And then I waited. The cattails blown back and forth above my head. Them stringy blue herons was spearing up their prey. The thing I know how to do best in this world, the thing I been training for all my life, is to wait. Sitting there and sitting there was no hardship on me. I got to thinking about some funny things that happened. There was this one time that Lulu Lamartine's little blue tweety bird, a paraclete, I guess you'd call it, flown up inside her dress and got lost within there. I recalled her running out into the hallway trying to yell something, shaking. She was doing a right good jig there, cutting the rug for sure, and the thing is it *never* flown out. To this day people speculate where it went. They fear she might perhaps of crushed it in her corsets. It sure hasn't ever yet been seen alive. I thought of funny things for a while, but then I used them up, and strange things that happened started weaseling their way into my mind.

60     I got to thinking quite naturally of the Lamartine's cousin named Wristwatch. I never knew what his real name was. They called him Wristwatch because he got his father's broken wristwatch as a young boy when his father passed on. Never in his whole life did Wristwatch take his father's watch off. He didn't care if it worked, although after a while he got sensitive when people

asked what time it was, teasing him. He often put    listening to the tick. But it was broken for good and f   least that's what they thought.

    Well I saw Wristwatch smoking in his pickup one a   that evening he was dead.

    He died sitting at the Lamartine's table, too. As she told   just eaten himself a good-size dinner and she said would he tak  hot dish when he fell over to the floor. They turnt him over. He  here's the strange thing: when the Senior Citizens' orderly took  noticed that the wristwatch Wristwatch wore was now working.  he died the wristwatch started keeping perfect time. They buried hi  watch still ticking on his arm.

    I got to thinking. What if some gravediggers dug up Wristwatch's  in two hundred years and that watch was still going? I thought what qu  they would ask and it was this: Whose hand wound it?

    I started shaking like a piece of grass at just the thought.

    Not to get off the subject or nothing. I was still hunkered in the slough.  was passing late into the afternoon and still no honkers had touched down. Now  I don't need to tell you that the waiting did not get to me, it was the chill. The  rushes was very soft, but damp. I was getting cold and debating to leave, when  they landed. Two geese swimming here and there as big as life, looking deep  into each other's little pinhole eyes. Just the ones I was looking for. So I lifted  Grandpa's gun to my shoulder and I aimed perfectly, and *blam! Blam!* I delivered  two accurate shots. But the thing is, them shots missed. I couldn't hardly believe  it. Whether it was that the stock had warped or the barrel got bent someways, and  I don't quite know, but anyway them geese flown off into the dim sky, and his two  Lipsha Morrissey was left there in the rushes with evening fallen and his two  cold hands empty. He had before him just the prospect of another day of  bone-cracking chill in them rushes, and the thought of it got him depressed.

    Now it isn't my style, in no way, to get depressed.

    So I said to myself, Lipsha Morrissey, you're a happy S.O.B. who could be  covered up with weeds by now down at the bottom of this slough, but instead  you're alive to tell the tale. You might have problems in life, but you still got  the touch. You got the power, Lipsha Morrissey. Can't argue that. So put your  mind to it and figure out how not to be depressed.

    I took my advice. I put my mind to it. But I never saw at the time how my  thoughts led me astray toward a tragic outcome none could have known. I  ignored all the danger, all the limits, for I was tired of sitting in the slough and  my feet were numb. My face was aching. I was chilled, so I played with fire. I  told myself love medicine was simple. I told myself the old superstitions was  just that—strange beliefs. I told myself to take the ten dollars Mary MacDonald  had paid me for putting the touch on her arthritis joint, and the other five I  hadn't spent yet from winning bingo last Thursday. I told myself to go down  to the Red Owl store.

She squinted up at me.  86

"Oh yes," she said after a moment. "I'm sorry, you're the youngest of the  87
Kashpaws. Gordie's brother."

Her faced warmed up.  88

"Lipsha," I said, "that's my name."  89

"Well, Lipsha," she said, smiling broadly at me now, "what can I do for  90
you?"

They always said she was the kindest-hearted of the Sisters up the hill, and  91
she was. She brought me back into their own kitchen and made me take a big
yellow wedge of cake and a glass of milk.

"Now tell me," she said, nodding at my package. "What have you got  92
wrapped up so carefully in those handkerchiefs?"

Like before, I answered honestly.  93

"Ah," said Sister Martin. "Turkey hearts." She waited.  94

"I hoped you could bless them."  95

She waited some more, smiling with her eyes. Kindhearted though she was,  96
I began to sweat. A person could not pull the wool down over Sister Martin. I
stumbled through my mind for an explanation, quick, that wouldn't scare her
off.

"They're a present," I said, "for Saint Kateri's statue."  97

"She's not a saint yet."  98

"I know," I stuttered on. "In the hopes they will crown her."  99

"Lipsha," she said, "I never heard of such a thing."  100

So I told her. "Well the truth is," I said, "it's a kind of medicine."  101

"For what?"  102

"Love."  103

"Oh Lipsha," she said after a moment, "you don't need any medicine. I'm  104
sure any girl would like you exactly the way you are."

I just sat there. I felt miserable, caught in my pack of lies.  105

"Tell you what," she said, seeing how bad I felt, "my blessing won't make  106
any difference anyway. But there is something you can do."

I looked up at her, hopeless.  107

"Just be yourself."  108

I looked down at my plate. I knew I wasn't much to brag about right then,  109
and I shortly became even less. For as I walked out the door I stuck my fingers
in the cup of holy water that was sacred from their touches. I put my fingers in
and blessed the hearts, quick, with my own hand.

I went back to Grandma and sat down in her little kitchen at the Senior Citizens.  110
I unwrapped them hearts on the table, and her hard agate eyes went soft. She
said she wasn't even going to cook those hearts up but eat them raw so their
power would go down strong as possible.

I couldn't hardly watch when she munched hers. Now that's true love. I  111
was worried about how she would get Grandpa to eat his, but she told me she'd

think of something and don't worry. So I did not. I was supposed to hide off in her bedroom while she put dinner on a plate for Grandpa and fixed up the heart so he'd eat it. I caught a glint of the plate she was making for him. She put that heart smack on a piece of lettuce like in a restaurant and then attached to it a little heap of boiled peas.

112 He sat down. I was listening in the next room.

113 She said, "Why don't you have some mash potato?" So he had some mash potato. Then she gave him a little piece of boiled meat. He ate that. Then she said, "Why you didn't never touch your salad yet. See that heart? I'm feeding you it because the doctor said your blood needs building up."

114 I couldn't help it, at that point I peeked through a crack in the door.

115 I saw Grandpa picking at that heart on his plate with a certain look. He didn't look appetized at all, is what I'm saying. I doubted our plan was going to work. Grandma was getting worried, too. She told him one more time, loudly, that he had to eat that heart.

116 "Swallow it down," she said. "You'll hardly notice it."

117 He just looked at her straight on. The way he looked at her made me think I was going to see the smokescreen drop a second time, and sure enough it happened.

118 "What you want me to eat this for so bad?" he asked her uncannily.

119 Now Grandma knew the jig was up. She knew that he knew she was working medicine. He put his fork down. He rolled the heart around his saucer plate.

120 "I don't want to eat this," he said to Grandma. "It don't look good."

121 "Why it's fresh grade-A," she told him. "One hundred percent."

122 He didn't ask percent what, but his eyes took on an even more warier look.

123 "Just go on and try it," she said, taking the salt shaker up in her hand. She was getting annoyed. "Not tasty enough? You want me to salt it for you?" She waved the shaker over his plate.

124 "All right, skinny white girl!" She had got Grandpa mad. Oopsy-daisy, he popped the heart into his mouth. I was about to yawn loudly and come out of the bedroom. I was about ready for this crash of wills to be over, when I saw he was still up to his old tricks. First he rolled it into one side of his cheek. "Mmmmm," he said. Then he rolled it into the other side of his cheek. "Mmmmmmm," again. Then he stuck his tongue out with the heart on it and put it back, and there was no time to react. He had pulled Grandma's leg once too far. Her goat was got. She was so mad she hopped up quick as a wink and slugged him between the shoulderblades to make him swallow.

125 Only thing is, he choked.

126 He choked real bad. A person can choke to death. You ever sit down at a restaurant table and up above you there is a list of instructions what to do if something slides down the wrong pipe? It sure makes you chew slow, that's for damn sure. When Grandpa fell off his chair better believe me that little graphic illustrated poster fled into my mind. I jumped out the bedroom. I done everything within my power that I could do to unlodge what was choking him. I

squeezed underneath his rib cage. I socked him in the back. I was desperate. But here's the factor of decision: he wasn't choking on the heart alone. There was more to it than that. It was other things that choked him as well. It didn't seem like he wanted to struggle or fight. Death came and tapped his chest, so he went just like that. I'm sorry all through my body at what I done to him with that heart, and there's those who will say Lipsha Morrissey is just excusing himself off the hook by giving song and dance about how Grandpa gave up.

Maybe I can't admit what I did. My touch had gone worthless, that is true. But here is what I seen while he lay in my arms.    127

You hear a person's life will flash before their eyes when they're in danger. It was him in danger, not me, but it was *his* life come over me. I saw him dying, and it was like someone pulled the shade down in a room. His eyes clouded over and squeezed shut, but just before that I looked in. He was still fishing in the middle of Matchimanito. Big thoughts was on his line and he had half a case of beer in the boat. He waved at me, grinned, and then the bobber went under.    128

Grandma had gone out of the room crying for help. I bunched my force up in my hands and I held him. I was so wound up I couldn't even breathe. All the moments he had spent with me, all the times he had hoisted me on his shoulders or pointed into the leaves was concentrated in that moment. Time was flashing back and forth like a pinball machine. Lights blinked and balls hopped and rubber bands chirped, until suddenly I realized the last ball had gone down the drain and there was nothing. I felt his force leaving him, flowing out of Grandpa never to return. I felt his mind weakening. The bobber going under in the lake. And I felt the touch retreat back into the darkness inside my body, from where it came.    129

One time, long ago, both of us were fishing together. We caught a big old snapper what started towing us around like it was a motor. "This here fishline is pretty damn good," Grandpa said. "Let's keep this turtle on and see where he takes us." So we rode along behind that turtle, watching as from time to time it surfaced. The thing was just about the size of a washtub. It took us all around the lake twice, and as it was traveling, Grandpa said something as a joke. "Lipsha," he said, "we are glad your mother didn't want you because we was always looking for a boy like you who would tow us around the lake."    130

"I ain't no snapper. Snappers is so stupid they stay alive when their head's chopped off," I said.    131

"That ain't stupidity," said Grandpa. "Their brain's just in their heart, like yours is."    132

When I looked up, I knew the fuse had blown between my heart and my mind and that a terrible understanding was to be given.    133

Grandma got back into the room and I saw her stumble. And then she went down too. It was like a house you can't hardly believe has stood so long, through years of record weather, suddenly goes down in the worst yet. It makes sense, is what I'm saying, but you still can't hardly believe it. You think a person you know has got through death and illness and being broke and living on commod-    134 ity rice will get through anything. Then they fold and you see how fragile were the stones that underpinned them. You see how instantly the ground can shift you thought was solid. You see the stop signs and the yellow dividing markers of roads you traveled and all the instructions you had played according to vanish. You see how all the everyday things you counted on was just a dream you had been having by which you run your whole life. She had been over me, like a sheer overhang of rock dividing Lipsha Morrissey from outer space. And now she went underneath. It was as though the banks gave way on the shores of Matchimanito, and where Grandpa's passing was just the bobber swallowed under by his biggest thought, her fall was the house and the rock under it sliding after, sending half the lake splashing up to the clouds.

135     Where there was nothing.

136     You play them games never knowing what you see. When I fell into the dream alongside of both of them I saw that the dominions I had defended myself from anciently was but delusions of the screen. Blips of light. And I was scot-free now, whistling through space.

137     I don't know how I come back. I don't know from where. They was slapping my face when I arrived back at Senior Citizens and they was oxygenating her. I saw her chest move, almost unwilling. She sighed the way she would when somebody bothered her in the middle of a row of beads she was counting. I think it irritated her to no end that they brought her back. I knew from the way she looked after they took the mask off, she was not going to forgive them disturbing her restful peace. Nor was she forgiving Lipsha Morrissey. She had been stepping out onto the road of death, she told the children later at the funeral. I asked was there any stop signs or dividing markers on that road, but she clamped her lips in a vise the way she always done when she was mad.

138     Which didn't bother me. I knew when things had cleared out she wouldn't have no choice. I was not going to speculate where the blame was put for Grandpa's death. We was in it together. She had slugged him between the shoulders. My touch had failed him, never to return.

139     All the blood children and the took-ins, like me, came home from Minneapolis and Chicago, where they had relocated years ago. They stayed with friends on the reservation or with Aurelia or slept on Grandma's floor. They were struck down with grief and bereavement to be sure, every one of them. At the funeral I sat down in the back of the church with Albertine. She had gotten all skinny and ragged haired from cramming all her years of study into two or three. She had decided that to be a nurse was not enough for her so she was going to be a doctor. But the way she was straining her mind didn't look too hopeful. Her eyes were bloodshot from driving and crying. She took my hand. From the back we watched all the children and the mourners as they hunched over their prayers, their hands stuffed full of Kleenex. It was someplace in that long sad service that my vision shifted. I began to see things different, more clear. The family kneeling down turned to rocks in a field. It struck me how strong and reliable grief was, and death. Until the end of time, death would be our rock.

So I had perspective on it all, for death gives you that. All the Kashpaw 140
children had done various things to me in their lives—shared their folks with
me, loaned me cash, beat me up in secret—and I decided, because of death, then
and there I'd call it quits. If I ever saw King again, I'd shake his hand. Forgiving
somebody else made the whole thing easier to bear.

Everybody saw Grandpa off into the next world. And then the Kashpaws 141
had to get back to their jobs, which was numerous and impressive. I had a few
beers with them and I went back to Grandma, who had sort of got lost in the
shuffle of everybody being sad about Grandpa and glad to see one another.

Zelda had sat beside her the whole time and was sitting with her now. I 142
wanted to talk to Grandma, say how sorry I was, that it wasn't her fault, but
only mine. I would have, but Zelda gave me one of her looks of strict warning
as if to say, "I'll take care of Grandma. Don't horn in on the women."

If only Zelda knew, I thought, the sad realities would change her. But of 143
course I couldn't tell the dark truth.

It was evening, late. Grandma's light was on underneath a crack in the door. 144
About a week had passed since we buried Grandpa. I knocked first but there
wasn't no answer, so I went right in. The door was unlocked. She was there but
she didn't notice me at first. Her hands were tied up in her rosary, and her gaze
was fully absorbed in the easy chair opposite her, the one that had always been
Grandpa's favorite. I stood there, staring with her, at the little green nubs in
the cloth and plastic armrest covers and the sad little hair-tonic stain he had
made on the white doily where he laid his head. For the life of me I couldn't
figure what she was staring at. Thin space. Then she turned.

"He ain't gone yet," she said. 145

Remember that chill I luckily didn't get from waiting in the slough? I got 146
it now. I felt it start from the very center of me, where fear hides, waiting to
attack. It spiraled outward so that in minutes my fingers and teeth were shaking
and clattering. I knew she told the truth. She seen Grandpa. Whether or not
he had been there is not the point. She had *seen* him, and that meant anybody
else could see him, too. Not only that but, as is usually the case with these
ghosts, he had a certain uneasy reason to come back. And of course Grandma
Kashpaw had scanned it out.

I sat down. We sat together on the couch watching his chair out of the 147
corner of our eyes. She had found him sitting in his chair when she walked in
the door.

"It's the love medicine, my Lipsha," she said. "It was stronger than we 148
thought. He came back even after death to claim me to his side."

I was afraid. "We shouldn't have tampered with it," I said. She agreed. For 149
a while we sat still. I don't know what she thought, but my head felt screwed
on backward. I couldn't accurately consider the situation, so I told Grandma to
go to bed. I would sleep on the couch keeping my eye on Grandpa's chair.
Maybe he would come back and maybe he wouldn't. I guess I feared the one
as much as the other, but I got to thinking, see, as I lay there in darkness, that

perhaps even through my terrible mistakes some good might come. If Grandpa did come back, I thought he'd return in his right mind. I could talk with him. I could tell him it was all my fault for playing with power I did not understand. Maybe he'd forgive me and rest in peace. I hoped this. I calmed myself and waited for him all night.

150    He fooled me though. He knew what I was waiting for, and it wasn't what he was looking to hear. Come dawn I heard a blood-splitting cry from the bedroom and I rushed in there. Grandma turnt the lights on. She was sitting on the edge of the bed and her face looked harsh, pinched-up, gray.

151    "He was here," she said. "He came and laid down next to me in bed. And he touched me."

152    Her heart broke down. She cried. His touch was so cold. She laid back in bed after a while, as it was morning, and I went to the couch. As I lay there, falling asleep, I suddenly felt Grandpa's presence and the barrier between us like a swollen river. I felt how I had wronged him. How awful was the place where I had sent him. Behind the wall of death, he'd watched the living eat and cry and get drunk. He was lonesome, but I understood he meant no harm.

153    "Go back," I said to the dark, afraid and yet full of pity. "You got to be with your own kind now," I said. I felt him retreating, like a sigh, growing less. I felt his spirit as it shrunk back through the walls, the blinds, the brick courtyard of Senior Citizens. "Look up Aunt June," I whispered as he left.

154    I slept late the next morning, a good hard sleep allowing the sun to rise and warm the earth. It was past noon when I awoke. There is nothing, to my mind, like a long sleep to make those hard decisions that you neglect under stress of wakefulness. Soon as I woke up that morning, I saw exactly what I'd say to Grandma. I had gotten humble in the past week, not just losing the touch but getting jolted into the understanding that would prey on me from here on out. Your life feels different on you, once you greet death and understand your heart's position. You wear your life like a garment from the mission bundle sale ever after—lightly because you realize you never paid nothing for it, cherishing because you know you won't ever come by such a bargain again. Also you have the feeling someone wore it before you and someone will after. I can't explain that, not yet, but I'm putting my mind to it.

155    "Grandma," I said, "I got to be honest about the love medicine."

156    She listened. I knew from then on she would be listening to me the way I had listened to her before. I told her about the turkey hearts and how I had them blessed. I told her what I used as love medicine was purely a fake, and then I said to her what my understanding brought me.

157    "Love medicine ain't what brings him back to you, Grandma. No, it's something else. He loved you over time and distance, but he went off so quick he never got the chance to tell you how he loves you, how he doesn't blame you, how he understands. It's true feeling, not no magic. No supermarket heart could have brung him back."

She looked at me. She was seeing the years and days I had no way of   158
knowing, and she didn't believe me. I could tell this. Yet a look came on her
face. It was like the look of mothers drinking sweetness from their children's
eyes. It was tenderness.

"Lipsha," she said, "you was always my favorite."   159

She took the beads off the bedpost, where she kept them to say at night,   160
and she told me to put out my hand. When I did this, she shut the beads inside
of my fist and held them there a long minute, tight, so my hand hurt. I almost
cried when she did this. I don't really know why. Tears shot up behind my
eyelids, and yet it was nothing. I didn't understand, except her hand was so
strong, squeezing mine.

The earth was full of life and there were dandelions growing out the window,   161
thick as thieves, already seeded, fat as big yellow plungers. She let my hand go.
I got up. "I'll go out and dig a few dandelions," I told her.

Outside, the sun was hot and heavy as a hand on my back. I felt it flow   162
down my arms, out my fingers, arrowing through the ends of the fork into the
earth. With every root I prized up there was return, as if I was kin to its secret
lesson. The touch got stronger as I worked through the grassy afternoon.
Uncurling from me like a seed out of the blackness where I was lost, the touch
spread. The spiked leaves full of bitter mother's milk. A buried root. A nuisance
people dig up and throw in the sun to wither. A globe of frail seeds that's
indestructible. ✜

---

RESPONDING

1.  In a journal entry, discuss Lipsha's understanding of "the Higher Power."
    Is he referring to God in the Old Testament? Chippewa Gods? Something
    else?

2.  Lipsha Morrissey describes human behavior by comparing it to things he
    sees in the world around him. Working individually or in a group, find some
    of his descriptions and discuss what they tell you about his daily life. Replace
    some of his descriptions with ones of your own that reflect your under-
    standing of human behavior. How does your understanding differ from his?

3.  The Catholic Church and the traditional beliefs of the Chippewa provide
    a great deal of Lipsha's worldview. In an essay, examine how the two belief
    systems influence his thinking and behavior and how he combines the two.
    Use examples from the story to support your assertions.

4. Grandpa Kashpaw's death gives Lipsha a new understanding of life, death, and love. Using examples from the reading, write an essay discussing the changes that take place in his understanding of life's milestones.

---

# PAULA GUNN ALLEN

*The novelist, essayist, and poet Paula Gunn Allen was born in 1939 in Cubero, New Mexico, of Laguna-Sioux and Lebanese-Jewish ancestry. She holds a doctorate from the University of New Mexico. In addition to serving as editor for* Studies in American Indian Literature: Critical Essays and Course Designs *(1983) and editing* Spider Woman's Granddaughters: Traditional Tales and Contemporary Writing by Native American Women *(1989) and* Voice of the Turtle: American Indian Literature, 1900–1970 *(1994), she has published a novel,* The Woman Who Owned the Shadows *(1983), a book-length study,* The Sacred Hoop: Recovering the Feminine in American Indian Traditions *(1986),* Wyrds *(1987),* Grandmothers of the Light: A Medicine Woman's Sourcebook *(1991), and several volumes of poetry. She also has been awarded a grant for creative writing from the National Endowment for the Arts and a fellowship for Native American Studies from the University of California at Los Angeles.*

*The poem "Pocahontas to Her English Husband, John Rolfe" confronts and refashions popular mythology about the friendship between the Indian woman and her spouse. In this version of the tale, we are shown the importance of female agency and the strength that can come from silence.*

✤

# POCAHONTAS TO HER ENGLISH HUSBAND, JOHN ROLFE

Had I not cradled you in my arms,
oh beloved   perfidious one,
you would have died.
And how many times did I pluck you
5    from certain death in the wilderness—
my world through which you stumbled
as though blind?
Had I not set you tasks
your masters far across the sea
10    would have abandoned you—

did abandon you, as many times they
left you to reap the harvest of their lies;
still you survived   oh my fair husband
and brought them gold
wrung from a harvest I taught you                                    15
to plant: Tobacco.  It
is not without irony that by this crop
your descendants die, for other powers
than those you know take part in this.
And indeed I did rescue you                                          20
not once but a thousand thousand times
and in my arms you slept, a foolish child,
and beside me you played,
chattering nonsense about a God
you had not wit to name;                                            25
and wondered you at my silence—
simple foolish wanton maid you saw,
dusky daughter of heathen sires
who knew not the ways of grace—
no doubt, no doubt.                                                 30
I spoke little, you said.
And you listened less.
But played with your gaudy dreams
and sent ponderous missives to the throne
striving thereby to curry favor                                     35
with your king.  I saw you well.  I
understood the ploy and still protected you,
going so far as to die in your keeping—
a wasting, putrifying death, and you,
deceiver, my husband, father of my son,                             40
survived, your spirit bearing crop
slowly from my teaching, taking
certain life from the wasting of my bones.  ✥

---

## RESPONDING

1. In a journal entry, discuss your thoughts about Pocahontas. What do you know about Pocahontas, and where did your knowledge come from? Is your information limited to the Disney movie *Pocahontas*?

2. Working individually or in a group, compare the legendary figure of Pocahontas with the Pocahontas we meet in this poem.

3. In an essay, discuss Pocahontas's attitude toward her husband. Be sure to include evidence from the text to support your conclusions. You might also consider when she is speaking and what her language reveals about her feelings.

4. Write an essay arguing why it is or is not important to know the historical facts behind a legend. You might want to discuss other myths in our society, such as the Alamo, the contented slave, or George Washington and the cherry tree, to support your point.

# SIMON J. ORTIZ

*A poet and short-story writer of Acoma Pueblo heritage, Simon J. Ortiz was born in 1941 at the Pueblo of Acoma, near Albuquerque, New Mexico, where he was raised. He received a bachelor's degree from the University of New Mexico (1968) and a master's degree in fine arts from the University of Iowa (1969). Ortiz has served in the U.S. Army and has been on the faculty at institutions such as the University of New Mexico and Sinte Gleska College in South Dakota, teaching creative writing. Ortiz's publications include the collections of short fiction* Howbah Indians *(1978) and* Fightin': New and Collected Stories *(1983) as well as the poetry collections* Going for the Rain *(1976),* A Good Journey *(1977),* From Sand Creek *(1981),* Woven Stone *(1991),* and After and Before the Lightning *(1994). He has also edited a collection of short fiction entitled* Earth Power Coming *(1983) and a collection of essays,* Speaking for the Generations: Native Writers on Writing *(1998).*

*In the essay that follows, Ortiz explores how heritage is defined through language; further, his essay reveals the ability of language to express natural beauty and artistic vision.*

⊞

# THE LANGUAGE WE KNOW

1 I DON'T REMEMBER a world without language. From the time of my earliest childhood, there was language. Always language, and imagination, speculation, utters of sound. Words, beginnings of words. What would I be without language? My existence has been determined by language, not only the spoken but the unspoken, the language of speech and the language of motion. I can't remember a world without memory. Memory, immediate and far away in the

past, something in a sinew, blood, ageless cell. Although I don't recall the exact moment I spoke or tried to speak, I know the feeling of something tugging at the core of the mind, something unutterable uttered into existence. It is language that brings us into existence. It is language that brings us into being in order to know life.

My childhood was the oral tradition of the Acoma Pueblo people—Aaquumeh     2
hano—which included my immediate family of three older sisters, two younger sisters, two younger brothers, and my mother and father. My world was our world of the Aaquumeh in McCartys, one of the two villages descended from the ageless mother pueblo of Acoma. My world was our Eagle clan-people among other clans. I grew up in Deetziyamah, which is the Aaquumeh name for McCartys, which is posted at the exit off the present interstate highway in western New Mexico. I grew up within a people who farmed small garden plots and fields, who were mostly poor and not well schooled in the American system's education. The language I spoke was that of a struggling people who held ferociously to a heritage, culture, language, and land despite the odds posed them by the forces surrounding them since A.D. 1540, the advent of Euro-American colonization. When I began school in 1948 at the BIA (Bureau of Indian Affairs) day school in our village, I was armed with the basic ABC's and the phrases "Good morning, Miss Oleman" and "May I please be excused to go to the bathroom," but it was an older language that was my fundamental strength.

In my childhood, the language we all spoke was Acoma, and it was a struggle     3
to maintain it against the outright threats of corporal punishment, ostracism, and the invocation that it would impede our progress towards Americanization. Children in school were punished and looked upon with disdain if they did not speak and learn English quickly and smoothly, and so I learned it. It has occurred to me that I learned English simply because I was forced to, as so many other Indian children were. But I know, also, there was another reason, and this was that I loved language, the sound, meaning, and magic of language. Language opened up vistas of the world around me, and it allowed me to discover knowledge that would not be possible for me to know without the use of language. Later, when I began to experiment with and explore language in poetry and fiction, I allowed that a portion of that impetus was because I had come to know English through forceful acculturation. Nevertheless, the underlying force was the beauty and poetic power of language in its many forms that instilled in me the desire to become a user of language as a writer, singer, and storyteller. Significantly, it was the Acoma language, which I don't use enough of today, that inspired me to become a writer. The concepts, values, and philosophy contained in my original language and the struggle it has faced have determined my life and vision as a writer.

In Deetziyamah, I discovered the world of the Acoma land and people firsthand     4
through my parents, sisters, and brothers, and my own perceptions, voiced

through all that encompasses the oral tradition, which is ageless for any culture. It is a small village, even smaller years ago, and like other Indian communities it is wealthy with its knowledge of daily events, history, and social system, all that make up a people who have a many-dimensioned heritage. Our family lived in a two-room home (built by my grandfather some years after he and my grandmother moved with their daughters from Old Acoma), which my father added rooms to later. I remember my father's work at enlarging our home for our growing family. He was a skilled stoneworker, like many other men of an older Pueblo generation who worked with sandstone and mud mortar to build their homes and pueblos. It takes time, persistence, patience, and the belief that the walls that come to stand will do so for a long, long time, perhaps even forever. I like to think that by helping to mix mud and carry stone for my father and other elders I managed to bring that influence into my consciousness as a writer.

5   Both my mother and my father were good storytellers and singers (as my mother is to this day—my father died in 1978), and for their generation, which was born soon after the turn of the century, they were relatively educated in the American system. Catholic missionaries had taken both of them as children to a parochial boarding school far from Acoma, and they imparted their discipline for study and quest for education to us children when we started school. But it was their indigenous sense of gaining knowledge that was most meaningful to me. Acquiring knowledge about life was above all the most important item; it was a value that one had to have in order to be fulfilled personally and on behalf of his community. And this they insisted upon imparting through the oral tradition as they told their children about our native history and our community and culture and our "stories." These stories were common knowledge of act, event, and behavior in a close-knit pueblo. It was knowledge about how one was to make a living through work that benefited his family and everyone else.

6   Because we were a subsistence farming people, or at least tried to be, I learned to plant, hoe weeds, irrigate and cultivate corn, chili, pumpkins, beans. Through counsel and advice I came to know that the rain which provided water was a blessing, gift, and symbol and that it was the land which provided for our lives. It was the stories and songs which provided the knowledge that I was woven into the intricate web that was my Acoma life. In our garden and our cornfields I learned about the seasons, growth cycles of cultivated plants, what one had to think and feel about the land; and at home I became aware of how we must care for each other: All of this was encompassed in an intricate relationship which had to be maintained in order that life continue. After supper on many occasions my father would bring out his drum and sing as we, the children, danced to themes about the rain, hunting, land, and people. It was all that is contained within the language of oral tradition that made me explicitly aware of a yet unarticulated urge to write, to tell what I had learned and was learning and what it all meant to me.

7   My grandfather was old already when I came to know him. I was only one

of his many grandchildren, but I would go with him to get wood for our households, to the garden to chop weeds, and to his sheep camp to help care for his sheep. I don't remember his exact words, but I know they were about how we must sacredly concern ourselves with the people and the holy earth. I know his words were about how we must regard ourselves and others with compassion and love; I know that his knowledge was vast, as a medicine man and an elder of his kiva, and I listened as a boy should. My grandfather represented for me a link to the past that is important for me to hold in my memory because it is not only memory but knowledge that substantiates my present existence. He and the grandmothers and grandfathers before him thought about us as they lived, confirmed in their belief of a continuing life, and they brought our present beings into existence by the beliefs they held. The consciousness of that belief is what informs my present concerns with language, poetry, and fiction.

My first poem was for Mother's Day when I was in the fifth grade, and it was [8] the first poem that was ever published, too, in the Skull Valley School newsletter. Of course I don't remember how the juvenile poem went, but it must have been certain in its expression of love and reverence for the woman who was the most important person in my young life. The poem didn't signal any prophecy of my future as a poet, but it must have come from the forming idea that there were things one could do with language and writing. My mother, years later, remembers how I was a child who always told stories—that is, tall tales—who always had explanations for things probably better left unspoken, and she says that I also liked to perform in school plays. In remembering, I do know that I was coming to that age when the emotions and thoughts in me began to boil to the surface. There was much to experience and express in that age when youth has a precociousness that is broken easily or made to flourish. We were a poor family, always on the verge of financial disaster, though our parents always managed to feed us and keep us in clothing. We had the problems, unfortunately ordinary, of many Indian families who face poverty on a daily basis, never enough of anything, the feeling of a denigrating self-consciousness, alcoholism in the family and community, the feeling that something was falling apart though we tried desperately to hold it all together.

My father worked for the railroad for many years as a laborer and later as [9] a welder. We moved to Skull Valley, Arizona, for one year in the early 1950s, and it was then that I first came in touch with a non-Indian, non-Acoma world. Skull Valley was a farming and ranching community, and my younger brothers and sisters and I went to a one-room school. I had never really had much contact with white people except from a careful and suspicious distance, but now here I was, totally surrounded by them, and there was nothing to do but bear the experience and learn from it. Although I perceived there was not much difference between *them* and *us* in certain respects, there was a distinct feeling that we were not the same either. This thought had been inculcated in me, especially by an Acoma expression—*Gaimuu Mericano*—that spoke of the "fortune" of being an American. In later years as a social activist and committed writer, I would try to offer a strong positive view of our collective Indianness through my writing. Nevertheless, my father was an inadequately paid laborer, and we were far from our home land for economic-social reasons, and my feelings and thoughts about that experience during that time would become a part of how I became a writer.

10    Soon after, I went away from my home and family to go to boarding school, first in Santa Fe and then in Albuquerque. This was in the 1950s, and this had been the case for the past half-century for Indians: We had to leave home in order to become truly American by joining the mainstream, which was deemed to be the proper course of our lives. On top of this was termination, a U.S. government policy which dictated that Indians sever their relationship to the federal government and remove themselves from their lands and go to American cities for jobs and education. It was an era which bespoke the intent of U.S. public policy that Indians were no longer to be Indians. Naturally, I did not perceive this in any analytical or purposeful sense; rather, I felt an unspoken anxiety and resentment against unseen forces that determined our destiny to be un-Indian, embarrassed and uncomfortable with our grandparents' customs and strictly held values. We were to set our goals as American working men and women, singlemindedly industrious, patriotic, and unquestioning, building for a future which ensured that the United States was the greatest nation in the world. I felt fearfully uneasy with this, for by then I felt the loneliness, alienation, and isolation imposed upon me by the separation from my family, home, and community.

11    Something was happening; I could see that in my years at Catholic school and the U.S. Indian school. I remembered my grandparents' and parents' words: Educate yourself in order to help your people. In that era and the generation who had the same experience I had, there was an unspoken vow: We were caught in a system inexorably, and we had to learn that system well in order to fight back. Without the motive of a fight-back we would not be able to survive as the people our heritage had lovingly bequeathed us. My diaries and notebooks began then, and though none have survived to the present, I know they contained the varied moods of a youth filled with loneliness, anger, and discomfort that seemed to have unknown causes. Yet at the same time, I realize now, I was coming to know myself clearly in a way that I would later articulate in writing. My love of language, which allowed me to deal with the world, to delve into it, to experiment and discover, held for me a vision of awe and wonder, and by then grammar teachers had noticed I was a good speller, used verbs and tenses correctly, and wrote complete sentences. Although I imagine that they might have surmised this as unusual for an Indian student whose original language was not English, I am grateful for their perception and attention.

12    During the latter part of that era in the 1950s of Indian termination and the Cold War, a portion of which still exists today, there were the beginnings of a

bolder and more vocalized resistance against the current U.S. public policies of repression, racism, and cultural ethnocide. It seemed to be inspired by the civil rights movement led by black people in the United States and by decolonization and liberation struggles worldwide. Indian people were being relocated from their rural homelands at an astonishingly devastating rate, yet at the same time they resisted the U.S. effort by maintaining determined ties with their heritage, returning often to their native communities, and establishing Indian centers in the cities they were removed to. Indian rural communities, such as Acoma Pueblo, insisted on their land claims and began to initiate legal battles in the areas of natural and social, political and economic human rights. By the retention and the inspiration of our native heritage, values, philosophies, and language, we would know ourselves as a strong and enduring people. Having a modest and latent consciousness of this as a teenager, I began to write about the experience of being Indian in America. Although I had only a romanticized image of what a writer was, which came from the pulp rendered by American popular literature, and I really didn't know anything about writing, I sincerely felt a need to say things, to speak, to release the energy of the impulse to help my people.

My writing in my late teens and early adulthood was fashioned after the American short stories and poetry taught in the high schools of the 1940s and 1950s, but by the 1960s, after I had gone to college and dropped out and served in the military, I began to develop topics and themes from my Indian background. The experience in my village of Deetziyamah and Acoma Pueblo was readily accessible. I had grown up within the oral tradition of speech, social and religious ritual, elders' counsel and advice, countless and endless stories, everyday event, and the visual art that was symbolically representative of life all around. My mother was a potter of the well-known Acoma clayware, a traditional art form that had been passed to her from her mother and the generations of mothers before. My father carved figures from wood and did beadwork. This was not unusual, as Indian people know; there was always some kind of artistic endeavor that people set themselves to, although they did not necessarily articulate it as "Art" in the sense of Western civilization. One lived and expressed an artful life, whether it was in ceremonial singing and dancing, architecture, painting, speaking, or in the way one's social-cultural life was structured. When I turned my attention to my own heritage, I did so because this was my identity, the substance of who I was, and I wanted to write about what that meant. My desire was to write about the integrity and dignity of an Indian identity, and at the same time I wanted to look at what this was within the context of an America that had too often denied its Indian heritage.

To a great extent my writing was a natural political-cultural bent simply because I was nurtured intellectually and emotionally within an atmosphere of Indian resistance. Aacquu did not die in 1598 when it was burned and razed by European conquerors, nor did the people become hopeless when their children were taken away to U.S. schools far from home and new ways were imposed upon them. The *Aaquumeh hano,* despite losing much of their land and surrounded by a foreign civilization, have not lost sight of their native heritage. This is the factual case with most other Indian peoples, and the clear explanation for this has been the fight-back we have found it necessary to wage. At times, in the past, it was outright armed struggle, like that of present-day Indians in Central and South America with whom we must identify; currently, it is often in the legal arena, and it is in the field of literature. In 1981, when I was invited to the White House for an event celebrating American poets and poetry, I did not immediately accept the invitation. I questioned myself about the possibility that I was merely being exploited as an Indian, and I hedged against accepting. But then I recalled the elders going among our people in the poor days of the 1950s, asking for donations—a dollar here and there, a sheep, perhaps a piece of pottery—in order to finance a trip to the nation's capital. They were to make another countless appeal on behalf of our people, to demand justice, to reclaim lost land even though there was only spare hope they would be successful. I went to the White House realizing that I was to do no less than they and those who had fought in the Pueblo Revolt of 1680, and I read my poems and sang songs that were later described as "guttural" by a Washington, D.C., newspaper. I suppose it is more or less understandable why such a view of Indian literature is held by many, and it is also clear why there should be a political stand taken in my writing and those of my sister and brother Indian writers.

15    The 1960s and afterward have been an invigorating and liberating period for Indian people. It has been only a little more than twenty years since Indian writers began to write and publish extensively, but we are writing and publishing more and more; we can only go forward. We come from an ageless, continuing oral tradition that informs us of our values, concepts, and notions as native people, and it is amazing how much of this tradition is ingrained so deeply in our contemporary writing, considering the brutal efforts of cultural repression that was not long ago outright U.S. policy. We were not to speak our languages, practice our spiritual beliefs, or accept the values of our past generations; and we were discouraged from pressing for our natural rights as Indian human beings. In spite of the fact that there is to some extent the same repression today, we persist and insist in living, believing, hoping, loving, speaking, and writing as Indians. This is embodied in the language we know and share in our writing. We have always had this language, and it is the language, spoken and unspoken, that determines our existence, that brought our grandmothers and grandfathers and ourselves into being in order that there be a continuing life.  ✠

---

## RESPONDING

1.  When do you have the urge or the need to express yourself in writing? Do you write only when forced to do so by necessity or a class assignment? Do you write to communicate or for your own pleasure? Given a choice, would

you prefer all your communication to be oral? In a journal entry, speculate about when and why you write.

2. Working individually or in a group, think about a recent event in your school, city, or country. Tell your version of the event to your group. Then write a version of the event. Compare the written and the spoken versions. How are they similar? In what ways are they different? What are the advantages and disadvantages of the written version?

3. Ortiz says that the "oral tradition . . . made me explicitly aware of a yet unarticulated urge to write" (paragraph 6). In an essay, explain and illustrate the influence of that tradition on his writing. Do you find it unusual that the spoken word was the stimulus for writing? What could he gain by writing that he couldn't achieve through telling a story aloud?

4. Ortiz believes Indians need a mainstream education in order to effect social change. In an essay, clarify Ortiz's views and give specific examples of the way in which he visualizes Indians using their education to fight injustice and preserve their cultural heritage. Then argue for or against his position.

---

# VINE DELORIA JR. AND CLIFFORD M. LYTLE

*A member of the Sioux tribe, Vine Deloria Jr. was born in Martin, South Dakota, in 1933. He earned his bachelor's degree from Iowa State University (1958), his master's from the Lutheran School of Theology (1963), and his law degree from the University of Colorado (1970). Since serving as director of the National Congress of American Indians, he has held teaching and research positions at several colleges and universities, including Colorado College, the University of Arizona, and the University of Colorado. His publications include* Custer Died for Your Sins: An Indian Manifesto *(1969),* We Talk, You Listen: New Tribes, New Turf *(1970),* God Is Red *(1973), and* Behind the Trail of Broken Treaties: An Indian Declaration of Independence *(1974). With Clifford M. Lytle, he has coauthored* American Indians, American Justice *(1983) and* The Nations Within: The Past and Future of American Indian Sovereignty *(1984), among others.*

*Clifford M. Lytle, who was born in 1932, has written extensively on issues related to constitutional law and the history of the American justice system. He holds a bachelor's degree from Denison University, a law degree from Case Western University, and a doctorate from the University of Pittsburgh. In addition to the books he has coauthored with Vine Deloria Jr., Lytle has also written* The Warren Court and Its Critics *(1968) and coauthored, with* Richard Cortner, Modern Constitutional Law *(1971) and* Constitutional Politics in Arizona *(1969), among other works.*

*The selection that follows, from* The Nations Within, *explores some of the negotiations that have taken place between the federal government and the American Indian tribes. As it examines the difference between nationhood and self-government, the selection assesses the implications of that distinction for American Indians and members of the dominant culture as well.*

# A STATUS HIGHER THAN STATES

1   IT MUST BE A BIT DISCONCERTING when the average American on vacation out west suddenly encounters a sign that boldly proclaims that the highway is entering an Indian "nation." We like to think of nations on a much larger scale—preferably an ocean away, with all the hustle and bustle of modern, industrial, institutional life. Nations have different languages, religions, customs, and holidays from our own; they represent a mass of people who have struggled for centuries to create institutions that presently serve them. Indian tribes have some of the attributes we find familiar in other nations; language, religion, and social customs certainly set them apart from other Americans. But we miss the massive crowd of people, the well-developed lands, the military and economic power that we see in larger nations. And so, when the idea of Indian tribes as nations is voiced, many Americans laugh at the pretension, convinced that Indians have some primitive delusion of grandeur that has certainly been erased by history.

2   Indian affairs constitute but a minute part of the domestic American scene— so small a share, in fact, that federal Indian legislation no longer even rates a permanent subcommittee in either house of Congress. It is not difficult to see that although Indians are poor and generally live in isolated places in rural America, they are not in most respects radically different from other Americans living in the same circumstances. In fact, one might observe, most Indians are not distinguishable from other Americans except on those occasions when they shed working clothes and perform dances in fancy costumes for tourists—for a small entrance fee, of course. If this occasional ceremonial, the meaning of which has been lost in the past century and replaced by the commercial powwow, is all that distinguishes Indians from other Americans, why do Indians believe they are different? And why does the United States government treat them differently?

3   Modern social reality and historical political reality are rarely consonant with each other. Contemporary Indian communities, both reservation and ur-

ban, represent the continuing existence of a particular group of people who have traditionally had a moral and legal claim against the United States. The fact that many Indian tribes continue to exist unassimilated is not due to the practice of traditional ceremonies as much as it testifies to the complex of legal and political ideas that have surrounded Indians for two centuries and made them understand the world in much different terms from any other group of American citizens.

American Indians are unique in the world in that they represent the only   4 aboriginal peoples still practicing a form of self-government in the midst of a wholly new and modern civilization that has been transported to their lands. Early in the period of discovery of the New World, the papacy articulated the Doctrine of Discovery, which announced that Christian princes discovering new lands had a recognized title to them, subject only to the willingness of the original inhabitants to sell their lands to the discoverer. Because of such principles—and in spite of the history of exploitation and conquest represented by American settlement of North America—American Indians have actually been treated considerably better than any other aboriginal group on any other continent.

The United States, after successfully revolting against the king of England,   5 claimed to inherit Great Britain's right to buy the lands of the Indians, and this doctrine, modified to fit the internal, domestic law of the United States, has been the primary conceptual focus for all subsequent federal Indian law. Every legal doctrine that today separates and distinguishes American Indians from other Americans traces its conceptual roots back to the Doctrine of Discovery and the subsequent moral and legal rights and responsibilities of the United States with respect to Indians.

Under the Constitutions, Congress is given exclusive power to regulate   6 commerce with foreign nations, among the several states, and with the Indian tribes.[1] Among other powers and privileges ceded to the national government with the adoption of the Constitution was the surrender by the states of the subject of Indians. New York State and several other former colonies—specifically, Virginia and Massachusetts—preserved the right to continue to deal with Indian tribes for whom they had already assumed some responsibility. But these relationships were themselves based upon the old Doctrine of Discovery and represented a long series of treaty agreements in which the colonies—now states, with the adoption of the Constitution—agreed to protect the tribes from the depredations of their own citizens. There is no inherent power in any of the fifty states to deal with Indians at all.

One good way to view the subsequent history of the United States is   7 through the eyes of the federal government in dealing with Indians and Indian rights. Much of the federal-state conflict has revolved around the role of the federal government in protecting its primacy with respect to Indian affairs.

1. U.S., *Constitution*, Art. 1, sec. 8, clause 3.

Pressures on the frontier for free lands, the extension of slavery into land unsuitable for cotton production, the aggressive gold rushes, the need for a suitable water law on western lands, and the authorization and construction of railroads—all these activities were hampered by and influenced by the role of the federal government toward Indians. Settlement was chaotic, but in a sense systematically so, in that many activities were delayed while the government dealt with the tribes who occupied and defended various parts of the continent.

8      The Constitution mentions Indians as an identifiable group twice: once in the provision for determining representation in the Congress and the second time when this phrase is repeated in the Fourteenth Amendment. Indians in these instances are viewed as individuals: "Indians not taxed," a phrase that testifies to the idea that Indians, as individuals, could be assimiliated into the body politic, providing they assumed the ordinary citizenship responsibilities. In the world of Anglo-Saxon property owners this meant paying taxes. Indians not paying taxes are not to be enumerated when determining the population of each state, and the presumption is that those Indians immune from state and federal taxes are in some kind of political allegiance to their own tribes, submitting to whatever strictures that tribe or society is able to impose on its members. Therefore these Indians are outside the reach of American sovereignty and its taxing power.

9      This interpretation is further supported by the language of the Indian Citizenship Act of 1924,[2] which gives all Indians born within the territorial limits of the United States full citizenship but adds that such status does not infringe upon the rights to tribal and other property that Indians enjoy as members of their tribes. A dual citizenship exists here, which is not to be hindered in either respect: Indians are not to lose civil rights because of their status as members of a tribe, and members of a tribe are not to be denied their tribal rights because of their American citizenship. Unfortunately, this distinction has not often been preserved, and in the 1920s, and again in the 1950s, Congress attempted to sever unilaterally the political relationship between Indian tribes and the United States, using the citizenship of individual Indians as its excuse.

10     For a long time after the United States assumed primary control over its portion of North America, Indian tribes maintained their own civil and criminal jurisdiction. Tribal traditions and customs prevailed in instances of civil and social disorder. Some treaties—most notably those signed in 1867 and 1868 with the large tribes of the West (the Sioux, Cheyenne, Navajo, Ute, Crow, and Arapaho)—made provision for the Indians to continue to govern themselves according to ancient ways. The first article of these treaties generally recites a formula to the effect that the tribes can punish their own wrongdoers and they can pay indemnities to the United States instead of surrendering tribal members who have performed bad or injurious acts against citizens of the United States or members of other tribes.

2. U.S., *Statutes at Large*, 43:253.

In 1882 the Brule Sioux medicine man Crow Dog killed Spotted Tail, leader  11
of the band and a chief who had counseled accommodation with the United
States. Under traditional Sioux customs the relatives of the two men arranged
for compensation for the death of Spotted Tail. Presents were exchanged, and
the families believed they had solved the problems created by the killing. The
federal attorney for Dakota Territory was aghast at the seemingly casual manner
in which the Sioux dealt with this killing, and he soon charged Crow Dog with
murder. The case reached the Supreme Court in 1883, and the conviction of
Crow Dog by the territorial court was reversed on the grounds that the 1868
treaty had preserved for the Sioux the right to punish tribal members who had
committed serious crimes. A great public outcry followed the decision, and in
1885 Congress passed the Seven Major Crimes Act,[3] which took away major
criminal jurisdiction from Indian tribes.

Although the Seven Major Crimes Act was phrased to apply to all Indian  12
tribes in their capacity as governments, it was not so applied. The Five Civilized
Tribes—the Cherokee, Choctaw, Creek, Chickasaw, and Seminole—did not
legally come under its provisions because of special laws which applied only to
them. Neither, as a matter of practical fact, was it applied to the small groups
of Indians in the Great Basin who had not yet moved to a reservation. Nevertheless, for the majority of Indians living on the reservations, the passage of this
act, coupled with a new aggressive attitude on the part of Indian agents assigned
to them, quickly eroded the social cement that tribal custom had provided to
tribal societies. Some tribes were able to maintain a form of religious continuity
in ceremonies, but the major strength of tribal political unity was broken by the
assumption of jurisdiction by federal and territorial courts over offenses committed by one Indian against another on the reservation.

In 1887 the General Allotment Act was passed, and shortly thereafter most  13
of the reservations were subdivided into 160-acre tracts, which were distributed
to tribal members. The remaining tribal lands were purchased by the United
States at a minimum price and opened to settlement by whites, the purchase
price sometimes deposited in the United States Treasury but more often distributed on a per-capita basis among tribal members. Allotment redirected the
thrust of the federal-Indian relationship to that of property management, and
with the need for supervision over the use of property came the expansion of
the administrative structure of the Bureau of Indian Affairs. Tribal status became
less important, and natural resources became the major concern of both Indians
and federal bureaucrats.

In 1934, as a part of the New Deal efforts to grapple with the economic  14
depression that had brought the country to a standstill, John Collier, commissioner of Indian Affairs, presented to Congress a major piece of reform legislation popularly called the Indian Reorganization Act (IRA). Under the provisions
of this act any tribe or the people of any reservation could organize themselves

3. Ibid., 23:362.

as a business corporation, adopt a constitution and bylaws, and exercise certain forms of self-government. Although the IRA was designed to permit tribal governments to engage in some kinds of economic development and business enterprise, the failure of Congress to appropriate sufficient funds made the economic recovery of the tribes difficult and blunted their progress.

15    The postwar retrenchment of domestic social programs made it exceedingly difficult for tribes to continue the progress they had made under the IRA before the Second World War. In 1954, under the urging of Senator Arthur Watkins, Congress adopted a program of termination of federal supervision of Indians. In reality this policy meant termination of federal services to Indians; most of the tribes who lost their federal status did not escape from the burdens of wardship. They were usually placed under the supervision of one of the larger banks in the state in which they were located, and their property was managed for them by it.

16    With the advent of the New Frontier and Great Society programs, Indian tribes were declared eligible as local sponsoring agencies for the multitude of social welfare programs authored by Congress. The sixties' War on Poverty required that the poor be organized into Community Action Program (CAP) areas and that a CAP agency administer programs designed to eliminate poverty. The poverty programs were a welcome respite from decades of neglect. Educational services were expanded, some modern forms of economic development were made available to the reservations, and housing was built for the first time since the Great Depression. By the early 1970s, tribes felt so confident in their own talents in management and political organization that they began to pressure the federal government to give them more flexibility in controlling the activities on their reservations. The 1972 Indian Education Act[4] and the Indian Self-determination and Education Act of 1975[5] were legislative expressions of the Indian desire for more freedom in the activities of government.

17    The major thrust of recent contemporary reform in Indian affairs was represented by the American Policy Review Commission resolution,[6] which established the American Indian Policy Review Commission (AIPRC), charged with surveying the conditions of Indians in the United States and making recommendations on how to improve federal Indian policy. The commission, popularly nicknamed the Abourezk Commission after the senator from South Dakota who had sponsored the measure in the Senate and had become co-chairman of the body, was subdivided into eleven task forces that investigated various topical subjects of importance to Indians—treaties, tribal government, economic development, education, and so forth.

18    The AIPRC devoted two years to this study and produced a massive report,

4. Ibid., 86:334.
5. Ibid., 88:2203.
6. Ibid., 1910.

running close to two thousand pages. The final report contained over two-hundred separate recommendations, the majority of which were simple house-keeping corrections that reflected the orientation of Bureau of Indian Affairs employees who had been borrowed to write the final draft of the commission's findings. The tone of the Abourezk Commission was very aggressive, and consequently the final report was divided into a majority and minority opinion, the conflict revolving around the degree to which the commission should endorse the idea of tribal sovereignty. Many of the Indians who had worked for the commission wanted a strong posture that conceived of tribes as dependent domestic nations. The minority, led by Congressman Lloyd Meeds of Washington, recognizing that the political climate was shifting away from militancy, sought to blunt the impact of the report. Shortly after the Abourezk Commission report was issued, the Indian subcommittees in the Senate and House Interior committees were abolished, making it difficult, if not impossible, to carry out the recommendations of the commission.

With the advent of the Carter and later Reagan administrations, Indian  19
tribes shifted their attention to more practical programmatic considerations. Declining federal budgets for domestic social programs meant a drastic cutback in funds available to operate reservation programs, and unemployment rose swiftly on most reservations, which had depended on an expanding number of federal programs for meeting the employment needs of the tribe. Neither Carter nor Reagan disturbed the status of tribal governments with new policy consid-erations. They were content to admonish the tribes to enter the world of private enterprise and reduce their dependence on federal largess.

Recent federal policy has featured the slogan of a "government-to-  20
government relationship," which is intended to represent the older idea that tribes have a special political status with respect to the United States. Few Indians or bureaucrats know exactly what this recent phrase is supposed to represent. Since tribes are very much dependent upon the federal government for their operating funds and for permission to exploit the natural resources present on their reservations, the idea of two governments meeting in some kind of contemporary contractual arrangement on anything approaching an equal bargaining position itself seems ludicrous. Nevertheless, the Indian leadership has insisted that this description of the federal-tribal relationship is accurate and describes precisely the framework they believe exists. It is no mistake, in view of the accommodations the tribes and the United States have worked out, that many tribes have erected signs proclaiming their nationhood, that traditional Indians believe themselves to be sovereign entities endowed with almost mystical political powers, and that groups of Indians have recently appeared on the world scene demanding some form of representation in the United Nations.

When we look back at the treaty negotiations between the United States and  21
the respective Indian tribes, there is little mention of the complex of ideas that

constitutes nationhood. Indeed, we find very little awareness in either the Indians or the American treaty commissioners that an important status was being changed by the agreement that people were then making. During the 1868 treaty negotiations with the Sioux and Arapaho, at times the American commissioners speak of the Sioux as a small nation that can be totally destroyed by the kind of warfare the United States was willing to wage were peace not forthcoming from the talks. Strangely, the Indians were not cowed by the threats of the treaty commissioners; they knew so little about the white man that they believed they could prevail if the whites wished to make war on them. So finally the United States signed the treaty and agreed to one of the most humiliating provisions it ever accepted. The forts on the Bozeman Trail were abandoned at the demand of Red Cloud that the Sioux hunting lands be kept inviolate, and as the soldiers departed, the Indians rushed into the stockades and burned them to the ground.

22    In almost every treaty, however, the concern of the Indians was the preservation of the people, and it is in this concept of the people that we find both the psychological and the political keys that unlock the puzzling dilemma of the present and enable us to understand why American Indians view the world as they do today. When we understand the idea of the people, we can also learn how the idea of the treaty became so sacred to Indians that even today, more than a century after most of the treaties were made, Indians still refer to the provisions as if the agreement were made last week. The treaty, for most tribes, was a sacred pledge made by one people to another and required no more than the integrity of each party for enforcement. That the United States quickly insisted that the treaties should be interpreted rigidly as strictly legal documents has galled succeeding generations of Indians and made permanent peace between Indians and the federal government impossible.

23    The idea of the people is primarily a religious conception, and with most American Indians tribes it begins somewhere in the primordial mists. In that time the people were gathered together but did not yet see themselves as a distinct people. A holy man had a dream or a vision; quasi-mythological figures of cosmic importance revealed themselves, or in some other manner the people were instructed. They were given ceremonies and rituals that enabled them to find their place on the continent. Quite often they were given prophecies that informed them of the historical journey ahead. In some instances the people were told to migrate until a special place was revealed; in the interim, as with the Hebrews wandering in the deserts of Sinai, the older generation, which had lost faith, and the cynics and skeptics in the group would be eliminated until the people were strong enough to receive the message.

24    Tribal names generally reflect the basic idea that these particular people have been chosen from among the various peoples of the universe—including mammals, birds, and reptiles, as well as other humans—to hold a special relationship with the higher powers. Thus, most tribal names can be interpreted simply to mean "the people." There are, of course, some variations that have

arisen in the course of the Indian historical journey. The people who pierced their noses have now become the Nez Perce; the prosperous people have become the Gros Ventres; the allies, or friends, have become the Sioux; and some tribes have called themselves after the holy location where they finally came to rest— they are now the people who live at the lake, on the river, and so forth.

Because the tribes understood their place in the universe as one given        25 specifically to them, they had no need to evolve special political institutions to shape and order their society. A council at which everyone could speak, a council to remind the people of their sacred obligations to the cosmos and to themselves, was sufficient for most purposes. The tribes needed no other form of government except the gentle reminder by elders of the tribe when the people were assembled to maintain their institutions. Indians had a good idea of nationhood, but they had no knowledge of the other attributes of political existence that other people saw as important. Most of all, Indians had no awareness of the complexity that plagued the lives of other peoples, in particular the Europeans.

First contact with Europeans shocked both the Indians and the explorers.        26 The Indians watched without understanding as the residents in the European settlements, bowed before arbitrary authority with a meekness that the Indians loathed. They believed that the whites had surrendered all moral substance in exchange for security in the anonymity of institutional life. Many Indian nicknames spoke derisively of the whites as "people who take orders," or "people who march in a straight line." And most Indians had little respect for white military leaders who commanded their soldiers to go to war while remaining safely in the rear. They might fear a white general, but they respected very few of them.

To the Europeans, Indians appeared as the lowest form of man. No formal        27 institutions were apparent. Leaders seemed to come and go almost whimsically. One might be negotiating with one chief on one occasion and be faced with a different person for no apparent reason except that the Indian council had designated the new man to speak for them. In tracing the source of political authority, whites were really baffled. No one seemed to be in charge of anything. A promise need not even be written down, and there seemed to be no appeal to any formal authority when things went wrong. In frustration, an early painter designated the Iroquois chiefs "kings," because there seemed no way to describe their status within the tribe except through the medium of familiar English feudal terminology.

It was difficult for whites not to conclude that chiefs had some mystical but        28 absolute power over other members of the tribe. Most important social/political positions of leadership in tribes depended upon the personal prestige and charisma of the individual. Even where a position as chief was a lifetime office, qualifications for filling the post were primarily those of personal integrity and honesty, so that respect rather than popularity was the criterion by which Indians selected who would lead them. When whites faced an Indian war party, they would note that the Indians fought with great vigor until their leader was killed. More often than not, the Indian spirit for the fight declined swiftly upon the death of the war chief, and the whites would win the day. This kind of behavior suggested an influence far beyond that of the hereditary European monarchs over their subjects.

29      The truth, not surprisingly, was somewhat less mysterious. Indian war parties most often were composed of individuals who had volunteered upon hearing the announcement, made by the village crier, that a certain warrior was thinking about leading a war party. No one had to go; there was never a draft in Indian society. But if the warrior had a good reputation and the adventure promised others a chance to distinguish themselves, and if they had confidence in the warrior, then a lot of men, particularly younger warriors, would clamor to be a part of the expedition. It is not difficult to imagine the trauma of seeing the leader of the war party, a man in whom the rest of the party had placed implicit trust, killed in a skirmish. Having lost their leader, the chances were that the Indians would quickly leave the field of combat, disheartened at the turn of events. Whites interpreted this kind of Indian behavior as a political/military defeat rather than the personal loss to the members of the war party that it really represented.

30      This kind of leadership and these kinds of informal governing institutions existed long ago, when Indian tribes were free to live as they wished. The substance of those days remained in Indian memories, but the political institutions and social customs changed quite rapidly as more contact with whites occurred, so that we can speak of these things now as the spiritual but not the practical heritage of Indians. The important thing is that there was no doubt in the minds of most Indians that, whatever the Europeans might say or do, they were still a free people, that they controlled certain lands and territories, and that they had the capability of punishing their enemies for any transgressions they might suffer. With respect to the lands they lived on, many Indians felt a strong religious duty to protect their territory. Future generations would need the lands to live on, many previous generations had migrated long distances to arrive finally at the place where the people were intended to live. One could sell neither the future nor the past, and land cessions represented the loss of both future and past to most Indians.

31      The expanding white population did not see it the same way, however, and when faced with the unpleasant choice of ceding their lands or drowning in the tidal wave of settlers who stood poised on their borders, the Indians wisely surrendered their lands and reluctantly moved west, hoping to escape white civilization by staying away from it. The course of American history demonstrated that even this faint hope was illusory, and the result of constant moves and land cessions is our scattered bits and pieces of reservation land that dot the maps of western states today.

32      Although Indians surrendered the physical occupation and ownership of their ancestral lands, they did not abandon the spiritual possession that had been

a part of them. Even today most Indians regard their homeland as the area where their tribe originally lived. The Cherokees recently filed suit to prevent the flooding of a part of the Little Tennessee River where the old Cherokee town of Tellico once stood. To most Americans, and certainly to the federal courts who heard the case, the claim of the Indians was remote, if it existed at all, geographical proximity being more tangible and comprehensible than spiritual beliefs. To the Cherokees who opposed the flooding of the area, however, there was no responsible course except to fight as best they were able to prevent the destruction of their town site.

Today a terrible divisiveness exists in many Indian tribes. After almost a 33 century of regarding their reservations as a place to live, Indians are discovering that they are being prodded into leasing large portions of their lands so that others can exploit the mineral wealth that lies underneath the ground. Sometimes it is coal deposits, often oil or natural gas, and occasionally uranium and molybdenum. All of these resources bring immense wealth, and their removal always leaves some desolation that cannot easily be corrected. Sacredness and utility confront each other within the tribal psyche, and it is not at all certain how Indians will decide the issue. Most Indians are so desperately poor that any kind of income seems a godsend. On the other hand, ancient teachings inform Indians that the true mark of a civilization is its ability to live in a location with a minimum disruption of its features.

Strangely, in the old prophecies in many tribes the conditions of today are 34 accurately forecast. "A time will come," these prophecies begin, and they speak of the total desolation of the land and the abandonment of ceremonials and rituals. Religious gifts of power seem not to be eternal but only to be used within this particular segment of cosmic time. As this cycle of planetary history ends, the culture and traditions that enabled the people to live are changed, distorted, and worn out. When all resources are exhausted, there will be tremendous cosmic upheaval and a new heaven and earth will be created. The survivors of the catastrophe will then receive new prophecies and ceremonies that will enable the people to prosper in the radically changed world that has come to pass. While traditional Indians mourn each step of dissolution, they are also comforted with the thought that a completely new world is in the process of being created. The fact remains, however, that the experience of this generation is one of transformation, heartbreak, and confusion.

The idea of peoplehood, of nationality, has gradually been transformed over the 35 past two centuries into a new idea, one derived primarily from the European heritage, and with a singular focus distinct from the old Indian culture and traditions. It is also important to understand the primacy of land in the Indian psychological makeup, because, as land is alienated, all other forms of social cohesion also begin to erode, land having been the context in which the other forms have been created. In such ideas lie the conceptual keys to understanding how the Indian experiences the world today.

36       With such understanding, we can see that the occupation of Wounded Knee in 1973 was far more traumatic for Indians than it was for whites, who might have felt a little disturbed at the idea of Indian militants taking up arms against the United States. Wounded Knee is symbolic of the conflict that is raging in Indian hearts everywhere. It arose basically over the question of how the Sioux, and by extension other Indians, should deal with the untenable situation created by the federal government in their communities. The tribes faced seemingly insoluble problems involving the form of tribal government; the claims filed against the United States that were not moving toward resolution; the use of land, tribal and individual, on the reservation; and the nature of education that Indians were receiving. Above all was the perennial dilemma of how Indians could pursue their own religious traditions in a world that refused to recognize the essential spiritual nature of life.

37       Politically the Wounded Knee occupation pitted traditional Indians and militants against the established tribal government, which had adopted a constitution and bylaws during the New Deal under somewhat less than promising circumstances. The traditional Sioux had always been suspicious of the new tribal government and frequently voiced their opposition to it. But since the tribal government was the only form of political participation that the United States government would recognize and deal with, the traditionals had little choice except to boycott the tribal government and then hope that some crumbs would fall from the table of government largess, which had become available because of the existence of the tribal government—an uncomfortable dilemma, to be sure.

38       From the perspective of the protestors, the point at issue in Wounded Knee was the *form of government* that the Sioux would use to direct their own destiny. From the perspective of the established tribal government—and, by extension, the federal government—the point at issue was *the direction that the existing tribal government would take.* For the traditionals the issue was philosophical and, by extension, theological and sociological; for the tribal government the issue was pragmatic, programmatic, and operational. They believed that the larger questions were considered settled by the passage of time and by the changes that had already been wrought in many of the tribal members.

39       Supporters of the tribal government argued that only through the Indian Reorganization Act did the Indians have self-government and that attacking the existing tribal government was in essence advocating anarchy, a condition that the United States could not allow under any circumstances. The response of those people who supported the traditionals and militants was that self-government was a delusion, because the existing tribal government had been created by the United States simply to serve its own purposes, supplanting the traditional government and customs with an alien institution and its rules and regulations. Where, one Sunday during the seventy-one-day occupation, the Indian protestors announced that they constituted the "independent Oglala Nation" and declared that a state of war existed between that nation and the

United States, few Americans realized that it represented deep and persistent conviction among the Oglalas.

Wounded Knee, in the end, represented the philosophical divisions within all Indian tribes, the collision between the political dilemma of nationhood and the adoption of self-government within the existing federal structure. The traditionals certainly focused on the morality of the case, but the incumbent tribal government, for all its faults, spoke with a bitter contemporary pragmatism that could not be ignored. Wounded Knee could have happened on any Indian reservation, and while the occupation was dragging out to its final spasms, even many a conservative Indian suggested that maybe such activities were necessary to awaken the bureau and the president to their responsibilities.   40

When we distinguish between nationhood and self-government, we speak of two entirely different positions in the world. *Nationhood* implies a process of decision making that is free and uninhibited within the community, a community in fact that is almost completely insulated from external factors as it considers its possible options. *Self-government*, on the other hand, implies a recognition by the superior political power that some measure of local decision making is necessary but that this process must be monitored very carefully so that its products are compatible with the goals and policies of the larger political power. *Self-government* implies that the people were previously incapable of making any decisions for themselves and are now ready to assume some, but not all, of the responsibilities of a municipality. Under self-government, however, the larger moral issues that affect a *people's* relationship with other people are presumed to be included within the responsibilities of the larger nation.   41

The postwar generation of Indians had been enthusiastic about self-government because it has represented a step forward from the absolute prostration the tribes suffered when the federal bureaucracy preempted all social and political functions on the reservations after the passage of the General Allotment Act. Thus, having a tribal government that did have minimum respect accorded it by the federal agencies that were charged with providing services to the tribe did help Indians regain a measure of self-respect that had been lacking for several generations.   42

It is a long step from a small group of people living in a rather primitive fashion on an undisturbed and undiscovered continent to the present immensely complicated network of reservations that constitutes the homelands of American Indians. Nevertheless, Indian tribal governments, as presently constituted, have many of the powers of nations and, more important, have the expectation that they will continue to enhance the political status they enjoy. With some exceptions, such as jurisdiction over major crimes, now fourteen in number, a standing army, coinage and postage, and other attributes of the truly independent nations, Indian tribes exercise in some respects more governing powers than local non-Indian municipalities and in other respects more important powers than the states themselves.   43

44 But such privileges do not assuage the needs of a spiritual tradition that remains very strong within most tribes and that needs to express itself in ways familiar to the people. Thus, Wounded Knee was the inevitable product of the experiment in self-government because it represented the first effort to establish the dignity of the tribe in a manner consonant with the people's memories of their older way of life.

45 To suggest now that the movement for self-government was wrong may shatter modern Indian beliefs and cause great consternation. Self-government was not wrong; it was simply inadequate. It was limited in a fundamental way because it circumscribed the area in which the people's aspirations could express themselves. Hence we *do not* say that the movement for self-government was wrong or misguided; it certainly led to the present situation, which has both positive and negative dimensions. The task that Indians face today is tracing the roots of the idea of self-government to discover how and where it relates to the present aspirations of Indians and Indian tribes.

46 Self-government is not an Indian idea. It originates in the minds of non-Indians who have reduced the traditional ways to dust, or believe they have, and now wish to give, as a gift, a limited measure of local control and responsibility. Self-government is an exceedingly useful concept for Indians to use when dealing with the larger government because it provides a context within which negotiations can take place. Since it will never supplant the intangible, spiritual, and emotional aspirations of American Indians, it cannot be regarded as the final solution to Indian problems. Because self-government is such a complex idea, because it has been a product of the historical process, and because it has received much of its substance from Indians in the course of its development, it is important that we trace the genesis and development of this idea and discover how it manifests itself in our lives today. ✤

---

## RESPONDING

1. In a journal entry, rewrite in your own words the provisions of the agreements between the U.S. government and the Indian tribes presented in this reading.

2. Working individually or in a group, construct a time line that outlines the historical relationship between the American government and the Indian tribes. Place all the treaties and agreements on the time line.

3. The reading explains the differing points of view between traditional and militant Indians. Imagine that you are the spokesperson for either group and write a letter to uncommitted Indians trying to persuade them to adopt your point of view.

4.  In an essay, agree or disagree that self-rule is an important component of Indian life. Be sure to support your argument with specific examples from the readings or with outside knowledge.

# LINDA HOGAN

*A poet, novelist, and essayist, Linda Hogan was born in Denver, Colorado, in 1947. After receiving her master's degree from the University of Colorado in 1978, she taught at several institutions, including the University of Denver, Colorado College, and the University of Minnesota. She currently holds an English professorship at the University of Colorado, Boulder. Hogan's publi-cations—which include the poetry collections* Eclipse *(1983),* The Book of Medicines *(1993), and* Seeing Through the Sun *(1995); the novels* Mean Spirit *(1990),* Solar Storms *(1995), and* Power *(1998); and the essay collection* Dwellings: A Spiritual History of the Living World *(1995)— have won her several significant awards, among them an American Book Award (1985), a grant from the National Endowment for the Arts (1986), a Guggenheim Fellowship (1990), and a grant from the Lannon Foundation (1994).*

*"Crossings," from* The Book of Medicines, *explores some of the ways in which elements of the physical world can suggest connections between personal and collective histories.*

✣

# CROSSINGS

There is a place at the center of earth
where one ocean dissolves inside the other
in a black and holy love;
It's why the whales of one sea
know songs of the other,                                                    5
why one thing becomes something else
and sand falls down the hourglass
into another time.

Once I saw a fetal whale
on a block of shining ice.                                                  10
Not yet whale, it still wore the shadow
of a human face, and fingers

that had grown before the taking
back and turning into fin.
15    It was a child from the curving world
of water turned square,
cold, small.

Sometimes the longing in me
comes from when I remember
20    the terrain of crossed beginnings
when whales lived on land
and we stepped out of water
to enter our lives in air.

Sometimes it's from the spilled cup of a child
25    who passed through all the elements
into the human fold,
but when I turned him over
I saw that he did not want to live
in air. He'd barely lost
30    the trace of gill slits
and already he was a member of the clan of crossings.
Like tides of water,
he wanted to turn back.

I spoke across elements
35    as he was leaving
and told him, Go.
It was like the wild horses
that night when fog lifted.
They were swimming across the river.
40    Dark was that water,
darker still the horses,
and then they were gone. ✠

---

## RESPONDING

1. In a journal entry, describe some aspect of the natural world that particularly interests or intrigues you. Do you feel separated from or connected to the natural world around you?

2. Working individually or in a group, discuss the connection of the American Indian to the land and its creatures. List all of your beliefs about American Indians and explain the source of these beliefs. How much of what you

know about American Indians comes from reliable sources and how much comes from films? Use the Internet to investigate whether your information reflects reality or is a myth.

3.  Hogan writes about a boy who wants to return to the sea (line 33). Write a story about what might happen to humans if they could adapt to living in the sea. Consider why humans might make such a choice, and its advantages and disadvantages.

4.  The poem suggests an interconnectedness between all creatures. In an essay, explain how embracing such a position would affect your daily life in a modern industrialized country.

# NICOLE BRODEUR

*Journalist Nicole Brodeur, who received her bachelor's degree from Glassboro (NJ) State College in 1984, has written for newspapers in four states. From 1985 to 1986 she covered four cities and wrote feature stories for* The Philadelphia Inquirer. *From 1986 to 1994 she had several assignments covering both news and feature stories at* The Orange County (CA) Register, *including first bureau reporter, general assignment reporter, and religion writer, before being assigned a weekly features column in 1994. She is currently a metro columnist for* The Seattle Times *and* The (Raleigh, NC) News *and* Observer, *where she covers social issues, politics, and human interest stories. In 1998 she was awarded first place in the National Headliner Award Competition.*

*In the essay that follows, Brodeur considers the term "endangered" as a focal point as well as an ironic metaphor as she describes a whale hunt.*

# THE MEANING OF THE HUNT

IF WE ARE A NATION THAT TRULY "CELEBRATES" DIVERSITY, then this week the   1
Makah reservation was a proving ground—a party that tests the depths of our acceptance.

Watching the hunt of a gray whale from our comfy homes in Seattle, it was   2
easy to be outraged by the bloodshed and the cheering.

3    But there had to be something more at the heart of what seemed like senseless murder.

4    So I drove to Neah Bay, at the far corner of the country, where this ramshackle community sits like a bedsheet that won't stay tucked under—a lack of order that somehow offends a lot of us.

5    By the time I arrived, the whale was just a bloody carcass. A sour smell hung in the air. Kids jiggled the flesh with sticks. Blood-caked knives still sat in the cedar-bark canoes.

6    I was searching for spirit, but saw only spoils.

7    Then a group of men circled the remains, chanting and drumming.

8    I heard a voice behind me: "That's so the soul of the whale will rest in peace," whispered Janet Elofson, 38, a Makah now living in Port Angeles.

9    When the drumming ended, there was silence, save for the grinding of the TV trucks that lined the road.

10   "His spirit has gone now, to his ancestors," said drummer Spencer McCarty, 39, stepping back from the circle. "It's an expression of respect."

11   It was a respect I had missed from afar.

12   The hunt offers the tribe a chance to transform the future, McCarty said; it was healing to honor the traditions of the past.

13   "That part of it has been a really positive influence for a lot of people," McCarty said.

14   The tribe started to fracture when whaling was outlawed in the 1920s. The culture crumbled even more in 1930, when the U.S. government forced Makah families to dismantle their longhouses, saying that communal living was against the law.

15   Crime and drug problems set in, McCarty said, as members lost their spiritual mooring.

16   Perhaps the Makahs needed an act as profound as this kill to end their 70-year cultural coma.

17   The problem is that in that same time, whales became hallowed creatures to the rest of us—the revered subject of murals, museum exhibits, even the ballads of Crosby, Stills and Nash.

18   And the Makahs, strangely, became more like us.

19   So of course whalers called in the kill on a cell phone. Of course they stood atop the whale as it was hauled into the bay, arms stabbing at the sky, a visual echo of Monday Night Football.

20   Two generations of Makahs never had a chance to see the traditional way to whale. Imagine a young boy trying to carve the Thanksgiving turkey like his grandfather did, when his father never learned.

21   Yes, the hunt was violent and bloody. It made schoolchildren cry. It made me sick.

But it made Kathryn Gyori, a 14-year-old Makah, proud.                              22

"People don't understand what being native really is," she told me. "You            23
can't understand this feeling. The tribe is getting back to the old ways of its
ancestors. . . . I feel peaceful."

Consider this: As long as the whales were endangered, so was the heart of          24
the Makahs. We should not judge what we can't understand.

"We will be the last people to want whales not to survive," McCarty said.          25
"Because whatever happens to them will happen to us, too." ✠

---

## RESPONDING

1. In a journal entry, describe a tradition that has been handed down in your
   family from one generation to the next, or describe a cultural tradition with
   which you are familiar.

2. Working in a group, compare the traditions described in your journal entries
   and discuss what they have in common. How did the traditions originate?
   How have they changed over time? Alternatively, consider a tradition or
   celebration in American culture, such as Thanksgiving or the Fourth of July,
   and discuss its origins and development. What rituals are part of the
   traditional celebration?

3. Kathryn Gyori, a 14-year-old Makah, proudly states, "People don't understand what being native really is. . . . The tribe is getting back to the old
   ways of its ancestors. . . . I feel peaceful." In an essay, explain why going
   back to the old ways might be helpful for the Makah. Why might it be
   harmful? Discuss some of the advantages and disadvantages of the old ways,
   or use this theme to examine American culture. For example, are there old
   ways in American culture that we should or should not return to? You might
   consider family life, gender roles, and other similar topics.

4. In an essay, discuss the problems groups encounter when trying to maintain
   their traditional cultural values and practices while being dominated by
   another culture. Consider, for example, the Makahs, the early Mormons,
   recent immigrants, or any other group you have some knowledge about.

# JERRY LARGE

*The journalist Jerry Large was born in Clovis, New Mexico, in 1954. He and his brothers were raised by a mother "who picked cotton just across the border in the Texas Panhandle and [worked] as a maid in Clovis." He earned a bachelor's degree in journalism and mass communication from New Mexico State University in 1976 and worked for newspapers in New Mexico, Texas, and California before joining the* Seattle Times *in 1981, where he is currently a regular columnist.*

*In the essay that follows, Large examines the competing interests in both the current whaling controversy and its coverage in the media.*

⁜

# CONCERNING A WHALE

1   WHAT AN INTERESTING CULTURE we have here in the United States. I suppose it's no less logical than most other human societies, except that it is burdened with a belief in its own superiority that makes it hard to tolerate sometimes.

2   I watched some white folks on TV the other day yelling "whale killer!" at a bunch of Indians, and I was struck by the absurdity of the scene. Saving whales was the least of what this was about.

3   Like a lot of people in this culture, I regard whales as special animals. There is little logic in it, but each culture makes its own sense of the world.

4   There are people who want to protect cows and pigs, too, but we like whales better and so we pay more attention to people who want to protect them.

5   Of course we think some animals are better than others. We think some people are better than others, don't we?

6   Monday the Makahs killed their first whale in generations. Those members of the tribe who wanted to resume the hunt after a 70-year hiatus saw it as a way to reconnect with their cultural roots. I suspect that what they really wanted to harpoon was cultural domination.

7   Members of the culture most responsible for the decline of whales and the demise of untold other species, not to mention the decimation of the Indians, chastised the Makahs for their incivility. The sight of yelling protesters made me grind my teeth.

I was reminded of news coverage several years ago when a group of whales      8
were trapped under polar ice at the same time that an African village was
surrounded by rising floodwaters.

Which story do you think got daily front-page play in most newspapers?      9
Just before the whales were trapped, floods killed about 300 people in India.
We ran a 5-inch-long story. As the whale drama came to a close, flooding in
Thailand claimed nearly 1,000 lives. We ran a 4-inch story.

There were stories about the whales for a month. Whales have a greater      10
claim on kinship to many Westerners than do Africans or Indians, or any number
of other peoples who don't make the cut.

That doesn't make me like whales any less, but it does give me a visceral      11
and negative reaction to those who champion the cause of whales and scorn
their two-legged brethren.

The entire Euro-American environmental movement has a lot of work to      12
do to win the favor of people who are tired of being told what to do by a culture
that believes the planet belongs to it alone.

Consciously or not, a lot of people seemed to be ticked off that the Indians      13
weren't behaving the way this culture wants them to. How dare they!

The hundreds of messages phoned and e-mailed to newspapers and TV      14
stations often got ugly.

One message to KIRO said, "Any culture that regains its pride by killing      15
is, at best, primitive." Does NATO know that? How did this culture come to
dominate the globe?

There seemed to be three kinds of protesters: people who just love whales      16
and were torn by their concern for the rights of Indians; people who like animals
and couldn't care less about the Makahs; and people who don't particularly like
animals but really don't like Indians.

Many people who are against whaling saw this mess as a distraction. Norway      17
and Japan kill well more than 1,000 whales every year. Alaskans eat whales. The
Makah whaling quota came out of the number allotted to the Russians. But this
one whale was intolerable to some folks.

The lovable icon of environmental caring, U.S. Rep. Jack Metcalf, R-Wash.,      18
called the hunt "barbaric."

U.S. Sen. Slade Gorton, who needs no introduction to Indians, said he was      19
"outraged and saddened."

As in most conflicts, the ones yelling the loudest were the most unreason-      20
able. There were death threats. How civilized. One caller claimed to have
planted a bomb in an Indian school.

Ours is a culture far removed from its food supply and far removed from      21
its soul. It is a culture that tries to kill everything animal in humanity, and to
make individuals pieces of efficient machinery. It is an odd champion of nature.

22    None of this is to say that Indian cultures are superior. Indians are humans (after reading some of the protest messages, it is clear this needs to be repeated) and humans exploit their environments, and often each other. Some humans have just been more efficient at that than others.

23    Pre-industrial village culture as it has existed on every continent has been, out of necessity, in tune with nature in ways that are forever lost to us.

24    The Makahs can't go back to a village culture any more than the rest of us can, but they do need to believe in themselves. This defiance may be part of a process that leads them back to some of what was taken from them.

25    If that whale is a martyr, it died for the sins of our culture. ✣

---

RESPONDING

1.  In a journal entry, discuss your feelings about the protection of endangered species.

2.  Working individually or in a group, use the Internet to research the history of whale hunting.

3.  Write an essay explaining what Large means when he says that the Makahs really wanted to harpoon "cultural domination" (paragraph 6). Do you agree with his analysis of their motives?

4.  In an essay, agree or disagree with Large's assertion that the American public is more concerned about the killing of one whale than about the devastation of non–Euro American peoples.

✜

# CONNECTING

## Critical Thinking and Writing

1.  Critics have called the period during which the readings in this chapter were written the American Indian Renaissance. Define *renaissance*. How do the readings in this chapter exemplify a renaissance?

2.  For many groups, tradition shapes understanding of the present. Using the readings in this chapter and your own experience, describe occasions in which traditional beliefs have helped individuals solve current problems or have created problems.

3.  The earth itself is an important force in American Indian culture. Write an essay describing the role of the earth in the life of one or more of the characters in these readings.

4.  Compare Lipsha Morrissey's understanding and acceptance of events at the end of the excerpt from *Love Medicine* with Ayah's understanding at the end of "Lullaby." What aspects of their responses are based on the teachings of their cultures? What might be considered universal? What aspects might be attributed to differences in personality or experience?

5.  Ortiz praises the oral tradition. Orality, for him, is a positive. Is this always the case? Write an essay comparing the value of orality with the difficulties encountered by Ayah in "Lullaby" because of her reliance on orality alone.

6.  Write an essay discussing the contributions American Indians made to new immigrants to America.

7.  Refer to the pre-reading assignment and review the characteristics the media currently attributes to American Indians. Now that you have read the selections in this chapter, discuss the accuracy of these portrayals.

8.  Storytelling and the oral tradition are an important part of many cultures. Discuss the importance of storytelling within a particular culture and support your points with examples from some of the readings in this text. Or compare the role of storytelling in American Indian culture with that of another culture such as the Chinese (see chapter 4).

9. Ayah in the story "Lullaby" expresses the point of view that having contact with mainstream culture is dangerous when she says "learning their language or any of their ways: it endangered you" (paragraph 12). Explain her fears. What compromise do you think might exist between a position that advocates total isolation from mainstream culture and a position that accepts total loss of native culture? How could such a compromise be implemented?

10. Welch's poem reflects the pressure on American Indians to assimilate into mainstream society and culture. Describe ways in which the pressure American Indians feel differs from and is similar to that experienced by early-twentieth-century European immigrants or other groups.

11. Design your own essay question, relating a theme that emerges from the concerns of American Indians to a theme that is important to another group. You can use examples from the readings in this text or from outside knowledge and research.

### For Further Research

1. Research the life of an American Indian leader such as Black Elk, Chief Joseph, or Geronimo. Look at novels and films treating events in that person's life. Compare the portrayals that emerge from the two forms of inquiry.

2. Many American Indians still live on reservations. Research the political, social, and economic structure of the reservation.

3. More than half of American Indians now live in cities. Research their social and economic situation. What factors cause people to leave the reservation? How successful are they in integrating into mainstream culture within urban areas? Are American Indians able to live in cities and still maintain their culture?

## REFERENCES AND ADDITIONAL SOURCES

Apes, William (Pequot). *A Son of the Forest: The Experience of William Apes, a Native of the Forest, Comprising a Notice of the Pequot Tribe of Indians.* New York: published by author, 1829. Republished as *A Son of the Forest: The Experience of William Apes, a Native of the Forest,* 2nd ed. rev. and corr. New York: published by author, 1831.

Axtell, James. *The European & the Indian: Essays in the Ethnohistory of Colonial North America.* New York: Oxford University Press, 1981.

Champagne, Duane, ed. *The Native North American Almanac: A Reference Work on Native North Americans in the United States and Canada.* Detroit: Gale Research, 1994.

Debo, Angie. *A History of the Indian in the United States,* vol. 106. The Civilizations of the American Indian Series. Norman, Okla.: University of Oklahoma Press, 1970.

Deloria, Vine, Jr. *Custer Died for Your Sins: An Indian Manifesto.* New York: Macmillan, 1969.

Deloria, Vine, Jr., and Clifford M. Lytle. *American Indians, American Justice.* Austin: University of Texas Press, 1983.

Donovan, Kathleen M. *Feminist Readings of Native American Literature: Coming to Voice.* Tucson: University of Arizona Press, 1998.

Eagle, Adam Fortunate. *Alcatraz! Alcatraz!: The Indian Occupation of 1969–1971.* Berkeley, Calif.: Heyday Books, 1992.

Fixico, Donald L. *Termination and Relocation: Federal Indian Policy, 1945–1960.* Albuquerque: University of New Mexico Press, 1986.

Green, Rayna, ed. *That's What She Said: Contemporary Poetry and Fiction by Native American Women.* Bloomington: Indiana University Press, 1984.

Hagan, William T. *The Indian in American History.* New York: Macmillan, 1963. Series: Service Center for Teachers of History. Vol. 50.

Hobson, Geary, ed. *The Remembered Earth. An Anthology of Contemporary Native American Literature.* Albuquerque: University of New Mexico Press, 1981.

Jaskoski, Helen, ed. *Early Native American Writing: New Critical Essays.* New York: Cambridge University Press, 1996.

Josephy, Alvin M., Jr. *The Nez Perce Indians and the Opening of the Northwest.* Boston: Houghton Mifflin, 1965.

Kehoe, Alice Beck. *North American Indians: A Comprehensive Account.* Englewood Cliffs, N.J.: Prentice-Hall, 1992.

Larson, Charles. *American Indian Fiction.* Albuquerque: University of New Mexico Press, 1978.

Lerner, Andrea, ed. *Dancing on the Rim of the World: An Anthology of Contemporary Northwest Native American Writing.* Tucson: University of Arizona Press, 1990.

Lindquist, Mark A., and Martin Zanger, eds. *Buried Roots and Indestructible Seeds: The Survival of American Indian Life in Story, History, and Spirit.* Madison: University of Wisconsin Press, 1994.

McNickle, D'Arcy. *Native American Tribalism: Indian Survivals and Renewals*. New York: Institute of Race Relations for Oxford University Press, 1973.

Mitchell, Lee C. *Witnesses to a Vanishing America: The Nineteenth-Century Response*. Princeton, N.J.: Princeton University Press, 1981.

Nagel, Joane. *American Indian Ethnic Renewal: Red Power and the Resurgence of Identity and Culture*. New York: Oxford University Press, 1996.

Neihardt, John G. *Black Elk Speaks: Being the Life Story of a Holy Man of the Ogala Sioux*. Lincoln: University of Nebraska Press, 1961.

Niatum, Duane, ed. *Carriers of the Dream Wheel: Contemporary Native American Poetry*. New York: Harper & Row, 1975, 1981.

Oswalt, Wendell H. *This Land Was Theirs: A Study of the North American Indian*. New York: Wiley, 1966.

Prucha, Francis P. *The Great Father: The United States Government and the American Indians*. Lincoln: University of Nebraska Press, 1984.

Rainwater, Catherine. *Dreams of Fiery Stars: The Transformations of Native American Fiction*. Philadelphia: University of Pennsylvania Press, 1999.

Rosen, Charles. *The Man to Send the Rain Clouds*. New York: Vintage, 1975.

Ruoff, A. Lavonne Brown. *American Indian Literatures: An Introduction, Bibliographic Review, and Selected Bibliography*. New York: Modern Language Association, 1990.

Sarris, Greg. *Keeping the Slug Woman Alive*. Berkeley: University of California Press, 1993.

Starr, G. A. *Defoe and Spiritual Autobiography*. Princeton, N.J.: Princeton University Press, 1965.

Sturtevant, William C., and Wilcomb E. Washburn, eds. *History of Indian-White Relations*, Vol. 4, Handbook of North American Indians series. Washington, D.C.: Smithsonian, 1988 edition, 1989 edition.

Swann, Brian. *Song of the Sky: Versions of Native American Songs and Poems*. Ashuelot, N.H.: Four Zoahs Night House, 1985, rev. ed. Amherst: University of Massachusetts Press, 1993.

Thernstrom, Stephen, et al., eds. "American Indians," in *Harvard Encyclopedia of American Ethnic Groups*. Cambridge, Mass.: Harvard University Press, 1980.

Tyler, S. Lyman. *A History of Indian Policy*. Washington, D.C.: Government Printing Office, 1973.

Vogel, Virgil J. *This Country Was Ours: A Documentary History of the American Indian.* New York: Harper & Row, 1972.

Walker, Cheryl. *Indian Nation: Native American Literature and Nineteenth-Century Nationalisms.* Durham, N.C.: Duke University Press, 1997.

Ward, Geoffrey C. *The West: An Illustrated History.* Boston: Little, Brown, 1996

Warren, Robert Penn. *Chief Joseph of the Nez Perce.* New York: Random House, 1983.

Welch, James. *Fools Crow.* New York: Viking, 1986.

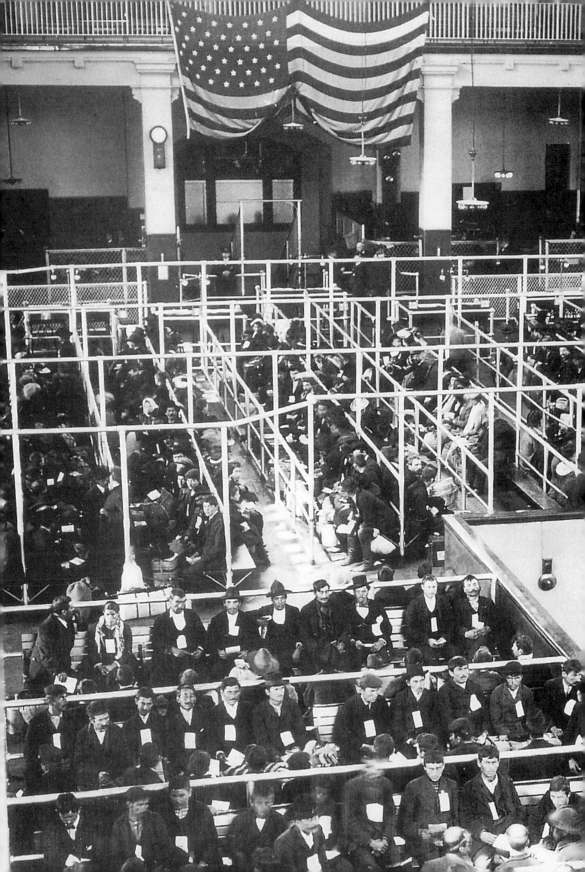

# 3

## EARLY IMMIGRANTS

### *In Search of the Land of Milk and Honey*

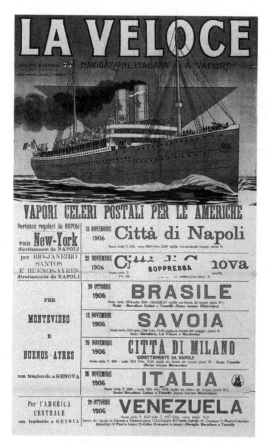

*Above:* Italian poster advertising sailings to the Western Hemisphere, 1906. *(RG85: 51411/53 oversize. National Archives)*
*Opposite:* Ellis Island, circa 1910. Newly arrived immigrants wait to be processed in the Great Hall, before being permitted entry into the United States. *(William Williams Collection, United States History, Local History & Genealogy Division, The New York Public Library/Astor, Lenox and Tilden Foundations)*

# SETTING THE HISTORICAL AND CULTURAL CONTEXT

Since its founding, the United States has been a land of immigrants. With the exception of American Indians, all persons who consider themselves Americans have been immigrants or descendents of immigrants. From colonial times, the process of immigration and resettlement has been ongoing, but the nineteenth century witnessed two notable waves of immigration. From 1820 to 1860, social and economic conditions in Europe—specifically, urban overcrowding, economic depression, and a series of bad harvests—prompted thousands to emigrate to the United States. Protestants and Catholics from northern and western Europe, most of these immigrants settled in the urban areas of the Northeast. Between 1880 and 1920, a second wave of immigration occurred. Catholics from southern Europe and Jews from eastern Europe fled religious persecution as well as economic strife and political upheaval. Many Jews, particularly those from Russia, hastened to escape the violent anti-Semitic attacks known as *pogroms;* Armenians fled the oppressive regimes of the Turks.

Influenced by advertisements and stories in European newspapers and by encouraging letters from friends and family members already settled in America, immigrants came to the United States expecting to find vast farmlands, theirs for the taking, and cites that would welcome even unskilled workers. The newcomers' expectations were often violated by the immigration process itself—the so-called Ellis Island experience, which has become a part of the nation's collective memory.

As soon as they arrived, immigrant families were detained at the immigration center for a series of debasing questions and medical examinations. They were asked their names and nationality; if the name were long or too difficult for the immigration official to spell, it might be changed on the spot. Those who failed the mandatory medical examinations were subject to detention or immediate deportation; often this resulted in families being separated for long periods. More than three fourths of the people who attempted to immigrate were admitted to the country; the other 20 to 25 percent were sent back to their homelands.

New immigrants were vulnerable to exploitation, both by government officials and by other immigrants themselves. An investigation of Ellis Island during Theodore Roosevelt's administration exposed the corrupt practices of some immigration officials as well as those of commercial enterprises that had used unfair currency exchange rates to cheat immigrants. Unprincipled attorneys would claim to work for the best interests of immigrants, only to charge them exorbitant fees. As Constantine Panunzio reports, *padroni* or other middle men would also exploit immigrants, promising them impressive employment opportunities that turned out to be "pick and shovel" work for little money.

But all was not grim. Some "in-country" immigrants offered encouragement and support to new arrivals and worked to protect their rights. Maxine Seller's essay recounts the efforts of three women immigrants to improve the quality of life for those who followed them.

After being admitted to the United States, most newcomers settled in the northeastern and midwestern states. Some took advantage of the Homestead Act of 1862, which guaranteed that those who lived on a parcel of land for five years could eventually claim ownership. Still a larger percentage settled in urban areas, where they established small shops or, more often, took jobs in factories. Many immigrants found work in the garment industry of New York City and in the slaughterhouses and meat-packing firms of Chicago.

Without question, life in both urban and rural areas was more difficult than most immigrants had expected. In cities, they lived in crowded apartments in equally crowded tenement buildings, where sanitation, heat, and even light were at a premium. The depth of poverty and deprivation is revealed in Anzia Yezierska's story "The Fat of the Land," where neighbors talk to each other across a narrow air shaft and children routinely fight over a potato.

In addition to Yezierska's fictional representation of immigrant life, several other selections in this chapter examine the living and working conditions encountered by newcomers. Jacob Riis, one of New York City's early reformers, used prose and photography to make the American public more aware of the troubling conditions of the immigrant. In the section included from the important work *How the Other Half Lives*, Riis explains how urban dwellings were converted to tenements. In the language of his day, Riis brands tenements with "the mark of Cain" and goes on to present a history in which individual desire for personal profit outweighed any consideration of public good. Though Riis's writing increased public concern about the general welfare and working conditions of immigrants, elements of his prose betrayed a condescending attitude toward its subject, as when he speaks of "a promiscuous crowd" or people "from whom nothing was expected." By supporting his arguments with equally deprecatory quotations, such as the description of the city as "a general asylum for vagrants," Riis seems implicitly to validate the judgment, as if he, too, were blaming the immigrant. As James West Davidson and Mark Hamilton Lytle point out in their analysis of Riis's work, "Images of the Other Half," not only does his use of language reveal ethnic and class biases, Riis's photography also raises questions about his methodology. The authors conclude by asserting "Riis did not simply want us to see the poor or the slums; he wanted us to see them as he saw them." These factors notwithstanding, Riis's investigative work was clearly influential in making the main-stream public more aware of these abuses, and establishing a climate for reform.

Working conditions were also substandard. Many urban immigrants were forced to work in overcrowded "sweatshops" without adequate facilities. Men often worked sixteen-hour shifts; everyone worked long hours for low pay. As Alan Kraut points out in *The Huddled Masses*—his study of Euro American immigrants—"No single development galvanized workers more than the Triangle Shirtwaist fire of 1911." As the fire spread through the overcrowded sweatshop, doors that were routinely locked from the outside prevented escape. Robert Pinsky recounts in his poem: "One hundred and forty-six died in the flames / On the ninth floor, no hydrants, no escapes."

Although some labor reform began in the mid-nineteenth century, with new laws prohibiting women from working more than ten consecutive hours, it was not until the first decades of the twentieth century that child labor laws were passed to protect the rights of children and make the education of minors compulsory. Unions became increasingly influential in this regard, yet the relationships between unions and immigrant groups remained problematic. Initially, workers had little power to influence the conditions of their employment because they received no help from organized labor unions. Many unions, in turn, considered immigrants a threat because they were sometimes recruited by employers as contract laborers and had been used, often unwittingly, to break up strikes. As time passed, some unions began to recognize the potential of immigrant workers as a labor force. The Irish immigrant Elizabeth Gurley Flynn, whose writing is included in this chapter, was a major force in the American labor movement.

The immigrants' struggle for acceptance by the unions and therefore a more secure place in the economy, mirrors the immigrants' struggle for a more secure place in society. Many U.S. citizens and established immigrants believed that newcomers could best ensure their success in this country by becoming "Americanized," or incorporated into the mainstream American culture. Writers such as philosopher John Dewey and journalist Abraham Cahan wrote essays and articles advocating assimilation. Israel Zangwill's play, *The Melting Pot*, provided a term for the process of assimilation that would be used liberally throughout the period and long after. Writings and cartoons of the period encouraged assimilation by mocking the *greenhorn*—the person who, naively or not, clings to the trappings of the Old Country. In addition, the educational system contributed to the assimilation process by familiarizing immigrants with the English language and indoctrinating them about the necessity of becoming Americanized.

Assimilation was not accomplished, however, without loss and pain. In her story, "Fat of the Land," Anzia Yezierska explores the cost of acculturation and economic success for an immigrant mother, her family, and friends. Acculturation often meant the loss of the comfort and sense of identity associated with a traditional way of life. In the story we see the main character's need for family rituals and old friends, and we discover the alienation and self-doubt that assimilation can bring.

Even during this early period some social critics objected to the assimilationist view. As David Fine makes clear, some who reviewed Zangwill's *Melting Pot* objected to the intermarriage of a Jew and a Gentile that takes place at the play's end, for this would constitute a violation of Jewish law. And while some reformers such as Jacob Riis advocated assimilation, Jane Addams, who had founded Hull House (an important Chicago settlement house), in 1889 took a different view. Addams believed that for acculturation to be successful, a two-way exchange had to take place: not only would the immigrant learn the ways of the new country, but the new country would be enriched by cultural contributions made by the newcomer. Maxine Seller's essay illustrates how this ideal was fulfilled in the work of Josephine Zeman, an eastern European immigrant who was educated at Hull House and went on to become an important social worker, author, journalist, and advocate for the rights of other immigrants.

Although many writers and reformers celebrated the arrival of the immigrants, many other members of society did not. Indeed, during the 1880s, at the height of the nation's second wave of immigration, much of the country's attention was focused on exclusionist legislation and nativist doctrines, which promoted the rights and interests of self-described "native" inhabitants over the rights and interests of immigrants. Ironically, these so-called native inhabitants were immigrants, too; they had simply arrived in the United States earlier than those whom they were trying to keep out.

The rejection of immigrants took several forms. Some members of the labor force regarded immigrants as a source of competition for jobs. Others, even government officials, entertained stereotypical notions about immigrants, believing that some groups included dangerous radicals. Other nativists subscribed to a theory of eugenics, which asserted the innate superiority of some groups. Still others claimed that the national identity might be diluted if the country were allowed to become a "melting pot." As a result of nativist pressure, Congress passed exclusionist legislation, establishing immigration quotas that favored Protestant immigrants from northern and western Europe over immigrants from other areas who often held other religious beliefs. Congress also instituted a *head tax*, a one-time charge for entering the country; each subsequent piece of exclusionist legislation was accompanied by an increase in rate of the head tax.

Despite these many obstacles, immigrants continued to come. They settled in urban areas, either working in factories or establishing small businesses. They formed civic organizations, built synagogues and churches, and dreamed of providing their children with better lives. Robert Pinsky's poem, "Shirt," which concludes the chapter, establishes a connection between the modern-day garment worker and the many immigrants—whether voluntary or not—who came before them: "The planter, the picker, the sorter / Sweating . . . / As slaves in calico headrags sweated in fields." Pondering the "inspected by" label on his shirt, the poet calls attention to the individual named therein:

> . . . her name is Irma
> And she inspected my shirt. Its color and fit
>
> And feel and its clean smell have satisfied
> Both her and me. . . .

In reflecting metaphysically about a humble object, its parts and its origin, Pinsky honors the individual who is part of the collective, and affirms the dignity of her labors, her hardships, and her dreams.

## BEGINNING: Pre-reading/Writing

*Working in a group, use the knowledge you have gained from reading the introduction to this chapter or from your own experience to list the possible reasons that immigrants flocked to America during the period between 1820 and 1920. Share your list with the class. How do you think these reasons compare with those motivating immigrants today? Use the Internet to investigate current immigration issues.*

*The Bill of Rights comprises the first ten amendments to the Constitution of the United States. They resulted from an agreement between those who wanted a strong federal government and those who sought to restrict the power of the government. These amendments, added in 1791, were designed to prevent the federal government from making laws that violated such basic rights as freedom of speech, press, assembly, expression of religious faith, and trial by jury. The Supreme Court later extended the power of the Bill of Rights by applying the document to state governments as well.*

*The Bill of Rights clearly articulates the rights guaranteed to each individual. As such it has assumed a special importance for many immigrants who have fled repressive regimes or religious persecution in their homelands.*

✤

# THE BILL OF RIGHTS

ARTICLES IN ADDITION TO, and Amendment of the Constitution of the United States of America, proposed by Congress, and ratified by the Legislatures of the several States, pursuant to the fifth Article of the original Constitution.

## *Art. I*

Congress shall make no law respecting an establishment of religion, or prohibiting the free exercise thereof; or abridging the freedom of speech, or of the press; or the right of the people peaceably to assemble, and to petition the government for a redress of grievances.

## *Art. II*

A well regulated Militia, being necessary to the security of a free State, the right of the people to keep and bear Arms, shall not be infringed.

## *Art. III*

No Soldier shall, in time of peace be quartered in any house, without the consent of the Owner, nor in time of war, but in a manner to be prescribed by law.

## *Art. IV*

The right of the people to be secure in their persons, houses, papers, and effects, against unreasonable searches and seizures, shall not be violated, and no

Warrants shall issue, but upon probable cause, supported by Oath or affirmation, and particularly describing the place to be searched, and the persons or things to be seized.

## Art. V

No person shall be held to answer for a capital, or otherwise infamous crime, unless on a presentment or indictment of a Grand Jury, except in cases arising in the land or naval forces, or in the Militia, when in actual service in time of War or public danger; nor shall any person be subject for the same offence to be twice put in jeopardy of life or limb; nor shall be compelled in any criminal case to be a witness against himself, nor be deprived of life, liberty, or property, without due process of law; nor shall private property be taken for public use, without just compensation.

## Art. VI

In all criminal prosecutions, the accused shall enjoy the right to a speedy and public trial, by an impartial jury of the State and district wherein the crime shall have been committed, which district shall have been previously ascertained by law, and to be informed of the nature and cause of the accusation; to be confronted with the witnesses against him; to have compulsory process for obtaining witnesses in his favor, and to have the Assistance of Counsel for his defence.

## Art. VII

In Suits at common law, where the value in controversy shall exceed twenty dollars, the right of trial by jury shall be preserved, and no fact tried by a jury, shall be otherwise re-examined in any Court of the United States, than according to the rules of the common law.

## Art. VIII

Excessive bail shall not be required, nor excessive fines imposed, nor cruel and unusual punishments inflicted.

## Art. IX

The enumeration in the Constitution, of certain rights, shall not be construed to deny or disparage others retained by the people.

## *Art. X*

The powers not delegated to the United States by the Constitution, nor prohibited by it to the States, are reserved to the States respectively, or to the people. ✠

---

## RESPONDING

1. Choose one of the provisions of the Bill of Rights that is particularly important to you. In a journal entry, explain in your own words what it promises or implies and why you chose it.

2. Working individually or in a group, rewrite all of the provisions of the Bill of Rights in less technical language.

3. Choose one of the rights that you think would have been particularly important to early immigrants and write an essay explaining your choice. Use information from the introduction to the chapter, other sources, and your own knowledge.

---

# CONSTANTINE PANUNZIO

*Constantine Panunzio, who was born in Bari, Italy, in 1884, arrived in the United States on July 3, 1902. After completing studies in theology at Wesleyan University, Boston University, and New York University, he earned a doctorate from the Brookings Institution in 1925. During the period between 1915 and 1920, Panunzio was active in the immigrant community, working at settlement houses and at the YMCA; in 1919 he became the superintendent of immigrant labor for the Interchurch World Movement. After 1920 he devoted most of his time to teaching, serving on the sociology faculty of several universities, including the State University of New York and the University of California, Los Angeles. Many of Panunzio's published works treated the issues of immigration and deportation. He died in 1964.*

*Panunzio's book* The Soul of an Immigrant *(1922) recounts the author's experiences and celebrates his assimilation into his new culture. Despite the text's general optimism, the excerpt that follows tells of his struggles to find housing and work just after arriving in America.*

⁜

# IN THE AMERICAN STORM

*Not that they starve, but starve so dreamlessly,*
*Not that they sow, but that they seldom reap,*
*Not that they serve, but have no gods to serve,*
*Not that they die, but that they die like sheep.*
　　　　　　　　　—VACHEL LINDSAY

1　THE *Francesco* put out to sea from Trapani, Sicily, on May 3, 1902, and a week or so later passed the Pillars of Hercules. Then she plunged into the wake of the trade winds and for about three weeks she sailed majestically before them like a gull, stirring not a sail all the while. Then followed a period of varying weather, which in turn was succeeded by a few days when the ocean was breathless and motionless. Frequently we could see whole schools of dolphins as they came to the surface, or monster whales spurting pillars of water into the air, a sight especially beautiful on calm moonlit nights.

2　The little brig had reached a distance of about three hundred miles from the coast of North America, when one day the very weight of heaven seemed to be pressing down upon her. The clouds were yellow, sullen and angry-looking; the air was breathless with pent-up power. As the day advanced the barometer went lower and lower, and with the approach of evening this invisible, uncontrollable power seemed to be seizing the little ship as if with mighty claws. The sea rumbled beneath her, the thick masses of clouds pressed closer upon her, the waters became deep-dyed black. At five-thirty we heard the call: "All hands on deck," and a few moments later: "All sails in but lower-topsail and jib." Climbing like monkeys after coconuts, we made short work of the task. We knew, however, that something more strenuous was coming. At six, just as the four bells were striking, the very bowels of sea and sky opened upon us with amazing suddenness and force. The seasoned Tuscan sailor, whose every word was wont to be an oath, struck with sudden fear, fell upon his knees by the bulwark and began to say his prayers. Some one kicked him as you would a dog. The moment the terrific gale struck the ship it tore the heavy lower-topsail and flapped it madly in the air as if it were a piece of tissue paper. The brave little ship beat pitifully beneath the gale; its mainroyalmast was broken like a reed; its cargo was shifted to one side like a handful of pebbles, and its hull sprung a leak. The blast was over in an hour or so, but all hands worked steadily for three days and nights to shift the cargo back in place, while four men were kept at the hand-pump night and day until we reached shore a week or more later.

3　Some years afterward an American friend, reflecting upon this incident as I had described it to him remarked, "That storm was indeed prophetic of your early experiences in America, was it not?" It may be that it was, and perhaps we shall soon discover the analogy as it appeared in my friend's mind.

On July 3rd, 1902, after a voyage of sixty-one days, the *Francesco* anchored in Boston Harbor. As the next day was the "Fourth," the city was already decked in festal array. The captain hastened to register his arrival. A boat was lowered, and I was ordered to take him ashore; thus it was my good fortune to be the first to touch land. "America!" I whispered to myself as I did so.

In a day or two the ship was towed to a pier in Charlestown, where it lay until its cargo of salt was unloaded and a cargo of lumber consigned to Montevideo was put on board of her.

In the meantime a desire had arisen within me to return home. There were several reasons for this. In the first place, it was becoming increasingly unpleasant for me to remain in the midst of that crew. It chanced that I was the only person on board hailing from southern Italy; the rest of the men were mostly Genoese, with one or two Tuscans. Now, the feeling of sectional provincialism between north and south Italy is still so strong, and the North always assumes such airs of superiority, that I had become the butt of every joke and the scapegoat of every occasion. This was becoming more and more unbearable, and as time went on I decided that my self-respect could not and would not stand it. To this was added the fact that the captain was one of those creatures who seem to be more brute than man, especially in dealing with youth. During that voyage he had more than once beaten me in a way that would have made the hardest punishments of my father blush. He was so cruel and unreasonable that before he left Boston several of the crew, including the first mate, left him.

In the face of these circumstances I began to think that if the captain would only let me go, I would return home. Accordingly, one day I went to him and very respectfully told him of my intention to return to Italy immediately if he would permit me, and would pay me the money which was due me. The stern, sea-hardened sailor brushed me aside without even an answer. A day or so later I again went to him; this time he drove me from his presence with a sharp kick. Whatever manhood there ever was in my being rose up and stood erect within me; with a determination as quick and as sharp as his kick had been, I decided I would now go at any cost.

I began to look about for ways and means to carry out my determination. On the pier was an elderly watchman, an Italian by birth, who had been in America for several years. To him I confided my difficulties. He was a sane and conservative man, cautious in giving advice. My desire was to find a ship which was returning to some European port. He did not know of any, but one evening he suggested that if worse came to worst, I could do some kind of work for a few days and thereby earn enough money to buy a third-class passage back to Naples, which at that time cost only fifty or sixty dollars. This gave me a new idea. I decided to take my destiny in my own hands and in some way find my way back to Italy. Two months had already passed since our arrival in Boston, and almost any day now the vessel would take to sea. If I were to act it must be now or never. I had been ashore twice and had become acquainted with a barber near the pier. To him I also confided my troubles, and he offered to keep my few belongings for me, should I finally decide to leave the ship.

9 Late in the evening of September 8, 1902, when the turmoil of the street traffic was subsiding, and the silence of the night was slowly creeping over the city, I took my sea chest, my sailor bag and all I had and set foot on American soil. I was in America. Of immigration laws I had not even a knowledge of their existence; of the English language I knew not a word; of friends I had none in Boston or elsewhere in America to whom I might turn for counsel or help. I had exactly fifty cents remaining out of a dollar which the captain had finally seen fit to give me. But as I was soon to earn money and return to Molfetta, I felt no concern.

10 My Charlestown barber friend took me in that first night with the distinct understanding that I could stay only one night. So the next morning bright and early, leaving all my belongings with the barber, I started out in search of a job. I roamed about the streets, not knowing where or to whom to turn. That day and the next four days I had one loaf of bread each day for food and at night, not having money with which to purchase shelter, I stayed on the recreation pier on Commercial Street. One night, very weary and lonely, I lay upon a bench and soon dozed off into a light sleep. The next thing I knew I cried out in bitter pain and fright. A policeman had stolen up to me very quietly and with his club had dealt me a heavy blow upon the soles of my feet. He drove me away, and I think I cried; I cried my first American cry. What became of me that night I cannot say. And the next day and the next. . . . I just roamed aimlessly about the streets, between the Public Garden with its flowers and the water-side, where I watched the children at play, even as I had played at the water's brink in old Molfetta.

11 Those first five days in America have left an impression upon my mind which can never be erased with the years, and which gives me a most profound sense of sympathy for immigrants as they arrive. On the fifth day, by mere chance, I ran across a French sailor on the recreation pier. We immediately became friends. His name was Louis. Just to look at Louis would make you laugh. He was over six feet tall, lank, queer-shaped, freckle-faced, with small eyes and a crooked nose. I have sometimes thought that perhaps he was the "missing link" for which the scientist has been looking. Louis could not speak Italian; he had a smattering of what he called "italien," but I could not see it his way. On the other hand, I kept imposing upon his good nature by giving a nasal twang to Italian words and insisting on calling it "francese." We had much merriment. Two facts, however, made possible a mutual understanding. Both had been sailors and had traveled over very much of the same world; this made a bond between us. Then too, we had an instinctive knowledge of "esperanto," a strange capacity for gesticulation and facial contortion, which was always our last "hope" in making each other understand.

Not far from the recreation pier on which we met is located the Italian   12
colony of "North End," Boston. To this Louis and I made our way, and to an
Italian boarding house. How we happened to find it and to get in I do not now
recall. It was a "three-room apartment" and the landlady informed us that she
was already "full," but since we had no place to go, she would take us in. Added
to the host that was already gathered there, our coming made fourteen people.
At night the floor of the kitchen and the dining table were turned into beds.
Louis and I were put to sleep in one of the beds with two other men, two facing
north and two south. As I had slept all my life in a bed or bunk by myself this
quadrupling did not appeal to me especially. But we could not complain. We
had been taken in on trust, and the filth, the smells and the crowding together
were a part of the trust.

We began to make inquiries about jobs and were promptly informed that   13
there was plenty of work at "pick and shovel." We were also given to understand
by our fellow-boarders that "pick and shovel" was practically the only work
available to Italians. Now these were the first two English words I had heard
and they possessed great charm. Moreover, if I were to earn money to return
home and this was the only work available for Italians, they were very weighty
words for me, and I must master them as soon and as well as possible and then
set out to find their hidden meaning. I practised for a day or two until I could
say "peek" and "shuvle" to perfection. Then I asked a fellow-boarder to take
me to see what the work was like. He did. He led me to Washington Street,
not far from the colony, where some excavation work was going on, and there
I did see, with my own eyes, what the "peek" and "shuvle" were about. My heart
sank within me, for I had thought it some form of office work; but I was game
and since this was the only work available for Italians, and since I must have
money to return home, I would take it up. After all, it was only a means to an
end, and would last but a few days.

It may be in place here to say a word relative to the reason why this idea   14
was prevalent among Italians at the time, and why so many Italians on coming
to America find their way to what I had called "peek and shuvle." It is a matter
of common knowledge, at least among students of immigration, that a very large
percentage of Italian immigrants were "contadini" or farm laborers in Italy.
American people often ask the question, "Why do they not go to the farms in
this country?" This query is based upon the idea that the "contadini" were
farmers in the sense in which we apply that word to the American farmer. The
facts in the case are that the "contadini" were not farmers in that sense at all,
but simply farm-laborers, more nearly serfs, working on landed estates and
seldom owning their own land. Moreover, they are not in any way acquainted
with the implements of modern American farming. Their farming tools consisted generally of a "zappa," a sort of wide mattock; an ax and the wooden plow
of biblical times. When they come to America, the work which comes nearest
to that which they did in Italy is not farming, or even farm labor, but excavation
work. This fact, together with the isolation which inevitably would be theirs on

an American farm, explains, in a large measure, why so few Italians go to the farm and why so many go into excavation work. There is another factor to be considered, and that is that the "padrone" perhaps makes a greater per capita percentage in connection with securing and managing workers for construction purposes than in any other line, and therefore he becomes a walking delegate about the streets of Italian colonies spreading the word that only "peek and shuvle" is available.

15　　Now, though Louis and I had never done such work, because we were Italians we must needs adapt ourselves to it and go to work with "peek and shuvle." (I should have stated that Louis, desiring to be like the Romans while living with them, for the time being passed for an Italian.)

16　　So we went out to hunt our first job in America. For several mornings Louis and I went to North Square, where there were generally a large number of men loitering in groups discussing all kinds of subjects, particularly the labor market. One morning we were standing in front of one of those infernal institutions which in America are permitted to bear the name of "immigrant banks," when we saw a fat man coming toward us. "Buon giorno, padrone," said one of the men. "Padrone?" said I to myself. Now the word "padrone" in Italy is applied to a proprietor, generally a respectable man, at least one whose dress and appearance distinguish him as a man of means. This man not only showed no signs of good breeding in his face, but he was unshaven and dirty and his clothes were shabby. I could not quite understand how he could be called "padrone." However, I said nothing, first because I wanted to get back home, and second because I wanted to be polite when I was in *American* society!

17　　The "padrone" came up to our group and began to wax eloquent and to gesticulate (both in Sicilian dialect) about the advantages of a certain job. I remember very clearly the points which he emphasized: "It is not very far, only twelve miles from Boston. For a few cents you can come back any time you wish, to see 'i parenti e gli amici,' your relatives and friends. The company has a 'shantee' in which you can sleep, and a 'storo' where you can buy your 'grosserie' all very cheap. 'Buona paga,'" he continued, "(Good pay), $1.25 per day, and you only have to pay me fifty cents a week for having gotten you this 'gooda jobba.' I only do it to help you and because you are my countrymen. If you come back here at six o'clock to-night with your bundles, I myself will take you out."

18　　The magnanimity of this man impressed Louis and me very profoundly; we looked at each other and said, "Wonderful!" We decided we would go; so at the appointed hour we returned to the very spot. About twenty men finally gathered there and we were led to North Station. There we took a train to some suburban place, the name of which I have never been able to learn. On reaching our destination we were taken to the "shantee" where we were introduced to long open bunks filled with straw. These were to be our beds. The "storo" of which we had been told was at one end of the shanty. The next morning we were taken out to work. It was a sultry autumn day. The "peek" seemed to grow heavier at every stroke and the "shuvle" wider and larger in its capacity to hold the gravel. The second day was no better than the first, and the third was worse than the second. The work was heavy and monotonous to Louis and myself especially, who had never been "contadini" like the rest. The "padrone" whose magnanimity had so stirred us was little better than a brute. We began to do some simple figuring and discovered that when we had paid for our groceries at the "storo," for the privilege of sleeping in the shanty, and the fifty cents to the "padrone" for having been so condescending as to employ us, we would have nothing left but sore arms and backs. So on the afternoon of the third day Louis and I held a solemn conclave and decided to part company with "peek and shuvle,"—for ever. We left, without receiving a cent of pay, of course.

Going across country on foot we came to a small manufacturing village. We [19] decided to try our luck at the factory, which proved to be a woolen mill, and found employment. Our work was sorting old rags and carrying them in wheelbarrows into a hot oven, in which the air was almost suffocating. Every time a person went in it he was obliged to run out as quickly as possible, for the heat was unbearable. Unfortunately for us, the crew was composed almost entirely of Russians, who hated us from the first day, and called us "dagoes." I had never heard the word before; I asked Louis if he knew its meaning, but he did not. In going in and out of the oven the Russians would crowd against us and make it hard for us to pass. One morning as I was coming out, four of the men hedged me in. I thought I would suffocate. I finally succeeded in pushing out, my hand having been cut in the rush of the wheelbarrows.

The superintendent of the factory had observed the whole incident. He was [20] a very kindly man. From his light complexion I think he was a Swede. He came to my rescue, reprimanded the Russians, and led me to his office, where he bandaged my hand. Then he called Louis and explained the situation to us. The Russians looked upon us as intruders and were determined not to work side by side with "the foreigners," but to drive them out of the factory. Therefore, much as he regretted it, the superintendent was obliged to ask us to leave, since there were only two of us, as against the large number of Russians who made up his unskilled crew.

So we left. My bandaged hand hurt me, but my heart hurt more. This kind [21] of work was hard and humiliating enough, but what went deeper than all else was the first realization that because of race I was being put on the road. And often since that day I have felt the cutting thrusts of race prejudice. They have been dealt by older immigrants, who are known as "Americans," as well as by more recent comers. All have been equally heart-rending and head-bending. I hold no grudge against any one; I realize that it is one of the attendant circumstances of our present nationalistic attitude the world over, and yet it is none the less saddening to the human heart. I have seen prejudice, like an evil shadow, everywhere. It lurks at every corner, on every street and in every mart. I have seen it in the tram and on the train; I have felt its dreaded power in school and college, in clubs and churches. It is an ever-present evil spirit, felt though unseen, wounding hearts, cutting souls. It passes on its poison like a serpent from generation to generation, and he who would see the fusion of the various elements into a truly American type must ever take into cognizance its presence in the hearts of some human beings. ✠

## RESPONDING

1. In a journal entry, compare Panunzio's experiences in a new situation and country to the experience of your family when they first came to the United States or moved to another part of the country or to your own experience in any new environment.

2. Working individually or in a group, use examples from Panunzio's autobiography to illustrate how the storm he encountered on his journey to America was "indeed prophetic of [his] early experiences in America" (paragraph 3). Which of those conditions would you have found most intolerable?

3. Write an essay discussing Panunzio's attitude toward prejudice. Do you agree that prejudice "passes on its poison like a serpent from generation to generation" (paragraph 21)? And what do you think of Panunzio's statement "I hold no grudge against any one" (paragraph 21)? Is this an effective response to prejudice or are there other strategies that might work better? Consider your own experience, the selection, and any other relevant reading.

4. In an essay, compare Panunzio's experiences working in Boston in 1902 with the experiences of new immigrants today. Base your response on your own knowledge, observations, and reading as well as on any news coverage, documentaries, or films you may have seen on this subject. How have employment opportunities and working conditions for new immigrants changed? Have they improved?

# OLE EDVART RÖLVAAG

*Ole Edvart Rölvaag was born in Norway in 1876. After immigrating in 1896, he spent his early years in the United States working on his uncle's farm in South Dakota. He later earned undergraduate and advanced degrees from Augustana College (in South Dakota), St. Olaf College (in Minnesota), and the University of Oslo. From 1906 to 1931 Rölvaag served as professor of Norwegian letters and literature at St. Olaf College. His publications* include Giants in the Earth: A Saga of the Prairie *(1924–1925, Norwegian; 1927, English);* Peder Victorious *(1929),* Their Father's God *(1931), and* Boat of Longings *(1933), published after his death in 1931.*

*Giants in the Earth has been praised for its psychological realism and for the intensity with which it depicts a pioneer family's struggles with the isolation of their environment. The excerpt that follows explores the tensions experienced by the woman of the family, who is in many ways a reluctant pioneer.*

✠

# FACING THE GREAT DESOLATION

## *VI*

THE DAYS WERE LONG for the boys during their father's absence. Ole soon tired of standing at the chopping block without the company of his brother; he idled aimlessly about, and made frequent errands into the house to see whether he couldn't hatch up something to break the monotony. Store-Hans wasn't much better off; the secret which his father had entrusted to him was certainly interesting; but it wasn't quite fascinating enough to hold its own with the vision of the ducks out there in the swamps. The father would surely bring something home from town to solve this problem; he and his brother ought to be over west reconnoitering every spare minute of the time. And now the Irish had all gone away, too; their sod huts were standing empty; there would be many curious things to look at and pry into! . . . Besides, their mother said so little these days; it was no fun to be with her any longer. Often when he spoke to her she was not there; she neither saw nor heard him, said only yes and no, which seemed to come from far away. . . . Probably she was brooding over the strange thing about to happen, Store-Hans told himself; he often looked wonderingly at her, thinking many thoughts beyond his years. . . . He remembered his father's words, and never left her for long, although it was very lonesome for him in the house.

2    A couple of days after the men's departure, she sent the boy over to Kjersti to borrow a darning needle; she had hidden her own away so carefully that she could not find it. Such things occurred commonly now; she would put something away, she could not remember where, and would potter around looking for it without really searching; at last, she would forget altogether what she was about, and would sit down with a peculiarly vacant look on her face; at such times she seemed like a stranger. . . . Ole was sitting in the house that morning, finishing a sling-shot which he had just made.

3    Suddenly Store-Hans came darting back with the needle; he had run until he was all out of breath. He burst out with the strangest news, of Tönseten's having killed a big animal; it was awfully big—almost like a bear! . . . Tönseten said it *was* a bear, so it must be true! Tönseten and Kjersti were skinning him right now; Kjersti had told him that if he would bring a pail, they could have fresh meat for supper. Both boys immediately began pleading for permission to go and see the animal; their mother scarcely answered; she gave them a pail and asked them not to stay long.

4    The boys came running down the hill just as Kjersti was cutting up the carcass; Tönseten was struggling with the hide, trying to stretch it on the barn door; his mouth bristled with nails, his hands were bloody—he was a frightful spectacle!

5    "What's that you've got?" asked Ole.

6    "Bear, my boy—bear!" . . . Tönseten wagged his head, took the nails out of his mouth, and spat a gob of tobacco juice.

7    "Bear!" snorted Ole, scornfully.

8    "That's no bear!" put in Store-Hans, though less doubtingly.

9    "By George! boys, to-day he had to bite the dust!" . . .

10   "But there aren't any bears out here, I tell you!" Ole protested.

11   "Is that so—huh? . . . There isn't an animal living that you can't find out here!" Tönseten spoke with such certainty that it was difficult for the boys to gainsay him.

12   "Where did you get him?" Store-Hans asked.

13   "Out west of the Irish a little way. . . . There were two of 'em; they had gone into the ground for the winter; this is the young one, you see—the old mammy got away from me!"

14   "But you didn't have any gun!" was Ole's next objection.

15   "Better than that, my boy! . . . I went for him with the crowbar!" Tönseten spat fiercely and looked at the boys. . . . "I smashed in his skull! . . . With that old bar I'd tackle either a tiger or a rhinoceros!"

16   "What became of the old she-bear?" Ole asked, falling under the spell of Tönseten's enthusiasm.

17   "She went north across the prairie, lickety-split! . . . Come here, now—take some of these chunks of meat home with you. . . . This will make delicious stew, let me tell you!"

18   "Is it fit to eat?" asked Store-Hans, still doubting.

"Fit to eat? No finer meat to be found than bear meat—don't you know     19
that?"

The boys followed him over to where Kjersti was still cutting up the animal;     20
it must have been a large carcass, for the cut meat made a sizable heap.

"Is it . . . is it really bear?" asked Ole, in a more humble tone.     21

"He's meaty enough for it! . . . Here, give me the pail; Beret needs some     22
good, strengthening food. . . . Maybe you'll take a little to Sörrina, too; you can
stop in with it on the way. . . . Careful—don't spill it, now!"

The boys loitered along on the way home; from time to time they had to     23
put down the pail, in order to discuss this extraordinary event. . . . So there
actually were bears slinking about this country! . . . If bears, there must be lions
and tigers and other such wild beasts; this was worth while!·. . . Suppose they
were to go home and get Old Maria, hunt up the she-bear herself, and put a
big bullet through her head? They thrilled with excitement. . . . "Do you dare
to shoot her off?" Store-Hans demanded of his brother; Ole scowled ominously
and clenched his fists. . . . "*I!* . . . I'd aim straight for her temple, and she'd drop
deader than a herring!" . . . "Yes, aim at her *temple!*" Store-Hans advised soberly.
"And if it's close range, you must draw the bead very fine!" . . . "Fine as a hair!"
said Ole, excitedly.

They picked up the pail at last, and finally succeeded in reaching Sörine's,     24
where there was another long delay; a detailed account had to be given of the
marvellous feat which Tönseten had performed.

When they were about to leave Sofie came out and wanted to know if they     25
weren't frightened; maybe the old mother bear was slinking about the prairie
right now looking for her cub! The boys lingered to talk with her; they drew a
glowing picture for the girl of how they were going home this minute to
get Old Maria, and then go hunting for the she-bear herself . . . just watch
them bring home a real roast pretty soon! . . . But weren't they scared? she
asked. . . . "Scared?" exclaimed Store-Hans. . . . "Oh, fiddle-sticks!" cried Ole.
"Only girls and old women get scared!"

Sofie only laughed; at which they affected a swaggering gruffness and tried     26
to spit like Tönseten—but theirs wouldn't come brown. . . .

They were gone such a long time that their mother grew anxious; when     27
they came over from Sörine's at last she stood outside the door watching for
them. She had dressed And-Ongen, and was almost on the point of starting out
to search; the boys were too preoccupied to notice this; Store-Hans spoke first:

"Just think, there's a big she-bear over there to the westward!" . . .     28

"We're going to take the gun and shoot her!" exclaimed Ole, gleefully.     29

"We'll aim straight for her temple!" Store-Hans assured his mother.     30

"Now we'll have plenty of bear meat!" continued Ole in the next breath,     31
with absolute confidence.

The boys were all raging excitement; their mood frightened Beret still more;     32
she grasped them frantically, one hand on the shoulder of each, and gave them
a hard shake. . . . They were to go inside this very minute, and take their books!

They weren't going out of this house to-day! . . . "Go in, don't you hear me! . . . Go in!" . . .

33     . . . But this wasn't fair! Ole began reasoning with his mother; he used strong words, his eyes flaming. . . . Didn't she realize that there was a real bear over to the westward—a real full-grown *grizzly* bear! . . . Mother . . . please . . . *please!* . . . Dad wasn't home, but the gun was all loaded and ready; they could easily manage the rest of it! In an hour's time they would have that bear's hide! Store-Hans even thought that he could go straight to the lair. . . . *Right through the temple* they would put the bullet! . . . The boys carried on like a raging hurricane.

34     The mother had to use force to get them indoors. . . . "Go in, I say, and take your books! Can't you hear what I'm saying?" . . .

35     This was hard on them; they burst into the house like two mad bull calves; she had to repeat the order several times more before they finally submitted and began to hunt for their books. At last Ole snatched up the "Epitome," his brother the "Bible History." They sat down to read by the table in front of the window, in a state of mutinous rebellion.

36     Trouble soon arose. Each wanted the seat immediately in front of the window, where the most light fell; and neither would give up the position. A terrible battle broke out; Ole was the stronger, but his brother the quicker. On account of his age and size Ole considered himself the legitimate master of the house in the absence of his father, and therefore had the right to do anything; he now burst out with words which he had heard in the mouths of the men when something went wrong with their work. As soon as Store-Hans heard this he too began to use vile language; if Ole dared, he certainly did; he knew those words, and plenty more! . . . The boys kept up the scrimmage until they almost upset the table; their books suffered bad treatment and lay scattered about on the floor. And-Ongen watched them open-mouthed until she suddenly grew frightened and set up a howl.

37     Over by the stove the mother was washing the meat, putting it into a kettle which she had placed on the fire. . . . Although she heard every word, she kept on working in silence; but her face turned ashen grey.

38     When she had finished the task she went out hurriedly; in a moment she came back with a willow switch in her hand. Going straight over to the table, she began to lay about her with the switch; she seemed beside herself, struck out blindly, hit whatever she happened to aim at, and kept it up without saying a word. The switch whizzed and struck; shrieks of pain arose. The boys at once stopped fighting and gazed horror-stricken at their mother; they could not remember that she had ever laid a hand on them before. . . . And now there was such a strange, unnatural look in her eyes! . . .

39     They flew out on the floor to gather up their books, while the blows continued to rain down upon them; And-Ongen stood in the middle of the floor, screaming with terror. . . .

40     Not until the mother struck amiss, breaking the switch against the edge of

the table, did she stop. . . . Suddenly she seemed to come to her senses; she left the child screaming in the middle of the floor, went out of the house, and was gone a long time. When she came back, she carried an armful of wood; she went over to the stove and fed the fire; then she picked up And-Ongen, and lay down on the bed with her. . . . The boys sat quietly at the table reading; neither of them had the courage to look up. . . .

The house seemed strangely still after the passage of the storm. Ole put his fingers into his ears to shut out the terrible silence; his brother began to read aloud. It was bad enough for Ole, but worse for Store-Hans; he now recalled clearly what his father had confided in him; he thought of his own solemn promise; here he had been away from the house nearly the whole day! He felt burning hot all over his body. . . . He had opened the book where it told about the choosing of the twelve disciples, and now he tried to read; but *that* wasn't the stuff for him just now! . . . He turned the pages forward to the story of Samson, and read it diligently; then to David and Goliath; then to the story about Joseph and his brethren. The last eased his heart somewhat. . . . Joseph was just the sort of boy that he longed to be! 41

Ole had felt ashamed at the sight of his mother bringing in the wood, though that was not his task; his brother was to be the hired girl! . . . Suddenly anger seized him; this time it certainly was the fault of Store-Hans—he should have given him the place! . . . He dragged himself through the *Third Article*, which he knew perfectly well already; when the tumult within him had somewhat subsided he sat there thinking of how shamefully Tönseten must have deceived them. . . . *He* kill a bear! It was nothing but a measly old badger! And now this nasty stuff was cooking on the stove—they were going to have it for supper! And mother was so angry that one would never dare to explain it to her! . . . There sat his younger brother, snuffling and reading his brains out; plain to be seen that he would never amount to anything! . . . Ole closed his book with a bang, got up, and went outdoors to chop more wood; but he did not dare to look at the bed as he passed. . . . 42

Store-Hans sat over his book until it grew so dark that he could no longer distinguish the letters. . . . From time to time he looked up; his mother lay on the bed perfectly still; he could not see her face; And-Ongen was fast asleep with her head high on the pillow. The boy rose quietly, looked around—then took an empty pail and went out for water. He left the pailful of water outside the door; then he brought Rosie and Injun and the two oxen into the stable, and tied them up for the night. He spoke loudly and gruffly to the animals; mother should hear that he was tending to business! . . . When he finally brought in the water his mother was up again; he could see nothing unusual about her. 43

. . . No, she hadn't been crying this time! The thought made Store-Hans so happy that he went straight to his brother, who was toiling over the chopping block as if possessed, and made friends with him again. The boys stayed outside until it was pitch dark; they talked fast and nervously, about a multitude of 44 things; but that which weighed most heavily on their hearts—the way their mother's face had looked when she whipped them—they could not mention.

45    Inside the house the lamp had been lit. And-Ongen toddled about the floor, busy over her own little affairs; the boys came in quietly and sat down to their books again; but very little reading was done now. . . . At last the kettle of meat that had been boiling on the stove was ready; the mother put the food on the table; the boys drew up, Ole somewhat reluctantly. . . . "You get that troll stuff down!" he whispered to his brother, making a wry face. To this command Store-Hans made no answer; he had stuck his spoon into a crack between the boards of the table; they were large, those cracks—he could see a broad section of floor when he laid his eye down close. The earthen floor had such a rich brown colour in the dim sheen of the lamp; the cracks in the table made stripes across the shadow down there; it looked pretty, too—and just then it had occurred to Store-Hans how nice it would be if they could only have the floor looking like that by daylight.

46    The mother filled the big bowl from the kettle and put it on the table; she had made a thick stew, with potatoes, carrots, and pieces of the meat; it looked appetizing enough but somehow the boys felt in no hurry to start. The mother came and sat down, bringing And-Ongen with her; the child was so delighted over the holiday fare they had to-night that she hurried to say grace.

47    She and the mother immediately began to eat; the boys no longer had an excuse to sit watching. Store-Hans dipped up a spoonful of stew, blew on it, closed his eyes, and gulped it down. Ole did the same, but coughed as if he had swallowed the wrong way; then he leaned under the table and spat it out. . . .

48    The mother asked quietly how they liked the supper. . . . At that, Ole could no longer restrain himself; he looked at his mother imploringly, and said in a tear-choked voice as he laid his spoon aside:

49    "It tastes like dog to me!"

50    To Store-Hans it seemed a shameful thing for Ole to speak that way of food which their mother had prepared for them; he swallowed spoonful after spoonful, while sweat poured from him.

51    "I have heard it said many times," the mother went on, quietly, "that bear meat is all right. . . . The stew has a tangy taste, I notice, but not so bad that it can't be eaten. . . . You'd better leave the meat if you don't like it."

52    "It isn't bear at all!" Ole blurted out.

53    "What?" cried the mother in alarm, lowering her spoon.

54    "It's only a lousy old badger! . . . I've heard dad say often that they aren't fit to eat!" . . .

55    "It's true, every word of it!" cried Store-Hans, suddenly feeling frightened and jamming his spoon farther down into the crack. . . . "I could tell it by his tail—Syvert had forgotten to cut it off! . . . Oh, I'm going to be sick—I can feel it coming!"

56    Beret got up, trembling in every limb; she took the bowl and carried it out into the darkness; a long way from the house she emptied it on the ground;

And-Ongen cried and toddled after her. . . . The boys sat on the table glaring reproachfully at each other; in the eyes of both blazed the same accusation:

"A nice mess you've made of things! Why didn't you keep your mouth 57 shut?"

The mother came in again; she set the empty kettle on the stove and scoured 58 it out carefully. . . .Then she cooked porridge for them, but when it was ready she could eat nothing herself. . . .

. . . That night she hung still more clothes over the window than she had 59 the evening before. She sat up very late; it seemed as if she was unable to go to bed.

## *VII*

She had been lying awake a long time; sleep would not come. Her thoughts 60 drifted. . . .

. . . So it had come to this; they were no longer ashamed to eat troll food; 61 they even sent it from house to house, as lordly fare!

All night long as she tossed in bed, bitter revolt raged within her. *They* 62 *should not stay here through the winter!* . . . As soon as Per Hansa came home they must start on the journey back east; he, too, ought to be able to see by this time that they would all become wild beasts if they remained here much longer. Everything human in them would gradually be blotted out. . . . They saw nothing, learned nothing. . . . It would be even worse for their children—and what of their children's children? . . . Couldn't he understand that if the Lord God had intended these infinities to be peopled, He would not have left them desolate down through all the ages . . . until now, when the end was nearing? . . .

After a while the bitterness of her revolt began to subside; her thoughts 63 became clear and shrewd, she tried to reason out the best way of getting back to civilization. That night she did not sleep at all.

The next morning she got up earlier than usual, kindled the fire, got the 64 breakfast and waked the children. The food was soon prepared; first she poured some water into the pot, put in a spoonful or two of molasses, and added a few pieces of cinnamon; then she cut into bits the cold porridge from last night, and put them into the big bowl; when the sweetened water was hot she poured it over the porridge. . . . This was all they had—and no one asked for more.

While she ate she looked repeatedly at the big chest, trying to recall how 65 everything had been packed when they came out last summer. Where did she keep all the things now? She had better get the packing done at once—then that job would be out of the way when he came home. . . .

The greatest difficulty would be to obtain wagons. . . . Alas! those old 66 wagons! The smaller one he had taken apart and used in making the very table around which they were now seated; as for the larger wagon, she knew only too well that it would never hang together through the long journey back; only the other day she had heard Per Hansa mention that he intended to break it up, and see if he couldn't make something or other out of it. . . . Well—how to get the wagons would be his business! They certainly couldn't perish out here for want of a wagon or two! Was there not One who once upon a time had had mercy on a great city full of wicked people, only because one just human being interceded?

67     . . . One just human being. . . . Alas! . . . Beret sighed heavily and put her hand up under her breast.

68     When there was no more porridge left in the bowl she rose, washed the dish, and put it away on the shelf. Ole had nothing to do in the house that morning; he walked toward the door, motioning to his brother to follow; but Store-Hans shook his head. Then Ole went out; the other boy sat there looking at his mother, not knowing what to do, unhappy and heavy-hearted; he felt a sudden impulse to throw himself down on the floor and weep aloud.

69     The mother was pottering about at some trifles, her thoughts constantly occupied with the idea of returning to civilization. Into her serious, grey-pale face, still soft and beautiful, had crept an expression of firmness and defiance; soon this aspect grew so marked that her face appeared to simulate anger, like that of one playing at being ferocious with a child.

70     As soon as she had finished her housework she went over to the big chest, opened the lid, sank down on her knees beside it, and began to rearrange the contents. The task was quickly done; then she took the clothes from the last washing, folded them up, and laid them carefully in the chest; there weren't many clothes left now! He ought to realize that they would soon be naked if they stayed here much longer! And where were they to get money for everything they needed out here? . . . Beret stood up and looked around the room, trying to decide what to pack first. On the shelf above the window lay an old Bible, a gift to her from her grandfather; it was so old that it was hard to read now, because of the many changes the language had undergone since then; but it was the only one they had. This book had been in her family many generations; her great-grandfather had owned it before her grandfather; from her it should pass on to Store-Hans; thus she had always determined when she thought of the matter. On top of the Bible lay the hymn book, in which she had read a little every Sunday since their arrival here. . . .

71     She put both books in the chest.

72     Again Beret rose and glanced around the room. Perhaps she had better take the school books, too; the boys were none too eager to use them; they might as well be excused for the rest of the day; either that day or the next the father would surely come. . . . She asked Store-Hans to bring the books to her so that she could pack them.

73     Not until then did the boy fully take in what his mother was doing; it startled him so that for a moment he could not get up.

74     "Mother, what are you doing?" . . .

75     "We must begin to get ready!" . . . She sighed, and pressed her hands tightly under her burden; it was painful to her, stooping over so long at a time.

"Get ready? Are . . . are we going *away?*" . . . Store-Hans's throat con-    76
tracted; his eyes stared big and terror-stricken at his mother.

"Why, yes, Hansy-boy—we had better be going back where people live    77
before the winter is upon us," she told him, sadly.

The boy had risen, and now stood at the end of the table; he wanted to go    78
to his mother but fear chained him to the spot; he stared at her with his mouth
wide open. At last he got out:

"What will dad say?" . . . The words came accusingly but there were tears    79
in them.

She looked at him like one in a dream; again she looked, but could not utter    80
a word. . . . The sheer impossibility of what she was about to do was written as
if in fire on the face and whole body of the boy—as if in rays that struck her,
lighted everything up with an awful radiance, and revealed the utter futility of
it all. . . . She turned slowly toward the chest, let down the lid, and sank on it
in untold weariness. . . . Again the child stirred within her, kicking and twisting,
so that she had to press her hand hard against it.

. . . O God! . . . now *he* was protesting, too! Was it only by ruthless sacrifice    81
of life that this endless desolation could ever be peopled?

. . . "Thou canst not be so cruel!" she moaned. . . . "Demand not this awful    82
sacrifice of a frail human being!" . . .

She rose slowly from the chest; as she walked across the floor and opened    83
the door she felt as if she were dragging leaden weights. . . . Her gaze flitted
fearfully toward the sky line—reached it, but dared not travel upward. . . .

Store-Hans remained at the end of the table, staring after her; he wanted    84
to scream, but could not utter a sound. Then he ran to her, put his arms around
her, and whispered hoarsely between sobs:

"Mother, are you . . . are you . . . getting sick now?"    85

Beret stroked the head that was pressed so hard against her side; it had such    86
a vigorous, healthy warmth, the hair was soft and pleasant to the touch; she had
to run her fingers through it repeatedly. . . . Then she stooped over and put her
arm around the boy; his response to her embrace was so violent that it almost
choked her. . . . O God! how sorely she needed some one to be kind to her
now! . . . She was weeping; Store-Hans, too, was struggling with wild, tearing
sobs. Little And-Ongen, who could not imagine what the two were doing over
there by the door, came toddling to them and gazed up into their faces; then
she opened her mouth wide, brought her hand up to it, and shrieked aloud. . . .
At that moment Ole came running down the hill, his feet flying against the sky,
and shouted out to them:

"They are coming! . . . Get the coffee on!"    87

. . . Gone was the boy like a gust of wind; he threw himself on the pony    88
and galloped away to meet the returning caravan.

Beret and Store-Hans had both sprung to their feet and stood looking across    89
the prairie. . . . Yes, there they were, away off to the southeast! . . . And now
Store-Hans, also, forgot himself; he glanced imploringly into his mother's face,
his eyes eagerly questioning:

90     "Would it be safe to leave you while I run to meet dad?"

91     She smiled down into the eager face—a benign, spreading smile.

92     "Don't worry about me. . . . Just run along." . . .

## VIII

93     The father sat at the table eating, with And-Ongen on his knee, the boys stood opposite him, listening enthusiastically to the story of his adventures along the way; the mother went to and fro between the stove and the table. There was an enchanting joyousness about Per Hansa to-day which coloured all he said; no matter how much he told, it always sounded as if he were keeping back the best till later on. This had a positively intoxicating effect on the boys; it made them impatient and eager for more, and caused a steady flood of fresh questions.

94     Even Beret was smiling, though her hand trembled.

95     At last the boys had to give an account of how they had managed affairs at home. When, after much teasing and banter, Per Hansa had finally heard the whole absurd story—it came little by little, in disjointed outbursts—of Tönseten and the bear, and their ill-starred badger stew of the night before, he laughed until the tears came and he had to stop eating. His mirth was so free and hearty that the boys, too, began to see the real fun of the incident, and joined in boisterously. Beret stood over by the stove, listening to it all; their infectious merriment carried her away, but at the same time she had to wipe her eyes. . . . She was glad that she had remembered to take out of the chest the things that she had begun to pack awhile before!

96     "Come here, Store-Hans," said the father, still laughing. "What's that across the back of your neck?"

97     The question caught the boy unawares; he ran over and stood beside his father.

98     "Why, it's a big red welt! . . . Have you been trying to hang yourself, boy?"

99     Store-Hans turned crimson; he suddenly remembered the fearful blows of last night.

100     Ole glanced quickly at his mother. . . . "Oh, pshaw!" he said with a manly air. . . . "That was only Hans and me fighting!"

101     "Ah-ha!" exclaimed the father, with another laugh. "So that's the way you two have been acting while I was away? Mother couldn't manage you, eh? . . . Well, now you'll soon be dancing to a different tune; we've got so much work on our hands that there won't be any peace here day or night. . . . Thanks for good food, Beret-girl!"

102     He got up, took the boys with him, and began to carry things in from the wagon. Most of the load they stored away in the house; some extra things, however, had to find a temporary place in the stable.

103     At length Per Hansa brought in a small armful of bottles and set them on the table.

104     "Come here, Beret-girl of mine! You have earned a good drink, and a good drink you shall have!" . . . He went over to the water pail with the coffee cup

from which he had just been drinking, rinsed it out with a little water, and emptied it on the floor; then he poured out a good half cupful of whisky and offered it to her. She put out her hand as if to push him away. . . . Yes, indeed, she would have to take it, he told her, putting his arm around her waist and lifting the cup to her lips. She took the cup and emptied it in one draught. . . . "There, that's a good little wife! . . . You're going to have just another little drop!" He went to the table again and poured out a second drink, but not so much this time. "Two legs, and one for each! Just drink it down! . . . And now you take care of the bottles!"

That was a busy day in the humble dwelling of Per Hansa. First of all, he had promised a load of potatoes to the Hallings, who waited back east somewhere under a bleak sky, without even a potato peeling to put in their pot; he must carry food to them. When Beret heard how poorly things were in that hut—about the woman with the drawn cheeks and the starved look in her eyes—she straightway began to hurry him up; he must go while he had the horses and wagon here. Couldn't he get started to-day? 105

"Not so hasty there, my girl, not so hasty!" laughed Per Hansa, his face beaming. . . . "I'm not going to sleep with any *Halling woman* to-night—that I can tell you!" 106

Now he was his old irresistible self again. How strong, how precious to her, he seemed! . . . She felt a loving impulse to grasp his hair and shake him. . . . 107

Ole was immediately put to work knitting the net. The father had already knitted four fathoms of it, by the light of the camp fire the night before; he had sat up working over the net long after the others had turned in. . . . The boys grew wild with enthusiasm at the sight of the net; were they going fishing in the Sioux River? Both of them immediately began begging to be taken along. . . . "Just keep your fingers moving, Olamand—hurry them up, I tell you!" . . . The father made a great mystery of it, and refused to give any further explanation. 108

As for himself and Store-Hans, they busied themselves over the line; it was all carried inside and placed in a corner where no moisture could reach it. The preparations for the mixing required a good deal of work; the first thing was to make a wooden box sufficiently tight to hold water. Well, there was plenty of lumber now, at any rate! Per Hansa built the box and carried it down to the creek; there he placed it under water, hoping that it would swell enough to be tight by the time he needed it. 109

Evening fell all too soon on a wonderfully busy and joyful day. The boys were at last in bed, fast asleep. 110

But Per Hansa had no time for rest; to-night that net simply had to be finished. He finally made Beret go to bed, but she wasn't a bit sleepy; she lay there talking to him and filling the shuttles whenever they were empty. He explained fully to her how he intended to use the net; first he would set it in the Sioux River as he passed by there to-morrow; he knew of just the place; he would leave it there until he came back from the Hallings'. Unless the cards were stacked against him he would bring back a nice mess of fish. . . . That, 111 however, wasn't his great plan with the net, he told her; but she mustn't say a word about this to the boys. It was to be a big surprise for them; they were such brave fellows! The fact of the matter was, he planned to catch *ducks* with that net; that had been the real reason for his buying the twine; there would be other fare than badger stew in this hut, he would just let her know, if the weather only held a few days more!

112 All at once it occurred to Beret that she had forgotten to cover up the windows to-night; she smiled to herself at the discovery. . . . What was the need of it, anyway? Cover the windows . . . what nonsense! . . . She smiled again, feeling a languorous drowsiness creep over her.

113 Per Hansa knit away on the net, chatting happily with her as he worked; a confident ring of joy sounded in all he said. He had fastened the net to the bedpost, just as her father always had done. She listened peacefully to his warm, cheerful voice, which after a while began to sound more distant, like the indolent swish and gurgle of lapping ocean waves on a fair summer's night. Gradually she was borne away on this sound, and slept the whole night through without stirring.

114 When she awoke next morning Per Hansa, still fully dressed, lay beside her, over against the wall; he evidently had thrown himself down to rest only a little while before. Light was creeping into the room; directly in front of the bed lay a big white heap of something. . . . Those careless boys—had they thrown their clothes on the floor again? . . . She stooped over to pick the clothes up and put them on the bench; she grasped hold of the heap—and it was a new net, sheeted and fully rigged, as a new net ought to be!

115 . . . Poor man!—he must have sat up all night! . . . She spread the quilt carefully over him.

116 That morning Beret took some of the precious white flour and made a batch of pancakes. He deserved to have one good meal before he went away again!

117 He left right after breakfast. Beret worked industriously throughout the day, while many thoughts came and went. . . . It must be her destiny, this! There was One who governed all things. . . . He knew what was best, and against His will it was useless to struggle! . . .

118 . . . Often that day she went to the window to look eastward. Every time she looked, it seemed to be growing darker over there. . . .

119 . . . That evening she again covered the window. . . .

## RESPONDING

1. Analyze Beret's response to the boys' fight. What pressures produced her reaction? What was she thinking and feeling when she "left the child screaming in the middle of the floor, went out of the house, and was gone a long time" (paragraph 40)? Imagine that your journal is Beret's diary and write an entry about the event.

2.  Working in two groups, discuss the behaviors and duties Ole and Store-Hans expect from women and men. One group should list these behaviors for women; the other should do the same for men. Put the lists on the board. Are they the same for men and women? Discuss the gender roles the children have internalized.

3.  Write an essay comparing Beret's and Per Hansa's attitudes toward life in the wilderness. How do you explain the differences? Some factors to consider are personal temperament, gender, upbringing, activities, responsibilities, ambitions, and expectations for the future.

4.  Beret has great difficulty with life on the prairie. Using your own knowledge, describe the pioneer heroine so often portrayed in stories and film. In an essay, compare her character and behavior with Beret's. What might account for the differences between Beret and the pioneer heroine?

# ANZIA YEZIERSKA

*Anzia Yezierska was born in Poland in 1885, the daughter of a Talmudic scholar. Her family immigrated to the United States during the 1890s. After attending night school, she graduated from the Teachers College of Columbia University in 1904. Her publications include* The Free Vacation House *(1915),* "The Fat of the Land" *(1919),* Salome of the Tenements *(1922),* Children of Loneliness *(1923),* The Bread Givers *(1925),* The Arrogant Beggar *(1927),* All I Could Never Be *(1932), and* The Red Ribbon on a White Horse *(1950).* "The Fat of the Land" *was awarded the O. Henry Prize for the best story of 1919; Yezierska's other literary prizes included the 1929–1930 Zora Gale Fellowship at the University of Wisconsin and two awards from the National Institute of Arts and Letters (1962 and 1965).*

*In the early part of Yezierska's career, her work enjoyed great popularity. She was friendly with many of the leading intellectuals of the day, including the philosopher John Dewey. In 1918 she was invited to Hollywood by film producer Sam Goldwyn to adapt one of her stories for the screen. Later in her life Yezierska had more difficulty getting her work published. She died in 1970.*

*Many of Yezierska's works explore elements of the immigrant experience. The selection that follows depicts the life of an immigrant from two perspec-*

*tives—during the period just after she settles in this country and twenty-five years later—and invites us to compare the quality of her life and her assessment of her place in the world from those perspectives. The story also raises interesting questions about the expectations placed on immigrant parents by their children.*

⊹

# THE FAT OF THE LAND

1   IN AN AIR-SHAFT so narrow that you could touch the next wall with your bare hands, Hanneh Breineh leaned out and knocked on her neighbor's window.

2   "Can you loan me your wash-boiler for the clothes?" she called.

3   Mrs. Pelz threw up the sash.

4   "The boiler? What's the matter with yours again? Didn't you tell me you had it fixed already last week?"

5   "A black year on him, the robber, the way he fixed it! If you have no luck in this world, then it's better not to live. There I spent out fifteen cents to stop up one hole, and it runs out another. How I ate out my gall bargaining with him he should let it down to fifteen cents! He wanted yet a quarter, the swindler. Gottuniu! My bitter heart on him for every penny he took from me for nothing!"

6   "You got to watch all those swindlers, or they'll steal the whites out of your eyes," admonished Mrs. Pelz. "You should have tried out your boiler before you paid him. Wait a minute till I empty out my dirty clothes in a pillow-case; then I'll hand it to you."

7   Mrs. Pelz returned with the boiler and tried to hand it across to Hanneh Breineh, but the soap-box refrigerator on the window-sill was in the way.

8   "You got to come in for the boiler yourself," said Mrs. Pelz.

9   "Wait only till I tie my Sammy on to the high-chair he shouldn't fall on me again. He's so wild that ropes won't hold him."

10   Hanneh Breineh tied the child in the chair, stuck a pacifier in his mouth, and went in to her neighbor. As she took the boiler Mrs. Pelz said:

11   "Do you know Mrs. Melker ordered fifty pounds of chicken for her daughter's wedding? And such grand chickens! Shining like gold! My heart melted in me just looking at the flowing fatness of those chickens."

12   Hanneh Breineh smacked her thin, dry lips, a hungry gleam in her sunken eyes.

13   "Fifty pounds!" she gasped. "It ain't possible. How do you know?"

14   "I heard her with my own ears. I saw them with my own eyes. And she said she will chop up the chicken livers with onions and eggs for an appetizer, and then she will buy twenty-five pounds of fish, and cook it sweet and sour with raisins, and she said she will bake all her shtrudels on pure chicken fat."

15   "Some people work themselves up in the world," sighed Hanneh Breineh.

"For them is America flowing with milk and honey. In Savel Mrs. Melker used to get shriveled up from hunger. She and her children used to live on potato-peelings and crusts of dry bread picked out from the barrels; and in America she lives to eat chicken, and apple shtrudels soaking in fat."

"The world is a wheel always turning," philosophized Mrs. Pelz. "Those who were high go down low, and those who've been low go up higher. Who will believe me here in America that in Poland I was a cook in a banker's house? I handled ducks and geese every day. I used to bake coffee-cake with cream so thick you could cut it with a knife." 16

"And do you think I was a nobody in Poland?" broke in Hanneh Breineh, tears welling in her eyes as the memories of her past rushed over her. "But what's the use of talking? In America money is everything. Who cares who my father or grandfather was in Poland? Without money I'm a living dead one. My head dries out worrying how to get for the children the eating a penny cheaper." 17

Mrs. Pelz wagged her head, a gnawing envy contracting her features. 18

"Mrs. Melker had it good from the day she came," she said, begrudgingly. "Right away she sent all her children to the factory, and she began to cook meat for dinner every day. She and her children have eggs and buttered rolls for breakfast each morning like millionaires." 19

A sudden fall and a baby's scream, and the boiler dropped from Hanneh Breineh's hands as she rushed into her kitchen, Mrs. Pelz after her. They found the high-chair turned on top of the baby. 20

"Gewalt! Save me! Run for a doctor!" cried Hanneh Breineh, as she dragged the child from under the high-chair. "He's killed! He's killed! My only child! My precious lamb!" she shrieked as she ran back and forth with the screaming infant. 21

Mrs. Pelz snatched little Sammy from the mother's hands. 22

"Meshugneh! What are you running around like a crazy, frightening the child? Let me see. Let me tend to him. He ain't killed yet." She hastened to the sink to wash the child's face, and discovered a swelling lump on his forehead. "Have you a quarter in your house?" she asked. 23

"Yes, I got one," replied Hanneh Breineh, climbing on a chair. "I got to keep it on a high shelf where the children can't get it." 24

Mrs. Pelz seized the quarter Hanneh Breineh handed down to her. 25

"Now pull your left eyelid three times while I'm pressing the quarter, and you'll see the swelling go down." 26

Hanneh Breineh took the child again in her arms, shaking and cooing over it and caressing it. 27

"Ah-ah-ah, Sammy! Ah-ah-ah-ah, little lamb! Ah-ah-ah, little bird! Ah-ah-ah-ah, precious heart! Oh, you saved my life; I thought he was killed," gasped Hanneh Breineh, turning to Mrs. Pelz. "Oi-i!" she sighed, "a mother's heart! Always in fear over her children. The minute anything happens to them all life goes out of me. I lose my head and I don't know where I am any more." 28

"No wonder the child fell," admonished Mrs. Pelz. "You should have a red 29 ribbon or red beads on his neck to keep away the evil eye. Wait. I got something in my machine-drawer."

30     Mrs. Pelz returned, bringing the boiler and a red string, which she tied about the child's neck while the mother proceeded to fill the boiler.

31     A little later Hanneh Breineh again came into Mrs. Pelz's kitchen, holding Sammy in one arm and in the other an apronful of potatoes. Putting the child down on the floor, she seated herself on the unmade kitchen-bed and began to peel the potatoes in her apron.

32     "Woe to me!" sobbed Hanneh Breineh. "To my bitter luck there ain't no end. With all my other troubles, the stove got broke. I lighted the fire to boil the clothes, and it's to get choked with smoke. I paid rent only a week ago, and the agent don't want to fix it. A thunder should strike him! He only comes for the rent, and if anything has to be fixed, then he don't want to hear nothing."

33     "Why comes it to me so hard?" went on Hanneh Breineh, the tears streaming down her cheeks. "I can't stand it no more. I came into you for a minute to run away from my troubles. It's only when I sit myself down to peel potatoes or nurse the baby that I take time to draw a breath, and beg only for death."

34     Mrs. Pelz, accustomed to Hanneh Breineh's bitter outbursts, continued her scrubbing.

35     "Ut!" exclaimed Hanneh Breineh, irritated at her neighbor's silence, "what are you tearing up the world with your cleaning? What's the use to clean up when everything only gets dirty again?"

36     "I got to shine up my house for the holidays."

37     "You've got it so good nothing lays on your mind but to clean your house. Look on this little blood-sucker," said Hanneh Breineh, pointing to the wizened child, made prematurely solemn from starvation and neglect. "Could anybody keep that brat clean? I wash him one minute, and he is dirty the minute after." Little Sammy grew frightened and began to cry. "Shut up!" ordered the mother, picking up the child to nurse it again. "Can't you see me take a rest for a minute?"

38     The hungry child began to cry at the top of its weakened lungs.

39     "Na, na, you glutton." Hanneh Breineh took out a dirty pacifier from her pocket and stuffed it into the baby's mouth. The grave, pasty-faced infant shrank into a panic of fear, and chewed the nipple nervously, clinging to it with both his thin little hands.

40     "For what did I need yet the sixth one?" groaned Hanneh Breineh, turning to Mrs. Pelz. "Wasn't it enough five mouths to feed? If I didn't have this child on my neck, I could turn myself around and earn a few cents." She wrung her hands in a passion of despair. "Gottuniu! The earth should only take it before it grows up!"

41     "Shah! Shah!" reproved Mrs. Pelz. "Pity yourself on the child. Let it grow up already so long as it is here. See how frightened it looks on you." Mrs. Pelz took the child in her arms and petted it. "The poor little lamb! What did it done you should hate it so?"

Hanneh Breineh pushed Mrs. Pelz away from her.                                    42

"To whom can I open the wounds of my heart?" she moaned. "Nobody has       43
pity on me. You don't believe me, nobody believes me until I'll fall down like
a horse in the middle of the street. Oi weh! Mine life is so black for my eyes!
Some mothers got luck. A child gets run over by a car, some fall from a window,
some burn themselves up with a match, some get choked with diphtheria; but
no death takes mine away."

"God from the world, stop cursing!" admonished Mrs. Pelz. "What do you      44
want from the poor children? Is it their fault that their father makes small wages?
Why do you let it all out on them?" Mrs. Pelz sat down beside Hanneh Breineh.
"Wait only till your children get old enough to go to the shop and earn money,"
she consoled. "Push only through those few years while they are yet small; your
sun will begin to shine; you will live on the fat of the land, when they begin to
bring you in the wages each week."

Hanneh Breineh refused to be comforted.                                           45

"Till they are old enough to go to the shop and earn money they'll eat the      46
head off my bones," she wailed. "If you only knew the fights I got by each meal.
Maybe I gave Abe a bigger piece of bread than Fanny. Maybe Fanny got a little
more soup in her plate than Jake. Eating is dearer than diamonds. Potatoes went
up a cent on a pound, and milk is only for millionaires. And once a week, when
I buy a little meat for the Sabbath, the butcher weighs it for me like gold, with
all the bones in it. When I come to lay the meat out on a plate and divide it
up, there ain't nothing to it but bones. Before, he used to throw me in a piece
of fat extra or a piece of lung, but now you got to pay for everything, even for
a bone to the soup."

"Never mind; you'll yet come out from all your troubles. Just as soon as       47
your children get old enough to get their working papers the more children you
got, the more money you'll have."

"Why should I fool myself with the false shine of hope? Don't I know it's      48
already my black luck not to have it good in this world? Do you think American
children will right away give everything they earn to their mother?"

"I know what is with you the matter," said Mrs. Pelz. "You didn't eat yet      49
to-day. When it is empty in the stomach, the whole world looks black. Come,
only let me give you something good to taste in the mouth; that will freshen
you up." Mrs. Pelz went to the cupboard and brought out the saucepan of gefülte
fish that she had cooked for dinner and placed it on the table in front of Hanneh
Breineh. "Give a taste my fish," she said, taking one slice on a spoon, and
handing it to Hanneh Breineh with a piece of bread. "I wouldn't give it to you
on a plate because I just cleaned up my house, and I don't want to dirty up more
dishes."

"What, am I stranger you should have to serve me on a plate yet!" cried       50
Hanneh Breineh, snatching the fish in her trembling fingers.

"Oi weh! How it melts through all the bones!" she exclaimed, brightening       51
as she ate. "May it be for good luck to us all!" she exulted, waving aloft the last
precious bite.

52    Mrs. Pelz was so flattered that she even ladled up a spoonful of gravy.

53    "There is a bit of onion and carrot in it," she said, as she handed it to her neighbor.

54    Hanneh Breineh sipped the gravy drop by drop, like a connoisseur sipping wine.

55    "Ah-h-h! A taste of that gravy lifts me up to heaven!" As she disposed leisurely of the slice of onion and carrot she relaxed and expanded and even grew jovial. "Let us wish all our troubles on the Russian Czar! Let him burst with our worries for rent! Let him get shriveled with our hunger for bread! Let his eyes dry out of his head looking for work!"

56    "Shah! I'm forgetting from everything," she exclaimed, jumping up. "It must be eleven or soon twelve, and my children will be right away out of school and fall on me like a pack of wild wolves. I better quick run to the market and see what cheaper I can get for a quarter."

57    Because of the lateness of her coming, the stale bread at the nearest bakeshop was sold out, and Hanneh Breineh had to trudge from shop to shop in search of the usual bargain, and spent nearly an hour to save two cents.

58    In the meantime the children returned from school, and, finding the door locked, climbed through the fire-escape, and entered the house through the window. Seeing nothing on the table, they rushed to the stove. Abe pulled a steaming potato out of the boiling pot, and so scalded his fingers that the potato fell to the floor; whereupon the three others pounced on it.

59    "It was my potato," cried Abe, blowing his burned fingers, while with the other hand and his foot he cuffed and kicked the three who were struggling on the floor. A wild fight ensued, and the potato was smashed under Abe's foot amid shouts and screams. Hanneh Breineh, on the stairs, heard the noise of her famished brood, and topped their cries with curses and invectives.

60    "They are here already, the savages! They are here already to shorten my life! They heard you all over the hall, in all the houses around!"

61    The children, disregarding her words, pounced on her market-basket, shouting ravenously: "Mamma, I'm hungry! What more do you got to eat?"

62    They tore the bread and herring out of Hanneh Breineh's basket and devoured it in starved savagery, clamoring for more.

63    "Murderers!" screamed Hanneh Breineh, goaded beyond endurance. "What are you tearing from me my flesh? From where should I steal to give you more? Here I had already a pot of potatoes and a whole loaf of bread and two herrings, and you swallowed it down in the wink of an eye. I have to have Rockefeller's millions to fill your stomachs."

64    All at once Hanneh Breineh became aware that Benny was missing. "Oi weh!" she burst out, wringing her hands in a new wave of woe, "where is Benny? Didn't he come home yet from school?"

65    She ran out into the hall, opened the grime-coated window, and looked up and down the street; but Benny was nowhere in sight.

66    "Abe, Jake, Fanny, quick, find Benny!" entreated Hanneh Breineh, as she

rushed back into the kitchen. But the children, anxious to snatch a few minutes' play before the school-call, dodged past her and hurried out.

With the baby on her arm, Hanneh Breineh hastened to the kindergarten.  67

"Why are you keeping Benny here so long?" she shouted at the teacher as  68
she flung open the door. "If you had my bitter heart, you would send him home long ago and not wait until I got to come for him."

The teacher turned calmly and consulted her record-cards.  69

"Benny Safron? He wasn't present this morning."  70

"Not here?" shrieked Hanneh Breineh. "I pushed him out myself he should  71
go. The children didn't want to take him, and I had no time. Woe is me! Where is my child?" She began pulling her hair and beating her breast as she ran into the street.

Mrs. Pelz was busy at a pushcart, picking over some spotted apples, when  72
she heard the clamor of an approaching crowd. A block off she recognized Hanneh Breineh, her hair disheveled, her clothes awry, running toward her with her yelling baby in her arms, the crowd following.

"Friend mine," cried Hanneh Breineh, falling on Mrs. Pelz's neck, "I lost  73
my Benny, the best child of all my children." Tears streamed down her red, swollen eyes as she sobbed. "Benny! mine heart, mine life! Oi-i-i!"

Mrs. Pelz took the frightened baby out of the mother's arms.  74

"Still yourself a little! See how you're frightening your child."  75

"Woe to me! Where is my Benny? Maybe he's killed already by a car. Maybe  76
he fainted away from hunger. He didn't eat nothing all day long. Gottuniu! Pity yourself on me!"

She lifted her hands full of tragic entreaty.  77

"People, my child! Get me my child! I'll go crazy out of my head! Get me  78
my child, or I'll take poison before your eyes!"

"Still yourself a little!" pleaded Mrs. Pelz.  79

"Talk not to me!" cried Hanneh Breineh, wringing her hands. "You're  80
having all your children. I lost mine. Every good luck comes to other people. But I didn't live yet to see a good day in my life. Mine only joy, mine Benny, is lost away from me."

The crowd followed Hanneh Breineh as she wailed through the streets,  81
leaning on Mrs. Pelz. By the time she returned to her house the children were back from school; but seeing that Benny was not there, she chased them out in the street, crying:

"Out of here, you robbers, gluttons! Go find Benny!" Hanneh Breineh  82
crumpled into a chair in utter prostration. "Oi weh! he's lost! Mine life; my little bird; mine only joy! How many nights I spent nursing him when he had the measles! And all that I suffered for weeks and months when he had the whooping-cough! How the eyes went out of my head till I learned him how to walk, till I learned him how to talk! And such a smart child! If I lost all the others, it wouldn't tear me so by the heart."

She worked herself up into such a hysteria, crying, and tearing her hair, and  83 hitting her head with her knuckles, that at last she fell into a faint. It took some time before Mrs. Pelz, with the aid of neighbors, revived her.

84     "Benny, mine angel!" she moaned as she opened her eyes.

85     Just then a policeman came in with the lost Benny.

86     "Na, na, here you got him already!" said Mrs. Pelz. "Why did you carry on so for nothing? Why did you tear up the world like a crazy?"

87     The child's face was streaked with tears as he cowered, frightened and forlorn. Hanneh Breineh sprang toward him, slapping his cheeks, boxing his ears, before the neighbors could rescue him from her.

88     "Woe on your head!" cried the mother. "Where did you lost yourself? Ain't I got enough worries on my head than to go around looking for you? I didn't have yet a minute's peace from that child since he was born!"

89     "See a crazy mother!" remonstrated Mrs. Pelz, rescuing Benny from another beating. "Such a mouth! With one breath she blesses him when he is lost, and with the other breath she curses him when he is found."

90     Hanneh Breineh took from the window-sill a piece of herring covered with swarming flies, and putting it on a slice of dry bread, she filled a cup of tea that had been stewing all day, and dragged Benny over to the table to eat.

91     But the child, choking with tears, was unable to touch the food.

92     "Go eat!" commanded Hanneh Breineh. "Eat and choke yourself eating!"

93     "Maybe she won't remember me no more. Maybe the servant won't let me in," thought Mrs. Pelz, as she walked by the brownstone house on Eighty-Fourth Street where she had been told Hanneh Breineh now lived. At last she summoned up enough courage to climb the steps. She was all out of breath as she rang the bell with trembling fingers. "Oi weh! even the outside smells riches and plenty! Such curtains! And shades on all windows like by millionaires! Twenty years ago she used to eat from the pot to the hand, and now she lives in such a palace."

94     A whiff of steam-heated warmth swept over Mrs. Pelz as the door opened, and she saw her old friend of the tenements dressed in silk and diamonds like a being from another world.

95     "Mrs. Pelz, is it you!" cried Hanneh Breineh, overjoyed at the sight of her former neighbor. "Come right in. Since when are you back in New York?"

96     "We came last week," mumbled Mrs. Pelz, as she was led into a richly carpeted reception-room.

97     "Make yourself comfortable. Take off your shawl," urged Hanneh Breineh.

98     But Mrs. Pelz only drew her shawl more tightly around her, a keen sense of her poverty gripping her as she gazed, abashed by the luxurious wealth that shone from every corner.

99     "This shawl covers up my rags," she said, trying to hide her shabby sweater.

100     "I'll tell you what; come right into the kitchen," suggested Hanneh Breineh. "The servant is away for this afternoon, and we can feel more comfortable there. I can breathe like a free person in my kitchen when the girl has her day out."

Mrs. Pelz glanced about her in an excited daze. Never in her life had she 101
seen anything so wonderful as a white-tiled kitchen, with its glistening porcelain
sink and the aluminum pots and pans that shone like silver.

"Where are you staying now?" asked Hanneh Breineh, as she pinned an 102
apron over her silk dress.

"I moved back to Delancey Street, where we used to live," replied Mrs. 103
Pelz, as she seated herself cautiously in a white enameled chair.

"Oi weh! What grand times we had in that old house when we were 104
neighbors!" sighed Hanneh Breineh, looking at her old friend with misty eyes.

"You still think on Delancey Street? Haven't you more high-class neighbors 105
uptown here?"

"A good neighbor is not to be found every day," deplored Hanneh Breineh. 106
"Uptown here, where each lives in his own house, nobody cares if the person
next door is dying or going crazy from loneliness. It ain't anything like we used
to have it in Delancey Street, when we could walk into one another's rooms
without knocking, and borrow a pinch of salt or a pot to cook in."

Hanneh Breineh went over to the pantry-shelf. 107

"We are going to have a bite right here on the kitchen-table like on 108
Delancey Street. So long there's no servant to watch us we can eat what we
please."

"Oi! How it waters my mouth with appetite, the smell of the herring and 109
onion!" chuckled Mrs. Pelz, sniffing the welcome odors with greedy pleasure.

Hanneh Breineh pulled a dish-towel from the rack and threw one end of it 110
to Mrs. Pelz.

"So long as there's no servant around, we can use it together for a napkin. 111
It's dirty, anyhow. How it freshens up my heart to see you!" she rejoiced as she
poured out her tea into a saucer. "If you would only know how I used to beg
my daughter to write for me a letter to you; but these American children, what
is to them a mother's feelings?"

"What are you talking!" cried Mrs. Pelz. "The whole world rings with you 112
and your children. Everybody is envying you. Tell me how began your luck?"

"You heard how my husband died with consumption," replied Hanneh 113
Breineh. "The five hundred dollars lodge money gave me the first lift in life,
and I opened a little grocery store. Then my son Abe married himself to a girl
with a thousand dollars. That started him in business, and now he has the biggest
shirt-waist factory on West Twenty-Ninth Street."

"Yes, I heard your son had a factory." Mrs. Pelz hesitated and stammered; 114
"I'll tell you the truth. What I came to ask you—I thought maybe you would
beg your son Abe if he would give my husband a job."

"Why not?" said Hanneh Breineh. "He keeps more than five hundred 115
hands. I'll ask him if he should take in Mr. Pelz."

"Long years on you, Hanneh Breineh! You'll save my life if you could only 116
help my husband get work."

"Of course my son will help him. All my children like to do good. My 117 daughter Fanny is a milliner on Fifth Avenue, and she takes in the poorest girls in her shop and even pays them sometimes while they learn the trade." Hanneh Breineh's face lit up, and her chest filled with pride as she enumerated the successes of her children. "And my son Benny he wrote a play on Broadway and he gave away more than a hundred free tickets for the first night."

118     "Benny! The one who used to get lost from home all the time? You always did love that child more than all the rest. And what is Sammy your baby doing?"

119     "He ain't a baby no longer. He goes to college and quarterbacks the football team. They can't get along without him.

120     "And my son Jake, I nearly forgot him. He began collecting rent in Delancey Street, and now he is boss of renting the swellest apartment-houses on Riverside Drive."

121     "What did I tell you? In America children are like money in the bank," purred Mrs. Pelz, as she pinched and patted Hanneh Breineh's silk sleeve. "Oi weh! How it shines from you! You ought to kiss the air and dance for joy and happiness. It is such a bitter frost outside; a pail of coal is so dear, and you got it so warm with steam heat. I had to pawn my feather bed to have enough for the rent, and you are rolling in money."

122     "Yes, I got it good in some ways, but money ain't everything," sighed Hanneh Breineh.

123     "You ain't yet satisfied?"

124     "But here I got no friends," complained Hanneh Breineh.

125     "Friends?" queried Mrs. Pelz. "What greater friend is there on earth than the dollar?"

126     "Oi! Mrs. Pelz; if you could only look into my heart! I'm so choked up! You know they say a cow has a long tongue, but can't talk." Hanneh Breineh shook her head wistfully, and her eyes filmed with inward brooding. "My children give me everything from the best. When I was sick, they got me a nurse by day and one by night. They bought me the best wine. If I asked for dove's milk, they would buy it for me; but—but—I can't talk myself out in their language. They want to make me over for an American lady, and I'm different." Tears cut their way under her eyelids with a pricking pain as she went on: "When I was poor, I was free, and could holler and do what I like in my own house. Here I got to lie still like a mouse under a broom. Between living up to my Fifth-Avenue daughter and keeping up with the servants, I am like a sinner in the next world that is thrown from one hell to another." The doorbell rang, and Hanneh Breineh jumped up with a start.

127     "Oi weh! It must be the servant back already!" she exclaimed, as she tore off her apron. "Oi weh! Let's quickly put the dishes together in a dish-pan. If she sees I eat on the kitchen table, she will look on me like the dirt under her feet."

128     Mrs. Pelz seized her shawl in haste.

129     "I better run home quick in my rags before your servant sees me."

"I'll speak to Abe about the job," said Hanneh Breineh, as she pushed a bill   130
into the hand of Mrs. Pelz, who edged out as the servant entered.

"I'm having fried potato lotkes special for you, Benny," said Hanneh Breineh,   131
as the children gathered about the table for the family dinner given in honor of
Benny's success with his new play. "Do you remember how you used to lick the
fingers from them?"

"Oh, mother!" reproved Fanny. "Anyone hearing you would think we were   132
still in the pushcart district."

"Stop your nagging, sis, and let ma alone," commanded Benny, patting his   133
mother's arm affectionately. "I'm home only once a month. Let her feed me
what she pleases. My stomach is bomb-proof."

"Do I hear that the President is coming to your play?" said Abe, as he stuffed   134
a napkin over his diamond-studded shirt-front.

"Why shouldn't he come?" returned Benny. "The critics say it's the greatest   135
antidote for the race hatred created by the war. If you want to know, he is coming
to-night; and what's more, our box is next to the President's."

"Nu, mammeh," sallied Jake, "did you ever dream in Delancey Street that   136
we should rub sleeves with the President?"

"I always said that Benny had more head than the rest of you," replied the   137
mother.

As the laughter died away, Jake went on:   138

"Honor you are getting plenty; but how much mezummen does this play   139
bring you? Can I invest any of it in real estate for you?"

"I'm getting ten per cent royalties of the gross receipts," replied the youthful   140
playwright.

"How much is that?" queried Hanneh Breineh.   141

"Enough to buy up all your fish-markets in Delancey Street," laughed Abe   142
in good-natured raillery at his mother.

Her son's jest cut like a knife-thrust in her heart. She felt her heart ache   143
with the pain that she was shut out from their successes. Each added triumph
only widened the gulf. And when she tried to bridge this gulf by asking
questions, they only thrust her back upon herself.

"Your fame has even helped me get my hat trade solid with the Four   144
Hundred," put in Fanny. "You bet I let Mrs. Van Suyden know that our box is
next to the President's. She said she would drop in to meet you. Of course she
let on to me that she hadn't seen the play yet, though my designer said she saw
her there on the opening night."

"Oh, Gosh, the toadies!" sneered Benny. "Nothing so sickens you with   145
success as the way people who once shoved you off the sidewalk come crawling
to you on their stomachs begging you to dine with them."

"Say, that leading man of yours he's some class!" cried Fanny. "That's the   146
man I'm looking for. Will you invite him to supper after the theater?"

147    The playwright turned to his mother.

148    "Say, ma," he said, laughingly, "how would you like a real actor for a son-in-law?"

149    "She should worry," mocked Sam. "She'll be discussing with him the future of the Greek drama. Too bad it doesn't happen to be Warfield, or mother could give him tips on the 'Auctioneer.'"

150    Jake turned to his mother with a covert grin.

151    "I guess you'd have no objection if Fanny got next to Benny's leading man. He makes at least fifteen hundred a week. That wouldn't be such a bad addition to the family, would it?"

152    Again the bantering tone stabbed Hanneh Breineh. Everything in her began to tremble and break loose.

153    "Why do you ask me?" she cried, throwing her napkin into her plate. "Do I count for a person in this house? If I'll say something, will you even listen to me? What is to me the grandest man that my daughter could pick out? Another enemy in my house! Another person to shame himself from me!" She swept in her children in one glance of despairing anguish as she rose from the table. "What worth is an old mother to American children? The President is coming to-night to the theater, and none of you asked me to go." Unable to check the rising tears, she fled toward the kitchen and banged the door.

154    They all looked at one another guiltily.

155    "Say, sis," Benny called out sharply, "what sort of frame-up is this? Haven't you told mother that she was to go with us to-night?"

156    "Yes—I—" Fanny bit her lips as she fumbled evasively for words. "I asked her if she wouldn't mind my taking her some other time."

157    "Now you have made a mess of it!" fumed Benny. "Mother'll be too hurt to go now."

158    "Well, I don't care," snapped Fanny. "I can't appear with mother in a box at the theater. Can I introduce her to Mrs. Van Suyden? And suppose your leading man should ask to meet me?"

159    "Take your time, sis. He hasn't asked yet," scoffed Benny.

160    "The more reason I shouldn't spoil my chances. You know mother. She'll spill the beans that we come from Delancey Street the minute we introduce her anywhere. Must I always have the black shadow of my past trailing after me?"

161    "But have you no feelings for mother?" admonished Abe.

162    "I've tried harder than all of you to do my duty. I've *lived* with her." She turned angrily upon them. "I've borne the shame of mother while you bought her off with a present and a treat here and there. God knows how hard I tried to civilize her so as not to have to blush with shame when I take her anywhere. I dressed her in the most stylish Paris models, but Delancey Street sticks out from every inch of her. Whenever she opens her mouth, I'm done for. You fellows had your chance to rise in the world because a man is free to go up as high as he can reach up to; but I, with all my style and pep, can't get a man my equal because a girl is always judged by her mother."

They were silenced by her vehemence, and unconsciously turned to Benny.   163

"I guess we all tried to do our best for mother," said Benny, thoughtfully.   164
"But wherever there is growth, there is pain and heartbreak. The trouble with
us is that the ghetto of the Middle Ages and the children of the twentieth century
have to live under one roof, and—"

A sound of crashing dishes came from the kitchen, and the voice of Hanneh   165
Breineh resounded through the dining-room as she wreaked her pent-up fury
on the helpless servant.

"Oh, my nerves! I can't stand it any more! There will be no girl again for   166
another week!" cried Fanny.

"Oh, let up on the old lady," protested Abe. "Since she can't take it out on   167
us any more, what harm is it if she cusses the servants?"

"If you fellows had to chase around employment agencies, you wouldn't see   168
anything funny about it. Why can't we move into a hotel that will do away with
the need of servants altogether?"

"I got it better," said Jake, consulting a notebook from his pocket. "I have   169
on my list an apartment on Riverside Drive where there's only a small kitchenette; but we can do away with the cooking, for there is a dining service in the
building."

The new Riverside apartment to which Hanneh Breineh was removed by her   170
socially ambitious children was for the habitually active mother an empty desert
of enforced idleness. Deprived of her kitchen, Hanneh Breineh felt robbed of
the last reason for her existence. Cooking and marketing and puttering busily
with pots and pans gave her an excuse for living and struggling and bearing up
with her children. The lonely idleness of Riverside Drive stunned all her senses
and arrested all her thoughts. It gave her that choked sense of being cut off
from air, from life, from everything warm and human. The cold indifference,
the each-for-himself look in the eyes of the people about her were like stinging
slaps in the face. Even the children had nothing real or human in them. They
were starched and stiff miniatures of their elders.

But the most unendurable part of the stifling life on Riverside Drive was   171
being forced to eat in the public dining-room. No matter how hard she tried
to learn polite table manners, she always found people staring at her, and her
daughter rebuking her for eating with the wrong fork or guzzling the soup or
staining the cloth.

In a fit of rebellion Hanneh Breineh resolved never to go down to the public   172
dining-room again, but to make use of the gas-stove in the kitchenette to cook
her own meals. That very day she rode down to Delancey Street and purchased a new market-basket. For some time she walked among the haggling
pushcart venders, relaxing and swimming in the warm waves of her old familiar
past.

A fish-peddler held up a large carp in his black, hairy hand and waved it   173
dramatically:

174     "Women! Women! Fourteen cents a pound!"

175     He ceased his raucous shouting as he saw Hanneh Breineh in her rich attire approach his cart.

176     "How much?" she asked, pointing to the fattest carp.

177     "Fifteen cents, lady," said the peddler, smirking as he raised his price.

178     "Swindler! Didn't I hear you call fourteen cents?" shrieked Hanneh Breineh, exultingly, the spirit of the penny chase surging in her blood. Diplomatically, Hanneh Breineh turned as if to go, and the fisherman seized her basket in frantic fear.

179     "I should live; I'm losing money on the fish, lady," whined the peddler. "I'll let it down to thirteen cents for you only."

180     "Two pounds for a quarter, and not a penny more," said Hanneh Breineh, thrilling again with the rare sport of bargaining, which had been her chief joy in the good old days of poverty.

181     "Nu, I want to make the first sale for good luck." The peddler threw the fish on the scale.

182     As he wrapped up the fish, Hanneh Breineh saw the driven look of worry in his haggard eyes, and when he counted out the change from her dollar, she waved it aside. "Keep it for your luck," she said, and hurried off to strike a new bargain at a pushcart of onions.

183     Hanneh Breineh returned triumphantly with her purchases. The basket under her arm gave forth the old, homelike odors of herring and garlic, while the scaly tail of a four-pound carp protruded from its newspaper wrapping. A gilded placard on the door of the apartment-house proclaimed that all merchandise must be delivered through the trade entrance in the rear; but Hanneh Breineh with her basket strode proudly through the marble-paneled hall and rang nonchalantly for the elevator.

184     The uniformed hall-man, erect, expressionless, frigid with dignity, stepped forward:

185     "Just a minute, madam. I'll call a boy to take up your basket for you."

186     Hanneh Breineh, glaring at him, jerked the basket savagely from his hands. "Mind your own business!" she retorted. "I'll take it up myself. Do you think you're a Russian policeman to boss me in my own house?"

187     Angry lines appeared on the countenance of the representative of social decorum.

188     "It is against the rules, madam," he said, stiffly.

189     "You should sink into the earth with all your rules and brass buttons. Ain't this America? Ain't this a free country? Can't I take up in my own house what I buy with my own money?" cried Hanneh Breineh, reveling in the opportunity to shower forth the volley of invectives that had been suppressed in her for the weeks of deadly dignity of Riverside Drive.

190     In the midst of this uproar Fanny came in with Mrs. Van Suyden. Hanneh Breineh rushed over to her, crying:

191     "This bossy policeman won't let me take up my basket in the elevator."

    The daughter, unnerved with shame and confusion, took the basket in her   192

white-gloved hand and ordered the hall-boy to take it around to the regular
delivery entrance.

Hanneh Breineh was so hurt by her daughter's apparent defense of the
hall-man's rules that she utterly ignored Mrs. Van Suyden's greeting and walked
up the seven flights of stairs out of sheer spite.

"You see the tragedy of my life?" broke out Fanny, turning to Mrs. Van
Suyden.

"You poor child! You go right up to your dear, old lady mother, and I'll
come some other time."

Instantly Fanny regretted her words. Mrs. Van Suyden's pity only roused
her wrath the more against her mother.

Breathless from climbing the stairs, Hanneh Breineh entered the apartment
just as Fanny tore the faultless millinery creation from her head and threw it
on the floor in a rage.

"Mother, you are the ruination of my life! You have driven away Mrs. Van
Suyden, as you have driven away all my best friends. What do you think we got
this apartment for but to get rid of your fish smells and your brawls with the
servants? And here you come with a basket on your arm as if you had just landed
from steerage! And this afternoon, of all times, when Benny is bringing his
leading man to tea. When will you ever stop disgracing us?"

"When I'm dead," said Hanneh Breineh, grimly. "When the earth will cover
me up, then you'll be free to go your American way. I'm not going to make
myself over for a lady on Riverside Drive. I hate you and all your swell friends.
I'll not let myself be choked up here by you or by that hall-boss policeman that
is higher in your eyes than your own mother."

"So that's your thanks for all we've done for you?" cried the daughter.

"All you've done for me!" shouted Hanneh Breineh. "What have you done
for me? You hold me like a dog on a chain! It stands in the Talmud; some
children give their mothers dry bread and water and go to heaven for it, and
some give their mother roast duck and go to Gehenna because it's not given
with love."

"You want me to love you yet?" raged the daughter. "You knocked every
bit of love out of me when I was yet a kid. All the memories of childhood I
have is your everlasting cursing and yelling that we were gluttons."

The bell rang sharply, and Hanneh Breineh flung open the door.

"Your groceries, ma'am," said the boy.

Hanneh Breineh seized the basket from him, and with a vicious fling sent
it rolling across the room, strewing its contents over the Persian rugs and inlaid
floor. Then seizing her hat and coat, she stormed out of the apartment and down
the stairs.

Mr. and Mrs. Pelz sat crouched and shivering over their meager supper
when the door opened, and Hanneh Breineh in fur coat and plumed hat charged
into the room.

"I come to cry out to you my bitter heart," she sobbed. "Woe is me! It is
so black for my eyes!"

208 "What is the matter with you, Hanneh Breineh?" cried Mrs. Pelz in bewildered alarm.

209 "I am turned out of my own house by the brass-buttoned policeman that bosses the elevator. Oi-i-i-i! Weh-h-h-h! What have I from my life? The whole world rings with my son's play. Even the President came to see it, and I, his mother, have not seen it yet. My heart is dying in me like in a prison," she went on wailing. "I am starved out for a piece of real eating. In that swell restaurant is nothing but napkins and forks and lettuce-leaves. There are a dozen plates to every bite of food. And it looks so fancy on the plate, but it's nothing but straw in the mouth. I'm starving, but I can't swallow down their American eating."

210 "Hanneh Breineh," said Mrs. Pelz, "you are sinning before God. Look on your fur coat; it alone would feed a whole family for a year. I never had yet a piece of fur trimming on a coat, and you are in fur from the neck to the feet. I never had yet a piece of feather on a hat, and your hat is all feathers."

211 "What are you envying me?" protested Hanneh Breineh. "What have I from all my fine furs and feathers when my children are strangers to me? All the fur coats in the world can't warm up the loneliness inside my heart. All the grandest feathers can't hide the bitter shame in my face that my children shame themselves from me."

212 Hanneh Breineh suddenly loomed over them like some ancient, heroic figure of the Bible condemning unrighteousness.

213 "Why should my children shame themselves from me? From where did they get the stuff to work themselves up in the world? Did they get it from the air? How did they get all their smartness to rise over the people around them? Why don't the children of born American mothers write my Benny's plays? It is I, who never had a chance to be a person, who gave him the fire in his head. If I would have had a chance to go to school and learn the language, what couldn't I have been? It is I and my mother and my mother's mother and my father and father's father who had such a black life in Poland; it is our choked thoughts and feelings that are flaming up in my children and making them great in America. And yet they shame themselves from me!"

214 For a moment Mr. and Mrs. Pelz were hypnotized by the sweep of her words. Then Hanneh Breineh sank into a chair in utter exhaustion. She began to weep bitterly, her body shaking with sobs.

215 "Woe is me! For what did I suffer and hope on my children? A bitter old age—my end. I'm so lonely!"

216 All the dramatic fire seemed to have left her. The spell was broken. They saw the Hanneh Breineh of old, ever discontented, ever complaining even in the midst of riches and plenty.

217 "Hanneh Breineh," said Mrs. Pelz, "the only trouble with you is that you got it too good. People will tear the eyes out of your head because you're complaining yet. If I only had your fur coat! If I only had your diamonds! I have nothing. You have everything. You are living on the fat of the land. You go right back home and thank God that you don't have any bitter lot."

"You got to let me stay here with you," insisted Hanneh Breineh. "I'll not    218
go back to my children except when they bury me. When they will see my dead
face, they will understand how they killed me."

Mrs. Pelz glanced nervously at her husband. They barely had enough    219
covering for their one bed; how could they possibly lodge a visitor?

"I don't want to take up your bed," said Hanneh Breineh. "I don't care if    220
I have to sleep on the floor or on the chairs, but I'll stay here for the night."

Seeing that she was bent on staying, Mr. Pelz prepared to sleep by putting    221
a few chairs next to the trunk, and Hanneh Breineh was invited to share the
rickety bed with Mrs. Pelz.

The mattress was full of lumps and hollows. Hanneh Breineh lay cramped    222
and miserable, unable to stretch out her limbs. For years she had been accustomed to hair mattresses and ample woolen blankets, so that though she covered
herself with her fur coat, she was too cold to sleep. But worse than the cold
were the creeping things on the wall. And as the lights were turned low, the
mice came through the broken plaster and raced across the floor. The foul odors
of the kitchen-sink added to the night of horrors.

"Are you going back home?" asked Mrs. Pelz, as Hanneh Breineh put on    223
her hat and coat the next morning.

"I don't know where I'm going," she replied, as she put a bill into Mrs.    224
Pelz's hand.

For hours Hanneh Breineh walked through the crowded ghetto streets. She    225
realized that she no longer could endure the sordid ugliness of her past, and yet
she could not go home to her children. She only felt that she must go on and
on.

In the afternoon a cold, drizzling rain set in. She was worn out from the    226
sleepless night and hours of tramping. With a piercing pain in her heart she at
last turned back and boarded the subway for Riverside Drive. She had fled from
the marble sepulcher of the Riverside apartment to her old home in the ghetto;
but now she knew that she could not live there again. She had outgrown her
past by the habits of years of physical comforts, and these material comforts that
she could no longer do without choked and crushed the life within her.

A cold shudder went through Hanneh Breineh as she approached the    227
apartment-house. Peering through the plate glass of the door she saw the face
of the uniformed hall-man. For a hesitating moment she remained standing in
the drizzling rain, unable to enter, and yet knowing full well that she would
have to enter.

Then suddenly Hanneh Breineh began to laugh. She realized that it was    228
the first time she had laughed since her children had become rich. But it was
the hard laugh of bitter sorrow. Tears streamed down her furrowed cheeks as
she walked slowly up the granite steps.

"The fat of the land!" muttered Hanneh Breineh, with a choking sob as the    229
hall-man with immobile face deferentially swung open the door—"the fat of the
land!" ✥

RESPONDING

1. We see Hanneh Brieneh from the author's point of view, but the other characters in the story see her differently. Imagine that you are one of her children and write a letter to a friend explaining your mother's behavior. Or write a journal entry about a time when you were torn between loyalty to a parent, sibling, or friend and embarrassment about his or her behavior in front of someone you wanted to impress.

2. Working individually or in a group, write a moral to this story. Share the morals in class. Consider whether the main character learns something. If the answer is yes, what does she learn?

3. Write an essay comparing Hanneh Breineh's life before and after her husband's death. Consider both her physical and emotional circumstances.

4. Hanneh Breineh's friend and old neighbor Mrs. Pelz says that in America money is everything and "What greater friend is there on earth than the dollar" (paragraph 125). She believes that the only trouble with Hanneh Breineh is that she's "got it too good" (paragraph 217). Do you agree or disagree? Support your argument with evidence from the story as well as from your own experience.

# Elizabeth Gurley Flynn

*The author and labor organizer Elizabeth Gurley Flynn (1890–1964) was the child of Irish political and economic refugees. From her teenage years, Flynn showed much of the same activism, devoting most of her life to calling attention to poverty and deprivation and what she perceived as the other injustices of capitalism. In 1906 she helped organize the Industrial Workers of the World; she later became a prominent figure in the Workers Defense Union and helped found the American Civil Liberties Union in 1920. She continued to be involved in controversial political activities even into her old age. In 1961 she became the first woman to chair the American Communist Party. Her publications include* Women in the War *(1942),* Women Have a Date with Destiny *(1944),* The Plot to Gag America *(1950),* Communists and the People *(1953), and* I Speak My Own Piece: Autobiography of "The Rebel Girl" *(1955).*

*The excerpt that follows, taken from* I Speak My Own Piece, *addresses both the political and economic factors that caused Flynn's family to leave Ireland and the poverty that turn-of-the-century immigrants often found in American cities.*

⊞

## *From* I SPEAK MY OWN PIECE

BY BIRTH I AM A NEW ENGLANDER, though not of Mayflower stock. My ancestors were "immigrants and revolutionists"—from the Emerald Isle. I was born in 1890, at the end of a most tragic century for "that most distressful country," which had suffered under British rule for over 700 years. There was an uprising in each generation in Ireland, and forefathers of mine were in every one of them. The awareness of being Irish came to us as small children, through plaintive song and heroic story. The Irish people fought to wrest their native soil from foreign landlords, to speak their native Gaelic tongue, to worship in the church of their choice, to have their own schools, to be independent and self-governing. As children, we drew in a burning hatred of British rule with our mother's milk. Until my father died, at over eighty, he never said *England* without adding, "God damn her!" Before I was ten I knew of the great heroes—Robert Emmet, Wolfe Tone, Michael Davitt, Parnell, and O'Donovan Rossa, who was chained hand and foot, like a dog, and had to eat from a tin plate on the floor of a British prison.

When the French army landed at Killalla Bay in 1798, on an expedition planned by Wolfe Tone, to help free Ireland, all four of my great grandfathers—Gurley, Flynn, Ryan and Conneran—joined them. They were members of the Society of United Irishmen, dedicated to set up an Irish Republic. Fired with enthusiasm over the French revolution and the success of the American colonies, they were determined to follow their examples. Young Irishmen for miles around dropped their potato digging when they heard "the French are in the Bay." The French armed the Irish, who had only pikes for weapons, and together they defeated the British garrison at Castlebar. The story is that Paddy Flynn of Mayo County, known far and wide as "Paddy the Rebel," led the French eighteen miles around through the mountains, to attack the British from the rear. The Irish revolution was finally crushed in a sea of blood by General Cornwallis, who had surrendered to George Washington at Yorktown.

A reign of horrible terror and reprisal against the Irish followed—floggings, executions, massacres, exile. Paddy Flynn lay in a ditch near his home all night till he heard that a baby was born. Then he was "On the run!" again with a price on his head, fed and protected by the peasants, like hundreds of his countrymen. Others fled to France, some came to the Americas, others were shipped to Australian penal colonies. Irish songs reflect this period—"Who dares to speak of '98?" and "Here's a memory to the friends that are gone, boys—gone!" Paddy slipped around the hills he knew so well. Once he lay in the center of a ripe wheatfield, while the peasants, knowing he was there, slowly cut and reaped all around him, and the British soldiers rode past, looking for rebels. Finally he reached the home of his foster brother, who was a landlord, but one who had a loyalty to the son of his peasant wet-nurse, and with whom he grew up as a lad. So he hid him away safely in the barn.

4    But my bold adventurous great-grandfather-to-be had a gun, a blunderbuss it was called, that "shot a hatful of bullets." He couldn't resist taking aim at the wild geese as they flew over. A "loyal" (pro-British) weaver heard the shot and came after him with a shuttle board, demanding his surrender. "A fine challenge!" cried Paddy, and shot the king's spokesman. A neighbor digging peat nearby threw down his spade and rushed to town spreading the news: "Paddy Flynn is in the bog shooting yeomen!" All his friends rushed to his aid while the British sent out a searching party. But he was over the hills and far away again. After several years, pardons (amnesty) were granted, and he came home to live to a ripe old age. He had two wives and eighteen children, who later scattered as immigrants to all continents. When he was dying, his last words were—"I want to see the French land on this coast once more!"

5    My grandfather, Tom Flynn, was one of the many sons of Paddy the Rebel. He was arrested in Ireland as a boy of sixteen, when caught fishing for salmon on a Sunday morning, at an hour when everybody was expected to be in church. The river was considered the private property of the landlord. Enraged because hungry people could not have the fish for food in a famine year, Tom Flynn threw lime in the water so the fish floated bellies up, dead, to greet the gentry. Then he ran away to America. His widowed mother, with her other children, followed during the '40's. The widow Conneran, with her large family had come earlier in the '30's. They travelled on small sailing vessels that took three months, carrying their own pots and pans and doing their cooking on board. The ships were crowded and unsanitary. Cholera would break out and some were to be held in quarantine in St. John's, New Brunswick. Tom, who was there to meet his family, hired a row boat and rescued a brother and sister and as many others as he could load in the boat. He laid them in the bottom, covered them over and started away. A guard shouted, "What have ye there?" Tom boldly replied, "Fish, do you want some?" The guard replied, "No, just keep away from here!" which Tom gladly did, with a hearty "Go to Hell!" which was ever on his lips for a British uniform.

6    Life was hard and primitive for these early Irish immigrants in isolated settlements in the state of Maine. Grandfather Tom Flynn worked in lumber camps, on building railroads, as an expert river man driving logs, and in granite quarries of Maine and New Hampshire. The climate was more rigorous than

their own mild country. The work was harder than agriculture in Ireland. So many died from tuberculosis that it was called "the Irish disease."

Undoubtedly "stonecutter's consumption" was what we know today as silicosis. Grandfather Flynn had an obsession against living in another man's house. He built a new cabin wherever he moved by setting up a keg of whiskey and inviting all hands to help him. He became an American citizen in 1856. He voted for Abraham Lincoln in 1860. He married my grandmother at Machias, Maine, where my father was born in 1859. She was little and pretty and had a violent temper. (That's where we get it, Sister Kathie says.)

Grandfather died of consumption in 1877 at Pennacook, New Hampshire, then Fisherville, where he is buried. He was only forty-nine years old. He was ever a fighter for freedom, in the spirit of his father. Dissatisfied with the bad living and working conditions, the lack of education for his children, and the prejudice and discrimination against the Irish, he at one time joined with others in an expedition to overthrow the Canadian government and set up a republic there. They captured an armory from the surprised Canadian militia and then got drunk to celebrate. But when they had to return across the border for lack of supplies, their leaders were arrested by the American authorities. Again in 1870 and '71 my father remembered that similar attempted raids were made on Canada. Gay, fighting old Paddy the Rebel has lived on, even unto the third generation. . . .

The Irish who came to this country around the middle of the last century were far from happy. They sought but had not found freedom from religious and political persecution, nor a chance to earn a decent livelihood for their families. My father was very bitter about the hard conditions which prevailed here in his youth among the Irish. They were principally employed at manual labor—building railroads, canals, roads, and in mines and quarries. They lived in shanty towns, even in New York City. One such—consisting of 20,000 inhabitants—was located in what is now Central Park. They were excluded from the better residential areas. In my father's youth there were many signs on empty houses and factories seeking help: "No Irish Need Apply." They were ridiculed by the Protestant Yankees for their "Papist" religion, for their large families, their fighting and drinking—called dirty, ignorant, superstitious, lazy, and what not, as each immigrant group in turn has been similarly maligned. Nor were the Irish united. Bloody battles occurred in my father's youth between Catholic Irish and Orangemen, who were Protestant Irish. A narrow canal was pointed out to me in Lowell, Massachusetts, by an old man who said: "That stream was once red with blood after a battle between Orangemen and Catholics."

However, the Irish had one advantage which other immigrants did not share—they did not have to learn to speak English. They more easily became citizens. My father commented bitterly: "They soon become foremen, straw bosses, policemen and politicians, and forget the Irish traditions of struggle for freedom!" While this was true of many, it was an exaggeration. The majority of the Irish Americans remained workers—on the waterfront, in mining, transport, maritime, in the building trades, and in other basic industries. They played a heroic part in early American labor history—in the Knights of Labor, the Western Federation of Miners, and the American Federation of Labor. William Sylvis, Peter Maguire, Terence V. Powderly, Kate Mullaney, Leonora O'Reilly, T. B. Barry, John Collins, Martin A. Foran, J. P. McDonald, John Sincey—are a few of the Irish names appearing in early labor history. In fact, in the beginnings of organizing labor they defied their church to be union members. Finally, yielding to the inevitable, the Catholic Church gave its blessing to trade unionism in 1891. Terence V. Powderly in his autobiography, *The Path I Trod*, has an interesting chapter, "Ecclesiastic Opposition," in which he tells of his struggles to defend the Knights of Labor, of which he was the head, against the attacks of priests, bishops and archbishops. Cardinal Gibbons, in his recommendations to the Pope not to condemn the Knights of Labor, saw the danger to the church in the growing cleavage between it and the mass of Catholic workers, who were joining unions.

11    My father, who was then a laborer in the quarries, met my mother in the mid '80's. There were tight social lines drawn between the "lace curtain" Irish of my mother's family and the "shanty Irish" of my father's family. The difficulties he had in courting my mother are indicated by the fact that neither Gurleys nor Flynns came to their wedding. My father was determined to leave the quarry. All but one of his male relatives had died as a result of working there. My father carried the mark of the quarry to his grave. When he was a young boy, working in a quarry in Maine, carrying tools, the sight of one eye was destroyed by a flying chip of granite. He lived to be over eighty, "thanks to Mama," we always said, who encouraged him in his ambition. He had a keen mathematical mind and through self-study and tutoring, he passed the entry examinations at Dartmouth College in Hanover, New Hampshire. He attended the Thayer School of Engineering and made excellent progress. One of his classmates, later a professor at Ann Arbor, Michigan, told me of how he remembered Tom Flynn poring over his book in the failing light of evening, finally taking it to the window to catch the last rays of the sun.

12    He was suspended from college for a short interval, because he refused to give information as to who attended a secret meeting of Catholic students, who were organizing to protest the denial of the right of Catholic students to attend Catholic services. The New York *World* of that day had an article commending his stand, the student body supported him, and he was reinstated. I thought proudly of this family precedent in December, 1952, over sixty-five years later, when I entered the Women's House of Detention in New York City, to serve a thirty days' sentence for contempt of court, for refusal to "name names." His brother Pat died of consumption shortly before my father was to graduate. Pat was the breadwinner for his mother and three sisters, who demanded that Tom now go to work. His money gave out, trying to divide with them, and he was

compelled to leave college. He was sufficiently grounded, however, so that he worked from then on as a civil engineer.

When he married, his family was highly indignant, but Mama remained at   13
work, partially solving the economic problem for a few years. My father got work in 1896 in Manchester, New Hampshire, as a civil engineer for the Manchester Street Railroad Company, which was laying a track for a new mode of transportation, since torn up to make way for buses. "Frogs" and switches were his specialty then. This was eighteen miles south of Concord, and we moved there. Here he took his first flyer into politics. He ran independently for City Engineer. He had joined the "Ancient Order of Hibernians" (A.O.H.) and marched in the St. Patrick's Day parade. He sported white gloves and a green sash over his shoulder, with golden harps and green shamrocks on it. We children were terribly impressed. We organized parades and pranced around in that sash till we wore it out. Undoubtedly he got the Irish vote but it was not enough to elect him. He was convinced that he lost because he was Irish and looked around for a job outside of New England. He took a poorly paid map-making job in Cleveland, Ohio. It was an uncertain, seasonal type of work. Collecting his pay in full depended upon how many orders the canvassers received for the finished atlases. Sometimes the operating companies failed or were fly-by-night concerns and in the end nothing was forthcoming. Somebody was always "owing Papa money."

Yet he worked hard, was out tramping around in all kinds of weather, with   14
his small hand-drafting board, plotting in with red and blue pencils the streets, houses, etc. He worked at this for years, making maps of Cleveland, Boston, Baltimore, Newark, Trenton, Kentucky, Nova Scotia and many other places. At first we moved around as his jobs changed, from Concord to Manchester, to Cleveland, to Adams, Massachusetts, and finally to New York City. Our greatest fear was "Papa losing his job!" We enjoyed our peaceful life with Mama when she gave us all her attention. We knew that there would be no money when he was at home all day, and that he would become increasingly irritable and explosive. We were selfishly happy when Papa got a new job and went off to another town. . . .

We finally arrived in New York City at the turn of the century—in 1900.   15
My mother was tired of moving around and decided here we would stay. Our school terms had been interrupted and what little furniture we possessed was being smashed up in moving around. We came to Aunt Mary, a widow and a tailoress, who lived with her five children in the South Bronx. Soon they found a flat for us nearby. It was on the inside facing an airshaft, gas-lit, with cold water. The only heat was the kitchen stove. We three older children cried, we refused to unpack our toys, and were as heart-sick for the green hills of New England as any lonely immigrants for their pleasant native lands. We missed the fields, the flowers, the cows, and beautiful Greylock Mountain we had seen from our window. We hated the big crowded dirty city, where now our play-

grounds were empty lots with neither grass nor trees. The flats where we lived, at 833 East 133rd St., are still in use, for "welfare families," I understand, although for a while they were condemned and boarded up.

16    We were horrified, too, at the conditions we had never met in our travels elsewhere—the prevalence of pests in the old slum houses—mice, rats, cockroaches and bedbugs. My poor mother carried on a desperate struggle to rid us of these parasites. And then something horrible happened to us in school—pediculosis is the scientific term—"lousy" the children called it. One child can infect a whole classroom, as every teacher knows. Yet often you will hear a smug prosperous person say: "Well, at least the poor can keep clean." I remember my friend, Rose Pastor Stokes, answering a woman who said this: "Did your mother ever look at a nickel in her hand and decide between a loaf of bread and a cake of soap? Well, mine did!" To be clean requires soap, hot water, changes of underwear, stockings and handkerchiefs, enough sheets and pillow cases and heat in the bathroom. We had none of these in periods of stark poverty. Mama washed our underwear clothes at night to be ready for the next morning.

17    On cold winter days we'd huddle in the kitchen and shut off the rest of the house. We would do our lessons by a kerosene lamp, when the gas was shut off for non-payment. We'd undress in the kitchen, scurry to the cold bedrooms, all the children sleeping in one bed, where we put our coats over us to keep us warm. We might as well have lived on an isolated farm in the Dakotas for all the good the benefits of the great city did us then. Bill collectors harassed my gentle mother—the landlord, the gas man, the milk man, the grocer. Once she bought us an encyclopedia, on the installment plan. But she couldn't keep up the payments and our hearts were broken when we lost the beautiful books we treasured so highly.

18    Our front windows of this long tunnel-like apartment faced the smoky roundhouse of the New York, New Haven and Hartford Railroad. The great engines would chug in day and night and blow off steam there. Many railroad workers lived in the area. In particularly bad times they would throw off chunks of coal and then look the other way when local children came to pick up coal around the roundhouse. There were many accidents to railroad workers. Widows lived around us who had lost their husbands on that dangerous road, and their children starved while the road fought sometimes for years against paying damages.

19    There were many small factories, veritable sweatshops in the neighborhood, where children went to work as early as the law allowed and even younger. They made paper boxes, pencils, shirts, handkerchiefs (at three dollars a week and bring your own thread). There were larger factories employing adult labor—piano and refrigerator factories, a drug plant, and others. Mothers worked too and many children were left alone. Sometimes babies fell out of windows; one boy was killed when a huge sewer pipe rolled over him; a widow's only son fell from a swaying pole in a backyard, where he was putting up a clothes line and was killed. Children lost legs on the railroad and under trucks on the streets.

The wife of the corner saloon-keeper made huge kettles of soup for free lunch and sent bowls of it around to the poorest families. People helped each other as best they could. Truly, as some philosopher said, "Poverty is like a strange and terrible country. Only those who have been there can really speak of it with knowledge."

An unforgettable tragedy of our childhood was the burning of the excursion boat, the "General Slocum," in 1904. It had left the Lower East Side loaded with women and children on a Sunday school picnic of the Lutheran Church. When it reached Hellgate, a pot of fat upset and the kitchen took fire. The captain tried to reach a dock at 138th Street. By then the boat was an inferno. A thousand people died as a result of burns or drowning. The local undertakers' establishments were full of bodies. The Alexander Avenue Police Station was a temporary morgue, where grief-stricken fathers and husbands rushed up from the East Side to claim their dead. It was heartrending to all of us in the neighborhood, like a disaster in a mining town. Investigation showed that the boat was an old firetrap, with inadequate fire-fighting equipment and life-preservers. The Captain, who did his best, was sent to prison, which cleared the company of responsibility for negligence. It was considered one of the worst marine disasters up to that time. The lives of working-class mothers and children were sacrificed to greed and corruption. ✤

20

## RESPONDING

1. In a journal entry, discuss the phrase "No Irish Need Apply." Why do you think people used this phrase? What does it suggest about conditions in America during the mid-1850s? Are you aware of similar phrases and situations that exist today for some groups?

2. Working individually or in a group, construct a time line depicting important events in the author's family history in Ireland and America. If you are able, add events in your own family history to the time line. Compare your family's situation to that of the Flynns.

3. Write an essay describing the character of Tom Flynn. Pay particular attention to the adjectives you use to describe him. Support your description with evidence from the reading.

4. Flynn reports that conditions in the New York slums were horrendous; she refutes the attitude often expressed by prosperous people that the poor should at least be able to keep clean. Journalist Jacob Riis, however, quotes a report on slum conditions at the time that says, "The proprietors frequently urged the filthy habits of the tenants as an excuse for the condition

of their property, utterly losing sight of the fact that it was the tolerance of those habits which was the real evil, and that for this they themselves were alone responsible." In an essay that expresses your opinion, supported by evidence from the reading, discuss who is responsible for slum conditions: landlords, tenants, society in general.

# Maxine S. Seller

*Maxine S. Seller, an expert in immigration history and ethnic life, was born in 1935 in Wilmington, North Carolina. She received her bachelor's degree from Bryn Mawr College in 1956 and her doctorate from the University of Pennsylvania in 1965. Seller has taught history and education at various institutions, including Temple University, Bucks County Community College, and the State University of New York at Buffalo, where she is professor of educational administration, organization, and policy. She has written* To Seek America: A History of Ethnic Life in the United States *(1977); edited the essay collections* Immigrant Women *(1981) and* Ethnic Theater in the United States *(1982); and coedited* Identity, Community and Pluralism in American Life *(1997).*

*Seller's essay "Beyond the Stereotype" not only details the contributions of three generally unnoticed immigrant activists, but also suggests ways in which historians need to challenge the stereotyped, and often inaccurate, ways in which the roles of immigrant women are portrayed.*

⊹

# BEYOND THE STEREOTYPE:

## A NEW LOOK AT THE IMMIGRANT WOMAN, 1880–1924

1    MUCH HAS BEEN WRITTEN about the achievements and experiences of the men who came to the United States from Southern and Eastern Europe between 1880 and 1924. Much less has been written, however, about the achievements and experiences of the immigrant women of this period. It is my opinion that the relative lack of material about immigrant women is not the result of a lack of activity on the part of these women. Rather, it is the result of the persistence of old, negative stereotypes, stereotypes making it appear that women did little worth writing about.

2    According to her native born contemporaries, the immigrant woman from

Southern or Eastern Europe spent her life "confined within the four walls of her home and chained to her household routine."[1] According to a librarian, "(Immigrant) women are left behind in intelligence by the father and children. They do not learn English; they do not keep up with other members of the family."[2] The political influence of the foreign born woman was supposedly nil, both before and after the passage of the Women's Suffrage Amendment. As one observer put it, "The foreign born woman plays directly in American politics a part somewhat, but not much, more important than that played by snakes in the zoology of Ireland."[3] In summary, the native born who saw all immigrants as a threat to the American way of life, saw the immigrant woman in particular as backward, ignorant, and degraded. She was considered excellent raw material for the "uplift" programs of social workers and home missionary societies, but good for little else. To fervent advocates of Americanization of the immigrant mother was a "natural obstructionist" whose eventual death would enable the family to "move on much more victoriously to Americanization."[4]

These negative stereotypes from the early twentieth century have continued to influence our view of the immigrant woman. The second or third generation ethnic comedian romanticizes her as Super-Mom, a domestic wonder woman who solved the problems of the world with steaming bowls of chicken soup, spaghetti, or other appropriate ethnic food. Those less steeped in nostalgia are likely to think of her, if at all, as a shadowy, kerchiefed figure absorbed in the not very efficient care of a cluttered tenement apartment and an unending stream of offspring. If she had ambition, it was for her children, never for herself. Her own horizons were limited to the corner grocery and the parish church. 3

Historians, like others, have been influenced by these stereotypes. They have also been influenced by the knowledge that Southern and Eastern European immigrant groups usually had, and still have, a patriarchal family structure. Many share the general bias of our society that the activities of women are less important than those of men. Even in recent works on ethnic history far fewer women than men are mentioned by name, and women's organizations and activities are rarely treated as fully as the corresponding organizations and activities of men. 4

Is the stereotyped picture of the immigrant woman an accurate reflection of reality? There were women who did conform to the stereotype, but significant numbers did not. Women of energy and ability stepped outside the traditionally 5

1. John Palmer Gavit, *Americans By Choice*, Harper and Row 1922. Reprinted in *Americanization Studies: The Acculturation of Immigrant Groups into American Society*. Patterson Smith, Montclair, New Jersey, 1971, p. 318.
2. Gavit, p. 319.
3. Gavit, p. 318.
4. The Second Annual Report of the Commission of Immigration and Housing of California, California State Printing Office, San Francisco, 1916, pp. 151–2. See also Albert Kennedy and Robert Woods, *Handbook of Settlements*, Russell Sage Foundation, New York, 1911, pp. 16, 37, 191, 211, 245.

feminine spheres of home and child care to make a variety of contributions to their ethnic communities and to American life in general. Immigrant women built social, charitable, and educational institutions that spanned the neighborhood and the nation. They established day care centers, restaurants, hotels, employment agencies, and legal aid bureaus. They wrote novels, plays, and poetry. They campaigned for a variety of causes, from factory legislation to birth control, from cleaner streets to cleaner government.[5]

6      To illustrate the range of these activities, I will begin this paper with case studies of three non-traditional women, each from a different ethnic background, each making her contribution in a different area: Antonietta Pisanelli Alessandro, a founder of professional Italian theater in the United States; Josephine Humpel Zeman, Bohemian journalist, lecturer, and feminist; and Rose Pesotta, Russian Jewish labor organizer. After sketching the career of each of these undeservedly obscure women, I will explore how, coming from patriarchal ethnic cultures, they were able to achieve what they did. Then, by discussing briefly the activities of other immigrant women, I will show that these three were not unique. So many women's lives, traditional as well as non-traditional, departed from the stereotype in so many ways that much more research in this area is needed. As ethnic historian Rudolph Vecoli recently observed, the history of the immigrant woman remains to be written.[6]

7      Antonietta Pisanelli Alessandro came from Naples to New York as a child.[7] As a young woman, she made her living singing, dancing, and acting in the major eastern cities. She made her New York debut at an Italian benefit in Giambelli Hall. Then, as there were no professional Italian theaters in New York, she and some colleagues organized several. Personal tragedy marred her career, however; first her mother died, then her husband, then one of her two children.

8      With her remaining young son and few other resources but her ingenuity, she arrived in San Francisco in 1904. She assembled a group of amateur performers, rented a ramshackled hall, and opened an Italian theater. According

---

5. Information about immigrant women's organizations can be found in Sophonisba Breckenridge, *New Homes for Old* and John Daniels, *America Via the Neighborhood*, both reprinted in *Americanization Studies: The Acculturation of Immigrant Groups into American Society*, Patterson Smith, Montclair, New Jersey, 1971. Examples of individual women active in public life are Teofila Samolinska, Polish poet, dramatist, and community organizer; Anzia Yezierska, Jewish author of short stories and novels; and Mrs. Mantura Frangierea, Lebanese businesswoman and advocate for the early Arabic community of Boston. Perhaps the best known national figure was Emma Goldman, spokeswoman for unpopular causes such as anarchism, labor reform, birth control, and the complete equality of women. Of course there were many more.

6. Rudolph J. Vecoli, "European Americans: From Immigrants to Ethics," *The Reinterpretation of American History and Culture*, edited by William H. Cartwright and Richard L. Watson, Jr., National Council for the Social Studies, Washington, D.C., 1973, p. 104.

7. For a full account of Antonietta Pisanelli Alessandro's career, see Lawrence Estavan, *The Italian Theater in San Francisco*, United States Works Progress Administration, North California District, San Francisco, 1939. Typescript copy is available at the Lincoln Center Theater Library in New York City.

to an early patron, the settings were so crude they were liable to fall apart at any moment—as were the actors. But the performance earned $150. By the time the fire department closed the building, Pisanelli was able to open the more substantial Cafe Pisanelli Family Circle, a combination theater, club, opera house, and cafe. Featuring the finest actors and singers imported from Italy, the Circle was soon known as the liveliest theater in San Francisco. Through road tours as well as home performances, Antonietta Pisanelli Alessandro and her company brought Italian drama and Italian music, from folk songs to opera, to Italian Americans and others throughout the country.

Josephine Humpel Zeman was born in Bohemia (Czechoslovakia) in 1870 and immigrated to Chicago as a young girl.[8] There she met Mary Ingersoll, a social worker at Hull House who became, in Humpel's words, "my second mother." Recognizing the young girl's ability, Mary Ingersoll helped her learn English and get an education. In 1895 Josephine Humpel Zeman was a member of the staff of Hull House, devoting her time to the study of the Bohemian community of Chicago. She was especially sensitive to the problems of women. In a published Hull House paper she complained that "nothing whatsoever has been done for the Bohemian working woman. No one has deemed her worthy of any effort. This is an interesting fact; for as long as these hundreds of thousands of girls shall be unorganized and uninformed, they will always be a great stumbling block in the path of the working women of Chicago."[9]

As social worker, author, journalist, and lecturer (both in her native language and in English) Josephine Zeman showed her concern for the welfare of immigrants, of women, and of all who were at the bottom of the nation's socioeconomic pyramid. She wrote articles for the ethnic press, for American magazines such as *Commons*, and for the United States Industrial Commission on Immigration and Education. According to the Library of Congress catalog, a Josephine Zeman, presumably Josephine Humpel Zeman, wrote two novels, *The Victim Triumphs: A Panorama of Modern Society* published by Dillingham in 1903, and *My Crime*, published by Ogelvie in 1907. Thomas Capek, who described Zeman's career in his *History of the Czechs in the United States*, did not mention these novels, however, raising the question of whether she did in fact write them. He does mention her social critique of the United States, *America in Its True Light*, published in Prague in 1903. The book contained lectures she delivered on a tour to some thirty towns in Bohemia, and Silesia. Zeman's most important work was the founding of the Chicago-based Bohemian feminist journal *Zemske Listy, The Woman's Gazette*, in 1894. Written, edited, and even printed by an exclusively female staff, the paper circulated throughout the United States.

8. Information on Josephine Humpel Zeman can be found in Thomas Capek, *The Czechs in America*, Houghton Mifflin Company, New York, 1920. I received additional information from the Balch Institute in Philadelphia, for which I am grateful to the Institute's bibliographer, Glen Skillen.
9. Josephine Humpel Zeman, "The Bohemian People in Chicago," *Hull House Maps and Papers*, Boston, 1895. Reprinted by Arno Press, New York, 1970, p. 120.

Avoiding the household hints and beauty advice common to most women's publications, the paper stressed the need to improve the lot of the working woman and campaigned for the adoption of the Women's Suffrage Amendment.[10]

11     Rose Pesotta was born in 1896 in the Ukraine, in the pale of settlement where Russian Jews were forced by law to live.[11] At the age of seventeen she came to New York City, where her older sister, who had emigrated earlier, got her a job in a garment factory. Familiar with the ideas of various peasant and worker revolutionary groups in Russia, Pesotta joined Waistmakers Local 25 of the International Ladies Garment Workers Union almost immediately. On May Day, 1914 she marched with her co-workers in a mass parade past the scene of the Triangle Waist Factory fire—an industrial disaster in which 126 garment workers, mostly immigrant girls like herself, burned to death.

12     Inspired by stories of the great labor battles of the recent past and by the distress of working people she saw all around her, Pesotta became actively involved in the organizational work of her union. She learned English at night school and continued her education, under the auspices of the Union, at Brookwood Labor College and at the Bryn Mawr Summer School for Working Girls. According to Pesotta, the aim of the latter institution was "to stimulate an active and continuous interest in the problems of our economic life which vitally concern industrial women as wage earners."[12]

13     The Bryn Mawr Summer School realized its aim: Pesotta began by working to organize her fellow workers in New York, many of whom, like herself, were Jewish immigrants. Soon she was also organizing Italians and other workers of a wide variety of ethnic backgrounds. She traveled from coast to coast, unionizing garment workers in Los Angeles, San Francisco, Montreal, San Juan, and wherever else her services were needed. During the Great Depression of the 1930s she helped organize automobile and rubber workers also. She traveled in Europe and, upon her return, rallied aid for the cause of the Spanish Loyalists. In recognition of her valuable services, she was elected a vice president of the International Ladies Garment Workers Union for three consecutive terms. Rejecting the suggestion of a fourth term in 1944, she pointed out that a union with 300,000 members, 85% of whom were women, should have more than one token woman, herself, on its executive committee.[13]

14     The lives of Antonietta Pisanelli Alessandro, Josephine Humpel Zeman, and Rose Pesotta were not confined within the limits of customary women's activities. Why did these three women break with tradition? In the first place, like millions of other working women, immigrant and native born, they could

---

10. Emily Balch, *Our Slavic Fellow Citizens*, Charities Publications Committee, New York, 1910, p. 384.
11. For an account of Pesotta's career, see her autobiography, Rose Pesotta, *Bread Upon the Waters*, Dodd, Mead & Company, New York, 1945.
12. Pesotta, p. 15.
13. Pesotta, p. 395.

not afford the luxury of full-time domesticity. Alessandro was a widow with a child to support when she opened her first theater in San Francisco. An "unfortunate" marriage made it necessary for Zeman to support herself. Pesotta, too, worked throughout her life to earn her own living.

For all three of these women, however, economic necessity was a less important motivating force than their inner drives to do meaningful and challenging work in the larger world. Antoinetta Alessandro began organizing theaters in New York while her first husband was still alive and continued to run her theater in San Francisco after a second marriage relieved her of the necessity to earn her living. Even before she left Russia, Rose Pesotta had decided that the traditional woman's life would not meet her needs. In her own words, "I can see no future for myself except to marry some young man returned from his four years of military service and be a housewife. That is not enough. . . . In America things are different. A decent middle class girl can work without disgrace."[14]

In each of these women motivation was matched by energy and ability. Alessandro impressed all who met her with her business acumen and resourcefulness, as well as with her unfailing charm. A fellow journalist dubbed Zeman "Mrs. General," a derisive acknowledgement of her forceful manner.[15] A colleague and former teacher described Pesotta as "possessing built-in energy . . . talk with her a few minutes as casually as you may and strength is poured into you, as when a depleted battery is connected to a generator."[16]

All three of these women came from ethnic backgrounds in which men were the dominant sex and women were relegated to domestic duties. Why, then, despite their obvious abilities, did they aspire to non-traditional careers in the first place? The journey to America opened new possibilities to these women, as it did to all immigrants. Still, early twentieth century America was scarcely more liberal than Europe in the roles it assigned to women. Also, by the time these three women arrived in the United States, their personalities and aspirations had already been shaped by old world environments. Undoubtedly there must be intensive investigation on the status of women in the mother countries if the immigrant woman is to be fully understood. Even a cursory investigation reveals, however, that there were cross currents in European ethnic cultures that supported the achievements of women like Alessandro, Zeman, and Pesotta.

Alessandro grew up in Southern Italy, where women were taught to be subservient to their fathers, husbands, uncles, brothers, even their male cousins. Still, Southern Italian women were respected, even revered, in their roles as mothers—perhaps because of the religious veneration of Mary as the mother of Jesus, or perhaps because of the critical economic importance of their work in

15

16

17

18

14. Pesotta, p. 9.
15. Capek, p. 275.
16. Pesotta, p. vii.

a society where livelihood was marginal. Whatever the reasons, an Italian family could survive the death of the father, but not that of the mother.[17]

19   Alessandro was not above utilizing the respect due her as an Italian mother when it was to her advantage to do so. On one occasion, a road tour audience in St. Louis threatened to riot in the theater because of a misunderstanding about the program. (They had expected the opera *Carmen* instead of the folk song with a similar name that was actually presented.) Alesandro restored peace and probably saved the building from being torn apart by putting her young son on stage to sing "Wait Til the Sun Shines, Nellie"—while her husband slipped out of the back door to safety carrying with him the evening's cash receipts.

20   According to an old Slavic proverb, "the man who does not beat his wife is not a man." According to another, "one man is worth more than ten women." Women in the more remote areas of the Balkans were used, along with the animals, to carry the heavy burdens.[18] The Slavic societies of Eastern Europe were far from monolithic, however, in their views on religion, sex, or anything else. Josephine Humpel Zeman was from Bohemia, an area with a long tradition of opposition to established religious and political institutions.[19] The rationalism of Bohemian "free thinkers" was notorious both in the United States and in Europe, and provided a hospitable atmosphere for the radical social ideas and non-traditional behavior of someone like Josephine Zeman. Indeed, her lectures on feminism and social reform may have seemed less shocking in Bohemia than in Chicago.

21   Rose Pesotta, too, could find support for her chosen life work from within her own ethnic tradition. Sex roles were sharply defined in East European Jewish society, but not in precisely the same way as in Anglo Saxon society. In theory at least, the Jewish man was most admired for his religious scholarship rather than for his physical prowess or his economic achievement. It was not uncommon for a pious Jewish man to spend all his time in religious study, while his wife assumed full responsibility for earning the family livelihood. Thus, many East European Jewish women from religious backgrounds were at home in the world of the marketplace.[20]

22   In addition, by the turn of the century some young women had come under the influence of two new secular philosophies, socialism and zionism, both of which emphasized the equality of the sexes and offered a new range of roles for

17. Leonard Covello, *The Social Background of the Italian-American School Child*, Ph.D. Thesis, New York University, 1944. E. J. Brill, Leiden, 1967, p. 210.
18. Gerald Gilbert Govorchin, *Americans from Yugoslavia*, University of Florida Press, Gainesville, 1961, pp. 188–189.
19. Kenneth Miller, *The Czech-Slovaks in America*, George H. Doran Company, New York, 1922, pp. 128–130.
20. Mark Zborowski and Elizabeth Herzog, *Life Is with People: The Culture of the Shtetl*, New York, Schocken, 1962, p. 131.

women. In 1880 Russia opened its universities to women. Although the government allowed few Jewish women to take advantage of this opportunity, increasing numbers found their way to some secular education. The "new" Jewish woman, intellectual, aggressive, and self-sufficient, brought her new lifestyle with her to the United States. According to journalist Hutchins Hapgood, who described the Jewish quarter of New York City in 1902,

> there are successful female dentists, physicians, writers, and even lawyers by the score in East Broadway who have attained financial independence through their industry and intelligence. They are ambitious to a degree and often direct the careers of their husbands. . . . There is more than one case on record where a girl has compelled her recalcitrant lover to learn law, medicine, or dentistry, or submit to being jilted by her. . . . The description of this type of woman seems rather cold and forbidding in the telling, but such an impression is misleading. . . . The women . . . are strikingly interesting because of their warm temperaments. . . .[21]

Certainly the old, limiting stereotypes of immigrant women do not apply [23] to Alesandro, Zeman, and Pesotta. These three women were unusually able, but, as already suggested, they were not unique. The same combination of talents, motivations, necessities, and opportunities that turned these three to activities outside the traditional woman's sphere acted upon other immigrant women as well.

As many historians have noted, more men than women immigrated to the [24] United States between 1880 and 1924, husbands often coming first and then sending for their wives and children. Still, surprisingly large numbers of single women did immigrate independently. Between 1912 and 1917, half a million single women under the age of thirty entered the United States. Many, like Rose Pesotta, were in their teens. Of 120,000 Polish women who came during this period, 84,000 were under the age of twenty-one.[22] Undoubtedly some came to join fiancés, but others came entirely on their own. For them, the act of immigration itself was a breach of the stereotype.

In a family unit or on their own, immigrant women frequently became part [25] of the labor force. In 1910 about a million and a quarter foreign born women were gainfully employed. Thus, contrary to the stereotype of the homebound immigrant woman, large numbers spent the greater part of their time somewhere other than in their own homes. Nor was this necessarily a new experience.

21. Hutchins Hapgood, *The Spirit of the Ghetto: Studies of the Jewish Quarter of New York*, 1902. Schocken paperback edition, New York, 1965.
22. Grace Abbott, *The Immigrant and the Community*, The Century Company, New York, 1921, pp. 55.

The economic pressures that stimulated immigration had already forced tens of thousands of East European women into day labor fields or in the homes of the large landowners. Thus, even before immigration, many women were working outside the traditional family unit, beyond the immediate supervision of father or husband.

26    The women of Southern Italy were kept closer to home than their Slavic counterparts, but here too, economic pressures were causing breaks in the traditional patterns even before immigration. In the United States most Italian families preferred to have their women work at home, but the need to earn more money drove increasing numbers into the garment factories. So many entered the clothing industry that the Women's Trade Union League of New York found it worthwhile to establish a special Italian committee to organize Italian working women.[23]

27    Working outside the home did not always—or even often—lead to a new lifestyle. But the ability to earn money could be a first step toward change. New economic power among women caused an enormous change in the lifestyle of at least one immigrant group—those from the Middle East. Arabic immigrant men, who often earned their living peddling lace, underwear, and notions from door to door, discovered that their wives had easier access to American homes than they did. Arabic wives learned English quickly by peddling with or for their husbands. As the family fortunes advanced, some became active partners in large commercial enterprises. Such women moved in one generation from a subordinate, almost cloistered life in the old country to economic and social equality with their husbands in the United States and positions of importance in their communities.[24]

28    Whether an immigrant woman worked outside of her home or not, other aspects of life in the United States tended to break up traditional patterns. American courts could be appealed to prevent some of the abuses, such as repeated wife beating, against which there was no legal redress in many old world cultures. According to male Ukrainian immigrants, "the laws here are made for women."[25] In Middle Eastern societies the education and even the social life of the children had been controlled by their father. In the United States teachers, doctors, and social workers supported the mother in assuming control of these areas.[26]

29    Neighborhood problems pulled immigrant women into activities not traditionally associated with their homemaking and childbearing roles—politics, for example. An Italian woman, newly arrived in a Chicago neighborhood, was

23. Rudolph Glanz, *Jew and Italian, Historic Group Relations and the New Immigration 1881–1924*, New York, 1971, p. 47.
24. Sabia F. Haddad, "The Woman's Role in Socialization of Syrian-Americans in Chicago," *The Arab-American: Studies in Assimilation*, edited by Elaine Hogopian and Ann Paden. Medina University Press International, Wilmett, 1969, pp. 89–97.
25. Breckenridge, p. 215.
26. Haddad, pp. 97–100.

appalled at the presence of open ditches, a hazard to her young children. At the suggestion of a settlement worker, she canvassed the neighborhood to see how many other children were similarly endangered. Her survey led to a formal complaint to city hall, and the offending ditches were covered.[27]

Nor was this an isolated case. In Chicago Bohemian women organized to protest the use of open garbage wagons in their neighborhood. After the passing of the Nineteenth Amendment, Poles, Bohemians, and other immigrant women in Chicago helped organize a women's civic league, which registered five thousand women voters and campaigned against corrupt city administration. J. Joseph Huthmacher suggests that the success of Progressive Era reforms in urban states like Massachusetts and New York was at least partly the result of immigrant political pressure.[28] More investigation is needed on the role of immigrant women in these reforms. [30]

In a study of today's working-class women, Nancy Seifer suggests that "When a wife comes home after testifying at a City Council hearing, from a meeting of the local school or hospital board, or from helping to out-maneuver a local politician or win a vote for day care in her union, she is changing the balance of power in her marriage in the most fundamental way, often without realizing it."[29] Did the pioneering ventures of immigrant women into the public life of their day have a similar effect on their marriages? [31]

Immigrant women created a great variety of local organizations, sometimes with the aid of second generation women of their own ethnic group or sympathetic social workers from nearby settlements and sometimes entirely on their own. Singing societies and other cultural associations were common, but there were many others. In New York City a group of Finnish domestic servants pooled their money to rent a small apartment for use on their days off. Within a few years the Finnish Women's Cooperative Home, as it was called, grew into a four story building with sleeping accommodations for forty, lounges, clubrooms, a library, a restaurant, and an employment bureau—still owned and operated by the women themselves.[30] In Buffalo an immigrant Jewish women's club based on a settlement house bought and remodeled an old home where they established a day care center for their own children and the children of others.[31] [32]

Slovenes, Lithuanians, Poles, Ukrainians, Lebanese, Syrians, Jews, and other immigrant women formed organizations that often expanded to include regions, or even the entire nation, to pursue charitable and educational work among the women of their own communities. Some of these groups functioned as auxiliaries [33]

---

27. Daniels, p. 213.
28. J. Joseph Huthmacher, "Urban Liberalism and the Age of Reform," *Mississippi Valley Historical Review XLIX* (September 1962), pp. 231–241.
29. Nancy Seifer, *Absent From the Majority*, National Project on Ethnic America, American Jewish Committee, 1973, p. 45.
30. Daniels, pp. 78–81.
31. Daniels, pp. 185–186.

to men's organizations. Others were independent. The Polish National Alliance, for example, was organized as one unit in which men and women were to be equal members. In practice, however, the Polish women discovered themselves an ineffective minority in a male dominated organization. A group of women decided, therefore, to establish a completely independent organization, The Polish Women's Alliance, so that Polish women could develop their own self-confidence and leadership ability.[32]

34    The varied and wide ranging activities of ethnic women's organizations are an appropriate subject for more intensive investigation. The Polish Women's Protective League gave free legal advice and other aid to Polish working women.[33] The Ukrainian Women's Alliance published a magazine offering its members information on homemaking, childcare, and women's suffrage.[34] The Lithuanian Women's Alliance provided insurance policies as well as social and educational programs.[35] Syrian, Lebanese, and Armenian women's groups had a virtual monopoly of social and charitable services within their communities. Another group of immigrant women whose contributions were great, and often overlooked, are the members of religious orders. Among these women were capable organizers and administrators of badly needed schools, hospitals, or-phanages, and other social service institutions.

35    Contrary to the view expressed in the old stereotypes, then, many immigrant women had interests and commitments that extended beyond the care of their own homes and families. But what of those who did not? What of the very traditional wife and mother who had neither the time, the energy, the self-assurance, nor perhaps even the desire to participate in public life. The negative stereotypes are unfair to her too. They are unfair because they confuse illiteracy with ignorance and poverty with personal degradation. The woman who fed and clothed a large family on five dollars a week—to the astonishment of the social worker trained in home economics—may have been illiterate, but she was certainly not ignorant. The woman who worked a twelve hour night shift in a foundry and cared for her family and several boarders during the day had no time for the so-called "finer" things in life, but she was not therefore a degraded human being. To survive at all she must have possessed enormous inner re-sources.

36    Nor was the uneducated, homebound immigrant woman necessarily politi-cally naive. While many women, like many men, sold their votes or did not vote at all, others were remarkably conscientious and astute. According to Jane Addams, Italian women who came in to vote knew more about the city's problems than their husbands, who were often away on construction or railroad jobs six months of the year. Addams writes of an illiterate Irish woman whom

32. Breckenridge, pp. 205–209.
33. Breckenridge, p. 294.
34. Breckenridge, p. 215.
35. Breckenridge, p. 214.

she was allowed to help at the voting booth in a Chicago municipal election. "The first proposition was about bonds for a new hospital. The Irish woman said, 'Is the same bunch to spend the money that run the hospital we have now? Then I am against it'. . . . There were ten propositions to be acted upon. I was scrupulous not to influence her: Yet on nine of them she voted from her own common sense just as the Municipal League and the City Club had recommended as the result of painstaking research."[36]

Undoubtedly life was too much for some immigrant women. Broken homes, physical and mental illness, despair, even suicide were all too often present in the ethnic ghetto. The amazing thing is that, given the cultural shock of immigration and the problems of poverty, and discrimination, and survival in urban slums, so many women were able to keep themselves and their families from being defeated. An early social worker, Katherine Anthony, described one such woman, a Hungarian immigrant, Mrs. Mary Grubinsky. Mr. Grubinsky worked in a furniture factory. The couple had seven children. Mrs. Grubinsky worked "a day here, half a day there" returning to her jobs within a month after the birth of each of her children.

> In addition she helps her husband with chair caning, makes the children's clothes, mends for her own family and also for hire, cooks, washes, irons, scrubs, tends her window boxes, minds the children of a neighbor who is doing a day's work, fetches ice from the brewery where it is thrown away, forages for kindling around warehouses, runs to the school when the teacher summons her—but a list of all that Mrs. Grubinsky does in the course of a week would be quite impossible. In her home nothing is lost. Even the feathers from a Thanksgiving turkey were made into cushions and dust brushes.[37]

It would be understandable if such a busy woman would lag behind the rest of her family in learning English and adjusting to the United States. But according to Katherine Anthony, this was not the case with Mary Grubinsky.

> She takes the lead in Americanizing her husband and family. She insisted they move from a two to a three room apartment to have a sitting room. . . . Sees to it the girls have proper clothes, white shoes for confirmation. In these matters Mrs. Grubinsky feels that she must decide and that Martin must accommodate himself.

Like Alesandro, Humpel, and Pesotta, Mary Grubinsky was unusually capable. But also like them, she was not unique.

In conclusion, the current interest in ethnicity occurring simultaneously

36. Gavit, p. 324.
37. Katherine Anthony, *Mothers Who Must Earn*, New York, 1914, pp. 186–190.

with the new interest in the history of women makes this an opportune time for scholars to take a new look at the immigrant woman. "Forgotten" women, who like Alessandro, Humpel, and Pesotta, played an important role in the public life of their communities can be rediscovered by a careful study of the ethnic press and the papers of ethnic institutions (especially women's groups), labor unions, settlement houses, and political parties. The experiences of these women should become an integral part of our understanding of immigration history.

41   So, too, should the experiences of the more traditional women whose lives, like that of Mary Grubinsky, were centered around care of the home and the family. These women constituted too varied and complex a group to be ignored or dismissed with an inherited negative stereotype. More can be learned about them from their letters and diaries (where these exist), from the records of charities, hospitals, courts and other institutions, and from demographic sources such as census tracts and school surveys. Letters-to-the-editor columns in the ethnic press can be useful, as can the short stories, novels, and poetry of perspective immigrant writers.[38] Research is needed on the impact of immigration and acculturation on the lives of all immigrant women, on the institution of marriage, and on child-rearing practices.

42   In conclusion, sources are available for the study of the Southern and Eastern European immigrant woman. With the use of some ingenuity on the part of historians, many more can probably be uncovered. It is time to begin writing the story of the immigrant woman—beyond the stereotype. ✠

---

RESPONDING

1.   Write a journal entry describing an immigrant woman. You might talk about a family member, someone else you know, or someone you have read about. Does this woman fit the stereotype Seller describes?

2.   Working individually or in a group, examine the current expectations for women in your culture or another culture with which you are familiar. Compare these with the expectations for women in one of the cultures Seller discusses.

3.   List the relevant factors that influenced the lives of Antonietta Pisanelli Alessandro, Josephine Humpel Zeman, and Rose Pesotta. Write an essay comparing their experiences. Consider whether all three are the products of similar backgrounds. What factors or events facilitated their choices? Was each a product of a unique culture?

38. See, for example, the works of Anzia Yezierska, *Hungry Hearts, The Bread Winners, Salome of the Tenements,* and *All I Could Never Be.*

4. Seller's position is that the negative stereotype of immigrant women is incorrect. How do you think this stereotype came about? What might its function have been? Support your argument with evidence from the reading, outside information, and your own experience. Refer to your journal entry to get started.

# JACOB RIIS

*Jacob Riis, who was born in Denmark in 1849, immigrated to the United States in 1870. After working at various jobs in New York City, he became a police reporter for the* New York Tribune *in 1877; later he worked for the* Sun. *Riis was a strong believer in personal initiative. In the public lectures he held during the 1880s, he encouraged immigrants to learn the language of their adopted country and adapt themselves to its customs. Jacob Riis died in 1914.*

How the Other Half Lives *is the most famous of the ten books Riis wrote. The text and its accompanying photographs, both by Riis, were first published as a series in* Scribner's Magazine. *The work was praised by Theodore Roosevelt, who then served as police commissioner of New York City. Riis's publications are credited with helping to effect reform in the poorest sections of New York City.*

*The selection that follows describes the development of tenements, from once-ornate single-family homes of the well-to-do to the overcrowded dwellings of the very poor. The excerpt presents the squalor of these buildings in strongly visual terms and raises questions about the public's responsibility for those who find themselves destitute.*

⁜

# GENESIS OF THE TENEMENT

THE FIRST TENEMENT NEW YORK KNEW bore the mark of Cain from its birth, though a generation passed before the writing was deciphered. It was the "rear house," infamous ever after in our city's history. There had been tenant-houses before, but they were not built for the purpose. Nothing would probably have shocked their original owners more than the idea of their harboring a promiscuous crowd; for they were the decorous homes of the old Knickerbockers, the proud aristocracy of Manhattan in the early days.

It was the stir and bustle of trade, together with the tremendous immigration that followed upon the war of 1812 that dislodged them. In thirty-five years the city of less than a hundred thousand came to harbor half a million souls, for whom homes had to be found. Within the memory of men not yet in their prime, Washington had moved from his house on Cherry Hill as too far out of town to be easily reached. Now the old residents followed his example; but they moved in a different direction and for a different reason. Their comfortable dwellings in the once fashionable streets along the East River front fell into the hands of real-estate agents and boarding-house keepers; and here, says the report to the Legislature of 1857, when the evils engendered had excited just alarm, "in its beginning, the tenant-house became a real blessing to that class of industrious poor whose small earnings limited their expenses, and whose employment in workshops, stores, or about the warehouses and thoroughfares, render a near residence of much importance." Not for long, however. As business increased, and the city grew with rapid strides, the necessities of the poor became the opportunity of their wealthier neighbors, and the stamp was set upon the old houses, suddenly become valuable, which the best thought and effort of a later age has vainly struggled to efface. Their "*large* rooms were partitioned into *several smaller ones*, without regard to light or ventilation, the rate of rent being lower in proportion to space or height from the street; and they soon became filled from cellar to garret with a class of tenantry living from hand to mouth, loose in morals, improvident in habits, degraded, and squalid as beggary itself." It was thus the dark bedroom, prolific of untold depravities, came into the world. It was destined to survive the old houses. In their new rôle, says the old report, eloquent in its indignant denunciation of "evils more destructive than wars," "they were not intended to last. Rents were fixed high enough to cover damage and abuse from this class, from whom nothing was expected, and the most was made of them while they lasted. Neatness, order, cleanliness, were never dreamed of in connection with the tenant-house system, as it spread its localities from year to year; while reckless slovenliness, discontent, privation, and ignorance were left to work out their invariable results, until the entire premises reached the level of tenant-house dilapidation, containing, but sheltering not, the miserable hordes that crowded beneath smouldering, water-rotted roofs or burrowed among the rats of clammy cellars." Yet so illogical is human greed that, at a later day, when called to account, "the proprietors frequently urged the filthy habits of the tenants as an excuse for the condition of their property, utterly losing sight of the fact that it was the tolerance of those habits which was the real evil, and that for this they themselves were alone responsible."

3 Still the pressure of the crowds did not abate, and in the old garden where the stolid Dutch burgher grew his tulips or early cabbages a rear house was built, generally of wood, two stories high at first. Presently it was carried up another story, and another. Where two families had lived ten moved in. The front house followed suit, if the brick walls were strong enough. The question was not always asked, judging from complaints made by a contemporary witness,

that the old buildings were "often carried up to a great height without regard to the strength of the foundation walls." It was rent the owner was after; nothing was said in the contract about either the safety or the comfort of the tenants. The garden gate no longer swung on its rusty hinges. The shell-paved walk had become an alley; what the rear house had left of the garden, a "court." Plenty such are yet to be found in the Fourth Ward, with here and there one of the original rear tenements.

Worse was to follow. It was "soon perceived by estate owners and agents of property that a greater percentage of profits could be realized by the conversion of houses and blocks into barracks, and dividing their space into smaller proportions capable of containing human life within four walls. . . . Blocks were rented of real estate owners, or 'purchased on time,' or taken in charge at a percentage, and held for under-letting." With the appearance of the middleman, wholly irresponsible, and utterly reckless and unrestrained, began the era of tenement building which turned out such blocks as Gotham Court, where, in one cholera epidemic that scarcely touched the clean wards, the tenants died at the rate of one hundred and ninety-five to the thousand of population; which forced the general mortality of the city up from 1 in 41.83 in 1815, to 1 in 27.33 in 1855, a year of unusual freedom from epidemic disease, and which wrung from the early organizers of the Health Department this wail: "There are numerous examples of tenement-houses in which are lodged several hundred people that have a *pro rata* allotment of ground area scarcely equal to two square yards upon the city lot, court-yards and all included." The tenement-house population had swelled to half a million souls by that time, and on the East Side, in what is still the most densely populated district in all the world, China not excluded, it was packed at the rate of 290,000 to the square mile, a state of affairs wholly unexampled. The utmost cupidity of other lands and other days had never contrived to herd much more than half that number within the same space. The greatest crowding of Old London was at the rate of 175,816. Swine roamed the streets and gutters as their principal scavengers.[1] The death of a child in a tenement was registered at the Bureau of Vital Statistics as "plainly due to suffocation in the foul air of an unventilated apartment," and the Senators, who had come down from Albany to find out what was the matter with New York, reported that "there are annually cut off from the population by disease and death enough human beings to people a city, and enough human labor to sustain it." And yet experts had testified that, as compared with uptown, rents were from twenty-five to thirty per cent. higher in the worst slums of the lower wards, with such accommodations as were enjoyed, for instance, by a "family with boarders" in Cedar Street, who fed hogs in the cellar that contained eight or ten loads of manure; or "one room 12 × 12 with five families living in it, comprising twenty persons of both sexes and all ages, with only two beds,

1. It was not until the winter of 1867 that owners of swine were prohibited by ordinance from letting them run at large in the built-up portions of the city. [Author's note]

without partition, screen, chair, or table." The rate of rent has been successfully maintained to the present day, though the hog at least has been eliminated.

5   Lest anybody flatter himself with the notion that these were evils of a day that is happily past and may safely be forgotten, let me mention here three very recent instances of tenement-house life that came under my notice. One was the burning of a rear house in Mott Street, from appearances one of the original tenant-houses that made their owners rich. The fire made homeless ten families, who had paid an average of $5 a month for their mean little cubby-holes. The owner himself told me that it was *fully* insured for $800, though it brought him in $600 a year rent. He evidently considered himself especially entitled to be pitied for losing such valuable property. Another was the case of a hard-working family of man and wife, young people from the old country, who took poison together in a Crosby Street tenement because they were "tired." There was no other explanation, and none was needed when I stood in the room in which they had lived. It was in the attic with sloping ceiling and a single window so far out on the roof that it seemed not to belong to the place at all. With scarcely room enough to turn around in they had been compelled to pay five dollars and a half a month in advance. There were four such rooms in that attic, and together they brought in as much as many a handsome little cottage in a pleasant part of Brooklyn. The third instance was that of a colored family of husband, wife, and baby in a wretched rear rookery in West Third Street. Their rent was eight dollars and a half for a single room on the top-story, so small that I was unable to get a photograph of it even by placing the camera outside the open door. Three short steps across either way would have measured its full extent.

6   There was just one excuse for the early tenement-house builders, and their successors may plead it with nearly as good right for what it is worth. "Such," says an official report, "is the lack of house-room in the city that any kind of tenement can be immediately crowded with lodgers, if there is space offered." Thousands were living in cellars. There were three hundred underground lodging-houses in the city when the Health Department was organized. Some fifteen years before that the old Baptist Church in Mulberry Street, just off Chatham Street, had been sold, and the rear half of the frame structure had been converted into tenements that with their swarming population became the scandal even of that reckless age. The wretched pile harbored no less than forty families, and the annual rate of deaths to the population was officially stated to be 75 in 1,000. These tenements were an extreme type of very many, for the big barracks had by this time spread east and west and far up the island into the sparsely settled wards. Whether or not the title was clear to the land upon which they were built was of less account than that the rents were collected. If there were damages to pay, the tenant had to foot them. Cases were "very frequent when property was in litigation, and two or three different parties were collecting rents." Of course under such circumstances "no repairs were ever made."

7   The climax had been reached. The situation was summed up by the Society for the Improvement of the Condition of the Poor in these words: "Crazy old

buildings, crowded rear tenements in filthy yards, dark, damp basements, leaking garrets, shops, outhouses, and stables[2] converted into dwellings, though scarcely fit to shelter brutes, are habitations of thousands of our fellow-beings in this wealthy, Christian city." "The city," says its historian, Mrs. Martha Lamb, commenting on the era of aqueduct building between 1835 and 1845, "was a general asylum for vagrants." Young vagabonds, the natural offspring of such "home" conditions, overran the streets. Juvenile crime increased fearfully year by year. The Children's Aid Society and kindred philanthropic organizations were yet unborn, but in the city directory was to be found the address of the "American Society for the Promotion of Education in Africa." ✠

## RESPONDING

1. In a journal entry, compare Riis's description of the New York City tenements of the 1880s to any part of your own or a nearby city today.

2. Working individually or in a group, list the rights and responsibilities of landlords and tenants. Whose rights have primary importance if there is a conflict? Share your lists with the class.

3. Consider the statement that "experts had testified that, as compared with uptown, rents were from twenty-five to thirty per cent. higher in the worst slums of the lower wards" (paragraph 4). How do you account for that difference? In an essay, compare that situation to conditions in a city you know. Are rents, goods, and services more expensive in poor neighborhoods than in middle-class or rich neighborhoods?

4. Riis quotes a report on slum conditions that says, "the proprietors frequently urged the filthy habits of the tenants as an excuse for the condition of their property, utterly losing sight of the fact that it was the tolerance of those habits which was the real evil, and that for this they themselves were alone responsible" (paragraph 2). Write an essay in which you agree or disagree.

2. "A lot 50 × 60, contained twenty stables, rented for dwellings at $15 a year each; cost of the whole $600." [Author's note]

# JAMES WEST DAVIDSON AND
# MARK HAMILTON LYTLE

*James West Davidson, who was born in 1946, earned his bachelor's degree from Haverford College in 1968 and his doctorate from Yale University in 1973. His publications include* The Logic of Millennial Thought: Eighteenth Century New England *(1977), as well as* After the Fact: The Art of Historical Detection *(1982; 1986) and* The United States: A History of a Republic *(1982), both of which he cowrote with Mark Hamilton Lytle.*

*Mark Hamilton Lytle received his bachelor's degree from Cornell University in 1966 and his doctorate from Yale University in 1973. He has published studies on American history as well as* The Origins of the Iranian-American Alliance, 1941–1953 *(1986). He has been on the faculty at Yale University and Bard College, where he has taught since 1980. He is currently Associate Professor of History and Chairman of the American Studies Program.*

*The following excerpt, from the second edition of* After the Fact, *explores the issues of objectivity and subjectivity in the literary and photographic representation and construction of the immigrant within the journalism of Jacob Riis.*

⁜

# IMAGES OF THE OTHER HALF

1   JACOB RIIS WAS AN IMMIGRANT TO AMERICA, like so many of those he wrote about. He had tasted poverty and hardship. Yet in a curious way, Riis the social reformer might best be understood as a tourist of the slums, wandering from tenement to tenement, camera in hand. To classify him as such is to suggest that despite his immigrant background, he maintained a distance between himself and his urban subjects.

2   In part, that distance can be explained by Riis's own background as an immigrant. Despite his tribulations, he came from a middle-class family, which made it easy to choose journalism as a career. As a boy, in fact, Riis had helped his father prepare copy for a weekly newspaper. Once established in a job commensurate with his training, Riis found it easy to accomplish the goal of so many immigrants—to rise to middle-class dignity and prosperity and to become, in the most respectable sense, not a newcomer but an American.

3   Furthermore, because Riis emigrated from Denmark, his northern European background made it more difficult for him to empathize with the immigrant cultures of southern and eastern Europe, increasingly the source of new

immigrants in the 1880s and 1890s. Like many native-born Americans, Riis found most of their customs distasteful and doubted whether they could successfully learn the traditional American virtues. As Sam Warner remarked, Riis ascribed a "degree of opprobrium to each group directly proportional to the distance from Denmark. . . ."

Yet for all that, Riis retained a measure of sympathy and understanding for the poor. He did not work his way out of poverty only to find a quiet house far from the turmoil of the urban scene. He was unable to ignore the squalor that so evidently needed the attention of concerned Americans. Thus an ambivalence permeated Riis's writings. On the one hand he sympathized with the plight of the poor and recognized how much they were the victims of their slum environment. "In the tenements all the elements make for evil," he wrote. He struggled to maintain a distinction between the "vicious" classes of beggars, tramps, and thieves, and the working poor who made the slum their home because they had no other choice. On the other hand, Riis could not avoid using language that continuously dismissed whole classes of immigrants as inherently unable to adapt themselves to what he considered acceptable American behavior.

When he visited "Jewtown," for example, Riis scarcely commented on the strong bonds of faith and loyalty that held families and groups together in the face of all the debilitating aspects of slum life. Instead, he dwelt on the popular "Shylock" stereotype. "Money is their God," he wrote. "Life itself is of little value compared to even the leanest bank account." Upon the Irish, of course, he bestowed a talent for politics and drink. "His genius runs to public affairs rather than domestic life," said Riis of the Irish politician; "wherever he is mustered in force the saloon is the gorgeous center of political activity."

To southern and eastern Mediterranean people, Riis was least understanding. The "happy-go-lucky" Italians he observed were "content to live in a pig sty." Not only did they "come in at the bottom," but also they managed to stay there. They sought to reproduce the worst of life in Italy by flocking to slum tenements. When an Italian found better housing, "he soon reduced what he did find to his own level, if allowed to follow his natural bent." These affable and malleable souls "learned slowly, if at all." And then there was the passion for gambling and murder: "[The Italian's] soul is in the game from the moment the cards are on the table, and very frequently his knife is in it too before the game is ended." Such observations confirm our sense of Riis as a tourist in the slums, for he seemed only to have educated his prejudices without collecting objective information.

A second quality that strikes the reader of *How the Other Half Lives* is its tone of Christian moralism. Riis blamed the condition of the urban poor on the sins of individuals—greedy landlords, petty grafters, corrupt officials, the weak character of the poor, and popular indifference. Insensitive to the economic forces that had transformed cities, he never attempted a systematic analysis of urban classes and institutional structures. Instead, he appealed to moral regeneration as the means of overcoming evil, and approvingly cited the plea of a philanthropic tenement builder: "How are these men and women to understand the love of God you speak of, when they see only the greed of men?" In his own ominous warning to his fellow New Yorkers, Riis struck an almost apocalyptic note. "When another generation shall have double the census of our city," he warned, "and to the vast army of workers held captive by poverty, the very name of home shall be a bitter mockery, what will the harvest be?" If conditions worsened, the violence of labor strikes during the 1870s and 1880s might seem quite tame in comparison.

8      Given those predispositions, how do we interpret Riis's photographs? Like the arrangers of family albums, his personal interests dictated the kind of photographs he included in his books. And as with the family albums, by being aware of these predispositions we can both understand Riis better by consciously examining his photographic messages and at the same time transcend the original intent of the pictures.

9      For example, Riis's Christian moralism led him to emphasize the need for stable families as a key to ameliorating slum conditions. Many American Protestants in his audience thought of the home and family as a "haven" from the

**Bohemian Cigarmakers at Work in Their Tenement.** *(Museum of the City of New York/The Jacob A. Riis Collection)*

bustle of the working world, as well as a nursery of piety and good morals. Fathers could return at the end of the day to the warm, feminine environment in which their children were carefully nurtured. . . . It is not simply the lack of cleanliness or space that would make such an apartment appalling to many viewers, but the corrosive effect of such conditions on family life. Yet this was a family dwelling, for Riis heard a baby crying in the adjoining hall-room. How could a family preserve any semblance of decency, Riis asked his readers, in a room occupied by twelve single men and women?

Let us turn from that photograph to another, [on page 232] which is much more obviously a family portrait. The middle-class Protestant viewer of Riis's day would have found this picture shocking for the same reasons. The home was supposed to be a haven away from the harsh workaday world, yet here the factory has invaded the home. This is the small room of an immigrant Bohemian family, crowded with the tools and supplies needed to make a living. The business is apparently a family enterprise, since the husband, wife, and at least one child assist in the work. . . .

The room speaks of a rather single-minded focus on making a living. All the furnishings are used for cigarmaking, not for creature comforts or living after work. The only light comes from a small kerosene lamp and the indirect sunlight from two windows facing out on the wall of another building. Yet Riis had a stronger message for the picture to deliver. The text stresses the exploitation of Bohemians in New York, most of whom worked at cigarmaking in apartments owned by their employers, generally Polish Jewish immigrants.

The cigar trade dominated all aspects of life: "The rank smell that awaited us on the corner of the block follows us into the hallways, penetrates every nook and cranny of the house." This particular family, he noted, turned out 4,000 cigars a week, for which it was paid fifteen dollars. Out of that amount the landlord-employer deducted $11.75 in rent for three small rooms, two of which had no windows for light or air. The father was so tied to his workbench that in six years he had learned no English and, therefore, made no attempt to assimilate into American life.

It is interesting to contrast the portrait of the Bohemian family with a different family portrait, this one taken by another reforming photographer, but still often published in reprints of *How the Other Half Lives*.[1] Unlike the photograph of the cigarmakers' lodgings, this is a more formal family portrait. Very much aware of the camera's presence, everyone is looking directly at the lens. Perhaps the photographer could gain consent to intrude on their privacy only by agreeing to do a formal photograph. The children have been scrubbed and dressed in what appear to be their good clothes—the oldest son in his shirt and

10

11

12

13

---

1. The photographer is Jessie Tarbox Beals and the picture was taken in 1910. Although not included in the original edition of *How the Other Half Lives*, it is among the photographs in the Riis collection held by the Museum of the City of New York.

**Room in Tenement Flat, 1910.** *(Museum of the City of New York/The Jacob A. Riis Collection)*

tie, his sister in a taffeta dress, and a younger girl in a frock. . . . [H]ere the family china is proudly displayed in the cabinet. Perhaps it was a valued possession carefully guarded on the journey from Europe.

14    Other details in the picture suggest that this family enjoyed a more pleasant environment than seen in the previous photos. Moving from left to right, we notice first a gas stove, a relatively modern improvement in an age when coal and wood were still widely used for heating and cooking. Perhaps these people had found a room in a once-elegant home divided by the realtor into a multiple dwelling. Certain details suggest that may be the case. Few tenements would have gas, much less built-in cupboards or the finished moldings around doors and windows. The window between the kitchen/bedroom and closet/bedroom indicates that the room may have once looked out on open space.

15    By contrast, the picture communicates a sense of crowding. This hardly seems an accident. Had the photographer wished to take only a family portrait, she could have clustered her subjects in the center of her lens. Instead, she placed them around the room, so that the camera would catch all the details of their domestic circumstance. We see not just a family, but the conditions of their lives

in an area far too small for their needs. Each space and almost all the furnishings are used for more than one purpose. The wash tub just before the window and washboard behind it indicate that the kitchen doubles as laundry room—and the tub was probably used for baths as well. The bed serves during the day as a sofa. To gain a measure of privacy the parents have crowded their bed into a closet stuffed with family possessions. Seven people seem to share a room perhaps no more than 250 square feet in total. The children appear to range in age from one to twelve. If the mother is again pregnant as the picture hints, that means every two years another person enters that cramped space.

This portrait, then, does not conform to the typical stereotype we would expect to find of urban immigrant slum dwellers. In the first place, many immigrants came to America without families. Of those, a majority were young men who hoped to stay just long enough to accumulate a small savings with which to improve their family fortunes upon returning to Europe. On the other hand, immigrant families tended to be much larger than those of middle-class native-born Americans. Rather than evoking a sympathetic response among an American audience, the picture might, instead, reinforce the widespread fear that prolific breeding among foreign elements threatened white Protestant domination of American society.

What then does the modern viewer derive from this family portrait? Over all, it seems to say that immigrants, like other Americans, prized family life. The father perches at the center almost literally holding his family together, though with a rather tenuous grip. The son with his tie appears to embody the family's hopes for a better future. His mother securely holds the baby in her arms. Each element, in fact, emphasizes the virtues of the domestic family as it was traditionally conceived in America. The picture, while sending a mixed message, conveys less a sense of terrible slum conditions than a sense of the middle-class aspirations among those forced to live in inadequate housing.

Does the fact that this picture is posed make it less useful as historical evidence? Not at all. Even when people perform for the camera, they communicate information about themselves. There is no hiding the difficulty of making a decent life for seven people in a small space. Nor can the viewer ignore the sense of pride of person and place, no matter how limited the resources. What remains uncertain, however, is what message the photographer meant to convey. The scene could serve equally well to arouse nativist prejudice or to extol the strength of family ties in the immigrant community. Both were concerns that Riis addressed in his writing and photographs.

Concern over the breakdown of family life drew Riis to children. They are among his most frequently photographed subjects. He shared the Victorian notion of childhood innocence and, therefore, understood that nothing could be more disturbing to his middle-class audience than scenes of homeless children, youth gangs, and "street arabs" sleeping in alleys, gutters, and empty stairways. At first glance, the three "street arabs" on this page appear as if they might even be dead. A closer look suggests helpless innocence—children alone

**Street Arabs in Sleeping Quarters.** *(Museum of the City of New York/The Jacob A. Riis Collection)*

and unprotected as they sleep. Their ragged clothes and bare feet advertise poverty and the absence of parents to care for them. In each other, though, they seem to have extracted a small measure of warmth, belonging, and comfort. It would be almost impossible for any caring person to view the picture without empathy for its subjects and anger at a society that cares so little for its innocent creatures.

20      Riis hints at his sympathies through the location of the camera. He did not stand over the boys to shoot the picture from above. That angle would suggest visually the superiority of the photographer to his subjects. From ground level, however, observer and subject are on the same plane. We look at the boys, not down on them. And should we dismiss as accidental his inclusion of the prison-like bars over the small window? From another angle Riis could have eliminated that poignant symbol from his frame.

21      Certainly, we know that Riis feared that all too soon those "innocents" would become the members of slum gangs, operating outside the law with

brazen disregard for society or its values. In this second picture of lost innocence [below] Riis persuaded some gang members to demonstrate how they "did the trick"—that is, robbed the pockets of a drunk lying in an alley. The mere fact that Riis had obviously arranged the content of the picture, indicating that some relationship existed between the photographer and his subjects, would have made the image even more shocking. These young men were clearly proud of their acts and so confident that they were beyond the reach of the law that they could show off for the camera. . . . Riis's audience would have understood quite clearly that the slums as breeding grounds for crime drove the innocence out of childhood.

Space was not only scarce in the homes of the poor. Crowding extended into public places as well. Without parks or wide streets children were forced to play in filthy alleys and garbage heaps. Adults had no decent communal space in which to make contact with the community. The picture of a tenement yard [page 238] immediately reveals a scene of chaos and crowding. As in slum

22

**Hell's Kitchen Boys—"Showing Their Tricks."** *(Museum of the City of New York/The Jacob A. Riis Collection)*

Tenement-house Yard. *(Museum of the City of New York/The Jacob A. Riis Collection)*

❖

# SHIRT

The back, the yoke, the yardage. Lapped seams,
The nearly invisible stitches along the collar
Turned in a sweatshop by Koreans or Malaysians

Gossiping over tea and noodles on their break
Or talking money or politics while one fitted
This armpiece with its overseam to the band

Of cuff I button at my wrist. The presser, the cutter,
The wringer, the mangle. The needle, the union,
The treadle, the bobbin. The code. The infamous blaze

At the Triangle Factory in nineteen-eleven.
One hundred and forty-six died in the flames
On the ninth floor, no hydrants, no fire escapes—

The witness in a building across the street
Who watched how a young man helped a girl to step
Up to the windowsill, then held her out

Away from the masonry wall and let her drop.
And then another. As if he were helping them up
To enter a streetcar, and not eternity.

A third before he dropped her put her arms
Around his neck and kissed him. Then he held
Her into space, and dropped her. Almost at once

He stepped to the sill himself, his jacket flared
And fluttered up from his shirt as he came down,
Air filling up the legs of his gray trousers—

Like Hart Crane's Bedlamite, "shrill shirt ballooning."
Wonderful how the pattern matches perfectly
Across the placket and over the twin bar-tacked

Corners of both pockets, like a strict rhyme
Or a major chord. Prints, plaids, checks,
Houndstooth, Tattersall, Madras. The clan tartans

**"Bottle Alley."** (*Museum of the City of New York/The Jacob A. Riis Collection*)

apartments, every open area had to serve more than one purpose. Women doing the wash and children playing appear to fall all over one another. The fire escape doubles as a balcony. Any readers with a small yard, separate laundry room or laundress, and nearby park surely thanked their good fortune not to be part of this confusion.

Once again, however, closer scrutiny may lead us to reconsider our initial impressions. This place seems alive with energy. We see that the women and children are all part of a community. They have given their common space, restricted as it may be, to shared activities. Everyone seems to have a place in the scheme of things. All that laundry symbolizes community concern with cleanliness and decency. On the balcony some people have flower boxes to add a touch of color and freshness to a drab landscape. Our initial shock gives way to a more complex set of feelings. We come to respect the durability of spirit that allowed people to struggle for a small measure of comfort amid such harsh surroundings. The message which at first seemed obvious is not so clear after all.

In the picture of "Bottle Alley," Riis has editorialized on the same theme with more telling effect. In this dingy slum, along the infamous Bend, we are still among tenements. Laundry again hangs from the balcony. A few isolated men look upon the camera as it takes in the scene. Their presence during the day suggests they are among the army of unemployed who sit aimlessly waiting for time to pass. They seem oblivious to the filth that surrounds them. We cannot help but feel that they are as degraded as the conditions in which they live. The dilapidated buildings and rickety stairs create an overall sense of decay; nothing in the picture relieves the image of poverty and disorder Riis wanted to capture. The message is all too clear.

25    As the case of Jacob Riis demonstrates, photography is hardly a simple "mirror of reality." The meanings behind each image must be uncovered through careful exploration and analysis. On the surface, certainly, photographs often provide the historian with a wealth of concrete detail. In that sense they do convey the reality of a situation with some objectivity. Yet Riis's relative inexperience with a camera did not long prevent him from learning how to frame the content to create a powerful image. The photographic details communicate a stirring case for social reform, full of subjective as well as objective intent. Riis did not simply want us to see the poor or the slums; he wanted us to see them as he saw them. His view was that of a partisan, not an unbiased observer.

26    In that sense the photographic "mirror," is silvered on both sides: catching the reflections of its user as well as its subjects. The prints which emerge from the twilight of the darkroom must be read by historians as they do all evidence— appreciating messages that may be simple and obvious or complex and elusive. Once these evidentiary limits are appreciated and accepted, one can recognize the rueful justice in Oliver Wendell Holmes's definition of a photograph: an illusion with the "appearance of reality that cheats the senses with its seeming truth." ✺

---

RESPONDING

1. In a journal entry, analyze a photograph in the text or from a newspaper. Does the photographer have an agenda that he or she is trying to promote?

2. Working individually or in a group, find examples that explain why Davidson and Lytle call Riis "a tourist in the slums" (paragraph 6). Are they being fair?

3. In an essay, agree or disagree with Oliver Wendell Holmes's definition of a photograph: an illusion with the "appearance of reality that cheats the senses with its seeming truth" (paragraph 26). Use examples from the text or evidence from your own experience to support your point. You might want to include and analyze some photographs in your essay.

4. Davidson and Lytle cite several examples of Riis's stereotypical thinking. Using information from the reading or from your own knowledge and experience, write an essay discussing how stereotypes can distort our view of individuals and events. You might consider, for example, whether the media shapes our thinking about social issues.

---

# ROBERT PINSKY

*Born in 1940, Robert Pinsky earned his doctorate from Stanford University in 1966. He has held teaching positions at Stanford, Wellesley College, University of Chicago, and Boston University. His publications include poetry collections* Sadness and Happiness, The Want Bone, *and* Figured Wheel; *several works of prose; the interactive fiction* Mindscape; *a translation of Dante's* Divine Comedy; *and a general introduction to poetry entitled* The Sounds of Poetry: A Brief Guide. *He was named poet laureate of the United States for an unprecedented [. . .] April 1999, overseeing an ambitious 100 Favorite Poems [. . .] also served as poetry editor for* The New Republic. *He [. . .] editor of* Slate, *an on-line magazine.*

*"Shirt" uses a mundane object to prompt a meditation [. . .] and the worker. Referring to the seventeenth-century [. . .] whose lyrics often used simple language and imagery [. . .] thought, Pinsky's poem invites us to consider a [. . .] work and an earlier form of poetry, but [. . .] sociohistorical context in which it is placed [. . .]*

Invented by mill-owners inspired by the hoax of Ossian,
To control their savage Scottish workers, tamed
By a fabricated heraldry: MacGregor,

Bailey, MacMartin. The kilt, devised for workers
To wear among the dusty clattering looms.                                    35
Weavers, carders, spinners. The loader,

The docker, the navvy. The planter, the picker, the sorter
Sweating at her machine in a litter of cotton
As slaves in calico headrags sweated in fields:

George Herbert, your descendant is a Black                                   40
Lady in South Carolina, her name is Irma
And she inspected my shirt. Its color and fit

And feel and its clean smell have satisfied
Both her and me. We have culled its cost and quality
Down to the buttons of simulated bone,                                       45

The buttonholes, the sizing, the facing, the characters
Printed in black on neckband and tail. The shape,
The label, the labor, the color, the shade. The shirt.  ✦

---

RESPONDING

1. Imagine that you are a new immigrant to the United States. In a journal entry, describe the kinds of employment opportunities that are open to you. What factors would influence the type of work you would be able to do?

2. Working individually or in a group, research the Triangle Factory fire of 1911. Discuss any parallels between it and sweatshop conditions that exist in our country or in overseas factories where our clothes are made.

3. In an essay, discuss the images of the immigrant worker that Pinsky creates. Is there a connection between the victims of the Triangle Factory fire and the woman who inspected his shirt? Alternatively, compare job opportunities and working conditions for recent U.S. immigrants with those available to European immigrants in the 1890s.

4.   Pinsky wants us to think of the producers of the clothing that we wear. In an essay, discuss the ethical considerations of buying clothing that is produced under substandard working conditions. How do you feel knowing that low clothing costs sometimes result because workers are paid low wages? Do you feel any guilt saving money on clothing, in effect profiting from the poor working conditions of new immigrants or from the low standard of living in developing countries? Or do you believe that manufacturers have the right to keep costs low by employing undocumented or nonunion workers or moving factories to countries where labor is cheaper?

‡

# CONNECTING

### *Critical Thinking and Writing*

1.   Write an essay that explores the difficulties of adjusting to life in a new country. You can use examples from the readings as well as from personal experience.

2.   Compare characters from two stories in this chapter to show the variety of ways early immigrants reacted to the challenges of living in a new country. Analyze the circumstances and the personal qualities of the characters to explain their methods of coping.

3.   An American clergyman, Canon Barnett (1844–1913), stated that "the things which make men alike are finer and better than the things that keep them apart, and that these basic likenesses, if they are properly accentuated, easily transcend the less essential differences of race, language, creed and tradition." Agree or disagree with this statement using evidence from the readings in this chapter as well as from your own experience.

4.   Research your family history and write the story of your family's journey to the United States and their experiences when they arrived in this country. Alternatively, discuss the circumstances surrounding your family's move to the place where they currently live. What were their experiences like?

5.   First- and second-generation Americans often criticize new immigrants for failing to learn English and failing to adopt the American way of doing things. They frequently cite their own parents or grandparents as examples of immigrants who assimilated easily. Write an essay supporting or refuting the idea

that early immigrant groups were more easily absorbed into the country than recent ones. Use examples from your own knowledge and experience as well as evidence from the readings in this chapter.

6. Seller describes a prevalent negative stereotype of immigrant women. Argue that the women portrayed in the other readings in this chapter are or are not modeled on the stereotype.

7. Design your own essay topic that analyzes or compares some aspect from two or more readings in this chapter. Then write an essay on your topic.

8. For some immigrants, Ellis Island was an "Island of Tears," for others "The House of Freedom." Explain the significance of the two names and discuss the selection process that took place at Ellis Island. Was the American government too harsh in its treatment of arriving immigrants? What rationale might there have been for the selection process?

9. Write an essay discussing the difficulties and misunderstandings that can occur between foreign-born parents and children raised in America. Support your points with examples from at least two readings in this book as well as from your own knowledge and experience. See, for example, "The Fat of the Land" and "Facing the Great Desolation" from this chapter, and No-no Boy from chapter 7.

10. Discuss the problems European immigrants faced in the late 1800s and early 1900s, such as poor working and living conditions, difficulty learning the language, lack of government support, and prejudice. Compare their hardships with those of other immigrant groups such as the Japanese, Chinese, Puerto Ricans, or Chicanos.

11. Evidence of folk beliefs and practices occurs when characters prepare love potions, wear charms to ward off evil, or behave in certain ways to avoid bad luck. Compare folk beliefs that appear in "The Fat of the Land" (in this chapter) and Love Medicine (in chapter 2) with those of your own culture. Argue that such beliefs and practices are or are not an important part of all or most cultures.

### For Further Research

1. Review current immigration laws and compare them to laws in the late 1800s and early 1900s. Some issues to consider are the ways in which attitudes have changed as the United States has become more populated, who currently makes up the largest group of immigrants, whether certain groups are more welcome than others, and what policies we should have in the future.

2. Research social legislation that existed to protect children and adults in the United States in the late 1800s and early 1900s. Some questions to consider include:

    a. What were the child labor laws?
    b. Was there compulsory education?
    c. Were unemployment benefits available?
    d. Were working conditions regulated?
    e. Was there a minimum wage?

Expand this topic further by comparing the working person's rights in the late 1800s and early 1900s with workers' rights today. What laws have been enacted to guarantee those rights?

## REFERENCES AND ADDITIONAL SOURCES

Addams, Jane. *Twenty Years at Hull House: With Autobiographical Notes.* New York: Macmillan, 1910, 1967.

———. *Forty Years at Hull House.* New York: Macmillan, 1935.

Barnett, Canon. *Practical Socialism: Essays in Social Reform by the Reverend and Mrs. Samuel A. Barnett.* Freeport, N.Y.: Books for Libraries Press, 1972.

———. *The Ideal City.* Ed. Helen Miller. Leicester University Press, 1979.

Barolini, Helen. *The Dream Book: An Anthology of Writings by Italian American Women.* New York: Shocken, 1985.

Cahan, Abraham. *The Education of Abraham Cahan.* Trans. Leo Stein et al. Philadelphia: Jewish Publication Society of America, 1969.

Daniels, Roger. *Not Like Us: Immigrants and Minorities in America, 1890–1924.* Chicago: Ivan R. Dee, 1997.

Dewey, John. *Democracy and Education: An Introduction to the Philosophy of Education.* New York: The Free Press, 1966.

Dunne, Finley Peter. *Observations by Mr. Dooley.* New York: R. H. Russell, 1902; Harper, 1906.

Ferraro, Thomas. *Ethnic Passages: Literary Immigrants in Twentieth-Century America.* Chicago: University of Chicago Press, 1993.

Fine, David M. "Attitudes Toward Acculturation in the English Fiction of the Jewish Immigrant, 1900–1917." American Jewish Historical Society, Waltham, Mass.

Gardaphe, Fred L. "Italian American Literature." *New Immigrant Literatures in the United States: A Sourcebook to Our Multicultural Literary Heritage.* Ed. Alpana Sharma Knippling. Westport, Conn.: Greenwood Press, 1996, 281–294.

Glenn, Susan Anita. *Daughters of the Shtetl: Life and Labor in the Immigrant Generation.* Ithaca, N.Y.: Cornell University Press, 1990.

Handlin, Oscar. *Race and Nationality in American Life.* Garden City, N.Y.: Doubleday, 1957.

————. *Uprooted: The Epic Story of the Great Migrations That Made the American People.* Boston: Little, Brown, 1951; New York: Grosset & Dunlap, 1957.

Heinze, Andrew R. *Adapting to Abundance: Jewish Immigrants, Mass Consumption, and the Search for American Identity.* New York: Columbia University Press, 1990.

Hoerder, Dirk, ed. *American Labor and Immigration History, 1877–1920s: Recent European Research.* Urbana: University of Illinois Press, 1983.

Jacobson, Matthew Frye. *Special Sorrows: The Diasporic Imagination of Irish, Polish, and Jewish Immigrants in the United States.* Cambridge: Harvard University Press, 1995.

Jones, Maldwyn Allen. *American Immigration.* Chicago: University of Chicago Press, 1960; 2nd ed. 1992.

Kraut, Alan M. *The Huddled Masses: The Immigrant in American Society, 1880–1921.* Arlington Heights, Ill.: Harlan Davidson, 1982.

Luebke, Frederick C. *Germans in the New World: Essays in the History of Immigration.* Urbana: University of Illinois Press, 1990.

Marcuson, Lewis R. *The Stage Immigrant: The Irish, Italians, and Jews in American Drama, 1920–1960.* New York: Garland, 1990.

Matza, Diane, ed. *Sephardic-American Voices: Two Hundred Years of a Literary Legacy.* Hanover, N.H.: University Press of New England for Brandeis University Press, 1997.

McCaffrey, Lawrence J. *The Irish Catholic Diaspora in America.* Washington, D.C.: Catholic University of America Press, 1997.

Miller, Kerby A. *Emigrants and Exiles: Ireland and the Irish Exodus to North America.* New York: Oxford University Press, 1985.

Miller, Wayne Charles. *A Gathering of Ghetto Writers: Irish, Italian, Jewish, Black, and Puerto Rican.* New York: New York University Press, 1972.

Mindel, Charles H., and Robert W. Haberstein, eds. *Ethnic Families in America: Patterns and Variations.* New York: Elsevier, 1976; 3rd ed. 1988.

Sorin, Gerald. *A Time for Building: The Third Migration, 1880–1920.* Baltimore, Md.: Johns Hopkins University Press, 1992.

Taylor, Philip. *The Distant Magnet: European Emigration to the U.S.A.* New York: Harper & Row, 1921; 1972.

Tifft, Wilton, and Thomas Dunne. *Ellis Island.* New York: Norton, 1971.

Yans-McLaughlin, Virginia, ed. *Immigration Reconsidered: History, Sociology, and Politics.* New York: Oxford University Press, 1990.

Zangwill, Israel. *The Melting Pot: Drama in Four Acts.* New York: Arno, 1975.

# 4

# EARLY CHINESE AMERICANS

## *The Lure of the Gold Mountain*

*Above:* Chinese immigrants building the transcontinental railroad,
circa 1866.  *(Asian American Studies Library, University of California at
Berkeley)*
*Opposite:* Chinese immigrants detained at the Angel Island
Immigrants Station.  *(California Historical Society, San Francisco.
FN-18240)*

# SETTING THE HISTORICAL AND CULTURAL CONTEXT

In "Gold Mountain," a poem written by a Chinese immigrant, we hear a warning to others who might want to follow: "Return to the old country quickly / to avoid going astray." These verses, and much of the other writing of the period of early Chinese immigration, establish a clear contrast between the promise of the Gold Mountain—the term applied by the Chinese to California, or more generally, to America itself—and its cost in human terms. Although the Gold Mountain was generally interpreted as representing a land of opportunity that offered an escape from the poverty of China, the term could also suggest more than financial success. Many immigrants planned to return to China after spending time in the United States; the journey to the Gold Mountain provided each sojourner with an opportunity to improve his social position at home. Too often, however, their dreams were unfulfilled. As the Gold Mountain poems in this chapter suggest, rather than finding riches in the United States, many immigrants found themselves targets of prejudice and often treated like criminals. Despite these challenges, Chinese immigrants did more than survive: they helped enrich the cultural heritage of the United States. In order to understand these pressures and the Chinese immigrant community's response to them, we need to examine briefly the circumstances of the immigrants' arrival in America.

The Chinese first arrived in the United States in great numbers between 1849 and 1870. Most came from the area of Kwangtung, a province on China's south coast and a noted commercial region. Because Kwangtung was a port city, its residents were kept informed about distant events through contact with people from around the world. Upon hearing about the gold rush in California, many residents decided to leave Kwangtung to seek out new opportunities for success in America. A large percentage of those who emigrated were young men who had left their families behind, hoping to return within a few years to share their newly acquired prosperity.

Emigration often involved considerable risk and hardship. Until 1860 the act of emigration violated both Chinese custom and imperial law; those apprehended were subject to capital punishment. Once under way, life aboard ship tested the passengers' endurance—quarters were cramped and food supplies were often inadequate. For many immigrants the struggle did not end when they arrived in California; like the newcomers discussed in chapter 1, Chinese immigrants typically underwent a series of medical tests and interrogation sessions at the immigration headquarters. As Sui Sin Far's story "In the Land of the Free" and Connie Young Yu's essay about her grandmother make clear, the intake process itself, with its apparently arbitrary laws, made immigrants endure lengthy periods of separation from their children and other forms of exploitation.

During the first twenty years of Chinese immigration, many new arrivals moved quickly from the West Coast to jobs inland. Generally, they served first as contract workers, laboring to repay sponsoring managers for the costs of their passage. Although a small number of Chinese workers found employment in New England or in the South, most remained in the West, journeying inland to the gold mines of the Sierra Nevada Mountains. Many Chinese immigrants worked in the mines; others provided laundry and cooking services at the mining camps.

Though there were wages to be made, the Chinese experienced great hardship in the mining camps. Maxine Hong Kingston's narrative reveals the dehumanizing nature of the work required of the sojourners, who were sent down mountains in baskets to plant explosives and, later, into the mines to "bite like a rat through that mountain." Moreover, the tensions between immigrants and whites at work sites sometimes became violent.

In the society at large, Chinese immigrant workers were subjected to unfair legislation. Discriminatory taxes, later ruled unconstitutional by the U.S. Supreme Court, were levied by the state of California on the income of Chinese workers. Despite these obstacles, many Chinese contributed significantly to the labor force at the time. They earned the praise of business and governmental leaders alike for their ability to perform difficult and dangerous tasks. In 1871, for example, a U.S. commission designated to report on the mining industry praised the efficiency and courage of Chinese immigrant workers.

After the gold rush had ended, some immigrants found work in other kinds of mines, but many more immigrants were employed in building the transcontinental railroad. Railroad executives were so impressed by the efficiency and high standards of the Chinese workers that they sent emissaries to Kwangtung province to recruit additional workers. During the last years of the construction (1865–1869), the great majority of railroad construction workers were Chinese immigrants. Although there was some acknowledgement of the contributions made by the Chinese laborers, their images are absent from the photographs made to commemorate the completion of the transcontinental railroad. The issue of recognition is examined in the piece by Maxine Hong Kingston, while she also explores conflicts between agency and ownership, self-sacrifice and reward. Moreover, as several of the selections suggest, an individual's success was often determined less by his or her own ambition than by the judgments and prejudices of others.

When the railroad construction project concluded, Chinese immigrants sought other work. Some moved to the San Joaquin Valley, where they applied their skills to a large land reclamation project. Others working in agriculture helped to cultivate California's citrus crops and to develop new strains of fruit. Still other immigrants settled on the coast, where they worked to establish fisheries. By the 1870s, however, the vast majority of Chinese immigrants had settled in urban areas.

The most important of these urban areas during the nineteenth century was San Francisco's Chinatown. This section underwent dramatic growth during the period after the completion of the Union Pacific Railroad. Chinatown offered a place to live during times when immigrants were able to find work in the larger society. It also offered a place of refuge during times of persecution. When immigrants were forced out of other areas of employment, Chinatown provided them with a place where they could establish their own small businesses and enterprises.

But Chinatown was more than a refuge. It was a social, political, and cultural center. By the mid-1850s it had its own theater. By the 1890s Chinatown had, in addition to its many bookstores and locally published periodicals, the first bilingual daily newspaper in the nation. Literary societies and political, fraternal, and social organizations flourished. Other Chinatowns developed in other urban centers as Chinese settlers moved down the California coast and took the railroad east to New York City and Boston.

Like many other communities settled right after the gold rush, Chinatown also had its share of social problems, specifically prostitution, gambling, and the opium trade. The circumstances of the immigrants' lives sometimes exacerbated common problems. The immigrants' resort to prostitutes can be partially attributed to state and federal laws barring Chinese men from having their wives join them in the United States or from marrying non-Asians.

Although Chinatown provided a community based on shared language and tradition, it could offer its inhabitants little protection from the virulent anti-Chinese sentiment that had become more pronounced at the end of the nineteenth century. This backlash was in part the result of an economic depression. With the mines exhausted and railroad construction completed, there was less work for the pool of available laborers. The railroad the Chinese immigrants had helped to construct added to their problems by bringing to the West Coast many workers who were not able to find work in the east. As in other periods, those who were unemployed sometimes blamed their situation not on the economics of the day, but on the Chinese immigrants, who they claimed would work for a cheaper wage. As a result of this misperception and the widely held prejudices of the time, Chinese immigrants continued to be scapegoated for economic problems that were out of their control.

The prevalent atmosphere allowed nativist and protectionist organizations to be formed throughout the west. These groups exerted pressure on governmental officials at all levels to exclude Chinese immigrants, who had already settled in the United States, from employment and to bar new Chinese immigrants from entering the country. Ironically, this call for sanctions was sometimes led by persons who had immigrated to America only years before, the most notable example of whom was Denis Kearney, an Irish immigrant who had founded the Workingmen's Party. This San Francisco–based organization had as its goal the exclusion of Asian workers from American commerce.

Media coverage intensified prevailing exclusionary sentiments. Historians have traced anti-immigrant news stories as far back as the Civil War period— the *New York Times*, for example, ran a series of purported news stories in the 1860s, warning about the influx of Chinese immigrants. By the 1890s, western papers, including the *San Francisco Chronicle*, further sensationalized the issue by advertising and then offering in-depth coverage of rallies and other media events organized by nativist and protectionist factions such as the Workingmen's Party.

The pressure exerted by media and special-interest groups was felt by many politicians of the period. Some ran on nativist or exclusionary platforms; others became more exclusionary over time. Leland Stanford, who, as the head of the Union Pacific Railroad, had praised Chinese workers, became less tolerant of immigrants when he served as California governor and U.S. senator.

Exclusionary legislation was passed at the local, state, and federal levels. In San Francisco, for example, schools were ordered to be racially segregated. In addition to leveling discriminatory taxes against the Chinese, the state of California passed laws prohibiting Asians from obtaining business licenses or owning real estate. On the federal level, the Scott Act (1888) prohibited Chinese laborers who had returned to China from being readmitted to the United States.

The most damaging piece of discriminatory legislation passed during this period, however, was the federal Exclusion Act of 1882, which prohibited Chinese nationals from entering the United States. After the Exclusion Act's passage, some immigrants entered the country from Mexico or Canada; a small number of others claimed to be among those categories of immigrants exempted from the Exclusion Act. By and large, however, the Exclusion Act virtually halted immigration to the United States from China until 1943.

The passage of the Exclusion Act was particularly deplorable, given the way in which the Chinese government had welcomed American nationals as early as the 1840s. Indeed, in 1841 the Chinese granted rather extensive unilateral rights to American citizens entering China; the Americans were not required to reciprocate. Later, however, negotiators representing the Chinese government insisted that their subjects be guaranteed certain basic rights in America. The Burlingame Treaty, negotiated in the 1860s, provided Chinese nationals with the immigration and employment rights accorded to persons from "a most favored nation." The Exclusion Act was thus a clear violation of the Burlingame Treaty.

After the passage of the Exclusion Act, Chinese nationals who had attempted to enter the United States legally were routinely detained for questioning; after 1910 they were held at Angel Island in San Francisco Bay. During their detention at the facility, the immigrants were examined and questioned. Those who were able to convince the examiners of their right to be in the country were admitted; those who could not were deported. The process of examining immigrants often took months. Whatever the duration, detainees were forced to live in squalid quarters and eat substandard food. Family members were separated by gender for the duration of the stay, and detainees were allowed no visitors. Even though the Angel Island facility had been declared "uninhabitable" as early as 1920, it remained in operation until the 1940s. Inmates protested the deplorable living conditions in poems written on the barrack walls. These works, first transcribed in 1910, provide a record of the suffering endured by many Chinese nationals. In many of these poems, the promise of America is contrasted with the intolerance that immigrants encountered upon arrival.

The image of Angel Island has an important place both in the writing of nineteenth-century Chinese immigrants and in that of their descendents. In the selection from *Homebase* included in this chapter, Shawn Wong describes his return to the island that he calls his "grandfather's land." He offers images of chain-link fences, broken windows, and glass underfoot. His connection with the poetry of Angel Island is tactile:

> If you run your fingers across the walls at night in the dark, your fingers will
> be filled with the splinters of poems carved into the walls. Maybe there is
> a dim light to help see what your fingers feel. But you can only read, "Staying
> on this island, my sorrow increases with the days / my face is growing sallow
> and body is getting thin," before your fingers give out following the grooves
> and gouges of the characters. (184)

As the narrative continues the speaker assumes the role of his grandfather, who has testified before two immigration officials. In this way, the speaker uses refashioned and reimagined images of the homeland to reflect on the reciprocal roles of the insider and the exiled.

The Exclusion Act, which was renewed in 1892, remained in effect until 1943. It was not until that late date that the U.S. government altered its treatment of immigrants from China, and even then, this change was due less to a change of heart than a change in strategic interests. As the entry of the United States into World War II became more likely, American military strategists sought to strengthen its alliances in Asia. Improvement of relations with China thus became extremely important. The repeal of the Exclusion Act was thus a part of the nation's attempt to improve its international strategic position.

During the first years after the repeal of the Exclusion Act, however, only a token number of Chinese—approximately one hundred—were allowed to immigrate to the United States each year. In 1945 immigration laws were relaxed somewhat to allow the foreign spouses of American soldiers to immigrate. Another law, passed in 1947, allowed approximately one thousand more Chinese nationals entry into the United States. During the next forty years these numbers increased dramatically with the easing of American immigration restrictions and the change of government in China. Some Chinese fled their homeland after the Communist victory in 1949; others left during the Cultural Revolution of the 1970s. More recently, Chinese young people who had come to the United States to study sought and were granted political asylum after the massacre at Tiananmen Square in 1989.

Several of the works included in this chapter highlight the literary production of Chinese Americans from their earliest work in English to the fiction of Maxine Hong Kingston, Shawn Wong, and Amy Tan. In "In the Land of the Free," a short story published as part of a collection in 1912, Sui Sin Far contrasts the promise of America with the actual experience of newcomers. Amy Ling's essay, included in this chapter, raises the issues of context and identity by reflecting on the use of pseudonyms for both Sui Sin Far and her sister and the ways in which such roles affect their writing and its reception by a variety of audiences. Maxine Hong Kingston has achieved both critical and commercial success for several decades; this notwithstanding, her work has also been criticized by some, most notably perhaps Frank Chin for its construction of its audience and its representation of males. Amy Tan's first novel, *The Joy Luck Club*, was commercially successful, and was made into a feature-length film directed by Ang Lee. The appeal of both the book and the film was intercultural, though also not without its critics. Whether written a century ago or during more recent times, the works included in this chapter invite us to consider both the key issues raised by each author and the sense of an audience that each work projects.

## BEGINNING: Pre-reading/Writing

*Working in a group, use your knowledge of early Chinese immigrants gained from the introduction to this chapter, other books, media, or the Internet, as well as personal experience, to try to construct profiles of some of the first Chinese immigrants to California. Consider gender, age, marital status, economic status, skills or profession, and reasons for immigrating. Share your profiles with the class. What type of person do you think would have made the journey from China to a foreign land in the mid-1800s?*

*The Chinese Exclusion Act barred Chinese nationals, with very few exceptions, from entering the United States. For the first time in American history, immigrants were excluded because of their country of origin. Congress passed the Act after much lobbying by nativist and protectionist groups such as Denis Kearney's Workingmen's Party. The Chinese Exclusion Act was later renewed and remained in effect until 1943.*

⁜

# *From* THE CHINESE EXCLUSION ACT

## *May 6, 1882. CHAP. 126.—An act to execute certain treaty stipulations relating to Chinese.*

1  WHEREAS, IN THE OPINION OF THE Government of the United States the coming of Chinese laborers to this country endangers the good order of certain localities within the territory thereof: Therefore,

2  *Be it enacted by the Senate and House of Representatives of the United States of America in Congress assembled,* That from and after the expiration of ninety days next after the passage of this act, and until the expiration of ten years next after the passage of this act, the coming of Chinese laborers to the United States be, and the same is hereby, suspended; and during such suspension it shall not be lawful for any Chinese laborer to come, or, having so come after the expiration of said ninety days, to remain within the United States.

3  SEC. 2. That the master of any vessel who shall knowingly bring within the United States on such vessel, and land or permit to be landed, any Chinese laborer, from any foreign port or place, shall be deemed guilty of a misdemeanor, and on conviction thereof shall be punished by a fine of not more than five hundred dollars for each and every such Chinese laborer so brought, and may also be imprisoned for a term not exceeding one year.

4  SEC. 3. That the two foregoing sections shall not apply to Chinese laborers who were in the United States on the seventeenth day of November, eighteen hundred and eighty, or who shall have come into the same before the expiration of ninety days next after the passage of this act, and who shall produce to such master before going on board such vessel, and shall produce to the collector of the port in the United States at which such vessel shall arrive, the evidence hereinafter in this act required of his being one of the laborers in this section mentioned; nor shall the two foregoing sections apply to the case of any master whose vessel, being bound to a port not within the United States, shall come within the jurisdiction of the United States by reason of being in distress or in stress of weather, or touching at any port of the United States on its voyage to

any foreign port or place: *Provided*, That all Chinese laborers brought on such vessel shall depart with the vessel on leaving port.

### *April 29, 1902. CHAP. 641.—An act to prohibit the coming into and to regulate the residence within the United States, its Territories, and all territory under its jurisdiction, and the District of Columbia, of Chinese and persons of Chinese descent.*

*Be it enacted by the Senate and House of Representatives of the United States of America in Congress assembled,* That all laws now in force prohibiting and regulating the coming of Chinese persons, and persons of Chinese descent, into the United States, and the residence of such persons therein, including sections five, six, seven, eight, nine, ten, eleven, thirteen, and fourteen of the Act entitled "An Act to prohibit the coming of Chinese laborers into the United States" approved September thirteenth, eighteen hundred and eighty-eight, be, and the same are hereby, re-enacted, extended, and continued so far as the same are not inconsistent with treaty obligations, until otherwise provided by law, and said laws shall also apply to the island territory under the jurisdiction of the United States, and prohibit the immigration of Chinese laborers, not citizens of the United States, from such island territory to the mainland territory of the United States, whether in such island territory at the time of cession or not, and from one portion of the island territory of the United States to another portion of said island territory: *Provided, however,* That said laws shall not apply to the transit of Chinese laborers from one island to another island of the same group; and any islands within the jurisdiction of any State or the District of Alaska shall be considered a part of the mainland under this section.

SEC. 2. That the Secretary of the Treasury is hereby authorized and empowered to make and prescribe, and from time to time to change, such rules and regulations not inconsistent with the laws of the land as he may deem necessary and proper to execute the provisions of this Act and of the Acts hereby extended and continued and of the treaty of December eighth, eighteen hundred and ninety-four, between the United States and China, and with the approval of the President to appoint such agents as he may deem necessary for the efficient execution of said treaty and said Acts.

SEC. 3. That nothing in the provisions of this Act or any other Act shall be construed to prevent, hinder, or restrict any foreign exhibitor, representative, or citizen of any foreign nation, or the holder, who is a citizen of any foreign nation, of any concession or privilege from any fair or exposition authorized by Act of Congress from bringing into the United States, under contract, such mechanics, artisans, agents, or other employees, natives of their respective foreign countries, as they or any of them may deem necessary for the purpose of making preparation for installing or conducting their exhibits or of preparing for installing or conducting any business authorized or permitted under or by virtue of or pertaining to any concession or privilege which may have been or may be granted by any said fair or exposition in connection with such exposition, under such rules and regulations as the Secretary of the Treasury may prescribe, both as to the admission and return of such person or persons.

8    SEC. 4. That it shall be the duty of every Chinese laborer, other than a citizen, rightfully in, and entitled to remain in any of the insular territory of the United States (Hawaii excepted) at the time of the passage of this Act, to obtain within one year thereafter a certificate of residence in the insular territory wherein he resides, which certificate shall entitle him to residence therein, and upon failure to obtain such certificate as herein provided he shall be deported from such insular territory; and the Philippine Commission is authorized and required to make all regulations and provisions necessary for the enforcement of this section in the Philippine Islands, including the form and substance of the certificate of residence so that the same shall clearly and sufficiently identify the holder thereof and enable officials to prevent fraud in the transfer of the same: *Provided, however,* That if said Philippine Commission shall find that it is impossible to complete the registration herein provided for within one year from the passage of this Act, said Commission is hereby authorized and empowered to extend the time for such registration for a further period not exceeding one year.

9    Approved, April 29, 1902. ✢

---

## RESPONDING

1.  Imagine that you are a Chinese immigrant in San Francisco in the late 1800s with a wife in China. Write a letter to your wife explaining the impact of the Chinese Exclusion Act on your life.

2.  Using material from the introduction to this chapter, your own knowledge, the Internet, or sources in your school library, gather information to answer the following questions:

    a. Why were the Chinese invited to the United States in the 1800s?
    b. How many laborers were imported from China?
    c. On what projects did they primarily work?

    Working individually or in a group, use the information gained from the research into the importation of laborers to speculate about the reactions of other groups already in the West.

3.  Write an essay discussing the ways in which the Exclusion Act of 1882 tried to curtail Chinese immigration. Discuss the effect the passage of this act might have had on the Chinese view of America as a land of opportunity.

# *From* THE GOLD MOUNTAIN POEMS

*The Gold Mountain poems are anonymous works written by some of the earliest Chinese immigrants to the United States. It was not until several generations later that the poems were edited by Marlon K. Hom and published by the University of California Press.*

*These three poems express the hardship and discrimination the immigrants faced when arriving in America.*

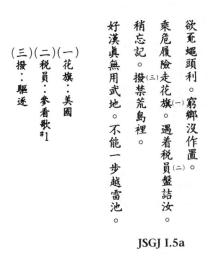

JSGJ I.5a

In search of a pin-head gain,
I was idle in an impoverished village.
I've risked a perilous journey to come to the Flowery
    Flag Nation.
Immigration officers interrogated me:             5
And, just for a slight lapse of memory,
I am deported, and imprisoned in this barren
    mountain.
A brave man cannot use his might here,
And he can't take one step beyond the confines.    10

家貧與米患。貸本來金山(一)。
關員審問脫身難。撥往埃崙(三)如監犯(二)。
到此間。闇室長嗟嘆。
國弱被人多辱慢。儼然畜類任摧殘。

（一）金山：美國
（二）撥：參看歌 #3
（三）埃崙：音譯「島」；
　　　　指天使島

**JSGJ I.14a**

At home I was in poverty,
　　constantly worried about firewood and rice.
I borrowed money
　　to come to Gold Mountain.
5　Immigration officers cross-examined me;
　　no way could I get through.
Deported to this island,
　　like a convicted criminal.
Here—
10　Mournful sighs fill the gloomy room.
A nation weak; her people often humiliated
Like animals, tortured and destroyed at others'
　　whim.

JSGJ I.13b

So, liberty is your national principle;
Why do you practice autocracy?
You don't uphold justice, you Americans,
You detain me in prison, guard me closely.
Your officials are wolves and tigers,                    5
All ruthless, all wanting to bite me.
An innocent man implicated, such an injustice!
When can I get out of this prison and free
    my mind? ✙

---

RESPONDING

1.  Unlike most of the poetry in this book, these poems were not written by
    professional poets who wanted to publish their work but by immigrants who
    used poetry as a way of understanding their own experiences and expressing
    their feelings about them. Write a poem about some experience that affected
    you strongly, or write a journal entry discussing the benefits of writing as
    an emotional outlet.

2.  Working in groups, discuss the attitude of the speakers in each of these
    poems. How does each feel about the U.S. government? Report your
    findings to the class.

3.  We don't know why the speaker in the second poem is imprisoned. Using
    material from the chapter introduction and your own knowledge, write a

story about the circumstances that might have caused him to be "deported to this island, like a convicted criminal."

4.   Drawing on your knowledge, the chapter introduction, or other sources, write a letter from a government official to a San Francisco newspaper justifying the imprisonment of the speaker in the second poem. Or write an editorial for a San Francisco newspaper condemning the treatment of prisoners held on Angel Island.

# SUI SIN FAR

*Sui Sin Far is a pseudonym assumed by the writer Edith Maude Eaton. Born in 1867, Edith Eaton was the eldest of fourteen children of a Chinese mother and an English father. Her earliest jobs included work in stenography and in the advertising department of a railroad company. Most of her stories were published in such magazines as* The Overland Monthly, Century, *and* Good Housekeeping. *She died in 1909.*

*The stories of Sui Sin Far are among the first works published by an Asian American author. "In the Land of the Free," which explores the consequences of the immigration process for one family, also depicts the family's vulnerability to exploitation by unscrupulous people.*

⁜

# IN THE LAND OF THE FREE

## *I*

1   "SEE, LITTLE ONE—the hills in the morning sun. There is thy home for years to come. It is very beautiful and thou wilt be very happy there."

2   The Little One looked up into his mother's face in perfect faith. He was engaged in the pleasant occupation of sucking a sweetmeat; but that did not prevent him from gurgling responsively.

3   "Yes, my olive bud; there is where thy father is making a fortune for thee. Thy father! Oh, wilt thou not be glad to behold his dear face. 'Twas for thee I left him."

4   The Little One ducked his chin sympathetically against his mother's knee. She lifted him on to her lap. He was two years old, a round, dimple-cheeked boy with bright brown eyes and a sturdy little frame.

5   "Ah! Ah! Ah! Ooh! Ooh! Ooh!" puffed he, mocking a tugboat steaming by.

San Francisco's waterfront was lined with ships and steamers, while other   6
craft, large and small, including a couple of white transports from the Philippines, lay at anchor here and there off shore. It was some time before the *Eastern
Queen* could get docked, and even after that was accomplished, a lone Chinaman
who had been waiting on the wharf for an hour was detained that much longer
by men with the initials U.S.C. on their caps, before he could board the steamer
and welcome his wife and child.

"This is thy son," announced the happy Lae Choo.   7

Hom Hing lifted the child, felt of his little body and limbs, gazed into his   8
face with proud and joyous eyes; then turned inquiringly to a customs officer at
his elbow.

"That's a fine boy you have there," said the man. "Where was he born?"   9

"In China," answered Hom Hing, swinging the Little One on his right   10
shoulder, preparatory to leading his wife off the steamer.

"Ever been to America before?"   11

"No, not he," answered the father with a happy laugh.   12

The customs officer beckoned to another.   13

"This little fellow," said he, "is visiting America for the first time."   14

The other customs officer stroked his chin reflectively.   15

"Good day," said Hom Hing.   16

"Wait!" commanded one of the officers. "You cannot go just yet."   17

"What more now?" asked Hom Hing.   18

"I'm afraid," said the customs officer, "that we cannot allow the boy to go   19
ashore. There is nothing in the papers that you have shown us—your wife's
papers and your own—having any bearing upon the child."

"There was no child when the papers were made out," returned Hom Hing.   20
He spoke calmly; but there was apprehension in his eyes and in his tightening
grip on his son.

"What is it? What is it?" quavered Lae Choo, who understood a little   21
English.

The second customs officer regarded her pityingly.   22

"I don't like this part of the business," he muttered.   23

The first officer turned to Hom Hing and in an official tone of voice, said:   24

"Seeing that the boy has no certificate entitling him to admission to this   25
country you will have to leave him with us."

"Leave my boy!" exclaimed Hom Hing.   26

"Yes; he will be well taken care of, and just as soon as we can hear from   27
Washington, he will be handed over to you."

"But," protested Hom Hing, "he is my son."   28

"We have no proof," answered the man with a shrug of his shoulders; "and   29
even if so we cannot let him pass without orders from the Government."

"He is my son," reiterated Hom Hing, slowly and solemnly. "I am a Chinese   30
merchant and have been in business in San Francisco for many years. When my
wife told to me one morning that she dreamed of a green tree with spreading

branches and one beautiful red flower growing thereon, I answered her that I wished my son to be born in our country, and for her to prepare to go to China. My wife complied with my wish. After my son was born my mother fell sick and my wife nursed and cared for her; then my father, too, fell sick, and my wife also nursed and cared for him. For twenty moons my wife care for and nurse the old people, and when they did they bless her and my son, and I send for her to return to me. I had no fear of trouble. I was a Chinese merchant and my son was my son."

31  "Very good, Hom Hing," replied the first officer. "Nevertheless, we take your son."

32  "No, you not take him; he my son too."

33  It was Lae Choo. Snatching the child from his father's arms she held and covered him with her own.

34  The officers conferred together for a few moments; then one drew Hom Hing aside and spoke in his ear.

35  Resignedly Hom Hing bowed his head, then approached his wife. "'Tis the law," said he, speaking in Chinese, "and 'twill be but for a little while—until tomorrow's sun arises."

36  "You, too," reproached Lae Choo in a voice eloquent with pain. But accustomed to obedience she yielded the boy to her husband, who in turn delivered him to the first officer. The Little One protested lustily against the transfer; but his mother covered her face with her sleeve and his father silently led her away. Thus was the law of the land complied with.

## II

37  Day was breaking. Lae Choo, who had been awake all night, dressed herself, then awoke her husband.

38  "'Tis the morn," she cried. "Go, bring our son."

39  The man rubbed his eyes and arose upon his elbow so that he could see out of the window. A pale star was visible in the sky. The petals of a lily in a bowl on the windowsill were unfurled.

40  "'Tis not yet time," said he, laying his head down again.

41  "Not yet time. Ah, all the time that I lived before yesterday is no so much as the time that has been since my Little One was taken from me."

42  The mother threw herself down beside the bed and covered her face.

43  Hom Hing turned on the light, and touching his wife's bowed head with a sympathetic hand inquired if she had slept.

44  "Slept!" she echoed, weepingly. "Ah, how could I close my eyes with my arms empty of the little body that has filled them every night for more than twenty moons! You do not know—man—what it is to miss the feel of the little fingers and the little toes and the soft round limbs of your little one. Even in the darkness his darling eyes used to shine up to mine, and often have I fallen into slumber with his pretty babble at my ear. And now, I see him not; I touch him not; I hear him not. My baby, my little fat one!"

"Now! Now! Now!" consoled Hom Hing, patting his wife's shoulder re-   45
assuringly; "there is no need to grieve so; he will soon gladden you again. There
cannot be any law that would keep a child from its mother!"

Lae Choo dried her tears.   46

"You are right, my husband," she meekly murmured. She arose and stepped   47
about the apartment, setting things to rights. The box of presents she had
brought for her California friends had been opened the evening before; and
silks, embroideries, carved ivories, ornamental lacquer-ware, brasses, camphor-
wood boxes, fans, and chinaware were scattered around in confused heaps. In
the midst of unpacking the thought of her child in the hands of strangers had
overpowered her, and she had left everything to crawl into bed and weep.

Having arranged her gifts in order she stepped out on to the deep balcony.   48

The star had faded from view and there were bright streaks in the western   49
sky. Lae Choo looked down the street and around. Beneath the flat occupied
by her and her husband were quarters for a number of bachelor Chinamen, and
she could hear them from where she stood, taking their early morning breakfast.
Below their dining-room was her husband's grocery store. Across the way was
a large restaurant. Last night it had been resplendent with gay colored lanterns
and the sound of music. The rejoicings over "the completion of the moon," by
Quong Sum's firstborn, had been long and loud, and had caused her to tie a
handkerchief over her ears. She, a bereaved mother, had it not in her heart to
rejoice with other parents. This morning the place was more in accord with her
mood. It was still and quiet. The revellers had dispersed or were asleep.

A roly-poly woman in black sateen, with long pendant earrings in her ears,   50
looked up from the street below and waved her a smiling greeting. It was her
old neighbor, Kuie Hoe, the wife of the gold embosser, Mark Sing. With her
was a little boy in yellow jacket and lavender pantaloons. Lae Choo remembered
him as a baby. She used to like to play with him in those days when she had no
child of her own. What a long time ago that seemed! She caught her breath in
a sigh, and laughed instead.

"Why are you so merry?" called her husband from within.   51

"Because my Little One is coming home," answered Lae Choo. "I am a   52
happy mother—a happy mother."

She pattered into the room with a smile on her face.   53

The noon hour had arrived. The rice was steaming in the bowls and a fragrant   54
dish of chicken and bamboo shoots was awaiting Hom Hing. Not for one
moment had Lae Choo paused to rest during the morning hours; her activity had been ceaseless. Every now and again, however, she had raised her eyes
to the gilded clock on the curiously carved mantelpiece. Once, she had exclaimed:

"Why so long, oh! why so long?" Then, apostrophizing herself: "Lae Choo,   55
be happy. The Little One is coming! The Little One is coming!" Several times
she burst into tears, and several times she laughed aloud.

Hom Hing entered the room; his arms hung down by his side.   56

57    "The Little One!" shrieked Lae Choo.

58    "They bid me call tomorrow."

59    With a moan the mother sank to the floor.

60    The noon hour passed. The dinner remained on the table.

### III

61    The winter rains were over: the spring had come to California, flushing the hills with green and causing an ever-changing pageant of flowers to pass over them. But there was no spring in Lae Choo's heart, for the Little One remained away from her arms. He was being kept in a mission. White women were caring for him, and though for one full moon he had pined for his mother and refused to be comforted he was now apparently happy and contented. Five moons or five months had gone by since the day he had passed with Lae Choo through the Golden Gate; but the great Government at Washington still delayed sending the answer which would return him to his parents.

62    Hom Hing was disconsolately rolling up and down the balls in his abacus box when a keen-faced young man stepped into his store.

63    "What news?" asked the Chinese merchant.

64    "This!" The young man brought forth a typewritten letter. Hon Hing read the words:

65    "Re Chinese child, alleged to be the son of Hom Hing, Chinese merchant, doing business at 425 Clay Street, San Francisco.

66    "Same will have attention as soon as possible."

67    Hom Hing returned the letter, and without a word continued his manipulation of the counting machine.

68    "Have you anything to say?" asked the young man.

69    "Nothing. They have sent the same letter fifteen times before. Have you not yourself showed it to me?"

70    "True!" The young man eyed the Chinese merchant furtively. He had a proposition to make and was pondering whether or not the time was opportune.

71    "How is your wife?" he inquired solicitously—and diplomatically.

72    Hom Hing shook his head mournfully.

73    "She seems less every day," he replied. "Her food she takes only when I bid her and her tears fall continuously. She finds no pleasure in dress or flowers and cares not to see her friends. Her eyes stare all night. I think before another moon she will pass into the land of spirits."

74    "No!" exclaimed the young man, genuinely startled.

75    "If the boy not come home I lose my wife sure," continued Hom Hing with bitter sadness.

76    "It's not right," cried the young man indignantly. Then he made his proposition.

77    The Chinese father's eyes brightened exceedingly.

78    "Will I like you to go to Washington and make them give you the paper

to restore my son?" cried he. "How can you ask when you know my heart's desire?"

"Then," said the young fellow, "I will start next week. I am anxious to see this thing through if only for the sake of your wife's peace of mind."                    79

"I will call her. To hear what you think to do will make her glad," said Hom Hing.                    80

He called a message to Lae Choo upstairs through a tube in the wall.                    81

In a few moments she appeared, listless, wan, and hollow-eyed; but when her husband told her the young lawyer's suggestion she became electrified; her form straightened, her eyes glistened; the color flushed to her cheeks.                    82

"Oh," she cried, turning to James Clancy. "You are a hundred man good!"                    83

The young man felt somewhat embarrassed; his eyes shifted a little under the intense gaze of the Chinese mother.                    84

"Well, we must get your boy for you," he responded. "Of course"—turning to Hom Hing—"it will cost a little money. You can't get fellows to hurry the Government for you without gold in your pocket."                    85

Hom Hing stared blankly for a moment. Then: "How much do you want, Mr. Clancy?" he asked quietly.                    86

"Well, I will need at least five hundred to start with."                    87

Hom Hing cleared his throat.                    88

"I think I told to you the time I last paid you for writing letters for me and seeing the Custom boss here that nearly all I had was gone!"                    89

"Oh, well then we won't talk about it, old fellow. It won't harm the boy to stay where he is, and your wife may get over it all right."                    90

"What that you say?" quavered Lae Choo.                    91

James Clancy looked out of the window.                    92

"He says," explained Hom Hing in English, "that to get our boy we have to have much money."                    93

"Money! Oh, yes."                    94

Lae Choo nodded her head.                    95

"I have not got the money to give him."                    96

For a moment Lae Choo gazed wonderingly from one face to the other; then, comprehension dawning upon her, with swift anger, pointing to the lawyer, she cried: "You not one hundred man good; you just common white man."                    97

"Yes, ma'am," returned James Clancy, bowing and smiling ironically.                    98

Hom Hing pushed his wife behind him and addressed the lawyer again: "I might try," said he, "to raise something; but five hundred—it is not possible."                    99

"What about four?"                    100

"I tell you I have next to nothing left and my friends are not rich."                    101

"Very well!"                    102

The lawyer moved leisurely toward the door, pausing on its threshold to light a cigarette.                    103

"Stop, white man; white man, stop!"                    104

105     Lae Choo, panting and terrified, had started forward and now stood beside him, clutching his sleeve excitedly.

106     "You say you can go to get paper to bring my Little One to me if Hom Hing give you five hundred dollars?"

107     The lawyer nodded carelessly; his eyes were intent upon the cigarette which would not take the fire from the match.

108     "Then you go get paper. If Hom Hing not can give you five hundred dollars—I give you perhaps what more that much."

109     She slipped a heavy gold bracelet from her wrist and held it out to the man. Mechanically he took it.

110     "I go get more!"

111     She scurried away, disappearing behind the door through which she had come.

112     "Oh, look here, I can't accept this," said James Clancy, walking back to Hom Hing and laying down the bracelet before him.

113     "It's all right," said Hom Hing, seriously, "pure China gold. My wife's parent give it to her when we married."

114     "But I can't take it anyway," protested the young man.

115     "It is all same as money. And you want money to go to Washington," replied Hom Hing in a matter-of-fact manner.

116     "See, my jade earrings—my gold buttons—my hairpins—my comb of pearl and my rings—one, two, three, four, five rings; very good—very good—all same much money. I give them all to you. You take and bring me paper for my Little One."

117     Lae Choo piled up her jewels before the layer.

118     Hom Hing laid a restraining hand upon her shoulder. "Not all, my wife," he said in Chinese. He selected a ring—his gift to Lae Choo when she dreamed of the tree with the red flower. The rest of the jewels he pushed toward the white man.

119     "Take them and sell them," said he. "They will pay your fare to Washington and bring you back with the paper."

120     For one moment James Clancy hesitated. He was not a sentimental man; but something within him arose against accepting such payment for his services.

121     "They are good, good," pleadingly asserted Lae Choo, seeing his hesitation.

122     Whereupon he seized the jewels, thrust them into his coat pocket, and walked rapidly away from the store.

## *IV*

123     Lae Choo followed after the missionary woman through the mission nursery school. Her heart was beating so high with happiness that she could scarcely breathe. The paper had come at last—the precious paper which gave Hom Hing and his wife the right to the possession of their own child. It was ten months now since he had been taken from them—ten months since the sun had ceased to shine for Lae Choo.

The room was filled with children—most of them wee tots, but none so    124
wee as her own. The mission woman talked as she walked. She told Lae Choo
that little Kim, as he had been named by the school, was the pet of the place,
and that his little tricks and ways amused and delighted every one. He had been
rather difficult to manage at first and had cried much for his mother; "but
children so soon forget, and after a month he seemed quite at home and played
around as bright and happy as a bird."

"Yes," responded Lae Choo. "Oh, yes, yes!"    125

But she did not hear what was said to her. She was walking in a maze of    126
anticipatory joy.

"Wait here, please," said the mission woman, placing Lae Choo in a chair.    127
"The very youngest ones are having their breakfast."

She withdrew for a moment—it seemed like an hour to the mother—then    128
she reappeared leading by the hand a little boy dressed in blue cotton overalls
and white-soled shoes. The little boy's face was round and dimpled and his eyes
were very bright.

"Little One, ah, my Little One!" cried Lae Choo.    129

She fell on her knees and stretched her hungry arms toward her son.    130

But the Little One shrunk from her and tried to hide himself in the folds    131
of the white woman's skirt.

"Go 'way, go 'way!" he bade his mother.  ✠    132

---

RESPONDING

1.  Although the language and writing style of the story is dated, the theme of
    being caught in the trap of official bureaucracy is current. Rewrite the story
    with a contemporary setting. Or write a journal entry about a time when
    you or someone you know had to fight what seemed to be endless red tape.

2.  Working individually or in a group, analyze the motivation and behavior of
    James Clancy. Do you think he is sincerely trying to help Hom Hing? He
    hesitates before taking the jewels in payment for his services. What do you
    think is going through his mind at that moment? Why does he accept them
    as payment? What do you think he should have done? Share your conclu-
    sions with the class.

3.  In an essay, explain the author's choice for the title. What was she trying
    to convey to her readers about America? Is the title ironic? Consider the
    possible response of different readers: readers of the story when it was
    published, native Americans and immigrants, and modern readers.

4.  Write an essay analyzing the way the story illustrates the fears of loss of
    culture and identity that plague many new immigrants to the United States.

# Shawn Wong

*The novelist Shawn Wong, who was born in Oakland, California, in 1949, received his bachelor's degree from the University of California at Berkeley in 1971 and a master's degree from San Francisco State University in 1974. His publications include* Homebase *(1979) and* American Knees *(1995), as well as several important literature anthologies. He was coeditor with Frank Chin and others of the ground-breaking* Aiiieeeee! *(1973), which has been published in several editions. He published* An American Literature: A Brief Introduction and Anthology *in 1995.*

*The following selection from* Homebase *depicts the speaker's present experience in terms of his personal memories and the collective experiences of his descendents. The journey becomes not a single spatial one but a temporal one as well, a pilgrimage to the place of his ancestors' detention.*

⊞

## *From* HOMEBASE

1    THE NIGHT TRAIN STOPPED at the edge of the ocean, the engine steaming into the waves that lapped against the iron wheels. The ocean was humbled in front of the great steaming engine, its great noise was iron; the moonlight on the ocean gave the sea its place, made the water look like waves of rippling steel. There was a low mumble heard beneath the sound of the waves, whose constant voice muted itself against fine sand; the voices of the men came towards me. I could not see their faces smeared with soot, charcoal faces. Their voices moved past me, towards the ocean, yet I was not afraid, I knew them. They had worked all day on the railroad, but at night they built the great iron engine that brought them to the sea's edge, pointed them home, the way west. They climbed down from the engine, faces black with soot, disguised, to dive into the ocean and swim home, but the moonlight hit the waves and made the surf like bones, white in their faces. Their swimming was useless, their strokes made in a desert of broken bones, of bone hitting bone, hollow noises to men who believed in home and hollow noises to men whose black faces held in their souls. But the engine waited in the iron night. And by morning the sun came up like the hot pulsating engine, the earth steams dry as I walk and kneel and wash my face with the earth's breathing, and the Chinamen rise all around me, their faces clean and grim, rising like swiftly rising steam to walk farther into their forest.

2    They go back to work, their eyes red with sea salt, their hands red from

swimming with the broken bone sea. The black from the iron rails comes off on their hands.

I run through a thick night, that night of black soot mixing with my sweat 3 to drip like tears from my face; my heart is the engine's red iron and if I stop running I will be burned. Now the night driver is me. The old night train filled with Chinamen, my grandfathers, fathers, all without lovers, without women, struggling against black iron with hands splintered from coarse cross ties. I am driving my car, moving out of a narrow side road at ninety onto a highway. With my father's spirit I am driving at night. No music. No more dreams. There is only the blur of the white line, the white guard rail at the edges of my sight as I outrun the yellow glare of lights, an ache at the temples and a pulse in the whites of my palms, knowing what is in front of me. I am speaking to the road with the green lights of the car's instruments touching my face, no dreams, just talk, like an ocean's talk, constant, muted against sand, immediate, suffocating. My fingers moving from the steering wheel, through glass, to grab at the blurs of white at one hundred miles an hour. My hands lift me out of my seat to stoop over and grab at the bleached bones of the road. I reach out to take the road in my hands, the blur of bones, no blood, someone speaks and I do not recognize the voice. Piano music rising in my ears like the winds that move across the plains and sweep like rivers, its waves of voice nearing my ear. The memorized picture fades and I am again speaking to myself with my lovers there, mother and father, and I remind myself what I call them. They begin to move. I give her all my weight, my father gives me his hand to hold saying, "We have to run, hold on." And I hold on for the chase, flying, my feet touching ground every six feet, like giants marching over the earth, my father, the track star, the runner giving me all the soul of his life.

I was never old enough to write a letter to my father to tell him how he 4 had shaped my life. So on a night like this I write him a letter. Standing there on the beach, the night train easing up to me, the engine blacker than the night, is blowing steam out to sea. So I write. Dear Father, I am now at home. At our home on the range, our place. It is April. Tonight I remember a humid night on Guam when I held your forehead in my small hands as I rode on your shoulders. My hands felt your ears, the shape of your chin, and the shape of your nose until you became annoyed and placed my hands back on your forehead and shifted my weight on your shoulders. Like a blind man, I remember your face in the darkness. I remember you now with urgency. In this night here I heard the same sounds of a tropical night; the clicking of insects, the scrape of a lizard's claws on the screen door. Because I am now the same age as you are, Father, I remember how you showed me the button holes and buttons of my clothes, the loops needed to tie my shoes. I do not remember whether you admired me then, or remarked to yourself how much I looked like you, or felt satisfied that I would grow into the athlete you were. Tonight I took a long look into your face and saw you smiling. You are twenty-eight years old. At fifteen, when my mother died, I thought my terror would increase with age. The terror that I would not be like you, the terror that I would never admit where my home stood rooted. A woman I love, Father, told me that identity is a word full of the home. Identity is a word that whispers, not whispers, but *gets* you to say, "ever, ever yours."

5      The night train is beside me, spewing steam. I hear iron gates and doors opening and closing, I feel the heat of the engine beside me. The cold ocean waves boil against the hot iron beneath the engine. The waves wet my shoes and my pants at the ankles. The train fills the whole night. It is a wall between the dry beach and the edge of the ocean. Under the legend of this train, the heart of this country lies in immovable granite mountains, and lies in the roots of giant trees. Those roots are sharp talons in the earth of my country. I stand my ground and wave the train on. The train inches by me, heaving up steam, heat, sand, and sea water. The last thing I remember doing tonight is raising my hand to signal the train on. I walk back to the dock where I am making my stand in the night and see the train gather speed, feel it brush by me. I count every car pulled by the engine until all the noise of the night is gone.

6      Now I have the loneliness of fathers. To work from my soul, the heart speaking and pledging a feeling and commitment that gives like my father's giving to his lover, my mother. Not in self-pity, since the dream of Great-Grand-father, whose crying left scars on his face, Dear Father, I say, I write, I sing, I give you my love, this is a letter whispering those words, "ever, ever yours." But you are dead, there is nothing that keeps me, no voice, except that voice plagued by memory and objects of no value, a watch, a ring, a sweater, no movement, "keep it close to the skin," I say to myself. Father, I have dreams of departures, people leaving me, of life losing ground. I cannot control the blood that rushes to my head in the night and makes my dreams red.

7      I am driving at night and the whine of the car's engine rips through second and third gears. The straight road at last, that familiar white blur. A shift at a hundred and ten, deafening my ears. No sound now except for the building whine of my engine, my knees go weak, no blood there. I am too busy for fear, checking oil, rpm's, engine heat, speed at a glance, hands and arms working at the wheel, correcting for wind gusts.

8      I am pointing the car's sloping blue nose at a hundred into the blur of moons. What my eye sees becomes a scream, the scream of moonlight. I take my hands off the road, out of the ocean of bones, my sight returns to that yellow glare of headlights, the car slows to a stop, trembling like the blood at my knees. I move across America picking up ghosts. . . .

9      In the late nights of spring, 1957, my mother drove home from Oak Knoll Naval Hospital, thrashing the night traffic, pushing the little car through its gears, and somehow returned home away from the sleepless daze and the edge of crash. She came home joking about amazing dog stories, traveling across the

desert, oceans, freezing mountains all in the night without food. Her driving at night seemed to her like swimming the currents of a flooded street, her eyes unfocused on the black night, still seeing the white hospital bed, father's pale skin and the light in the hospital's solarium that signaled his dying.

And one night she came home early, not joking, not ready to gather me up in her arms to play. She asked what color I wanted my room painted. And in her black expression I knew that father had died. I started crying. She became angry, not looking at me, and started calling out colors.

My mother taught me how to iron clothes that night. She had a basket full of clothes that had been around for years. The basket never grew or decreased in size. She ironed only what we needed. So when I was seven she told me to iron the back of the collar on my shirt so that the collar won't show wrinkles on the top part that shows. Next, to iron the shoulder area. Then the sleeves. The flap that the buttons are sewn to. Then the left front, the back, and the right front. Hang it up and button the top two buttons. A family tradition had been passed on to me. I don't remember how long I was ironing that night but I ironed all my own shirts. When I had finished ironing my shirts I noticed she had fallen asleep on the couch. I could see her from the kitchen. That was when I started ironing my father's shirts. Most of them were at the bottom of the basket. My father used to send his shirts out to be cleaned and ironed. He would let me put on his huge shirt before he put it on so that I could hear the sound of my hand working its way down the sleeve with that tearing sound because the starch had glued the sleeves shut. He had shirt pockets that held both my hands. I didn't have any starch that night so I ironed his shirts like mine. I folded them all neatly on the kitchen table, ten white shirts, five light blue shirts, two khaki work shirts, two plaid ones. I reached down into the basket and found myself a set of flannel pajamas. I ironed them and put them on. I took the blanket off my bed and squeezed into a small space next to my mother on the couch and fell asleep with her, the blanket trapped the smells of clean and warm cotton with her perfume and her warm breath.

I had said before that I am violent, that I had become a father to myself. But it was my mother that controlled my growing until she too died eight years after my father's death. Not a startling revelation except when I saw her burial and I discovered that she had shaped the style of my manhood in accordance with her own competitive and ambitious self. I grew up watching my mother's face for direction, the movements of her body. The features of her face shaped me. She was thirty-two years old when my father died and I was seven, and when I think of her now I remember her as a young woman and how her growing kept pace with mine. She would not let me be present at my father's funeral, she did not want to be the object of everyone's pity, the mother of a fatherless child, and she did not want my childhood shaped around the ceremony and ritual of a funeral. And now, after I had witnessed her dying in another hospital eight years later and became the prominent figure at her funeral, I did not cry. I did not want everyone's pity for an orphaned fifteen-year-old boy, but kept my eyes on the casket, kept my hands in my pockets and walked quickly through the ceremony of her death.

13 After she died I was no longer anyone's son . . . I was alone, but I did not cry. My sleep tore me apart, and gave her flesh back to me in pieces, her voice with no substance, and finally nothing but a hollow sound would wake me, her jade bracelet knocking against the house as she moved around, cleaning, cooking, writing. It had become for me, in those dreams, the rhythmic beating of her heart. There was no need for me to put my head against her chest to hear the beating of her heart; the cold stone, jade in my eyes, filled my youth and kept time with the unsteady beating of my own heart. . . .

*"Drifting alone in the ocean it suddenly passed autumn."*
—ANGEL ISLAND

14 Now after seeking out all the wrong names to call myself, I've been to those places that can destroy me, I've felt those places overcome me without violence, only my own dreaming brought it on until I was able to say that I am violent and I sought out these places, making them mine.

15 Now I knew that my grandfather's land was an island. He was born in San Francisco but his father, my great-grandfather, sent him back to China for safety. It was 1917 when he came back. And in 1917 Grandfather's island was called Angel Island.

16 My grandfather's land sits in the middle of San Francisco Bay directly in the path of the fog that flows in from the Golden Gate. The fog meets Angel Island and moves around it to hold it and silence it. When the fog lifts and retreats to the sea it will often leave a halo around the peaks of Angel Island.

17 On the north side of the island at Winslow Cove there is a building called P-317—the U.S. Justice Department Immigration detention center for Chinese immigrants. A chain link fence surrounds the building. All the windows are broken yet the frames for the small panes of glass are still in position. Some windows are half open.

18 There is a movement about the place that gives off sound like sleeping gives off dreams, like a haunted house moves people to realize that life still exists within. The sounds I heard as a child in dreams made me deaf but never woke me. Hearing voices waked me.

19 I have to bend back the fence to get near the building. I walk through and release the fence and it springs back into place and rattles against the pole that holds it. There is broken glass everywhere, even on the stairs leading to the door. After I make my way past the sounds under my feet of old wood rotten from the ocean air mixed with breaking glass, I am standing at an open door looking in.

20 Once inside, you will see that the room is lit with bare bulbs hung from the ceiling. You will see that the room is filled with men, women, and children.

There are two lines—men and young boys in one and women and a few very young children in the other. An officer stands between the two lines. Behind a large counter there is an officer for each line. There is some shuffling but no talking except for the two officers behind the counter. You will see that we are dressed in drab jackets, some men are wearing long coats with black pants underneath, others are wearing regular work clothes, and many are wearing flat brim black hats.

You will know why you're standing in line with me. I am my grandfather 21 come back to America after having been raised in China. My father is dead so I've had to assume someone else's name and family in order to legally enter the country. All this information about my new family has been memorized. All my sons after me will have my assumed name.

I was not allowed to ever leave the building, even to go outside. Husbands 22 were not allowed to see their wives or children, who were kept in another part of the building. We ate in different shifts. There were riots in the mess hall and the main building. We had given up everything to come to this country. Many were former citizens. If you run your fingers across the walls at night in the dark, your fingers will be filled with the splinters of poems carved into the walls. Maybe there is a dim light to help see what your fingers feel. But you can only read, "Staying on this island, my sorrow increases with the days / my face is growing sallow and body is getting thin," before your fingers give out following the grooves and gouges of the characters.

Sometimes the morning will show you someone has hung themselves in the 23 night, someone who could no longer bear the waiting, or the interrogation, or failing the interrogation—someone waiting to be sent back to China. Everyone knows how to hang yourself. There are no nails or hooks high enough to hang a piece of cloth from and leap from a stool to a quick death. There is only one way—to tie your piece of cloth on one of those big nails about four and a half feet off the floor, lean against the wall to brace yourself, and bend your knees and hold them up off the floor. Then your bones will be collected and placed on the open seas.

I have memorized someone else's family history, taken someone else's name, 24 and suppressed everything that I have chronicled for myself. The questions begin in the Interrogation Room. It is a room blocked off from the light. The windows are painted black. One immigration officer has a list of questions in his hand and the other has a file folder in front of him with the data given by relatives years ago.

Question:  How large is your village?
Answer:    It has fifty houses.
Question:  How many rows of houses are there?
Answer:    Ten rows.

Question:   Which way does the village face and where is the head?
Answer:     It faces east and the head is south.
Question:   Where is your house located?
Answer:     Second house, third row, counting from the south.
Question:   Do you know who lived in that house before your family?
Answer:     I do not remember.
Question:   How many houses in your row?
Answer:     Five.
Question:   Do all of the houses in your row touch each other?
Answer:     None of them do.
Question:   How far apart are they?
Answer:     About six feet.
Question:   What were the sleeping arrangements in your house when you were
            last in China?
Answer:     My mother, all my brothers, and I occupied the south bedroom.
Question:   How many beds are in the south bedroom?
Answer:     Sometimes two, and sometimes three.
Question:   Please explain that statement.
Answer:     When the weather gets warm, we use three.
Question:   How many steps lead to your front door?
Answer:     None.
Question:   Is there a clock in your house?
Answer:     Yes.
Question:   Describe it.
Answer:     It is wood on the outside. It is brass with a white porcelain face. It
            has brass numbers.
Question:   Where did your mother buy provisions?
Answer:     She buys at the Tin Wo Market.
Question:   How far and in what direction is that from your village?
Answer:     One or two lis west.
Question:   How many of your brothers have attended school?
Answer:     All my brothers.
Question:   Did they attend the same school with you?
Answer:     Yes.
Question:   When did your youngest brother start school?
Answer:     The beginning of this year.
Question:   When did your oldest brother start school?
Answer:     When he was eleven years old.
Question:   When did you quit school?
Answer:     I attended school for six months this year, then I quit.

Question:   Who told you to quit?

Answer:    My mother. She told me to prepare myself to go to the United States.

Question:   When did you first learn that you were to come to the United States of America?

Answer:    About the time my mother told me to quit school.

The officer asking the questions stops for a moment. He puts down the   25
paper he's been reading from and draws out a tobacco pouch and begins to roll a cigarette for himself. He rises from his chair and goes to the window. He licks his cigarette and draws a match out from his pocket and lights his cigarette. The second officer has stopped writing whatever he was writing and puts down his pencil. The first one begins scraping the black paint from a small section of the window. He pulls out his pocket knife, unfolds it, and continues scraping until he has a small peephole. "It's a nice day outside," he says to no one. The room fills with the cigarette smoke. He continues to look out the hole in the window and, absentmindedly, is folding and unfolding his pocket knife. "Where does your mother receive her mail?" He asks with his back still turned to me.

"I don't know."   26

"Who goes after the mail?"   27

"My mother."   28

"Where do you suppose she goes to get it?"   29

"I don't know."   30

"Describe your mother."   31

"She is medium in height and slim in build. She has black hair. She is   32
exuberant, graceful, and stubborn." I see her on no particular day in my mind. Her hair is set in a fashionable wave. She always wore red lipstick, not brilliant red but a darker shade. She used eyebrow pencil even though she didn't need it. She was always looking at her clothes to see if everything was in place, picking lint off, brushing her hand over the material as if to smooth out a wrinkle. She was doing that now as she crossed the street. She had extravagant taste in clothes, not flashy, but suits made of Italian knits, cashmere sweaters, elegant slips.

"Does your mother wear any jewelry?"   33

"Yes."   34

"Describe it."   35

"It is a dark green jade bracelet. She wears it on her right wrist. I can hear   36
her working around the house when she has it on because it knocks against everything she touches. I've felt it touching my skin many times."

The officer turns from the window to face me. He steps towards me, but I   37
do not see him move towards me. I'm gazing out of the small hole he's carved in the window.

"Have you ever seen a photograph of your father?"   38

"Yes. Yes, it was taken on a day like today. He is seated in a wooden chair   39 on a lawn somewhere next to a wooden table with a heart-shaped hole. . . ." I see my father sleeping on a cot. It is night and the air around me is brilliantly cold. There is snow outside.

40    Then the poor men filled the island with their smells, filled the yellow glow of the bare light in the building. Their fists rose like clubs. Then I smelled the rotting wood of the building and I rose with them. I moved with them through the barracks screaming at the doors until the taste of metal came to my tongue. We beat at the steel doors until they broke loose from the wooden building. Then water came rushing in pushing us back. Ocean water from a fire hose pushed at us until we were all huddled in the corners of the bunk room. The doors closed again.

41    After the riot of blood, a man was beaten and thrown into isolation. And beaten again and again until I could hear his flesh break like glass, cutting him deeper and the salt of his sweat moved like dark worms in his wound.

42    On days like today, the glass is merely under my feet and I pick the pieces up like I'm collecting bones. This is my home base, my Rainsford, California. I place the glass in a small pile on the floor and rise up to the window. On days like today, I will remember the time I took the rotting wooden windowsill in my hands and tore it to shreds. It crumbled like bone marrow. The window is open.

43    On days like today, I hear someone moving through the chain link fence, something she's wearing strikes a note on the fence post and as the vibration fades away, she moves through. ✛

---

RESPONDING

1.  In a journal entry, describe a significant member of your family. Explain how he or she influences your thinking or way of looking at the world.

2.  Working individually or in a group, outline the important events in the history of the Chinese in the United States. Use information from the readings, the Internet, or your own knowledge.

3.  In an essay, describe the physical and psychological characteristics of the narrator of this story. Consider when and where the story is taking place.

4.  In this excerpt Wong creates a world where the past and present intersect. Choose some people or events from your past to write a similar piece that illuminates something from your personal history.

# MAXINE HONG KINGSTON

*Maxine Hong Kingston was born in Stockton, California, in 1940, the daughter of Chinese immigrants. Kingston attended the University of California at Berkeley, earning her bachelor's degree in 1962 and later a teaching certificate. After college she taught high school English in California and Hawaii, then college English in Hawaii.*

*Kingston's first book,* The Woman Warrior: Memoirs of a Girlhood Among Ghosts, *was published in 1976. Combining realism and fantasy,* The Woman Warrior *tells Kingston's mother's story, describing her life as a medical student in China and then as an immigrant to the United States. It was awarded the National Book Critics Circle Award in 1976. Kingston has also published the novel* Tripmaster Monkey: His Fake Book *(1989), which is set in Berkeley, California, during the 1960s.*

*Kingston considers* China Men *the companion volume to* The Woman Warrior. China Men *relates some of the experiences of the male family members who often immigrated first to make a home for their families in the new land. This volume received the American Book Award in 1981. The following chapter from* China Men *describes Kingston's grandfather's experiences while working in the mines and building the railroads. In fictional and nonfictional episodes, the chapter dramatizes the immigrants' struggles for success. In describing the sacrifice and determination required of these men, it also reflects on the legacy they have left their descendents.*

╬

# THE GRANDFATHER OF THE SIERRA NEVADA MOUNTAINS

THE TRAINS USED TO CROSS THE SKY. The house jumped and dust shook down from the attic. Sometimes two trains ran parallel going in opposite directions; the railroad men walked on top of the leaning cars, stepped off one train onto the back of the other, and traveled the opposite way. They headed for the caboose while the train moved against their walk, or they walked toward the engine while the train moved out from under their feet. Hoboes ran alongside, caught the ladders, and swung aboard. I would have to learn to ride like that, choose my boxcar, grab a ladder at a run, and fling myself up and sideways into an open door. Elsewhere I would step smoothly off. Bad runaway boys lost their legs trying for such rides. The train crunched past—pistons stroking like elbows and knees, the coal cars dropping coal, cows looking out between the slats of the cattlecars, the boxcars almost stringing together sentences—Hydro-Cushion, Georgia Flyer, Route of the Eagle—and suddenly sunlight filled the windows again, the slough wide again and waving with tules, for which the city was once named; red-winged blackbirds and squirrels settled. We children ran to the tracks and found the nails we'd placed on them; the wheels had flattened them into knives that sparked.

2     Once in a while an adult said, "Your grandfather built the railroad." (Or "Your grandfathers built the railroad." Plural and singular are by context.) We children believed that it was that very railroad, those trains, those tracks running past our house; our own giant grandfather had set those very logs into the ground, poured the iron for those very spikes with the big heads and pounded them until the heads spread like that, mere nails to him. He had built the railroad so that trains would thunder over us, on a street that inclined toward us. We lived on a special spot of the earth, Stockton, the only city on the Pacific coast with three railroads—the Santa Fe, Southern Pacific, and Western Pacific. The three railroads intersecting accounted for the flocks of hoboes. The few times that the train stopped, the cows moaned all night, their hooves stumbling crowdedly and banging against the wood.

3     Grandfather left a railroad for his message: We had to go somewhere difficult. Ride a train. Go somewhere important. In case of danger, the train was to be ready for us.

4     The railroad men disconnected the rails and took the steel away. They did not come back. Our family dug up the square logs and rolled them downhill home. We collected the spikes too. We used the logs for benches, edged the yard with them, made bases for fences, embedded them in the ground for walkways. The spikes came in handy too, good for paperweights, levers, wedges, chisels. I am glad to know exactly the weight of ties and the size of nails.

5     Grandfather's picture hangs in the dining room next to an equally large one of Grandmother, and another one of Guan Goong, God of War and Literature. My grandparents' similarity is in the set of their mouths; they seem to have hauled with their mouths. My mouth also feels the tug and strain of weights in its corners. In the family album, Grandfather wears a greatcoat and Western shoes, but his ankles show. He hasn't shaved either. Maybe he became sloppy after the Japanese soldier bayoneted his head for not giving directions. Or he was born slow and without a sense of direction.

6     The photographer came to the village regularly and set up a spinet, potted trees, an ornate table stacked with hardbound books of matching size, and a backdrop with a picture of paths curving through gardens into panoramas; he lent his subjects dressy ancient mandarin clothes, Western suits, and hats. An aunt tied the fingers of the lame cousin to a book, the string leading down his sleeve; he looks like he's carrying it. The family hurried from clothes chests to mirrors without explaining to Grandfather, hiding Grandfather. In the family album are group pictures with Grandmother in the middle, the family arranged on either side of her and behind her, second wives at the ends, no Grandfather.

Grandmother's earrings, bracelets, and rings are tinted jade green, everything and everybody else black and white, her little feet together neatly, two knobs at the bottom of her gown. My mother, indignant that nobody had readied Grandfather, threw his greatcoat over his nightclothes, shouted, "Wait! Wait!" and encouraged him into the sunlight. "Hurry," she said, and he ran, coat flapping, to be in the picture. She would have slipped him into the group and had the camera catch him like a peeping ghost, but Grandmother chased him away. "What a waste of film," she said. Grandfather always appears alone with white stubble on his chin. He was a thin man with big eyes that looked straight ahead. When we children talked about overcoat men, exhibitionists, we meant Grandfather, Ah Goong, who must have yanked open that greatcoat—no pants.

MaMa was the only person to listen to him, and so he followed her 7 everywhere, and talked and talked. What he liked telling was his journeys to the Gold Mountain. He wasn't smart, yet he traveled there three times. Left to himself, he would have stayed in China to play with babies or stayed in the United States once he got there, but Grandmother forced him to leave both places. "Make money," she said. "Don't stay here eating." "Come home," she said.

Ah Goong sat outside her open door when MaMa worked. (In those days 8 a man did not visit a good woman alone unless married to her.) He saw her at her loom and came running with his chair. He told her that he had found a wondrous country, really gold, and he himself had gotten two bags of it, one of which he had had made into a ring. His wife had given that ring to their son for his wedding ring. "That ring on your finger," he told Mother, "proves that the Gold Mountain exists and that I went there."

Another of his peculiarities was that he heard the crackles, bangs, gunshots 9 that go off when the world lurches; the gears on its axis snap. Listening to a faraway New Year, he had followed the noise and come upon the blasting in the Sierras. (There is a Buddhist instruction that that which is most elusive must, of course, be the very thing to be pursued; listen to the farthest sound.) The Central Pacific hired him on sight; chinamen had a natural talent for explosions. Also there were not enough workingmen to do all the labor of building a new country. Some of the banging came from the war to decide whether or not black people would continue to work for nothing.

Slow as usual, Ah Goong arrived in the spring; the work had begun in 10 January 1863. The demon that hired him pointed up and up, east above the hills of poppies. His first job was to fell a redwood, which was thick enough to divide into three or four beams. His tree's many branches spread out, each limb like a little tree. He circled the tree. How to attack it? No side looked like the side made to be cut, nor did any ground seem the place for it to fall. He axed for almost a day the side he'd decided would hit the ground. Halfway through, imitating the other lumberjacks, he struck the other side of the tree, above the cut, until he had to run away. The tree swayed and slowly dived to earth, creaking and screeching like a green animal. He was so awed, he forgot he was supposed to yell. Hardly any branches broke; the tree sprang, bounced, pushed at the ground with its arms. The limbs did not wilt and fold; they were a small forest, which he chopped. The trunk lay like a long red torso; sap ran from its cuts like crying blind eyes. At last it stopped fighting. He set the log across sawhorses to be cured over smoke and in the sun.

11      He joined a team of men who did not ax one another as they took alternate hits. They blew up the stumps with gunpowder. "It was like uprooting a tooth," Ah Goong said. They also packed gunpowder at the roots of a whole tree. Not at the same time as the bang but before that, the tree rose from the ground. It stood, then plunged with a tearing of veins and muscles. It was big enough to carve a house into. The men measured themselves against the upturned white roots, which looked like claws, a sun with claws. A hundred men stood or sat on the trunk. They lifted a wagon on it and took a photograph. The demons also had their photograph taken.

12      Because these mountains were made out of gold. Ah Goong rushed over to the root hole to look for gold veins and ore. He selected the shiniest rocks to be assayed later in San Francisco. When he drank from the streams and saw a flash, he dived in like a duck; only sometimes did it turn out to be the sun or the water. The very dirt winked with specks.

13      He made a dollar a day salary. The lucky men gambled, but he was not good at remembering game rules. The work so far was endurable. "I could take it," he said.

14      The days were sunny and blue, the wind exhilarating, the heights godlike. At night the stars were diamonds, crystals, silver, snow, ice. He had never seen diamonds. He had never seen snow and ice. As spring turned into summer, and he lay under that sky, he saw the order in the stars. He recognized constellations from China. There—not a cloud but the Silver River, and there, on either side of it—Altair and Vega, the Spinning Girl and the Cowboy, far, far apart. He felt his heart breaking of loneliness at so much blue-black space between star and star. The railroad he was building would not lead him to his family. He jumped out of his bedroll. "Look! Look!" Other China Men jumped awake. An accident? An avalanche? Injun demons? "The stars," he said. "The stars are here." "Another China Man gone out of his mind," men grumbled. "A sleep-walker." "Go to sleep, sleepwalker." "There. And there," said Ah Goong, two hands pointing. "The Spinning Girl and the Cowboy. Don't you see them?" "Homesick China Man," said the China Men and pulled their blankets over their heads. "Didn't you know they were here? I could have told you they were here. Same as in China. Same moon. Why not same stars?" "Nah. Those are American stars."

15      Pretending that a little girl was listening, he told himself the story about the Spinning Girl and the Cowboy: A long time ago they had visited earth, where they met, fell in love, and married. Instead of growing used to each other, they remained enchanted their entire lifetimes and beyond. They were too happy. They wanted to be doves or two branches of the same tree. When they

returned to live in the sky, they were so engrossed in each other that they neglected their work. The Queen of the Sky scratched a river between them with one stroke of her silver hairpin—the river a galaxy in width. The lovers suffered, but she did devote her time to spinning now, and he herded his cow. The King of the Sky took pity on them and ordered that once each year, they be allowed to meet. On the seventh day of the seventh month (which is not the same as July 7), magpies form a bridge for them to cross to each other. The lovers are together for one night of the year. On their parting, the Spinner cries the heavy summer rains.

Ah Goong's discovery of the two stars gave him something to look forward to besides meals and tea breaks. Every night he located Altair and Vega and gauged how much closer they had come since the night before. During the day he watched the magpies, big black and white birds with round bodies like balls with wings; they were a welcome sight, a promise of meetings. He had found two familiars in the wilderness: magpies and stars. On the meeting day, he did not see any magpies nor hear their chattering jaybird cries. Some black and white birds flew overhead, but they may have been American crows or late magpies on their way. Some men laughed at him, but he was not the only China Man to collect water in pots, bottles, and canteens that day. The water would stay fresh forever and cure anything. In ancient days the tutelary gods of the mountains sprinkled corpses with this water and brought them to life. That night, no women to light candles, burn incense, cook special food, Grandfather watched for the convergence and bowed. He saw the two little stars next to Vega—the couple's children. And bridging the Silver River, surely those were black flapping wings of magpies and translucent-winged angels and faeries. Toward morning, he was awakened by rain, and pulled his blankets into his tent. 16

The next day, the fantailed orange-beaked magpies returned. Altair and Vega were beginning their journeys apart, another year of spinning and herding. Ah Goong had to find something else to look forward to. The Spinning Girl and the Cowboy met and parted six times before the railroad was finished. 17

When cliffs, sheer drops under impossible overhangs, ended the road, the workers filled the ravines or built bridges over them. They climbed above the site for tunnel or bridge and lowered one another down in wicker baskets made stronger by the lucky words they had painted on four sides. Ah Goong got to be a basketman because he was thin and light. Some basketmen were fifteen-year-old boys. He rode the basket barefoot, so his boots, the kind to stomp snakes with, would not break through the bottom. The basket swung and twirled, and he saw the world sweep underneath him; it was fun in a way, a cold new feeling of doing what had never been done before. Suspended in the quiet sky, he thought all kinds of crazy thoughts, that if a man didn't want to live any more, he could just cut the ropes or, easier, tilt the basket, dip, and never have to worry again. He could spread his arms and the air would momentarily hold him before he fell past the buzzards, hawks, and eagles, and landed impaled on the tip of a sequoia. This high and he didn't see any gods, no Cowboy, no 18

Spinner. He knelt in the basket though he was not bumping his head against the sky. Through the wickerwork, slivers of depths darted like needles, nothing between him and air but thin rattan. Gusts of wind spun the light basket. "Aiya," said Ah Goong. Winds came up under the basket, bouncing it. Neighboring baskets swung together and parted. He and the man next to him looked at each other's faces. They laughed. They might as well have gone to Malaysia to collect bird nests. Those who had done high work there said it had been worse; the birds screamed and scratched at them. Swinging near the cliff, Ah Goong stood up and grabbed it by a twig. He dug holes, then inserted gunpowder and fuses. He worked neither too fast nor too slow, keeping even with the others. The basketmen signaled one another to light the fuses. He struck match after match and dropped the burnt matches over the sides. At last his fuse caught; he waved, and the men above pulled hand over hand hauling him up, pulleys creaking. The scaffolds stood like a row of gibbets. Gallows trees along a ridge. "Hurry, hurry," he said. Some impatient men clambered up their ropes. Ah Goong ran up the ledge road they'd cleared and watched the explosions, which banged almost synchronously, echoes booming like war. He moved his scaffold to the next section of cliff and went down in the basket again, with bags of dirt, and set the next charge.

19    This time two men were blown up. One knocked out or killed by the explosion fell silently, the other screaming, his arms and legs struggling. A desire shot out of Ah Goong for an arm long enough to reach down and catch them. Much time passed as they fell like plummets. The shreds of baskets and a cowboy hat skimmed and tacked. The winds that pushed birds off course and against mountains did not carry men. Ah Goong also wished that the conscious man would fall faster and get it over with. He hands gripped the ropes, and it was difficult to let go and get on with the work. "It can't happen twice in a row," the basketmen said the next trip down. "Our chances are very good. The trip after an accident is probably the safest one." They raced to their favorite basket, checked and double-checked the four ropes, yanked the strands, tested the pulleys, oiled them, reminded the pulleymen about the signals, and entered the sky again.

20    Another time, Ah Goong had been lowered to the bottom of a ravine, which had to be cleared for the base of a trestle, when a man fell, and he saw his face. He had not died of shock before hitting bottom. His hands were grabbing at air. His stomach and groin must have felt the fall all the way down. At night Ah Goong woke up falling, though he slept on the ground, and heard other men call out in their sleep. No warm women tweaked their ears and hugged them. "It was only a falling dream," he reassured himself.

21    Across a valley, a chain of men working on the next mountain, men like ants changing the face of the world, fell, but it was very far away. Godlike, he watched men whose faces he could not see and whose screams he did not hear roll and bounce and slide like a handful of sprinkled gravel.

22    After a fall, the buzzards circled the spot and reminded the workers for days

that a man was dead down there. The men threw piles of rocks and branches to cover bodies from sight.

The mountainface reshaped, they drove supports for a bridge. Since ham-  23
mering was less dangerous than the blowing up, the men played a little; they rode the baskets swooping in wide arcs; they twisted the ropes and let them unwind like tops. "Look at me," said Ah Goong, pulled open his pants, and pissed overboard, the wind scattering the drops. "I'm a waterfall," he said. He had sent a part of himself hurtling. On rare windless days he watched his piss fall in a continuous stream from himself almost to the bottom of the valley.

One beautiful day, dangling in the sun above a new valley, not the desire  24
to urinate but sexual desire clutched him so hard he bent over in the basket. He curled up, overcome by beauty and fear, which shot to his penis. He tried to rub himself calm. Suddenly he stood up tall and squirted out into space. "I am fucking the world," he said. The world's vagina was big, big as the sky, big as a valley. He grew a habit: whenever he was lowered in the basket, his blood rushed to his penis, and he fucked the world.

Then it was autumn, and the wind blew so fiercely, the men had to postpone  25
the basketwork. Clouds moved in several directions at once. Men pointed at dust devils, which turned their mouths crooked. There was ceaseless motion; clothes kept moving; hair moved; sleeves puffed out. Nothing stayed still long enough for Ah Goong to figure it out. The wind sucked the breath out of his mouth and blew thoughts from his brains. The food convoys from San Francisco brought tents to replace the ones that whipped away. The baskets from China, which the men saved for high work, carried cowboy jackets, long underwear, Levi pants, boots, earmuffs, leather gloves, flannel shirts, coats. They sewed rabbit fur and deerskin into the linings. They tied the wide brims of their cowboy hats over their ears with mufflers. And still the wind made confusing howls into ears, and it was hard to think.

The days became nights when the crews tunneled inside the mountain,  26
which sheltered them from the wind, but also hid the light and sky. Ah Goong pickaxed the mountain, the dirt filling his nostrils through a cowboy bandanna. He shoveled the dirt into a cart and pushed it to a place that was tall enough for the mule, which hauled it the rest of the way out. He looked forward to cart duty to edge closer to the entrance. Eyes darkened, nose plugged, his windy cough worse, he was to mole a thousand feet and meet others digging from the other side. How much he'd pay now to go swinging in a basket. He might as well have gone to work in a tin mine. Coming out of the tunnel at the end of a shift, he forgot whether it was supposed to be day or night. He blew his nose fifteen times before the mucus cleared again.

The dirt was the easiest part of tunneling. Beneath the soil, they hit granite.  27
Ah Goong struck it with his pickax, and it jarred his bones, chattered his teeth. He swung his sledgehammer against it, and the impact rang in the dome of his skull. The mountain that was millions of years old was locked against them and was not to be broken into. The men teased him, "Let's see you fuck the world

now." "Let's see you fuck the Gold Mountain now." But he no longer felt like it. "A man ought to be made of tougher material than flesh," he said. "Skin is too soft. Our bones ought to be filled with iron." He lifted the hammer high, careful that it not pull him backward, and let it fall forward of its own weight against the rock. Nothing happened to that gray wall; he had to slam with strength and will. He hit at the same spot over and over again, the same rock. Some chips and flakes broke off. The granite looked everywhere the same. It had no softer or weaker spots anywhere, the same hard gray. He learned to slide his hand up the handle, lift, slide and swing, a circular motion, hammering, hammering, hammering. He would bite like a rat through that mountain. His eyes couldn't see; his nose couldn't smell; and now his ears were filled with the noise of hammering. This rock is what is real, he thought. This rock is what real is, not clouds or mist, which make mysterious promises, and when you go through them are nothing. When the foreman measured at the end of twenty-four hours of pounding, the rock had given a foot. The hammering went on day and night. The men worked eight hours on and eight hours off. They worked on all eighteen tunnels at once. While Ah Goong slept, he could hear the sledgehammers of other men working in the earth. The steady banging reminded him of holidays and harvests; falling asleep, he heard the women chopping mincemeat and the millstones striking.

28     The demons in boss suits came into the tunnel occasionally, measured with a yardstick and shook their heads. "Faster," they said. "Faster. Chinamen too slow. Too slow." "Tell us we're slow," the China Men grumbled. The ones in top tiers of scaffolding let rocks drop, a hammer drop. Ropes tangled around the demons' heads and feet. The cave China Men muttered and flexed, glared out of the corners of their eyes. But usually there was no diversion—one day the same as the next, one hour no different from another—the beating against the same granite.

29     After tunneling into granite for about three years, Ah Goong understood the immovability of the earth. Men change, men die, weather changes, but a mountain is the same as permanence and time. This mountain would have taken no new shape for centuries, ten thousand centuries, the world a still, still place, time unmoving. He worked in the tunnel so long, he learned to see many colors in black. When he stumbled out, he tried to talk about time. "I felt time," he said. "I saw time. I saw world." He tried again, "I saw what's real. I saw time, and it doesn't move. If we break through the mountain, hollow it, time won't have moved anyway. You translators ought to tell the foreigners that."

30     Summer came again, but after the first summer, he felt less nostalgia at the meeting of the Spinning Girl and the Cowboy. He now knew men who had been in this country for twenty years and thirty years, and the Cowboy's one year away from his lady was no time at all. His own patience was longer. The stars were meeting and would meet again next year, but he would not have seen his family. He joined the others celebrating Souls' Day, the holiday a week later, the fourteenth day of the seventh month. The supply wagons from San Francisco

and Sacramento brought watermelon, meat, fish, crab, pressed duck. "There, ghosts, there you are. Come and get it." They displayed the feast complete for a moment before falling to, eating on the dead's behalf.

In the third year of pounding granite by hand, a demon invented dynamite. The railroad workers were to test it. They had stopped using gunpowder in the tunnels after avalanches, but the demons said that dynamite was more precise. They watched a scientist demon mix nitrate, sulphate, and glycerine, then flick the yellow oil, which exploded off his fingertips. Sitting in a meadow to watch the dynamite detonated in the open, Ah Goong saw the men in front of him leap impossibly high into the air; then he felt a shove as if from a giant's unseen hand—he fell backward. The boom broke the mountain silence like fear breaking inside stomach and chest and groin. No one had gotten hurt; they stood up laughing and amazed, looking around at how they had fallen, the pattern of the explosion. Dynamite was much more powerful than gunpowder. Ah Goong had felt a nudge, as if something kind were moving him out of harm's way. "All of a sudden I was sitting next to you." "Aiya. If we had been nearer, it would have killed us." "If we were stiff, it would have gone through us." "A fist." "A hand." "We leapt like acrobats." Next time Ah Goong flattened himself on the ground, and the explosion rolled over him.

He never got used to the blasting; a blast always surprised him. Even when he himself set the fuse and watched it burn, anticipated the explosion, the bang—*bahng* in Chinese—when it came, always startled. It cleaned the crazy words, the crackling, and bingbangs out of his brain. It was like New Year's, when every problem and thought was knocked clean out of him by firecrackers, and he could begin fresh. He couldn't worry during an explosion, which jerked every head to attention. Hills flew up in rocks and dirt. Boulders turned over and over. Sparks, fires, debris, rocks, smoke burst up, not at the same time as the boom (*bum*) but before that—the sound a separate occurrence, not useful as a signal.

The terrain changed immediately. Streams were diverted, rockscapes exposed. Ah Goong found it difficult to remember what land had looked like before an explosion. It was a good thing the dynamite was invented after the Civil War to the east was over.

The dynamite added more accidents and ways of dying, but if it were not used, the railroad would take fifty more years to finish. Nitroglycerine exploded when it was jounced on a horse or dropped. A man who fell with it in his pocket blew himself up into red pieces. Sometimes it combusted merely standing. Human bodies skipped through the air like puppets and made Ah Goong laugh crazily as if the arms and legs would come together again. The smell of burned flesh remained in rocks.

In the tunnels, the men bored holes fifteen to eighteen inches deep with a power drill, stuffed them with hay and dynamite, and imbedded the fuse in sand. Once, for extra pay, Ah Goong ran back in to see why some dynamite had not gone off and hurried back out again; it was just a slow fuse. When the explosion settled, he helped carry two-hundred-, three-hundred-, five-hundred-pound boulders out of the tunnel.

36     As a boy he had visited a Taoist monastery where there were nine rooms, each a replica of one of the nine hells. Lifesize sculptures of men and women were spitted on turning wheels. Eerie candles under the suffering faces emphasized eyes poked out, tongues pulled, red mouths and eyes, and real hair, eyelashes, and eyebrows. Women were split apart and men dismembered. He could have reached out and touched the sufferers and the implements. He had dug and dynamited his way into one of these hells. "Only here there are eighteen tunnels, not nine, plus all the tracks between them," he said.

37     One day he came out of the tunnel to find the mountains white, the evergreens and bare trees decorated, white tree sculptures and lace bushes everywhere. The men from snow country called the icicles "ice chopsticks." He sat in his basket and slid down the slopes. The snow covered the gouged land, the broken trees, the tracks, the mud, the campfire ashes, the unburied dead. Streams were stilled in mid-run, the water petrified. That winter he thought it was the task of the human race to quicken the world, blast the freeze, fire it, redden it with blood. He had to change the stupid slowness of one sunrise and one sunset per day. He had to enliven the silent world with sound. "The rock," he tried to tell the others. "The ice." "Time."

38     The dynamiting loosed blizzards on the men. Ears and toes fell off. Fingers stuck to the cold silver rails. Snowblind men stumbled about with bandannas over their eyes. Ah Goong helped build wood tunnels roofing the track route. Falling ice scrabbled on the roofs. The men stayed under the snow for weeks at a time. Snowslides covered the entrances to the tunnels, which they had to dig out to enter and exit, white tunnels and black tunnels. Ah Goong looked at his gang and thought, if there is an avalanche, these are the people I'll be trapped with, and wondered which ones would share food. A party of snowbound barbarians had eaten the dead. Cannibals, thought Ah Goong, and looked around. Food was not scarce; the tea man brought whiskey barrels of hot tea, and he warmed his hands and feet, held the teacup to his nose and ears. Someday, he planned, he would buy a chair with metal doors for putting hot coal inside it. The magpies did not abandon him but stayed all winter and searched the snow for food.

39     The men who died slowly enough to say last words said, "Don't leave me frozen under the snow. Send my body home. Burn it and put the ashes in a tin can. Take the bone jar when you come down the mountain." "When you ride the fire car back to China, tell my descendants to come for me." "Shut up," scolded the hearty men. "We don't want to hear about bone jars and dying." "You're lucky to have a body to bury, not blown to smithereens." "Stupid man to hurt yourself," they bawled out the sick and wounded. How their wives would scold if they brought back deadmen's bones. "Aiya. To be buried here, no-where." "But this is somewhere," Ah Goong promised. "This is the Gold Mountain. We're marking the land now. The track sections are numbered, and

your family will know where we leave you." But he was a crazy man, and they didn't listen to him.

Spring did come, and when the snow melted, it revealed the past year, what had happened, what they had done, where they had worked, the lost tools, the thawing bodies, some standing with tools in hand, the bright rails. "Remember Uncle Long Winded Leong?" "Remember Strong Back Wong?" "Remember Lee Brother?" "And Fong Uncle?" They lost count of the number dead; there is no record of how many died building the railroad. Or maybe it was demons doing the counting and chinamen not worth counting. Whether it was good luck or bad luck, the dead were buried or cairned next to the last section of track they had worked on. "May his ghost not have to toil," they said over graves. (In China a woodcutter ghost chops eternally; people have heard chopping in the snow and in the heat.) "Maybe his ghost will ride the train home." The scientific demons said the transcontinental railroad would connect the West to Cathay. "What if he rides back and forth from Sacramento to New York forever?" "That wouldn't be so bad. I hear the cars will be like houses on wheels." The funerals were short. "No time. No time," said both China Men and demons. The railroad was as straight as they could build it, but no ghosts sat on the tracks; no strange presences haunted the tunnels. The blasts scared ghosts away.

When the Big Dipper pointed east and the China Men detonated nitro-glycerine and shot off guns for the New Year, which comes with the spring, these special bangs were not as loud as the daily bangs, not as numerous as the bangs all year. Shouldn't the New Year be the loudest day of all to obliterate the noises of the old year? But to make a bang of that magnitude, they would have to blow up at least a year's supply of dynamite in one blast. They arranged strings in chain reactions in circles and long lines, banging faster and louder to culminate in a big bang. And most importantly, there were random explosions— surprise. Surprise. SURPRISE. They had no dragon, the railroad their dragon.

The demons invented games for working faster, gold coins for miles of track laid, for the heaviest rock, a grand prize for the first team to break through a tunnel. Day shifts raced against night shifts, China Men against Welshmen, China Men against Irishmen, China Men against Injuns and black demons. The fastest races were China Men against China Men, who bet on their own teams. China Men always won because of good teamwork, smart thinking, and the need for the money. Also, they had the most workers to choose teams from. When-ever his team won anything, Ah Goong added to his gold stash. The Central Pacific or Union Pacific won the land on either side of the tracks it built.

One summer day, demon officials and China Man translators went from group to group and announced, "We're raising the pay—thirty-five dollars a month. Because of your excellent work, the Central Pacific Railroad is giving you a four-dollar raise per month." The workers who didn't know better cheered. "What's the catch?" said the smarter men. "You'll have the opportunity to put in more time," said the railroad demons. "Two more hours per shift."

Ten-hour shifts inside the tunnels. "It's not ten hours straight," said the demons. "You have time off for tea and meals. Now that you have dynamite, the work isn't so hard." They had been working for three and a half years already, and the track through the Donner Summit was still not done.

44       The workers discussed the ten-hour shift, swearing their China Man obscenities. "Two extra hours a day—sixty hours a month for four dollars." "Pig catcher demons." "Snakes." "Turtles." "Dead demons." "A human body can't work like that." "The demons don't believe this is a human body. This is a chinaman's body." To bargain, they sent a delegation of English speakers, who were summarily noted as troublemakers, turned away, docked.

45       The China Men, then, decided to go on strike and demand forty-five dollars a month and the eight-hour shift. They risked going to jail and the Central Pacific keeping the pay it was banking for them. Ah Goong memorized the English, "Forty-five dollars a month—eight-hour shift." He practiced the strike slogan: "Eight hours a day good for white man, all the same good for China Man."

46       The men wrapped barley and beans in ti leaves, which came from Hawai'i via San Francisco, for celebrating the fifth day of the fifth month (not May but mid-June, the summer solstice). Usually the way the red string is wound and knotted tells what flavors are inside—the salty barley with pickled egg, or beans and pork, or the gelatin pudding. Ah Goong folded ti leaves into a cup and packed it with food. One of the literate men slipped in a piece of paper with the strike plan, and Ah Goong tied the bundle with a special pattern of red string. The time and place for the revolution against Kublai Khan had been hidden inside autumn mooncakes. Ah Goong looked from one face to another in admiration. Of course, of course. No China Men, no railroad. They were indispensable labor. Throughout these mountains were brothers and uncles with a common idea, free men, not coolies, calling for fair working conditions. The demons were not suspicious as the China Men went gandying up and down the tracks delivering the bundles tied together like lines of fish. They had exchanged these gifts every year. When the summer solstice cakes came from other camps, the recipients cut them into neat slices by drawing the string through them. The orange jellies, which had a red dye stick inside soaked in lye, fell into a series of sunrises and sunsets. The aged yolks and the barley also looked like suns. The notes gave a Yes strike vote. The yellow flags to ward off the five evils—centipedes, scorpions, snakes, poisonous lizards, and toads—now flew as banners.

47       The strike began on Tuesday morning, June 25, 1867. The men who were working at that hour walked out of the tunnels and away from the tracks. The ones who were sleeping slept on and rose as late as they pleased. They bathed in streams and shaved their moustaches and wild beards. Some went fishing and hunting. The violinists tuned and played their instruments. The drummers beat theirs at the punchlines of jokes. The gamblers shuffled and played their cards and tiles. The smokers passed their pipes, and the drinkers bet for drinks by

making figures with their hands. The cooks made party food. The opera singers' falsettos almost perforated the mountains. The men sang new songs about the railroad. They made up verses and shouted Ho at the good ones, and laughed at the rhymes. Oh, they were madly singing in the mountains. The storytellers told about the rise of new kings. The opium smokers when they roused themselves told their florid images. Ah Goong sifted for gold. All the while the English-speaking China Men, who were being advised by the shrewdest bargainers, were at the demons' headquarters repeating the demand: "Eight hours a day good for white man, all the same good for China Man." They had probably negotiated the demons down to nine-hour shifts by now.

The sounds of hammering continued along the tracks and occasionally there 48 were blasts from the tunnels. The scabby white demons had refused to join the strike. "Eight hours a day good for white man, all the same good for China Man," the China Men explained to them. "Cheap John Chinaman," said the demons, many of whom had red hair. The China Men scowled out of the corners of their eyes.

On the second day, artist demons climbed the mountains to draw the China 49 Men for the newspapers. The men posed bare-chested, their fists clenched, showing off their arms and backs. The artists sketched them as perfect young gods reclining against rocks, wise expressions on their handsome noble-nosed faces, long torsos with lean stomachs, a strong arm extended over a bent knee, long fingers holding a pipe, a rope of hair over a wide shoulder. Other artists drew faeries with antennae for eyebrows and brownies with elfish pigtails; they danced in white socks and black slippers among mushroom rings by moonlight.

Ah Goong acquired another idea that added to his reputation for craziness: 50 The pale, thin Chinese scholars and the rich men fat like Buddhas were less beautiful, less manly than these brown muscular railroad men, of whom he was one. One of ten thousand heroes.

On the third day, in a woods—he would be looking at a deer or a rabbit or 51 an Injun watching him before he knew what he was seeing—a demon dressed in a white suit and tall hat beckoned him. They talked privately in the wilderness. The demon said, "I Citizenship Judge invite you to be U.S. citizen. Only one bag gold." Ah Goong was thrilled. What an honor. He would accept this invitation. Also what advantages, he calculated shrewdly; if he were going to be jailed for this strike, an American would have a trial. The Citizenship Judge unfurled a parchment sealed with gold and ribbon. Ah Goong bought it with one bag of gold. "You vote," said the Citizenship Judge. "You talk in court, buy land, no more chinaman tax." Ah Goong hid the paper on his person so that it would protect him from arrest and lynching. He was already a part of this new country, but now he had it in writing.

The fourth day, the strikers heard that the U.S. Cavalry was riding single 52 file up the tracks to shoot them. They argued whether to engage the Army with dynamite. But the troops did not come. Instead the cowardly demons blockaded the food wagons. No food. Ah Goong listened to the optimistic China Men, who said, "Don't panic. We'll hold out forever. We can hunt. We can last fifty days on water." The complainers said, "Aiya. Only saints can do that. Only magic men and monks who've practiced." The China Men refused to declare a last day for the strike.

53       The foresighted China Men had cured jerky, fermented wine, dried and strung orange and grapefruit peels, pickled and preserved leftovers. Ah Goong, one of the best hoarders, had set aside extra helpings from each meal. This same quandary, whether to give away food or to appear selfish, had occurred during each of the six famines he had lived through. The foodless men identified themselves. Sure enough, they were the shiftless, piggy, arrogant type who didn't worry enough. The donors scolded them and shamed them the whole while they were handing them food: "So you lived like a grasshopper at our expense." "Fleaman." "You'll be the cause of our not holding out long enough." "Rich man's kid. Too good to hoard." Ah Goong contributed some rice crusts from the bottoms of pans. He kept how much more food he owned a secret, as he kept the secret of his gold. In apology for not contributing richer food, he repeated a Mohist saying that had guided him in China: "'The superior man does not push humaneness to the point of stupidity.'" He could hear his wife scolding him for feeding strangers. The opium men offered shit and said that it calmed the appetite.

54       On the fifth and sixth days, Ah Goong organized his possessions and patched his clothes and tent. He forebore repairing carts, picks, ropes, baskets. His work-habituated hands arranged rocks and twigs in designs. He asked a reader to read again his family's letters. His wife sounded like herself except for the polite phrases added professionally at the beginnings and the ends. "Idiot," she said, "why are you taking so long? Are you wasting the money? Are you spending it on girls and gambling and whiskey? Here's my advice to you: Be a little more frugal. Remember how it felt to go hungry. Work hard." He had been an idle man for almost a week. "I need a new dress to wear to weddings. I refuse to go to another banquet in the same old dress. If you weren't such a spendthrift, we could be building the new courtyard where we'll drink wine among the flowers and sit about in silk gowns all day. We'll hire peasants to till the fields. Or lease them to tenants, and buy all our food at market. We'll have clean fingernails and toenails." Other relatives said, "I need a gold watch. Send me the money. Your wife gambles it away and throws parties and doesn't disburse it fairly among us. You might as well come home." It was after one of these letters that he had made a bonus checking on some dud dynamite.

55       Ah Goong did not spend his money on women. The strikers passed the word that a woman was traveling up the railroad and would be at his camp on the seventh and eighth day of the strike. Some said she was a demoness and some that she was a Chinese and her master a China Man. He pictured a nurse coming to bandage wounds and touch foreheads or a princess surveying her subjects; or perhaps she was a merciful Jesus demoness. But she was a pitiful woman, led on a leash around her waist, not entirely alive. Her owner sold

lottery tickets for the use of her. Ah Goong did not buy one. He took out his penis under his blanket or bared it in the woods and thought about nurses and princesses. He also just looked at it, wondering what it was that it was for, what a man was for, what he had to have a penis for.

There was a rumor also of an Injun woman called Woman Chief, who led a nomadic fighting tribe from the eastern plains as far as these mountains. She was so powerful that she had four wives and many horses. He never saw her though.

The strike ended on the ninth day. The Central Pacific announced that in its benevolence it was giving the workers a four-dollar raise, not the fourteen dollars they had asked for. And that the shifts in the tunnels would remain eight hours long. "We were planning to give you the four-dollar raise all along," the demons said to diminish the victory. So they got thirty-five dollars a month and the eight-hour shift. They would have won forty-five dollars if the thousand demon workers had joined the strike. Demons would have listened to demons. The China Men went back to work quietly. No use singing and shouting over a compromise and losing nine days' work.

There were two days that Ah Goong did cheer and throw his hat in the air, jumping up and down and screaming Yippee like a cowboy. One: the day his team broke through the tunnel at last. Toward the end they did not dynamite but again used picks and sledgehammers. Through the granite, they heard answering poundings, and answers to their shouts. It was not a mountain before them any more but only a wall with people breaking through from the other side. They worked faster. Forward. Into day. They stuck their arms through the holes and shook hands with men on the other side. Ah Goong saw dirty faces as wondrous as if he were seeing Nu Wo, the creator goddess who repairs cracks in the sky with stone slabs; sometimes she peeks through and human beings see her face. The wall broke. Each team gave the other a gift of half a tunnel, dug. They stepped back and forth where the wall had been. Ah Goong ran and ran, his boots thudding to the very end of the tunnel, looked at the other side of the mountain, and ran back, clear through the entire tunnel. All the way through.

He spent the rest of his time on the railroad laying and bending and hammering the ties and rails. The second day the China Men cheered was when the engine from the West and the one from the East rolled toward one another and touched. The transcontinental railroad was finished. They Yippee'd like madmen. The white demon officials gave speeches. "The Greatest Feat of the Nineteenth Century," they said. "The Greatest Feat in the History of Mankind," they said. "Only Americans could have done it," they said, which is true. Even if Ah Goong had not spent half his gold on Citizenship Papers, he was an American for having built the railroad. A white demon in top hat tap-tapped on the gold spike, and pulled it back out. Then one China Man held the real spike, the steel one, and another hammered it in.

While the demons posed for photographs, the China Men dispersed. It was dangerous to stay. The Driving Out had begun. Ah Goong does not appear in railroad photographs. Scattering, some China Men followed the north star in the constellation Tortoise the Black Warrior to Canada, or they kept the constellation Phoenix ahead of them to South America or the White Tiger west or the Wolf east. Seventy lucky men rode the Union Pacific to Massachusetts for jobs at a shoe factory. Fifteen hundred went to Fou Loy Company in New Orleans and San Francisco, several hundred to plantations in Mississippi, Georgia, and Arkansas, and sugarcane plantations in Louisiana and Cuba. (From the South, they sent word that it was a custom to step off the sidewalk along with the black demons when a white demon walked by.) Seventy went to New Orleans to grade a route for a railroad, then to Pennsylvania to work in a knife factory. The Colorado State Legislature passed a resolution welcoming the railroad China Men to come build the new state. They built railroads in every part of the country—the Alabama and Chattanooga Railroad, the Houston and Texas Railroad, the Southern Pacific, the railroads in Louisiana and Boston, the Pacific Northwest, and Alaska. After the Civil War, China Men banded the nation North and South, East and West, with crisscrossing steel. They were the binding and building ancestors of this place.

61    Ah Goong would have liked a leisurely walk along the tracks to review his finished handiwork, or to walk east to see the rest of his new country. But instead, Driven Out, he slid down mountains, leapt across valleys and streams, crossed plains, hid sometimes with companions and often alone, and eluded bandits who would hold him up for his railroad pay and shoot him for practice as they shot Injuns and jackrabbits. Detouring and backtracking, his path wound back and forth to his railroad, a familiar silver road in the wilderness. When a train came, he hid against the shaking ground in case a demon with a shotgun was hunting from it. He picked over camps where he had once lived. He was careful to find hidden places to sleep. In China bandits did not normally kill people, the booty the main thing, but here the demons killed for fun and hate. They tied pigtails to horses and dragged chinamen. He decided that he had better head for San Francisco, where he would catch a ship to China.

62    Perched on hillsides, he watched many sunsets, the place it was setting, the direction he was going. There were fields of grass that he tunneled through, hid in, rolled in, dived and swam in, suddenly jumped up laughing, suddenly stopped. He needed to find a town and human company. The spooky tumbleweeds caught in barbed wire were peering at him, waiting for him; he had to find a town. Towns grew along the tracks as they did along rivers. He sat looking at a town all day, then ducked into it by night.

63    At the familiar sight of a garden laid out in a Chinese scheme—vegetables in beds, white cabbages, red plants, chives, and coriander for immortality, herbs boxed with boards—he knocked on the back door. The China Man who answered gave him food, the appropriate food for the nearest holiday, talked story, exclaimed at how close their ancestral villages were to each other. They exchanged information on how many others lived how near, which towns had Chinatowns, what size, two or three stores or a block, which towns to avoid. "Do you have a wife?" they asked one another. "Yes. She lives in China. I have

been sending money for twenty years now." They exchanged vegetable seeds, slips, and cuttings, and Ah Goong carried letters to another town or China.

Some demons who had never seen the likes of him gave him things and touched him. He also came across lone China Men who were alarmed to have him appear, and, unwelcome, he left quickly; they must have wanted to be the only China Man of that area, the special China Man. 64

He met miraculous China Men who had produced families out of no-where—a wife and children, both boys and girls. "Uncle," the children called him, and he wanted to stay to be the uncle of the family. The wife washed his clothes, and he went on his way when they were dry. 65

On a farm road, he came across an imp child playing in the dirt. It looked at him, and he looked at it. He held out a piece of sugar; he cupped a grassblade between his thumbs and whistled. He sat on the ground with his legs crossed, and the child climbed into the hollow of his arms and legs. "I wish you were my baby," he told it. "My baby." He was very satisfied sitting there under the humming sun with the baby, who was satisfied too, no squirming. "My daugh-ter," he said. "My son." He couldn't tell whether it was a boy or a girl. He touched the baby's fat arm and cheeks, its gold hair, and looked into its blue eyes. He made a wish that it not have to carry a sledgehammer and crawl into the dark. But he would not feel sorry for it; other people must not suffer any more than he did, and he could endure anything. Its mother came walking out into the road. She had her hands above her like a salute. She walked tentatively towards them, held out her hand, smiled, spoke. He did not understand what she said except "Bye-bye." The child waved and said, "Bye-bye," crawled over his legs, and toddled to her. Ah Goong continued on his way in a direction she could not point out to a posse looking for a kidnapper chinaman. 66

Explosions followed him. He heard screams and went on, saw flames out-lining black windows and doors, and went on. He ran in the opposite direction from gunshots and the yell—*eeha awha*—the cowboys made when they herded cattle and sang their savage songs. 67

Good at hiding, disappearing—decades unaccounted for—he was not work-ing in a mine when forty thousand chinamen were Driven Out of mining. He was not killed or kidnapped in the Los Angeles Massacre, though he gave money toward ransoming those whose toes and fingers, a digit per week, and ears grotesquely rotting or pickled, and scalped queues, were displayed in China-towns. Demons believed that the poorer a chinaman looked, the more gold he had buried somewhere, that chinamen stuck together and would always ransom one another. If he got kidnapped, Ah Goong planned, he would whip out his Citizenship Paper and show that he was an American. He was lucky not to be in Colorado when the Denver demons burned all chinamen homes and busi-nesses, nor in Rock Springs, Wyoming, when the miner demons killed twenty-eight or fifty chinamen. The Rock Springs Massacre began in a large coal mine owned by the Union Pacific; the outnumbered chinamen were shot in the back as they ran to Chinatown, which the demons burned. They forced chinamen out into the open and shot them; demon women and children threw the 68 wounded back in the flames. (There was a rumor of a good white lady in Green Springs who hid China Men in the Pacific Hotel and shamed the demons away.) The hunt went on for a month before federal troops came. The count of the dead was inexact because bodies were mutilated and pieces scattered all over the Wyoming Territory. No white miners were indicted, but the government paid $150,000 in reparations to victims' families. There were many family men, then. There were settlers—abiding China Men. And China Women. Ah Goong was running elsewhere during the Drivings Out of Tacoma, Seattle, Oregon City, Albania, and Marysville. The demons of Tacoma packed all its chinamen into boxcars and sent them to Portland, where they were run out of town. China Men returned to Seattle, though, and refused to sell their land and stores but fought until the army came; the demon rioters were tried and acquitted. And when the Boston police imprisoned and beat 234 chinamen, it was 1902, and Ah Goong had already reached San Francisco or China, and perhaps San Francisco again.

69    In Second City (Sacramento), he spent some of his railroad money at the theater. The main actor's face was painted red with thick black eyebrows and long black beard, and when he strode onto the stage, Ah Goong recognized the hero, Guan Goong; his puppet horse had red nostrils and rolling eyes. Ah Goong's heart leapt to recognize hero and horse in the wilds of America. Guan Goong murdered his enemy—crash! bang! of cymbals and drum—and left his home village—sad, sad flute music. But to the glad clamor of cymbals entered his friends—Liu Pei (pronounced the same as Running Nose) and Chang Fei. In a joyful burst of pink flowers, the three men swore the Peach Garden Oath. Each friend sang an aria to friendship; together they would fight side by side and live and die one for all and all for one. Ah Goong felt as warm as if he were with friends at a party. Then Guan Goong's archenemy, the sly Ts'ao Ts'ao, captured him and two of Liu Pei's wives, the Lady Kan and the Lady Mi. Though Ah Goong knew they were boy actors, he basked in the presence of Chinese ladies. The prisoners traveled to the capital, the soldiers waving horse-hair whisks, signifying horses, the ladies walking between horizontal banners, signifying palanquins. All the prisoners were put in one bedroom, but Guan Goong stood all night outside the door with a lighted candle in his hand, singing an aria about faithfulness. When the capital was attacked by a common enemy, Guan Goong fought the biggest man in one-to-one combat, a twirling, jumping sword dance that strengthened the China Men who watched it. From afar Guan Goong's two partners heard about the feats of the man with the red face and intelligent horse. The three friends were reunited and fought until they secured their rightful kingdom.

70    Ah Goong felt refreshed and inspired. He called out Bravo like the demons in the audience, who had not seen theater before. Guan Goong, the God of War, also God of War and Literature, had come to America—Guan Goong, Grandfather Guan, our own ancestor of writers and fighters, of actors and

gamblers, and avenging executioners who mete out justice. Our own kin. Not a distant ancestor but Grandfather.

In the Big City (San Francisco), a goldsmith convinced Ah Goong to have his gold made into jewelry, which would organize it into one piece and also delight his wife. So he handed over a second bag of gold. He got it back as a small ring in a design he thought up himself, two hands clasping in a handshake. "So small?" he said, but the goldsmith said that only some of the ore had been true gold.    71

He got a ship out of San Francisco without being captured near the docks, where there was a stockade full of jailed chinamen; the demonesses came down from Nob Hill and took them home to be servants, cooks, and baby-sitters.    72

Grandmother liked the gold ring very much. The gold was so pure, it squished to fit her finger. She never washed dishes, so the gold did not wear away. She quickly spent the railroad money, and Ah Goong said he would go to America again. He had a Certificate of Return and his Citizenship Paper.    73

But this time, there was no railroad to sell his strength to. He lived in a basement that was rumored to connect with tunnels beneath Chinatown. In an underground arsenal, he held a pistol and said, "I feel the death in it." "The holes for the bullets were like chambers in a beehive or wasp nest," he said. He was inside the earth when the San Francisco Earthquake and Fire began. Thunder rumbled from the ground. Some say he died falling into the cracking earth. It was a miraculous earthquake and fire. The Hall of Records burned completely. Citizenship Papers burned, Certificates of Return, Birth Certificates, Residency Certificates, passenger lists, Marriage Certificates—every paper a China Man wanted for citizenship and legality burned in that fire. An authentic citizen, then, had no more papers than an alien. Any paper a China Man could not produce had been "burned up in the Fire of 1906." Every China Man was reborn out of that fire a citizen.    74

Some say the family went into debt and sent for Ah Goong, who was not making money; he was a homeless wanderer, a shiftless, dirty, jobless man with matted hair, ragged clothes, and fleas all over his body. He ate out of garbage cans. He was a louse eaten by lice. A fleaman. It cost two thousand dollars to bring him back to China, his oldest sons signing promissory notes for one thousand, his youngest to repay four hundred to one neighbor and six hundred to another. Maybe he hadn't died in San Francisco, it was just his papers that burned; it was just that his existence was outlawed by Chinese Exclusion Acts. The family called him Fleaman. They did not understand his accomplishments as an American ancestor, a holding, homing ancestor of this place. He'd gotten the legal or illegal papers burned in the San Francisco Earthquake and Fire; he appeared in America in time to be a citizen and to father citizens. He had also been seen carrying a child out of the fire, a child of his own in spite of the laws against marrying. He had built a railroad out of sweat, why not have an American child out of longing? ✠    75

RESPONDING

1.  Maxine Hong Kingston calls her grandfather "an American ancestor, a holding, homing ancestor of this place" (paragraph 75), even though he was never legally an American citizen. Explain his contribution to the United States in a journal entry.

2.  Working in a group, discuss the ways in which Kingston's grandfather's life was shaped by the place where he was living and the opportunities available to him. Write a journal entry or an essay about the ways in which you or any of your relatives have been directly affected by the period or place in which you happen to have been born or live.

3.  Imagine that you are a reporter for a San Francisco newspaper in the late 1800s. You have just returned from interviewing Chinese railroad workers. Write a feature story for your newspaper arguing that they are being exploited and mistreated by the "demon" bosses. Or write a story from the bosses' point of view about working conditions on the railroad.

4.  Choose one of the atrocities Kingston writes about and expand your knowledge of the circumstances by researching the incident. Write an account of the events and share it with the class.

# CONNIE YOUNG YU

*Born in Los Angeles in 1941, Connie Young Yu is a specialist in Asian American immigration history and culture. One of the founders of the Angel Island Immigration Station Historical Advisory Committee, she has also played active roles in the Santa Clara County Asian Health Needs Assessment Study and the Chinatown Housing and Health Resource Project of San Francisco. Her 1969 article, "The Unsung Heroes of the Golden Spikes," which appeared in the* San Francisco Examiner, *brought her work to national attention. Since then, her research has appeared in such publications as* The Civil Rights Digest, Amerasia, *and the anthology* Working It Out. *More recently, she has published* Profiles in Excellence *(1986), a series of biographies of Asian American women, and* Chinatown, San Jose, USA *(1991).*

*In the essay that follows Young Yu examines how the experiences of her grandmother provide a special perspective on the history of her family and the larger community.*

⊹

# THE WORLD OF OUR GRANDMOTHERS

IN ASIAN AMERICA there are two kinds of history. The first is what is written   1
about us in various old volumes on immigrants and echoed in textbooks, and
the second is our own oral history, what we learn in the family chain of
generations. We are writing this oral history ourselves. But as we research the
factual background of our story, we face the dilemma of finding sources. Worse
than burning the books is not being included in the record at all, and in
American history—traditionally viewed from the white male perspective—
minority women have been virtually ignored. Certainly the accomplishments
and struggles of early Chinese immigrants, men as well as women, have been
obscured.

Yet for a period in the development of the West, Chinese immigration was   2
a focus of prolonged political and social debate and a subject of daily news.
When I first began searching into the background of my people, I read this
nineteenth-century material with curious excitement, grateful for any information on Chinese immigration.

Looking for the history of Chinese pioneer women, I began with the first   3
glimpses of Chinese in America—newspaper accounts found in bound volumes
of the *Alta California* in the basement of a university library. For Chinese
workers, survival in the hostile and chaotic world of Gum San, or Gold Mountain, as California was called by Chinese immigrants, was perilous and a constant
struggle, leaving little time or inclination for reflection or diary writing. So for
a look into the everyday life of early arrivals from China, we have only the
impressions of white reporters on which to depend.

The newspapers told of the comings and goings of "Chinamen," their   4
mining activities, new Chinese settlements, their murders by claim-jumpers, and
assaults by whites in the city. An item from 17 August 1855, reported a "dis-
graceful outrage": Mr. Ho Alum was setting his watch under a street clock when
a man called Thomas Field walked up and deliberately dashed the timepiece to
the pavement. "Such unprovoked assaults upon unoffending Chinamen are not
of rare occurrence. . . ." On the same day the paper also reported the suicide
of a Chinese prostitute. In this item no name, details, or commentary were given,
only a stark announcement. We can imagine the tragic story behind it: the short
miserable life of a young girl sold into slavery by her impoverished parents and
taken to Gum San to be a prostitute in a society of single men.

An early history of this period, *Lights and Shades in San Francisco* by   5
B. E. Lloyd (1878), devoted ten chapters to the life of California Chinese,
describing in detail "the subjects of the Celestial Kingdom." Chinese women,
however, are relegated to a single paragraph:

Females are little better than slaves. They are looked upon as merchantable property, and are bought and sold like any other article of traffic, though their value is not generally great. A Chinese woman never gains any distinction until after death. . . . Considering the humble position the women occupy in China, and the hard life they therefore lead, it would perhaps be better (certainly more merciful) were they all slain in infancy, and better still, were they never born.[1]

6    Public opinion, inflamed by lurid stories of Chinese slave girls, agreed with this odious commentary. The only Chinese women whose existence American society acknowledged were the prostitutes who lived miserable and usually short lives. Senate hearings on Chinese immigration in 1876 resounded with harangues about prostitutes and slave girls corrupting the morals of young white boys. "The Chinese race is debauched," claimed one lawyer arguing for the passage of the Chinese Exclusion Law: "They bring no decent women with them." This stigma on the Chinese immigrant woman remained for many decades, causing unnecessary hardships for countless wives, daughters, and slave girls.

7    Chinese American society finally established itself as families appeared, just as they did in the white society of the forty-niners who arrived from the East Coast without bringing "decent women" with them. Despite American laws intended to prevent the "settlement" of Chinese, Chinese women did make the journey and endured the isolation and hostility, braving it for future generations here.

8    Even though Chinese working men were excluded from most facets of American society and their lives were left unrecorded, their labors bespoke their existence—completed railroads, reclaimed lands, and a myriad of new industries. The evidence of women's lives seems less tangible. Perhaps the record of their struggles to immigrate and overcome discriminatory barriers is their greatest legacy. Tracing that record therefore becomes a means of recovering our history.

9    Our grandmothers are our historical links. As a fourth-generation Chinese American on my mother's side, and a third-generation on my father's, I grew up hearing stories about ancestors coming from China and going back and returning again. Both of my grandmothers, like so many others, spent a lot of time waiting in China.

10    My father's parents lived with us when I was growing up, and through them I absorbed a village culture and the heritage of my pioneer Chinese family. In the kitchen my grandmother told repeated stories of coming to America after

---

1. B. E. Lloyd, *Lights and Shades in San Francisco* (San Francisco: San Francisco Press, 1878).

waiting for her husband to send for her. (It took sixteen years before Grandfather could attain the status of merchant and only then arrange for her passage to this country.)[2] She also told stories from the village about bandits, festivals, and incidents showing the tyranny of tradition. For example, Grandma was forbidden by her mother-in-law to return to her own village to visit her mother: A married woman belonged solely within the boundaries of her husband's world.

Sometimes I was too young to understand or didn't listen, so my mother— who knew all the stories by heart—told me those stories again later. We heard over and over how lucky Grandpa was to have come to America when he was eleven—just one year before the gate was shut by the exclusion law banning Chinese laborers. Grandpa told of his many jobs washing dishes, making bricks, and working on a strawberry farm. Once, while walking outside Chinatown, he was stoned by a group of whites and ran so fast he lost his cap. Grandma had this story to tell of her anger and frustration: "While I was waiting in the immigration shed,[3] Grandpa sent in a box of *dim sum*.[4] I was still waiting to be released. I would have jumped in the ocean if they decided to deport me." A woman in her position was quite helpless, but she still had her pride and was not easily pacified. "I threw the box of *dim sum* out the window."

Such was the kind of history I absorbed. I regret deeply that I was too young to have asked the questions about the past that I now want answered; all my grandparents are now gone. But I have another chance to recover some history from my mother's side. Family papers, photographs, old trunks that have traveled across the ocean several times filled with clothes, letters, and mementos provide a documentary on our immigration. My mother—and some of my grandmother's younger contemporaries—fill in the narrative.

A year before the Joint Special Committee of Congress to investigate Chinese immigration met in San Francisco in 1876, my great-grandmother, Chin Shee, arrived to join her husband, Lee Wong Sang, who had come to America a decade earlier to work on the transcontinental railroad. Chin Shee arrived with two brides who had never seen their husbands. Like her own, their marriages had been arranged by their families. The voyage on the clipper ship was rough and long. Seasick for weeks, rolling back and forth as she lay in the bunk, Chin Shee lost most of her hair. The two other women laughed, "Some newlywed you'll make!" But the joke was on them as they mistakenly set off

11

12

13

2. Under the Chinese Exclusion Act of 1882, Chinese laborers could no longer immigrate to America. Until the act was repealed in 1943, only merchants, diplomats, students, and visitors were allowed to enter.
3. Between 1910 and 1940 Chinese immigrants arriving in the port of San Francisco were detained at the Angel Island Immigration Station to await physical examinations and interrogation to determine their right to enter this country. Prior to 1910 immigrants were detained in a building on the wharf known as "the shed."
4. Chinese pastries.

with the wrong husbands, the situation realized only when one man looked at his bride's normal-sized feet and exclaimed, "But the letter described my bride as having bound feet!" Chin Shee did not have her feet bound because she came from a peasant family. But her husband did not seem to care about that nor that the back of her head was practically bald. He felt himself fortunate just to be able to bring his wife to Gum San.

14    Chin Shee bore six children in San Francisco, where her husband assisted in the deliveries. They all lived in the rear of their grocery store, which also exported dried shrimp and seaweed to China. Great-Grandma seldom left home; she could count the number of times she went out. She and other Chinese wives did not appear in the streets even for holidays, lest they be looked upon as prostitutes. She took care of the children, made special cakes to sell on feast days, and helped with her husband's work. A photograph of her shows a middle-aged woman with a kindly, but careworn face, wearing a very regal brocade gown and a long, beaded necklace. As a respectable, well-to-do Chinese wife in America, married to a successful Chinatown merchant, with children who were by birthright American citizens, she was a rarity in her day. (In contrast, in 1884 Mrs. Jew Lim, the wife of a laborer, sued in federal court to be allowed to join her husband, but was denied and deported.)

15    In 1890 there were only 3,868 Chinese women among 103,620 Chinese males in America. Men such as Lee Yoke Suey, my mother's father, went to China to marry. He was one of Chin Shee's sons born in the rear of the grocery store, and he grew up learning the import and export trade. As a Gum San merchant, he had money and status and was able to build a fine house in Toishan. Not only did he acquire a wife but also two concubines. When his wife became very ill after giving birth to an infant who soon died, Yoke Suey was warned by his father that she was too weak to return to America with him. Reminding Yoke Suey of the harsh life in Gum San, he advised his son to get a new wife.

16    In the town of Foshan, not far from my grandfather's village, lived a girl who was recommended to him by his father's friend. Extremely capable, bright, and with some education, she was from a once prosperous family that had fallen on hard times. A plague had killed her two older brothers, and her heartbroken mother died soon afterwards. She was an excellent cook and took good care of her father, an herb doctor. Her name was Jeong Hing Tong, and she was pretty, with bound feet only three and a half inches long. Her father rejected the offer of the Lee family at first; he did not want his daughter to be a concubine, even to a wealthy Gum San merchant. But the elder Lee assured him this girl would be the wife, the one who would go to America with her husband.

17    So my maternal grandmother, bride of sixteen, went with my grandfather, then twenty-six, to live in America. Once in San Francisco, Grandmother lived a life of confinement, as did her mother-in-law before her. When she went out, even in Chinatown, she was ridiculed for her bound feet. People called out mockingly to her, "Jhat!" meaning bound. She tried to unbind her feet by soaking them every night and putting a heavy weight on each foot. But she was

already a grown woman, and her feet were permanently stunted, the arches bent and the toes crippled. It was hard for her to stand for long periods of time, and she frequently had to sit on the floor to do her chores. My mother comments: "Tradition makes life so hard. My father traveled all over the world. There were stamps all over his passport—London, Paris—and stickers all over his suitcases, but his wife could not go into the street by herself."

Their first child was a girl, and on the morning of her month-old "red eggs 18 and ginger party" the earth shook 8.3 on the Richter scale. Everyone in San Francisco, even Chinese women, poured out into the streets. My grandmother, babe in arms, managed to get a ride to Golden Gate Park on a horse-drawn wagon. Two other Chinese women who survived the earthquake recall the shock of suddenly being out in the street milling with thousands of people. The elderly goldsmith in a dimly lit Chinatown store had a twinkle in his eye when I asked him about the scene after the quake. "We all stared at the women because we so seldom saw them in the streets." The city was soon in flames. "We could feel the fire on our faces," recalls Lily Sung, who was seven at the time, "but my sister and I couldn't walk very fast because we had to escort this lady, our neighbor, who had bound feet." The poor woman kept stumbling and falling on the rubble and debris during their long walk to the Oakland-bound ferry.

That devastating natural disaster forced some modernity on the San Fran- 19 cisco Chinese community. Women had to adjust to the emergency and makeshift living conditions and had to work right alongside the men. Life in America, my grandmother found, was indeed rugged and unpredictable.

As the city began to rebuild itself, she proceeded to raise a large family, 20 bearing four more children. The only school in San Francisco admitting Chinese was the Oriental school in Chinatown. But her husband felt, as did most men of his class, that the only way his children could get a good education was for the family to return to China. So they lived in China and my grandfather traveled back and forth to the United States for his trade business. Then suddenly, at the age of forty-three, he died of an illness on board a ship returning to China. After a long and painful mourning, Grandmother decided to return to America with her brood of now seven children. That decision eventually affected immigration history.

At the Angel Island immigration station in San Francisco Bay, Grandmother 21 went through a physical examination so thorough that even her teeth were checked to determine whether she was the age stated on her passport. The health inspector said she had filariasis, liver fluke, a common ailment of Asian immigrants which caused their deportation by countless numbers. The authorities thereby ordered Grandmother to be deported as well.

While her distraught children had to fend for themselves in San Francisco 22 (my mother, then fifteen, and her older sister had found work in a sewing factory), a lawyer was hired to fight for Grandmother's release from the detention barracks. A letter addressed to her on Angel Island from her attorney, C. M. Fickert, dated 24 March 1924, reads: "Everything I can legitimately do will be done on your behalf. As you say, it seems most inhuman for you to be separated from your children who need your care. I am sorry that the immigration officers will not look at the human side of your case."

23    Times were tough for Chinese immigrants in 1924. Two years before, the federal government had passed the Cable Act, which provided that any woman born in the United States who married a man "ineligible for citizenship" (including the Chinese, whose naturalization rights had been eliminated by the Chinese Exclusion Act) would lose her own citizenship. So, for example, when American-born Lily Sung, whom I also interviewed, married a Chinese citizen she forfeited her birthright. When she and her four daughters tried to re-enter the United States after a stay in China, they were denied permission. The immigration inspector accused her of "smuggling little girls to sell." The Cable Act was not repealed until 1930.

24    The year my grandmother was detained on Angel Island, a law had just taken effect that forbade all aliens ineligible for citizenship from landing in America.[5] This constituted a virtual ban on the immigration of all Chinese, including Chinese wives of U.S. citizens.

25    Waiting month after month in the bleak barracks, Grandmother heard many heart-rending stories from women awaiting deportation. They spoke of the suicides of several despondent women who hanged themselves in the shower stalls. Grandmother could see the calligraphy carved on the walls by other detained immigrants, eloquent poems expressing homesickness, sorrow, and a sense of injustice.

26    Meanwhile, Fickert was sending telegrams to Washington (a total of ten the bill stated) and building up a case for the circuit court. Mrs. Lee, after all, was the wife of a citizen who was a respected San Francisco merchant, and her children were American citizens. He also consulted a medical authority to see about a cure for liver fluke.

27    My mother took the ferry from San Francisco twice a week to visit Grand-mother and take her Chinese dishes such as salted eggs and steamed pork because Grandmother could not eat the beef stew served in the mess hall. Mother and daughter could not help crying frequently during their short visits in the administration building. They were under close watch of both a guard and an interpreter.

28    After fifteen months the case was finally won. Grandmother was easily cured of filariasis and was allowed—with nine months probation—to join her children in San Francisco. The legal fees amounted to $782.50, a fortune in those days.

29    In 1927 Dr. Frederick Lam in Hawaii, moved by the plight of Chinese families deported from the islands because of the liver fluke disease, worked to convince federal health officials that the disease was noncommunicable. He used

5. The Immigration Act of 1924 affected all Asians who sought to immigrate to the United States. Congress repealed the law as to Chinese in 1943, and then in 1952 through the McCarran-Walter Act as to other Asian ethnic groups.

the case of Mrs. Lee Yoke Suey, my grandmother, as a precedent for allowing an immigrant to land with such an ailment and thus succeeded in breaking down a major barrier to Asian immigration.

My most vivid memory of Grandmother Lee is when she was in her seventies and studying for her citizenship. She had asked me to test her on the three branches of government and how to pronounce them correctly. I was a sophomore in high school and had entered the "What American Democracy Means To Me" speech contest of the Chinese American Citizens Alliance. When I said the words "judicial, executive, and legislative," I looked directly at my grandmother in the audience. She didn't smile, and afterwards, didn't comment much on my patriotic words. She had never told me about being on Angel Island or about her friends losing their citizenship. It wasn't in my textbooks either. I may have thought she wanted to be a citizen because her sons and sons-in-law had fought for this country, and we lived in a land of freedom and opportunity, but my guess now is that she wanted to avoid any possible confrontation—even at her age—with immigration authorities. The bad laws had been repealed, but she wasn't taking any chances.

I think a lot about my grandmother now and can understand why, despite her quiet, elegant dignity, an aura of sadness always surrounded her. She suffered from racism in the new country, as well as from traditional cruelties in the old. We, her grandchildren, remember walking very slowly with her, escorting her to a family banquet in Chinatown, hating the stares of tourists at her tiny feet. Did she, I wonder, ever feel like the victim of a terrible hoax, told as a small weeping girl that if she tried to untie the bandages tightly binding her feet she would grow up ugly, unwanted, and without the comforts and privileges of the wife of a wealthy man?

We seemed so huge and clumsy around her—a small, slim figure always dressed in black. She exclaimed once that the size of my growing feet were "like boats." But she lived to see some of her granddaughters graduate from college and pursue careers and feel that the world she once knew with its feudal customs had begun to crumble. I wonder what she would have said of my own daughter who is now attending a university on an athletic scholarship. Feet like boats travel far?

I keep looking at the artifacts of the past: the photograph of my grandmother when she was an innocent young bride and the sad face in the news photo taken on Angel Island. I visit the immigration barracks from time to time, a weather-beaten wooden building with its walls marked by calligraphy bespeaking the struggles of our history. I see the view of sky and water from the window out of which my grandmother gazed. My mother told me how, after visiting hours, she would walk to the ferry and turn back to see her mother waving to her from this window. This image has been passed on to me like an heirloom of pain and of love. When I leave the building, emerging from the darkness into the glaring sunlight of the island, I too turn back to look at my grandmother's window. ✙

## RESPONDING

1. Connie Young Yu expresses the wish that she had asked her grandmother more about her history. Write a journal entry either presenting the history of your own grandparents or formulating the questions you would like to ask your parents or grandparents.

2. Working individually or in a group, list the immigration laws to which Young Yu refers. Do you think those laws were appropriate and necessary? Compare them to our current immigration policies, reviewing these first in the library or on the Internet if necessary. Share your conclusions with the class or organize a class debate.

3. Explain in an essay why Young Yu's mother believes that "Tradition makes life so hard" (paragraph 17). Do you agree or disagree? Support your point of view with evidence from the reading and other sources, as well as your own knowledge.

4. Imagine that you are the attorney representing Mrs. Lee. Write the appeal you will present to the circuit court arguing that she should be admitted to the country.

# Amy Tan

*Amy Tan, the daughter of Chinese immigrants, was born in Oakland, California, in 1952. She received her bachelor's and master's degrees from San Jose State University in 1973 and 1974, respectively. Her publications include the novels* The Joy Luck Club *(1989), which received several major awards,* The Kitchen God's Wife *(1991),* The Hundred Secret Senses *(1995), and* The Year of No Flood *(1995).*

*In* The Joy Luck Club, *Tan uses the voices of various characters to reflect on the relationship between acculturation and heritage. The chapter "Lindo Jong: Double Face," included here, is an account of a mother's first days in the United States, her work in a fortune cookie factory, and her early attempts to translate words and experiences from Chinese into English. In telling this story, Tan also explores the family's reasons for emigrating from China and the challenges they would face upon returning, if only for a visit.*

�֎

# LINDO JONG: DOUBLE FACE

MY DAUGHTER WANTED TO GO TO CHINA for her second honeymoon, but now 1
she is afraid.

"What if I blend in so well they think I'm one of them?" Waverly asked 2
me. "What if they don't let me come back to the United States?"

"When you go to China," I told her, "you don't even need to open your 3
mouth. They already know you are an outsider."

"What are you talking about?" she asked. My daughter likes to speak back. 4
She likes to question what I say.

"Aii-ya," I said. "Even if you put on their clothes, even if you take off your 5
makeup and hide your fancy jewelry, they know. They know just watching the
way you walk, the way you carry your face. They know you do not belong."

My daughter did not look pleased when I told her this, that she didn't look 6
Chinese. She had a sour American look on her face. Oh, maybe ten years ago,
she would have clapped her hands—hurray!—as if this were good news. But
now she wants to be Chinese, it is so fashionable. And I know it is too late. All
those years I tried to teach her! She followed my Chinese ways only until she
learned how to walk out the door by herself and go to school. So now the only
Chinese words she can say are *sh-sh, houche, chr fan,* and *gwan deng shweijyau.*
How can she talk to people in China with these words? Pee-pee, choo-choo
train, eat, close light sleep. How can she think she can blend in? Only her skin
and her hair are Chinese. Inside—she is all American-made.

It's my fault she is this way. I wanted my children to have the best combi- 7
nation: American circumstances and Chinese character. How could I know these
two things do not mix?

I taught her how American circumstances work. If you are born poor here, 8
it's no lasting shame. You are first in line for a scholarship. If the roof crashes
on your head, no need to cry over this bad luck. You can sue anybody, make
the landlord fix it. You do not have to sit like a Buddha under a tree letting
pigeons drop their dirty business on your head. You can buy an umbrella. Or
go inside a Catholic church. In America, nobody says you have to keep the
circumstances somebody else gives you.

She learned these things, but I couldn't teach her about Chinese character. 9
How to obey parents and listen to your mother's mind. How not to show your
own thoughts, to put your feelings behind your face so you can take advantage
of hidden opportunities. Why easy things are not worth pursuing. How to know
your own worth and polish it, never flashing it around like a cheap ring. Why
Chinese thinking is best.

No, this kind of thinking didn't stick to her. She was too busy chewing gum, 10
blowing bubbles bigger than her cheeks. Only that kind of thinking stuck.

11     "Finish your coffee," I told her yesterday. "Don't throw your blessings away."

12     "Don't be so old-fashioned, Ma," she told me, finishing her coffee down the sink. "I'm my own person."

13     And I think, How can she be her own person? When did I give her up?

14     My daughter is getting married a second time. So she asked me to go to her beauty parlor, her famous Mr. Rory. I know her meaning. She is ashamed of my looks. What will her husband's parents and his important lawyer friends think of this backward old Chinese woman?

15     "Auntie An-mei can cut me," I say.

16     "Rory is famous," says my daughter, as if she had no ears. "He does fabulous work."

17     So I sit in Mr. Rory's chair. He pumps me up and down until I am the right height. Then my daughter criticizes me as if I were not there. "See how it's flat on one side," she accuses my head. "She needs a cut and a perm. And this purple tint in her hair, she's been doing it at home. She's never had anything professionally done."

18     She is looking at Mr. Rory in the mirror. He is looking at me in the mirror. I have seen this professional look before. Americans don't really look at one another when talking. They talk to their reflections. They look at others or themselves only when they think nobody is watching. So they never see how they really look. They see themselves smiling without their mouth open, or turned to the side where they cannot see their faults.

19     "How does she want it?" asked Mr. Rory. He thinks I do not understand English. He is floating his fingers through my hair. He is showing how his magic can make my hair thicker and longer.

20     "Ma, how do you want it?" Why does my daughter think she is translating English for me? Before I can even speak, she explains my thoughts: "She wants a soft wave. We probably shouldn't cut it too short. Otherwise it'll be too tight for the wedding. She doesn't want it to look kinky or weird."

21     And now she says to me in a loud voice, as if I had lost my hearing, "Isn't that right, ma? Not too tight?"

22     I smile, I use my American face. That's the face Americans think is Chinese, the one they cannot understand. But inside I am becoming ashamed. I am ashamed she is ashamed. Because she is my daughter and I am proud of her, and I am her mother but she is not proud of me.

23     Mr. Rory pats my hair more. He looks at me. He looks at my daughter. Then he says something to my daughter that really displeases her: "It's uncanny how much you two look alike!"

24     I smile, this time with my Chinese face. But my daughter's eyes and her smile become very narrow, the way a cat pulls itself small just before it bites.

Now Mr. Rory goes away so we can think about this. I hear him snap his fingers, "Wash! Mrs. Jong is next!"

So my daughter and I are alone in this crowded beauty parlor. She is   25
frowning at herself in the mirror. She sees me looking at her.

"The same cheeks," she says. She points to mine and then pokes her cheeks.   26
She sucks them outside in to look like a starved person. She puts her face next
to mine, side by side, and we look at each other in the mirror.

"You can see your character in your face," I say to my daughter without   27
thinking. "You can see your future."

"What do you mean?" she says.   28

And now I have to fight back my feelings. These two faces, I think, so much   29
the same! The same happiness, the same sadness, the same good fortune, the
same faults.

I am seeing myself and my mother, back in China, when I was a young girl.   30

My mother—your grandmother—once told me my fortune, how my character   31
could lead to good and bad circumstances. She was sitting at her table with the
big mirror. I was standing behind her, my chin resting on her shoulder. The
next day was the start of the new year. I would be ten years by my Chinese age,
so it was an important birthday for me. For this reason maybe she did not
criticize me too much. She was looking at my face.

She touched my ear. "You are lucky," she said. "You have my ears, a big   32
thick lobe, lots of meat at the bottom, full of blessings. Some people are born
so poor. Their ears are so thin, so close to their head, they can never hear luck
calling to them. You have the right ears, but you must listen to your opportunities."

She ran her thin finger down my nose. "You have my nose. The hole is not   33
too big, so your money will not be running out. The nose is straight and smooth,
a good sign. A girl with a crooked nose is bound for misfortune. She is always
following the wrong things, the wrong people, the worst luck."

She tapped my chin and then hers. "Not too short, not too long. Our   34
longevity will be adequate, not cut off too soon, not so long we become a
burden."

She pushed my hair away from my forehead. "We are the same," concluded   35
my mother. "Perhaps your forehead is wider, so you will be even more clever.
And your hair is thick, the hairline is low on your forehead. This means you
will have some hardships in your early life. This happened to me. But look at
my hairline now. High! Such a blessing for my old age. Later you will learn to
worry and lose your hair, too."

She took my chin in her hand. She turned my face toward her, eyes facing   36
eyes. She moved my face to one side, then the other. "The eyes are honest,
eager," she said. "They follow me and show respect. They do not look down in

shame. They do not resist and turn the opposite way. You will be a good wife, mother, and daughter-in-law."

37 When my mother told me these things, I was still so young. And even though she said we looked the same, I wanted to look more the same. If her eye went up and looked surprised, I wanted my eye to do the same. If her mouth fell down and was unhappy, I too wanted to feel unhappy.

38 I was so much like my mother. This was before our circumstances separated us: a flood that caused my family to leave me behind, my first marriage to a family that did not want me, a war from all sides, and later, an ocean that took me to a new country. She did not see how my face changed over the years. How my mouth began to droop. How I began to worry but still did not lose my hair. How my eyes began to follow the American way. She did not see that I twisted my nose bouncing forward on a crowded bus in San Francisco. Your father and I, we were on our way to church to give many thanks to God for all our blessings, but I had to subtract some for my nose.

39 It's hard to keep your Chinese face in America. At the beginning, before I even arrived, I had to hide my true self. I paid an American-raised Chinese girl in Peking to show me how.

40 "In America," she said, "you cannot say you want to live there forever. If you are Chinese, you must say you admire their schools, their ways of thinking. You must say you want to be a scholar and come back to teach Chinese people what you have learned."

41 "What should I say I want to learn?" I asked. "If they ask me questions, if I cannot answer . . ."

42 "Religion, you must say you want to study religion," said this smart girl. "Americans all have different ideas about religion, so there are no right and wrong answers. Say to them, I'm going for God's sake, and they will respect you."

43 For another sum of money, this girl gave me a form filled out with English words. I had to copy these words over and over again as if they were English words formed from my own head. Next to the word NAME, I wrote *Lindo Sun*. Next to the word BIRTHDATE, I wrote *May 11, 1918*, which this girl insisted was the same as three months after the Chinese lunar new year. Next to the word BIRTHPLACE, I put down *Taiyuan, China*. And next to the word OCCUPATION, I wrote *student of theology*.

44 I gave the girl even more money for a list of addresses in San Francisco, people with big connections. And finally, this girl gave me, free of charge, instructions for changing my circumstances. "First," she said, "you must find a husband. An American citizen is best."

45 She saw my surprise and quickly added, "Chinese! Of course, he must be Chinese. 'Citizen' does not mean Caucasian. But if he is not a citizen, you should immediately do number two. See here, you should have a baby. Boy or girl, it doesn't matter in the United States. Neither will take care of you in your old age, isn't that true?" And we both laughed.

"Be careful, though," she said. "The authorities there will ask you if you have children now or if you are thinking of having some. You must say no. You should look sincere and say you are not married, you are religious, you know it is wrong to have a baby." 46

I must have looked puzzled, because she explained further: "Look here now, how can an unborn baby know what it is not supposed to do? And once it has arrived, it is an American citizen and can do anything it wants. It can ask its mother to stay. Isn't that true?" 47

But that is not the reason I was puzzled. I wondered why she said I should look sincere. How could I look any other way when telling the truth? 48

See how truthful my face still looks. Why didn't I give this look to you? Why do you always tell your friends that I arrived in the United States on a slow boat from China? This is not true. I was not that poor. I took a plane. I had saved the money my first husband's family gave me when they sent me away. And I had saved money from my twelve years' work as a telephone operator. But it is true I did not take the fastest plane. The plane took three weeks. It stopped everywhere: Hong Kong, Vietnam, the Philippines, Hawaii. So by the time I arrived, I did not look sincerely glad to be here. 49

Why do you always tell people that I met your father in the Cathay House, that I broke open a fortune cookie and it said I would marry a dark, handsome stranger, and that when I looked up, there he was, the waiter, your father. Why do you make this joke? This is not sincere. This was not true! Your father was not a waiter, I never ate in that restaurant. The Cathay House had a sign that said "Chinese Food," so only Americans went there before it was torn down. Now it is a McDonald's restaurant with a big Chinese sign that says *mai dong lou*—"wheat," "east," "building." All nonsense. Why are you attracted only to Chinese nonsense? You must understand my real circumstances, how I arrived, how I married, how I lost my Chinese face, why you are the way you are. 50

When I arrived, nobody asked me questions. The authorities looked at my papers and stamped me in. I decided to go first to a San Francisco address given to me by this girl in Peking. The bus put me down on a wide street with cable cars. This was California Street. I walked up this hill and then I saw a tall building. This was Old St. Mary's. Under the church sign, in handwritten Chinese characters, someone had added: "A Chinese Ceremony to Save Ghosts from Spiritual Unrest 7 A.M. and 8:30 A.M." I memorized this information in case the authorities asked me where I worshipped my religion. And then I saw another sign across the street. It was painted on the outside of a short building: "Save Today for Tomorrow, at Bank of America." And I thought to myself, This is where American people worship. See, even then I was not so dumb! Today that church is the same size, but where that short bank used to be, now there is a tall building, fifty stories high, where you and your husband-to-be work and look down on everybody. 51

My daughter laughed when I said this. Her mother can make a good joke. 52

So I kept walking up this hill. I saw two pagodas, one on each side of the street, as though they were the entrance to a great Buddha temple. But when I 53 looked carefully, I saw the pagoda was really just a building topped with stacks of tile roofs, no walls, nothing else under its head. I was surprised how they tried to make everything look like an old imperial city or an emperor's tomb. But if you looked on either side of these pretend-pagodas, you could see the streets became narrow and crowded, dark, and dirty. I thought to myself, Why did they choose only the worst Chinese parts for the inside? Why didn't they build gardens and ponds instead? Oh, here and there was the look of a famous ancient cave or a Chinese opera. But inside it was always the same cheap stuff.

54    So by the time I found the address the girl in Peking gave me, I knew not to expect too much. The address was a large green building, so noisy, children running up and down the outside stairs and hallways. Inside number 402, I found an old woman who told me right away she had wasted her time waiting for me all week. She quickly wrote down some addresses and gave them to me, keeping her hand out after I took the paper. So I gave her an American dollar and she looked at it and said, "*Syaujye*"—Miss—"we are in America now. Even a beggar can starve on this dollar." So I gave her another dollar and she said, "Aii, you think it is so easy getting this information?" So I gave her another and she closed her hand and her mouth.

55    With the addresses this old woman gave me, I found a cheap apartment on Washington Street. It was like all the other places, sitting on top of a little store. And through this three-dollar list, I found a terrible job paying me seventy-five cents an hour. Oh, I tried to get a job as a salesgirl, but you had to know English for that. I tried for another job as a Chinese hostess, but they also wanted me to rub my hands up and down foreign men, and I knew right away this was as bad as fourth-class prostitutes in China! So I rubbed that address out with black ink. And some of the other jobs required you to have a special relationship. They were jobs held by families from Canton and Toishan and the Four Districts, southern people who had come many years ago to make their fortune and were still holding onto them with the hands of their great-grandchildren.

56    So my mother was right about my hardships. This job in the cookie factory was one of the worst. Big black machines worked all day and night pouring little pancakes onto moving round griddles. The other women and I sat on high stools, and as the little pancakes went by, we had to grab them off the hot griddle just as they turned golden. We would put a strip of paper in the center, then fold the cookie in half and bend its arms back just as it turned hard. If you grabbed the pancake too soon, you would burn your fingers on the hot, wet dough. But if you grabbed too late, the cookie would harden before you could even complete the first bend. And then you had to throw these mistakes in a barrel, which counted against you because the owner could sell those only as scraps.

57    After the first day, I suffered ten red fingers. This was not a job for a stupid person. You had to learn fast or your fingers would turn into fried sausages. So the next day only my eyes burned, from never taking them off the pancakes. And the day after that, my arms ached from holding them out ready to catch

the pancakes at just the right moment. But by the end of my first week, it became mindless work and I could relax enough to notice who else was working on each side of me. One was an older woman who never smiled and spoke to herself in Cantonese when she was angry. She talked like a crazy person. On my other side was a woman around my age. Her barrel contained very few mistakes. But I suspected she ate them. She was quite plump.

"Eh, *Syaujye*," she called to me over the loud noise of the machines. I was grateful to hear her voice, to discover we both spoke Mandarin, although her dialect was coarse-sounding. "Did you ever think you would be so powerful you could determine someone else's fortune?" she asked.

I didn't understand what she meant. So she picked up one of the strips of paper and read it aloud, first in English: "Do not fight and air your dirty laundry in public. To the victor go the soils." Then she translated in Chinese: "You shouldn't fight and do your laundry at the same time. If you win, your clothes will get dirty."

I still did not know what she meant. So she picked up another one and read in English: "Money is the root of all evil. Look around you and dig deep." And then in Chinese: "Money is a bad influence. You become restless and rob graves."

"What is this nonsense?" I asked her, putting the strips of paper in my pocket, thinking I should study these classical American sayings.

"They are fortunes," she explained. "American people think Chinese people write these sayings."

"But we never say such things!" I said. "These things don't make sense. These are not fortunes, they are bad instructions."

"No, Miss," she said laughing, "it is our bad fortune to be here making these and somebody else's bad fortune to pay to get them."

So that is how I met An-mei Hsu. Yes, yes, Auntie An-mei, now so old-fashioned. An-mei and I still laugh over those bad fortunes and how they later became quite useful in helping me catch a husband.

"Eh, Lindo," An-mei said to me one day at our workplace. "Come to my church this Sunday. My husband has a friend who is looking for a good Chinese wife. He is not a citizen, but I'm sure he knows how to make one." So that is how I first heard about Tin Jong, your father. It was not like my first marriage, where everything was arranged. I had a choice. I could choose to marry your father, or I could choose not to marry him and go back to China.

I knew something was not right when I saw him: He was Cantonese! How could An-mei think I could marry such a person? But she just said: "We are not in China anymore. You don't have to marry the village boy. Here everybody is now from the same village even if they come from different parts of China." See how changed Auntie An-mei is from those old days.

So we were shy at first, your father and I, neither of us able to speak to each other in our Chinese dialects. We went to English class together, speaking to each other in those new words and sometimes taking out a piece of paper to write a Chinese character to show what we meant. At least we had that, a piece of paper to hold us together. But it's hard to tell someone's marriage intentions when you can't say things aloud. All those little signs—the teasing, the bossy, scolding words—that's how you know if it is serious. But we could talk only in the manner of our English teacher. I see cat. I see rat. I see hat.

69      But I saw soon enough how much your father liked me. He would pretend he was in a Chinese play to show me what he meant. He ran back and forth, jumped up and down, pulling his fingers through his hair, so I knew—*mangjile!*— what a busy, exciting place this Pacific Telephone was, this place where he worked. You didn't know this about your father—that he could be such a good actor? You didn't know your father had so much hair?

70      Oh, I found out later his job was not the way he described it. It was not so good. Even today, now that I can speak Cantonese to your father, I always ask him why he doesn't find a better situation. But he acts as if we were in those old days, when he couldn't understand anything I said.

71      Sometimes I wonder why I wanted to catch a marriage with your father. I think An-mei put the thought in my mind. She said, "In the movies, boys and girls are always passing notes in class. That's how they fall into trouble. You need to start trouble to get this man to realize his intentions. Otherwise, you will be an old lady before it comes to his mind."

72      That evening An-mei and I went to work and searched through strips of fortune cookie papers, trying to find the right instructions to give to your father. An-mei read them aloud, putting aside ones that might work: "Diamonds are a girl's best friend. Don't ever settle for a pal." "If such thoughts are in your head, it's time to be wed." "Confucius say a woman is worth a thousand words. Tell your wife she's used up her total."

73      We laughed over those. But I knew the right one when I read it. It said: "A house is not home when a spouse is not at home." I did not laugh. I wrapped up this saying in a pancake, bending the cookie with all my heart.

74      After school the next afternoon, I put my hand in my purse and then made a look, as if a mouse had bitten my hand. "What's this?" I cried. Then I pulled out the cookie and handed it to your father. "Eh! So many cookies, just to see them makes me sick. You take this cookie."

75      I knew even then he had a nature that did not waste anything. He opened the cookie and he crunched it in his mouth, and then read the piece of paper.

76      "What does it say?" I asked. I tried to act as if it did not matter. And when he still did not speak, I said, "Translate, please."

77      We were walking in Portsmouth Square and already the fog had blown in and I was very cold in my thin coat. So I hoped your father would hurry and ask me to marry him. But instead he kept his serious look and said, "I don't know this word 'spouse.' Tonight I will look in my dictionary. Then I can tell you the meaning tomorrow."

78      The next day he asked me in English, "Lindo, can you spouse me?" And I laughed at him and said he used that word incorrectly. So he came back and

made a Confucius joke, that if the words were wrong, then his intentions must also be wrong. We scolded and joked with each other all day long like this, and that is how we decided to get married.

One month later we had a ceremony in the First Chinese Baptist Church, where we met. And nine months later your father and I had our proof of citizenship, a baby boy, your big brother Winston. I named him Winston because I liked the meaning of those two words "wins ton." I wanted to raise a son who would win many things, praise, money, a good life. Back then, I thought to myself, At last I have everything I wanted. I was so happy, I didn't see we were poor. I saw only what we had. How did I know Winston would die later in a car accident? So young! Only sixteen! 79

Two years after Winston was born, I had your other brother, Vincent. I named him Vincent, which sounded like "win cent," the sound of making money, because I was beginning to think we did not have enough. And then I bumped my nose riding on the bus. Soon after that you were born. 80

I don't know what caused me to change. Maybe it was my crooked nose that damaged my thinking. Maybe it was seeing you as a baby, how you looked so much like me, and this made me dissatisfied with my life. I wanted everything for you to be better. I wanted you to have the best circumstances, the best character. I didn't want you to regret anything. And that's why I named you Waverly. It was the name of the street we lived on. And I wanted you to think, This is where I belong. But I also knew if I named you after this street, soon you would grow up, leave this place, and take a piece of me with you. 81

Mr. Rory is brushing my hair. Everything is soft. Everything is black. 82

"You look great, Ma," says my daughter. "Everyone at the wedding will think you're my sister." 83

I look at my face in the beauty parlor mirror. I see my reflection. I cannot see my faults, but I know they are there. I gave my daughter these faults. The same eyes, the same cheeks, the same chin. Her character, it came from my circumstances. I look at my daughter and now it is the first time I have seen it. 84

"Ai-ya! What happened to your nose?" 85

She looks in the mirror. She sees nothing wrong. "What do you mean? Nothing happened," she says. "It's just the same nose." . . . ✛ 86

---

RESPONDING

1. In a journal entry explain what, according to Mrs. Jong, are "American circumstances and Chinese character" (paragraph 7)?

2. Working individually or in a group, list the characteristics that Mrs. Jong believes are American and those that she believes are Chinese. Share your list with the class and discuss her conclusions.

3. In an essay, agree or disagree with the narrator's statement: "In America, nobody says you have to keep the circumstances somebody else gives you" (paragraph 8).

4. Write an essay analyzing the relationship between Mrs. Jong and her daughter, Waverly. Using examples from the reading, explain the ways in which the culture of the country where each was raised influences her attitudes and behavior.

---

# AMY LING

*Amy Ling, who was born in Beijing, China, in 1939, received her doctorate from New York University in 1979. She held teaching and research positions at several institutions, including Rutgers University, Harvard University, and the University of Wisconsin, where she served as Director of Asian American Studies. Ling wrote, edited, and coedited several critical works treating immigrant experience and Asian American life and culture, including* Imagining America, *with Wesley Brown (1990),* Between Worlds: Women Writers of Chinese Ancestry *(1990),* Reading the Literature of Asian America, *with Shirley Geok-lin Lim (1992), and* Mrs. Spring Fragrance and Other Writings, *with Annette-White Parks (1995). She was also coeditor with Paul Lauter and others of the* Heath Anthology of American Literature. *Amy Ling died in 1999.*

*The following essay, from* Reading the Literature of Asian America, *explores the Eaton sisters' adoption of a pseudonym as a response to prevalent prejudices of the time.*

✤

# CREATING ONE'S SELF: THE EATON SISTERS

*The story is no longer about the things that have happened to men and women and how they have reacted to them; instead it is about how the subjective and collective meanings of women and men as categories of identity have been constructed. If identities change over time and are relative to different contexts, then we cannot use simple models of socialization that see gender as the more or less stable product of early childhood education in the family and the school.*

—JOAN WALLACE SCOTT

*Consciousness is never fixed, never attained once and for all because discursive boundaries change with historical conditions.*

—Teresa de Laurentis

*Selves which are coherent, seamless, bounded, and whole are indeed illusions. . . . You are not an "I" untouched by context, rather you are defined by context. One could argue that identity and context are inseparable.*

—Dorinne Kondo

These three feminist scholars—a historian, a film theoretician, and an anthropologist—all iterate what has by now become almost a truism: that the self is not a fixed entity but a fluid, changing construct or creation determined by context or historical conditions and particularly by power relationships.

Nowhere do we find this phenomenon more clearly, even literally, demonstrated than in the choice of identity made by persons of mixed race. Unhampered by physical features which may declare a particular exterior identity at odds with interior realities, mixed-race people, particularly those combining Caucasian and Asian races, are free to choose the identity or identities that suit a particular historical moment. Not only are more choices open to them than to people of monoracial ancestry, but these choices are fluid and may change during one lifetime. The story of the Eaton sisters provides a striking illustration of identity as a conscious creation of the self.

As far as our research has uncovered to date, Asian American fiction may be said to have had its beginning with the publication of Sui Sin Far's first short story, "The Gamblers," in the February 1896 issue of *Fly Leaf* and with Onoto Watanna's first novel *Miss Numè of Japan* in 1899.[1] If we use an author's ethnic origin as an identifying criterion to classify her writing, then we may say, without qualms, that Chinese American fiction began with Sui Sin Far, but we may not say that Japanese American literature began with Onoto Watanna. In fact, we would have to say that *Miss Numè of Japan* was the first Chinese American novel and that the twelve other "Japanese" novels of Onoto Watanna should be classified, despite their themes and settings, as Chinese American fiction (Cheung and Yogi ix), for Sui Sin Far and Onoto Watanna were two of the fourteen children of a Chinese woman, Grace Trefusis, and her English husband, Edward Eaton. Sui Sin Far was the pseudonym of Edith Maude Eaton, and Onoto

---

1. I am indebted to Annette-White Parks for this correction. In an earlier article, "Revelation and Mask: Autobiographies of the Eaton Sisters" I mistakenly cited "A Chinese Ishmael" (*Overland Monthly*, July 1899) as Sui Sin Far's first story.

Watanna was her younger sister (Lillie) Winnifred Eaton (Babcock) (Reeve).[2] Thus, it is a fact that the two texts named above were published in the years cited and that Asian American fiction, as far as we know, had its start with those texts, but it is also a fact that the ethnicity of one of the authors was very much a fiction.

4      The lesson of the Eaton sisters is a lesson in the permeability of the boundaries of the self. In *Between Worlds: Women Writers of Chinese Ancestry*, I have traced the context and historical conditions of the turn of the century as background to a discussion of the Eaton sisters' autobiographical and fictional writing. A brief review may be necessary and useful, but this paper will focus on the creation of the sisters' separate identities through their individual choices of pseudonyms and persona. Setting Winnifred Eaton into the context of contemporaneous pseudonymous writers will shed new light on her choice of a persona and enable us to read this choice as a biographical enactment of the literary trickster.

5      The choice of a pseudonym is an act of self-creation, a choice of identity. Pseudonyms are chosen for a variety of reasons, as Joseph Clarke has pointed out in the brief introduction to his reference book on the subject. In theater and film, a stage name is chosen because it conveys more glamour, a more attractive image than the name one was born with, such as Marilyn Monroe for Norma Jean Mortenson and Cary Grant instead of Archibald Leach. In politics, one may be motivated by fear of persecution or discovery, as was Dzhugashvili when he took the name Stalin. Among writers, particularly prevalent in the nineteenth century, one could change one's sex and be more readily published. More women took men's names, of course, than vice versa; however, Clarke mentions one William Sharp who published romantic novels as Fiona Macleoud. Sharp fabricated a biographical entry for Macleoud that was published in *Who's Who* at the turn of the century, as Winnifred Eaton would later do for Onoto Watanna. Literary historian Karl Miller has described the 1880s and 1890s as "an age tormented by genders and pronouns, by pen-names, by the identity of authors" (209).

6      For both of the Eaton sisters, the choice of a pseudonym was a cloak to mask their patronymic and to emphasize their matronymic and for both, even Edith, though to a lesser extent than her sister, the pen-name was a contextual construct. Though biologically half Chinese through their mother, the Eaton sisters were culturally English and Canadian. In her 1909 autobiographical essay

2. Lillie appears on her birth certificate as her first name with Winnifred as a middle name; however, she apparently never used Lillie. Her grandson, Paul Rooney, who lived with her, was surprised to learn of this first name when Winnifred's birth certificate was retrieved in the spring of 1990. Bertrand Whitcomb Babcock was Winnifred Eaton's first husband, from 1901–17; the marriage ended in divorce. Her marriage to Francis Fournier Reeve lasted from 1917 until her death in 1954.

"Leaves from the Mental Portfolio of an Eurasian," Edith relates that their mother as a child was adopted by an English couple, educated in English schools and always dressed in Western clothes. Edith and five siblings were born in England before the family immigrated to America, arriving in Hudson City, New York in the early 1870s and finally settling in Montreal, Quebec, where Winnifred was born. Edith writes that at age six when she saw her first Chinese workmen, "uncouth specimens of their race, dressed in working blouses and pantaloons with queues hanging down their backs, I recoil with a sense of shock" (126). In their childhood home in Montreal, their mother read them Tennyson's *Idylls of the King;* the children took parts and performed minidramas. Several children wrote poetry, but all communication within the family was in English. Edith notes that when she began her work in the Chinese community, one drawback was that "save for a few phrases, I am unacquainted with my mother tongue." Furthermore, "the Americanized Chinamen actually laugh in my face when I tell them that I am of their race" (131).

Nonetheless, since only three Chinese women resided in Montreal in the 1870s, Grace Eaton's ethnicity colored all, and the perception of outsiders was that this was a Chinese family. To be Chinese at this period and for several preceding decades was to be considered subhuman by the dominant society. After the Civil War had abolished black slave labor, workers by the thousands were imported from China to complete the transcontinental railroad and to supply agricultural labor. However, in the 1870s, when an economic depression ensued, Chinese laborers became the scapegoat. The ambivalence of North America's attitude toward the Chinese is clear in the words of a Montana journalist, published in *The Mountanian,* March 27, 1873: "We don't mind hearing of a Chinaman being killed now and then, but it has been coming too thick of late. . . . Soon there will be a scarcity of Chinese cheap labor in the country. . . . Don't kill them unless they deserve it, but when they do—why kill 'em lots" (Lyman 165). On the one hand, the Chinese were desirable as cheap labor; on the other hand, they were like vermin, deserving of extermination.

In this hostile climate, prevalent throughout Canada and the United States, the Eaton sisters grew to maturity. Perceived as Chinese, they were subject to all the abuse heaped on that group. One sister, Grace, reported that a girl at school refused to sit next to her because she was Chinese. A young man in their dancing class said he'd "rather marry a pig than a girl with Chinese blood in her veins" (Far 130). Years later, a dinner conversation recorded in Edith's autobiographical essay demonstrates the continued persistence of sinophobia. Edith, then in the United States, had just obtained a position "in a little [midwest] town away off on the north shore of a big lake." Among those at the dinner table were her new employer, her new landlady, the town clerk, and a young girl. A trainload of Chinese workers passing through the town sparked the ensuing conversation:

My employer shakes his rugged head. "Somehow or other," says he, "I cannot reconcile myself to the thought that the Chinese are humans like ourselves. They may have immortal souls, but their faces seem so utterly devoid of expression that I cannot help but doubt."

"Souls," echoes the town clerk. "Their bodies are enough for me. A Chinaman is, in my eyes, more repulsive than a nigger."

"They always give me such a creepy feeling," puts in the young girl with a laugh.

"Now I wouldn't have one in my house," declares my landlady.

"Now the Japanese are different altogether. There is something bright and likeable about those men," continues Mr. K. (Far 129)

9    Edith, though tempted to keep silent after this conversation, spoke out, identified herself as Chinese and left that town—an act of courage and defiance. She made it her life's work to defend her mother's much maligned race, and a Chinese pen-name served her purpose well. Winnifred, however, chose to be the admired "oriental."

10    To understand why the Japanese were admired, we have only to look at a few facts of history. First, there were few Japanese in the United States in the late nineteenth century and therefore they were not an alternate labor source posing an economic threat to white workers. Second, Japan, an island empire, had fought and defeated two large continental nations—China in 1895 and Russia in 1905. Japanese militarism was seen as the noble embodiment of the samurai tradition until it was directed against the United States decades later, at Pearl Harbor.

11    Since the Chinese and Japanese were indistinguishable to Western eyes and since Edith was already mining the Chinese vein, Winnifred Eaton chose to be Japanese. Her choice paid off, in the form of astonishing success. She published hundreds of short stories in national magazines and two dozen novels that were nearly all best-sellers, most published by Harpers. Several novels were translated into many European languages. Her second novel, *A Japanese Nightingale* (1901), was adapted as a play and performed on Broadway in 1903 to compete with David Belasco's long-running *Madame Butterfly*.[3] From 1924 to 1931 Onoto Watanna wrote scripts for Hollywood and for a period was chief scenarist for Universal Studios. She had a play produced in Paris, "The Road to Honor," and worked on such early films as "Show Boat," "Phantom of the Opera," and "Shanghai Lady" before retiring with her second husband, Francis Reeve, to Calgary, Alberta.

3. It is not generally known that Puccini's popular opera began as a short story by John Luther Long that appeared in *Century* magazine in 1898. From Long's story, David Belasco created a one-act curtain raiser, "Madame Butterfly," so popular that it remained in production at different theaters in New York City from 1900 until 1905. Enchanted by the play, Puccini bought the rights and created his world famous opera.

Winnifred Eaton was the author of her own life story in supplying *Who's* 12
*Who* with the following "facts": born in 1879 in Nagasaki, Japan to a Japanese
noblewoman. Her actual birth year was 1875, her birthplace Montreal and her
mother, of course, Chinese. In a very literal way, Winnifred created herself,
drawing no distinctions between her books and her life, and in fact, extending
her fiction-making skills into her life. Her keen marketing instinct and sense of
timing were precisely accurate, for orientalism was in full flower at the turn of
the century. Her sense of the importance of ethnic validity as manifested in a
name, however, was so strong that it overshadowed her belief in her imagination
and her storytelling powers, both of which were considerable. In midcareer, for
example, Winnifred submitted a novel in Irish American dialect, *The Diary of
Delia*, under the name Winnifred Mooney. The publisher, Doubleday, chose to
publish this book under her well-known pseudonym, Onoto Watanna. Thus,
for the first, and undoubtedly only, time in literary history, we have a novel
written in Irish American dialect by a Chinese Eurasian Canadian published
under a Japanese name. (In so blatantly disregarding boundaries and facts, she
has given literary scholars a major headache: how do we classify this anomaly?)

In her excellent study, *Dark Twins: Imposture and Identity in Mark Twain's* 13
*America*, Susan Gillman differentiates between British writers whose pen-names
were neutral and innocuous, such as George Eliot or Acton, Currer and Ellis
Bell, and Americans who chose names that dramatized and fostered a personality
cult, such as Artemus Ward, Petroleum V. Nasby, Josh Billings, and Mark
Twain. She quotes Walter Benjamin, who criticized this tendency still manifested in our present-day film industry: "The cult of the movie star . . . preserves
not the unique aura of the person but 'the spell of the personality,' the phony
spell of a commodity" (29). Clearly Onoto Watanna's name had become a
commodity too valuable to ignore.

Sui Sin Far is Cantonese for narcissus, also known as "Chinese Lily." Onoto 14
Watanna sounds Japanese but is not a legitimate Japanese name.[4] Each sister
selected a pseudonym to authenticate the subject matter she had chosen to make
her own. It was a choice not all of their siblings made. With English names and
racially indeterminate facial features, the racial identification of the Eaton offspring, on reaching adulthood, varied. The eldest son, Edward, denied his

---

4. Onoto was the name of a pen made in London or the United States (the archival materials contain
contradictory information) and imported to Japan from 1907 until 1955, except during World War II
(says one source) and sold in the Maruzen Book Store 1923–27 (says another). According to Yoshiro
Ando, a scholar from Fujisawa City, Japan who wrote a thesis on Onoto Watanna and began a
correspondence with Doris Rooney, Winnifred Eaton's daughter, the Onoto pen was used by
"almost all novelists and poets in the Meiji era. . . . A professor of English wrote me that 'Onoto
pens produced the westernized culture in our country'" (letter from Yoshiro Ando to Doris Rooney,
dated June 17, 1971). In his thesis, Ando wrote that Onoto was the name of a character in "From
the Eastern Country," a work by another Eurasian writer, Lafcadio Hearn. Ando goes on to say,
presumably receiving his information from Doris Rooney, that Winnifred Eaton was asked by the
manufacturer of the pen, Thomas de la Rue Company, for permission to use her name; she gave
them permission and disclaimed any credit or royalties.

Chinese heritage, marrying an aristocratic white woman who had little to do with her parents-in-law and joining a Montreal rifle club whose members were exclusively Anglo-Canadian. One sister, May, is believed to be the Eurasian described in "Leaves" in this fashion:[5]

> Her face is plastered with a thick white coat of paint and her eyelids and eyebrows are blackened so that the shape of her eyes and the whole expression of her face is changed. . . . Living for many years among the working class, she had heard little but abuse of the Chinese. It is not difficult in a land like California, for a half Chinese, half white girl to pass as one of Spanish or Mexican origin. This the poor child does, tho she lives in nervous dread of being "discovered." (131)

Though their specific choices differed, all of the Eaton children were responding to the same hostile environment. Despite the differences in their specific choices—passing as Mexican, as English, as Japanese, as Chinese—there were essentially only two responses to their embattled position: resistance or accommodation. Edith was the only one among fourteen children to choose resistance, the more difficult and more noble path.

15    Conventional wisdom decrees that "honesty is the best policy," that integrity and truthfulness are noble while lying and accommodation are cowardly and condemnable. And yet, should accommodation always be condemned? If we look more closely at the situation, can we not deconstruct this hierarchy?

16    We can begin by noting that in nature and in warfare, for example, the fittest survive, and survival depends on adaptation to one's environment. Camouflage is not only a legitimate strategy but a clever and critical one. Was it not the British soldiers' red coats and straight military lines that made them easy targets during the Revolutionary War? Is not the broad-leaved, thick-trunked oak that stands firm against the wind more easily blown over and uprooted than the thin, pliant, hollow-centered bamboo? Ironically, Edith in asserting her Chinese ancestry was like the English oak, while Winnifred, in assuming a Japanese persona, was more like the bamboo, regarded by the Chinese as a symbol of nobility. What Rosenblatt noted as true of Afro-Americans like Malcolm X also held true for Asian Americans like Winnifred Eaton: "Recognizing an elusive and unpredictable situation, they adapt to it for survival, becoming masters of both physical and psychological disguise, in part to avoid their hunters" (175).

17    In *Dark Twins*, Gillman represents "that process of continual self-construction and destruction by someone who is both critic and child of his culture"

5. This is the hypothesis of L. Charles Laferriere, grandson of Edith and Winnifred's sister Agnes. A photograph of May in his possession, shows a young woman with heavily darkened eyelids, which would seem to corroborate M. Laferriere's theory.

(13). Though Gillman is writing of Samuel Clemens, this was equally true of Winnifred Eaton. In assuming a Japanese persona, and making liberal use of orientalist materials in her novels, she was a child of her culture and yet, since all was a conscious fantasy and in time a disillusionment, she was a critic of it as well.[6] The dark twin is a trope for the Other within the Self, and the pseudonym is a manifestation of that inner split. Though Gillman recognizes the moral dimensions of imposture, she sees it primarily as a useful strategy for the writer:

> Since "posture" already implies posing or faking, "imposture" is the pose of a pose, the fake of a fake. The word implies no possible return to any point of origin. Synonyms for imposture complicate this ambiguity by distinguishing degrees of intentionality on the part of the impostor. "Deceit" is strongly condemnatory because it refers to "purposeful" deceiving or misleading, whereas "counterfeit" and "fake" may or may not condemn "depending on culpable intent to deceive." Thus imposture raises but does not resolve complex connections between morality and intentionality. Its multiple confusions leave room for lawyers, confidence men, and, ultimately, the writer himself to erase boundaries and circumvent the law, making suspect the premise that knowledge is possible—by legal or any other means. (6)

Further, Gillman writes: "The confidence man presides over the comic tale as hero, not villain. Simon Suggs, a character created by Johnson J. Hooper, another humorist, proclaims in his favorite motto, 'It is good to be shifty in a new country'" (22).

It is crucial to remember that the trickster figure from the perspective of the disempowered is a hero, not a villain. In situations when power is unequal and legally obtained justice is impossible, outsmarting the system is the only means of resistance available. In folk tales of Native Americans and African Americans, the trickster figure—despite what would normally be considered faults—chicanery, cheating, and lying—has the sympathy of the audience because it is through this clever deviousness and deception that unjust situations too large and too difficult for the small person to handle are overcome and victory or a balance of the scales is achieved. In this inversion of established power, the powerless person may take vicarious delight. Furthermore, in contrast to the flexibility and variousness of the trickster, the morally sanctioned stance of his/her opponent at the top of the established hierarchy appears foolishly rigid. Thus, we may read the novels of Onoto Watanna as the brain children of Asian America's first trickster hero.

---

6. I use the term "orientalist" in the sense defined and discussed by Edward Said in his classic study of cultural imperialism, *Orientalism* (New York, 1978). See also Zhang Longxi, "The Myth of the Other: China in the Eyes of the West" in *Critical Inquiry* 15 (1988) 108–131. Zhang takes Foucault and Borges, among others, to task for perpetuating the myth of the strangeness and illogicality of the Chinese.

19    Undoubtedly Suggs was not the only person who realized that a new country provides a fresh start, releasing one from the constraints of the past, from the restraints of family and of history. One has the freedom to create oneself anew, and the West, both in Canada and the United States, in the late nineteenth and early twentieth centuries was still a relatively "new" country. Under the big tolerant skies of the prairies, and in valleys protected by tall mountains, anything seemed possible; one had only to assert it. Winnifred Eaton had at least two well-known contemporaries in Western Canada who, like her, assumed personaes unsubstantiated or not wholly substantiated by facts.

20    The first of these was Grey Owl (1888–1938). He claimed to be the son of an Apache Indian and a Scot and achieved an international reputation as a writer/naturalist, whom the London *Times* called a Canadian Thoreau. Unlike Thoreau, who spent only two years at Walden Pond and was always within walking distance of Concord, Grey Owl lived much of his adult life far from civilization and in close harmony with the animals of the woods, particularly beavers. His love of beavers and their regard for him were captured, incredibly, on film that showed the beavers swimming back and forth bringing sticks to repair his cabin. Initially a trapper, he was convinced by his Iroquois wife, Anahareo, of the need for conservation, the central theme of his writing and of their work. The couple's success in creating a sanctuary for beavers in northern Quebec, described in Grey Owl's book, *Pilgrims of the Wild* (1930), attracted the attention of the Canadian government, which then appointed him Honorary Park Warden and built a home for Anahareo, Grey Owl, and their beavers at Lake Ajawaan in Prince Albert National Park, Saskatchewan. His many articles and four books were so popular that he made two highly successful lecture tours of England and the United States in 1935–36 and 1937–38, concluding with a lecture before the royal family at Buckingham Palace. After his death in 1938, a great public furor followed the discovery that Grey Owl had had no Indian blood at all and was born Archibald Stansfeld Belany in Hastings, England.

21    Reared by two maiden aunts and his grandmother, Belany had an unhappy childhood and a passion for North American Indians. In his late teens, he immigrated to Canada, became a guide and packer in Northern Ontario, and lived six years with a band of Ojibwa Indians on Bear Island in Lake Temagami. By his own account, he was adopted into this tribe and given the name Grey Owl. In 1910 he married an Ojibwa woman, Angela Eguana, but left the tribe in 1912 to serve in World War I and was wounded in service. While recuperating in England in 1917, he married his childhood sweetheart, Constance Holmes. This marriage was brief, for he soon returned to Canada where, in 1926 he married Anahareo. This marriage was the turning point of his life. After his death, Anahareo wrote two books about him, *My Life with Grey Owl* (1940) and the more revealingly titled *Devil in Deerskins* (1972). His grave is beside his cabin on Lake Ajawaan in Prince Albert National Park. The original cross with his English name was replaced with a stone bearing the name Grey Owl, as if to assert that the identity he had chosen and created was of greater lasting significance than the one thrust upon him at birth.

The other notable persona of this period was Long Lance, another cele-  22
brated Indian, whose years (1919–27) in Calgary overlapped with Winnifred's.
He like Sui Sin Far, began as a journalist. In Calgary, he discovered his calling
when he began to visit Indian reserves in the outskirts of Calgary and then
published articles about the plight of the various Indian tribes of western
Canada. In 1922 he was adopted into the Blackfoot tribe and given the name
Buffalo Child, a warrior known for his bravery. In 1923, Long Lance staged a
kidnapping of the mayor of Calgary as a publicity stunt for the Calgary Stam-
pede. His biographer, Donald Smith, describes the event in this way:

> Long Lance with seven chiefs and a healthy assortment of Blackfoot, Stoney
> and Sarcee warriors all painted and feathered and mounted on war ponies
> charged down 7th Avenue to City Hall. Led by Long Lance, they entered the
> mayor's office, ordered him to vacate his chair and installed Running Rabbit
> (who spoke no English) as mayor. Photographers recorded the "event." Mayor
> Webster was tied to a horse and ridden to the center of the city (8th Avenue
> and 1st Street West). The Indian mayor officially adopted the captive white
> mayor as Blackfoot, naming him Chief Crowfoot, and then returned the charge
> of the city to the white chief who was now one of them. (110)

Though one cannot help thinking of this as an elaborate charade invented  23
and relished by boys who have refused to grow up, Long Lance carried off the
stunt with such aplomb that the story "made a great splash in Eastern Canada"
and in the United States (Smith 106). He had himself photographed astride an
Indian pinto attired in white buckskins, mocassins, and full feather war head-
dress. When an Indian was sought to play the starring role in "The Silent
Enemy," a silent film about Indians, Long Lance was called to Hollywood.
Despite his public high jinks and celebrity, his private life was unfulfilled; he
never married, cut himself off from his family, had no close friends, and shot
himself on March 20, 1932 at the estate of Anita Baldwin, a rich philanthropist,
outside Los Angeles. He was forty-two years old.

Long Lance was born Sylvester Long in Winston-Salem, North Carolina  24
on December 1, 1890 to parents who claimed exclusively white and Indian
blood. His mother was three-quarters white and one-quarter Croatan. Despite
the family's denial, however, photographs of his father and brother show them
to have strongly African features, though Long Lance himself, in the photographs, seemed to have straight hair. Smith explains that discrimination against
black people in the American south was so oppressive that Sylvester Long "got
out and asserted his Indian heritage." Claiming Cherokee blood, Sylvester Long
gained admission to Carlyle Indian School, though when Carlyle School investigated further, the Cherokee nation disclaimed any knowledge of him. After
graduation, he applied to West Point but decided instead to join the Royal
Canadian Air Force. Here, again, he ran into difficulties concerning his claim
of an Indian identity and finally decided to go west in search of his fortune.

25     What all four—Mark Twain, Onoto Watanna, Grey Owl, and Long Lance—had in common, in addition to the use of pseudonyms, of course, was the means by which all made their living. To be a good writer, one must be a good storyteller. Where does one draw the boundary between fiction and lying? And, to play the devil's advocate, why must storytelling cease when one's own life is concerned? Who among us does not enjoy the pleasures of "hamming it up" and role-playing?

26     Furthermore, according to William James humbugging may be a universal trait. In "Final Impressions of a Psychic Researcher," James asserts that the medium's "will to personate" raises "questions about our subconscious constitution and its curious tendency to humbug." He tentatively concludes that far from being uncommon, "every sort of person is liable to it [humbugging], or to something equivalent to it" (Gilman 163–64). Is this statement an indictment of the human race or a description of one of our imaginative and unique pleasures? Is the assumption of a persona merely telling a useless lie or is it pointing out a useful truth about the values of the society in which we live?

27     I would argue that, in cases where no harm to others is done by the deception, assuming a persona is a form of defiance to free one's self from the fetters applied by a society concerned with the insignificancies of skin color and eye shape. To exploit, consciously and cynically, the prejudices and stereotypes of the dominent society in its misperceptions of the racial minority in its midst is one step toward exploding the prejudices. As the grandfather in Ellison's *Invisible Man* advised his grandson, "Agree 'em to death and destruction" (497). Clearly, though her own personal stance differed from her younger sister's, Edith Eaton wrote in her defense in "Leaves":

> The Americans, having for many years manifested a much higher regard for the Japanese than for the Chinese, several half Chinese young men and women, thinking to advance themselves, both in a social and business sense, pass as Japanese. They continue to be known as Eurasians; but a Japanese Eurasian does not appear in the same light as a Chinese Eurasian. The unfortunate Chinese Eurasians! Are not those who compel them to thus cringe more to be blamed than they? (Far 131)

Edith Eaton makes a strong and irrefutable point. The creation of a more acceptable identity, particularly in the cases of Winnifred Eaton/Onoto Watanna and Sylvester Long/Long Lance, is indeed a defensive reaction to an unacceptable embattled situation: the rejection and devaluation of the biological self. For this provocation, the society that made such harsh judgments in the first place should be called to account. ✢

## *Works Cited*

Cheung, King-Kok and Stan Yogi. *Asian American Literature: An Annotated Bibliography*. New York: Modern Language Association, 1988.

Clarke, Joseph F. *Pseudonyms*. Nashville: T. Nelson, 1977.

De Laurentis, Teresa. *Feminist Studies/Critical Studies.* Bloomington: Indiana University Press, 1988.

Ellison, Ralph. *Invisible Man.* New York: Signet, 1952.

Far, Sui Sin. "Leaves from the Mental Portfolio of an Eurasian." *Independent,* January 21, 1909. 125–32.

Gillman, Susan. *Dark Twins: Imposture and Identity in Mark Twain's America.* Chicago: University of Chicago Press, 1989.

Kondo, Dorinne. *Crafting Selves: Power, Gender, and Discourses of Identity in a Japanese Workplace.* Chicago: University of Chicago Press, 1990.

Ling, Amy. *Between Worlds: Women Writers of Chinese Ancestry.* New York: Pergamon Press, 1990.

Lyman, Stanford. "Strangers in the City: The Chinese in the Urban Frontier." In *Roots: An Asian American Reader,* ed. Amy Tachiki, Eddie Wong, Franklin Odo, Buck Wong. Los Angeles: University of California, Los Angeles Asian American Studies Center, 1971. 159–87.

Miller, Karl. *Doubles: Studies in Literary History.* New York: Oxford University Press, 1985.

*Oxford Companion to Canadian Literature,* ed. William Toye. Toronto/New York/Oxford: Oxford University Press, 1983.

Rosenblatt, Roger. "Black Autobiography: Life as the Death Weapon." In *Autobiography: Essays Theoretical and Critical,* ed. James Olney. Princeton, N.J.: Princeton University Press, 1980.

Said, Edward. *Orientalism.* New York: Vintage, 1979.

Scott, Joan Wallach. *Gender and the Politics of History.* New York: Columbia University Press, 1988.

Smith, Donald. *Long Lance: The True Story of an Imposter.* Lincoln: University of Nebraska Press, 1983.

Watanna, Onoto. *The Diary of Delia.* New York: Page, 1907.

———. *A Japanese Nightingale.* New York: Harper, 1901.

———. *Marion: A Story of an Artist's Model by Herself and the Author of Me.* New York: Watt, 1916.

———. *Me, A Book of Remembrance.* New York: Century, 1915.

———. *Miss Nume of Japan.* Chicago: Rand, McNally, 1899.

White-Parks, Annette. "Sui Sin Far: Writer on the Chinese-Anglo Borders of North America, 1885–1914." Ph.D. dissertation, Washington State University, Program in American Studies, 1991.

## RESPONDING

1.  How do you define yourself? Write a journal entry in which you construct your own identity. In your opinion, does that identity come from biological factors or is it determined by your environment?

2.  Working individually or in a group, paraphrase and explain the quotations that begin the essay.

3.  Ling states that Edith Eaton chose "resistance, the more difficult and more

noble path" (paragraph 14). But then she questions whether "accommodation should always be condemned" (paragraph 15). Using evidence from the reading, write an essay tracing the history of the Eaton sisters and analyzing the reasons for their different choices. In your opinion, which sister made the wiser choice?

4. American society is just beginning to encourage people to identify all of the various ethnicities that contribute to their ethnic identity. Write an essay agreeing or disagreeing that people shouldn't have to choose only one part of their heritage but should be able to acknowledge all aspects of their background, not just the obvious physical characteristics. Think about how this issue applies to people of mixed ethnic origins.

✜

# CONNECTING

### *Critical Thinking and Writing*

1. Write an essay speculating on the possible social, psychological, and economic effects of the Exclusion Act on Chinese already in the United States when it was passed. Use examples from the readings to support your opinions.

2. Using the readings as a resource, compile a list of the customs and folklore that were a part of Chinese culture in the late 1800s. Write an essay discussing the folklore of your family or culture or of another culture with which you are familiar.

3. Discuss the lives of the women portrayed in this section. What opportunities were available for Chinese women of the period? What obligations did they have to fulfill? In an essay, compare their situation to that of Chinese men.

4. The year is 1882. Choose an identity for yourself. Perhaps you are a worker, a merchant, a factory owner, or a wife and mother. Take a position for or against the importation of Chinese workers, and write a letter to the editor of a San Francisco newspaper presenting your position. Support your ideas with examples from the readings, material from other sources, or your own knowledge.

5. The authors of the Gold Mountain poems in this chapter are men. Compare the authors' experiences at Angel Island with the experience of Connie Young Yu's grandmother, Mrs. Lee. What thoughts or feelings might Mrs. Lee have put in a poem?

6. Consider the similar ways in which Sui Sin Far uses the phrase "the land of the free" and Connie Young Yu uses the phrase "a land of freedom." Write an essay arguing that Young Yu's essay does or does not validate the events presented in Sin Far's short story.

7. According to the readings, what aspects of Chinese culture and character helped the Chinese become successful in America? After isolating those characteristics, list the values that seemed to be important to Chinese culture. Compare these values to your own. Are these values important to you and to contemporary American society?

8. Using information from these readings, describe the role of women in traditional Chinese culture. Compare the Chinese woman immigrant of the late 1800s to women from other immigrant groups of the same period, such as those from Europe.

9. Many Chinese came to the United States in the late 1800s. Using evidence from the readings, write an essay comparing their reasons for immigrating with those of other groups who came during the same period.

10. Compare the working conditions of the Chinese on the railway as described by Kingston to the working conditions of other groups described in readings by Panunzio in chapter 3 and Chavez in chapter 8, among others. How was each group treated? You may compare the treatment of the group or the experiences of individuals.

11. Discuss the causes and effects of organized resistance among the Chinese railroad workers that Kingston reports and compare those to Chavez's description in chapter 8 of Chicano efforts to organize almost one hundred years later.

12. The theme of parents wishing to maintain a native culture while raising their children in an alien culture recurs throughout these readings. Some parents find it easier to accept the assimilation of their children than others. Compare the reactions of any two families in this or other chapters when their children begin to become Americanized.

13. Trace the struggles for civil rights and acceptance that faced the immigrant Chinese in America. Using information from this chapter and from chapter 7 about Japanese American experiences during World War II, compare the problems facing the Chinese during the late 1800s with those of the Japanese during the 1940s.

14. Discuss the influence of the American school system on the children of immigrants. Is education a force that melds society? Is it a force that separates parents and children?

15. Discuss the relationship between parents and children portrayed in this chapter. What duties did a Chinese child in the past owe to parents and to the rest of the family? What duties does a Chinese child have today?

### For Further Research

1.  Angel Island has been called the Ellis Island of the West Coast. Research and compare the situations at the two ports of entry to the United States.

2.  Research the changes in family life that have taken place in Chinese families living in America during the past sixty years.

## REFERENCES AND ADDITIONAL SOURCES

Barth, Gunther. *Bitter Strength: A History of the Chinese in the United States, 1850–1870.* Cambridge: Harvard University Press, 1964.

Chan, Sucheng, ed. *Entry Denied: Exclusion and the Chinese Community in America, 1882–1943.* Philadelphia: Temple University Press, 1991.

———. *This Bittersweet Soil: The Chinese in California Agriculture, 1860–1910.* Berkeley: University of California Press, 1986.

Chan, Sucheng, and K. Scott Wong, eds. *Claiming America: Constructing Chinese American Identities During the Exclusion Era.* Philadelphia: Temple University Press, 1998.

Char, Tin Yuke. *The Sandalwood Mountains: Readings and Stories of the Early Chinese in Hawaii.* Honolulu: The University Press of Hawaii, 1975.

Chin, Frank. "Come All Ye Asian American Writers of the Real and the Fake," in *The Big Aiiieeeee!* Jeffrey Paul Chan, et al. New York: Meridian, 1991. 1–94.

Chinn, Thomas, et al. *A History of the Chinese in California: A Syllabus.* San Francisco: Chinese Historical Society of America, 1969, 1973.

Genthe, Arnold, and John K. Tchen. *Genthe's Photographs of San Francisco's Old Chinatown.* New York: Dover, 1984.

Gyory, Andrew. *Closing the Gate: Race, Politics, and the Chinese Exclusion Act.* Chapel Hill: University of North Carolina Press, 1998.

Hom, Marlon K. *Songs of the Gold Mountain: Cantonese Rhymes from San Francisco Chinatown.* Berkeley and Los Angeles: University of California Press, 1987.

Hwang, David Henry. *The Dance and the Railroad and Family Devotions: Two Plays by David Henry Hwang.* New York: Dramatists Play Service Inc., 1983.

Kim, Elaine. *Asian American Literature: An Introduction to Their Writings and Their Social Context.* Philadelphia: Temple University Press, 1982.

Kim, Hyung-Chan, ed. *Dictionary of Asian American History.* Westport, Conn.: Greenwood, 1986.

Lai, Him Mark, et al. *Island: Poetry and History of Chinese Immigrants on Angel Island, 1910–1940*. San Francisco: HOC DOI Project, 1980. Seattle: University of Washington Press, 1991.

Lim, Genny. *The Chinese American Experience: Papers for the Second National Conference on Chinese American Studies (1980)*. San Francisco: The Chinese Historical Society of America and the Chinese Culture Foundation of San Francisco, 1984.

Ling, Amy. *Between Worlds: Women Writers of Chinese Ancestry*. New York: Pergamon Press, 1990.

Mark, Diane Mei Lin, and Ginger Chih. *A Place Called Chinese America*. Dubuque, Iowa, 1982.

McClain, Charles J. *In Search of Equality: The Chinese Struggle Against Discrimination in Nineteenth-Century America*. Berkeley: University of California Press, 1994.

Miller, Stuart C. *The Unwelcome Immigrant: The American Image of the Chinese, 1785–1882*. Berkeley: University of California Press, 1969.

Natividad, Irene, ed. *The Asian American Almanac: A Reference Work*. Detroit: Gale, 1995.

Salyer, Lucy E. *Laws Harsh as Tigers: Chinese Immigrants and the Shaping of Modern Immigration Law*. Chapel Hill: University of North Carolina Press, 1995.

Saxton, Alexander. *The Indispensable Enemy: Labor and the Anti-Chinese Movement in California*. Berkeley: University of California Press, 1971.

Solberg, S. E. "Sui, Storyteller: Sui Sin Far," in *Turning Shadows into Light: Art and Culture of the Northwest's Early Asian/Pacific Community*, Muyami Tsutakawa and Alan Chong Lau, eds. Seattle: Young Pine Press, Asian Multi-Media Center, 1982.

———. "Sui Sin Far/Edith Eaton: First Chinese American Fictionalist," in *Melus* 8:1 (1981), 27–39.

Takaki, Ronald. *Strangers from a Different Shore: A History of Asian Americans*. Boston: Little, Brown, 1989. Penguin, 1990.

Tsai, Shih Shan Henry. *The Chinese Experience in America*. Bloomington: Indiana University Press, 1986.

Tung, William L. *The Chinese in America 1820–1973: A Chronology and Fact Book*. Dobbs Ferry, N.Y.: Oceana, 1974.

Wong, Sau-ling Cynthia. "Chinese American Literature," in *An Interethnic Companion to Asian American Literature*, King-Kok Cheung, ed. Cambridge, Engl., and New York: Cambridge University Press, 1997. 39–61.

Yung, Judy. "Chinese," in *A Nation of Peoples: A Sourcebook on America's Multicultural Heritage*, Elliot Robert Barkan, ed. Westport, Conn.: Greenwood, 1999. 119–137.

———. *Chinese Women of America: A Pictorial History*. Seattle: University of Washington Press, 1986.

# 5

## AFRICAN AMERICANS

*The Migration North and the
Journey Toward Civil Rights*

*Above:* From Jacob Lawrence  *The migrants arrived in great numbers,*
plate 40 from *The Migration of the Negro.*  (*Courtesy the artist and
Francine Seders Gallery*)
*Opposite:* March from Selma to Montgomery, in summer of 1965.
(*© James H. Karales*)

# SETTING THE HISTORICAL AND CULTURAL CONTEXT

In Gwendolyn Brooks's poem "The Chicago Defender Sends a Man to Little Rock," the speaker begins by describing what might be considered a typical community of the late 1950s:

> In Little Rock the people bear
> Babes, and comb and part their hair
> And watch the want ads, put repair
> To roof and latch. While wheat toast burns
> A woman waters multiferns. . . .
>
> In Little Rock the people sing
> Sunday hymns like anything,
> Through Sunday pomp and polishing. . . .

It becomes all the more inexplicable that this community, which seemed so "like people everywhere," engaged in a kind of unspeakable cruelty toward a group of African American students who, supported by the U.S. Supreme Court's ruling against segregated schools, had sought admission to the local high school. As the speaker of the poem, a reporter who was himself injured while covering the event, recounts:

> And true, they are hurling spittle, rock,
> Garbage and fruit in Little Rock.
> And I saw coiling storm a-writhe
> On bright madonnas. And a scythe
> Of men harassing brownish girls.
> (The bows and barrettes in the curls
> And braids declined away from joy.)
>
> I saw a bleeding brownish boy. . . .

In the poem, people who observe conventions of duty and civility with members of their own race seem to think little of committing acts of brutality in their dealings with people not of their kind.

In a literal sense, Brooks's poem has its grounding in the incidents of 1957, when a group of African American students was beaten by an angry mob after they had attempted to gain admission to Little Rock's formerly segregated Central High School. In another sense, the poem also reflects the injustices that prompted many African Americans, both adults and children, to work for civil rights. This struggle involved local and federal courts, Congress, and the White House; it took place in offices, in churches, and in the streets; and it brought together people from different backgrounds who were willing to sacrifice their social position and their very lives for their ideals.

This chapter isolates two generative periods in the construction of African American identity and the establishment of the African American canon of literary work: the Harlem Renaissance period of the 1920s and the civil rights movement of the 1950s and 1960s. To trace the patterns of segregation and discrimination that existed in various regions of the United States for more than a century is a complex task. In this introduction, we can highlight only a few of the important pieces of legislation passed on the federal level and some of the laws made by states to weaken and to codify discriminatory practices. Although the North was not immune from discriminatory practices, much repressive legislation was drafted in the South, where state legislatures allowed racial considerations to take precedence over constitutional guarantees.

The Reconstruction Act of 1867 and, later, the Fourteenth and Fifteenth Amendments to the Constitution were intended to guarantee African Americans full citizenship and participation in the electoral process—specifically, to enable African Americans to vote, hold office, participate in state constitutional conventions, and establish schools. But Reconstruction was only a small step toward overcoming the legacy of slavery. Without federal resettlement or land redistribution programs, African Americans remained economically subservient to landowning whites. Moreover, they had to endure the persecution, harassment, and terror of such racist organizations as the Ku Klux Klan, which were determined to limit the rights of African Americans at all costs.

The period after Reconstruction (1877–1896) witnessed a dramatic erosion in the federal government's commitment to the rights of African Americans. Federal laws were less strenuously enforced, and the federal government provided fewer obstacles to those state governments intent on limiting the rights of African Americans. A new low point was reached in the U.S. Supreme Court's 1896 decision in *Plessy* v. *Ferguson*, which upheld segregation by establishing the "separate but equal" doctrine.

Throughout the 1880s, southern legislatures were drafting measures that would limit African Americans' access to such public facilities as streetcars, waiting rooms, water fountains, and restrooms. Vital institutions, such as schools and hospitals, were now to be run on a segregated basis as well. One southern state after another altered its constitution in order to segregate and exclude African Americans. By 1907, all southern states had adopted segregation measures.

But how was this possible? Southern states instituted and maintained seg-regation by eliminating the voting rights of many African Americans. This process, known as *disfranchisement*, began in the late 1890s; it required that citizens pay poll taxes, pass literacy tests, or prove that they owned property before they would be allowed to vote. Often, applicants were also quizzed on whatever sections of the state constitution that the examiner deemed appro-priate. When legislators discovered that some whites were having difficulty passing these tests, they found another way in which to give whites preferen-tial treatment: they instituted *grandfather clauses*, which exempted from test-ing and property requirements any man whose father or grandfather had been eligible to vote in the state on a given date, usually during the early 1860s. Because African Americans had not been allowed to vote during the years of slavery, their descendents were effectively prevented from voting as well.

The "Letter from Birmingham Jail" notes "privileged groups rarely give up their privileges voluntarily." For over a century, African Americans at-tempted to gain the rights guaranteed them by federal law. In many places throughout the South there were sporadic demonstrations against discrimina-tory legislation and attempts to mobilize through boycott. The migration north of large numbers of African Americans created in urban areas concen-trated populations with a strengthened sense of political purpose. Organiza-tions such as the NAACP and the National Urban League were established. Their publications, begun during the Harlem Renaissance of the 1920s, an-nounced a new political and cultural awakening.

Although there had been earlier periods of migration, the so-called Great Migration took place during the first two decades of the twentieth cen-tury, particularly during and after World War I, as a reaction to the poor eco-nomic and sociopolitical conditions blacks experienced in the South.

African Americans migrated—in small numbers to the West, and in large numbers to the urban centers of the North. With the increased concentra-tion of African Americans in cities, there were greater opportunities for po-litical dialogue and debate. The New Negro movement of the 1920s rejected an earlier attitude toward racial advancement that had been popularized by educator Booker T. Washington during the late nineteenth century. Washing-ton had exhorted African Americans to earn the respect of whites by pursu-ing moral, educational, and occupational self-improvement; the latter could be gained, for example, by mastering skills that would lead to better-paying jobs in existing industries and, by extension, a better place in white society. Historian and scholar W. E. B. Du Bois challenged Washington's beliefs, maintaining that his accommodationist position would only perpetuate the status of African Americans as second-class citizens. At the Niagara Confer-ence for equal rights held in Niagara Falls, New York, in 1905, Du Bois as-serted that African Americans should instead develop their own society and culture as they pressed for full rights as American citizens. Du Bois soon became a founding member of the National Association for the Advancement of Colored People (NAACP) and editor of *The Crisis,* one of the most influential periodicals of the Harlem Renaissance period.

Other African American leaders also worked within their communities to achieve social justice. A. Philip Randolph organized and unionized the Brotherhood of Sleeping Car Porters; his organization published *The Messenger,* a magazine critical of both Washington and Du Bois. Marcus Garvey, born in Jamaica, founded the Universal Negro Improvement Association (UNIA) in 1914, before immigrating to the United States in 1916. The UNIA sought equality for blacks through social, political, and economic independence from whites. In the United States, Garvey, who advocated separatism, called on African Americans to unite to promote the liberation and development of the African homeland. Garvey received some support from African Americans and whites before being imprisoned for mail fraud and then deported from the United States. Garvey's advocacy of separatism continues to influence some African American leaders today.

In the words of Alain Locke, the Harlem Renaissance movement attempted to address "the discrepancy between the American social creed and American social practice." Although the American social creed purported to advocate freedom and justice for all, its social practices still disclosed prejudice and discrimination; lynchings also persisted. The questionable status of African Americans in their own country, then, led to conflicts within the African American community about its proper role in World War I. Although they were at first hesitant, many community leaders—Du Bois among them—encouraged African Americans to support the war effort as a means of improving their status at home. Despite their distinguished service, however, African American soldiers returning from World War I found that conditions in the United States had improved little; in fact, in some places they had worsened. Even before the end of the war the Wilson administration, in an effort to appease southerners, had begun segregating all public facilities within the District of Columbia. African Americans in other urban centers continued to face restrictive housing covenants and discriminatory employment practices. There was also a dramatic increase in racially motivated violence: historians estimate that between forty and two hundred people were killed during the East St. Louis, Illinois, riots of 1917, and twenty-five cities and towns had violent confrontations over race.

Leading periodicals such as *The Crisis* and *Opportunity* addressed the rising violence by printing monthly reports of the number of African Americans who had been lynched. These periodicals also provided a forum for literary work that expressed the anger of the period. One of the earliest poems of the Harlem Renaissance, Claude McKay's "If We Must Die," decries the continued violation of basic rights:

If we must die—oh, let us nobly die,
So that our precious blood may not be shed
In vain; then even that monsters we defy
Shall be constrained to honor us though dead!
Oh, Kinsmen! We must meet the common foe;
Though far outnumbered, let us show us brave.
And for their thousand blows deal one deathblow!
What though before us lies the open grave?
Like men we'll face the murderous, cowardly pack.
Pressed to the wall, dying, but fighting back.

While McKay's poem focuses on the relationship between the African American and white communities, the works of other Harlem Renaissance writers focus on African American culture itself. Wallace Thurman's novel *The Blacker the Berry*, for example, suggests that members of the African American community were not immune to another form of prejudice known as *colorism*, part of a system in which one's skin color determines social standing. The system privileged lighter-skinned blacks.

Although some of the writing produced during the Harlem Renaissance addresses social conditions, other works present a vision of a future with great possibilities. Alain Locke's extremely influential *The New Negro*, for example, offers an explicit program for educational advancement. Moreover, the work of poets such as Langston Hughes stresses both recovery and re-awakening. In Hughes's "Afro American Fragment," the landscape evokes a sense of collective memory:

. . . Subdued and time-lost
Are the drums—and yet
Through some vast mist of race
There comes this song
I do not understand
This song of atavistic land . . .

Hughes's poem stresses the importance of recovering a sense of history, a past that had been lost for too long.

The Harlem Renaissance period ended abruptly, with the stock market crash of 1929 and the Depression that followed. Even as the movement asserted the black community's political and cultural awakening, it remained separate from African American communities in both the North and South, which experienced regular patterns of discrimination.

During the period just before World War II, several segments of the African American community increased their demands for equal treatment under the law. Much of the political action of the 1940s can be credited to the work of A. Philip Randolph, who, as editor of *The Messenger* and president of the Brotherhood of Sleeping Car Porters, had been politically active since the Harlem Renaissance. In 1940 Randolph organized 100,000 people to march on Washington, D.C., in protest of segregation in the government and discriminatory hiring practices in the defense industries. This group called off its march only after it had received a commitment from President Franklin D. Roosevelt to the cause of civil rights. Executive Order 8802, issued by Roosevelt, outlawed discrimination in defense industries and in government hiring. Later that year the federal government established the Fair Employment Practices Commission. Full integration of the armed forces was not accomplished, however, until the Korean War.

For generations, African Americans had been excluded from many educational and employment opportunities. Despite the state governments' assertion that black and white schools were "separate but equal," the facilities for African Americans were clearly inferior to those for whites. The passage from Ernest Gaines's novel included in this chapter, and set in New Orleans in the 1940s, reflects some of the inequities: hand-me-down books that are outdated and lacking pages, not enough paper, not enough chalk, not enough pencils, not enough heat. As the narrative unfolds, it becomes increasingly clear that the lack of supplies is but one inequity that is experienced: the superintendent, having arrived for his annual visit, examines the children's teeth "as they used to do at the time of slavery"; counsels the children on the benefits of "exercise," including picking cotton; and chastises the teacher for asking for books with all the pages.

During the 1940s and 1950s, organizations such as the NAACP began to challenge the legality of "separate but equal" schools that was first established in the 1896 U.S. Supreme Court *Plessy* v. *Ferguson* decision. Civil rights groups gained some encouragement from the Court's 1950 *Sweatt* v. *Painter* ruling that a separate law school for African Americans that had been established in Texas was unconstitutional. It was in the 1954 case of *Brown* v. *The Board of Education of Topeka* that the doctrine of separate but equal was successfully challenged for the first time. Led by Thurgood Marshall (who would later become a justice of the U.S. Supreme Court), the plaintiffs argued against the doctrine in *Plessy* on educational, psychological, and economic grounds. In a unanimous ruling, the U.S. Supreme Court reversed the *Plessy* decision, declaring that separate educational facilities were inherently unequal and therefore unconstitutional.

The *Brown* decision, important as it was, did not end racial segregation in schools. Many southerners protested against the ruling; others sought ways to evade or defer it. More than one hundred southern congressmen wrote letters denouncing the decision, and several southern governors attempted to block its implementation. In 1957 Governor Orval Faubus ordered the Arkansas National Guard to prevent the court-ordered integration of Little Rock's Central High; after President Eisenhower forced him to rescind the order, an angry mob formed to take the guardsmen's place, and several African American students were severely beaten (see Gwendolyn Brooks, "The Chicago Defender Sends a Man to Little Rock"). In 1962, as James Meredith, aided by Medgar Evers and others from the NAACP, attempted to register at the University of Mississippi, a mob, incited by the defiant speeches of Governor Ross Barnett, rioted; federal troops had to be called in to quell the unrest. In 1963 Alabama's governor, George Wallace, stood in a doorway, barring two students from registering at the University of Alabama; it took the intervention of the Justice Department before the students could be admitted. In the South, school districts encouraged white parents to send their children to private schools, which could remain segregated. In Virginia, the public schools were closed and much of their property was given to private schools; as a result, many African American children were kept out of school for up to two years.

African Americans also had to demand their rights to public transportation. Although the U.S. Supreme Court had outlawed segregation in interstate transportation, most public transportation within individual southern states remained segregated. African Americans, who paid the same fares as whites, were required to sit in the back of the bus; worse, when there was a shortage of seats for whites, African American passengers were expected to give up their seats without question. On December 1, 1955, Mrs. Rosa Parks protested this form of discrimination by refusing to give her seat to a white. Her nonviolent civil disobedience led to her arrest and imprisonment; it also marked the beginning of a long boycott of the bus system. There had been earlier protests against such discrimination, including a boycott of a Louisiana bus system. The Montgomery boycott of 1955, however, was the first demonstration of its kind to succeed. Its success led to the founding of the Southern Christian Leadership Conference in 1957. During the early 1960s, Freedom Riders—African Americans and whites organized by the Congress of Racial Equality (CORE)—rode southern buses to protest the continued illegal segregation in interstate transportation. Freedom Riders also participated in education and voter registration drives.

During the 1950s and early 1960s, African Americans were still refused service at the lunch counters of many department stores. Martin Luther King Jr. reflected on the grim irony of this daily humiliation in his "Letter from Birmingham Jail": "The nations of Asia and Africa are moving with jetlike speed toward gaining political independence, but we still creep at horse-and-buggy pace toward gaining a cup of coffee at a lunch counter." Even before King wrote his letter, however, students had begun to protest these inequities with some success. In 1960, members of the Student Nonviolent Coordinating Committee had a "sit-in" at a local lunch counter in Greensboro, North Carolina. They manned the counters in shifts around the clock until they were finally served. This type of sit-in protest, begun by four college freshmen, was repeated with success at lunch counters, libraries, swimming pools, theaters, and other public facilities throughout the South.

In these protests and others, African Americans made use of nonviolent direct action. The strategies of direct action are outlined in "Letter from Birmingham Jail," which Martin Luther King Jr. composed after being arrested for leading a boycott of stores in Birmingham, Alabama. While being held in solitary confinement, King uses the letter as an opportunity not only to answer his critics, but also to explain and to justify the important role of civil disobedience and nonviolent protest in the cause of equality. The letter establishes philosophical, theological, and historical grounds for such protest and supplements formal argument with concrete images that still create an affective appeal for readers more than thirty years after the letter was written.

The protests against desegregation culminated in the March on Washington in August 1963, which brought together more than a quarter of a million people. Organized to promote congressional passage of the Civil Rights Act, the march featured addresses by activists John Lewis and Bayard Rustin, among others, and Martin Luther King Jr.'s now-famous "I Have a Dream" speech. The major television and radio networks provided extensive coverage of the event. When the Civil Rights Act was passed in 1964, it was considered the farthest-reaching legislation in the nation's history. The Voting Rights Act the following year established federal offices to monitor the registration of African American voters, as well as to regulate and to prevent abuses by registrars.

Each victory in the struggle for civil rights was achieved because of the courage of the activists involved. Those sitting in at lunch counters were subjected to beatings and arrest; activists had food, ammonia, and other substances poured on them, and lit cigarettes ground into their backs. Leaders of the civil rights movement found their homes, churches, and families threatened and at times attacked. Freedom Riders traveling throughout the South by bus were stoned and beaten; their buses were burned by angry mobs. In Birmingham during the administration of Mayor Eugene "Bull" Connor, police fought protesters—both adults and children—with fire hoses and attack dogs, and then savagely beat them. In 1965, demonstrators marching through Selma, Alabama, were driven back by tear gas and then attacked by sheriff's officers. Such events, which were often televised, revealed the brutality with which civil rights activists were treated in the South and prompted national outrage and action.

Many civil rights workers were martyred as a result of their activism and honored because of their activism. In 1963, Medgar Evers, who had helped James Meredith gain admission to the University of Mississippi, was shot in front of his home. (Although authorities at the time suspected Byron De La Beckwith of his murder, it took thirty years for the suspect to be brought to justice, when the defendant was convicted and sentenced to life in prison.) A year later, also in Mississippi, three Freedom Riders—Andrew Goodman, Michael Schwerner, and James Chaney: two whites and an African American—disappeared; they were later discovered to have been murdered. They had been investigating a church fire when they were apprehended by local authorities; after being turned over to a mob, they were tortured and murdered. In 1968, while leading a strike of workers in Memphis, Martin Luther King Jr. was assassinated.

In her poetry Gwendolyn Brooks celebrates people of vision and courage—Medgar Evers, Malcolm X, and the children of Little Rock, all of whom suffered in the name of civil rights. Martin Luther King Jr. received the Nobel Peace Prize in 1964. A year before his death in 1999, James Farmer was awarded the Medal of Freedom, the highest award presented to a civilian, for his work on behalf of civil rights. In 1999 Rosa Parks was also honored for her courage with the Congressional Gold Medal. In Brooks's words, each of these people "leaned against tomorrow."

After the passage of the Civil Rights Act, there was division in the civil rights movement. The nonviolent action advocated by the Southern Christian Leadership Conference and CORE was rejected by Stokley Carmichael and other African American leaders. Malcolm X, one of the most influential of these, questioned the achievements of the civil rights movement. In the selection that follows in this chapter, Malcolm X returns to questions of justice and dignity. In his words, "A desegregated cup of coffee, a theater, public toilets—the whole range of hypocritical 'integration'" could be seen as inadequate "atonement" for the nation's treatment of African Americans.

Despite its many accomplishments, the civil rights movement has yet to achieve its goals. As activists point out, the rates of poverty, unemployment, infant mortality, and crime remain higher in African American communities than in the dominant culture. African Americans now have greater opportunities to serve in public office and to participate in the political process, but neither the government nor the private sector has been able to stop the deterioration of many American urban areas or to counteract the extreme poverty of many rural areas. Despite the victories of the 1960s, African Americans in the new millennium still have to demand the right to join exclusive business and social clubs. Medgar Evers's murder remains unsolved. And cities from Brooklyn to Los Angeles have been scarred by racial violence. As President Clinton commissions a National Dialogue on Race and national pundits repeat the question of Rodney King—"Can't we all get along?"—it becomes more apparent that the struggle against prejudice and injustice is far from being won.

## BEGINNING: Pre-reading/Writing

*Before reading the selections in this chapter, try to determine how much you already know about the civil rights movement of the 1960s and its leaders by listing events that led to and took place during the struggle for civil rights. Working with the class, construct a time line of significant events. As you read the selections in this chapter and learn more about the civil rights movement, revise your time line as necessary. Then compare your time line to a time line in a book or on the Internet.*

*The Constitution of South Carolina (1895) illustrates a trend that began in southern states in the 1880s and 1890s. In a process known as disfranchisement, the state legislature set limits on voting rights, based on such criteria as the applicant's ownership of property, payment of a poll tax, and ability to pass a literacy test. Such laws effectively excluded most African Americans from the voting process. It was not until the 1960s that these laws were repealed. Disfranchisement is considered one of the primary causes of the great migration of African Americans from the South.*

⁜

# *From* THE CONSTITUTION OF SOUTH CAROLINA

## *Article II: Right of Suffrage*

SECTION 1. All elections by the people shall be by ballot, and elections shall never be held or the ballots counted in secret. 1

SEC. 2. Every qualified elector shall be eligible to any office to be voted for, unless disqualified by age, as prescribed in this Constitution. But no person shall hold two offices of honor or profit at the same time: *Provided,* That any person holding another office may at the same time be an officer in the militia or a Notary Public. 2

SEC. 3. Every male citizen of this State and of the United States twenty-one years of age and upwards, not laboring under the disabilities named in this Constitution and possessing the qualifications required by it, shall be an elector. 3

SEC. 4. The qualifications for suffrage shall be as follows: 4

(*a*) Residence in the State for two years, in the County one year, in the polling precinct in which the elector offers to vote four months, and the payment 5 six months before any election of any poll tax then due and payable: *Provided,* That ministers in charge of an organized church and teachers of public schools shall be entitled to vote after six months' residence in the State, otherwise qualified.

6     (*b*) Registration, which shall provide for the enrollment of every elector once in ten years, and also an enrollment during each and every year of every elector not previously registered under the provisions of this Article.

7     (*c*) Up to January 1st 1898, all male persons of voting age applying for registration who can read any Section in this Constitution submitted to them by the registration officer, or understand and explain it when read to them by the registration officer, shall be entitled to register and become electors. A separate record of all persons registered before January 1st, 1898, sworn to by the registration officer, shall be filed, one copy with the Clerk of Court and one in the office of the Secretary of State, on or before February 1st, 1898, and such persons shall remain during life qualified electors unless disqualified by the other provisions of this Article. The certificate of the Clerk of Court or Secretary of State shall be sufficient evidence to establish the right of said citizens to any subsequent registration and the franchise under the limitations herein imposed.

8     (*d*) Any person who shall apply for registration after January 1st, 1898, if otherwise qualified, shall be registered: *Provided,* That he can both read and write any Section of this Constitution submitted to him by the registration officer or can show that he owns, and has paid all taxes collectible during the previous year on property in this State assessed at three hundred dollars ($300) or more.

9     (*e*) Managers of election shall require of every elector offering to vote at any election, before allowing him to vote, proof of the payment of all taxes, including poll tax, assessed against him and collectible during the previous year. The production of a certificate or of the receipt of the officer authorized to collect such taxes shall be conclusive proof of the payment thereof.

10     (*f*) The General Assembly shall provide for issuing to each duly registered elector a certificate of registration, and shall provide for the renewal of such certificate when lost, mutilated or destroyed, if the applicant is still a qualified elector under the provisions of this Constitution, or if he has been registered as provided in subsection (*c*). ✜

---

## RESPONDING

1. Find the provisions in the section of the Constitution of South Carolina that could be used to keep someone from voting. In a journal entry, discuss who has the discretion to grant someone the right to vote and the implications of that power.

2.  Working in a group, discuss the ways in which the power structure in a society can work to disfranchise certain citizens.

3.  Are you surprised that such laws were not challenged in the courts? Write an essay comparing these provisions with the guarantees in the Bill of Rights. Argue that the provisions do or do not violate the rights guaranteed in the U.S. Constitution.

---

*In 1954 the Supreme Court ruled that the school board of Topeka, Kansas, had violated the law when it had ordered children to attend racially segregated schools. In their unanimous decision, the justices said that segregation by race violated the constitutional guarantee of equal protection under the law. The Court reversed the earlier decision of* Plessy v. Ferguson *(1896), which had permitted "separate but equal" schools.*

❖

# *From* BROWN v. THE BOARD OF EDUCATION OF TOPEKA

THESE CASES COME TO US from the States of Kansas, South Carolina, Virginia, and Delaware. They are premised on different facts and different local conditions, but a common legal question justifies their consideration together in this consolidated opinion. 1

In approaching this problem, we cannot turn the clock back to 1868 when the Amendment was adopted, or even to 1896 when *Plessy* v. *Ferguson* was written. We must consider public education in the light of its full development and its present place in American life throughout the Nation. Only in this way can it be determined if segregation in public schools deprives these plaintiffs of the equal protection of the laws. 2

Today, education is perhaps the most important function of state and local governments. Compulsory school attendance laws and the great expenditures for education both demonstrate our recognition of the importance of education to our democratic society. It is required in the performance of our most basic public responsibilities, even service in the armed forces. It is the very foundation of good citizenship. Today it is a principal instrument in awakening the child to cultural values, in preparing him for later professional training, and in helping him to adjust normally to his environment. In these days, it is doubtful that any child may reasonably be expected to succeed in life if he is denied the oppor- 3 tunity of an education. Such an opportunity, where the state has undertaken to provide it, is a right which must be made available to all on equal terms.

4    We come then to the question presented: Does segregation of children in public schools solely on the basis of race, even though the physical facilities and other "tangible" factors may be equal, deprive the children of the minority group of equal educational opportunities? We believe that it does.

5    In *Sweatt* v. *Painter*, . . . in finding that a segregated law school for Negroes could not provide them equal educational opportunities, this Court relied in large part on "those qualities which are incapable of objective measurement but which make for greatness in a law school." In *McLaurin* v. *Oklahoma State Regents*, . . . the Court, in requiring that a Negro admitted to a white graduate school be treated like all other students, again resorted to intangible considerations: ". . . his ability to study, to engage in discussions and exchange views with other students, and, in general, to learn his profession." Such considerations apply with added force to children in grade and high schools. To separate them from others of similar age and qualifications solely because of their race generates a feeling of inferiority as to their status in the community that may affect their hearts and minds in a way unlikely ever to be undone. The effect of this separation on their educational opportunities was well stated by a finding in the Kansas case by a court which nevertheless felt compelled to rule against the Negro plaintiffs:

> Segregation of white and colored children in public schools has a detrimental effect upon the colored children. The impact is greater when it has the sanction of the law; for the policy of separating the races is usually interpreted as denoting the inferiority of the Negro group. A sense of inferiority affects the motivation of a child to learn. Segregation with the sanction of the law, therefore, has a tendency to retard the educational and mental development of Negro children and to deprive them of some of the benefits they would receive in a racially integrated school system.

Whatever may have been the extent of psychological knowledge at the time of *Plessy* v. *Ferguson*, this finding is amply supported by modern authority. Any language in *Plessy* v. *Ferguson* contrary to this finding is rejected.

6    We conclude that in the field of public education the doctrine of "separate but equal" has no place. Separate educational facilities are inherently unequal. Therefore, we hold that the plaintiffs and others similarly situated for whom the actions have been brought are, by reason of the segregation complained of, deprived of the equal protection of the laws guaranteed by the Fourteenth Amendment. . . . ✠

## RESPONDING

1. In a journal entry, explain the significance of the Fourteenth Amendment to the Constitution in your own words.

2. Working individually or in a group, define "segregation," "*de facto* segregation," and "separate but equal." Discuss the ways in which these policies were implemented in many school systems.

3. List the reasons that the justices give to support their statement that "today, education is perhaps the most important function of state and local·governments" (paragraph 3). Which of these reasons do you think is most persuasive and important? Write an essay supporting your choice.

4. Using arguments from the decision as well as your own knowledge and experience, write an essay in which you agree or disagree that "in the field of public education the doctrine of 'separate but equal' has no place" (paragraph 6). Consider, as well, whether the same arguments apply to private education.

# LANGSTON HUGHES

*Langston Hughes, who was born in Joplin, Missouri, in 1902, studied at Columbia University and Lincoln University. During a literary career of more than forty years, he wrote poetry, fiction, drama, and a two-volume autobiography,* The Big Sea *(1940) and* I Wonder as I Wander *(1956). His work has been praised for its simplicity and its wit. During the 1920s, Hughes participated in many of the editorial activities and the lively debates of the Harlem Renaissance. He died in 1967.*

*The poem that follows explores the issues of heritage, identity, and ambition. It invites us to consider the relationships between individuals and groups and the power that each of us has to make others feel accepted or rejected.*

⁜

# THEME FOR ENGLISH B

THE INSTRUCTOR SAID,

> *Go home and write*
> *a page tonight.*
> *And let that page come out of you—*
> 5 *Then, it will be true.*

I wonder if it's that simple?

I am twenty-two, colored, born in Winston-Salem.
I went to school there, then Durham, then here
to this college on the hill above Harlem.
10 I am the only colored student in my class.
The steps from the hill lead down into Harlem,
through a park, then I cross St. Nicholas,
Eighth Avenue, Seventh, and I come to the Y,
the Harlem Branch Y, where I take the elevator
15 up to my room, sit down, and write this page:

It's not easy to know what is true for you or me
at twenty-two, my age. But I guess I'm what
I feel and see and hear. Harlem, I hear you:
hear you, hear me—we two—you, me, talk on this page.
20 (I hear New York, too.) Me—who?

Well, I like to eat, sleep, drink, and be in love.
I like to work, read, learn, and understand life.
I like a pipe for a Christmas present,
or records—Bessie, bop, or Bach.
25 I guess being colored doesn't make me *not* like
the same things other folks like who are other races.

So will my page be colored that I write?
Being me, it will not be white.
But it will be
30 a part of you, instructor.
You are white—
yet a part of me, as I am a part of you.
That's American.
Sometimes perhaps you don't want to be a part of me.

Nor do I often want to be a part of you.                                      35
But we are, that's true!
As I learn from you,
I guess you learn from me—
although you're older—and white—
and somewhat more free.                                                      40

This is my page for English B.  ✠

---

## RESPONDING

1.  The speaker is the only "colored student" in his university class (line 10). How do you think he feels about that situation? Write a journal entry about a time when you or a relative or friend were the only representative of a group, for example, the only woman or man, the only American, the only northerner, among a group of "others." How did you respond in that situation? How did the "others" treat you?

2.  Working individually or in a group, list the ways in which the speaker sees himself as similar to everyone else in his class and the ways in which he sees himself as different.

3.  Write an essay explaining what the speaker means when he says, "you are . . . / a part of me, as I am a part of you. / That's American" (lines 31–33). You might want to include your own prose version of the lines.

---

# WALLACE THURMAN

*Wallace Thurman was born in Salt Lake City in 1902. After studying at the University of Southern California, he settled in Harlem, where he worked on several of the important periodicals of the Harlem Renaissance period, including* The Messenger. *He collaborated with many of the foremost writers of the movement: with W. J. Rapp he wrote the play* Harlem, *and with Zora Neale Hurston and Langston Hughes he edited the literary publication* Fire!!! *Thurman also wrote two novels,* The Blacker the Berry *(1929) and* Infants of the Spring *(1932). The second novel satirized some of the pretensions of the Harlem Renaissance itself. Thurman died of tuberculosis at the age of thirty-two.*

   *The following excerpt, from* The Blacker the Berry, *examines the influence of unconscious prejudices on first impressions.*

✠

## *From* THE BLACKER THE BERRY

1   SUMMER VACATION WAS NEARLY OVER and it had not yet been decided what to do with Emma Lou now that she had graduated from high school. She herself gave no help nor offered any suggestions. As it was, she really did not care what became of her. After all it didn't seem to matter. There was no place in the world for a girl as black as she anyway. Her grandmother had assured her that she would never find a husband worth a dime, and her mother had said again and again, "Oh, if you had only been a boy!" until Emma Lou had often wondered why it was that people were not able to effect a change of sex or at least a change of complexion.

2   It was her Uncle Joe who finally prevailed upon her mother to send her to the University of Southern California in Los Angeles. There, he reasoned, she would find a larger and more intelligent social circle. In a city the size of Los Angeles there were Negroes of every class, color, and social position. Let Emma Lou go there where she would not be as far away from home as if she were to go to some eastern college.

3   Jane and Maria, while not agreeing entirely with what Joe said, were nevertheless glad that at last something which seemed adequate and sensible could be done for Emma Lou. She was to take the four year college course, receive a bachelor degree in education, then go South to teach. That, they thought, was a promising future, and for once in the eighteen years of Emma Lou's life every one was satisfied in some measure. Even Emma Lou grew elated over the prospects of the trip. Her Uncle Joe's insistence upon the differences of social contacts in larger cities intrigued her. Perhaps he was right after all in continually reasserting to them that as long as one was a Negro, one's specific color had little to do with one's life. Salvation depended upon the individual. And he also told Emma Lou, during one of their usual private talks, that it was only in small cities one encountered stupid color prejudice such as she had encountered among the blue vein circle in her home town.

4   "People in large cities," he had said, "are broad. They do not have time to think of petty things. The people in Boise are fifty years behind the times, but you will find that Los Angeles is one of the world's greatest and most modern cities, and you will be happy there."

5   On arriving in Los Angeles, Emma Lou was so busy observing the colored inhabitants that she had little time to pay attention to other things. Palm trees and wild geraniums were pleasant to behold, and such strange phenomena as pepper trees and century plants had to be admired. They were very obvious and they were also strange and beautiful, but they impinged upon only a small corner of Emma Lou's consciousness. She was minutely aware of them, necessarily took them in while passing, viewing the totality without pondering over or

lingering to praise their stylistic details. They were, in this instance, exquisite theatrical props, rendered insignificant by a more strange and a more beautiful human pageant. For Emma Lou, who, in all her life, had never seen over five hundred Negroes, the spectacle presented by a community containing over fifty thousand, was sufficient to make relatively commonplace many more important and charming things than the far famed natural scenery of Southern California.

She had arrived in Los Angeles a week before registration day at the university, and had spent her time in being shown and seeing the city. But whenever these sightseeing excursions took her away from the sections where Negroes lived, she immediately lost all interest in what she was being shown. The Pacific Ocean in itself did not cause her heart beat to quicken, nor did the roaring of its waves find an emotional echo within her. But on coming upon Bruce's Beach for colored people near Redondo, or the little strip of sandied shore they had appropriated for themselves at Santa Monica, the Pacific Ocean became an intriguing something to contemplate as a background for their activities. Everything was interesting as it was patronized, reflected through, or acquired by Negroes.

Her Uncle Joe had been right. Here, in the colored social circles of Los Angeles, Emma Lou was certain that she would find many suitable companions, intelligent, broad-minded people of all complexions, intermixing and being too occupied otherwise to worry about either their own skin color or the skin color of those around them. Her Uncle Joe had said that Negroes were Negroes whether they happened to be yellow, brown, or black, and a conscious effort to eliminate the darker elements would neither prove nor solve anything. There was nothing quite so silly as the creed of the blue veins: "Whiter and whiter, every generation. The nearer white you are the more white people will respect you. Therefore all light Negroes marry light Negroes. Continue to do so generation after generation, and eventually white people will accept this racially bastard aristocracy, thus enabling those Negroes who really matter to escape the social and economic inferiority of the American Negro."

Such had been the credo of her grandmother and of her mother and of their small circle of friends in Boise. But Boise was a provincial town, given to the molding of provincial people with provincial minds. Boise was a backward town out of the mainstream of modern thought and progress. Its people were cramped and narrow, their intellectual concepts stereotyped and static. Los Angeles was a happy contrast in all respects.

On registration day, Emma Lou rushed out to the campus of the University of Southern California one hour before the registrar's office was scheduled to open. She spent the time roaming around, familiarizing herself with the layout of the campus and learning the names of the various buildings, some old and vineclad, others new and shiny in the sun, and watching the crowds of laughing students, rushing to and fro, greeting one another and talking over their plans for the coming school year. But her main reason for such an early arrival on the campus had been to find some of her fellow Negro students. She had heard that there were to be quite a number enrolled, but in all her hour's stroll she saw not one, and finally somewhat disheartened she got into the line stretched out in front of the registrar's office, and, for the moment, became engrossed in becoming a college freshman.

10      All the while, though, she kept searching for a colored face, but it was not until she had been duly signed up as a student and sent in search of her advisor that she saw one. Then three colored girls had sauntered into the room where she was having a conference with her advisor, sauntered in, arms interlocked, greeted her advisor, then sauntered out again. Emma Lou had wanted to rush after them—to introduce herself, but of course it had been impossible under the circumstances. She had immediately taken a liking to all three, each of whom was what is known in the parlance of the black belt as high brown, with modishly-shingled bobbed hair and well formed bodies, fashionably attired in flashy sport garments. From then on Emma Lou paid little attention to the business of choosing subjects and class hours, so little attention in fact that the advisor thought her exceptionally tractable and somewhat dumb. But she liked students to come that way. It made the task of being advisor easy. One just made out the program to suit oneself, and had no tedious explanations to make as to why the student could not have such and such a subject at such and such an hour, and why such and such a professor's class was already full.

11      After her program had been made out, Emma Lou was directed to the bursar's office to pay her fees. While going down the stairs she almost bumped into two dark-brown-skinned boys, obviously brothers if not twins, arguing as to where they should go next. One insisted that they should go back to the registrar's office. The other was being equally insistent that they should go to the gymnasium and make an appointment for their required physical examination. Emma Lou boldly stopped when she saw them, hoping they would speak, but they merely glanced up at her and continued their argument, bringing cards and pamphlets out of their pockets for reference and guidance. Emma Lou wanted to introduce herself to them, but she was too bashful to do so. She wasn't yet used to going to school with other Negro students, and she wasn't exactly certain how one went about becoming acquainted. But she finally decided that she had better let the advances come from the others, especially if they were men. There was nothing forward about her, and since she was a stranger it was no more than right that the old-timers should make her welcome. Still, if these had been girls . . . , but they weren't, so she continued her way down the stairs.

12      In the bursar's office, she was somewhat overjoyed at first to find that she had fallen into line behind another colored girl who had turned around immediately, and, after saying hello, announced in a loud, harsh voice:

"My feet are sure some tired!"                                                    13

Emma Lou was so taken aback that she couldn't answer. People in college    14
didn't talk that way. But meanwhile the girl was continuing:

"Ain't this registration a mess?"                                                  15

Two white girls who had fallen into line behind Emma Lou snickered.        16
Emma Lou answered by shaking her head. The girl continued:

"I've been standin' in line and climbin' stairs and talkin' and a-signin' till   17
I'm just 'bout done for."

"It is tiresome," Emma Lou returned softly, hoping the girl would take a    18
hint and lower her own strident voice. But she didn't.

"Tiresome ain't no name for it," she declared more loudly than ever before,   19
then, "Is you a new student?"

"I am," answered Emma Lou, putting much emphasis on the "I am."           20

She wanted the white people who were listening to know that she knew her   21
grammar if this other person didn't. "Is you," indeed! If this girl was a specimen
of the Negro students with whom she was to associate, she most certainly did
not want to meet another one. But it couldn't be possible that all of them—those
three girls and those two boys for instance—were like this girl. Emma Lou was
unable to imagine how such a person had ever gotten out of high school. Where
on earth could she have gone to high school? Surely not in the North. Then
she must be a southerner. That's what she was, a southerner—Emma Lou curled
her lips a little—no wonder the colored people in Boise spoke as they did about
southern Negroes and wished that they would stay South. Imagine anyone
preparing to enter college saying "Is you," and, to make it worse, right before
all these white people, these staring white people, so eager and ready to laugh.
Emma Lou's face burned.

"Two mo', then I goes in my sock."                                                22

Emma Lou was almost at the place where she was ready to take even this     23
statement literally, and was on the verge of leaving the line. Supposing this
creature did "go in her sock"! God forbid!

"Wonder where all the spades keep themselves? I ain't seen but two 'sides    24
you."

"I really do not know," Emma Lou returned precisely and chillily. She had    25
no intentions of becoming friendly with this sort of person. Why she would be
ashamed even to be seen on the street with her, dressed as she was in a
red-striped sport suit, a white hat, and white shoes and stockings. Didn't she
know that black people had to be careful about the colors they affected?

The girl had finally reached the bursar's window and was paying her fees,    26
and loudly differing with the cashier about the total amount due.

"I tell you it ain't that much," she shouted through the window bars. "I      27
figured it up myself before I left home."

The cashier obligingly turned to her adding machine and once more ob-      28
tained the same total. When shown this, the girl merely grinned, examined the
list closely, and said:

29     "I'm gonna' pay it; but I still think you're wrong."

30     Finally she moved away from the window, but not before she had turned to Emma Lou and said,

31     "You're next," and then proceeded to wait until Emma Lou had finished.

32     Emma Lou vainly sought some way to escape, but was unable to do so, and had no choice but to walk with the girl to the registrar's office where they had their cards stamped in return for the bursar's receipt. This done, they went onto the campus together. Hazel Mason was the girl's name. Emma Lou had fully expected it to be either Hyacinth or Geranium. Hazel was from Texas, Prairie Valley, Texas, and she told Emma Lou that her father, having become quite wealthy when oil had been found on his farm lands, had been enabled to realize two life ambitions—obtain a Packard touring car and send his only daughter to a "fust-class" white school.

33     Emma Lou had planned to loiter around the campus. She was still eager to become acquainted with the colored members of the student body, and this encounter with the crass and vulgar Hazel Mason had only made her the more eager. She resented being approached by any one so flagrantly inferior, any one so noticeably a typical southern darky, who had no business obtruding into the more refined scheme of things. Emma Lou planned to lose her unwelcome companion somewhere on the campus so that she could continue unhindered her quest for agreeable acquaintances.

34     But Hazel was as anxious to meet one as was Emma Lou, and having found her was not going to let her get away without a struggle. She, too, was new to this environment and in a way was more lonely and eager for the companionship of her own kind than Emma Lou, for never before had she come into such close contact with so many whites. Her life had been spent only among Negroes. Her fellow pupils and teachers in school had always been colored, and as she confessed to Emma Lou, she couldn't get used "to all these white folks."

35     "Honey, I was just achin' to see a black face," she had said, and, though Emma Lou was experiencing the same ache, she found herself unable to sympathize with the other girl, for Emma Lou classified Hazel as a barbarian who had most certainly not come from a family of best people. No doubt her mother had been a washerwoman. No doubt she had innumerable relatives and friends all as ignorant and as ugly as she. There was no sense in any one having a face as ugly as Hazel's, and Emma Lou thanked her stars that though she was black, her skin was not rough and pimply, nor was her hair kinky, nor were her nostrils completely flattened out until they seemed to spread all over her face. No wonder people were prejudiced against dark skin people when they were so ugly, so haphazard in their dress, and so boisterously mannered as was this present specimen. She herself was black, but nevertheless she had come from a good family, and she could easily take her place in a society of the right sort of people.

36     The two strolled along the lawn-bordered gravel path which led to a vine-covered building at the end of the campus. Hazel never ceased talking. She kept shouting at Emma Lou, shouting all sorts of personal intimacies as if she

were desirous of the whole world hearing them. There was no necessity for her to talk so loudly, no necessity for her to afford every one on the crowded campus the chance to stare and laugh at them as they passed. Emma Lou had never before been so humiliated and so embarrassed. She felt that she must get away from her offensive companion. What did she care if she had to hurt her feelings to do so? The more insulting she could be now, the less friendly she would have to be in the future.

"Good-bye," she said abruptly, "I must go home." With which she turned away and walked rapidly in the opposite direction. She had only gone a few steps when she was aware of the fact that the girl was following her. She quickened her pace, but the girl caught up with her and grabbing hold of Emma Lou's arm, shouted, 37

"Whoa there, Sally." 38

It seemed to Emma Lou as if every one on the campus was viewing and enjoying this minstrel-like performance. Angrily she tried to jerk away, but the girl held fast. 39

"Gal, you sure walk fast. I'm going your way. Come on, let me drive you home in my buggy." 40

And still holding on the Emma Lou's arm, she led the way to the side street where the students parked their cars. Emma Lou was powerless to resist. The girl didn't give her a chance, for she held tight, then immediately resumed the monologue which Emma Lou's attempted leave-taking had interrupted. They reached the street, Hazel still talking loudly, and making elaborate gestures with her free hand. 41

"Here we are," she shouted, and releasing Emma Lou's arm, salaamed before a sport model Stutz roadster. "Oscar," she continued, "meet the new girl friend. Pleased to meetcha, says he. Climb aboard." 42

And Emma Lou had climbed aboard, perplexed, chagrined, thoroughly angry, and disgusted. What was this little black fool doing with a Stutz roadster? And of course, it would be painted red—Negroes always bedecked themselves and their belongings in ridiculously unbecoming colors and ornaments. It seemed to be a part of their primitive heritage which they did not seem to have sense enough to forget and deny. Black girl—white hat—red and white striped sport suit—white shoes and stockings—red roadster. The picture was complete. All Hazel needed to complete her circus-like appearance, thought Emma Lou, was to have some purple feathers stuck in her hat. 43

Still talking, the girl unlocked and proceeded to start the car. As she was backing it out of the narrow parking space, Emma Lou heard a chorus of semi-suppressed giggles from a neighboring automobile. In her anger she had failed to notice that there were people in the car parked next to the Stutz. But as Hazel expertly swung her machine around, Emma Lou caught a glimpse of them. They were all colored and they were all staring at her and at Hazel. She thought she recognized one of the girls as being one of the group she had seen earlier that morning, and she did recognize the two brothers she had passed on 44 the stairs. And as the roadster sped away, their laugher echoed in her ears, although she hadn't actually heard it. But she had seen the strain in their faces, and she knew that as soon as she and Hazel were out of sight, they would give free rein to their suppressed mirth.

45 Although Emma Lou had finished registering, she returned to the university campus on the following morning in order to continue her quest for collegiate companions without the alarming and unwelcome presence of Hazel Mason. She didn't know whether to be sorry for that girl and try to help her or to be disgusted and avoid her. She didn't want to be intimately associated with any such vulgar person. It would damage her own position, cause her to be classified with some one who was in a class by herself, for Emma Lou was certain that there was not, and could not be, any one else in the university just like Hazel. But despite her vulgarity, the girl was not all bad. Her good nature was infectious, and Emma Lou had surmised from her monologue on the day before how utterly unselfish a person she could be and was. All of her store of the world's goods were at hand to be used and enjoyed by her friends. There was not, as she had said "a selfish bone in her body." But even that did not alter the disgusting fact that she was not one who would be welcome by the "right sort of people." Her flamboyant style of dress, her loud voice, her raucous laughter, and her flagrant disregard or ignorance of English grammar seemed inexcusable to Emma Lou, who was unable to understand how such a person could stray so far from the environment in which she rightfully belonged to enter a first-class university. Now Hazel, according to Emma Lou, was the type of Negro who should go to a Negro college. There were plenty of them in the South whose standard of scholarship was not beyond her ability. And, then, in one of those schools, her darky-like clownishness would not have to be paraded in front of white people, thereby causing discomfort and embarrassment to others of her race, more civilized and circumspect than she.

46 The problem irritated Emma Lou. She didn't see why it had to be. She had looked forward so anxiously, and so happily to her introductory days on the campus, and now her first experience with one of her fellow colored students had been an unpleasant one. But she didn't intend to let that make her unhappy. She was determined to return to the campus alone, seek out other companions, see whether they accepted or ignored the offending Hazel, and govern herself accordingly.

47 It was early and there were few people on the campus. The grass was still wet from a heavy overnight dew, and the sun had not yet dispelled the coolness of the early morning. Emma Lou's dress was of thin material and she shivered as she walked or stood in the shade. She had no school business to attend to; there was nothing for her to do but to walk aimlessly about the campus.

48 In another hour, Emma Lou was pleased to see that the campus walks were becoming crowded, and that the side streets surrounding the campus were now heavy with student traffic. Things were beginning to awaken. Emma Lou became jubilant and walked with jaunty step from path to path, from building to building. It then occurred to her that she had been told that there were more

Negro students enrolled in the School of Pharmacy than in any other department of the university, so finding the Pharmacy building she began to wander
through its crowded hallways.

Almost immediately, she saw a group of five Negro students, three boys    49
and two girls, standing near a water fountain. She was both excited and perplexed, excited over the fact that she was so close to those she wished to find,
and perplexed because she did not know how to approach them. Had there been
only one person standing there, the matter would have been comparatively easy.
She could have approached with a smile and said, "Good morning." The person
would have returned her greeting, and it would then have been a simple matter
to get acquainted.

But five people in one bunch all known to one another and all chatting    50
intimately together!—it would seem too much like an intrusion to go bursting
into their gathering—too forward and too vulgar. Then, there was nothing she
could say after having said "good morning." One just didn't break into a group
of five and say, "I'm Emma Lou Morgan, a new student, and I want to make
friends with you." No, she couldn't do that. She would just smile as she passed,
smile graciously and friendly. They would know that she was a stranger, and her
smile would assure them that she was anxious to make friends, anxious to become
a welcome addition to their group.

One of the group of five had sighted Emma Lou as soon as she had sighted    51
them:

"Who's this?" queried Helen Wheaton, a senior in the College of Law.    52

"Some new 'pick,' I guess," answered Bob Armstrong, who was Helen's    53
fiance and a senior in the School of Architecture.

"I bet she's going to take Pharmacy," whispered Amos Blaine.    54

"She's hottentot enough to take something," mumbled Tommy Brown.    55
"Thank God, she won't be in any of our classes, eh Amos?" ✤

---

## RESPONDING

1.  Emma Lou is a victim of prejudice within her family. Yet when she goes to
    college, she is prejudiced against Hazel Mason. Why is Emma Lou's family
    biased against her, and why is she biased against Hazel? Emma Lou is aware
    of her victimization but unaware of her victimizing. In contemporary terms,
    Emma Lou needs her consciousness raised. Write her a letter making her
    aware of what she is doing.

2.  Working individually or in a group, list all of Hazel Mason's good and bad
    qualities according to Emma Lou's assessment. From Emma Lou's point of
    view, consider whether she should befriend Hazel. Do you think the two
    young women will become friends? Share your reasons with the class.

3. Thurman takes his title *The Blacker the Berry* from the folk saying "The blacker the berry, the sweeter the juice." In an essay, explain what this title reveals about Thurman's attitudes toward racial characteristics. Speculate about what he will have Emma Lou come to realize by the end of the novel.

4. Emma Lou is rejected by the students she wishes to befriend. Why are they laughing at her? Whose criteria are the group members using as their model? Using examples from the selection, your own experience, or sources such as Spike Lee's film *School Daze*, write an essay explaining the ways in which prejudice within a racial group can distort relationships and undermine the members of the group.

# RALPH ELLISON

*Ralph Ellison, who was born in Oklahoma City, Oklahoma, in 1914, studied at the Tuskegee Institute in Alabama and served in the merchant marines during World War II. After the war he taught at several major universities, including the University of Chicago, UCLA, Yale, New York University, and Bard College. His publications included the novel* Invisible Man *(1952), the essay collections* Shadow and Art *(1964) and* Going to the Territory *(1986), as well as essays, articles, and short stories in many periodicals. Ralph Ellison died in 1994.*

*In the following excerpt from* Invisible Man, *the narrator describes his feelings as he joins a group of people witnessing the eviction of an elderly couple. In its depiction of the couple's attempt to retain their dignity at this moment of crisis, the passage raises troubling questions about the nature of justice and leadership.*

❖

## From **INVISIBLE MAN**

1    THE WIND DROVE ME INTO A SIDE STREET where a group of boys had set a packing box afire. The gray smoke hung low and seemed to thicken as I walked with my head down and eyes closed, trying to avoid the fumes. My lungs began to pain; then emerging, wiping my eyes and coughing, I almost stumbled over it: It was piled in a jumble along the walk and over the curb into the street, like a lot of junk waiting to be hauled away. Then I saw the sullen-faced crowd, looking

at a building where two white men were toting out a chair in which an old woman sat; who, as I watched, struck at them feebly with her fists. A motherly-looking old woman with her head tied in a handkerchief, wearing a man's shoes and a man's heavy blue sweater. It was startling: The crowd watched silently, the two white men lugging the chair and trying to dodge the blows and the old woman's face streaming with angry tears as she thrashed at them with her fists. I couldn't believe it. Something, a sense of foreboding, filled me, a quick sense of uncleanliness.

"Leave us alone," she cried, "leave us alone!" as the men pulled their heads out of range and sat her down abruptly at the curb, hurrying back into the building.  2

What on earth, I thought, looking about me. What on earth? The old woman sobbed, pointing to the stuff piled along the curb. "Just look what they doing to us. Just look," looking straight at me. And I realized that what I'd taken for junk was actually worn household furnishings.  3

"Just look at what they doing," she said, her teary eyes upon my face.  4

I looked away embarrassed, staring into the rapidly growing crowd. Faces were peering sullenly from the windows above. And now as the two men reappeared at the top of the steps carrying a battered chest of drawers, I saw a third man come out and stand behind them, pulling at his ear as he looked out over the crowd.  5

"Shake it up, you fellows," he said, "shake it up. We don't have all day."  6

Then the men came down with the chest and I saw the crowd give way sullenly, the men trudging through, grunting and putting the chest at the curb, then returning into the building without a glance to left or right.  7

"Look at that," a slender man near me said. "We ought to beat the hell out of those paddies!"  8

I looked silently into his face, taut and ashy in the cold, his eyes trained upon the men going up the steps.  9

"Sho, we ought to stop 'em," another man said, "but ain't that much nerve in the whole bunch."  10

"There's plenty nerve," the slender man said. "All they need is someone to set it off. All they need is a leader. You mean *you* don't have the nerve."  11

"Who me?" the man said. "Who me?"  12

"Yes, you."  13

"Just look," the old woman said, "just look," her face still turned toward mine. I turned away, edging closer to the two men.  14

"Who are those men?" I said, edging closer.  15

"Marshals or something. I don't give a damn who they is."  16

"Marshals, hell," another man said. "Those guys doing all the toting ain't nothing but trusties. Soon as they get through they'll lock 'em up again."  17

"I don't care who they are, they got no business putting these old folks out on the sidewalk."  18

"You mean they're putting them out of their apartment?" I said. "They can do that up *here*?"  19

20    "Man, where *you* from?" he said, swinging toward me. "What does it look like they puttin' them out of, a Pullman car? They being evicted!"

21    I was embarrassed; others were turning to stare. I had never seen an eviction. Someone snickered.

22    "Where did *he* come from?"

23    A flash of heat went over me and I turned. "Look, friend," I said, hearing a hot edge coming into my voice. "I asked a civil question. If you don't care to answer, don't, but don't try to make me look ridiculous."

24    "Ridiculous? Hell, all scobos is ridiculous. Who the hell is you?"

25    "Never mind, I am who I am. Just don't beat up your gums at me," I said, throwing him a newly acquired phrase.

26    Just then one of the men came down the steps with an armful of articles, and I saw the old woman reach up, yelling, "Take your hands off my Bible!" And the crowd surged forward.

27    The white man's hot eyes swept the crowd. "Where, lady?" he said. "I don't see any Bible."

28    And I saw her snatch the Book from his arms, clutching it fiercely and sending forth a shriek. "They can come in your home and do what they want to you," she said. "Just come stomping in and jerk your life up by the roots! But this here's the last straw. They ain't going to bother with my Bible!"

29    The white man eyed the crowd. "Look, lady," he said, more to the rest of us than to her, "I don't want to do this, I *have* to do it. They sent me up here to do it. If it was left to me, you could stay here till hell freezes over . . ."

30    "These white folks, Lord. These white folks," she moaned, her eyes turned toward the sky, as an old man pushed past me and went to her.

31    "Hon, Hon," he said, placing his hand on her shoulder. "It's the agent, not these gentlemen. He's the one. He says it's the bank, but you know he's the one. We've done business with him for over twenty years."

32    "Don't tell me," she said. "It's all the white folks, not just one. They all against us. Every stinking low-down one of them."

33    "She's right!" a hoarse voice said. "She's right! They *all* is!"

34    Something had been working fiercely inside me, and for a moment I had forgotten the rest of the crowd. Now I recognized a self-consciousness about them, as though they, we, were ashamed to witness the eviction, as though we were all unwilling intruders upon some shameful event; and thus we were careful not to touch or stare too hard at the effects that lined the curb; for we were witnesses of what we did not wish to see, though curious, fascinated, despite our shame, and through it all the old female, mind-plunging crying.

35    I looked at the old people, feeling my eyes burn, my throat tighten. The old woman's sobbing was having a strange effect upon me—as when a child, seeing the tears of its parents, is moved by both fear and sympathy to cry. I turned away, feeling myself being drawn to the old couple by a warm, dark, rising whirlpool of emotion which I feared. I was wary of what the sight of them crying there on the sidewalk was making me begin to feel. I wanted to leave,

but was too ashamed to leave, was rapidly becoming too much a part of it to leave.

I turned aside and looked at the clutter of household objects which the two men continued to pile on the walk. And as the crowd pushed me I looked down to see looking out of an oval frame a portrait of the old couple when young, seeing the sad, stiff dignity of the faces there; feeling strange memories awakening that began an echoing in my head like that of a hysterical voice stuttering in a dark street. Seeing them look back at me as though even then in that nineteenth-century day they had expected little, and this with a grim, unillusioned pride that suddenly seemed to me both a reproach and a warning. My eyes fell upon a pair of crudely carved and polished bones, "knocking bones," used to accompany music at country dances, used in black-face minstrels; the flat ribs of a cow, a steer or sheep, flat bones that gave off a sound, when struck, like heavy castanets (had he been a minstrel?) or the wooden block of a set of drums. Pots and pots of green plants were lined in the dirty snow, certain to die of the cold; ivy, canna, a tomato plant. And in a basket I saw a straightening comb, switches of false hair, a curling iron, a card with silvery letters against a background of dark red velvet, reading "God Bless Our Home"; and scattered across the top of a chiffonnier were nuggets of High John the Conqueror, the lucky stone; and as I watched the white men put down a basket in which I saw a whiskey bottle filled with rock candy and camphor, a small Ethiopian flag, a faded tintype of Abraham Lincoln, and the smiling image of a Hollywood star torn from a magazine. And on a pillow several badly cracked pieces of delicate china, a commemorative plate celebrating the St. Louis World Fair . . . I stood in a kind of daze, looking at an old folded lace fan studded with jet and mother-of-pearl.

The crowd surged as the white men came back, knocking over a drawer that spilled its contents in the snow at my feet. I stooped and started replacing the articles: a bent Masonic emblem, a set of tarnished cuff links, three brass rings, a dime pierced with a nail hole so as to be worn about the ankle on a string for luck, an ornate greeting card with the message "Grandma, I love you" in childish scrawl; another card with a picture of what looked like a white man in black-face seated in the door of a cabin strumming a banjo beneath a bar of music and the lyric "Going back to my old cabin home"; a useless inhalant, a string of bright glass beads with a tarnished clasp, a rabbit foot, a celluloid baseball scoring card shaped like a catcher's mitt, registering a game won or lost years ago; an old breast pump with rubber bulb yellowed with age, a worn baby shoe and a dusty lock of infant hair tied with a faded and crumpled blue ribbon. I felt nauseated. In my hand I held three lapsed life insurance policies with perforated seals stamped "Void"; a yellowing newspaper portrait of a huge black man with the caption: MARCUS GARVEY[1] DEPORTED.

---

1. Marcus Garvey (1887–1940), Jamaican-born Black Nationalist leader deported to Jamaica for mail fraud.

38     I turned away, bending and searching the dirty snow for anything missed by my eyes, and my fingers closed upon something resting in a frozen footstep: a fragile paper, coming apart with age, written in black ink grown yellow. I read: FREE PAPERS. *Be it known to all men that my negro, Primus Provo, has been freed by me this sixth day of August, 1859. Signed: John Samuels. Macon . . .* I folded it quickly, blotting out the single drop of melted snow which glistened on the yellowed page, and dropped it back into the drawer. My hands were trembling, my breath rasping as if I had run a long distance or come upon a coiled snake in a busy street. *It has been longer than that, further removed in time,* I told myself, and yet I knew that it hadn't been. I replaced the drawer in the chest and pushed drunkenly to the curb.

39     But it wouldn't come up, only a bitter spurt of gall filled my mouth and splattered the old folk's possessions. I turned and stared again at the jumble, no longer looking at what was before my eyes, but inwardly-outwardly, around a corner in the dark, far-away-and-long-ago, not so much of my own memory as of remembered words, of linked verbal echoes, images, heard even when not listening at home. And it was as though I myself was being dispossessed of some painful yet precious thing which I could not bear to lose; something confounding, like a rotted tooth that one would rather suffer indefinitely than endure the short, violent eruption of pain that would mark its removal. And with this sense of dispossession came a pang of vague recognition: this junk, these shabby chairs, these heavy, old-fashioned pressing irons, zinc wash tubs with dented bottoms— all throbbed within me with more meaning than there should have been: *And why did I, standing in the crowd, see like a vision my mother hanging wash on a cold windy day, so cold that the warm clothes froze even before the vapor thinned and hung stiff on the line, and her hands white and raw in the skirt-swirling wind and her gray head bare to the darkened sky—why were they causing me discomfort so far beyond their intrinsic meaning as objects? And why did I see them now as behind a veil that threatened to lift, stirred by the cold wind in the narrow street?*

40     A scream, "I'm going in!" spun me around. The old couple were on the steps now, the old man holding her arm, the white men leaning forward above, and the crowd pressing me closer to the steps.

41     "You can't go in, lady," the man said.

42     "I want to pray!" she said.

43     "I can't help it, lady. You'll have to do your praying out here."

44     "I'm go'n in!"

45     "Not in here!"

46     "All we want to do is go in and pray," she said, clutching her Bible. "It ain't right to pray in the street like this."

47     "I'm sorry," he said.

48     "Aw, let the woman go in to pray," a voice called from the crowd. "You got all their stuff out here on the walk—what more do you want, blood?"

49     "Sure, let them old folks pray."

"That's what's wrong with us now, all this damn praying," another voice  50
called.

"You don't go back, see," the white man said. "You were legally evicted."  51

"But all we want to do is go in an' kneel on the floor," the old man said.  52
"We been living right here for over twenty years. I don't see why you can't let
us go just for a few minutes . . ."

"Look, I've told you," the man said. "I've got my orders. You're wasting  53
my time."

"We go'n in!" the woman said.  54

It happened so suddenly that I could barely keep up with it: I saw the old  55
woman clutching her Bible and rushing up the steps, her husband behind her
and the white man stepping in front of them and stretching out his arm. "I'll
jug you," he yelled, "by God, I'll jug you!"

"Take your hands off that woman!" someone called from the crowd.  56

Then at the top of the stairs they were pushing against the man and I saw  57
the old woman fall backwards, and the crowd exploded.

"Get that paddie sonofabitch!"  58

"He struck her!" a West Indian woman screamed into my ear. "The filthy  59
brute, he struck her!"

"Stand back or I'll shoot," the man called, his eyes wild as he drew a gun  60
and backed into the doorway where the two trusties stood bewildered, their
arms full of articles. "I swear I'll shoot. You don't know what you're doing, but
I'll shoot!"

They hesitated. "Ain't but six bullets in that thing," a little fellow called.  61
"Then what you going to do?"

"Yeah, you damn sho caint hide."  62

"I advise you to stay out of this," the marshal called.  63

"Think you can come up here and hit one of our women, you a fool."  64

"To hell with all this talk, let's rush that bastard!"  65

"You better think twice," the white man called.  66

I saw them start up the steps and felt suddenly as though my head would  67
split. I knew that they were about to attack the man and I was both afraid and
angry, repelled and fascinated. I both wanted it and feared the consequences,
was outraged and angered at what I saw and yet surged with fear; not for the
man or of the consequences of an attack, but of what the sight of violence might
release in me. And beneath it all there boiled up all the shock-absorbing phrases
that I had learned all my life. I seemed to totter on the edge of a great dark
hole.

"No, no," I heard myself yelling. "Black men! Brothers! Black Brothers!  68
That's not the way. We're law-abiding. We're a law-abiding people and a
slow-to-anger people."

Forcing my way quickly through the crowd, I stood on the steps facing  69
those in front, talking rapidly without thought but out of my clashing emotions.

"We're a law-abiding people and a slow-to-anger people . . ." They stopped, listening. Even the white man was startled.

70 "Yeah, but we mad now," a voice called out.

71 "Yes, you're right," I called back. "We're angry, but let us be wise. Let us, I mean let us not . . . Let us learn from that great leader whose wise action was reported in the newspaper the other day . . ."

72 "What, mahn? Who?" a West Indian voice shouted.

73 "Come on! To hell with this guy, let's get that paddie before they send him some help . . ."

74 "No, wait," I yelled. "Let's follow a leader, let's organize. *Organize.* We need someone like that wise leader, you read about him, down in Alabama. He was strong enough to choose to do the wise thing in spite of what he felt himself . . ."

75 "Who, mahn? Who?"

76 This was it, I thought, they're listening, eager to listen. Nobody laughed. If they laugh, I'll die! I tensed my diaphragm.

77 "That wise man," I said, "you read about him, who when that fugitive escaped from the mob and ran to his school for protection, that wise man who was strong enough to do the legal thing, the law-abiding thing, to turn him over to the forces of law and order . . ."

78 "Yeah," a voice rang out, "yeah, so they could lynch his ass."

79 Oh, God, this wasn't it at all. Poor technique and not at all what I intended.

80 "He was a wise leader," I yelled. "He was within the law. Now wasn't that the wise thing to do?"

81 "Yeah, he was wise all right," the man laughed angrily. "Now get out of the way so we can jump this paddie."

82 The crowd yelled and I laughed in response as though hypnotized.

83 "But wasn't that the human thing to do? After all, he had to protect himself because—"

84 "He was a handkerchief-headed rat!" a woman screamed, her voice boiling with contempt.

85 "Yes, you're right. He was wise and cowardly, but what about us? What are we to do?" I yelled, suddenly thrilled by the response. "Look at him," I cried.

86 "Yes, just look at him!" an old fellow in a derby called out as though answering a preacher in church.

87 "And look at that old couple . . ."

88 "Yeah, what about Sister and Brother Provo?" he said. "It's an ungodly shame!"

89 "And look at their possessions all strewn there on the sidewalk. Just look at their possessions in the snow. How old are you, sir?" I yelled.

90 "I'm eighty-seven," the old man said, his voice low and bewildered.

91 "How's that? Yell so our slow-to-anger brethren can hear you."

92 "I'm *eighty-seven years old!*"

93 "Did you hear him? He's eighty-seven. Eighty-seven and look at all he's

accumulated in eighty-seven years, strewn in the snow like chicken guts, and we're a law-abiding, slow-to-anger bunch of folks turning the other cheek every day in the week. What are we going to do? What would you, what would I, what would he have done? *What is to be done?* I propose we do the wise thing, the law-abiding thing. Just look at this junk! Should two old folks live in such junk, cooped up in a filthy room? It's a great danger, a fire hazard! Old cracked dishes and broken-down chairs. Yes, yes, yes! Look at that old woman, somebody's mother, somebody's grandmother, maybe. We call them 'Big Mama' and they spoil us and—*you* know, *you* remember . . . Look at her quilts and broken-down shoes. I know she's somebody's mother because I saw an old breast pump fall into the snow, and she's somebody's grandmother, because I saw a card that read 'Dear Grandma' . . . But we're law-abiding . . . I looked into a basket and I saw some bones, not neckbones, but rib bones, knocking bones . . . This old couple used to dance . . . I saw—What kind of work do you do, Father?" I called.

"I'm a day laborer . . ."                                                                  94

". . . A day laborer, you heard him, but look at his stuff strewn like chitter-    95
lings in the snow . . .Where has all his labor gone? Is he lying?"

"Hell, no, he ain't lying."                                                                96

"Naw, suh!"                                                                                97

"Then where did his labor go? Look at his old blues records and her pots      98
of plants, they're down-home folks, and everything tossed out like junk whirled eighty-seven years in a cyclone. Eighty-seven years, and *poof*! like a snort in a wind storm. Look at them, they look like my mama and my papa and my grandma and grandpa, and I look like you and you look like me. Look at them but remember that we're a wise, law-abiding group of people. And remember it when you look up there in the doorway at that law standing there with his forty-five. Look at him, standing with his blue steel pistol and his blue serge suit. Look at him! You don't see just one man dressed in one blue serge suit, or one forty-five, you see ten for every one of us, ten guns and ten warm suits and ten fat bellies and ten million laws. *Laws*, that's what we call them down South! Laws! And we're wise, and law-abiding. And look at this old woman with her dog-eared Bible. What's she trying to bring off here? She's let her religion go to her head, but we all know that religion is for the heart, not for the head. 'Blessed are the pure in heart,' it says. Nothing about the poor in head. What's she trying to do? What about the clear of head? And the clear of eye, the ice-water-visioned who see too clear to miss a lie? Look out there at her cabinet with its gaping drawers. Eighty-seven years to fill them, and full of brick and brack, a bricabrac, and she wants to break the law . . . What's happened to them? They're our people, your people and mine, your parents and mine. What's happened to 'em?"

"I'll tell you!" a heavyweight yelled, pushing out of the crowd, his face angry.    99
"Hell, they been dispossessed, you crazy sonofabitch, get out the way!"

"Dispossessed?" I cried, holding up my hand and allowing the word to          100 whistle from my throat. "That's a good word, 'Dispossessed'! 'Dispossessed,' eighty-seven years and dispossessed of what? They ain't *got* nothing, they caint *get* nothing, they never *had* nothing. So who was dispossessed?" I growled. "We're law-abiding. So who's being dispossessed? Can it be us? These old ones are out in the snow, but we're here with them. Look at their stuff, not a pit to hiss in, not a window to shout the news and us right with them. Look at them, not a shack to pray in or an alley to sing the blues! They're facing a gun and we're facing it with them. They don't want the world, but only Jesus. They only want Jesus, just fifteen minutes of Jesus on the rug-bare floor . . . How about it, Mr. Law? Do we get our fifteen minutes worth of Jesus? You got the world, can we have our Jesus?"

101     "I got my orders, Mac," the man called, waving the pistol with a sneer. "You're doing all right, tell 'em to keep out of this. This is legal and I'll shoot if I have to . . ."

102     "But what about the prayer?"

103     "They don't go back!"

104     "Are you positive?"

105     "You could bet your life," he said.

106     "Look at him," I called to the angry crowd. "With his blue steel pistol and his blue serge suit. You heard him, he's the law. He says he'll shoot us down because we're a law-abiding people. So we've been dispossessed, and what's more, he thinks he's God. Look up there backed against the post with a criminal on either side of him. Can't you feel the cold wind, can't you hear it asking, 'What did you do with your heavy labor? What did you do?' When you look at all you haven't got in eighty seven years you feel ashamed—"

107     "Tell 'em about it, brother," an old man interrupted. "It makes you feel you ain't a man."

108     "Yes, these old folks had a dream book, but the pages went blank and it failed to given them the number. It was called the Seeing Eye, The Great Constitutional Dream Book, The Secrets of Africa, The Wisdom of Egypt—but the eye was blind, it lost its luster. It's all cataracted like a cross-eyed carpenter and it doesn't saw straight. All we have is the Bible and this Law here rules that out. So where do we go? Where do we go from here, without a pot—"

109     "We going after that paddie," the heavyweight called, rushing up the steps.

110     Someone pushed me. "No, wait," I called.

111     "Get out the way now."

112     There was a rush against me and I fell, hearing a single explosion, backward into a whirl of milling legs, overshoes, the trampled snow cold on my hands. Another shot sounded above like a bursting bag. Managing to stand, I saw atop the steps the fist with the gun being forced into the air above the crowd's bobbing heads and the next instant they were dragging him down into the snow; punching him left and right, uttering a low tense swelling sound of desperate effort; a grunt that exploded into a thousand softly spat, hate-sizzling curses. I saw a woman striking with the pointed heel of her shoe, her face a blank mask

with hollow black eyes as she aimed and struck, aimed and struck, bringing spurts of blood, running along beside the man who was dragged to his feet now as they punched him gauntlet-wise between them. Suddenly I saw a pair of handcuffs arc gleaming into the air and sail across the street. A boy broke out of the crowd, the marshal's snappy hat on his head. The marshal was spun this way and that, then a swift tattoo of blows started him down the street. I was beside myself with excitement. The crowd surged after him, milling like a huge man trying to turn in a cubbyhole—some of them laughing, some cursing, some intently silent.

"The brute struck that gentle woman, poor thing!" the West Indian woman    113 chanted. "Black men, did you ever see such a brute? Is he a gentleman, I ask you? The brute! Give it back to him, black men. Repay the brute a thousandfold! Give it back to him unto the third and fourth generations. Strike him, our fine black men. Protect your black women! Repay the arrogant creature to the third and fourth generations!"

"We're dispossessed," I sang at the top of my voice, "dispossessed and we    114 want to pray. Let's go in and pray. Let's have a big prayer meeting. But we'll need some chairs to sit in . . . rest upon as we kneel. We'll need some chairs!"

"Here's some chairs down here," a woman called from the walk. "How 'bout    115 taking in some chairs?"

"Sure," I called, "take everything. Take it all, hide that junk! Put it back    116 where it came from. It's blocking the street and the sidewalk, and that's against the law. We're law-abiding, so clear the street of the debris. Put it out of sight! Hide it, hide their shame! Hide *our* shame!

"Come on, men," I yelled, dashing down the steps and seizing a chair and    117 starting back, no longer struggling against or thinking about the nature of my action. The others followed, picking up pieces of furniture and lugging it back into the building.

"We ought to done this long ago," a man said.    118

"We damn sho should."    119

"I feel so good," a woman said, "I feel so *good*!"    120

"Black men, I'm proud of you," the West Indian woman shrilled. "Proud!"    121

We rushed into the dark little apartment that smelled of stale cabbage and    122 put the pieces down and returned for more. Men, women and children seized articles and dashed inside shouting, laughing. I looked for the two trusties, but they seemed to have disappeared. Then, coming down into the street, I thought I saw one. He was carrying a chair back inside.

"So you're law-abiding too," I called, only to become aware that it was    123 someone else. A white man but someone else altogether.

The man laughed at me and continued inside. And when I reached the    124 street there were several of them, men and women, standing about, cheering whenever another piece of furniture was returned. It was like a holiday. I didn't want it to stop.

"Who are those people?" I called from the steps.    125

126     "What people?" someone called back.

127     *"Those,"* I said, pointing.

128     "You mean those ofays?"

129     "Yes, what do they want?"

130     "We're friends of the people," one of the white men called.

131     "Friends of what people?" I called, prepared to jump down upon him if he answered, *"You* people."

132     "We're friends of *all* the common people," he shouted. "We came up to help."

133     "We believe in brotherhood," another called.

134     "Well, pick up that sofa and come on," I called. I was uneasy about their presence and disappointed when they all joined the crowd and starting lugging the evicted articles back inside. Where had I heard of them?

135     "Why don't we stage a march?" one of the white men called, going past.

136     "Why don't we march!" I yelled out to the sidewalk before I had time to think.

137     They took it up immediately.

138     "Let's march . . ."

139     "It's a good idea."

140     "Let's have a demonstration . . ."

141     "Let's parade!"

142     I heard the siren and saw the scout cars swing into the block in the same instant. It was the police! I looked into the crowd, trying to focus upon their faces, hearing someone yell, "Here come the cops," and others answering, "Let 'em come!"

143     Where is all this leading? I thought, seeing a white man run inside the building as the policemen dashed from their cars and came running up.

144     "What's going on here?" a gold-shield officer called up the steps.

145     It had become silent. No one answered.

146     "I said, what's going on here," he repeated. "You," he called, pointing straight at me.

147     "We've . . . we've been clearing the sidewalk of a lot of junk," I called, tense inside.

148     "What's that?" he said.

149     "It's a clean-up campaign," I called, wanting to laugh. "These old folks had all their stuff cluttering up the sidewalk and we cleared the street . . ."

150     "You mean you're interfering with an eviction," he called, starting through the crowd.

151     "He ain't doing nothing," a woman called from behind me.

152     I looked around, the steps behind were filled with those who had been inside.

153     "We're all together," someone called, as the crowd closed in.

154     "Clear the streets," the officer ordered.

"That's what we were doing," someone called from back in the crowd. 155

"Mahoney!" he bellowed to another policeman, "send in a riot call!" 156

"What riot?" one of the white men called to him. "There's no riot." 157

"If I say there's a riot, there's a riot," the officer said. "And what are you 158
white people doing up here in Harlem?"

"We're citizens. We go anywhere we like." 159

"Listen! Here come some more cops!" someone called. 160

"Let them come!" 161

"Let the Commissioner come!" 162

It became too much for me. The whole thing had gotten out of hand. What 163
had I said to bring on all this? I edged to the back of the crowd on the steps
and backed into the hallway. Where would I go? I hurried up to the old couple's
apartment. But I can't hide here, I thought, heading back for the stairs.

"No. You can't go that way," a voice said. 164

I whirled. It was a white girl standing in the door. 165

"What are you doing in here?" I shouted, my fear turning to feverish anger. 166

"I didn't mean to startle you," she said. "Brother, that was quite a speech 167
you made. I heard just the end of it, but you certainly moved them to action . . ."

"Action," I said, "action—" 168

"Don't be modest, brother," she said, "I heard you." 169

"Look, Miss, we'd better get out of here," I said, finally controlling the 170
throbbing in my throat. "There are a lot of policemen downstairs and more
coming."

"Oh, yes. You'd better go over the roof," she said. "Otherwise, someone is 171
sure to point you out."

"Over the roof?" 172

"It's easy. Just go up to the roof of the building and keep crossing until you 173
reach the house at the end of the block. Then open the door and walk down as
though you've been visiting. You'd better hurry. The longer you remain unknown to the police, the longer you'll be effective."

Effective? I thought. What did she mean? And what was this "brother" 174
business?

"Thanks," I said, and hurried for the stairs. 175

"Good-bye," her voice rose fluidly behind me. I turned, glimpsing her white 176
face in the dim light of the darkened doorway.

I took the flight in a bound and cautiously opened the door, and suddenly 177
the sun flared bright on the roof and it was windy cold. Before me the low,
snow-caked walls dividing the buildings stretched hurdle-like the long length
of the block to the corner, and before me empty clotheslines trembled in the
wind. I made my way through the wind-carved snow to the next roof and then
to the next, going with swift caution. Planes were rising over an airfield far to
the southeast, and I was running now and seeing all the church steeples rising

and falling and stacks with smoke leaning sharp against the sky, and below in the street the sound of sirens and shouting. I hurried. Then, climbing over a wall I looked back, seeing a man hurrying after me, slipping, sliding, going over the low dividing walls of the roofs with puffing, bustling effort. I turned and ran, trying to put the rows of chimneys between us, wondering why he didn't yell "Halt!" or shout, or shoot. I ran, dodging behind an elevator housing, then dashing to the next roof, going down, the snow cold to my hands, knees striking, toes gripping, and up and running and looking back, seeing the short figure in black still running after. The corner seemed a mile away. I tried to count the number of roofs that bounced before me yet to be crossed. Getting to seven, I ran, hearing shouts, more sirens, and looking back and him still behind me, running in a short-legged scramble, still behind me as I tried to open the door of a building to go down and finding it stuck and running once more, trying to zig-zag in the snow and feeling the crunch of gravel underneath, and behind me still, as I swung over a partition and went brushing past a huge cote and arousing a flight of frantic white birds, suddenly as large as buzzards as they beat furiously against my eyes, dazzling the sun as they fluttered up and away and around in a furious glide and me running again and looking back and for a split second thinking him gone and once more seeing him bobbing after. Why doesn't he shoot? Why? If only it were like at home where I knew someone in *all* the houses, knew them by sight and by name, by blood and by background, by shame and pride, and by religion.

178      It was a carpeted hall and I moved down with pounding heart as a dog set up a terrific din within the top apartment. Then I moved quickly, my body like glass inside as I skipped downward off the edges of the stairs. Looking down the stairwell I saw pale light filtering through the door glass, far below. But what had happened to the girl, had she put the man on my trail? What was she doing there? I bounded down, no one challenging me, and I stopped in the vestibule, breathing deeply and listening for his hand upon the door above and brushing my clothing into order. Then I stepped into the street with a nonchalance copied from characters I had seen in the movies. No sound from above, not even the malicious note of the barking dog. ✢

---

## RESPONDING

1. In a journal entry, describe how the narrator's feelings about his identity change during the course of this incident.

2. Working individually or in a group, examine events in this narrative as they occur chronologically and explain how each subsequent event escalates hostilities. Identify the interchanges that particularly move the onlookers to anger.

3.  The narrator in this selection says, "it was as though I myself was being dispossessed of some painful yet precious thing which I could not bear to lose" (paragraph 39). In an essay, explain why the narrator identifies with the couple being evicted and feels himself to be dispossessed.

4.  Compare the narrator's speech to the crowd to Marc Antony's speech to the crowd in Shakespeare's *Julius Caesar*. What techniques do they both use to move the crowd to action?

Friends, Romans, countrymen, lend me your ears!
I come to bury Caesar, not to praise him.
The evil that men do lives after them,
The good is oft interred with their bones;
So are they all, all honorable men,                                                            5
Come I to speak of Caesar's funeral.
He was my friend, faithful and just to me;
But Brutus says he was ambitious,
And Brutus is an honorable man.
He hath brought many captives home to Rome,                                            10
Whose ransoms did the general coffers fill;
Did this in Caesar seem ambitious?
When that the poor have cried, Caesar hath wept;
Ambition should be made of sterner stuff:
Yet Brutus says he was ambitious,                                                              15
And Brutus is an honorable man.
You all did see that on the Lupercal
I thrice presented him a kingly crown,
Which he did thrice refuse. Was this ambition?
Yet Brutus says he was ambitious,                                                              20
And sure he is an honorable man.
I speak not to disprove what Brutus spoke,
But here I am to speak what I do know.
You all did love him once, not without cause;
What cause withholds you then to mourn for him?                                        25
O judgment! thou [art] fled to brutish beasts,
And men have lost their reason. Bear with me,
My heart is in the coffin there with Caesar,
And I must pause till it come back to me.
                                        —WILLIAM SHAKESPEARE

# ERNEST J. GAINES

*The novelist Ernest J. Gaines was born in Louisiana in 1933. He earned a
bachelor's degree from San Francisco State College in 1957 and took graduate
courses at Stanford University. His publications include* The Autobiography
of Miss Jane Pittman *(1971),* A Gathering of Old Men *(1983), and at
least a half dozen other publications. His work has been adapted for both film
and television. Gaines's work has won many awards, among them Stegner
and Guggenheim fellowships, and grants from the National Endowment for
the Arts and the MacArthur Foundation. Serving as writer-in-residence at
several institutions, including Stanford, he holds a professorship in the Department of English at the University of Southwestern Louisiana.*

*The following selection, from Gaines's 1993 novel* A Lesson Before
Dying, *reveals some of the inequities of the "separate but equal" doctrine, not
only in terms of the teaching environment, but also in terms of the assumptions
and value systems of the doctrine's proponents.*

⁜

## *From* A LESSON BEFORE DYING

1   TWO THINGS HAPPENED at the school during the weeks before I visited Jefferson
in jail. The superintendent of schools made his annual visit, and we got our first
load of wood for winter.

2   We heard on Monday by Farrell Jarreau, who had gotten the news from
Henri Pichot, that the superintendent was going to visit us sometime during
the week, but we didn't know what day or time. I told my students to take baths
each morning and wear their best clothes to school. After the Pledge of Allegiance in the yard and the recitation of Bible verses inside the church, I would
send a student back outside to look out for the superintendent. If the student
saw a car, any car, turn off the highway down into the quarter, he or she was
supposed to run inside and tell me.

3   The superintendent didn't show up until Thursday. By then we had had
many false alarms. The minister of the church, who didn't live in the quarter,
had made a couple of visits to church members. A doctor had come once, a
midwife had visited a young woman twice, an insurance man had shown up, a
bill collector from a furniture store had appeared, Henri Pichot had driven
through the quarter at least once each day, and family and friends of people in
the quarter had also visited. On Thursday, just before two o'clock, the boy I
had watching for cars ran into the church.

4   "Another one, Mr. Wiggins, another one."

5   "All right," I said to the class. "Keep those books opened and look sharp."

I passed my fingers over my shirt collar and checked the knot in my necktie.  6
I felt my jacket to be sure both flaps were outside the pockets. I had three
suits—navy blue, gray, and brown. I had on the blue one today. In the yard, I
passed the tips of my shoes over the backs of my pant legs. Now I was ready to
receive our guest.

This time it was the superintendent. He stopped his car before the door of  7
the church. A thick cloud of gray dust flew over the top of the car and down
into the quarter. The superintendent was a short, fat man with a large red face
and a double chin, and he needed all his energy to get out of the car.

"Dr. Joseph," I said.  8

"Hummmm. Stifling," he said.  9

I thought it was a little cool myself, but I figured that anyone as heavy as  10
he was must have felt stifled all the time. He wheezed his way across the shallow
ditch that separated the road from the churchyard. He looked up at me, but I
could tell he didn't remember my name, though he had visited the school once
each year since I had been teaching there.

"Grant Wiggins," I said.  11

"How are you, Higgins?"  12

"Wiggins, sir," I said. "I'm fine."  13

"Well, I'm not," he said. "All this running around. More schools to attend."  14

Dr. Joseph visited the colored schools once a year, the white schools prob-  15
ably twice—once each semester. There were a dozen schools in the parish to
visit, if that many.

"We're honored that you took this time for us, sir."  16

He grunted and looked around the yard. There was a good breeze coming  17
in from the direction of the cane fields, and it wavered the flag on the pole in
the yard.

"Place looks about the same," Dr. Joseph said.  18

"Things change very slowly around here, Dr. Joseph," I said.  19

"Hummmm," he said.  20

I motioned for him to precede me into the church. He needed all his  21
strength to go up the three wooden steps, and as he entered the doorway, I
heard Irene Cole, the sixth-grade student in charge, call out to the class: "Rise.
Shoulders back."

I followed Dr. Joseph down the aisle, and on either side of us, the students  22
from primer through sixth grade stood as still and as straight as soldiers for
inspection.

I nodded toward my desk for Dr. Joseph to take my chair. He grunted,  23
which meant thanks, and pulled the chair farther from the desk before he sat
down. He needed the extra distance for comfort.

Irene was watching me all the time, and when I nodded to her, she called  24
out to the classes: "Seats." And the whole school sat as one. We had been
rehearsing this, morning and afternoon, for the past three days.

"Students, I'm sure you all know Dr. Joseph Morgan," I told them. "Dr.  25
Joseph is our superintendent of schools here in St. Raphael Parish. He has taken

time out of a very busy schedule to visit us for a few minutes. Please respond loudly: 'Thank you, Dr. Joseph,'" Which they did, loudly.

26 Dr. Joseph acknowledged their greeting: "Hummmm."

27 "Dr. Joseph, we're at your service," I said, and sat down on one of the benches against the wall.

28 Dr. Joseph leaned back in the chair, and still his large stomach nearly touched the edge of the table. He looked over the classes from one side of the aisle to the other, as though he was trying to catch someone doing something improper.

29 "Primer, on your feet," he said.

30 They stood up, seven or eight of them. Dr. Joseph looked them over for a moment, then he told the little girl at the end to come forward. She took a deep breath and looked at the girl standing beside her before coming up to the desk. She was afraid, but she came up quickly and stood before the table with her little arms tight to her sides. She would not look up.

31 "Nothing to be afraid of, child," Dr. Joseph said to her. "What is your name?"

32 "Gloria Hebert," she said.

33 "I can't hear you if you keep your head down," Dr. Joseph told her.

34 She looked up, timidly. "Gloria Hebert."

35 "That's a pretty name," Dr. Joseph said. "Hold out your hands."

36 She must have thought she had said or done something wrong, because as she held her hands out across the table, palms up, I could see them trembling.

37 "Turn them over," Dr. Joseph told her.

38 She did.

39 "Uh-huh," he said. "Relax."

40 She did not know what he wanted her to do.

41 "Lower your arms, child," Dr. Joseph said.

42 She brought her arms back to her sides and lowered her eyes as well.

43 "Did you say your Bible verse this morning, Gloria?"

44 "Yes, sir, Dr. Joseph."

45 "Well, what did you say?" he asked her.

46 "I said, 'Lord is my shepherd, I shall not want,' Dr. Joseph."

47 "Hummm," Dr. Joseph said. "Seems I've heard that one before. But you're a bright little girl. You tell your folks Dr. Joseph said they ought to be proud of you. Go back to your seat."

48 "Thank you, Dr. Joseph," she said, bowing and turning away quickly. She smiled as she faced forward again. But no one else was smiling.

49 "Primers, take your seats," Dr. Joseph said. "First graders, on your feet."

50 And he called on the one boy in class who I wished had stayed home today. He was without doubt the worst child in the school. He came from a large family—thirteen, fourteen, fifteen: I don't know how many—and he had to fight for every crumb of food he got. At school he did the same. He fought if he played marbles, he fought if he played ball, he fought if he played hide-and-go-

seek, he fought if he played hide-the-switch. In class he fought with those who sat in front of him, beside him, behind him. I had punished him as much during the last month as I had all the other children put together.

Dr. Joseph asked his name, and he ran together three words even I couldn't 51 understand. His name was Louis Washington, Jr., but what he said didn't sound anything like that.

"Your hands," Dr. Joseph told him. 52

The hands had been cleaned an hour before, I was sure, because I had 53 checked each pair when the students came in from dinner. But now the palms of those same hands were as black and grimy as if he had been pitching coal all day.

"Did you pledge allegiance to the flag this morning?" Dr. Joseph asked him. 54

"Yazir," he said. Not "Yes, sir," as I had told him a hundred times to say. 55 "Yazir."

"Well?" Dr. Joseph said. 56

"Want me go stand outside and s'lute flag?" the boy asked. 57

"You don't have to go outside," Dr. Joseph said. "You can show me in here." 58

The boy raised his hand to his chest. 59

"Plege legen toda flag. Ninety state. 'Merica. Er—er—yeah, which it stand. 60 Visibly. Amen."

Dr. Joseph grunted. Several students giggled. Dr. Joseph seemed quite 61 satisfied. I would have to do a lot more work.

For the next half hour it continued. Dr. Joseph would call on someone who 62 looked half bright, then he would call on someone whom he felt was just the opposite. In the upper grades—fourth, fifth, and sixth—he asked grammatical, mathematical, and geographical questions. And besides looking at hands, now he began inspecting teeth. Open wide, say "Ahhh"—and he would have the poor children spreading out their lips as far as they could while he peered into their mouths. At the university I had read about slave masters who had done the same when buying new slaves, and I had read of cattlemen doing it when purchasing horses and cattle. At least Dr. Joseph had graduated to the level where he let the children spread out their own lips, rather than using some kind of crude metal instrument. I appreciated his humanitarianism.

Finally, when he felt that he had inspected enough mouths and hands, he 63 gave the school a ten-minute lecture on nutrition. Beans were good, he said. Not only just good, but very, very good. Beans, beans, beans—he must have said beans a hundred times. Then he said fish and greens were good. And exercise was good. In other words, hard work was good for the young body. Picking cotton, gathering potatoes, pulling onions, working in the garden—all of that was good exercise for a growing boy or girl.

"Higgins, I must compliment you. You have an excellent crop of students, 64 an excellent crop, Higgins. You ought to be proud."

He had said the same thing the year before, and he had called me Higgins 65 then too. And the year before that he had said the same thing, but he had called me Washington then. At least he was getting closer to my real name.

66     "Rise," Irene called to the class.

67     They came to their feet, their heads up, their arms clasped to their sides. But instead of feeling pride, I hated myself for drilling them as I had done.

68     Dr. Joseph and I went down the aisle. Outside, he looked up at the flag waving on its bamboo pole in the corner of the fence. I thought for a moment the superintendent was about to salute it, but he was either too tired or too lazy to raise his hand.

69     "Doing a good job, Higgins," he said.

70     "I do the best I can with what I have to work with, Dr. Joseph," I said. "I don't have all the books I need. In some classes I have two children studying out of one book. And even with that, some of the pages in the book are missing. I need more paper to write on, I need more chalk for the blackboards, I need more pencils, I even need a better heater."

71     "We're all in the same shape, Higgins," he said.

72     I didn't answer him.

73     "I said we're all in the same shape, Higgins, the white schools just as much as the colored schools. We take what the state gives us, and we make the best of it."

74     "Many of the books I have to use are hand-me-downs from the white schools, Dr. Joseph," I said. "And they have missing pages. How can I—"

75     "Are you questioning me, Higgins?"

76     "No sir, Dr. Joseph. I was just—"

77     "Thank you, Higgins."

78     He started to get back into his car. It was harder to do than getting out, because he was upset with me now.

79     "More drill on the flag, Higgins," he said, through the rolled-down window. "More emphasis on hygiene."

80     "Some of these children have never seen a toothbrush before coming to school, Dr. Joseph."

81     "Well, isn't that your job, Higgins?"

82     "Yes, sir, I suppose so. But then I would have to buy them."

83     "Can't they work?" he asked me. "Look at all the pecan trees." He waved his hand toward the yards. "I wager you can count fifty trees right here in the quarter. Back in the field, back in the pasture, you can count another hundred, two hundred trees. Get them off their lazy butts, they can make enough for a dozen toothbrushes in one evening."

84     "That money usually goes to helping the family, Dr. Joseph."

85     "Then you tell the family about health," he said, looking out of the rolled-down window to let me know that his visit was over. "I have another school to visit. All this running around 'nough to give a man a heart attack."

86     He drove away. I stood there until he had turned his car around and started back up the quarter. I waved at him, but he did not wave back. ✤

## RESPONDING

1. Write a journal entry about a time when your class was visited by someone in authority, perhaps your school principal or the superintendent of schools. How did you feel when that person was in the classroom? Was the situation tense? What, if anything, did the authority figure do to put you and your teacher at ease?

2. Working individually or in a group, discuss the concept of "separate but equal." Did the school in the reading seem to be equal to any school with which you are familiar?

3. Who has the power during the superintendent's visit to this rural segregated school? Write an essay illustrating how language reflects the power relationship between Grant Wiggins and Dr. Joseph.

4. We experience the episode from Grant Wiggins's point of view. What message do you imagine the children are receiving about their school and their place in society? Imagine that you are one of the students in the class, and tell the story of the superintendent's visit to your parents or a friend.

# GWENDOLYN BROOKS

*The poet Gwendolyn Brooks was born in Topeka, Kansas, in 1917. After graduating from Wilson Junior College, she worked as a book reviewer for the* New York Times *and the* New York Herald Tribune. *During the late 1930s she joined the NAACP; she has remained active in the civil rights movement since that time. Her publications include* A Street in Bronzeville *(1945),* Annie Allen *(1949),* The Bean Eaters *(1960),* Selected Poems *(1963),* In the Mecca *(1968),* Family Pictures *(1970),* To Disembark *(1981),* The Near-Johannesburg Boy and Other Poems *(1986),* Gottschalk and the Grande Tarantelle *(1988),* Winnie *(1988), and* Children Coming Home *(1991). Brooks's work has been awarded the prize of the American Academy of Arts and Letters (1946), Guggenheim fellowships (1946 and 1947), and the Pulitzer Prize for Poetry (1950)—Brooks is the first African American to be thus honored. In 1968 Brooks was named the poet laureate of Illinois. In that post, as writer-in-residence at several universities, and as professor at the City College of New York and Chicago State*

*University, she has worked tirelessly to make young people more aware of their talents as writers.*

*"The Chicago Defender Sends a Man to Little Rock" explores the effects of prejudice and injustice on the children who are its victims.*

⊹

# THE CHICAGO DEFENDER SENDS A MAN TO LITTLE ROCK

FALL, 1957

In Little Rock the people bear
Babes, and comb and part their hair
And watch the want ads, put repair
To roof and latch. While wheat toast burns
5      A woman waters multiferns.

Time upholds or overturns
The many, tight, and small concerns.

In Little Rock the people sing
Sunday hymns like anything,
10     Through Sunday pomp and polishing.
And after testament and tunes,
Some soften Sunday afternoons
With lemon tea and Lorna Doones.

I forecast
15     And I believe
Come Christmas Little Rock will cleave
To Christmas tree and trifle, weave,
From laugh and tinsel, texture fast.

In Little Rock is baseball; Barcarolle.
20     That hotness in July . . . the uniformed figures raw and
       implacable
And not intellectual,
Batting the hotness or clawing the suffering dust.
The Open Air Concert, on the special twilight green . . .
When Beethoven is brutal or whispers to lady-like air.
Blanket-sitters are solemn, as Johann troubles to lean      25
To tell them what to mean. . . .

There is love, too, in Little Rock. Soft women softly
Opening themselves in kindness,
Or, pitying one's blindness,
Awaiting one's pleasure                                             30
In azure
Glory with anguished rose at the root. . . .
To wash away old semi-discomfitures.
They re-teach purple and unsullen blue.
The wispy soils go. And uncertain                                   35
Half-havings have they clarified to sures.

In Little Rock they know
Not answering the telephone is a way of rejecting life,
That it is our business to be bothered, is our business
To cherish bores or boredom, be polite                             40
To lies and love and many-faceted fuzziness.

I scratch my head, massage the hate-I-had.
I blink across my prim and pencilled pad.
The saga I was sent for is not down.
Because there is a puzzle in this town.                             45
The biggest News I do not dare
Telegraph to the Editor's chair:
"They are like people everywhere."

The angry Editor would reply
In hundred harryings of Why.                                       50
And true, they are hurling spittle, rock,
Garbage and fruit in Little Rock.
And I saw coiling storm a-writhe
On bright madonnas. And a scythe
Of men harassing brownish girls.                                   55
(The bows and barrettes in the curls
And braids declined away from joy.)

I saw a bleeding brownish boy. . . .

The lariat lynch-wish I deplored.

The loveliest lynchee was our Lord. ✠                              60

## RESPONDING

1. In your journal, describe an incident of injustice about which you or someone you know became aware. What response did you or your friend have? Did you try to rectify what you felt was wrong? Were you successful or unsuccessful?

2. Working individually or in a group, describe the people to whom the poet refers. Do they include the entire population of Little Rock?

3. Write a profile of the speaker. Who is he? For whom does he work? Is the speaker white or African American? How does he feel about what is happening? Use evidence from the poem to support your claims.

4. Explain why the poem begins with the date "Fall, 1957." Is it necessary to know about the events in Little Rock in order to understand the poem? What else does the poet expect her audience to know? Review the introduction to the chapter and do outside research as needed. Then write an essay discussing the ways in which the additional knowledge informed your response to the poem.

# JAMES FARMER

*James Farmer was born in Marshall, Texas, in 1920. He studied at Wiley College in Texas before pursuing graduate studies in religion at Howard University, where he earned a degree in divinity in 1941.*

   *Even while attending school, Farmer was active in religious and civil rights groups, including the Christian Youth Movement, the National Council of Methodist Youth, and the Christian Youth Council of America. His involvement in civil rights led to his cofounding of the Congress of Racial Equality (CORE) in 1942, the first African American protest organization to adopt the methods of nonviolent resistance advocated by Gandhi. A year later, in a Chicago restaurant, Farmer organized the first successful sit-in demonstration. In 1961 CORE introduced the Freedom Ride to Alabama and Mississippi; during this period Farmer was imprisoned and had his life threatened. Farmer later worked as an adviser in the Johnson and Nixon administrations. In addition to teaching and lecturing on the civil rights movement he held a professorship at Mary Washington College in Virginia. His publications include* Freedom When? *(1965),* Lay Bare the Heart: The Autobiography of the Civil Rights Movement *(1986), and many magazine articles. He was awarded the Presidential Medal of Freedom in 1998. James Farmer died in 1999.*

*The following chapter from* Lay Bare the Heart *describes the way in which peaceful demonstrators sometimes met with violence. The passage serves as a reminder that some civil rights workers made the ultimate sacrifice for their beliefs.*

✠

# "TOMORROW IS FOR OUR MARTYRS"

I︎T HAD BEEN A CALM DAY in the office, if any days could be considered calm in the frenetic atmosphere in which we functioned. There had been no major crises; no mass arrests or calls for immediate bail money; no libel suits had been filed against any of our chapters; no scandals were threatening to erupt in the press; the sky had not fallen that day. Such tranquility was rare, particularly in the freedom summer of 1964 when CORE[1] and SNCC[2] had drawn hundreds of young volunteers into Mississippi, blanketing the state with voter registration workers.   1

I went home the evening of June 21, 1964, with a sense of well-being, cherishing the night of easy sleep that lay ahead.   2

Gretchen, now an old dog, labored to get on the bed and snuggle in her favorite spot on the pillows between Lula's head and mine. ("I always knew some bitch would come between us," Lula had once said.) At 3:00 A.M., the bedside phone rang. Cursing the intrusion, I growled hello into the receiver.   3

CORE's Mississippi field secretary, George Raymond, spoke into the phone: "Jim, three of our guys, Schwerner, Goodman, and Chaney, are missing. They left Meridian yesterday afternoon to go over to the town of Philadelphia in Neshoba County to look at the ruins of the church where they had been teaching voter registration courses. You know that church was burned down a week ago. They were supposed to return by sundown, but they're not back yet. Can you come down right away?"   4

"Don't jump to conclusions, George," I said. "It's only been a few hours. Maybe they stopped to visit some friends for dinner and decided to take a nap before driving home."   5

"Face facts, Jim," Raymond shouted into the phone. "Our guys and gals don't just stop over and visit friends or take a nap without calling in. Those   6

1. Congress of Racial Equality.
2. Student Nonviolent Coordinating Committee.

three are responsible guys; they wouldn't be nine hours late without calling us. That is, if they could call."

7   "Okay, I'll be on the next plane to Meridian," I said. "I'll call you back in a few minutes to let you know the time of arrival."

8   I wanted company going to Neshoba County, so I called Dick Gregory at his home in Chicago, waking him up. Before he answered the phone, I glanced at Lula and saw that she was wide awake, watching with no sign of emotion.

9   "Hey, big daddy," said Gregory. "What's happening?"

10   "Three of my guys are missing in Mississippi," I said.

11   After a brief silence, Gregory said, "Okay, I know you're going down there. I'll meet you there. What airport do I fly to?"

12   Meridian, though close to Neshoba County, was an island of relative sanity in Mississippi. At the airport when we arrived were a few dozen city policemen with rifles. They were there to ensure my safety. I was given a police escort to the small, unpretentious black hotel. Immediately, I was closeted with George Raymond; Mickey Schwerner's wife, Rita; and several other CORE people in Meridian.

13   It was early evening on the day after the disappearance, and still there was no word. We were certain our colleagues were dead. Rita, no more than five feet tall and less than a hundred pounds, was dry-eyed and rational. When Mickey had accepted the assignment, both of them were well aware of the risks. Mickey was a social worker from New York who had joined the CORE staff several months earlier. Rita intended to study law.

14   The local and state officials were showing no interest in locating the men or their bodies. We had alerted the FBI, but there was not yet any evidence of their involvement in the search. A nearby U.S. military unit had just been called in to search some of the swamps for bodies, but the results thus far were negative. The CORE car in which the men had been riding when last seen—a white Ford station wagon—had not been found.

15   As we discussed things that might be done to aid the search, Rita suggested that going through the ashes at the city dump where trash was burned might possibly yield some fragments of metal that could be identified as having belonged to one of the three men. Nothing more helpful than that came immediately to mind.

16   I told them that on the following morning, I intended to go into Philadelphia in Neshoba County to talk with Sheriff Lawrence Rainey and Deputy Sheriff Cecil Price about the disappearance of the men. Considering the racist reputation of the sheriff and his deputy, all agreed that one or both of them knew something about the disappearance of our friends.

17   George Raymond told us that Dick Gregory had called to say that he would be joining me in Meridian early the next morning.

18   "Good," I said. "Let's time my trip to Philadelphia so that Dick can go along with me."

19   Early the next morning, after Gregory's arrival, he and I sat in the small

hotel office on the ground floor with Raymond and one or two other CORE staffers. There was also a lieutenant of the Meridian City Police. Outside the building were several uniformed policemen and two squad cars, with others ready if needed.

The police official asked me what our plans were and I told him of my     20
intention to talk with Rainey and Price in their office. He let out a low whistle. "Farmer," he said, "you can't go over there. That's Neshoba County. That's real red-neck territory. We cain't protect you outside of Meridian."

"Lieutenant, we do appreciate the protection the city is giving us and we     21
want to thank you for it. However, we're not asking for protection, and certainly not from the Meridian police, when we go into Neshoba County. Mr. Gregory and I will go to Neshoba County this morning to try to see the sheriff and his deputy. That is our right and our duty, and we intend to exercise it."

The lieutenant shook his head and then made a phone call to a Mr.     22
Snodgrass, head of the Mississippi State Police. I knew Snodgrass and had always respected him. He was a conscientious law enforcement officer and, I felt, a humane one. At the various marches and demonstrations CORE had held in Mississippi, when Snodgrass personally was present, I had felt a little more at ease.

This time, I could hear Snodgrass shouting over the phone from ten feet     23
away: "He can't go over there. They'll kill him in that place. We can't protect him."

The lieutenant handed me the phone. "Mr. Snodgrass wants to talk to you."     24

Still shouting, Snodgrass said, "Farmer, don't go over there. That's one of     25
the worst red-neck areas in this state. They would just as soon kill you as look at you. We cannot protect you over there."

"Mr. Snodgrass, we have not asked for your protection. This is something     26
we have to do, protection or not."

"Okay, okay," Snodgrass replied. "What time are you going?"     27

"We're leaving here in about an hour and a half," I said and hung up.     28

We left Meridian in a caravan of five cars, with an escort of city police cars.     29
Dick Gregory and I were in the lead car. Our escort left us at the Meridian city limits.

At the Neshoba County line, there was a roadblock with two sheriff's cars     30
and one unmarked vehicle. A hefty middle-aged man, stereotypical of the "Negro-hating" southern sheriff of that day—chewing either a wad of tobacco or the end of a cigar, I forget which—swaggered up to our lead car. He was closely followed by an equally large but younger deputy sheriff.

The middle-aged man spoke to me: "Whut's yo' name?"     31

"James Farmer, and this gentleman is Mr. Dick Gregory, the entertainer     32
and social critic."

"Where yo' think you goin'?"     33

"Mr. Gregory and I are going to Philadelphia."     34

"Whut yo' gon' do there?"     35

36   "We are going to talk to Sheriff Rainey and Deputy Price."

37   "Whut yo' wanna talk ta them 'bout?"

38   "We are going to talk with them about the disappearance of three of the staff members of the organization I head: Michael Schwerner, Andrew Goodman, and James Chaney."

39   "Well, Ah'm Sheriff Rainey and this heah's mah deputy, Deputy Price. Y'all wanna talk ta us heah?"

40   "No. We want to talk to you in your office."

41   "Awright, folla me."

42   "Just a moment," I said, "let me pass the word back down the line that we're all going to Philadelphia."

43   "Naw. Jus' you and this heah man can come," he said, pointing to Gregory. "The rest of them boys'll have to wait heah."

44   I glanced at the unmarked car and saw that leaning against it was Mr. Snodgrass, watching the scene closely.

45   Gregory and I followed Rainey and Price into town. Outside the courthouse were several hundred shirt-sleeved white men, standing with assorted weapons in hand. Surrounding the courthouse, though, were state police with rifles pointed at the crowd. State police also flanked the sidewalk leading to the steps of the building.

46   Gregory and I followed Rainey and Price up those steps and into the courthouse. We followed them to an elevator, and as the doors closed behind us, we thought of the same thing simultaneously. We never should have gotten into that box with those two men. They could have killed us and said that we had jumped them and that they had to shoot us in self-defense. And there would have been no witnesses. But it was too late now. We shrugged our shoulders.

47   To our relief, the door opened on the second floor without event, and we followed the two men down the hallway to an office at its end. Rainey introduced the three men seated in that office as the city attorney of Philadelphia, the county attorney of Neshoba, and Mr. Snodgrass of the state police. Snodgrass merely nodded at the introduction, and looked sharply at the faces of the other men in the room.

48   Rainey cleared his throat and rasped, "Ah've got laryngitis or somethin'. This heah man will tall fer me." He was pointing at the county attorney. I nodded, but thought it strange that I had not noticed the impaired throat during our conversation at the roadblock.

49   The county attorney squinted his eyes, and said to me, "Well, we're all heah. What was it you wanted to talk to the sheriff and his deputy about?"

50   I told him that, as national director of CORE, I was charged with responsibility for the supervision of all members of the CORE staff. Three members of that staff had been missing for thirty-six hours. Mr. Gregory and I were there, I said, to try to find out what had happened to them and whether they were alive or dead. Specifically, I indicated I wanted to ask Deputy Price a question.

51   Price then sat upright in this seat. Deputy Price had given conflicting stories

to the press, I pointed out. First, he had said he never saw the men, then he said he had arrested them and released them in the evening. I wanted to know the true story.

The attorney looked at Price and the deputy spoke: "Ah'll tell ya the God's truth. Ah did see them boys. I arrested them for speedin' and took them ta jail—" 52

"What time did you arrest them?" I said. 53

"It was about three or three-thirty. Yeah, closer to three-thirty when Ah arrested them. Ah kept them in jail till 'bout six-thirty or seven in the evenin'—" 54

"Why would you keep men in jail for three and a half hours for speeding?" 55

"Ah had to find out how much the justice of the peace was gonna fine them. The justice of the peace was not at home, so Ah had to wait till he got home. He fined them fifteen dollars. That colored boy, Chaney, who wuz drivin' the car, didn't have no fifteen dollars, but one of them Jew boys, Schwerner, had fifteen an' he paid the fine. Then, I took them boys out to the edge of town and put them in their car and they headed for Meridian. Ah sat in mah car and watched their taillights as long as Ah could see them. An' they were goin' toward Meridian. Then Ah turned around and came back into town, and that was the last Ah seen of them boys. Now, that's the God's truth." 56

"At this moment," I said, "I have about fifteen young men waiting at the county line. They are friends and coworkers of Mickey Schwerner, Jim Chaney, and Andy Goodman. They want to join in the search for their missing colleagues." 57

"What would they do? Where would they look?" the county attorney asked, rather anxiously, I felt. Could it have been he thought we might have gotten some clue as to where the bodies could be found? 58

"They would look anywhere and everywhere that bodies could be hidden or disposed of—in the woods, the swamps, the rivers, whatever." 59

"No!" he said. "We can't let them go out there by themselves without any supervision." 60

"Oh, they'll be supervised," I replied. "I'll go with them." 61

"And I'll be with them, too," Gregory added. 62

"No, no! I can't let you do that. This is private property all around heah and the owners could shoot you for trespassing. We don't want anything to happen to you down here," he said. 63

"Something already *has* happened to three of our brothers. I'll take my chances," I said. 64

"No, these swamps around here are very dangerous," the attorney said. "They've got water moccasins, rattlesnakes, copperheads, and everything else in them. Like I said, we don't want anything to happen to you. We won't allow you to do it." 65

"Then," I said, "I have another question. We heard over the car radio coming here that the car in which the men were riding, that white Ford station wagon, has been found burned out on the other side of town, the opposite side 66 from Meridian. That automobile belonged to the organization I serve as national director, and I want to look at what is left of it."

67 "No," said the county lawyer emphatically. "We can't let you do that either. You might destroy fingerprints or some other evidence that will be useful to Sheriff Rainey or Deputy Price in solving this crime—if there has been a crime. You know, those boys may have decided to go up north or someplace and have a short vacation. They'll probably be coming back shortly."

68 Dick Gregory, who had shown masterful restraint thus far, rose to his feet. He began speaking to the assembled men, pointing his finger at them, looking at each one with sharp eyes, and speaking with an even sharper tongue. He made it clear that he thought someone there knew much more about the disappearance of the three men than was being told. He said that we were not going to let this matter rest but were going to get to the bottom of it, and the guilty persons were going to pay for their crimes.

69 I felt this was neither the time nor the place to have a showdown with Rainey and Price. Yet, I was struggling with my own feelings. I was not Christ. I was not Gandhi. I was not King. I wanted to kill those men—not with bullets, but with my fingers around their throats, squeezing tighter as I watched life ebb from their eyes.

70 Back in Meridian, I called a meeting of the CORE staff and summer volunteers. Our embattled southern staff evidenced little of the black/white tension so prevalent in the North. At the meeting, I announced that I wanted two volunteers for an extraordinarily important and dangerous mission. The qualifications for the volunteers were that they had to be black, male, and young. I wanted them to slip into Philadelphia in Neshoba County in the dead of night, not going by the main highway but by side routes. They would very quietly disappear into the black community of Philadelphia, see a minister, and ask if he could find a family for them to stay with.

71 They would have to do all they could to keep the officials from knowing that they were there or of their mission. I believed that the black community would take them in, for that is an old tradition among blacks—the extended family. They would have to try not to be conspicuous, but to disappear into the woodwork, so to speak, until they were trusted by the blacks in Philadelphia.

72 In all probability, George Raymond and I believed, some person or persons in the black community knew what had happened to the three men. Someone in that community always does, but no one would tell the FBI or any city or state officials, for fear of retribution.

73 When accepted and trusted, our men were to begin asking discreet questions. When any information was secured, they were to communicate that to me. If they did so by phone, it was to be from a phone booth and not the same one each time. If by letter, the message should be mailed from another town, and without a return address on the envelope. If they had any reason to believe that Rainey or Price knew of their presence or mission, they were to contact me immediately by phone.

Practically all hands went up. Everyone wanted to go. When George 74
Raymond and I selected two, most others felt let down and angry.

The two volunteers left the meeting, packed small suitcases, and surrepti- 75
tiously moved into Philadelphia. It was about two weeks before I began getting
reports. Those reports from eyewitnesses of various parts of the tragedy indicated a clear scenario, the stage for which had been set by an earlier report from
another source.

A black maid in Meridian had told us of overhearing a phone call from a 76
black Meridian man who was speaking in an open telephone booth. The man
allegedly fingered the three young CORE men. The maid, of course, did not
know to whom the call was made, but we suspected it was either to Sheriff
Rainey or Deputy Price. The caller said that the three guys, two Jews and one
colored, were in a white '62 Ford station wagon. He also gave the license number
of the car. He said the three had just left Meridian, heading for Philadelphia.

The scenario as told to the CORE volunteers by various eyewitnesses was 77
as follows: when Schwerner, Goodman, and Chaney entered Philadelphia, they
were trailed by Deputy Price, who kept his distance. When they stopped at the
charred ruins of the small black church on the other side of town, Price parked
at a distance and watched them. As they got back into the car to drive on, Deputy
Price, according to the witnesses, closed in on them.

James Chaney, who was driving the car, saw Price in his rearview mirror 78
and, knowing Price's reputation as a "nigger killer," sped up.

Price then shot a tire on the Ford wagon and it came to a halt. The men 79
were arrested and taken to jail, as Price had said. Also, as the deputy had told
us, he took them out of jail about sundown, but there the similarity between
the deputy's story and fact seemed to end.

He took them to the other side of town, not the Meridian side, and turned 80
them over to a waiting mob in a vacant field. The three men were pulled into
the field and pushed beneath a large tree. There, members of the mob held
Schwerner and Goodman while the other mobsters beat Chaney without mercy.
He was knocked down, stomped, kicked, and clubbed. Schwerner broke away
from his captives and tried to help Chaney. He was then clubbed once on the
head and knocked unconscious. Seconds later, he revived and was again held by
members of the mob while the beating of Chaney continued.

By this time Chaney appeared dead, and the beating stopped. Members of 81
the mob huddled, and then Deputy Price, who was also in the group, went back
to his car and drove away. The mob remained there, holding Schwerner and
Goodman and looking at the prone form of Chaney on the ground.

A little while later, Price returned and said something to the members of 82
the mob. They then dragged Schwerner and Goodman and Chaney's body to
a car and threw them into it. The car drove off.

The latter scene was allegedly witnessed by two blacks crossing different 83
corners of the field at about the same time, on the way to church for a prayer
meeting.

We turned this information over to the FBI. 84

85    It was weeks later—August fifth—when I received a call from Deke DeLoach, then assistant to the director at FBI headquarters in Washington, D.C.

86    DeLoach said, "Mr. Farmer, since Schwerner, Goodman, and Chaney were members of your staff, I wanted you to be the first to know. We have found the bodies. An informant told us to look under a fake dam. We drove in a bulldozer and with the first scoop of earth uncovered the three bodies. Though they were badly decomposed, there was every evidence that Chaney had received the most brutal beating imaginable. It seemed that every bone in his body was broken. He was beaten to death. Each of the other two was shot once in the heart."

87    Months later, on October 3, 1964, the FBI arrested a group of men and charged them with conspiracy to violate the civil rights of the dead trio—the only charge available to the federal government, since murder is a state charge. Mississippi never charged them with murder.

88    Among those arrested and convicted of conspiracy, in addition to Deputy Price, was a minister of the gospel. When he prayed to his God, did he feel remorse? Or had he silenced the still, small voice within his soul?

89    Evil societies always kill their consciences.

90    We, who are the living, possess the past. Tomorrow is for our martyrs. ✠

---

## RESPONDING

1. Imagine that you were James Farmer. What fears might you have had about going to Mississippi? Write a letter to your family explaining why you must go.

2. Members of the African American community possessed information about the killings of Chaney, Schwerner, and Goodman but didn't come forward immediately. Working individually or in a group, discuss the reasons why having such information would be dangerous. What difficulties would African Americans have in getting the information to someone they could trust? Farmer implies that the three civil rights workers were "fingered" by someone who was African American. What might explain such a betrayal? Why might some members of the African American community cooperate with a white sheriff?

3. Describe the circumstances when Farmer says, "I was not Christ. I was not Gandhi. I was not King" (paragraph 69). Why was it especially hard for him to practice nonviolence at that moment? Using your own knowledge and any relevant readings, write an essay speculating about the arguments that figures such as Christ, Gandhi, or King would present for "turning the other cheek."

4.  African American and white members of CORE and other groups that went into the South to register voters willingly risked their lives. Does such idealism exist in America today? In an essay, support your position using examples from the readings, current events, and personal knowledge and experiences.

# MARTIN LUTHER KING JR.

*Martin Luther King Jr., the son, grandson, and greatgrandson of Baptist ministers, was born in Atlanta, Georgia, in 1929. After graduating from Morehouse College in 1951, he earned a doctorate from Boston University in 1955. In that year he also led the Montgomery bus boycott; two years later he founded the Southern Christian Leadership Conference (SCLC). During this time and throughout the 1960s, King worked vigorously to organize and promote boycotts and voter registration drives in the South. Because of the leadership and self-sacrifice he displayed on behalf of the civil rights movement, he received the 1964 Nobel Prize for Peace, the youngest person ever to receive this honor. King was assassinated in 1968.*

*The "Letter from Birmingham Jail," which uses the techniques of deductive argument to outline his position, is one of Dr. King's most important works.*

# LETTER FROM BIRMINGHAM JAIL*

April 16, 1963

MY DEAR FELLOW CLERGYMEN:

WHILE CONFINED HERE IN THE BIRMINGHAM CITY JAIL, I came across your recent    1
statement calling my present activities "unwise and untimely." Seldom do I pause to answer criticism of my work and ideas. If I sought to answer all the criticisms that cross my desk, my secretaries would have little time for anything other than

---

*Author's Note: This response to a published statement by eight fellow clergymen from Alabama (Bishop C. C. J. Carpenter, Bishop Joseph A. Durick, Rabbi Hilton L. Grafman, Bishop Paul Hardin, Bishop Holan B. Harmon, the Reverend George M. Murray, the Reverend Edward V. Ramage and the Reverend Earl Stallings) was composed under somewhat constricting circumstances. Begun on the margins of the newspaper in which the statement appeared while I was in jail, the letter was continued on scraps of writing paper supplied by a friendly Negro trusty, and concluded on a pad my attorneys were eventually permitted to leave me. Although the text remains in substance unaltered, I have indulged in the author's prerogative of polishing it for publication.

such correspondence in the course of the day, and I would have no time for constructive work. But since I feel that you are men of genuine good will and that your criticisms are sincerely set forth, I want to try to answer your statement in what I hope will be patient and reasonable terms.

2     I think I should indicate why I am here in Birmingham, since you have been influenced by the view which argues against "outsiders coming in." I have the honor of serving as president of the Southern Christian Leadership Conference, an organization operating in every southern state, with headquarters in Atlanta, Georgia. We have some eighty-five affiliated organizations across the South, and one of them is the Alabama Christian Movement for Human Rights. Frequently we share staff, educational and financial resources with our affiliates. Several months ago the affiliate here in Birmingham asked us to be on call to engage in a nonviolent direct-action program if such were deemed necessary. We readily consented, and when the hour came we lived up to our promise. So I, along with several members of my staff, am here because I was invited here. I am here because I have organizational ties here.

3     But more basically, I am in Birmingham because injustice is here. Just as the prophets of the eighth century B.C. left their villages and carried their "thus said the Lord" far beyond the boundaries of their home towns, and just as the Apostle Paul left his village of Tarsus and carried the gospel of Jesus Christ to the far corners of the Greco-Roman world, so am I compelled to carry the gospel of freedom beyond my own home town. Like Paul, I must constantly respond to the Macedonian call for aid.

4     Moreover, I am cognizant of the interrelatedness of all communities and states. I cannot sit idly by in Atlanta and not be concerned about what happens in Birmingham. Injustice anywhere is a threat to justice everywhere. We are caught in an inescapable network of mutuality, tied in a single garment of destiny. Whatever affects one directly, affects all indirectly. Never again can we afford to live with the narrow, provincial "outside agitator" idea. Anyone who lives inside the United States can never be considered an outsider anywhere within its bounds.

5     You deplore the demonstrations taking place in Birmingham. But your statement, I am sorry to say, fails to express a similar concern for the conditions that brought about the demonstrations. I am sure that none of you would want to rest content with the superficial kind of social analysis that deals merely with effects and does not grapple with underlying causes. It is unfortunate that demonstrations are taking place in Birmingham, but it is even more unfortunate that the city's white power structure left the Negro community with no alternative.

6     In any nonviolent campaign there are four basic steps: collection of the facts to determine whether injustices exist; negotiation; self-purification; and direct action. We have gone through all these steps in Birmingham. There can be no gainsaying the fact that racial injustice engulfs this community. Birmingham is

probably the most thoroughly segregated city in the United States. Its ugly record of brutality is widely known. Negroes have experienced grossly unjust treatment in the courts. There have been more unsolved bombings of Negro homes and churches in Birmingham than in any other city in the nation. These are the hard, brutal facts of the case. On the basis of these conditions, Negro leaders sought to negotiate with the city fathers. But the latter consistently refused to engage in good-faith negotiation.

Then, last September, came the opportunity to talk with leaders of Birmingham's economic community. In the course of the negotiations, certain promises were made by the merchants—for example, to remove the stores' humiliating racial signs. On the basis of these promises, the Reverend Fred Shuttlesworth and the leaders of the Alabama Christian Movement for Human Rights agreed to a moratorium on all demonstrations. As the weeks and months went by, we realized that we were the victims of a broken promise. A few signs, briefly removed, returned; the others remained. 7

As in so many past experiences, our hopes had been blasted, and the shadow of deep disappointment settled upon us. We had no alternative except to prepare for direct action, whereby we would present our very bodies as a means of laying our case before the conscience of the local and the national community. Mindful of the difficulties involved, we decided to undertake a process of self-purification. We began a series of workshops on nonviolence, and we repeatedly asked ourselves: "Are you able to accept blows without retaliating?" "Are you able to endure the ordeal of jail?" We decided to schedule our direct-action program for the Easter season, realizing that except for Christmas, this is the main shopping period of the year. Knowing that a strong economic-withdrawal program would be the by-product of direct action, we felt that this would be the best time to bring pressure to bear on the merchants for the needed change. 8

Then it occurred to us that Birmingham's mayoral election was coming up in March, and we speedily decided to postpone action until after election day. When we discovered that the Commissioner of Public Safety, Eugene "Bull" Connor, had piled up enough votes to be in the run-off, we decided again to postpone action until the day after the run-off so that the demonstrations could not be used to cloud the issues. Like many others, we waited to see Mr. Connor defeated, and to this end we endured postponement after postponement. Having aided in the community need, we felt that our direct-action program could be delayed no longer. 9

You may well ask: "Why direct action? Why sit-ins, marches and so forth? Isn't negotiation a better path?" You are quite right in calling for negotiation. Indeed, this is the very purpose of direct action. Nonviolent direct action seeks to create such a crisis and foster such a tension that a community which has constantly refused to negotiate is forced to confront the issue. It seeks so to dramatize the issue that it can no longer be ignored. My citing the creation of tension as part of the work of the nonviolent-resister may sound rather shocking. 10

But I must confess that I am not afraid of the word "tension." I have earnestly opposed violent tension, but there is a type of constructive, nonviolent tension which is necessary for growth. Just as Socrates felt that it was necessary to create a tension in the mind so that individuals could rise from the bondage of myths and half-truths to the unfettered realm of creative analysis and objective appraisal, so must we see the need for nonviolent gadflies to create the kind of tension in society that will help men rise from the dark depths of prejudice and racism to the majestic heights of understanding and brotherhood.

11      The purpose of our direct-action program is to create a situation so crisis-packed that it will inevitably open the door to negotiation. I therefore concur with you in your call for negotiation. Too long has our beloved Southland been bogged down in a tragic effort to live in monologue rather than dialogue.

12      One of the basic points in your statement is that the action that I and my associates have taken in Birmingham is untimely. Some have asked: "Why don't you give the new city administration time to act?" The only answer that I can give to this query is that the new Birmingham administration must be prodded about as much as the outgoing one, before it will act. We are sadly mistaken if we feel that the election of Albert Boutwell as mayor will bring the millennium to Birmingham. While Mr. Boutwell is a much more gentle person than Mr. Connor, they are both segregationists, dedicated to maintenance of the status quo. I have hope that Mr. Boutwell will be reasonable enough to see the futility of massive resistance to desegregation. But he will not see this without pressure from devotees of civil rights. My friends, I must say to you that we have not made a single gain in civil rights without determined legal and nonviolent pressure. Lamentably, it is an historical fact that privileged groups seldom give up their privileges voluntarily. Individuals may see the moral light and voluntarily give up their unjust posture; but, as Reinhold Niebuhr has reminded us, groups tend to be more immoral than individuals.

13      We know through painful experience that freedom is never voluntarily given by the oppressor; it must be demanded by the oppressed. Frankly, I have yet to engage in a direct-action campaign that was "well timed" in the view of those who have not suffered unduly from the disease of segregation. For years now I have heard the word "Wait!" It rings in the ear of every Negro with piercing familiarity. This "Wait" has almost always meant "Never." We must come to see, with one of our distinguished jurists, that "justice too long delayed is justice denied."

14      We have waited for more than 340 years for our constitutional and God-given rights. The nations of Asia and Africa are moving with jetlike speed toward gaining political independence, but we still creep at horse-and-buggy pace toward gaining a cup of coffee at a lunch counter. Perhaps it is easy for those who have never felt the stinging darts of segregation to say, "Wait." But when you have seen vicious mobs lynch your mothers and fathers at will and drown your sisters and brothers at whim; when you have seen hate-filled policemen curse, kick and even kill your black brothers and sisters; when you see the vast

majority of your twenty million Negro brothers smothering in an airtight cage of poverty in the midst of an affluent society; when you suddenly find your tongue twisted and your speech stammering as you seek to explain to your six-year-old daughter why she can't go to the public amusement park that has just been advertised on television, and see tears welling up in her eyes when she is told that Funtown is closed to colored children, and see ominous clouds of inferiority beginning to form in her little mental sky, and see her beginning to distort her personality by developing an unconscious bitterness toward white people; when you have to concoct an answer for a five-year-old son who is asking: "Daddy, why do white people treat colored people so mean?"; when you take a cross-country drive and find it necessary to sleep night after night in the uncomfortable corners of your automobile because no motel will accept you; when you are humiliated day in and day out by nagging signs reading "white" and "colored"; when your first name becomes "nigger," your middle name becomes "boy" (however old you are) and your last name becomes "John," and your wife and mother are never given the respected title "Mrs."; when you are harried by day and haunted by night by the fact that you are a Negro, living constantly at tiptoe stance, never quite knowing what to expect next, and are plagued with inner fears and outer resentments; when you are forever fighting a degenerating sense of "nobodiness"—then you will understand why we find it difficult to wait. There comes a time when the cup of endurance runs over, and men are no longer willing to be plunged into the abyss of despair. I hope, sirs, you can understand our legitimate and unavoidable impatience.

You express a great deal of anxiety over our willingness to break laws. This 15 is certainly a legitimate concern. Since we so diligently urge people to obey the Supreme Court's decision of 1954 outlawing segregation in the public schools, at first glance it may seem rather paradoxical for us consciously to break laws. One may well ask: "How can you advocate breaking some laws and obeying others?" The answer lies in the fact that there are two types of laws: just and unjust. I would be the first to advocate obeying just laws. One has not only a legal but a moral responsibility to obey just laws. Conversely, one has a moral responsibility to disobey unjust laws. I would agree with St. Augustine that "an unjust law is no law at all."

Now, what is the difference between the two? How does one determine 16 whether a law is just or unjust? A just law is a man-made code that squares with the moral law or the law of God. An unjust law is a code that is out of harmony with the moral law. To put it in the terms of St. Thomas Aquinas: An unjust law is a human law that is not rooted in eternal law and natural law. Any law that uplifts human personality is just. Any law that degrades human personality is unjust. All segregation statutes are unjust because segregation distorts the soul and damages the personality. It gives the segregator a false sense of superiority and the segregated a false sense of inferiority. Segregation, to use the terminology of the Jewish philosopher Martin Buber, substitutes an "I—it" relationship for an "I—thou" relationship and ends up relegating persons to the status of things. Hence segregation is not only politically, economically and sociologically unsound, it is morally wrong and sinful. Paul Tillich has said that sin is separation. Is not segregation an existential expression of man's tragic separation, his awful estrangement, his terrible sinfulness? Thus it is that I can urge men to obey the 1954 decision of the Supreme Court, for it is morally right; and I can urge them to disobey segregation ordinances, for they are morally wrong.

17  Let us consider a more concrete example of just and unjust laws. An unjust law is a code that a numerical or power majority group compels a minority group to obey but does not make binding on itself. This is *difference* made legal. By the same token, a just law is a code that a majority compels a minority to follow and that it is willing to follow itself. This is *sameness* made legal.

18  Let me give another explanation. A law is unjust if it is inflicted on a minority that, as a result of being denied the right to vote, had no part in enacting or devising the law. Who can say that the legislature of Alabama which set up that state's segregation laws was democratically elected? Throughout Alabama all sorts of devious methods are used to prevent Negroes from becoming registered voters, and there are some counties in which, even though Negroes constitute a majority of the population, not a single Negro is registered. Can any law enacted under such circumstances be considered democratically structured?

19  Sometimes a law is just on its face and unjust in its application. For instance, I have been arrested on a charge of parading without a permit. Now, there is nothing wrong in having an ordinance which requires a permit for a parade. But such an ordinance becomes unjust when it is used to maintain segregation and to deny citizens the First-Amendment privilege of peaceful assembly and protest.

20  I hope you are able to see the distinction I am trying to point out. In no sense do I advocate evading or defying the law, as would the rabid segregationist. That would lead to anarchy. One who breaks an unjust law must do so openly, lovingly, and with a willingness to accept the penalty. I submit that an individual who breaks a law that conscience tells him is unjust, and who willingly accepts the penalty of imprisonment in order to arouse the conscience of the community over its injustice, is in reality expressing the highest respect for law.

21  Of course, there is nothing new about this kind of civil disobedience. It was evidenced sublimely in the refusal of Shadrach, Meshach and Abednego to obey the laws of Nebuchadnezzar, on the ground that a higher moral law was at stake. It was practiced superbly by the early Christians, who were willing to face hungry lions and the excruciating pain of chopping blocks rather than submit to certain unjust laws of the Roman Empire. To a degree, academic freedom is a reality today because Socrates practiced civil disobedience. In our own nation, the Boston Tea Party represented a massive act of civil disobedience.

22  We should never forget that everything Adolf Hitler did in Germany was "legal" and everything the Hungarian freedom fighters did in Hungary was "illegal." It was "illegal" to aid and comfort a Jew in Hitler's Germany. Even

so, I am sure that, had I lived in Germany at the time, I would have aided and comforted my Jewish brothers. If today I lived in a Communist country where certain principles dear to the Christian faith are suppressed, I would openly advocate disobeying that country's antireligious laws.

I must make two honest confessions to you, my Christian and Jewish 23 brothers. First, I must confess that over the past few years I have been gravely disappointed with the white moderate. I have almost reached the regrettable conclusion that the Negro's great stumbling block in his stride toward freedom is not the White Citizen's Counciler or the Ku Klux Klanner, but the white moderate, who is more devoted to "order" than to justice; who prefers a negative peace which is the absence of tension to a positive peace which is the presence of justice; who constantly says: "I agree with you in the goal you seek, but I cannot agree with your methods of direct action"; who paternalistically believes he can set the timetable for another man's freedom; who lives by a mythical concept of time and who constantly advises the Negro to wait for a "more convenient season." Shallow understanding from people of good will is more frustrating than absolute misunderstanding from people of ill will. Lukewarm acceptance is much more bewildering than outright rejection.

I had hoped that the white moderate would understand that law and order 24 exist for the purpose of establishing justice and that when they fail in this purpose they become the dangerously structured dams that block the flow of social progress. I had hoped that the white moderate would understand that the present tension in the South is a necessary phase of the transition from an obnoxious negative peace, in which the Negro passively accepted his unjust plight, to a substantive and positive peace, in which all men will respect the dignity and worth of human personality. Actually, we who engage in nonviolent direct action are not the creators of tension. We merely bring to the surface the hidden tension that is already alive. We bring it out in the open, where it can be seen and dealt with. Like a boil that can never be cured so long as it is covered up but must be opened with all its ugliness to the natural medicines of air and light, injustice must be exposed, with all the tension its exposure creates, to the light of human conscience and the air of national opinion before it can be cured.

In your statement you assert that our actions, even though peaceful, must 25 be condemned because they precipitate violence. But is this a logical assertion? Isn't this like condemning a robbed man because his possession of money precipitated the evil act of robbery? Isn't this like condemning Socrates because his unswerving commitment to truth and his philosophical inquiries precipitated the act by the misguided populace in which they made him drink hemlock? Isn't this like condemning Jesus because his unique God-consciousness and never-ceasing devotion to God's will precipitated the evil act of crucifixion? We must come to see that, as the federal courts have consistently affirmed, it is wrong to urge an individual to cease his efforts to gain his basic constitutional rights because the quest may precipitate violence. Society must protect the robbed and punish the robber.

26      I had also hoped that the white moderate would reject the myth concerning time in relation to the struggle for freedom. I have just received a letter from a white brother in Texas. He writes: "All Christians know that the colored people will receive equal rights eventually, but it is possible that you are in too great a religious hurry. It has taken Christianity almost two thousand years to accomplish what it has. The teachings of Christ take time to come to earth." Such an attitude stems from a tragic misconception of time, from the strangely irrational notion that there is something in the very flow of time that will inevitably cure all ills. Actually, time itself is neutral; it can be used either destructively or constructively. More and more I feel that the people of ill will have used time much more effectively than have the people of good will. We will have to repent in this generation not merely for the hateful words and actions of the bad people but for the appalling silence of the good people. Human progress never rolls in on wheels of inevitability; it comes through the tireless efforts of men willing to be co-workers with God, and without this hard work, time itself becomes an ally of the forces of social stagnation. We must use time creatively, in the knowledge that the time is always ripe to do right. Now is the time to make real the promise of democracy and transform our pending national elegy into a creative psalm of brotherhood. Now is the time to lift our national policy from the quicksand of racial injustice to the solid rock of human dignity.

27      You speak of our activity in Birmingham as extreme. At first I was rather disappointed that fellow clergymen would see my nonviolent efforts as those of an extremist. I began thinking about the fact that I stand in the middle of two opposing forces in the Negro community. One is a force of complacency, made up in part of Negroes who, as a result of long years of oppression, are so drained of self-respect and a sense of "somebodiness" that they have adjusted to segregation; and in part of a few middle-class Negroes who, because of a degree of academic and economic security and because in some ways they profit by segregation, have become insensitive to the problems of the masses. The other force is one of bitterness and hatred, and it comes perilously close to advocating violence. It is expressed in the various black nationalist groups that are springing up across the nation, the largest and best-known being Elijah Muhammad's Muslim movement. Nourished by the Negro's frustration over the continued existence of racial discrimination, this movement is made up of people who have lost faith in America, who have absolutely repudiated Christianity, and who have concluded that the white man is an incorrigible "devil."

28      I have tried to stand between these two forces, saying that we need emulate neither the "do-nothingism" of the complacent nor the hatred and despair of the black nationalist. For there is the more excellent way of love and nonviolent protest. I am grateful to God that, through the influence of the Negro church, the way of nonviolence became an integral part of our struggle.

29      If this philosophy had not emerged, by now many streets of the South

would, I am convinced, be flowing with blood. And I am further convinced that if our white brothers dismiss as "rabble-rousers" and "outside agitators" those of us who employ nonviolent direct action, and if they refuse to support our nonviolent efforts, millions of Negroes will, out of frustration and despair, seek solace and security in black-nationalist ideologies—a development that would inevitably lead to a frightening racial nightmare.

Oppressed people cannot remain oppressed forever. The yearning for free- 30 dom eventually manifests itself, and that is what has happened to the American Negro. Something within has reminded him of his birthright of freedom, and something without has reminded him that it can be gained. Consciously or unconsciously, he has been caught up by the *Zeitgeist*, and with his black brothers of Africa and his brown and yellow brothers of Asia, South America and the Caribbean, the United States Negro is moving with a sense of great urgency toward the promised land of racial justice. If one recognizes this vital urge that has engulfed the Negro community, one should readily understand why public demonstrations are taking place. The Negro has many pent-up resentments and latent frustrations, and he must release them. So let him march; let him make prayer pilgrimages to the city hall; let him go on freedom rides—and try to understand why he must do so. If his repressed emotions are not released in nonviolent ways, they will seek expression through violence; this is not a threat but a fact of history. So I have not said to my people: "Get rid of your discontent." Rather, I have tried to say that this normal and healthy discontent can be channeled into the creative outlet of nonviolent direct action. And now this approach is being termed extremist.

But though I was initially disappointed at being categorized as an extremist, 31 as I continued to think about the matter I gradually gained a measure of satisfaction from the label. Was not Jesus an extremist for love: "Love your enemies, bless them that curse you, do good to them that hate you, and pray for them which despitefully use you, and persecute you." Was not Amos an extremist for justice: "Let justice roll down like waters and righteousness like an ever-flowing stream." Was not Paul an extremist for the Christian gospel: "I bear in my body the marks of the Lord Jesus." Was not Martin Luther an extremist: "Here I stand; I cannot do otherwise, so help me God." And John Bunyan: "I will stay in jail to the end of my days before I make a butchery of my conscience." And Abraham Lincoln: "This nation cannot survive half slave and half free." And Thomas Jefferson: "We hold these truths to be self-evident, that all men are created equal . . ." So the question is not whether we will be extremists, but what kind of extremists we will be. Will we be extremists for hate or for love? Will we be extremists for the preservation of injustice or for the extension of justice? In that dramatic scene on Calvary's hill three men were crucified. We must never forget that all three were crucified for the same crime—the crime of extremism. Two were extremists for immorality, and thus fell below their environment. Two were extremists for immorality, and thus fell below their environment. The other, Jesus Christ, was an extremist for love, truth and goodness, and thereby rose above his environment. Perhaps the South, the nation and the world are in dire need of creative extremists.

32 I had hoped that the white moderate would see this need. Perhaps I was too optimistic; perhaps I expected too much. I suppose I should have realized that few members of the oppressor race can understand the deep groans and passionate yearnings of the oppressed race, and still fewer have the vision to see that injustice must be rooted out by strong, persistent and determined action. I am thankful, however, that some of our white brothers in the South have grasped the meaning of this social revolution and committed themselves to it. They are still all too few in quantity, but they are big in quality. Some—such as Ralph McGill, Lillian Smith, Harry Golden, James McBride Dabbs, Ann Braden and Sarah Patton Boyle—have written about our struggle in eloquent and prophetic terms. Others have marched with us down nameless streets of the South. They have languished in filthy, roach-infested jails, suffering the abuse and brutality of policemen who view them as "dirty nigger-lovers." Unlike so many of their moderate brothers and sisters, they have recognized the urgency of the moment and sensed the need for powerful "action" antidotes to combat the disease of segregation.

33 Let me take note of my other major disappointment. I have been so greatly disappointed with the white church and its leadership. Of course, there are some notable exceptions. I am not unmindful of the fact that each of you has taken some significant stands on this issue. I commend you, Reverend Stallings, for your Christian stand on this past Sunday, in welcoming Negroes to your worship service on a nonsegregated basis. I commend the Catholic leaders of this state for integrating Spring Hill College several years ago.

34 But despite these notable exceptions, I must honestly reiterate that I have been disappointed with the church. I do not say this as one of those negative critics who can always find something wrong with the church. I say this as a minister of the gospel, who loves the church; who was nurtured in its bosom; who has been sustained by its spiritual blessings and who will remain true to it as long as the cord of life shall lengthen.

35 When I was suddenly catapulted into the leadership of the bus protest in Montgomery, Alabama, a few years ago, I felt we would be supported by the white church. I felt that the white ministers, priests and rabbis of the South would be among our strongest allies. Instead, some have been outright opponents, refusing to understand the freedom movement and misrepresenting its leaders; all too many others have been more cautious than courageous and have remained silent behind the anesthetizing security of stained-glass windows.

36 In spite of my shattered dreams, I came to Birmingham with the hope that the white religious leadership of this community would see the justice of our cause and, with deep moral concern, would serve as the channel through which our just grievances could reach the power structure. I had hoped that each of you would understand. But again I have been disappointed.

I have heard numerous southern religious leaders admonish their worshippers to comply with a desegregation decision because it is the law, but I have longed to hear white ministers declare: "Follow this decree because integration is morally right and because the Negro is your brother." In the midst of blatant injustices inflicted upon the Negro, I have watched white churchmen stand on the sideline and mouth pious irrelevancies and sanctimonious trivialities. In the midst of a mighty struggle to rid our nation of racial and economic injustice, I have heard many ministers say: "Those are social issues, with which the gospel has no real concern." And I have watched many churches commit themselves to a completely otherworldly religion which makes a strange, un-Biblical distinction between body and soul, between the sacred and the secular. 37

I have traveled the length and breadth of Alabama, Mississippi and all the other southern states. On sweltering summer days and crisp autumn mornings I have looked at the South's beautiful churches with their lofty spires pointing heavenward. I have beheld the impressive outlines of her massive religious-education buildings. Over and over I have found myself asking: "What kind of people worship here? Who is their God? Where were their voices when the lips of Governor Barnett dripped with words of interposition and nullification? Where were they when Governor Wallace gave a clarion call for defiance and hatred? Where were their voices of support when bruised and weary Negro men and women decided to rise from the dark dungeons of complacency to the bright hills of creative protest?" 38

Yes, these questions are still in my mind. In deep disappointment I have wept over the laxity of the church. But be assured that my tears have been tears of love. There can be no deep disappointment where there is not deep love. Yes, I love the church. How could I do otherwise? I am in the rather unique position of being the son, the grandson and the great-grandson of preachers. Yes, I see the church as the body of Christ. But, oh! How we have blemished and scarred the body through social neglect and through fear of being nonconformists. 39

There was a time when the church was very powerful—in the time when the early Christians rejoiced at being deemed worthy to suffer for what they believed. In those days the church was not merely a thermometer that recorded the ideas and principles of popular opinion; it was a thermostat that transformed the mores of society. Whenever the early Christians entered a town, the people in power became disturbed and immediately sought to convict the Christians for being "disturbers of the peace" and "outside agitators." But the Christians pressed on, in the conviction that they were "a colony of heaven," called to obey God rather than man. Small in number, they were big in commitment. They were too God-intoxicated to be "astronomically intimidated." By their effort and example they brought an end to such ancient evils as infanticide and gladiatorial contests. 40

Things are different now. So often the contemporary church is a weak, ineffectual voice with an uncertain sound. So often it is an archdefender of the 41 status quo. Far from being disturbed by the presence of the church, the power structure of the average community is consoled by the church's silent—and often even vocal—sanction of things as they are.

42      But the judgment of God is upon the church as never before. If today's church does not recapture the sacrificial spirit of the early church, it will lose its authenticity, forfeit the loyalty of millions, and be dismissed as an irrelevant social club with no meaning for the twentieth century. Every day I meet young people whose disappointment with the church has turned into outright disgust.

43      Perhaps I have once again been too optimistic. Is organized religion too inextricably bound to the status quo to save our nation and the world? Perhaps I must turn my faith to the inner spiritual church, the church within the church, as the true *ekklesia* and the hope of the world. But again I am thankful to God that some noble souls from the ranks of organized religion have broken loose from the paralyzing chains of conformity and joined us as active partners in the struggle for freedom. They have left their secure congregations and walked the streets of Albany, Georgia, with us. They have gone down the highways of the South on tortuous rides for freedom. Yes, they have gone to jail with us. Some have been dismissed from their churches, have lost the support of their bishops and fellow ministers. But they have acted in the faith that right defeated is stronger than evil triumphant. Their witness has been the spiritual salt that has preserved the true meaning of the gospel in these troubled times. They have carved a tunnel of hope through the dark mountain of disappointment.

44      I hope the church as a whole will meet the challenge of this decisive hour. But even if the church does not come to the aid of justice, I have no despair about the future. I have no fear about the outcome of our struggle in Birmingham, even if our motives are at present misunderstood. We will reach the goal of freedom in Birmingham and all over the nation, because the goal of America is freedom. Abused and scorned though we may be, our destiny is tied up with America's destiny. Before the pilgrims landed at Plymouth, we were here. Before the pen of Jefferson etched the majestic words of the Declaration of Independence across the pages of history, we were here. For more than two centuries our forebears labored in this country without wages; they made cotton king; they built the homes of their masters while suffering gross injustice and shameful humiliation—and yet out of a bottomless vitality they continued to thrive and develop. If the inexpressible cruelties of slavery could not stop us, the opposition we now face will surely fail. We will win our freedom because the sacred heritage of our nation and the eternal will of God are embodied in our echoing demands.

45      Before closing I feel impelled to mention one other point in your statement that has troubled me profoundly. You warmly commended the Birmingham police force for keeping "order" and "preventing violence." I doubt that you would have so warmly commended the police force if you had seen its dogs sinking their teeth into unarmed, nonviolent Negroes. I doubt that you would so quickly commend the policemen if you were to observe their ugly and

inhuman treatment of Negroes here in the city jail; if you were to watch them push and curse old Negro women and young Negro girls; if you were to see them slap and kick old Negro men and young boys; if you were to observe them, as they did on two occasions, refuse to give us food because we wanted to sing our grace together. I cannot join you in your praise of the Birmingham police department.

It is true that the police have exercised a degree of discipline in handling the demonstrators. In this sense they have conducted themselves rather "non-violently" in public. But for what purpose? To preserve the evil system of segregation. Over the past few years I have consistently preached that nonviolence demands that the means we use must be as pure as the ends we seek. I have tried to make clear that it is wrong to use immoral means to attain moral ends. But now I must affirm that it is just as wrong, or perhaps even more so, to use moral means to preserve immoral ends. Perhaps Mr. Connor and his policemen have been rather nonviolent in public, as was Chief Pritchett in Albany, Georgia, but they have used the moral means of nonviolence to maintain the immoral end of racial injustice. As T. S. Eliot has said: "The last temptation is the greatest treason: To do the right deed for the wrong reason."  46

I wish you had commended the Negro sit-inners and demonstrators of Birmingham for their sublime courage, their willingness to suffer and their amazing discipline in the midst of great provocation. One day the South will recognize its real heroes. They will be the James Merediths, with the noble sense of purpose that enables them to face jeering and hostile mobs, and with the agonizing loneliness that characterizes the life of the pioneer. They will be old, oppressed, battered Negro women, symbolized in a seventy-two-year-old woman in Montgomery, Alabama, who rose up with a sense of dignity and with her people decided not to ride segregated buses, and who responded with ungrammatical profundity to one who inquired about her weariness: "My feets is tired, but my soul is at rest." They will be the young high school and college students, the young ministers of the gospel and a host of their elders, courageously and nonviolently sitting in at lunch counters and willingly going to jail for conscience' sake. One day the South will know that when these disinherited children of God sat down at lunch counters, they were in reality standing up for what is best in the American dream and for the most sacred values in our Judaeo-Christian heritage, thereby bringing our nation back to those great wells of democracy which were dug deep by the founding fathers in their formulation of the Constitution and the Declaration of Independence.  47

Never before have I written so long a letter. I'm afraid it is much too long to take your precious time. I can assure you that it would have been much shorter if I had been writing from a comfortable desk, but what else can one do when he is alone in a narrow jail cell, other than write long letters, think long thoughts and pray long prayers?  48

If I have said anything in this letter that overstates the truth and indicates  49 an unreasonable impatience, I beg you to forgive me. If I have said anything that understates the truth and indicates my having a patience that allows me to settle for anything less than brotherhood, I beg God to forgive me.

50      I hope this letter finds you strong in the faith. I also hope that circumstances will soon make it possible for me to meet each of you, not as an integrationist or a civil-rights leader but as a fellow clergyman and a Christian brother. Let us all hope that the dark clouds of racial prejudice will soon pass away and the deep fog of misunderstanding will be lifted from our fear-drenched communities, and in some not too distant tomorrow the radiant stars of love and brotherhood will shine over our great nation with all their scintillating beauty.

51      Yours for the cause of Peace and Brotherhood,

MARTIN LUTHER KING JR. ✚

## RESPONDING

1. In your opinion, has the hope Dr. King expressed in the penultimate paragraph of the letter been realized? Write a journal entry supporting your position with examples from your reading or personal experience or from television news reports or special programs.

2. Working individually or in a group, discuss the reasons that Dr. King was in jail if he was fighting injustice.

3. Argue for or against the following proposition: "an individual who breaks a law that conscience tells him is unjust, and who willingly accepts the penalty of imprisonment in order to arouse the conscience of the community over its injustice, is in reality expressing the highest respect for law" (paragraph 20).

4. Write an essay agreeing or disagreeing with the following statement: "Injustice anywhere is a threat to justice everywhere. We are caught in an inescapable network of mutuality, tied in a single garment of destiny. Whatever affects one directly, affects all indirectly" (paragraph 4).

# MALCOLM X

*Malcolm X was born Malcolm Little in Omaha, Nebraska, in 1925. When Little was only six years old, his father was murdered—apparently by members of the Ku Klux Klan. He left school in the eighth grade and became involved in crime; he was imprisoned for burglary and larceny in 1946. While in prison, Little studied the teachings of Mohammed and became a Black Muslim minister; he also changed his name to Malcolm X in order to eliminate his slave name. After his release from prison in 1952, he worked first as an evangelist for the Nation of Islam, and later as the leader of the Muslim Mosque and the Organization of Afro-American Unity. He also became a major spokesman for the Black separatist movement. In 1965, he was assassinated.*

*Alex P. Haley, with whom Malcolm X collaborated on his* Autobiography *(1965), was born in Ithaca, New York, in 1921. He served as a journalist in the Coast Guard for twenty years before beginning work as a freelance writer in 1959. His most famous work,* Roots *(1976), won a Pulitzer Prize. Alex Haley died in 1992.*

*This excerpt from Malcolm X's* Autobiography *examines the injustices endured by African Americans and takes issue with those who rely on nonviolence as a means of obtaining equality.*

## *From* THE AUTOBIOGRAPHY OF MALCOLM X

I MUST BE HONEST. Negroes—Afro-Americans—showed no inclination to rush to the United Nations and demand justice for themselves here in America. I really had known in advance that they wouldn't. The American white man has so thoroughly brainwashed the black man to see himself as only a domestic "civil rights" problem that it will probably take longer than I live before the Negro sees that the struggle of the American black man is international.

And I had known too, that Negroes would not rush to follow me into the orthodox Islam which had given me the insight and perspective to see that the black men and white men truly could be brothers. America's Negroes—especially older Negroes—are too indelibly soaked in Christianity's double standard of oppression.

So, in the "public invited" meetings which I began holding each Sunday afternoon or evening in Harlem's well-known Audubon Ballroom, as I addressed predominantly non-Muslim Negro audiences, I did not immediately attempt to press the Islamic religion, but instead to embrace all who sat before me:

"—not Muslim, nor Christian, Catholic, nor Protestant . . . Baptist nor Methodist, Democrat nor Republican, Mason nor Elk! I mean the black people of America—and the black people all over this earth! Because it is as this collective mass of black people that we have been deprived not only of our civil rights, but even of our human rights, the right to human dignity. . . ."

5    On the streets, after my speeches, in the faces and the voices of the people I met—even those who would pump my hands and want my autograph—I would feel the wait-and-see attitude. I would feel—and I understood—their uncertainty about where I stood. Since the Civil War's "freedom," the black man has gone down so many fruitless paths. His leaders, very largely, had failed him. The religion of Christianity had failed him. The black man was scarred, he was cautious, he was apprehensive.

6    I understood it better now than I had before. In the Holy World, away from America's race problem, was the first time I ever had been able to think clearly about the basic divisions of white people in America, and how their attitudes and their motives related to, and affected Negroes. In my thirty-nine years on this earth, the Holy City of Mecca had been the first time I had ever stood before the Creator of All and felt like a complete human being.

7    In that peace of the Holy World—in fact, the very night I have mentioned when I lay awake surrounded by snoring brother pilgrims—my mind took me back to personal memories I would have thought were gone forever . . . as far back, even, as when I was just a little boy, eight or nine years old. Out behind our house, out in the country from Lansing, Michigan, there was an old, grassy "Hector's Hill," we called it—which may still be there. I remembered there in the Holy World how I used to lie on top of Hector's Hill, and look up at the sky, at the clouds moving over me, and daydream, all kinds of things. And then, in a funny contrast of recollections, I remembered how years later, when I was in prison, I used to lie on my cell bunk—this would be especially when I was in solitary: what we convicts called "The Hole"—and I would picture myself talking to large crowds. I don't have any idea why such previsions came to me. But they did. To tell that to anyone then would have sounded crazy. Even I didn't have, myself, the slightest inkling. . . .

8    In Mecca, too, I had played back for myself the twelve years I had spent with Elijah Muhammad[1] as if it were a motion picture. I guess it would be impossible for anyone ever to realize fully how complete was my belief in Elijah Muhammad. I believed in him not only as a leader in the ordinary *human* sense, but also I believed in him as a *divine* leader. I believed he had no human weaknesses or fault, and that, therefore, he could make no mistakes and that he could do no wrong. There on a Holy World hilltop, I realized how very dangerous it is for people to hold any human being in such esteem, especially to consider anyone some sort of "divinely guided" and "protected" person.

9    My thinking had been opened up wide in Mecca. In the long letters I wrote to friends, I tried to convey to them my new insights into the American black man's struggle and his problems, as well as the depths of my search for truth and justice.

---

1. Elijah Mohammed (1896–1975), a leader of the Black Muslim faith in the United States Malcolm X began corresponding with him soon after his conversion.

"I've had enough of someone else's propaganda," I had written to these 10
friends. "I'm for truth, no matter who tells it. I'm for justice, no matter who it
is for or against. I'm a human being first and foremost, and as such I'm for
whoever and whatever benefits humanity *as a whole.*"

Largely, the American white man's press refused to convey that I was now 11
attempting to teach Negroes a new direction. With the 1964 "long, hot summer"
steadily producing new incidents, I was constantly accused of "stirring up
Negroes." Every time I had another radio or television microphone at my
mouth, when I was asked about "stirring up Negroes" or "inciting violence,"
I'd get hot.

"It takes no one to stir up the sociological dynamite that stems from the 12
unemployment, bad housing, and inferior education already in the ghettoes.
This explosively criminal condition has existed for so long, it needs no fuse; it
fuses itself; it spontaneously combusts from within itself. . . ."

They called me "the angriest Negro in America." I wouldn't deny that 13
charge. I spoke exactly as I felt. "I *believe* in anger. The Bible says there is a *time*
for anger." They called me a "teacher, a fomentor of violence." I would say point
blank, "That is a lie. I'm not for wanton violence, I'm for justice. I feel that if
white people were attacked by Negroes—if the forces of law prove unable, or
inadequate, or reluctant to protect those whites from those Negroes—then those
white people should protect and defend themselves from those Negroes, using
arms if necessary. And I feel that when the law fails to protect Negroes from
whites' attack, then those Negroes should use arms, if necessary, to defend
themselves."

"Malcolm X Advocates Armed Negroes!" 14

What was wrong with that? I'll tell you what was wrong. I was a black man 15
talking about physical defense against the white man. The white man can lynch
and burn and bomb and beat Negroes—that's all right: "Have patience" . . .
"The customs are entrenched" . . . "Things are getting better."

Well, I believe it's a crime for anyone who is being brutalized to continue 16
to accept that brutality without doing something to defend himself. If that's how
"Christian" philosophy is interpreted, if that's what Gandhian philosophy
teaches, well, then, I will call them criminal philosophies.

I tried in every speech I made to clarify my new position regarding white 17
people—"I don't speak against the sincere, well-meaning, good white people. I
have learned that there *are* some. I have learned that not all white people are
racists. I am speaking against and my fight is against the white *racists.* I firmly
believe that Negroes have the right to fight against these racists, by any means
that are necessary."

But the white reporters kept wanting me linked with that word "violence." 18
I doubt if I had one interview without having to deal with that accusation.

"I *am* for violence if non-violence means we continue postponing a solution 19
to the American black man's problem—just to *avoid* violence. I don't go for
non-violence if it also means a delayed solution. To me a delayed solution is a
non-solution. Or I'll say it another way. If it must take violence to get the black

man his human rights in this country, I'm *for* violence exactly as you know the Irish, the Poles, or Jews would be if they were flagrantly discriminated against. I am just as they would be in that case, and they would be for violence—no matter what the consequences, no matter who was hurt by the violence."

20      White society *hates* to hear anybody, especially a black man, talk about the crime the white man has perpetrated on the black man. I have always understood that's why I have been so frequently called "a revolutionist." It sounds as if *I* have done some crime! Well, it may be the American black man does need to become involved in a *real* revolution. The word for "revolution" in German is *Umwälzung*. What it means is a complete overturn—a complete change. The overthrow of King Farouk in Egypt and the succession of President Nasser is an example of a true revolution. It means the destroying of an old system, and its replacement with a new system. Another example is the Algerian revolution, led by Ben Bella; they threw out the French who had been there over 100 years. So how does anybody sound talking about the Negro in America waging some "revolution"? Yes, he is condemning a system—but he's not trying to overturn the system, or to destroy it. The Negro's so-called "revolt" is merely an asking to be *accepted* into the existing system! A *true* Negro revolt might entail, for instance, fighting for separate black states within this country—which several groups and individuals have advocated, long before Elijah Muhammad came along.

21      When the white man came into this country, he certainly wasn't demonstrating any "non-violence." In fact, the very man whose name symbolizes non-violence here today has stated:

22      "Our nation was born in genocide when it embraced the doctrine that the original American, the Indian, was an inferior race. Even before there were large numbers of Negroes on our shores, the scar of racial hatred had already disfigured colonial society. From the sixteenth century forward, blood flowed in battles over racial supremacy. We are perhaps the only nation which tried as a matter of national policy to wipe out its indigenous population. Moreover, we elevated that tragic experience into a noble crusade. Indeed, even today we have not permitted ourselves to reject or to feel remorse for this shameful episode. Our literature, our films, our drama, our folklore all exalt it. Our children are still taught to respect the violence which reduced a red-skinned people of an earlier culture into a few fragmented groups herded into impoverished reservations."

23      "Peaceful coexistence!" That's another one the white man has always been quick to cry. Fine! But what have been the deeds of the white man? During his entire advance through history, he has been waving the banner of Christianity . . . and carrying in his other hand the sword and the flintlock.

24      You can go right back to the very beginning of Christianity. Catholicism, the genesis of Christianity as we know it to be presently constituted, with its hierarchy, was conceived in Africa—by those whom the Christian church calls "The Desert Fathers." The Christian church became infected with racism when it entered white Europe. The Christian church returned to Africa under the

banner of the Cross—conquering, killing, exploiting, pillaging, raping, bullying, beating—and teaching white supremacy. This is how the white man thrust himself into the position of leadership of the world—through the use of naked physical power. And he was totally inadequate spiritually. Mankind's history has proved from one era to another that the true criterion of leadership is spiritual. Men are attracted by spirit. By power, men are *forced*. Love is engendered by spirit. By power, anxieties are created.

I am in agreement one hundred per cent with those racists who say that no  25 government laws ever can *force* brotherhood. The only true world solution today is governments guided by true religion—of the spirit. Here in race-torn America, I am convinced that the Islam religion is desperately needed, particularly by the American black man. The black man needs to reflect that he has been America's most fervent Christian—and where has it gotten him? In fact, in the white man's hands, in the white man's interpretation . . . where has Christianity brought this *world*?

It has brought the non-white two-thirds of the human population to rebel-  26 lion. Two-thirds of the human population today is telling the one-third minority white man, "Get out!" And the white man is leaving. And as he leaves, we see the non-white peoples returning in a rush to their original religions, which had been labeled "pagan" by the conquering white man. Only one religion—Islam— had the power to stand and fight the white man's Christianity for a *thousand years!* Only Islam could keep white Christianity at bay.

The Africans are returning to Islam and other indigenous religions. The  27 Asians are returning to being Hindus, Buddhists and Muslims.

As the Christian Crusade once went East, now the Islamic Crusade is going  28 West. With the East—Asia—closed to Christianity, with Africa rapidly being converted to Islam, with Europe rapidly becoming un-Christian, generally today it is accepted that the "Christian" civilization of America—which is propping up the white race around the world—is Christianity's remaining strongest bastion.

Well, if *this* is so—if the so-called "Christianity" now being practiced in  29 America displays the best that world Christianity has left to offer—no one in his right mind should need any much greater proof that very close at hand is the *end* of Christianity.

Are you aware that some Protestant theologians, in their writings, are using  30 the phrase "post-Christian era"—and they mean *now*?

And what is the greatest single reason for this Christian church's failure? It  31 is its failure to combat racism. It is the old "You sow, you reap" story. The Christian church sowed racism—blasphemously; now it reaps racism.

Sunday mornings in this year of grace 1965, imagine the "Christian con-  32 science" of congregations guarded by deacons barring the door to black would-be worshipers, telling them, "You can't enter *this* House of God!"

Tell me, if you can, a sadder irony than that St. Augustine, Florida—a city  33 named for the black African saint who saved Catholicism from heresy—was recently the scene of bloody race riots.

34      I believe that God now is giving the world's so-called "Christian" white society its last opportunity to repent and atone for the crimes of exploiting and enslaving the world's non-white peoples. It is exactly as when God gave Pharaoh a chance to repent. But Pharaoh persisted in his refusal to give justice to those whom he oppressed. And, we know, God finally destroyed Pharaoh.

35      Is white America really sorry for her crimes against the black people? Does white America have the capacity to repent—and to atone? Does the capacity to repent, to atone, exist in a majority, in one-half, in even one-third of American white society?

36      Many black men, the victims—in fact most black men—would like to be able to forgive, to forget, the crimes.

37      But most American white people seem not to have it in them to make any serious atonement—to do justice to the black man.

38      Indeed, how *can* white society atone for enslaving, for raping, for unmanning, for otherwise brutalizing *millions* of human beings, for centuries? What atonement would the God of Justice demand for the robbery of the black people's labor, their lives, their true identities, their culture, their history—and even their human dignity?

39      A desegregated cup of coffee, a theater, public toilets—the whole range of hypocritical "integration"—these are not atonement.

40      After a while in America, I returned abroad—and this time, I spent eighteen weeks in the Middle East and Africa.

41      The world leaders with whom I had private audiences this time included President Gamal Abdel Nasser, of Egypt; President Julius K. Nyerere, of Tanzania; President Nnamoi Azikiwe, of Nigeria; Osagyefo Dr. Kwame Nkrumah, of Ghana; President Sekou Touré, of Guinea; President Jomo Kenyatta, of Kenya; and Prime Minister Dr. Milton Obote, of Uganda.

42      I also met with religious leaders—African, Arab, Asian, Muslim, and non-Muslim. And in all of these countries, I talked with Afro-Americans and whites of many professions and backgrounds.

43      An American white ambassador in one African country was Africa's most respected American ambassador: I'm glad to say that this was told to me by one ranking African leader. We talked for an entire afternoon. Based on what I had heard of him, I had to believe him when he told me that as long as he was on the African continent, he never thought in terms of race, that he dealt with human beings, never noticing their color. He said he was more aware of language differences than of color differences. He said that only when he returned to America would he become aware of color differences.

44      I told him, "What you are telling me is that it isn't the American white *man* who is a racist, but it's the American political, economic, and social *atmosphere* that automatically nourishes a racist psychology in the white man." He agreed.

45      We both agreed that American society makes it next to impossible for humans to meet in America and not be conscious of their color differences. And

we both agreed that if racism could be removed, America could offer a society where rich and poor could truly live like human beings.

That discussion with the ambassador gave me a new insight—one which I like: that the white man is *not* inherently evil, but America's racist society influences him to act evilly. The society has produced and nourishes a psychology which brings out the lowest, most base part of human beings. 46

I had a totally different kind of talk with another white man I met in Africa—who, to me, personified exactly what the ambassador and I had discussed. Throughout my trip, I was of course aware that I was under constant surveillance. The agent was a particularly obvious and obnoxious one; I am not sure for what agency, as he never identified it, or I would say it. Anyway, this one finally got under my skin when I found I couldn't seem to eat a meal in the hotel without seeing him somewhere around watching me. You would have thought I was John Dillinger or somebody. 47

I just got up from my breakfast one morning and walked over to where he was and I told him I knew he was following me, and if he wanted to know anything, why didn't he ask me. He started to give me one of those too-lofty-to-descend-to-you attitudes. I told him then right to his face he was a fool, that he didn't know me, or what I stood for, so that made him one of those people who let somebody else do their thinking; and that no matter what job a man had, at least he ought to be able to think for himself. That stung him; he let me have it. 48

I was, to hear him tell it, anti-American, un-American, seditious, subversive, and probably Communist. I told him that what he said only proved how little he understood about me. I told him that the only thing the F.B.I., the C.I.A., or anybody else could ever find me guilty of, was being open-minded. I said I was seeking for the truth, and I was trying to weigh—objectively—everything in its own merit. I said what I was against was strait-jacketed thinking, and strait-jacketed societies. I said I respected every man's right to believe whatever his intelligence tells him is intellectually sound, and I expect everyone else to respect my right to believe likewise. ✤ 49

---

## RESPONDING

1. Clarify Malcolm X's position on nonviolence and on the appropriate use of violence. Write a journal entry responding to his statement that "when the law fails to protect Negroes from whites' attack, then those Negroes should use arms, if necessary, to defend themselves" (paragraph 13).

2. Individually or in a group, list Malcolm X's criticisms of the Christian church. Discuss the validity of his charges.

3. In an essay, discuss Malcolm X's solution to the problems of the "black man" worldwide. Analyze the strengths and weaknesses of that solution.

4.  Argue for or against the position that Malcolm X states in the following passage: "it's the American political, economic, and social *atmosphere* that automatically nourishes a racist psychology in the white man . . . American society makes it next to impossible for humans to meet in America and not be conscious of their color differences" (paragraphs 44–45).

---

# Mary Helen Washington

*Critic and theorist Mary Helen Washington earned her bachelor's degree from Notre Dame University (1962) and her doctorate from the University of Detroit (1976). She has held teaching positions at St. John's College in Cleveland, the University of Detroit, and the University of Massachusetts in Boston. Since 1989 she has held a faculty position at the University of Maryland, where she is currently a Professor of English. With a concentration in the literary production of African American women, she has written and edited several important studies, including* Black-Eyed Susans: Classic Stories by and About Black Women *(1975);* Midnight Birds: Stories of Contemporary Women Writers *(1980);* Invented Lives: Narratives of Black Women, *1860–1950 (1987); and* Memories of Kin: Stories About Family by Black Writers *(1991).*

*The following article explores the intersection of race and gender in the critical reception of two prominent African American writers.*

❖

# "THE DARKENED EYE RESTORED": NOTES TOWARD A LITERARY HISTORY OF BLACK WOMEN

1   When Gwendolyn Brooks won the Pulitzer prize for her second book of poems, *Annie Allen*, in 1950, *Negro Digest* sent a male reporter who covered the story and wrote a brief "homey" article about the life of a Pulitzer-prize-winning poet. The article begins with a list of people who didn't believe Brooks had won the prize—her son, her mother, her husband, friends—even the poet herself. It then catalogs all the negative experiences Brooks had after winning the prize— phones ringing, people dropping in, work interrupted, the family overwhelmed. It mentions her husband, Henry Blakely, as a poet who devotes only occasional time to poetry because "he feels no one family can support two poets." We also learn that the poet was "shy and self conscious" (her terms) until she married

Blakely, who helped her to lose some of her "social backwardness" (the reporter's terms). The last paragraph of the article, devoted to the poet's nine-year-old son, includes one of the boy's poems (but not a line from the poet who has just won the Pulitzer!) and ends with the son's rejection of his mother's fame because it has upset his life: "All the attention is wearing off now and I sure am glad. I don't like to be so famous. You have too many people talking to you. You never have any peace."[1] The entire article was an act of sabotage, situating Brooks in a domestic milieu where her "proper" role as wife and mother could be asserted and her role as serious artist—a role this reporter obviously found too threatening to even consider—could be undercut.

Three years later when Brooks published her first—and still her only novel—*Maud Martha* (1953), a novel about a woman's anger, repressions, and silences, the critical reviews were equally condescending and dismissive. Despite Brooks's stature as a Pulitzer-prize-winning poet, the reviews were short, ranging in length from one hundred and sixty to six hundred words, and many were unsigned. Here is a novel that deals with the most compelling themes in contemporary literature: the struggle to sustain one's identity against a racist and sexist society, the silences that result from repressed anger, the need to assert a creative life. Had *Maud Martha* been written by a man about a man's experience, it would have been considered a brilliant modernist text. But these reviewers, unable to place *Maud Martha* in any literary context, chose instead to concentrate on female cheerfulness, calling Maud Martha "a spunky and sophisticated Negro girl" who, they said, had a marvelous "ability to turn unhappiness and anger into a joke."[2]

Consider the way Ralph Ellison's first novel, *Invisible Man*, was received the year before *Maud Martha* when Ellison was still relatively unknown. *The New Republic*, *Crisis*, *The Nation*, *The New Yorker*, and *The Atlantic* published lengthy and signed reviews, ranging in length from six hundred to twenty-one hundred words. Wright Morris and Irving Howe were called in to write serious critical assessments for the *Times* and *The Nation*. Although Brooks's protagonist was never compared to any other literary character, Ellison's nameless hero was considered not only "the embodiment of the Negro race" but the "conscience of all races." The titles of Ellison's reviews—"Black & Blue," "Underground Notes," "Brother Betrayed," "Black Man's Burdens"—suggest the universality of the invisible man's struggle. The titles of Brooks's reviews—"Young Girl Growing Up" and "Daydreams of Flight," beside being misleading, deny any relationship between the protagonist's personal experiences and the historical experiences of her people. Ellison himself was compared to Richard Wright, Dostoyevski, and Faulkner; Brooks, only to the unspecified "imagists." Most critically, Ellison's work was placed in a tradition; it was described as an example of the "picaresque" tradition and the pilgrim/journey tradition by all reviews. (Later it would be considered a descendant of the slave narrative tradition.) *Maud Martha*, the reviewers said, "stood alone."[3]

Reading these reviews I was struck not only by their resistance to the deeper meaning in *Maud Martha* but by their absolute refusal to see Brooks's novel as part of any tradition in Afro-American or mainstream American literature. Is this because few critics could picture the questing figure, the powerful articulate voice in the tradition as a plain, dark-skinned housewife living in a kitchenette apartment on the south side of Chicago? As I have written earlier, I realize that the supreme confidence of the Ellison text—its epic sweep, its eloquent flow of words, its conscious manipulation of historical situations—invites its greater critical acceptance. By comparison, the *Maud Martha* text is hesitant, self-doubting, retentive, mute. Maud is restricted, for a good part of the novel, to a domestic life that seems narrow and limited—even to her. And, yet, if the terms *invisibility, double-consciousness, the black mask* have any meaning at all for the Afro-American literary tradition, then *Maud Martha*, whose protagonist is more intimately acquainted with the meanings of those words than any male character, belongs unquestionably to that tradition.

5      Tradition. Now there's a word that nags the feminist critic. A word that has so often been used to exclude or misrepresent women. It is always something of a shock to see black women, sharing equally (and sometimes more than equally) in the labor and strife of black people, expunged from the text when that history becomes shaped into what we call tradition. Why is the fugitive slave, the fiery orator, the political activist, the abolitionist always represented as a black *man?*[4] How does the heroic voice and heroic image of the black woman get suppressed in a culture that depended on her heroism for its survival? What we have to recognize is that the creation of the fiction of tradition is a matter of power, not justice, and that that power has always been in the hands of men—mostly white but some black. Women are the disinherited. Our "ritual journeys," our "articulate voices," our "symbolic spaces" are rarely the same as men's. Those differences and the assumption that those differences make women inherently inferior, plus the appropriation by men of the power to define tradition, account for women's absence from our written records.

6      In the early 1890s when a number of leading black intellectuals decided to form "an organization of Colored authors, scholars, and artists," with the expressed intent of raising "the standard of intellectual endeavor among American Negroes," one of the invited members wrote to declare himself "decidedly opposed to the admission of women to membership" because "literary matters and social matters do not mix." He need not have concerned himself since the distinguished luminaries, among them Alexander Crummell, Francis Grimké, and W.E.B. Du Bois, proposed from the beginning that the American Negro Academy—a kind of think tank for that intellectual black elite called the Talented Tenth—be open only to "*men* of African descent."[5] Imagine, if you can, black women intellectuals and activists, who in the 1890s had taken on such issues as the moral integrity of black women, lynching, and the education of black youth, being considered social decorations. I mention this egregious example of sexism in the black intellectual community—which by and large was

and still is far more egalitarian than their white counterparts—because it under-scores an attitude toward black women that has helped to maintain and perpetu-ate a male-dominated literary and critical tradition. Women have worked as-siduously in this tradition as writers, as editors, sometimes, though rarely, as critics, and yet every study of Afro-American narrative, every anthology of *the* Afro-American literary tradition has set forth a model of literary paternity in which each male author vies with his predecessor for greater authenticity, greater control over *his* voice, thus fulfilling the mission his *forefathers* left unfinished.

Women in this model are sometimes granted a place as a stepdaughter who prefigures and directs us to the real heirs (like Ellison and Wright) but they do not influence and determine the direction and shape of the literary canon.[6] Women's writing is considered singular and anomalous, not universal and representative, and for some mysterious reason, writing about black women is not considered as racially significant as writing about black men. Zora Neale Hurston was chastised by critic Benjamin Brawley because "Her interest . . . is not in solving problems, the chief concern being with individuals."[7] And, in his now-famous contemptuous review of Hurston's *Their Eyes Were Watching God*, Richard Wright objects to her novel because her characters (unlike his) live in a "safe and narrow orbit . . . between laughter and tears."[8] Male critics go to great lengths to explain the political naïveté or racial ambivalence of male writers while they harshly criticize women writers for the same kinds of shortcomings. In Wright's essay, "Literature of the Negro of the United States," he forgives George Moses Horton, an early black poet, for being "a split man," trapped in a culture of which he was not really a part; but Phillis Wheatley, he says, is fully culpable. She was, Wright claims, so fully at one with white colonial culture that she developed "innocently," free "to give utterance to what she felt without the humiliating pressure of the color line."[9]

Banished to the "nigger pews" in the Christian churches of Colonial Boston, deprived of the companionship of other blacks, totally under the control of whites, "torn by contrary instincts," Phillis Wheatley was never "at one with her culture." As a new generation of critics, led by William Robinson, Alice Walker, and Merle A. Richmond, has shown us, Phillis Wheatley was a young slave woman whose choice to be an artist in the repressive, racist era of Colonial America represents "the triumph of the artist amid catastrophe."[10]

> With the exception of a handful of autobiographical narratives from the nine-teenth century, the black woman's realities are virtually suppressed until the period of the Harlem Renaissance and later. Essentially the black woman as artist, as intellectual spokesperson for her own cultural apprenticeship, has not existed before, for anyone. At the source of her own symbol-making task, this community of writers confronts, therefore, a tradition of work that is quite recent, its continuities, broken and sporadic.[11]

9      Without exception Afro-American women writers have been dismissed by Afro-American literary critics until they were rediscovered and reevaluated by feminist critics. Examples: Linda Brent's slave narrative, *Incidents in the Life of a Slave Girl* (1860), was judged by male historians to be inauthentic because her story was "too melodramatic" and not "representative."[12] Contemporary feminist critics have documented Brent's life as not only entirely authentic but "representative" of the experience of many slave women. Except for Barbara Christian's *Black Women Novelists* and other texts that specifically deal with women writers, critical texts have never considered Frances Harper and Pauline Hopkins makers of early black literary traditions. Like many white women writers of the nineteenth century, they were dismissed as "sentimentalists," even though their male counterparts wrote similarly sentimental novels. Zora Hurston's *Their Eyes Were Watching God* was declared by Richard Wright to be a novel that carried "no theme, no message, no thought," and during the thirty years that Wright dominated the black literary scene, Hurston's novel was out of print.[13] Nella Larsen was also out of print for many years and was not until recently considered a major Harlem Renaissance writer. Ann Petry is usually analyzed as a disciple of Wright's school of social protest fiction, and Dorothy West has not been written about seriously since Robert Bone's *The Negro Novel in America* in 1965. Brooks's novel, *Maud Martha*, though it perfectly expresses the race alienation of the 1950s, was totally eclipsed by Ellison's *Invisible Man* and never considered a vital part of the Afro-American canon.

10      If there is a single distinguishing feature of the literature of black women—and this accounts for their lack of recognition—it is this: their literature is about black women; it takes the trouble to record the thoughts, words, feelings, and deeds of black women, experiences that make the realities of being black in America look very different from what men have written. There are no women in this tradition hibernating in dark holes contemplating their invisibility; there are no women dismembering the bodies or crushing the skulls of either women or men; and few, if any, women in the literature of black women succeed in heroic quests without the support of other women or men in their communities. Women talk to other women in this tradition, and their friendships with other women—mothers, sisters, grandmothers, friends, lovers—are vital to their growth and well-being. A common scene recurring in at least five of the eight fiction writers in this collection is one in which women (usually two) gather together in a small room to share intimacies that can be trusted only to a kindred female spirit. That intimacy is a tool, allowing women writers to represent women more fully. The friendship between Sappho and Dora in *Contending Forces*, Janie and Pheoby in *Their Eyes Were Watching God*, Linda and her grandmother in *Incidents in the Life of a Slave Girl*, Helga and Mrs. Hayes-Rore in *Quicksand*, Cleo and her sisters in *The Living Is Easy* emphasize this concern with female bonding and suggest that female relationships are an essential aspect of self-definition for women.

I do not want these writers to be misrepresented as apolitical because of their deep concern for the personal lives of their characters. All of these texts are clearly involved with issues of social justice: the rape of black women, the lynching of black men, slavery and Reconstruction, class distinctions among blacks, and all forms of discrimination against black people. No romantic heroines, all of these women work, and in nearly every one of these eight selections women experience discrimination against them in the workplace, a subject that almost never surfaces in the writings of men. At the beginning of *Contending Forces*, Sappho Clark brings her stenography work home with her because blacks are not allowed in the office. Iola Leroy is twice dismissed from jobs when her coworkers discover her race. The educated Helga Crane seeks work as a domestic in Chicago because black women are barred from the professions and from clerical work. Maud Martha also finds work as a domestic where she encounters the brutal condescension of her white employers. These examples have a special meaning for me because in the 1920s my mother and my five aunts migrated to Cleveland, Ohio, from Indianapolis and, in spite of their many talents, they found every door except the kitchen door closed to them. My youngest aunt was trained as a bookkeeper and was so good at her work that her white employer at Guardian Savings of Indianapolis allowed her to work at the branch in a black area. The Cleveland Trust Company was not so liberal, however, so in Cleveland (as Toni Morrison asks, "What could go wrong in Ohio?") she went to work in what is known in the black community as "private family." Her thwarted career is not simply a narrow personal tragedy. As these texts make clear to us—and they are the only texts that tell this story—several generations of competent and talented black women, all of whom *had* to work, were denied access to the most ordinary kind of jobs and therefore to any kind of economic freedom. 11

Women's sexuality is another subject treated very differently by women and men writers. In the male slave narrative, for example, sexuality is nearly always avoided, and when it does surface it is to report the sexual abuse of female slaves. The male slave narrator was under no compulsion to discuss his own sexuality nor that of other men. As far as we know, the only slave narrator forced to admit a sexual life was Linda Brent, who bore two children as a single woman rather than submit to forced concubinage. Her reluctance to publish *Incidents* because it was not the life of "a Heroine with no degradation associated with it" shows that sexuality literally made a woman an unfit subject for literature. In Harlem Renaissance literature, as Barbara Christian reminds us, only male writers felt free to celebrate exoticized sexuality: "The garb of uninhibited passion wears better on a male, who after all, does not have to carry the burden of the race's morality or lack of it."[14] In Renaissance literature, Nella Larsen does represent Helga as a sexual being but that treatment of sex is never celebratory. Helga's sexuality is constantly thwarted, ending as Hazel Carby notes, not in exotic passion but in biological entrapment. In *The Living Is Easy*, Cleo connects 12 sexuality to women's repression and refuses any kind of sexual life, preferring instead emotional intimacy with her sisters and their children. The only woman in these excerpts who revels in her sexuality is Janie Crawford in *Their Eyes Were Watching God*, and, significantly, even in this seemingly idyllic treatment of erotic love, female sexuality is always associated with violence. Janie's mother and grandmother are sexually exploited and Janie is beaten by her glorious lover, Tea Cake, so that he can prove his superiority to other men. What do these stories say about female sexuality? It seems to me that all of them point to the fundamental issue of whether or not women can exert control over their sexuality. Helga Crane, for example, fights against the sexual attraction she feels for Dr. Anderson because that attraction makes her feel out of control. Cleo, who is controlled by her husband in all other aspects of her life, controls him by refusing sex. In *Contending Forces*, Sappho forces her lover to undergo a series of tests in order to determine the constancy of his love. And surely the clearest statement of women's anxiety about sexuality and the need for control over one's female body is made by Linda Brent when she tries to explain to her white female audience why she deliberately chose to bear two children outside of marriage to a white man who was not her owner: "It seems less degrading to give one's self, than to submit to compulsion. There is something akin to freedom in having a lover *who has no control over you*, [emphasis mine] except that which he gains by kindness and attachment."[15] Given this deep alienation from and anxiety about heterosexual relationships, we might wonder if any of these women considered taking women as lovers. If they did, they wrote about such affairs in private places—letters, journals, diaries, poetry—if they wrote about them at all. In a diary, which she kept in the 1920s and 1930s, Alice Dunbar-Nelson is more explicit about sexual intimacy among black women than any writer of that period that I know, but even her revelations are quite guarded: "And Fay, lovely little Fay. One day we saw each other, *one day*, and a year has passed. And still we cannot meet again . . ."[16]

13     The anxiety of black women writers over the representation of sexuality goes back to the nineteenth century and the prescription for womanly "virtues" which made slave women automatically immoral and less "feminine than white women," but that anxiety is evident even in contemporary texts, many of which avoid any kind of sexual vulnerability or project the most extreme forms of sexual vulnerability onto children and poor women. Once again the issue is control, and control is bought by cordoning off those aspects of sexuality that threaten to make women feel powerless. If pleasure and danger are concomitant aspects of sexuality, it seems clear to me that black women writers have, out of historical necessity, registered far more of the latter than the former.

For a woman to write, she must experiment with "altering and adapting the current shape of her thought without crushing or distorting it."[17]

Although many writers in some way challenge conventional notions of what    14
is possible for women characters, "dissenting" from traditions that demand
female subordination, I want to single out Zora Neale Hurston and Gwendolyn
Brooks for creating narrative strategies whose major concern is the empowerment of women. Both Hurston and Brooks enter fiction through a side door:
Hurston was a folklorist and anthropologist; Brooks is primarily a poet. As
outsiders both were freer to experiment with fictional forms, the result being
that they were able to choose forms that resist female entrapment. Janie Crawford's quest in *Their Eyes Were Watching God* is to recover her own voice and
her own sense of autonomy. By framing the story with Janie telling her tale to
her friend Pheoby, Hurston makes Janie's self-conscious reflections on her life
the central narrative concern. Though Hurston often denies this quest story in
favor of the romantic plot, her interest in Janie's heroic potential is unmistakable.
In *Maud Martha* Brooks also dislodges the romance plot, first by inventing a
woman who does not fit the profile of a romantic heroine and then by making
the death of romance essential to Maud's growth. Being a wife, "in every way
considering and replenishing him," is in conflict with Maud's own desire for
what she vaguely terms "more life." And finally the narrative form itself, as it
enacts Maud's rage, her muteness, her indirection, places narrative emphasis on
the unsparing, meticulous, courageous consciousness of Maud Martha, making
that female consciousness the heroic center of the text. The text that was so
arrogantly dismissed in 1953 returns, subversively, in the 1980s, with its rejection
of male power, as a critique of the very patriarchal authority that sought its
dismissal.

Obviously we will have to learn to read the Afro-American literary tradition    15
in new ways, for continuing on in the old way is impossible. In the past ten or
fifteen years the crucial task of reconstruction has been carried on by a number
of scholars whose work has made it possible to document black women as artists,
as intellectuals, as symbol makers. The continuities of this tradition, as Hortense
Spillers tells us, are broken and sporadic, but the knitting together of these
fragments has begun. As I look around at my own library shelves I see the texts
that have helped to make my recent book, *Invented Lives*, possible. First those
pioneering studies undertaken to pave the way for the rest of us: Barbara
Christian's, *Black Women Novelists, The Development of a Tradition, 1892–1976;*
the invaluable sourcebook, *All the Women Are White, All the Blacks Are Men, But
Some of Us Are Brave*, edited by Gloria L. Hull, Patricia Bell Scott, and Barbara
Smith; Marilyn Richardson's bibliography, *Black Women and Religion;* Ora Wil-
liams's bibliography, *American Black Women:* those early anthologies of black
women's literature, *The Black Woman*, edited by Toni Cade Bambara; Pat
Crutchfield Exum's *Keeping the Faith;* and *Sturdy Black Bridges; Visions of Black
Women in Literature*, edited by Beverly Guy-Sheftall, Roseann P. Bell, and Bettye
J. Parker.

16    Robert Hemenway's biography, *Zora Neale Hurston: A Literary Biography*, and Alice Walker's *I Love Myself When I Am Laughing . . . And Then Again When I Am Looking Mean and Impressive: A Zora Neale Hurston Reader* are the major scholarly works that allowed us to reclaim Hurston. Two books on black women's spiritual autobiography, Jean McMahon Humez's *Gifts of Power*, an edition of the writings of Rebecca Jackson Cox, as well as William Andrews's *Sisters of the Spirit* have reclaimed a unique part of black women's early literary tradition. Gloria Hull's edition of Alice Dunbar-Nelson's diary, *Give Us Each Day*, and Dorothy Sterling's *We Are Your Sisters*, a documentary portrayal of nineteenth-century black women, provide evidence of the rich cultural history of black women that is to be found in nontraditional sources. Paula Giddings's history of black women, *When and Where I Enter: The Impact of Black Women on Race and Sex in America*, documents the political, social, and literary work of black women.

17    Deborah E. McDowell's Beacon Press series on black women's fiction has already reissued a number of out-of-print novels, for example, *The Street*, *Like One of the Family*, and *Iola Leroy*. Rutgers University Press has reissued *Quicksand* and *Passing*. In 1987 a number of important works on black women were published: Jean Fagan Yellin's definitive edition of Harriet Jacobs's *Incidents in the Life of a Slave Girl* and Hazel Carby's ground-breaking work on black women's narrative tradition: *Reconstructing Womanhood: The Emergence of the Afro-American Woman Novelist*.

18    As we continue the work of reconstructing a literary history that insists on black women as central to that history, as we reject the old male-dominated accounts of history, refusing to be cramped into the little spaces men have allotted women, we should be aware that this is an act of enlightenment, not simply repudiation. In her 1892 text on black women, *A Voice from the South*, Anna Julia Cooper says that a world in which the female is made subordinate is like a body with one eye bandaged. When the bandage is removed, the body is filled with light: "It sees a circle where before it saw a segment. The darkened eye restored, every member rejoices with it."[18] The making of a literary history in which black women are fully represented is a search for full vision, to create a circle where now we have but a segment. ✣

## Notes

1. Frank Harriott, "The Life of a Pulitzer Poet," *Negro Digest* (August 1950): 14–16.

2. 1953 reviews of *Maud Martha: The New Yorker* (October 10, 1953), unsigned, 160 words; Hubert Creekmore, "Daydreams in Flight, *New York Times Book*

*Review* (October 4, 1953), 400 words; Nicolas Monjo, "Young Girl Growing up," *Saturday Review* (October 31, 1953), 140 words; and Coleman Rosenberger, New York *Herald Tribune* (October 18, 1953), 600 words.

3. 1952 reviews of *Invisible Man:* George Mayberry, "Underground Notes," *The New Republic* (April 21, 1952), 600 words; Irving Howe, "A Negro in America," *The Nation* (May 10, 1952), 950 words; Anthony West, "Black Man's Burden," *The New Yorker* (May 31, 1952), 2,100 words; C. J. Rolo, "Candide in Harlem," *The Atlantic* (July 1952), 450 words; Wright Morris, "The World Below," *New York Times Book Review* (April 13, 1952), 900 words; "Black & Blue," *Time* (April 14, 1952), 850 words; and J. E. Cassidy, "A Brother Betrayed," *Commonweal* (May 2, 1952), 850 words.

1953 reviews of *Maud Martha: The New Yorker* (October 10, 1953), unsigned 160 words; Hubert Creekmore, "Daydreams in Flight," *New York Times Book Review* (October 4, 1953), 400 words; Nicolas Monjo, "Young Girl Growing Up," *Saturday Review* (October 31, 1953), 140 words; and Coleman Rosenberger, New York *Herald Tribune* (October 18, 1953), 600 words.

The diction of the reviews, too, is revealing. The tone of *Invisible Man* was defined as "vigorous, imaginative, violently humorous and quietly tragic" *(New Republic)*, "searing and exalted" *(The Nation);* while *Maud Martha* drew "freshness, warm cheerfulness . . . [and] vitality" *(New York Times)*, "ingratiating" *(Saturday Review)*. Several reviews of Ellison used "gusto," for Brooks, "liveliness." Brooks's "Negro heroine" *(New York Times)*, was characterized as a "young colored woman" *(Saturday Review)* and a "spunky and sophisticated Negro girl" *(New York Times);* Ellison's character as a "hero" and "pilgrim" *(New Republic)*.

Matters of style received mixed response in both novels. *Maud Martha's* "impressionistic style" was deemed "not quite sharp or firm enough" and her "remarkable gift" was seen (in the same review) as "mimicry" and an "ability to turn unhappiness and anger into a joke"—a gift that her style did not engender *(New York Times)*. The *Saturday Review* said: "Its form is no more than a random narration of loosely assembled incidents" and called its "framework . . . somewhat ramshackle." Only the *New York Times* noticed a significance in her style, and likened the "flashes . . . of sensitive lightness" to Imagist poetics, as well as commenting on the "finer qualities of insight and rhythm."

Both authors are criticized along the same lines concerning form and style, but in the reviews of Brooks, her style is the topic that draws the most attention, and the review is favorable or unfavorable depending upon whether or not the reviewer is personally attracted to "impressionism." Ellison's novel is treated more seriously than Brooks's because his novel is seen as addressing a broader range of issues, despite his sometimes "hysterical" style.

This position is most apparent in Howe's review in *The Nation.* Howe asks serious questions about traditional literary devices, such as narrative stance and voice, and method of characterization, despite the book's lack of "finish." (Ellison's first-person narration is discussed by all reviewers, while Brooks's narrative style is hardly mentioned in any review.) Implicit in Howe's stance toward *Invisible Man* is an assumption that this is a serious novel to be investigated rigorously in accordance with the (high) standards of the academy. Despite those qualities of tone and style that Howe criticizes it for, *Invisible Man* is important, finally, because it fits into the literary tradition of the epic journey of discovery. Howe calls it a "searing and exalted record of a Negro's journey toward contemporary America in search of success, companionship, and finally himself."

4. The extent to which black men are considered representative of the race was suggested to me most emphatically in *Black Women in Nineteenth-Century American Life: Their Words, Their Thoughts, Their Feelings,* ed. Bert James Loewenberg and Ruth Bogin (University Park: Pennsylvania State University Press, 1976). In their introduction, "Women, Blacks, History," the editors make this comment: "Not only do black women seldom appear in treatments of black history, but historians have been content to permit the male to represent the female in almost every significant category. Thus it is the male who is the representative abolitionist, fugitive slave, or political activist. The black male is the leader, the entrepreneur, the politician, the man of thought. When historians discuss black abolitionist writers and lecturers, they are men. David Walker, Charles Lenox Remond, and a procession of male stalwarts preempt the list in conventional accounts. Particularly later when black history was consciously written, it was the male, not the female, who recorded it. Women are conspicuous by their silence." (p. 4)

5. Alfred A. Moss, Jr., *The American Negro Academy: Voice of the Talented Tenth* (Baton Rouge: Louisiana State University Press, 1981). According to Moss, The American Negro Academy, the first major black American learned society, was founded March 5, 1897 in Washington, D.C. The constitution of the ANA defined it as "an organization of authors, scholars, artists, and those distinguished in other walks of life, men of African descent, for the promotion of Letters, Science, and Art." While Du Bois argued for a more democratic membership "because we find men who are not distinguished in science or

literature or art are just the men we want," he did not, apparently, argue for women. Theophilus G. Steward, one of the invited members, was the only one who specifically declared himself opposed to the admission of women. (pp. 38, 42)

6. Nearly every Afro-American literary history reads the tradition as primarily a male tradition, beginning with the male slave narrative as the source which generates the essential texts in the canon. With absolute predictability the Frederick Douglass 1845 *Narrative* is the text that issues the call, and the response comes back loud and clear from W. E. B. Du Bois, James Weldon Johnson, Richard Wright, James Baldwin, and Ralph Ellison. So firmly established is this male hegemony that even men's arguments with one another (Wright, Baldwin, Ellison) get written into the tradition as a way of interpreting its development. As most feminist critics have noted, women writers cannot simply be inserted into the gaps, or be used to prefigure male writers; the tradition has to be conceptualized from a feminist viewpoint.

7. Benjamin Brawley, *The Negro Genius: A New Appraisal of the Achievement of the American Negro in Literature and the Fine Arts* (New York: Bibb and Tannen, 1969), 258. Of the thirteen portraits of writers and artists in this book, only two are of women.

8. Richard Wright, "Between Laughter and Tears," *New Masses 5* (October 1937): 25–26.

9. Richard Wright, "The Literature of the Negro of the United States," in *White Man Listen!* (Garden City, N.Y.: Doubleday & Company, 1964), 76.

10. William Robinson, *Phillis Wheatley in the Black American Beginnings* (Detroit: Broadside Press, 1976); Alice Walker, "In Search of Our Mothers' Gardens," in *In Search of Our Mothers' Gardens: Womanist Prose* (New York: Harcourt Brace Jovanovich, 1983), 231–43; and M. A. Richmond, *Bid the Vassal Soar: Interpretive Essays on the Life and Poetry of Phillis Wheatley and George Moses Horton* (Washington, D.C.: Howard University Press, 1974).

11. Hortense J. Spillers, "A Hateful Passion, A Lost Love," *Feminist Studies 9*, no. 2 (Summer 1983): 297.

12. In *Reconstructing Womanhood: The Emergence of the Afro-American Woman Novelist* (New York: Oxford University Press, 1987). Hazel Carby discusses this dismissal of the Brent narrative by John Blassingame in *The Slave Community: Plantation Life in the Antebellum South* (New York: Oxford University Press, 1979).

13. Wright, "'Beyond Laughter and Tears.'"

14. Barbara Christian, *Black Women Novelists: The Development of a Tradition 1892–1976* (Westport, Conn.: Greenwood Press, 1980), 40.

15. Linda Brent, *Incidents in the Life of a Slave Girl*, ed. L. Maria Child (New York: Harcourt Brace Jovanovich, 1973), 55.

16. Gloria T. Hull, ed., *Give Us Each Day: The Diary of Alice Dunbar-Nelson* (New York: W. W. Norton & Company, 1984), 421–22.

17. In *Writing Beyond the Ending: Narrative Strategies of Twentieth-Century Women Writers* (Bloomington: Indiana University Press, 1985), p. 32. Rachel Blau DuPlessis quotes Virginia Woolf's prescription for women's writing, "Women and Fiction," in *Granite and Rainbow* (New York: Harcourt Brace and Company, 1958), 80.

18. Anna J. Cooper, *A Voice from the South by a Black Woman of the South* (Xenia, Oh.: Aldine Printing House, 1892), 123.

---

## RESPONDING

1. Do you think about the author of a book you are reading? Does it matter to you if you are reading something written by a man or a woman? Respond to these questions in a journal entry.

2. Working individually or in a group, define the following terms: invisibility, double-consciousness, the black mask, feminism. How do they fit in African American literary tradition?

3. Washington argues that "tradition" has often been used to "exclude or misrepresent women" (paragraph 5). In an essay, agree or disagree with this

statement. You may use examples from your own knowledge and experience as well as from the readings.

4.  Washington wrote this essay in the 1980s. Since then Toni Morrison, an African American woman writer, won the Nobel Prize for Literature. Does this change how African American women writers are perceived? In an essay, discuss the role and history of African American women writers and how that history has changed or remained the same in the past two decades.

⁜

# CONNECTING

1.  What's in a name? A great deal, especially if it's the name of a group you belong to. Write an essay discussing why the name of an ethnic group is a particularly sensitive issue for people within that group. Consider the ways in which ethnic group names are chosen. Who does the naming, and who uses the name? Why do groups sometimes decide that they prefer to be called by a new name? For example, why was the name "Negro" rejected by the African American community? What are the psychological effects of names with positive and names with negative connotations? Why are some names appropriate when used by group members but not by outsiders?

2.  Compare the situation for people of color in universities today with the situation for the speaker in "Theme for English B" or for Emma Lou in *The Blacker the Berry*. In what ways has your university tried to welcome and encourage students who are people of color? How successful have these attempts been?

3.  Characters such as Emma Lou in *The Blacker the Berry* and Hanneh Breineh in "The Fat of the Land" in chapter 3 are rejected by their own families. Compare their situations. Analyze what such a rejection reveals about the families themselves.

4.  Emma Lou has a problem in *The Blacker the Berry* because she is perceived by some as "too" dark. Compare her situation with the one Greg Sarris describes in "Battling Illegitimacy" in chapter 1.

5.   Argue for or against the position that though morality cannot be controlled by legislation, the passage of laws can gradually change attitudes.

6.   Write an essay discussing the shift in focus that took place in the civil rights movement after 1965. What civil rights issues seem most important today?

7.   Watch the 1988 film *Mississippi Burning*, which tells the story of the murders of Schwerner, Chaney, and Goodman, and compare its account of events with Farmer's. Some social and film critics were very unhappy with the movie version. Read reviews by both African American and white critics and summarize their comments. Write your own review of the film considering the reviews you read and Farmer's essay.

8.   Apply King's argument defending the breaking of an unjust law to a current issue. Present the case both for and against such an action. Be sure to consider the restrictions King placed on the lawbreaker.

9.   See Spike Lee's 1990 film *Do the Right Thing* and compare the circumstances surrounding the conflict in the film with the situation described by Ellison. Compare the origin of the conflict in these two cases. Should we view these disturbances as civil disobedience protests or criminal activities?

10.  Discuss the current status of African Americans in the United States. Argue that King's dream of an America where "all men are created equal" has or has not become a reality.

11.  Research the Black Power movement discussed in this chapter and the Red Power movement discussed in chapter 2. Discuss the parallels and differences between the movements.

12.  Using information from your reading in this text and elsewhere, argue that a nonviolent restructuring of society is or is not possible.

13.  Write about a time when you or someone you know has been torn between a violent and a nonviolent reaction to a situation or solution to a problem. What choice did you or your friend make? Was it the most effective choice? Why or why not?

14.  The theme of injustice runs through many of the selections in this book. Choose an individual or an ethnic group and write an essay about the suffering the person or the group endured as a victim of injustice. Then discuss the ways in which one or more groups in this text have tried to gain acceptance and equality.

## *For Further Research*

1. Compare the changes in living and working conditions, education, and political activity for an African American person living in Montgomery, Alabama, in 1965 and today. Research and describe the role of specific legislation in effecting changes in the living conditions for African Americans in the South.

2. Many of the readings in this chapter focus on the contributions of men, specifically African American leaders, or the role and fate of the African American man. Research and describe the role of women in the civil rights movement. Consider the contributions of Septima Clark, Rosa Parks, Fannie Lou Hamer, or Coretta King.

3. Research the history of civil disobedience both in the United States and around the world. Select a country such as India or South Africa and compare nonviolent protest in that country with the nonviolent movement in the United States.

4. Investigate the legacies of major civil rights figures such as Martin Luther King Jr., James Farmer, or Malcolm X. Compare their methods and discuss their relative successes and failures.

## REFERENCES AND ADDITIONAL SOURCES

Adera, Malaika. *Up South: Stories, Studies, and Letters of This Century's Black Migrations.* New York: The New Press, 1993.

Andrews, William L., et al., eds. *The Oxford Companion to African American Literature.* New York: Oxford University Press, 1997.

Baker, Houston A. Jr. *Afro-American Poetics: Revisions of Harlem and the Black Aesthetic.* Madison, Wis.: University of Wisconsin Press, 1987.

Bambara, Toni Cade. *Gorilla, My Love.* New York: Random House, 1981.

———. *The Sea Birds Are Still Alive.* New York: Random House, 1974.

Bates, Daisy. *The Long Shadow of Little Rock: A Memoir.* New York: David McKay, 1962; Fayetteville: University of Arkansas Press, 1987.

Bell, Bernard W. *The Afro-American Novel and Its Tradition.* Amherst: University of Massachusetts Press, 1987.

Berghahn, Marion. *Images of Africa in Black American Literature.* Totowa, N.J.: Rowman and Littlefield, 1977.

Bontemps, Arna, ed. *The Harlem Renaissance Remembered: Essays Edited with a Memoir by Arna Bontemps.* New York: Dodd, 1984.

Branch, Taylor. *Parting the Water: American in the King Years, 1954–63.* New York: Simon and Schuster, 1988, 1989 (1st Touchstone ed.).

Brooks, Thomas R. *Walls Come Tumbling Down: A History of the Civil Rights Movement: 1940–1970.* Englewood Cliffs, N.J.: Prentice-Hall, 1974.

Brown, Sterling. *Negro Poetry and Drama.* New York: Arno, 1969.

Buchanan, A. Russell. *Black Americans in World War II.* Claremont, Calif.: Regina Books, 1977; Santa Barbara: Clio Books, 1977.

Clark, B. Kenneth. *The Negro Protest.* Boston: Beacon Press, 1964.

Clark, Septima. *Echo in My Soul.* New York: Dutton, 1962.

Cruse, Harold. *The Crisis of the Negro Intellectual: A Historical Analysis of the Failure of Black Leadership.* New York: Morrow, 1967; New York: Quill, 1984.

Davis, Arthur P., and Michael Peplow, eds. *The New Negro Renaissance: An Anthology.* New York: Holt, Rinehart, and Winston, 1975.

De Jongh, James. *Vicious Modernism: Black Harlem and the Literary Imagination.* Cambridge: Cambridge University Press, 1990.

Farmer, James. *Lay Bare the Heart: The Autobiography of the Civil Rights Movement.* New York: New American Library, 1986.

Franklin, John Hope. *From Slavery to Freedom: A History of Negro Americans.* New York: Knopf, 1988.

Friedman, Lawrence M. *A History of American Law.* 2nd ed. New York: Simon and Schuster, Touchstone, 1973, 1986; New York: Oceana Publications, 1990.

Gabbin, Joanne V., ed. *The Furious Flowering of African American Poetry.* Charlottesville: University Press of Virginia, 1999.

Gates, Henry Louis Jr. *Figures in Black: Words, Signs, and the "Racial" Self.* New York: Oxford University Press, 1987.

Gates, Henry Louis Jr., and Nellie Y. McKay, eds. *The Norton Anthology of African American Literature.* New York: W.W. Norton, 1997.

George, Lynell. *No Crystal Stair: African American in the City of Angels.* New York: Verso, 1992.

Goldfield, David R. *Black, White and Southern.* Baton Rouge: Louisiana State University Press, 1990.

Griffin, Farah Jasmine. *"Who Set You Flowin'?": The African-American Migration Narrative.* New York: Oxford University Press, 1995.

Holt, Thomas C. *"Afro Americans," in Harvard Encyclopedia of American Ethnic Groups.* Cambridge: Harvard University Press, 1980.

Huggins, Nathan I. *Harlem Renaissance.* London: Oxford University Press, 1971, 1973.

———. *Revelations: American History, American Myths.* Ed. Brenda Smith Huggins. New York: Oxford University Press, 1995.

Hull, Gloria T., ed. *Color, Sex & Poetry: Three Women Writers of the Harlem Renaissance.* Bloomington: Indiana University Press, 1987.

Ikonné, Chidi. *From Du Bois to Van Vechten: The Early New Negro Literature, 1903–1926.* Westport, Conn.: Greenwood Press, 1981.

Johnson, James Weldon. *Black Manhattan.* New York: Knopf, 1930; New York: De Capo, 1991.

Jones, Jacqueline. *Labor of Love, Labor of Sorrow: Black Women, Work & the Family from Slavery to the Present.* New York: Basic Books, 1985; New York: Random House, 1986.

Killens, John Oliver, and Jerry W. Ward Jr., eds. *Black Southern Voices: An Anthology of Fiction, Poetry, Drama, Nonfiction, and Critical Essays.* New York: Meridian, 1992.

King, Martin Luther Jr. *A Testament of Hope: The Essential Writings of Martin Luther King Jr.* Ed. James Melvin Washington. San Francisco: Harper & Row, 1986.

———. *The Trumpet of Conscience.* New York: Harper & Row, 1967.

Kluger, Richard. *Simple Justice: The History of Brown v. Board of Education and Black America's Struggle for Equality.* New York: Knopf, 1976; New York: Vintage, 1977.

Lehman, Nicholas. *The Promised Land.* New York: Knopf, 1991.

Levy, Peter B. *The Civil Rights Movement*. Westport, Conn.: Greenwood Press, 1998.

Lewis, John, and Michael D'Orso. *Walking with the Wind: A Memoir of the Movement*. New York: Simon and Schuster, 1998.

Locke, Alain. *The New Negro*. New York: A and C Boni, 1925; New York: Maxwell Macmillan International (Introduction by Arnold Rampersad), 1992.

Malcolm X. *Malcolm X Speaks*. Ed. George Breitman. New York: Merit, 1965; New York: Grove Weidenfield, 1990.

Martin, Tony. *Literary Garveyism: Garvey, Black Arts, and the Harlem Renaissance*. Dover, Mass.: Majority Press, 1983.

Moody, Anne. *Coming of Age in Mississippi*. New York: Dell, 1976, 1980.

Morrison, Toni. *Jazz*. New York: Plume Books, 1992.

Oates, Stephen B. *Let the Trumpet Sound: The Life of Martin Luther King, Jr.* New York: Harper & Row, 1982; New York: New American Library, 1988.

Perry, Margaret. *Silence to the Drums: A Survey of the Literature of the Renaissance*. Westport, Conn.: Greenwood Press, 1976; New York: Garland, 1982.

Rodgers, Lawrence R. *Canaan Bound: The African-American Great Migration Novel*. Chicago: University of Illinois Press, 1997.

Roses, Lorraine Elena, and Ruth Elizabeth Randolph, eds. *Harlem's Glory: Black Women Writing, 1900–1950*. Cambridge: Harvard University Press, 1996.

Roses, Lorraine Elena, and Ruth Elizabeth Randolph. *Harlem Renaissance and Beyond: Literary Biographies of 100 Black Women Writers, 1900–1945*. Boston: G.K. Hall, 1990.

Sigler, Jay A. *Civil Rights in America: 1500 to the Present*. Detroit, Mich.: Gale, 1998.

Smythe, Mabel M. *The Black American Reference Book*. Englewood Cliffs, N.J.: Prentice-Hall, 1976.

Wagner, Jean. *Black Poets of the United States: From Paul Laurence Dunbar to Langston Hughes*. Trans. Kenneth Douglas. Champaign-Urbana: University of Illinois Press, 1973.

Williams, Juan. *Eyes on the Prize: America's Civil Rights Years, 1954–65*. New York: Viking, 1987; New York: Penguin, 1988.

Woodward, C. Vann. *The Strange Career of Jim Crow*. New York: Oxford University Press, 1955; 3rd rev. ed. 1974.

# 6

## PUERTO RICANS

### *The View from the Mainland*

*Above:* Puerto Rican immigrants arriving in the United States, 1945. First immigrants to arrive by air to the United States *(Culver Pictures, Inc.)*

*Opposite:* **La Fortaleza,** by Pedro Villarini. *(Photo courtesy of El Museo del Barrio)*

# SETTING THE CULTURAL AND HISTORICAL CONTEXT

I**N THE PREFACE** to her first short-story collection, *El Bronx Remembered*, the writer Nicholasa Mohr establishes a connection between the Puerto Rican community in which she situates her work and the larger experiences of migrants:

> There have been Puerto Ricans living in the mainland USA since the middle of the last century. But it was after the Second World War, when traveling became cheaper and easier that the great influx began. . . . As citizens [of the United States], they did not face immigration quotas or laws. . . . These migrants and their children, strangers in their own land, brought with them a different language, culture, and racial mixture. Like so many before them they hoped for a better life, a new future for their children, and a piece of that good life known as the "American Dream." (ix)

While Mohr's preface stresses the connection between migrant experience and the experiences of earlier immigrant groups, the poetry of Judith Ortiz Cofer often represents another side of migration; she considers it a form of exile that is both geographical and cultural in nature. Her poem, "Exile," begins with the following assertion:

> I left my home behind me
> but my past clings to my fingers
> so that every word I write
> bears the mark
> like a canceled postage stamp
> of my birthplace . . . (50)

Here the movement is temporal as well as spatial, conveying both the speaker's connection with the homeland as well as a separation from it. Even as the geographical and temporal distance widens, the poet's language brings the Island back to memory. The two works point to an important tension in the writing of many Puerto Rican mainland writers—a tension that affects one's sense of identity and affiliation on a personal level, as well as one's attitude toward the more public debates, such as the proper relationship between the Island and the U.S. mainland.

In 1493 Columbus claimed the Island, then inhabited by peaceful Taíno, for Spain. As a Spanish colony, Puerto Rico was eventually put under the *encomienda*, forced labor practiced until the nineteenth century. Exploited for its agricultural production and strategic importance, the Island remained under Spanish control until it was ceded to the United States in 1898, after the Spanish-American War. Liberal forces in Puerto Rico had campaigned throughout the nineteenth century for reform of the colonial government, ultimately achieving two major goals: the abolition of slavery and the institution of an autonomous island government. The second of these major reforms, however, was swept away when the United States established military control.

Several factors influenced the U.S. interest in Puerto Rico, among them the Island's economic potential and strategic importance. American corporations noted the Island's potential for agrarian production, specifically coffee and sugarcane crops. Strategically, Puerto Rico was considered important because of its proximity to the proposed Panama Canal, which would connect the Atlantic and Pacific Oceans. The Treaty of Paris (1898), which ended the Spanish-American War, made Puerto Rico—along with Cuba, Guam, and the Philippines—a territory of the United States. Arguments in Congress and elsewhere made use of the doctrine of manifest destiny to legitimize U.S. government's claims to the Island.

Puerto Rico became a U.S. territory, now subject to the U.S. Congress, which shaped policy through a series of legislative acts. The Foraker Act (1900) established a civil administration on the Island under a presidentially appointed governor. The Jones Act (1917) made the Island an "organized but unincorporated" territory of the United States and conferred U.S. citizenship on Puerto Ricans. The benefits of the act were, however, extremely limited. Puerto Ricans gained a representative in Congress, but that member was not permitted to vote. Although the Island would now have a civilian rather than a military governor, that person would continue to be an appointed official; Puerto Ricans would have no say in selecting him.

Although Puerto Ricans were not given all the rights and benefits of American citizenship, they were expected to meet many of the obligations of citizenship. Specifically, the Jones Act made all eligible citizens of Puerto Rico subject to the American military draft during the final months of World War I. Not until 1947 did Congress permit Puerto Ricans to elect their governor by popular vote, and not until 1950 did it permit them to write a constitution. Under their constitution, the Island became fully self-governing as the Commonwealth of Puerto Rico, while remaining in voluntary association with the United States.

U.S. government attempts at agrarian reform and industrialization on the Island were controversial. Generally, the policy had been to consolidate land and the means of production of food and other commodities—changes usually designed to benefit mainland investors. The most famous of these reforms, Operation Bootstrap, was begun on the Island during the 1940s as an extension of Franklin D. Roosevelt's New Deal. Under Operation Bootstrap, agricultural land in Puerto Rico was cleared for the development of industrial sites, and the U.S. government gave investors tax reductions and aided in the construction of hotels, factories, and other businesses. Many substandard housing units were replaced by concrete buildings, and roads were paved throughout the Island's countryside. Proponents of Operation Bootstrap point to the increased literacy, decreased infant mortality, and increased employment opportunities that accompanied the introduction of technology and industrialization. Critics charge that such controlled economic programs interfere with, rather than promote, local development, and that they displace agricultural workers without creating new employment for them. Emphasizing the negative effects of absentee land ownership and the urban congestion caused by the necessary migration from rural areas, critics contend that those who profited most by the rapid industrialization of Puerto Rico were not the people of the Island but corporations on the U.S. mainland.

Migration from Puerto Rico to the mainland of the United States began in the mid-nineteenth century. Sometimes people have migrated for political reasons, as when Puerto Ricans who participated in the unsuccessful rebellion against Spain in the 1870s sought refuge in New York City. More often, however, socioeconomic factors have taken precedence. Because of the increased prosperity brought about by mainland investment in the Island, migration has helped to reduce the pressure of overcrowding caused by a high birthrate and improved public health. Migration has been so important to the Island's economic stability, in fact, that the Puerto Rican government has long maintained an office in New York City to facilitate it. By 1930, a large majority of Puerto Rican migrants had settled in East Harlem (now called Spanish Harlem) and in parts of Brooklyn and the Bronx, often working in the garment and tobacco industries. The selection by Jesús Colón illustrates the struggles of the new arrivals not only to survive in the new surroundings, but also to educate themselves and to prosper.

The migration has also served American commercial interests. In the 1950s New York City Mayor Robert Wagner Jr. visited Puerto Rico to recruit workers, and American corporations routinely sent recruiters there as well. The most significant period of migration to the mainland, however, occurred during the late 1940s, just after World War II, when the postwar economic boom caused a demand for labor. This factor, combined with the introduction of cheap airfares to the mainland, resulted in a dramatic increase in the number of persons leaving for the mainland. Although some migrants were recruited for work in the western states and Hawaii, most settled in the northeastern United States, particularly New York City.

Although their social status was generally lower than it would have been in Puerto Rico, those living on the mainland were compensated by health and educational opportunities, increased wages, and a higher standard of living. Despite this, their increasing separation from Puerto Rican family members and religious and cultural values was a cause for concern. The selection from Piri Thomas's *Down These Mean Streets*, an early work by a Puerto Rican writer, conveys a sense of the nostalgia for the Island experienced by many. In Nicholasa Mohr's "The English Lesson," received notions of "the nation of immigrants," "the American Dream," and other doctrines are put to the test in an adult education classroom. The chapter from Judith Ortiz Cofer's *The Line of the Sun* explores how economic and cultural conflicts can be played out, not only in the larger society, but also within the family itself.

The erosion of the U.S. economy in the 1970s further undermined Puerto Ricans' social and economic position on the mainland. As the industries that required semiskilled labor began to close, automate, or relocate, many Puerto Rican migrants turned to the service economy, filling positions as maids, waiters, dishwashers, and busboys; they were often required to work long hours and at low wages. Even highly educated professionals found that the licenses they had held in Puerto Rico were not honored in the United States; as a result, many were forced to accept positions below their qualifications in order to remain employed.

Education, which has traditionally been considered a means for immigrant populations to improve their position in society, began to fail the Puerto Rican communities. Access to free university education and other social services was reduced as the economy deteriorated; moreover, the needs of Puerto Rican elementary and high school students were often neglected. The 1976 Report of the United States Civil Rights Commission concluded that in Puerto Rican communities, the conditions in public schools were substandard, and that opportunities for higher education were rare. The Civil Rights Commission also found that Puerto Rican children were often treated unfairly; because their first language was Spanish, they were frequently misidentified as slow learners and kept back. Students also complained of being pressured to select basic studies or vocational, rather than college preparatory, tracks. Although federal programs were started in the late 1960s to combat discrimination in education and employment, many were later abandoned because of funding and administrative problems.

In the early part of the twentieth century, Puerto Ricans attempted to address such socioeconomic problems in the United States by establishing and participating in political and labor organizations that worked for social change. Especially after gaining citizenship in 1917, Puerto Ricans became more involved in local government. In the 1940s and 1950s, social and cultural organizations were founded to help ease the tensions between those already settled on the mainland and the large numbers of new arrivals. In the 1960s, organizations such as the Puerto Rican Community Development Project were founded to unify old and new members of the community and to take advantage of federal programs and other opportunities for improvement and advancement.

Since the 1960s, Puerto Ricans increasingly have been integrated into the political mainstream. One example of this is the Democratic official Herman Badillo of New York, who, after serving in the U.S. Congress for eight years, held several offices in state government and in New York City, including that of deputy mayor. Badillo was elected chair of the City University of New York Board of Trustees in 1999. In the past forty years, some younger Puerto Ricans, especially college students who are restless with what they perceive to be the community's continued dependence on federal money and political alliances with other groups, have demonstrated increased militancy. Recently, protests about the U.S. government's use of the outlying island of Vieques for military exercises became more prevalent. While proponents pointed to national security issues, opponents argued that the threats to safety had not been given due consideration, citing the death of a civilian employee in 1999; others pointed to the potential ecological damage that sustained use might cause to the area.

In 1993 and 1998, Puerto Ricans on the Island voted to retain their status as a commonwealth. These votes, like that of the plebiscite of 1967, rejected two other alternatives: cultural autonomy or increased economic, political, and cultural affiliation with the United States. The chapter ends with two essays that highlight the opposing arguments on statehood.

As we see from several of the readings in this chapter, Puerto Rican migrants came to the United States anticipating new political and economic opportunities. For many, the dream of prosperity and a better life has not yet been realized.

---

## BEGINNING: Pre-reading/Writing

*In a class discussion, speculate about the political, economic, and personal reasons why Puerto Ricans emigrate to the United States. Consider whether the political relationship between Puerto Rico and the United States creates circumstances for Puerto Ricans that are different from those of immigrants from other countries.*

---

*The Foraker Act, which was passed in 1900, instituted a civil government for Puerto Rico, under the jurisdiction of an American military governor and an eleven-member executive council with an American majority. The act also designated English as the Island's official language. It remained in effect until 1917, when the Jones Act granted Island residents American citizenship. Puerto Ricans were not allowed to elect their own governor, however, until 1948; they were not permitted to vote until 1950.*

# From THE FORAKER ACT

## *The Governor*

Sec. 17. That the official title of the chief executive officer shall be "The Governor of Porto Rico." He shall be appointed by the President, by and with the advice and consent of the Senate; he shall hold his office for a term of four years and until his successor is chosen and qualified unless sooner removed by the President; he shall reside in Porto Rico during his official incumbency, and shall maintain his office at the seat of government; he may grant pardons and reprieves, and remit fines and forfeitures for offenses against the laws of Porto Rico, and respites for offenses against the laws of the United States, until the decision of the President can be ascertained; he shall commission all officers that he may be authorized to appoint, and may veto any legislation enacted, as hereinafter provided; he shall be the commander in chief of the militia, and shall at all times faithfully execute the laws, and he shall in that behalf have all the powers of governors of the Territories of the United States that are not locally inapplicable; and he shall annually, and at such other times as he may be required, make official report of the transactions of the government in Porto Rico, through the Secretary of State, to the President of the United States: *Provided,* That the President may, in his discretion, delegate and assign to him such executive duties and functions as may in pursuance with law be so delegated and assigned.

## *The Executive Council*

Sec. 18. That there shall be appointed by the President, by and with the advice and consent of the Senate, for the period of four years, unless sooner removed by the President, a secretary, an attorney-general, a treasurer, an auditor, a commissioner of the interior, and a commissioner of education, each of whom shall reside in Porto Rico during his official incumbency and have the powers and duties hereinafter provided for them, respectively, and who, together with five other persons of good repute, to be also appointed by the President for a like term of four years, by and with the advice and consent of the Senate, shall constitute an executive council, at least five of whom shall be native inhabitants of Porto Rico, and, in addition to the legislative duties hereinafter imposed upon them as a body, shall exercise such powers and perform such duties as are hereinafter provided for them, respectively, and who shall have power to employ all necessary deputies and assistants for the proper discharge of their duties as such officials and as such executive council. ✠

## RESPONDING

1. In a journal entry, summarize these provisions of the Foraker Act in your own words. What duties and responsibilities are given to the governor?

2. Working individually or in a group, discuss the way officials were chosen to govern Puerto Rico before 1948. Who made these appointments? What role did local Puerto Ricans play? Speculate on the reaction of local people to this situation.

3. Imagine that the year is 1947. You are a resident of Puerto Rico. Write a letter to the U.S. Congress detailing your opinion of the Foraker Act. Or write a letter arguing that Puerto Ricans should or should not be granted the rights and privileges of citizenship.

# JESUS COLON

*Jesús Colón, born in Puerto Rico, immigrated to the United States around 1916 as a stowaway aboard ship. He spent his early years working at odd jobs in order to support himself and later drew on these experiences for a column for the* Daily Worker. *His column became the source of many of the essays in* A Puerto Rican in New York.

*Throughout this collection, Colón explores the tension between what he expected to find in the United States and what he actually discovered. As a black Puerto Rican emigré, Colón had to confront American society's prejudices against his language and his race. In the following selection he describes his reaction to being judged not by the quality of his work but by the color of his skin.*

⊹

# KIPLING AND I

Sometimes I pass Debevoise Place at the corner of Willoughby Street. . . . I look at the old wooden house, gray and ancient, the house where I used to live some forty years ago. . . .

My room was on the second floor at the corner. On hot summer nights I would sit at the window reading by the electric light from the street lamp which was almost at a level with the window sill.

It was nice to come home late during the winter, look for some scrap of old newspaper, some bits of wood and a few chunks of coal and start a sparkling fire in the chunky fourlegged coal stove. I would be rewarded with an intimate warmth as little by little the pigmy stove became alive, puffing out its sides, hot and red, like the crimson cheeks of a Santa Claus.

My few books were in a soap box nailed to the wall. But my most prized possession in those days was a poem I had bought in a five and ten cent store on Fulton Street. (I wonder what has become of these poems, maxims and sayings of wise men that they used to sell at the five and ten cent stores?) The poem was printed on gold paper and mounted on a gilded frame ready to be hung in a conspicuous place in the house. I bought one of those fancy silken picture cords finishing in a rosette to match the color of the frame.

I was seventeen. This poem to me then seemed to summarize the wisdom of all the sages that ever lived in one poetical nutshell. It was what I was looking for, something to guide myself by, a way of life, a compendium of the wise, the true and the beautiful. All I had to do was to live according to the counsel of the poem and follow its instructions and I would be a perfect man—the useful, the good, the true human being. I was very happy that day, forty years ago.

The poem had to have the most prominent place in the room. Where could I hang it? I decided that the best place for the poem was on the wall right by the entrance to the room. No one coming in and out would miss it. Perhaps someone would be interested enough to read it and drink the profound waters of its message. . . .

Every morning as I prepared to leave, I stood in front of the poem and read it over and over again, sometimes half a dozen times. I let the sonorous music of the verse carry me away. I brought with me a handwritten copy as I stepped out every morning looking for work, repeating verses and stanzas from memory until the whole poem came to be part of me. Other days my lips kept repeating a single verse of the poem at intervals throughout the day.

In the subways I loved to compete with the shrill noises of the many wheels below by chanting the lines of the poem. People stared at me moving my lips as though I were in a trance. I looked back with pity. They were not so fortunate as I who had as a guide to direct my life a great poem to make me wise, useful and happy.

9    And I chanted:

> If you can keep your head when all about you
> Are losing theirs and blaming it on you . . .
>
> If you can wait and not be tired by waiting
> Or being hated don't give way to hating . . .
>
> If you can make one heap of all your winnings
> And risk it on a turn of pitch and toss . . .
> And lose and start again at your beginnings . . .

10    "If," by Kipling, was the poem. At seventeen, my evening prayer and my first morning thought. I repeated it every day with the resolution to live up to the very last line of that poem.

11    I would visit the government employment office on Jay Street. The conversations among the Puerto Ricans on the large wooden benches in the employment office were always on the same subject. How to find a decent place to live. How they would not rent to Negroes or Puerto Ricans. How Negroes and Puerto Ricans were given the pink slips first at work.

12    From the employment office I would call door to door at the piers, factories and storage houses in the streets under the Brooklyn and Manhattan bridges. "Sorry, nothing today." It seemed to me that "today" was a continuation and combination of all the yesterdays, todays and tomorrows.

13    From the factories I would go to the restaurants looking for a job as a porter or dishwasher. At least I would eat and be warm in a kitchen.

14    "Sorry" . . . "Sorry" . . .

15    Sometimes I was hired at ten dollars a week, ten hours a day including Sundays and holidays. One day off during the week. My work was that of three men: dishwasher, porter, busboy. And to clear the sidewalk of snow and slush "when you have nothing else to do." I was to be appropriately humble and grateful not only to the owner but to everybody else in the place.

16    If I rebelled at insults or at a pointed innuendo or just the inhuman amount of work, I was unceremoniously thrown out and told to come "next week for your pay." "Next week" meant weeks of calling for the paltry dollars owed me. The owners relished this "next week."

17    I clung to my poem as to a faith. Like a potent amulet, my precious poem was clenched in the fist of my right hand inside my second-hand overcoat. Again and again I declaimed aloud a few precious lines when discouragement and disillusionment threatened to overwhelm me.

> If you can force your heart and nerve and sinew
> To serve your turn long after you are gone . . .

The weeks of unemployment and hard knocks turned into months. I con-  18
tinued to find two or three days of work here and there. And I continued to be
thrown out when I rebelled at the ill treatment, overwork and insults. I kept
pounding the streets looking for a place where they would treat me half decently,
where my devotion to work and faith in Kipling's poem would be appreciated.
I remember the worn out shoes I bought in a second-hand store on Myrtle
Avenue at the corner of Adams Street. The round holes in the soles that I tried
to cover with pieces of carton were no match for the frigid knives of the
unrelenting snow.

One night I returned late after a long day of working for work. I was hungry.  19
My room was dark and cold. I wanted to warm my numb body. I lit a match
and began looking for some scraps of wood and a piece of paper to start a fire.
I searched all over the floor. No wood, no paper. As I stood up, the glimmering
flicker of the dying match was reflected in the glass surface of the framed poem.
I unhooked the poem from the wall. I reflected for a minute, a minute that felt
like an eternity. I took the frame apart, placing the square glass upon the small
table. I tore the gold paper on which the poem was printed, threw its pieces
inside the stove and placing the small bits of wood from the frame on top of
the paper I lit it, adding soft and hard coal as the fire began to gain strength
and brightness.

I watched how the lines of the poem withered into ashes inside the small  20
stove. ✠

---

## RESPONDING

1. Read the entire poem "If—," which appears below. In a journal entry, discuss
   how realistic you find its premise. Do you believe what the poem promises?
   Give examples to support your opinion.

### *If—*

> If you can keep your head when all about you
>    Are losing theirs and blaming it on you;
> If you can trust yourself when all men doubt you,
>    But make allowance for their doubting too:
> If you can wait and not be tired by waiting,                    5
>    Or being lied about, don't deal in lies,
> Or being hated, don't give way to hating,
>    And yet don't look too good, nor talk too wise;
>
> If you can dream—and not make dreams your master;
>    If you can think—and not make thoughts your aim,          10

If you can meet with Triumph and Disaster
    And treat those two impostors just the same:
If you can bear to hear the truth you've spoken
    Twisted by knaves to make a trap for fools,
15    Or watch the things you gave your life to, broken,
    And stoop and build 'em up with worn-out tools;

If you can make one heap of all your winnings
    And risk it on one turn of pitch-and-toss,
And lose, and start again at your beginnings
20    And never breathe a word about your loss:
If you can force your heart and nerve and sinew
    To serve your turn long after they are gone,
And so hold on when there is nothing in you
    Except the Will which says to them: "Hold on!"

25  If you can talk with crowds and keep your virtue,
    Or walk with Kings—nor lose the common touch,
If neither foes nor loving friends can hurt you,
    If all men count with you, but none too much:
If you can fill the unforgiving minute
30    With sixty seconds' worth of distance run,
Yours is the Earth and everything that's in it,
    And—which is more—you'll be a Man, my son!

2. Colón has many problems earning a living in New York City. Working individually or in a group, list Colón's difficulties living and working in New York. Use evidence from the reading to discuss the reasons for his problems. Share your conclusions with the class.

3. After reading Colón's work, one could argue that he must confront a system where material things are more important than human suffering. Write an essay agreeing or disagreeing with this view of American society. You may consider his experience and the historical period he wrote about or deal with the issue in relation to contemporary society.

4. Why does Colón burn the poem at the end of the selection? Write an essay explaining why a reader might claim that it is a symbolic as well as an actual act.

# PIRI THOMAS

*Piri Thomas, born in Spanish Harlem in 1928, began writing while in prison for armed robbery. His books include* Down These Mean Streets *(1967),* Savior, Savior Hold My Hand *(1972),* Seven Times Long *(1974), and* The View from El Barrio *(1978).*

*The excerpt that follows is from* Down These Mean Streets. *The stories in this book, describing Thomas's involvement with street gangs and drug addiction, are often raw in their use of language, sexually explicit, and violent. In this story, however, Thomas uses a more nostalgic, more pensive tone to describe gatherings in the small New York City apartment that his family shared. The passage has as its focus the author's mother and her memories of the Island she left behind.*

✜

## PUERTO RICAN PARADISE

Poppa didn't talk to me the next day. Soon he didn't talk much to anyone. He lost his night job—I forget why, and probably it was worth forgetting—and went back on home relief. It was 1941, and the Great Hunger called Depression was still down on Harlem. 1

But there was still the good old WPA. If a man was poor enough, he could dig a ditch for the government. Now Poppa was poor enough again. 2

The weather turned cold one more time, and so did our apartment. In the summer the cooped-up apartments in Harlem seem to catch all the heat and improve on it. It's the same in the winter. The cold, plastered walls embrace that cold from outside and make it a part of the apartment, till you don't know whether it's better to freeze out in the snow or by the stove, where four jets, wide open, spout futile, blue-yellow flames. It's hard on the rats, too. 3

Snow was falling. "My *Cristo*," Momma said, "*qué frío.* Doesn't that landlord have any *corazón?*[1] Why don't he give more heat?" I wondered how Pops was making out working a pick and shovel in that falling snow. 4

Momma picked up a hammer and began to beat the beat-up radiator that's copped a plea from so many beatings. Poor steam radiator, how could it give out heat when it was freezing itself? The hollow sounds Momma beat out of it brought echoes from other freezing people in the building. Everybody picked up the beat and it seemed a crazy, good idea. If everybody took turns beating on the radiators, everybody could keep warm from the exercise. 5

1. heart

6     We drank hot cocoa and talked about summertime. Momma talked about Puerto Rico and how great it was, and how she'd like to go back one day, and how it was warm all the time there and no matter how poor you were over there, you could always live on green bananas, *bacalao*,[2] and rice and beans. "*Dios mío*," she said, "I don't think I'll ever see my island again."

7     "Sure you will, Mommie," said Miriam, my kid sister. She was eleven. "Tell us, tell us all about Porto Rico."

8     "It's not P*o*rto Rico, it's P*ue*rto Rico," said Momma.

9     "Tell us, Moms," said nine-year-old James, "about P*ue*rto Rico."

10     "Yeah, Mommie," said six-year-old José.

11     Even the baby, Paulie, smiled.

12     Moms copped that wet-eyed look and began to dream-talk about her *isla verde*,[3] Moses' land of milk and honey.

13     "When I was a little girl," she said, "I remember the getting up in the morning and getting the water from the river and getting the wood for the fire and the quiet of the greenlands and the golden color of the morning sky, the grass wet from the *lluvia*[4] . . . *Ai, Dios*, the *coquís*[5] and the *pajaritos*[6] making all the *música* . . ."

14     "Mommie, were you poor?" asked Miriam.

15     "*Sí, muy pobre*, but very happy. I remember the hard work and the very little bit we had, but it was a good little bit. It counted very much. Sometimes when you have too much, the good gets lost within and you have to look very hard. But when you have a little, then the good does not have to be looked for so hard."

16     "Moms," I asked, "did everybody love each other—I mean, like if everybody was worth something, not like if some weren't important because they were poor—you know what I mean?"

17     "*Bueno hijo*, you have people everywhere who, because they have more, don't remember those who have very little. But in Puerto Rico those around you share *la pobreza*[7] with you and they love you, because only poor people can understand poor people. I like *los Estados Unidos*, but it's sometimes a cold place to live—not because of the winter and the landlord not giving heat but because of the snow in the hearts of the people."

18     "Moms, didn't our people have any money or land?" I leaned forward, hoping to hear that my ancestors were noble princes born in Spain.

19     "Your grandmother and grandfather had a lot of land, but they lost that."

20     "How come, Moms?"

21     "Well, in those days there was nothing of what you call *contratos*,[8] and when you bought or sold something, it was on your word and a handshake, and that's the way your *abuelos*[9] bought their land and then lost it."

---

2. codfish
3. green island
4. rain

5. small treetoads
6. little birds
7. poverty

8. contracts
9. grandparents

"Is that why we ain't got nuttin' now?" James asked pointedly.    22

"Oh, it—"    23

The door opened and put an end to the kitchen yak. It was Poppa coming    24
home from work. He came into the kitchen and brought all the cold with him.
Poor Poppa, he looked so lost in the clothes he had on. A jacket and coat,
sweaters on top of sweaters, two pairs of long johns, two pairs of pants, two
pairs of socks, and a woolen cap. And under all that he was cold. His eyes were
cold; his ears were red with pain. He took off his gloves and his fingers were
stiff with cold.

"*Cómo está?*"[10] said Momma. "I will make you coffee."    25

Poppa said nothing. His eyes were running hot frozen tears. He worked his    26
fingers and rubbed his ears, and the pain made him make faces. "Get me some
snow, Piri," he said finally.

I ran to the window, opened it, and scraped all the snow on the sill into    27
one big snowball and brought it to him. We all watched in frozen wonder as
Poppa took that snow and rubbed it on his ears and hands.

"Gee, Pops, don't it hurt?" I asked.    28

"*Sí,* but it's good for it. It hurts a little first, but it's good for the frozen    29
parts."

I wondered why.    30

"How was it today?" Momma asked.    31

"Cold. My God, ice cold."    32

Gee, I thought, *I'm sorry for you, Pops. You gotta suffer like this.*    33

"It was not always like this," my father said to the cold walls. "It's all the    34
fault of the damn depression."

"Don't say 'damn,'" Momma said.    35

"Lola, I say 'damn' because that's what it is—*damn.*"    36

And Momma kept quiet. She knew it was "damn."    37

My father kept talking to the walls. Some of the words came out loud, others    38
stayed inside. I caught the inside ones—the damn WPA, the damn depression,
the damn home relief, the damn poorness, the damn cold, the damn crummy
apartments, the damn look on his damn kids, living so damn damned and his
not being able to do a damn thing about it.

And Momma looked at Poppa and at us and thought about her Puerto Rico    39
and maybe being there where you didn't have to wear a lot of extra clothes and
feel so full of damns, and how when she was a little girl all the green was wet
from the *lluvias.*

And Poppa looking at Momma and us, thinking how did he get trapped    40
and why did he love us so much that he dug in damn snow to give us a piece
of chance? And why couldn't he make it from home, maybe, and keep running?

And Miriam, James, José, Paulie, and me just looking and thinking about    41

10. How are you?

snowballs and Puerto Rico and summertime in the street and whether we were gonna live like this forever and not know enough to be sorry for ourselves.

42 The kitchen all of a sudden felt warmer to me, like being all together made it like we wanted it to be. Poppa made it into the toilet and we could hear everything he did, and when he finished, the horsey gurgling of the flushed toilet told us he'd soon be out. I looked at the clock and it was time for "Jack Armstrong, the All-American Boy."

43 José, James, and I got some blankets and, like Indians, huddled around the radio digging the All-American Jack and his adventures, while Poppa ate dinner quietly. Poppa was funny about eating—like when he ate, nobody better bother him. When Poppa finished, he came into the living room and stood there looking at us. We smiled at him, and he stood there looking at us.

44 All of a sudden he yelled, "How many wanna play 'Major Bowes' Amateur Hour'?"

45 "Hoo-ray! Yeah, we wanna play," said José.

46 "Okay, first I'll make some taffy outta molasses, and the one who wins first prize gets first choice at the biggest piece, okay?"

47 "Yeah, hoo-ray, *chevere.*"

48 Gee, Pops, you're great, I thought, *you're the swellest, the bestest Pops in the whole world, even though you don't understand us too good.*

49 When the candy was all ready, everybody went into the living room. Poppa came in with a broom and put an empty can over the stick. It became a microphone, just like on the radio.

50 "Pops, can I be Major Bowes?" I asked.

51 "Sure, Piri," and the floor was mine.

52 "Ladies and gentlemen," I announced, "tonight we present 'Major Bowes' Amateur Hour,' and for our first number—"

53 "Wait a minute, son, let me get my ukulele," said Poppa. "We need music."

54 Everybody clapped their hands and Pops came back with his ukulele.

55 "The first con-tes-tant we got is Miss Miriam Thomas."

56 "Oh no, not me first, somebody else goes first," said Miriam, and she hid behind Momma.

57 "Let me! Let me!" said José.

58 Everybody clapped.

59 "What are you gonna sing, sir?" I asked.

60 "Tell the people his name," said Poppa.

61 "Oh yeah. Presenting Mr. José Thomas. And what are you gonna sing, sir?"

62 I handed José the broom with the can on top and sat back. He sang well and everybody clapped.

63 Everyone took a turn, and we all agreed that two-year-old Paulie's "gurgle, gurgle" was the best song, and Paulie got first choice at the candy. Everybody got candy and eats and thought how good it was to be together, and Moms thought that it was wonderful to have such a good time even if she wasn't in Puerto Rico where the grass was wet with *lluvia.* Poppa thought about how cold

it was gonna be tomorrow, but then he remembered tomorrow was Sunday and he wouldn't have to work, and he said so and Momma said "*Sí*," and the talk got around to Christmas and how maybe things would get better.

The next day the Japanese bombed Pearl Harbor. 64

"My God," said Poppa. "We're at war." 65

"*Dios Mío*," said Momma. 66

I turned to James. "Can you beat that," I said. 67

"Yeah," he nodded. "What's it mean?" 68

"What's it mean?" I said. "You gotta ask, dopey? It means a rumble is on, 69 and a big one, too."

I wondered if the war was gonna make things worse than they were for us. 70 But it didn't. A few weeks later Poppa got a job in an airplane factory. "How about that?" he said happily. "Things are looking up for us."

Things *were* looking up for us, but it had taken a damn war to do it. A lousy 71 rumble had to get called so we could start to live better. I thought, *How do you figure this crap out?*

I couldn't figure it out, and after a while I stopped thinking about it. Life 72 in the streets didn't change much. The bitter cold was followed by the sticky heat; I played stickball, marbles, and Johnny-on-the-Pony, copped girls' drawers and blew pot. War or peace—what difference did it really make? ✳

---

## RESPONDING

1. Sometimes when we are unhappy with our present circumstances we like to think about a time when we were happier. In a journal entry, describe a time when you compared your situation in the present to a happier time in the past. Were your memories accurate or did you idealize the past? Did your memories help you or hinder you in accepting conditions in the present? What role do such memories play in the Thomas family?

2. The Thomas family has few material comforts, but family members contribute to each other's comfort. Working individually or in a group, list the family's activities. Discuss how these compensate or fail to compensate for some of the difficulties of their living conditions. How does your family or the family of someone you know provide financial and emotional support for its members?

3. Using examples from the reading, write an essay describing Thomas's mother's life in Puerto Rico and contrast it with the situation she finds herself in in Harlem. Consider whether Thomas's mother's memories of Puerto Rico are realistic. He calls the chapter "Puerto Rican Paradise." Do you think this title is descriptive or ironic?

4. Mrs. Thomas said, "only poor people can understand poor people" (paragraph 17). Does this mean that only by being a member of a group can you understand the experience of someone in that group? In an essay, argue for or against this position.

# NICHOLASA MOHR

*Nicholasa Mohr, who was born in New York City in 1938, studied at the Brooklyn Museum Art School and the Pratt School. Between 1952 and 1967 she worked as a painter and printmaker and taught in the New York City public schools. Since 1972 she has held lectureships and visiting appointments in creative writing, Puerto Rican studies, and art at several universities, including the State University of New York at Stony Brook, the University of Illinois, and the University of Wisconsin. Mohr's publications include* Nilda *(1973),* El Bronx Remembered: A Novella and Stories *(1975),* In Nueva York *(1977),* Rituals of Survival: A Women's Portfolio *(1985),* Going Home *(1986), and* A Matter of Pride and Other Stories *(1997).*

*The story that follows, from* In Nueva York, *makes use of multiple points of view to contrast the expectations of the English-as-a-second-language (ESL) teacher with those of her adult students. In the story, both teacher and students are presented with learning opportunities, but perhaps in unexpected ways.*

⊕

# THE ENGLISH LESSON

1    "REMEMBER OUR ASSIGNMENT for today everybody! I'm so confident that you will all do exceptionally well!" Mrs. Susan Hamma smiled enthusiastically at her students. "Everyone is to get up and make a brief statement as to why he or she is taking this course in Basic English. You must state your name, where you originally came from, how long you have been here, and . . . uh . . . a little something about yourself, if you wish. Keep it brief, not too long; remember, there are twenty-eight of us. We have a full class, and everyone must have a chance." Mrs. Hamma waved a forefinger at her students. "This is, after all, a democracy, and we have a democratic class; fairness for all!"

2    Lali grinned and looked at William, who sat directly next to her. He winked and rolled his eyes toward Mrs. Hamma. This was the third class they had attended together. It had not been easy to persuade Rudi that Lali should learn better English.

3    "Why is it necessary, eh?" Rudi had protested. "She works here in the store

with me. She don't have to talk to nobody. Besides, everybody that comes in speaks Spanish—practically everybody, anyway."

But once William had put the idea to Lali and explained how much easier things would be for her, she kept insisting until Rudi finally agreed. "Go on, you're both driving me nuts. But it can't interfere with business or work—I'm warning you!"

Adult Education offered Basic English, Tuesday evenings from 6:30 to 8:00, at a local public school. Night customers did not usually come into Rudi's Luncheonette until after eight. William and Lali promised that they would leave everything prepared and make up for any inconvenience by working harder and longer than usual, if necessary.

The class admitted twenty-eight students, and because there were only twenty-seven registered, Lali was allowed to take the course even after missing the first two classes. William had assured Mrs. Hamma that he would help Lali catch up; she was glad to have another student to make up the full registration.

Most of the students were Spanish speaking. The majority were American citizens—Puerto Ricans who had migrated to New York and spoke very little English. The rest were immigrants admitted to the United States as legal aliens. There were several Chinese, two Dominicans, one Sicilian, and one Pole.

Every Tuesday Mrs. Hamma traveled to the Lower East Side from Bayside, Queens, where she lived and was employed as a history teacher in the local junior high school. She was convinced that this small group of people desperately needed her services. Mrs. Hamma reiterated her feelings frequently to just about anyone who would listen. "Why, if these people can make it to class after working all day at those miserable, dreary, uninteresting, and often revolting jobs, well, the least I can do is be there to serve them, making every lesson count toward improving their conditions! My grandparents came here from Germany as poor immigrants, working their way up. I'm not one to forget a thing like that!"

By the time class started most of the students were quite tired. And after the lesson was over, many had to go on to part-time jobs, some even without time for supper. As a result there was always sluggishness and yawning among the students. This never discouraged Mrs. Hamma, whose drive and enthusiasm not only amused the class but often kept everyone awake.

"Now this is the moment we have all been preparing for." Mrs. Hamma stood up, nodded, and blinked knowingly at her students. "Five lessons, I think, are enough to prepare us for our oral statements. You may read from prepared notes, as I said before, but please try not to read every word. We want to hear you speak; conversation is what we're after. When someone asks you about yourself, you cannot take a piece of paper and start reading the answers, now can you? That would be foolish. So . . ."

Standing in front of her desk, she put her hands on her hips and spread her feet, giving the impression that she was going to demonstrate calisthenics.

"Shall we begin?"

13    Mrs. Hamma was a very tall, angular woman with large extremities. She was the tallest person in the room. Her eyes roamed from student to student until they met William's.

14    "Mr. Colón, will you please begin?"

15    Nervously William looked around him, hesitating.

16    "Come on now, we must get the ball rolling. All right now . . . did you hear what I said? Listen, 'getting the ball rolling' means getting started. Getting things going, such as—" Mrs. Hamma swiftly lifted her right hand over her head, making a fist, then swung her arm around like a pitcher and, with an underhand curve, forcefully threw an imaginary ball out at her students. Trying to maintain her balance, Mrs. Hamma hopped from one leg to the other. Startled, the students looked at one another. In spite of their efforts to restrain themselves, several people in back began to giggle. Lali and William looked away, avoiding each other's eyes and trying not to laugh out loud. With assured countenance, Mrs. Hamma continued.

17    "An idiom!" she exclaimed, pleased. "You have just seen me demonstrate the meaning of an idiom. Now I want everyone to jot down this information in his notebook." Going to the blackboard, Mrs. Hamma explained, "It's something which literally says one thing, but actually means another. Idiom . . . idiomatic." Quickly and obediently, everyone began to copy what she wrote. "Has everyone got it? O.K., let's GET THE BALL ROLLING, Mr. Colón!"

18    Uneasily William stood up; he was almost the same height standing as sitting. When speaking to others, especially in a new situation, he always preferred to sit alongside those listening; it gave him a sense of equality with other people. He looked around and cleared his throat; at least everyone else was sitting. Taking a deep breath, William felt better.

19    "My name is William Horacio Colón," he read from a prepared statement. "I have been here in New York City for five months. I coming from Puerto Rico. My town is located in the mountains in the central part of the island. The name of my town is Aibonito, which means in Spanish 'oh how pretty.' It is name like this because when the Spaniards first seen that place they was very impressed with the beauty of the section and—"

20    "Make it brief, Mr. Colón," Mrs. Hamma interrupted, "there are others, you know."

21    William looked at her, unable to continue.

22    "Go on, go on, Mr. Colón, please!"

23    "I am working here now living with my mother and family in Lower East Side of New York City," William spoke rapidly. "I study Basic English por que . . . because my ambition is to learn to speak and read English very good. To get a better job. Y—y también, to help my mother y familia." He shrugged. "Y do better, that's all."

24    "That's all? Why, that's wonderful! Wonderful! Didn't he do well class?" Mrs. Hamma bowed slightly toward William and applauded him. The students

watched her and slowly each one began to imitate her. Pleased, Mrs. Hamma looked around her; all together they gave William a healthy round of applause.

Next, Mrs. Hamma turned to a Chinese man seated at the other side of the room.                                                                                          25

"Mr. Fong, you may go next."                                                                      26

Mr. Fong stood up; he was a man in his late thirties, of medium height and slight build. Cautiously he looked at Mrs. Hamma, and waited.                        27

"Go on, Mr. Fong. Get the ball rolling, remember?"                                     28

"All right. Get a ball rolling . . . is idiot!" Mr. Fong smiled.                        29

"No, Mr. Fong, idio*mmmmmm!*" Mrs. Hamma hummed her *m*'s, shaking her head. "Not an—It's idiomatic!"                                                           30

"What I said!" Mr. Fong responded with self-assurance, looking directly at Mrs. Hamma. "Get a ball rolling, idiomit."                                              31

"Never mind." She cleared her throat. "Just go on."                                   32

"I said O.K.?" Mr. Fong waited for an answer.                                           33

"Go on, please."                                                                                  34

Mr. Fong sighed, "My name is Joseph Fong. I been here in this country United States New York City for most one year." He too read from a prepared statement. "I come from Hong Kong but original born in city of Canton, China. I working delivery food business and live with my brother and his family in Chinatown. I taking the course in Basic English to speak good and improve my position better in this country. Also to be eligible to become American citizen."   35

Mrs. Hamma selected each student who was to speak from a different part of the room, rather than in the more conventional orderly fashion of row by row, or front to back, or even alphabetical order. This way, she reasoned, no one will know who's next; it will be more spontaneous. Mrs. Hamma enjoyed catching the uncertain looks on the faces of her students. A feeling of control over the situation gave her a pleasing thrill, and she made the most of these moments by looking at several people more than once before making her final choice.                                                                                            36

There were more men than women, and Mrs. Hamma called two or three men for each woman. It was her way of maintaining a balance. To her distress, most read from prepared notes, despite her efforts to discourage this. She would interrupt them when she felt they went on too long, then praise them when they finished. Each statement was followed by applause from everyone.          37

All had similar statements. They had migrated here in search of a better future, were living with relatives, and worked as unskilled laborers. With the exception of Lali, who was childless, every woman gave the ages and sex of her children; most men referred only to their "family." And, among the legal aliens, there was only one who did not want to become an American citizen, Diego Torres, a young man from the Dominican Republic, and he gave his reasons.      38

". . . and to improve my economic situation." Diego Torres hesitated, looking around the room. "But is one thing I no want, and is to become       39

American citizen"—he pointed to an older man with a dark complexion, seated a few seats away—"like my fellow countryman over there!" The man shook his head disapprovingly at Diego Torres, trying to hide his annoyance. "I no give up my country, Santo Domingo, for nothing," he went on, "nothing in the whole world. O.K., man? I come here, pero I cannot help. I got no work at home. There, is political. The United States control most the industry which is sugar and tourismo. Y—you have to know somebody. I tell you, is political to get a job, man! You don't know nobody and you no work, eh? So I come here from necessity, pero this no my country—"

40    "Mr. Torres," Mrs. Hamma interrupted, "we must be brief, please, there are—"

41    "I no finish lady!" he snapped. "You wait a minute when I finish!"

42    There was complete silence as Diego Torres glared at Susan Hamma. No one had ever spoken to her like that, and her confusion was greater than her embarrassment. Without speaking, she lowered her eyes and nodded.

43    "O.K., I prefer live feeling happy in my country, man. Even I don't got too much. I live simple but in my own country I be contento. Pero this is no possible in the situation of Santo Domingo now. Someday we gonna run our own country and be jobs for everybody. My reasons to be here is to make money, man, and go back home buy my house and property. I no be American citizen, no way. I'm Dominican and proud! That's it. That's all I got to say." Abruptly, Diego Torres sat down.

44    "All right." Mrs. Hamma had composed herself. "Very good; you can come here and state your views. That is what America is all about! We may not agree with you, but we defend your right to an opinion. And as long as you are in this classroom, Mr. Torres, you are in America. Now, everyone, let us give Mr. Torres the same courtesy as everyone else in this class." Mrs. Hamma applauded with a polite light clap, then turned to find the next speaker.

45    "Bullshit," whispered Diego Torres.

46    Practically everyone had spoken. Lali and the two European immigrants were the only ones left. Mrs. Hamma called upon Lali.

47    "My name is Rogelia Dolores Padillo. I come from Canovanas in Puerto Rico. Is a small village in the mountains near El Yunque Rain Forest. My family is still living there. I marry and live here with my husband working in his business of restaurant. Call Rudi's Luncheonette. I been here New York City Lower East Side since I marry, which is now about one year. I study Basic English to improve my vocabulario and learn more about here. This way I help my husband in his business and I do more also for myself, including to be able to read better in English. Thank you."

48    Aldo Fabrizi, the Sicilian, spoke next. He was a very short man, barely five feet tall. Usually he was self-conscious about his height, but William's presence relieved him of these feelings. Looking at William, he thought being short was no big thing; he was, after all, normal. He told the class that he was originally from Palermo, the capital of Sicily, and had gone to Milano, in the north of

Italy, looking for work. After three years in Milano, he immigrated here six months ago and now lived with his sister. He had a good steady job, he said, working in a copper wire factory with his brother-in-law in Brooklyn. Aldo Fabrizi wanted to become an American citizen and spoke passionately about it, without reading from his notes.

"I be proud to be American citizen. I no come here find work live good   49
and no have responsibility or no be grateful." He turned and looked threateningly at Diego Torres. "Hey? I tell you all one thing, I got my nephew right now fighting in Vietnam for this country!" Diego Torres stretched his hands over his head, yawning, folded his hands, and lowered his eyelids. "I wish I could be citizen to fight for this country. My whole family is citizens—we all Americans and we love America!" His voice was quite loud. "That's how I feel."

"Very good," Mrs. Hamma called, distracting Aldo Fabrizi. "That was well   50
stated. I'm sure you will not only become a citizen, but you will also be a credit to this country."

The last person to be called on was the Pole. He was always neatly dressed   51
in a business suit, with a shirt and tie, and carried a briefcase. His manner was reserved but friendly.

"Good evening fellow students and Madame Teacher." He nodded politely   52
to Mrs. Hamma. "My name is Stephan Paczkowski. I am originally from Poland about four months ago. My background is I was born in capital city of Poland, Warsaw. Being educated in capital and also graduating from the University with degree of professor of music with specialty in the history of music."

Stephan Paczkowski read from his notes carefully, articulating every word.   53
"I was given appointment of professor of history of music at University of Krakow. I work there for ten years until about year and half ago. At this time the political situation in Poland was so that all Jewish people were requested by the government to leave Poland. My wife who also is being a professor of economics at University of Krakow is of Jewish parents. My wife was told she could not remain in position at University or remain over there. We made arrangements for my wife and daughter who is seven years of age and myself to come here with my wife's cousin who is to be helping us.

"Since four months I am working in large hospital as position of porter in   54
maintenance department. The thing of it is, I wish to take Basic English to improve my knowledge of English language, and be able to return to my position of professor of history of music. Finally, I wish to become a citizen of United States. That is my reasons. I thank you all."

After Stephan Paczkowski sat down, there was a long awkward silence and   55
everyone turned to look at Mrs. Hamma. Even after the confrontation with Diego Torres, she had applauded without hesitation. Now she seemed unable to move.

"Well," she said, almost breathless, "that's admirable! I'm sure, sir, that you   56
will do very well . . . a person of your . . . like yourself, I mean . . . a professor, after all, it's really just admirable." Everyone was listening intently to what she

said. "That was well done, class. Now, we have to get to next week's assignment." Mrs. Hamma realized that no one had applauded Stephan Paczkowski. With a slightly pained expression, she began to applaud. "Mustn't forget Mr. Paczkowski; everybody here must be treated equally. This is America!" The class joined her in a round of applause.

57 As Mrs. Hamma began to write the next week's assignment on the board, some students looked anxiously at their watches and others asked about the time. Then they all quickly copied the information into their notebooks. It was almost eight o'clock. Those who had to get to second jobs did not want to be late; some even hoped to have time for a bite to eat first. Others were just tired and wanted to get home.

58 Lali looked at William, sighing impatiently. They both hoped Mrs. Hamma would finish quickly. There would be hell to pay with Rudi if the night customers were already at the luncheonette.

59 "There, that's next week's work, which is very important, by the way. We will be looking at the history of New York City and the different ethnic groups that lived here as far back as the Dutch. I can't tell you how proud I am of the way you all spoke. All of you—I have no favorites, you know."

60 Mrs. Hamma was interrupted by the long, loud buzzing sound bringing the lesson to an end. Quickly everyone began to exit.

61 "Good night, see you all next Tuesday!" Mrs. Hamma called out. "By the way, if any of you here wants extra help, I have a few minutes this evening." Several people bolted past her, excusing themselves. In less than thirty seconds, Mrs. Hamma was standing in an empty classroom.

62 William and Lali hurried along, struggling against the cold, sharp March wind that whipped across Houston Street, stinging their faces and making their eyes tear.

63 In a few minutes they would be at Rudi's. So far, they had not been late once.

64 "You read very well—better than anybody in class. I told you there was nothing to worry about. You caught up in no time."

65 "Go on. I was so nervous, honestly! But, I'm glad she left me for one of the last. If I had to go first, like you, I don't think I could open my mouth. You were so calm. You started the thing off very well."

66 "You go on now, I was nervous myself!" He laughed, pleased.

67 "Mira, Chiquitín," Lali giggled, "I didn't know your name was Horacio. William Horacio. Ave María, so imposing!"

68 "That's right, because you see, my mother was expecting a valiant warrior! Instead, well"—he threw up his hands—"no one warned me either. And what a name for a Chiquitín like me."

69 Lali smiled, saying nothing. At first she had been very aware of William's dwarfishness. Now it no longer mattered. It was only when she saw others

reacting to him for the first time that she was once more momentarily struck with William's physical difference.

"We should really try to speak in English, Lali. It would be good practice for us."                                                                        70

"Dios mío . . . I feel so foolish, and my accent is terrible!"                   71

"But look, we all have to start some place. Besides, what about the Americanos? When they speak Spanish, they sound pretty awful, but we accept it. You know I'm right. And that's how people get ahead, by not being afraid to try."   72

They walked in silence for a few moments. Since William had begun to work at Rudi's, Lali's life had become less lonely. Lali was shy by nature; making friends was difficult for her. She had grown up in the sheltered environment of a large family living in a tiny mountain village. She was considered quite plain. Until Rudi had asked her parents for permission to court her, she had only gone out with two local boys. She had accepted his marriage proposal expecting great changes in her life. But the age difference between her and Rudi, being in a strange country without friends or relatives, and the long hours of work at the luncheonette confined Lali to a way of life she could not have imagined. Every evening she found herself waiting for William to come in to work, looking forward to his presence.                                                            73

Lali glanced over at him as they started across the wide busy street. His grip on her elbow was firm but gentle as he led her to the sidewalk.          74

"There you are, Miss Lali, please to watch your step!" he spoke in English.   75

His thick golden-blond hair was slightly mussed and fell softly, partially covering his forehead. His wide smile, white teeth and large shoulders made him appear quite handsome. Lali found herself staring at William. At that moment she wished he could be just like everybody else.                        76

"Lali?" William asked, confused by her silent stare. "Is something wrong?"   77

"No." Quickly Lali turned her face. She felt herself blushing. "I . . . I was just thinking how to answer in English, that's all."                           78

"But that's it . . . don't think! What I mean is, don't go worrying about what to say. Just talk natural. Get used to simple phrases and the rest will come, you'll see."                                                                     79

"All right," Lali said, glad the strange feeling of involvement had passed, and William had taken no notice of it. "It's an interesting class, don't you think so? I mean—like that man, the professor. Bendito! Imagine, they had to leave because they were Jewish. What a terrible thing!"                              80

"I don't believe he's Jewish; it's his wife who is Jewish. She was a professor too. But I guess they don't wanna be separated . . . and they have a child."    81

"Tsk, tsk, los pobres! But, can you imagine, then? A professor from a university doing the job of a porter? My goodness!" Lali sighed. "I never heard of such a thing!"                                                                   82

"But you gotta remember, it's like Mrs. Hamma said, this is America, right? So . . . everybody got a chance to clean toilets! Equality, didn't she say that?"  83

84    They both laughed loudly, stepping up their pace until they reached Rudi's Luncheonette.

85    The small luncheonette was almost empty. One customer sat at the counter.

86    "Just in time," Rudi called out. "Let's get going. People gonna be coming in hungry any minute. I was beginning to worry about you two!"

87    William ran in the back to change into his workshirt.

88    Lali slipped into her uniform and soon was busy at the grill.

89    "Well, did you learn anything tonight?" Rudi asked her.

90    "Yes."

91    "What?"

92    "I don't know," she answered, without interrupting her work. "We just talked a little bit in English."

93    "A little bit in English—about what?"

94    Lali busied herself, ignoring him. Rudi waited, then tried once more.

95    "You remember what you talked about?" He watched her as she moved, working quickly, not looking in his direction.

96    "No." Her response was barely audible.

97    Lately Rudi had begun to reflect on his decision to marry such a young woman. Especially a country girl like Lali, who was shy and timid. He had never had children with his first wife and wondered if he lacked the patience needed for the young. They had little in common and certainly seldom spoke about anything but the business. Certainly he could not fault her for being lazy; she was always working without being asked. People would accuse him in jest of overworking his young wife. He assured them there was no need, because she had the endurance of a country mule. After almost one year of marriage, he felt he hardly knew Lali or what he might do to please her.

98    William began to stack clean glasses behind the counter.

99    "Chiquitín! How about you and Lali having something to eat? We gotta few minutes yet. There's some fresh rice pudding."

100    "Later . . . I'll have mine a little later, thanks."

101    "Ask her if she wants some." Rudi whispered, gesturing toward Lali.

102    William moved close to Lali and spoke softly to her.

103    "She said no." William continued his work.

104    "Listen, Chiquitín, I already spoke to Raquel Martinez who lives next door. You know, she's got all them kids? In case you people are late, she can cover for you and Lali. She said it was O.K."

105    "Thanks, Rudi, I appreciate it. But we'll get back on time."

106    "She's good, you know. She helps me out during the day whenever I need extra help. Off the books, I give her a few bucks. But, mira, I cannot pay you and Raquel both. So if she comes in, you don't get paid. You know that then, O.K.?"

107    "Of course. Thanks, Rudi."

108    "Sure, well, it's a good thing after all. You and Lali improving yourselves. Not that she really needs it, you know. I provide for her. As I said, she's my

wife, so she don't gotta worry. If she wants something, I'll buy it for her. I made it clear she didn't have to bother with none of that, but"—Rudi shrugged—"if that's what she wants, I'm not one to interfere."

The door opened. Several men walked in. 109

"Here they come, kids!" 110

Orders were taken and quickly filled. Customers came and went steadily 111 until about eleven o'clock, when Rudi announced that it was closing time.

The weeks passed, then the months, and this evening, William and Lali sat with 112 the other students listening to Mrs. Hamma as she taught the last lesson of the Basic English course.

"It's been fifteen long hard weeks for all of you. And I want you to know 113 how proud I am of each and every one here."

William glanced at Lali; he knew she was upset. He felt it too, wishing that 114 this was not the end of the course. It was the only time he and Lali had free to themselves together. Tuesday had become their evening.

Lali had been especially irritable that week, dreading this last session. For 115 her, Tuesday meant leaving the world of Rudi, the luncheonette, that street, everything that she felt imprisoned her. She was accomplishing something all by herself, and without the help of the man she was dependent upon.

Mrs. Hamma finally felt that she had spent enough time assuring her 116 students of her sincere appreciation.

"I hope some of you will stay and have a cup of coffee or tea, and cookies. 117 There's plenty over there." She pointed to a side table where a large electric coffeepot filled with hot water was steaming. The table was set for instant coffee and tea, complete with several boxes of assorted cookies. "I do this every semester for my classes. I think it's nice to have a little informal chat with one another; perhaps discuss our plans for the future and so on. But it must be in English! Especially those of you who are Spanish speaking. Just because you outnumber the rest of us, don't you think you can get away with it!" Mrs. Hamma lifted her forefinger threateningly but smiled. "Now, it's still early, so there's plenty of time left. Please turn in your books."

Some of the people said good-bye quickly and left, but the majority waited, 118 helping themselves to coffee or tea and cookies. Small clusters formed as people began to chat with one another.

Diego Torres and Aldo Fabrizi were engaged in a friendly but heated debate 119 on the merits of citizenship.

"Hey, you come here a minute, please," Aldo Fabrizi called out to William, 120 who was standing with a few people by the table, helping himself to coffee. William walked over to the two men.

"What's the matter?" 121

"What do you think of your paisano. He don't wanna be citizen. I say—my 122 opinion—he don't appreciate what he got in this country. This is a great country! You the same like him, what do you think?"

123     "Mira, please tell him we no the same," Diego Torres said with exasperation. "You a citizen, pero not me. Este tipo no comprende, man!"

124     "Listen, yo comprendo . . . yo capito! I know what you say. He be born in Puerto Rico. But you see, we got the same thing. I be born in Sicily—that is another part of the country, separate. But I still Italiano, capito?"

125     "Dios mío!" Diego Torres smacked his forehead with an open palm. "Mira"—he turned to William—"explain to him, por favor."

126     William swallowed a mouthful of cookies. "He's right. Puerto Rico is part of the United States. And Sicily is part of Italy. But not the Dominican Republic where he been born. There it is not the United States. I was born a citizen, do you see?"

127     "Sure!" Aldo Fabrizi nodded. "Capito. Hey, but you still no can vote, right?"

128     "Sure I can vote; I got all the rights. I am a citizen, just like anybody else," William assured him.

129     "You some lucky guy then. You got it made! You don't gotta worry like the rest of—"

130     "Bullshit," Diego Torres interrupted. "Why he got it made, man? He force to leave his country. Pendejo, you no capito nothing, man . . ."

131     As the two men continued to argue, William waited for the right moment to slip away and join Lali.

132     She was with some of the women, who were discussing how sincere and devoted Mrs. Hamma was.

133     "She's hardworking . . ."

134     "And she's good people . . ." an older woman agreed.

135     Mr. Fong joined them, and they spoke about the weather and how nice and warm the days were.

136     Slowly people began to leave, shaking hands with their fellow students and Mrs. Hamma, wishing each other luck.

137     Mrs. Hamma had been hoping to speak to Stephan Paczkowski privately this evening, but he was always with a group. Now he offered his hand.

138     "I thank you very much for your good teaching. It was a fine semester."

139     "Oh, do you think so? Oh, I'm so glad to hear you say that. You don't know how much it means. Especially coming from a person of your caliber. I am confident, yes, indeed, that you will soon be back to your profession, which, after all, is your true calling. If there is anything I can do, please . . ."

140     "Thank you, miss. This time I am registering in Hunter College, which is in Manhattan on Sixty-fifth Street in Lexington Avenue, with a course of English Literature for beginners." After a slight bow, he left.

141     "Good-bye." Mrs. Hamma sighed after him.

142     Lali, William, and several of the women picked up the paper cups and napkins and tossed them into the trash basket.

143     "Thank you so much, that's just fine. Luis the porter will do the rest. He takes care of these things. He's a lovely person and very helpful. Thank you."

William shook hands with Mrs. Hamma, then waited for Lali to say good-  144
bye. They were the last ones to leave.

"Both of you have been such good students. What are your plans? I hope  145
you will continue with your English."

"Next term we're taking another course," Lali said, looking at William.  146

"Yes," William responded, "it's more advance. Over at the Washington  147
Irving High School around Fourteenth Street."

"Wonderful." Mrs. Hamma hesitated. "May I ask you a question before you  148
leave? It's only that I'm a little curious about something."

"Sure, of course." They both nodded.  149

"Are you two related? I mean, you are always together and yet have different  150
last names, so I was just . . . wondering."

"Oh, we are just friends," Lali answered, blushing.  151

"I work over in the luncheonette at night, part-time."  152

"Of course." Mrs. Hamma looked at Lali. "Mrs. Padillo, your husband's  153
place of business. My, that's wonderful, just wonderful! You are all just so
ambitious. Very good . . ."

They exchanged farewells.  154

Outside, the warm June night was sprinkled with the sweetness of the new  155
buds sprouting on the scrawny trees and hedges planted along the sidewalks and
in the housing project grounds. A brisk breeze swept over the East River on to
Houston Street, providing a freshness in the air.

This time they were early, and Lali and William strolled at a relaxed pace.  156

"Well," Lali shrugged, "that's that. It's over!"  157

"Only for a couple of months. In September we'll be taking a more advanced  158
course at the high school."

"I'll probably forget everything I learned by then."  159

"Come on, Lali, the summer will be over before you know it. Just you wait  160
and see. Besides, we can practice so we don't forget what Mrs. Hamma taught
us."

"Sure, what do you like to speak about?" Lali said in English.  161

William smiled, and clasping his hands, said, "I would like to say to you  162
how wonderful you are, and how you gonna have the most fabulous future . . .
after all, you so ambitious!"

When she realized he sounded just like Mrs. Hamma, Lali began to laugh.  163

"Are you"—Lali tried to keep from giggling, tried to pretend to speak in  164
earnest—"sure there is some hope for me?"

"Oh, heavens, yes! You have shown such ability this"—William was begin-  165
ning to lose control, laughing loudly—"semester!"

"But I want"—Lali was holding her sides with laughter—"some guarantee  166
of this. I got to know."

"Please, Miss Lali." William was laughing so hard tears were coming to his  167
eyes. "After . . . after all, you now a member in good standing . . . of the promised
future!"

168    William and Lali broke into uncontrollable laughter, swaying and limping, oblivious to the scene they created for the people who stared and pointed at them as they continued on their way to Rudi's.  ✚

---

RESPONDING

1.  Adopt the persona of one of the characters in the story and, in your journal, write a letter telling friends or family about your English class and your future in America.

2.  Working individually or in a group, make a list of all the participants in Mrs. Hamma's class and identify them by gender, ethnicity, age (if possible), and class (level of education, economic status). What are their attitudes toward each other and the teacher? What do they have in common, and how are they different? Speculate about what the future in America holds for them.

3.  Mrs. Hamma claims that "everybody here must be treated equally. This is America!" (paragraph 56). Write an essay discussing how she treats her students. Is everyone in the class treated the same way, or does she treat some differently based on the students' ethnicity, class, and gender?

4.  In an essay, argue whether the story does or does not support the notion of the American dream, with equality and opportunity for all. Is the promise of America the same for all new immigrants?

---

# JUDITH ORTIZ COFER

*Born in Puerto Rico in 1952, Judith Ortiz Cofer immigrated to the United States with her family in 1956. After earning her bachelor's degree from Augusta College and her master's degree from Florida Atlantic University, she spent a year at Oxford University in 1977. Since then she has taught English and Spanish at several universities, including the University of Miami and the University of Georgia. Cofer's publications include the novel* The Line of the Sun *(1985), the essay collection* Silent Dancing *(1990),* The Latin Deli *(1993), An Island Like You *(1995),* The Year of Our Revolution *(1998), and several volumes of poetry.*

*The following excerpt from* The Line of the Sun *explores some of the contrasts between what the narrator calls life in "the tropical paradise" and life on the streets of Paterson, New Jersey. The narrator speculates on how her life would have been different if her family had remained in Puerto Rico. In so doing, the narrative suggests the importance of the imagination in fashioning one's view of both the present and the past.*

#### ⁜

# From THE LINE OF THE SUN

It was a bitter winter in Paterson. The snow fell white and dry as coconut shavings, but as soon as it touched the dirty pavement it turned into a muddy soup. Though we wore rubber boots, our feet stayed wet and cold all day. The bitter wind brought hot tears to our eyes, but it was so cold that we never felt them streaking our cheeks.

During Lent the nuns counted attendance at the seven o'clock mass and gave demerits if we did not take into our dry mouths Christ's warm body in the form of a wafer the priest held in his palm. The church was dark at that hour of the morning, and thick with the steaming garments of children dropped off by anxious mothers or, like us, numb from a seven-block walk.

In the hour of the mass, I thawed in the sweet unctuousness of the young Italian priest's voice chanting his prayers for the souls of these young children and their teachers, for their parents, for the dead and the living, for our deprived brothers and sisters, some of whom had not found comfort in Christ and were now in mortal danger of damning their souls to the raging fire of hell. He didn't really say hell, a word carefully avoided in our liturgy: it was all innuendo and Latin words that sounded like expletives. *Kyrie Eleison*, he would challenge; *Christe Eleison*, we would respond heartily, led by the strong voice of Sister Mary Beata, our beautiful homeroom teacher, whose slender body and perfect features were evident in spite of the layers of clothing she wore and the coif that surrounded her face. She was the envy of our freshman-class girls. In the classroom I sat in the back watching her graceful movements, admiring the translucent quality of her unblemished skin, wondering whether both her calm and her beauty were a gift from God, imagining myself in the medieval clothes of her nun's habit.

I sat in the last desk of the last row of the girl's side of the room, the smallest, darkest member of a class full of the strapping offspring of Irish immigrants with a few upstart Italians recently added to the roll. The blazing red hair of Jackie O'Connell drew my eyes like a flame to the center of the room, and the pattern of freckles on her nose fascinated me. She was a popular girl with the sisters; her father was a big-shot lawyer with political ambitions. Donna Finney was well developed for her age, her woman's body restrained within the angular lines of the green-and-white plaid uniform we would wear until our junior year, when we would be allowed to dress like young ladies in a pleated green skirt and white blouse. Donna sat in the row closest to the boys' side of the room.

5    The boys were taller and heavier than my friends at El Building; they wore their blue ties and opened doors for girls naturally, as if they did it at home too. At school we were segregated by sex: every classroom was divided into girlside and boyside, and even the playground had an imaginary line right down the middle, where the assigned nun of the day would stand guard at recess and lunchtime. There were some couples in the school, of course. Everyone knew Donna went with a junior boy, a basketball player named Mickey Salvatore, an Italian playing on our Fighting Irish team—and it was a known fact that they went out in his car. After school some girls met their boyfriends at Schulze's drugstore for a soda. I saw them go in on my way home. My mother, following Rafael's instructions, gave us thirty minutes to get home before she put on her coat and high heels and came looking for us. I had just enough time to round up my brother at the grammar-school building across the street and walk briskly the seven blocks home. No soda for me with friends at Schulze's.

6    Ramona had come looking for us one day when an afternoon assembly had held me up, and that episode had taught me a lesson. Her long black hair loose and wild from the wind, she was wearing black spiked shoes and was wrapped in a red coat and black shawl when she showed up outside the school building. The kids stared at her as if she were a circus freak, and the nuns looked doubtful, thinking perhaps they should ask the gypsy to leave the school grounds. One boy said something about her that made a hot blush of shame creep up my neck and burn my cheeks. They didn't know—couldn't know—that she was my mother, since Rafael made all our school arrangements every year, explaining that his wife could not speak English and therefore would not be attending PTA meetings and so forth. My mother looked like no other mother at the school, and I was glad she did not participate in school activities. Even on Sunday she went to the Spanish mass while we attended our separate service for children. My gypsy mother embarrassed me with her wild beauty. I wanted her to cut and spray her hair into a sculptured hairdo like the other ladies; I wanted her to wear tailored skirts and jackets like Jackie Kennedy; I even resented her youth, which made her look like my older sister. She was what I would have looked like if I hadn't worn my hair in a tight braid, if I had allowed myself to sway when I walked, and if I had worn loud colors and had spoken only Spanish.

7    I was beginning to understand why Rafael wanted to move us away from El Building. The older I got, the more embarrassed I felt about living in this crowded, noisy tenement, which the residents seemed intent on turning into a bizarre facsimile of an Island barrio. But for a while my fascination with Guzmán overpowered all other feelings, and when I came home from the organized, sanitized world of school, I felt drawn into his sickroom like an opium addict. I looked forward to the air thick with the smells of many cigarettes and of alcohol. More and more I took over the nursing duties which Ramona, with her

impatient hands, relished little. She was used to fast-healing children and an absent husband. Guzmán's bleeding wound and his careful movements tried her patience.

And so it happened that my uncle and I began talking. Guzmán told me          8
about his childhood on the Island in general terms, leaving out things he did not think I would understand, but his silences and omissions were fuel to my imagination and I filled in the details. I questioned him about his friend Rosa, whose name came up whenever he began to describe the Island. It was as if she were the embodiment of all that was beautiful, strange, and tempting about his homeland. He told me about her amazing knowledge of plants and herbs, how she knew what people needed just by talking to them. Once I asked him to describe her to me. His eyes had been closed as he spoke, seeing her, I suppose; but he opened them like one who slowly rises from a dream and looked at me, sitting by the side of his bed in my blue-and-white first Friday uniform, my hair pulled back in a tightly wound bun.

"Let your hair down," he said.          9

I reached back and pulled the long black pins out of my thick hair, letting          10
it fall over my shoulders. It was quite long, and I never wore it loose.

"She had long black hair like yours," he said rising on his elbows to look          11
intently into my face as if seeing me for the first time. I noticed his knuckles going white from the effort. "And she was light-complexioned like you." He fell back on the pillow, groaning a little. Ramona came in at that moment with fresh bandages and looked strangely at me sitting there with my hair undone, but did not say anything. Ordering Guzmán to shift to his side, she changed his bandage briskly.

"I need you to go to the bodega for me, Marisol," she said, not looking at          12
me. I hated going into the gloomy little Spanish grocery store with its fishy smell and loiterers who always had something smart to say to women.

"Why can't you send Gabriel?" I asked petulantly, feeling once again that          13
strain developing between my mother and me which kept getting more in the way of all our attempts at communication. She refused to acknowledge the fact that I was fast becoming too old to order around.

"He is doing his homework." Tucking the sheet around her brother as if          14
he were another child, she turned to me. "Just do what I tell you, niña, without arguments or back talk. It looks like we are going to have a serious discussion with your father when he comes home." She looked at me meaningfully.

When she left the room I braided my hair slowly. It was the new impasse          15
we had reached. I would obey her but I would take my time doing so, pushing her to a steady burning anger which could no longer be relieved by the familiar routine of spanking, tears, reconciliation. It was a contest of wills that I knew no one could win, but Ramona was still hoping Rafael would know how to mediate. He was the absent disciplinarian—Solomon, the wise judge, the threat and the promise that hung over us day after day in her constant "when your father comes home."

16    I couldn't understand how she continued to treat me like a child when she had not been much older than I when she married Rafael. If I were on the Island I would be respected as a young woman of marriageable age. I had heard Ramona talking with her friends about a girl's fifteenth year, the *Quinceañera*, when everything changes for her. She no longer plays with children; she dresses like a woman and joins the women at coffee in the afternoon; she is no longer required to attend school if there is more pressing need for her at home, or if she is engaged. I was almost fifteen now—still in my silly uniform, bobby socks and all; still not allowed to socialize with my friends, living in a state of limbo, halfway between cultures. No one at school asked why I didn't participate in the myriad parish activities. They all understood that Marisol was *different*.

17    Talking with my uncle, listening to stories about his life on the Island, and hearing Ramona's constant rhapsodizing about that tropical paradise—all conspired to make me feel deprived. I should have grown up there. I should have been able to play in emerald-green pastures, to eat sweet bananas right off the trees, to learn about life from the women who were strong and wise like the fabled Mamá Cielo. How could she be Ramona's mother? Ramona, who could not make a decision without invoking the name of our father, whose judgment we awaited like the Second Coming.

18    As I reached for the door to leave Guzmán's room, he stirred.

19    "Rosa," he said, groggy from medication.

20    "Do you need anything?" I was trembling.

21    Alert now, he pointed to the dresser against the wall. "Take my wallet from the top drawer and get me a carton of L&M's when you go to the bodega." He closed his eyes again, whispering, "Thanks, niña."

22    I took his wallet, unwilling to make more noise by looking through it for money. In the kitchen Ramona was washing dishes at the sink, her back to me, but she was aware of my presence, and her anger showed in the set of her shoulders. I suddenly remembered how much she used to laugh, and still did when she was around her women friends.

23    "The list and the money are on the table, Marisol. Don't take long. I need to start dinner soon."

24    I put my coat on and left the apartment. The smells of beans boiling in a dozen kitchens assailed my nostrils. Rice and beans, the unimaginative staple food of all these people who re-created every day the same routines they had followed in their mamá's houses so long ago. Except that here in Paterson, in the cold rooms stories about the frozen ground, the smells and sounds of a lost way of life could only be a parody.

25    Instead of heading out the front door and to the street, an impulse carried my feet down an extra flight of stairs to El Basement. It was usually deserted at this hour when everyone was preparing to eat. I sat on the bottom step and looked around me at the cavernous room. A yellow light hung over my head. I took Guzmán's wallet from my coat pocket. Bringing it close to my face, I smelled the old leather. Carefully I unfolded it flat on my lap. There were several photos in the plastic. On top was a dark Indian-looking woman whose features

looked familiar. Her dark, almond-shaped eyes were just like Ramona's, but her dark skin and high cheekbones were Guzmán's. I guessed this was an early picture of my grandmother, Mamá Cielo. Behind that there was one of two teenage boys, one dark, one blond. They were smiling broadly, arms on each other's shoulders. There was a fake moon in the background like the ones they use in carnival photo booths. Though the picture was bent, cutting the boys at the neck, and of poor quality, I recognized them: it was Guzmán and Rafael. I looked at it for a long time, especially at my father's face, almost unrecognizable to me with its unfamiliar look of innocent joy. Perhaps they had been drinking that night. I had often heard Ramona talking about the festivals dedicated to Our Lady of Salud, the famous smiling Virgin. Maybe they had the photo taken then. Was this the night that Guzmán had seen Rosa dressed like a gypsy at the fair? I had heard that story told late at night in my mother's kitchen, eavesdropping while I pretended to sleep. Did Rafael know Ramona then—was he happy because he was in love with the beautiful fourteen-year-old sister of his best friend?

In one of the plastic windows there was a newspaper clipping, yellow and torn, of a Spanish actress, wild black hair falling like a violent storm around a face made up to look glamorous, eyelashes thickened black, glossy lips parted in an open invitation. She was beautiful. I had seen her face often in the magazines my mother bought at the bodega, but why did Guzmán carry this woman's picture around? Was this what Rosa had looked like, or was she just his fantasy? 26

Deeply engrossed in my secret activity of going through my uncle's wallet, I was startled to hear men's voices approaching the top of the landing. I sat still waiting for them to go up the stairs, but they came down instead. There were four or five whose faces I recognized in the dim light as the working men of El Building, young husbands whose wives were Ramona's friends. I was not afraid, but I hid the wallet in my coat pocket and quickly got to my feet. My mind raced to come up with an excuse, though it was *their* presence in El Basement that was odd. The laundry room was used legitimately by women and otherwise by kids. The only other users, as I very well knew from my encounter with José and the woman, were people who wanted to hide what they were doing. 27

The voice I heard most clearly was that of Santiago, the only man from El Building ever to have been invited by Rafael into our apartment. After a severe winter week several years before, we had been left without heat until this man went down to city hall and got a judge to force the building superintendent to do something about the frozen heater pipes. Rafael had been in Europe at the time, but he obviously respected Santiago. 28

Coming down the steps, Santiago's voice directed the others. One man was to stand at the top and wait for the others, the rest were to follow him into the basement. He nearly stumbled over me in the dim light, not seeing me wrapped in my gray coat. 29

"Niña, *por Dios*, what are you doing here at this hour?" His voice was gentle but I detected irritation. 30

31     "My mother lost something here earlier and sent me down to try to find it." I explained rather rapidly in my awkward formal Spanish.

32     He took my elbow in a fatherly way: "Marisol, I don't believe your mother would be so careless as to send you down here to this dark place at the dinner hour alone. But I won't mention that I saw you here, and you must do the same for me, for us. These men and I want to have a private conversation. Do you understand?"

33     "Yes," I said quickly, wanting to be released from his firm grasp, "I won't say anything." He let go of my arm and I ran up the stairs. Several other men had arrived and were talking in hushed tones at the top of the steps. I managed to catch a few sentences as I slipped by their surprised faces and into the streets. It was the factory they were discussing. Someone had said *huelga*, a strike. They were planning a strike.

34     Outside it was cold, but not bitter; a hint of spring in the breeze cooled my cheeks without biting into my skin. For once I felt a sense of pride in my father, who had managed to escape the horrible trap of factory work, though he was paying a high price for it. Tonight I'd have something to talk about with Guzmán. He would be interested in the secret basement meeting and the strike. ✤

---

## RESPONDING

1. Discuss Marisol's reaction to her mother's visit to her school. What ideal image does she have in mind for her mother? In a journal entry, talk about a time when you (or someone you know) were in a situation where you felt out of place and wanted to fit in.

2. Working individually or in a group, discuss the conflict of wills between mother and daughter. List examples of their encounters and the reactions of each participant. How much of Marisol's behavior do you think is adolescent rebellion, and how much is a response to her mother's personality?

3. Describe Puerto Rico as Marisol pictures it. In what ways do you think Marisol might have idealized the Island? In an essay, discuss the role of Puerto Rico in helping Marisol deal with her everyday life.

4. Marisol describes herself as "halfway between cultures" (paragraph 16). Using information from this and other readings in this chapter as well as outside information, write an essay comparing her lifestyle at fifteen in Paterson, New Jersey, to what her life would have been like if she had been born and raised in Puerto Rico.

# Martin Espada

*The poet and lawyer Martín Espada was born in Brooklyn, New York, in 1957. He earned a bachelor's degree in history from the University of Wisconsin-Madison and a law degree from Northeastern University. Espada's poems, which have been published in many journals, are collected in his books* The Immigrant Iceboy's Bolero *(1982),* Trumpets from the Islands of Their Eviction *(1987),* Rebellion Is the Circle of a Lover's Hands *(1990),* City of Coughing and Dead Radiators *(1993), and* Imagine the Angels of Bread *(1996). He has also edited* Poetry Like Bread: Poets of the Political Imagination *(1996). Espada has received the PEN/Revsen Prize and the Paterson Poetry Prize as well as fellowships from the Massachusetts Artists' Foundation and the National Endowment for the Arts, among other awards. In addition to addressing the Nuyorican experience, Espada has traveled extensively in Puerto Rico and Nicaragua, writing about political issues there as well. Espada teaches literature and creative writing at the University of Massachusetts, Amherst.*

*The poem that follows, from Espada's first collection, addresses the ways in which people forced to live amidst urban decay and deterioration are robbed of their dignity. The poet has stressed the special role of language (what he has called "la fuerza moral de la palabra") for the poor, the oppressed, and the powerless.*[1]

⁜

# MRS. BAEZ SERVES COFFEE ON THE THIRD FLOOR

It hunches
with a brittle black spine
where they poured
gasoline on the stairs
and the bannister                                     5
and burnt it.

The fire went running
down the steps,
a naked lunatic,

---

1. Quotation from *Papiros de Babel: Antología de la poesía puertorriqueña en Nueva York.*

10
calling the names
of the neighbors,
cackling in the hall.

The immigrants
ate terror with their hands
15
and prayed to Catholic statues
as the fire company
pumped a million gallons in
and burst the roof,
as an old man
20
on the top floor
with no name known
to authorities
strangled on the smoke
and stopped breathing.

25
Some of the people left.
There's a room
on the third floor:
high-heeled shoes kicked off,
a broken dresser,
30
the saint's portrait
hanging where it looked on
shrugging shoulders for years,
soot, trash, burnt tile,
a perfect black light bulb
35
to remember everything.

And some stayed. The old men
barechested, squatting
on the milk crates to play dominoes
in the front-stoop sun;
40
the younger ones, the tigres,
watching the block with unemployed faces
bitter as bad liquor;
Mrs. Baez, who serves coffee
on the third floor
45
from tiny porcelain cups,
insisting that we stay;
the children who live
between narrow kitchens

and charred metal doors
and laugh anyway;                                                    50
the skinny man, the one
just arrived from Santo Domingo,
who cannot read or write,
with no hot water
for six weeks,                                                       55
telling us in the hallway
that the landlord set the fire
and everyone knows it,
the building's worth more empty.

The street organizer said it:                                       60
burn the building out,
blacken an old Dominicano's lungs
and sell
so that the money-people
can renovate                                                        65
and live here
where an old Dominicano died,
over the objections
of his choking spirit.

But some have stayed.                                               70
Stayed for the malicious winter,
stayed frightened
of the white man who comes
to collect rent
and borrowing from cousins                                          75
to pay it,
stayed waiting for the next fire,
and the siren,
hysterical and late.

Someone poured gasoline                                             80
on the steps outside her door,
but Mrs. Baez
still serves coffee
in porcelain cups
to strangers,                                                       85
coffee the color
of a young girl's skin
in Santo Domingo. ✠

## RESPONDING

1. In a journal entry, work through the poem and explain what is happening in prose.

2. Working individually or in a group, list the images (sensory description of places, people, and things) that give this poem its power. Divide your list into images you consider negative and those you consider positive. What is the overall emotional effect this poem has on you, and how do its images help create that effect?

3. The poem says, "building's worth more empty" (lines 58–59). Adopt the point of view of the landlord or one of the tenants and write a letter to the editor of the local newspaper explaining your reaction to that statement.

4. Imagine that you are one of the residents of the building. Write a story about what your home means to you. Why would you stay in this building after the fire? What might your options be?

# LINDA CHAVEZ

*Linda Chavez, who describes herself as the daughter of an Anglo mother and a "conservative Spanish American [father] whose family had roots in the Southwest dating back three hundred years," was born in Albuquerque, New Mexico, in 1947. After receiving a bachelor's degree from the University of Colorado in 1970, she pursued graduate study at the University of California at Los Angeles. She served as Director of the Commission on Civil Rights and later as Director of the White House Office of Public Liaison during the administration of President Ronald Reagan. Since 1986, Chavez has held positions in several private organizations. Until 1988, she was president of U.S. English, a group advocating English as the official language of the United States. Later, she became the director of the Center for the New American Community, a group opposed to multiculturalism. She is the author of* Out of the Barrio: Towards a New Politics of Hispanic Assimilation *(1991), as well as essays in the* New York Times, New Republic, *and* Washington Post, *among others.*

*In the following essay from* Human Events *(1998), Chavez states her arguments for opposing Puerto Rican statehood.*

❖

# NO TO PUERTO RICAN STATEHOOD

Republican leaders are about to do something so stupid and venal that maybe  1
they don't deserve to retain control of Congress in this year's election.

They want to make Puerto Rico the 51st state in the union, and this week,  2
the House will vote on a measure to start the process. Why? Expect to hear
plenty of platitudes about self-determination and full democracy for Puerto
Rico's 3.7 million people. But what the Republicans are really interested in is
the potential votes of some 25 million Hispanics on the U.S. mainland.

Only a fool or a desperate Republican could ever imagine that the average  3
Mexican-American in East Los Angeles or Cuban-American in Miami gives a
hoot about statehood for Puerto Rico. But the hope that Puerto Rican statehood
would entice more Hispanics into voting Republican is what is driving this
monumentally bad idea that could cost billions in increased federal aid and
permanently alter the culture of the United States.

Puerto Rico became an American territory in 1898 after the United States  4
won the Spanish-American War. Everyone born on the island is a U.S. citizen
by birth, and all males are subject to the draft. The island is currently considered
a "commonwealth," with its own elected government and laws, subject to the
U.S. Constitution and federal court jurisdiction.

On the other hand, Puerto Ricans living on the island do not pay federal  5
taxes, cannot vote in presidential elections and elect only a nonvoting member
(called resident commissioner) to the U.S. House of Representatives.

All that would change under the bill to be voted on this week. The proposed  6
legislation will allow Puerto Ricans to vote on whether they wish to become a
state. If a bare majority voting in the plebiscite support statehood, Congress will
be locked into a transition plan, making the island a state in 10 years.

So, what makes this such a bad idea? For starters, Puerto Rico is a linguis-  7
tically and culturally autonomous island with a rich modern history that dates
back nearly 100 years before Jamestown and Plymouth Rock. Puerto Ricans
don't consider themselves Americans even though they are U.S. citizens—only
16% defined themselves as Americans in one recent poll.

Fewer than 20% of Puerto Ricans speak English, and the bill does nothing  8
to ensure that Puerto Ricans—especially schoolchildren—learn English if
Puerto Rico becomes a state.

In fact, there is nothing Congress can do to force Puerto Ricans to learn  9
English, even if Congress makes the acceptance of English a condition of
statehood. As the current congressional delegate from Puerto Rico, Resident
Commissioner Carlos Romero-Barcelo, told me personally a few months ago,
once Puerto Rico becomes a state, the legislature would simply revoke English
as its official language and put in place Spanish or both Spanish and English.

10    The likely outcome for the rest of the nation would be increased pressure to make the United States bilingual—or at least those states with large Spanish-speaking populations, such as California, Texas, Florida, New York and Illinois. Hispanic activists have been promoting this agenda for years and already have succeeded in mandating Spanish language instruction for some two million Hispanic youngsters in public schools and bilingual ballots in federal elections.

11    As worrisome as the cultural implications for Puerto Rican statehood are, however, the dismal economy on the island should be cause for even greater alarm. In 1990, one-half of all Puerto Rican families earned less than $10,000 a year, 20% of Puerto Ricans were unemployed, and an additional 52% were out of the labor force altogether.

12    More than half the island's population already receives some form of public assistance, and 59% would qualify for the Earned Income Tax Credit once Puerto Rico becomes a state—at an estimated cost to American taxpayers of $18 billion in additional federal outlays.

13    As Romero-Barcelo, an avid statehood supporter, succinctly put it in his 1978 book *Statehood Is for the Poor:* "Puerto Rico's per capita contribution to the U.S. federal treasury, were we a state, would come to less than that of any other state in the Union. At the same time, the per capita benefits we'd reap from federal aid programs would be greater than those of any other state in the Union."

14    It is simply not in anyone's interest to grant statehood under these circumstances. When Puerto Ricans become economically self-sufficient and decide they want to learn English—as my Spanish-speaking ancestors did in New Mexico before it became a state in 1912—Republicans and everyone else should welcome them with open arms. But not until then. ✢

---

## RESPONDING

1. Imagine that you live in a territory of the United States. You are an American citizen, but you cannot vote. In a journal entry, write a letter to a politician telling her how you feel about the situation.

2. Working individually or in a group, list the arguments for and against statehood for Puerto Rico. Use information from this article and material from other sources, such as the Internet. Use the Internet to investigate the current state of the debate over Puerto Rico.

3. In an essay, explain why Chavez is opposed to Puerto Rican statehood at this time. Do you agree or disagree with her views?

# Rosario Ferre

*The novelist Rosario Ferre was born in San Juan, Puerto Rico, in 1938. She is the daughter of Lorenza Ramirez and Luis Ferre (the former governor of the Island). Rosario Ferre attended Manhattanville College. She earned her master's degree from the University of Puerto Rico and her doctorate from the University of Maryland (1986). She has held teaching positions at several institutions, including Georgetown University, the University of California— Berkeley, Johns Hopkins University, and the University of Puerto Rico. She has written several books, including* Sweet Diamond Dust *(1986),* The Youngest Doll *(1991),* House on the Lagoon *(1995), and* Eccentric Neighborhoods *(1999).*

*In the following essay, Ferre expresses her views in favor of Puerto Rican statehood.*

⌗

# PUERTO RICO, U.S.A.

. . . As a PUERTO RICAN WRITER, I constantly face the problem of identity. When I travel to the States I feel as Latina as Chita Rivera. But in Latin America, I feel more American than John Wayne. To be Puerto Rican is to be a hybrid. Our two halves are inseparable: we cannot give up either without feeling maimed.  1

For many years, my concern was to keep my Hispanic self from being stifled. Now I discover it's my American self that's being threatened.  2

I recently was on a book tour in the United States. Wherever I went, people who knew about the plebiscite asked, "Why do you want to be American?"  3

The question was unsettling. Puerto Ricans have been Americans for almost a hundred years. At least 6,000 Puerto Ricans, have died fighting for the United States, and many thousands more served in Korea and Vietnam. My son led a platoon of Puerto Rican soldiers in the Persian Gulf war. At the time, no one asked if he wanted to be an American. He simply did his duty.  4

Puerto Ricans living on the mainland think of the island in much the same way as African-Americans think of Africa—as an almost mythical place inhabited by ancestral gods. For those Puerto Ricans, the homeland is a place of origin, proof of a vital "difference" that sets them apart from what can seem the vast sameness of the United States.  5

6    Puerto Ricans living in the United States also point out that crime, drugs, AIDS and other ills are the result of too much American-style progress. They want us on the island to preserve the bucolic paradise they left behind, a place where one could drive lazily down half-deserted avenues, walk in the streets at night without feeling terrified, go for a drive in mountains still covered with lush vegetation.

7    But this paradise exists only in their minds. Puerto Ricans have already joined the first world, deeply involved with American interests.

8    Puerto Ricans have contributed more than $500,000 to political campaigns in the United States. We have our reasons. The outcome of the Senate vote could have a great impact. Since we have practically no natural resources, independence would be sure to hurt Puerto Rico's economy. It would mean poverty, deteriorated health care and education, a disintegrating infrastructure and, worst of all, the disappearance of the Puerto Rican middle class.

9    In 1976 I lived in Mexico for a year and learned what it was like to live in a country that called itself a democracy, but where a small class of the wealthy dominates the vast majority, which is poor. Puerto Rico is different. Its strong middle class sets it apart. Our average income per household is $27,000; our annual per-capita income is $8,500, compared with $4,000 for most of Latin America.

10   The majority of Puerto Ricans prize their American citizenship. It represents for us economic stability and the assurance of civil liberties and democracy. On the other hand, we also cherish our language and culture. Thus, Puerto Rico's situation has historically been a paradox.

11   Living on the island, I've witnessed our Catch-22 situation from up close. I've lived through two plebiscites, both of them nonbinding, and have voted for independence. It was the only honorable solution, because losing our language and culture would have been a form of spiritual suicide.

12   But conditions have changed. Latinos are the fastest growing minority in the United States; by 2010 their numbers are expected to reach 39 million— more than the population of most Latin American republics. Bilingualism and multiculturalism are vital aspects of American society. Florida's Dade County is about 60 percent Hispanic. New York City, Los Angeles, Houston and Chicago all have large Hispanic populations. The reality is that we can no longer "be disappeared."

13   President Clinton recently declared, in no uncertain terms, that in order to become a state, Puerto Rico should not be forced to adopt English as its only official language and thereby abandon, possibly, its Hispanic culture. The decision on language, he said, should be left to Puerto Ricans, just as it was in the

case of Hawaii, where both English and the Hawaiian dialect were made official tongues.

Mr. Clinton's remark acknowledged that ethnic diversity has become a 14 fundamental value in the United States.

Puerto Ricans have been Americans since 1898, and our culture and language remain as healthy as ever. We are no longer poor, undernourished or anemic. We are mulatto-mestizo, bilingual and proud of it. We no longer need fear that "el otro," the other, will swallow us up. 15

We have become the other. As a Puerto Rican and an American, I believe 16 our future as a community is inseparable from our culture and language, but I'm also passionately committed to the modern world. That's why I'm going to support statehood in the next plebiscite. ✤

## RESPONDING

1. In a journal entry, explore what you know about Puerto Rico's geography, economy, and society.

2. Working individually or in a group, compare your knowledge against the information in Ferre's essay. Use the Internet to find additional information about conditions in Puerto Rico.

3. Ferre talks about the Puerto Rican paradox (paragraph 10). Write an essay discussing her reasons for calling the situation a paradox and the conflict Puerto Ricans feel when considering their relationship to the United States.

4. President Clinton has stated that Puerto Rico should not be forced to adopt English as its only official language. In an essay, agree or disagree with that position.

⊞

# CONNECTING

## *Critical Thinking and Writing*

1.   For many Puerto Ricans on the mainland, Puerto Rico continues to occupy an important place in their thoughts and dreams. Compare the different attitudes toward Puerto Rico held by the characters in the selections by Thomas, Mohr, and Cofer.

2.   Families such as Thomas's support each other emotionally as well as economically. Using examples from the readings in this chapter, write an essay discussing the importance of this emotional support for family members.

3.   Many of the readings describe situations involving insider/outsider relationships. Write an essay discussing those relationships using specific examples from the readings in this chapter, especially those of Colón and Espada.

4.   Most Puerto Rican immigrants settled in New York City. Speculate about the attraction of that particular large urban area as compared to a smaller town or a rural area. Compare conditions and opportunities in the city with those encountered by groups such as the Mexican immigrants, who often settled in farming communities.

5.   Design your own essay topic based on an issue emerging from these readings that engaged your interest.

6.   People moving to a new country often have a difficult time adjusting because they speak a different language or dialect or have different customs or a different culture. Compare the experiences of European immigrants, such as Constantine Panunzio in chapter 3, with the experiences of Puerto Ricans, such as Colón.

7.   Many of the readings in this book describe situations in which workers are exploited or their opportunities are limited. Write an essay arguing for or against the idea that much of that exploitation was based on racism.

8.   Write an essay defining what it means to be educated and illustrating your definition with examples from the readings and from your own observations. In your definition, does being educated include being "street smart" as well as "book smart"? Consider basic skills learned in school and those learned through experience. For example, Piri Thomas's mother, although not formally educated, is well informed about her own culture.

9. Using examples from this reading as well as from other readings in this book and your own experience, write an essay discussing the role of language and culture in forging bonds between immigrant groups.

10. Compare the living conditions described by Espada with those of early European immigrants.

11. Write an essay describing the current political situation in Puerto Rico. Consider the likelihood of statehood as well as what other options are available for the territory.

### *For Further Research*

1. Use the Internet to compare current socioeconomic conditions for recent Puerto Rican immigrants with those that existed when Puerto Rican immigrants arrived in the 1950s and 1960s.

2. Investigate the current demographics of Puerto Ricans in the United States. How many Puerto Ricans come to the continental United States each year? Where do they settle? What reasons do they have for leaving the Island? Compare those reasons to those of other current immigrant groups, for example, those from Latin America.

## REFERENCES AND ADDITIONAL SOURCES

Acosta-Belén, Edna, and Barbara R. Sjöstrom, eds. *The Hispanic Experience in the United States: Contemporary Issues and Perspective.* New York: Praeger, 1988.

Algarin, Miguel, and Miguel Pinero, eds. *Nuyorican Poetry: An Anthology of Puerto Rican Words and Feelings.* New York: William Morrow, 1975.

Bramen, Carrie Tirado. *"Puerto Rican-American Literature,"* in *New Immigrant Literatures in the United States: A Sourcebook to Our Multicultural Literary Heritage*, Alpana Sharma Knippling, ed. Westport, Conn.: Greenwood Press, 1996. 221–242.

Centro de Estudios Puertorriqueños, Oral History Task Force. *Labor Migration Under Capitalism: The Puerto Rican Experience.* New York: Monthly Review Press, 1979.

Cordasco, Francesco, and Eugene Bucchioni, eds. *The Puerto Rican Experience: A Sociological Sourcebook.* Totowa, N.J.: Rowman and Littlefield, 1973.

———. *The Puerto Ricans, 1493–1973: A Chronology and Fact Book.* Dobbs Ferry, N.Y.: Oceana, 1973.

Dietz, James. *Economic History of Puerto Rico: Institutional Change and Capitalist Development.* Princeton, N.J.: Princeton University Press, 1986.

Fitzpatrick, Joseph P. Puerto *Rican Americans: The Meaning of Migration to the Mainland.* Englewood Cliffs, N.J.: Prentice-Hall, 1971; 2nd ed. 1987.

Garcia-Passalacqua, Juan Manuel. Puerto *Rico: Equality and Freedom at Issue.* New York: Praeger, 1984.

Hauberg, Clifford A. *Puerto Rico and the Puerto Ricans.* New York: Twayne, 1974; New York: Hippocrene Books, 1984.

Hernández, Alvarez José. *Return Migration to Puerto Rico.* Berkeley: Institute of International Studies, University of California, 1967; Westport, Conn.: Greenwood Press, 1976.

Hernandez, Carmen Dolores. *Puerto Rican Voices in English: Interviews with Writers.* Westport, Conn.: Praeger, 1997.

Jennings, James, and Monte Rivera. *Puerto Rican Politics in Urban America.* Westport, Conn.: Greenwood Press, 1984.

Kanellos, Nicholas, ed. *Biographical Dictionary of Hispanic Literature in the United States: The Literature of Puerto Ricans, Cuban Americans, and Other Hispanic Writers.* Westport, Conn.: Greenwood Press, 1989.

Lopez, Adalberto, ed. *The Puerto Ricans: Their History, Culture and Society.* Cambridge, Mass.: Schenkman, 1980.

Luis, William. "Puerto Rican American Poetry: Street Rhythms and Voices of the People" and "Puerto Ricans in New York: Memoirs of Bernardo Vega and Piri Thomas's *Down These Mean Streets,*" in *Dance Between Two Cultures: Latino Caribbean Literature Written in the United States.* Nashville, Tenn.: Vanderbilt University Press, 1997. 37–147.

Mohr, Eugene V. *The Nuyorican Experience: Literature of the Puerto Rican Minority.* Westport, Conn.: Greenwood Press, 1982.

Mohr, Nicholasa. *El Bronx Remembered: A Novella and Stories,* 2nd ed. Houston: Arte Publico, 1986.

Morales Carrión, Arturo. *Puerto Rico: A Political and Cultural History.* New York: Norton, 1983; Nashville, Tenn.: American Association for State and Local History, 1983.

Ocasio, Rafael. "From Nuyorican Barrio Literature to Issues on Puerto Rican Literature Outside New York City: Nicholasa Mohr and Judith Ortiz Cofer," in *Literature and Ethnic Discrimination,* Michael J. Meyer, ed. Atlanta, Georgia: Rodopi, 1997. 187–203.

Ortiz Cofer, Judith. "Exile," in *Terms of Survival.* Houston: Arte Publico, 1995. 50.

Padilla, Elena. *Up from Puerto Rico.* New York: Columbia University Press, 1958.

Rodriguez, Clara E., et al., eds. *The Puerto Rican Struggle: Essays on Survival in the U.S.* Maplewood, N.J.: Waterfront, 1984.

Rodriguez de Laguna, Asela. *Images and Identities: The Puerto Rican in Two World Contexts.* New York: Puerto Rican Migration Research Consortium, 1980; New Brunswick, N.J.: Transaction Books, 1987.

Sánchez Korrol, Virginia E. *From Colonia to Community: The History of Puerto Ricans in New York City, 1917–1948.* Westport, Conn.: Greenwood Press, 1983.

Santiago, Roberto, ed. *Boricuas: Influential Puerto Rican Writings: An Anthology.* New York: One World, 1995.

Steven-Arroyo, Anthony M., and Ana María Díaz Ramírez. "Puerto Ricans in the States," in *The Minority Report*, 2nd ed., A. G. Dworkin and R. J. Dworkin, eds. New York: Holt, Rinehart and Winston, 1999, 196–232.

Torres, Andres, and Jose E. Velazquez, eds. *The Puerto Rican Movement: Voices from the Diaspora.* Philadelphia: Temple University Press, 1998.

United States Commission on Civil Rights. *Puerto Ricans in the Continental United States: An Uncertain Future.* Washington, D.C.: Government Printing Office, The U.S. Commission on Civil Rights, 1976.

Weisskoff, Richard. *Factories and Food Stamps: The Puerto Rican Model of Development.* Baltimore: Johns Hopkins University Press, 1985.

Young Lords Party. *Palante: Young Lords Party.* New York: McGraw-Hill, 1971.

# 7

# JAPANESE AMERICANS

## *In Camp, In Community*

✛

*Above: The Evacuee by Tokio Ueyama. (Gift of Kayoko Tsukada, Japanese American National Museum, 92.20.3).*
*Opposite:* Heart Mountain, Wyoming. Japanese American internment camp, with tarpaper-covered barracks housing 10,000 citizens. *(National Archives)*

# SETTING THE HISTORICAL AND CULTURAL CONTEXT

IN HER BOOK *Nisei Daughter*, Monica Sone's brother asks, "Doesn't my citizenship mean a single blessed thing to anyone?" Rhetorical though it was, the question dramatizes the reaction many Japanese Americans had when they learned that they would have to leave their homes and businesses and move to remote camps, ostensibly to protect national security in the United States. This forced resettlement, known as the Internment, followed the U.S. declaration of war against Japan. The Internment affected both Japanese nationals and those persons of Japanese ancestry who were also American citizens. Many people, both within and outside the Japanese community, look back on this action, like the Japanese attack on Pearl Harbor itself, as an event that, in the words of President Franklin D. Roosevelt, "would live in infamy."

The Internment was not the first time that immigrants from Japan had suffered injustice because of their race and country of origin. Japanese nationals were prohibited by their government from immigrating to the United States until 1890. When the first group arrived, they encountered a nation reluctant to accept more foreigners. Exclusionists, including such influential people as writer Jack London and Senator Henry Cabot Lodge, campaigned to have quotas set on immigrants of non-European origin. They sought to extend to the Japanese the Exclusion Act of 1882, which had been targeted at Chinese immigration.

When those efforts were unsuccessful, exclusionists pressured the federal government to negotiate restrictive quotas with the emperor of Japan. These negotiations resulted in the Gentlemen's Agreement of 1907, which stipulated how many Japanese would be allowed to immigrate to the United States each year; it also prohibited unskilled workers—a large percentage of those who would typically emigrate—from coming to America.

Once in the United States, Japanese immigrants faced discrimination in employment and education. Not only did unions exclude them, but they were often barred from holding professional positions as well. In the first years of the twentieth century, school districts, such as those of San Francisco, segregated Japanese students from white students. San Francisco's segregation was opposed by President Theodore Roosevelt, who was concerned about its effect on U.S. strategic diplomatic relations with Japan. The issue became part of the negotiations surrounding the 1907 Gentleman's Agreement between the two nations. Between 1910 and 1920, self-described "protective" leagues further pressured the legislature to restrict the economic power of Japanese immigrants. In 1913, the California legislature passed the Alien Land Law, which forbade the Japanese as "aliens ineligible to citizenship" to own agricultural property in the state. Furthermore, they could only lease lands for three years, they could not bequeath their lands to other "aliens ineligible to citizenship," nor could they hold more than 50 percent of the stock in any landowning corporation. To get around this, the Japanese put the titles and leases into the names of their American-born children. As a result, in 1920, another law was passed which forbade the Japanese from putting the titles and leases under their American-born children's names.

Unlike European immigrants, Japanese immigrants were prohibited from becoming naturalized American citizens. Citing a 1790 law that restricted citizenship to whites, the courts and the U.S. Department of Justice denied citizenship to both the Chinese (in 1882) and the Japanese (in 1906); this restriction was upheld by the U.S. Supreme Court as late as 1922, when the Court ruled that Takao Ozawa was ineligible for citizenship because of his race. Congress passed the Johnson-Reed Act in 1924, which allowed only those immigrants considered "racially eligible" for citizenship to enter the country. This act cut off immigration from Japan almost completely.

Such legal and social restrictions affected the composition of the Japanese American community before World War II. The first wave of immigration, which occurred between 1898–1899 and 1907–1908, brought to America primarily unmarried, unskilled workers who planned to return to Japan after achieving economic success. Married immigrants frequently planned to settle in the United States and, later, to send to Japan for their wives. After the Gentlemen's Agreement of 1907, immigrants from Japan were primarily skilled workers who established themselves in business or in agriculture.

The Johnson-Reed Act of 1924 changed the demographics of the Japanese American community. Because no new Japanese immigrants were allowed to enter the United States, a gap in age and culture developed between the dwindling Issei (first-generation immigrants born in Japan) and the increasing Nisei (second-generation immigrants born in the United States). At the same time, the discrimination Japanese immigrants experienced in the larger society caused the Japanese community to isolate itself. For this reason the Japanese community retained much of its cultural heritage longer than many other immigrant groups. Children were taught Japanese language and culture in schools that were established and supported by their parents; many children also were sent to Japan to complete their education.

Despite restrictive laws and discriminatory practices, members of the Japanese community found employment. Many worked in agriculture, commercial fishing, and the canning industry. Japanese immigrants helped the fishing and canning industries thrive in southern California and throughout the Pacific Northwest; moreover, Japanese farmers were responsible for a large percentage of the berry and vegetable crops grown in California. Other Japanese immigrants helped to establish an urban service economy by working in and later founding their own small restaurants, hotels, and shops, which served the immigrant population primarily, and by offering gardening and laundry services to those outside their community. While some Japanese immigrants became wealthy as a result of wise financial investments, many other newcomers prospered in less dramatic ways. They saved money and, like other immigrants, maintained their belief that hard work and academic achievement would lead to success.

This belief was tested when the United States entered World War II on December 7, 1941. Anti-Japanese sentiment among whites, less often expressed since the passage of the Johnson-Reed Act, re-emerged. This sentiment affected the treatment of individuals of Japanese descent not only by the general public but by the U.S. government as well. Some special interest groups, as well as some members of Congress and of the American military, held Japanese Americans responsible for the Japanese government's surprise attack on Pearl Harbor, the American naval headquarters in Hawaii. Rumors circulated that Japanese immigrants, both in Hawaii and on the mainland, had communicated with the Japanese military forces, directing planes and transmitting classified information. Early victories in the Pacific by the Imperial army made some Americans fearful that the West Coast might be vulnerable to attack.

Fear, along with the prevalent racial stereotypes of the time, caused the U.S. government to treat Japanese Americans differently from German Americans and Italian Americans, even though the United States was also at war with Germany and Italy. Some military officers feared that Japanese Americans living on the West Coast could sabotage military installations. Pressured by the forces within the military, the press, and politicians, as well as so called "patriotic" associations such as the Native Sons and Daughters of the Golden West, the executive branch of the U.S. government denied Japanese Americans many of their constitutional rights. Despite the strong protests of the U.S. attorney general, the government authorized extensive searches of private residences and businesses for anything that might be considered contraband. The homes of Japanese immigrants and Japanese American citizens were searched, often in the middle of the night. As Monica Sone describes in "Pearl Harbor Echoes in Seattle," virtually all personal possessions were viewed with suspicion; the presence of cameras or radios, Japanese newspapers, books, or magazines—or the absence of such objects—made ordinary families subject to further government surveillance. Those who did not answer questions to the satisfaction of the authorities could be detained for further questioning. As a result, many Japanese and Japanese American heads of households, some of whom spoke little English, were rounded up and detained by the Federal Bureau of Investigation. As Garrett Hongo explains in "Kubota," some Japanese Americans and others living in Hawaii were rounded up and sent to "holding centers" on the island and to American Indian reservations and other remote locations on the U.S. mainland.

The search-and-seizure process was only a prelude to the more extensive violation of rights that members of the Japanese community would endure as the war continued. Some were subjected to verbal and physical abuse; others

had their homes and businesses vandalized and even destroyed. When the
U.S. military, wary of Japanese living along the Pacific coast, asked them to
move to areas farther inland, those who relocated were abused and threatened by the residents of the inland areas. Understandably, only a small number of Japanese Americans volunteered for the relocation program.

The military then asked President Roosevelt to begin a forced evacuation. General John DeWitt, an army officer with no combat experience,
called for internment. On February 19, 1942, Roosevelt signed Executive Order 9066, which authorized the removal of certain people from military areas. DeWitt, who was given the authority to oversee the evacuation of the
West Coast, stated that all persons of Japanese ancestry would be removed
from that area "in the interest of military necessity." On March 18, 1942,
Roosevelt established the War Relocation Authority (WRA) to coordinate
the evacuation.

Those subject to the internment order—both Japanese immigrants and
American citizens of Japanese descent or, in the contemporary vernacular,
"aliens" and "nonaliens"—were given only a few days to leave their homes
and move to designated camps. Because they were allowed to take with them
only their bedding and a few suitcases, the Japanese had to sell their homes,
businesses, and other property at great loss or to entrust them to neighbors.
After reporting to a local pick-up area, they were taken first by bus and then
by train to one of ten internment camps, located in remote sections of California and Arizona, and, later, in Colorado, Utah, Idaho, and Arkansas.

Life in the camps was dismal. Dwellings consisted of hastily constructed
barracks or other makeshift structures, such as recently cleared livestock exhi-
bition halls. Barbed wire and watchtowers marked the perimeters of the
camps. The barracks offered little comfort and lacked adequate heat and privacy; internees often had to use some of their blankets to shield windows
from searchlights. They stood in line for meals, eating in communal kitchens
where the food allotment was less than fifty cents per person per day. Bathroom facilities were often latrines without running water. As well as lacking
personal comforts, internees were subject to curfews, monitoring, and arbitrary searches. There were usually meager "work opportunities" for adults
and minimal educational opportunities for children. This environment and
the deprivation of basic rights it represented led to disillusionment. Hisaye
Yamamoto's story "The Legend of Miss Sasagawara" examines the effects of
camp life on one internee. As the story continues, one sees how the pressures
of regimented routine imposed by the government, the atmosphere of the
camp itself—the lack of privacy and the hunger for gossip—as well as pressures within the family can damage an individual's talent and sense of self-
worth. The narrative also invites us to consider how gender and class issues
were addressed within the camp structure.

In 1943—one year after the internment order—the U.S. Army invited
male internees eighteen years old or older to serve in special units of the

armed forces. When the army distributed loyalty questionnaires to all candi-
dates and to the rest of the interned population, it found more than 20,000
men eligible for service. Many of these recruits went on to fight in the war,
some earning medals of honor (the extent of their bravery was not fully acknowledged until June 2000, more than fifty years later, when President Clinton awarded fifteen surviving heroes the nation's highest medal for bravery).
Other young male internees refused military service, asserting that they
could not fight for a country that refused to recognize their rights as citizens.
These people, called "No-no Boys," were segregated from the rest of the internees. In the excerpt from his novel *No-no Boy*, John Okada—himself a
decorated war veteran—contrasts those who retained loyalty to the United
States with those who were so offended by having their loyalty questioned
that they renounced their American citizenship.

In 1945, in the case of *Endo* v. *the United States*, the U.S. Supreme Court
unanimously ruled that the prolonged internment of Japanese nationals who
posed no threat to national security had been unconstitutional. In the decision, Justice William O. Douglas asserts, "A citizen who is concededly loyal
presents no problem of espionage or sabotage. Loyalty is a matter of the
heart and the mind, not of race, creed or color."

The Endo decision brought an end to the Internment. As several of the
readings in the chapter suggest, however, Japanese Americans, as individuals
and as a community, continued to be affected by the camp experience
throughout the rest of their lives. When the internees returned from the
camps, they found much of their property gone, often sold to pay taxes.
Their businesses and farms often had been dissolved or were in other hands.
Beyond the loss of property, the Internment affected the community in less
tangible ways. It helped to shape the ways in which individuals interacted
within the Japanese American community and beyond it for many years to
come. As Garrett Hongo, reflecting on his own childhood in the 1950s, explains: "We avoided grief. We avoided government. . . . Once punished, we
tried to maintain a concerted emotional and social discipline and would not
willingly seek to fall out of the narrow margin of protective favor again."

In the 1980s and 1990s, in response to pressure from Japanese Americans seeking redress and an apology, the U.S. government officially began to
concede that the Internment was unjust. The Civil Liberties Act of 1988
awarded the 60,000 former internees alive on the day of its signing $1.25 bil-
lion in reparations. In October 1990, Attorney General Dick Thornburgh
presented to the Japanese Americans a formal apology signed by President
George Bush and the first set of reparation checks to members of the Japanese community who had been interned during World War II. In so doing,
he praised the efforts of Japanese Americans for "forcing us to reexamine our
history."

We might argue that the opposite of history is silence. For several of
the writers included in this chapter, the issue is not so much forcing a re-

examination as it is addressing issues of silence and shame. Later generations of Japanese Americans, as Hongo suggests, were often educated in classrooms where the Internment was never mentioned, from textbooks in which the Internment was not discussed: "It was as if we had no history for four years and the relocation was something unspeakable." In their essays, both Hongo and Ronald Takaki stress the importance of "overcoming [this] silence." In constructing one's history, in giving voice to the experiences of one's ancestors, one serves as a witness. In Lawson Fusao Inada's poem "Concentration Constellation," the points on the map that mark the sites of former internment camps compose a pattern:

> Now regard what sort of shape
> this constellation takes.
> It sits there like a jagged scar,
> massive, on the massive landscape.
> It lies there like the rusted wire
> of a twisted and remembered fence.

Here the poet bears witness for the silent ones who survived the camp and for those who had perished before any apology or redress was offered.

### BEGINNING: Pre-reading/Writing

*Imagine yourself in the following situation. A government agency has informed you that you must leave your home in seven days and go to an internment camp. You can bring only two small suitcases and a bag of bedding with you. How do you react to what is happening? What will you do? What will you take with you and why? Share your choices with the class.*

*Executive Order 9066, which was signed by President Franklin D. Roosevelt on February 19, 1942, gave the secretary of war the power to evacuate from specific military areas any residents who were considered to be risks to national security. Although the act did not mention any ethnic group, it was applied almost exclusively to Japanese Americans. Almost immediately after the order was signed, the military officer in charge ordered the evacuation of people of Japanese ancestry.*

*On March 18, Roosevelt established the War Relocation Authority (WRA) to take charge of this evacuation. The injustice of the Internment was not acknowledged by Congress until the 1980s, when it ordered that reparations be paid.*

⊹

# JAPANESE RELOCATION ORDER

### February 19, 1942
### (Federal Register, Vol. VII, No. 38)

1    ALARMED BY THE SUPPOSED DANGER of Japanese invasion of the Pacific coast after Pearl Harbor and under the apprehension that all persons of Japanese ancestry were a potential threat to the United States, the War Department persuaded the President to authorize the evacuation of some 112,000 West Coast Japanese, two-thirds of them American citizens to "relocation" centers. A Congressional Resolution of March 21, 1942, made it a misdemeanor "to knowingly enter, remain in, or leave prescribed military areas" contrary to the orders of the commanding officer of the area. This Act which, in perspective seems to have been wholly unnecessary, has been called by E. S. Corwin "the most drastic invasion of the rights of citizens of the U.S. by their own government that has thus far occurred in the history of our nation." See Doc. No. 547 and M. Grodzins, *Americans Betrayed*.

### Executive Order
### Authorizing the Secretary of War to Prescribe Military Areas

2    Whereas the successful prosecution of the war requires every possible protection against espionage and against sabotage to national-defense materials, national-defense premises, and national-defense utilities. . . .

3    Now, therefore, by virtue of the authority vested in me as President of the United States, and Commander in Chief of the Army and Navy, I hereby authorize and direct the Secretary of War, and the Military Commanders whom he may from time to time designate, whenever he or any designated Commander deems such action necessary or desirable, to prescribe military areas in such

places and of such extent as he or the appropriate Military Commander may determine, from which any or all persons may be excluded, and with respect to which, the right of any person to enter, remain in, or leave shall be subject to whatever restrictions the Secretary of War or the appropriate Military Commander may impose in his discretion. The Secretary of War is hereby authorized to provide for residents of any such area who are excluded therefrom, such transportation, food, shelter, and other accommodations as may be necessary, in the judgment of the Secretary of War or the said Military Commander, and until other arrangements are made, to accomplish the purpose of this order. The designation of military areas in any region or locality shall supersede designations of prohibited and restricted areas by the Attorney General under the Proclamations of December 7 and 8, 1941, and shall supersede the responsibility and authority of the Attorney General under the said Proclamations in respect of such prohibited and restricted areas.

I hereby further authorize and direct the Secretary of War and the said    4 Military Commanders to take such other steps as he or the appropriate Military Commander may deem advisable to enforce compliance with the restrictions applicable to each Military area hereinabove authorized to be designated, including the use of Federal troops and other Federal Agencies, with authority to accept assistance of state and local agencies.

I hereby further authorize and direct all Executive Departments, inde-    5 pendent establishments and other Federal Agencies, to assist the Secretary of War or the said Military Commanders in carrying out this Executive Order, including the furnishing of medical aid, hospitalization, food, clothing, transportation, use of land, shelter, and other supplies, equipment, utilities, facilities, and services. . . . �֍

FRANKLIN D. ROOSEVELT

---

## RESPONDING

1. Imagine that you are a native-born American of Japanese descent. The year is 1942 and you live in California. In a journal entry, write your reaction to the Japanese Relocation Order.

2. Working individually or in a group, list the powers that the order gives to the "appropriate Military Commander" (paragraph 3). Then explain the government's reasons for issuing the order. How does the act directly or indirectly indicate that the Japanese will be forced to live in relocation centers?

3. Legal historian E. S. Corwin has called this act "the most drastic invasion of the rights of citizens of the U.S. by their own government that has thus far occurred in the history of our nation." Explain this statement and argue

for or against its conclusion. Support your argument with examples from the introduction to the chapter and your own knowledge of history and current events.

# Monica Sone

*Monica Sone, born Kazuko Itoi in 1919, grew up in Seattle, Washington, where her family was in the hotel business until they were forced to evacuate. After World War II she attended Hanover College and did graduate work in psychology at Case Western Reserve University.*

*In the following selection from her book* Nisei Daughter *(1953), Sone recounts the changes in the country and in the Japanese American community after the attack on Pearl Harbor. The chapter also raises some uncomfortable questions about the relationship between national security and personal liberty during times of war.*

⁜

# PEARL HARBOR ECHOES IN SEATTLE

1   On a peaceful Sunday morning, December 7, 1941, Henry, Sumi and I were at choir rehearsal singing ourselves hoarse in preparation for the annual Christmas recital of Handel's "Messiah." Suddenly Chuck Mizuno, a young University of Washington student, burst into the chapel, gasping as if he had sprinted all the way up the stairs.

2   "Listen, everybody!" he shouted. "Japan just bombed Pearl Harbor . . . in Hawaii! It's war!"

3   The terrible words hit like a blockbuster, paralyzing us. Then we smiled feebly at each other, hoping this was one of Chuck's practical jokes. Miss Hara, our music director, rapped her baton impatiently on the music stand and chided him, "Now Chuck, fun's fun, but we have work to do. Please take your place. You're already half an hour late."

4   But Chuck strode vehemently back to the door. "I mean it, folks, honest! I just heard the news over my car radio. Reporters are talking a blue streak. Come on down and hear it for yourselves."

5   With that, Chuck swept out of the room, a swirl of young men following in his wake. Henry was one of them. The rest of us stayed, rooted to our places like a row of marionettes. I felt as if a fist had smashed my pleasant little existence, breaking it into jigsaw puzzle pieces. An old wound opened up again,

and I found myself shrinking inwardly from my Japanese blood, the blood of an enemy. I knew instinctively that the fact that I was an American by birthright was not going to help me escape the consequences of this unhappy war.

One girl mumbled over and over again, "It can't be, God, it can't be!" Someone else was saying, "What a spot to be in! Do you think we'll be considered Japanese or Americans?"  6

A boy replied quietly, "We'll be Japs, same as always. But our parents are enemy aliens now, you know."  7

A shocked silence followed. Henry came for Sumi and me. "Come on, let's go home," he said.  8

We ran trembling to our car. Usually Henry was a careful driver, but that morning he bore down savagely on the accelerator. Boiling angry, he shot us up Twelfth Avenue, rammed through the busy Jackson Street intersection, and rocketed up the Beacon Hill bridge. We swung violently around to the left of the Marine Hospital and swooped to the top of the hill. Then Henry slammed on the brakes and we rushed helter-skelter up to the house to get to the radio. Asthma skidded away from under our trampling feet.  9

Mother was sitting limp in the huge armchair as if she had collapsed there, listening dazedly to the turbulent radio. Her face was frozen still, and the only words she could utter were, "*Komatta neh, komatta neh.* How dreadful, how dreadful."  10

Henry put his arms around her. She told him she first heard about the attack on Pearl Harbor when one of her friends phoned her and told her to turn on the radio.  11

We pressed close against the radio, listening stiffly to the staccato outbursts of an excited reporter: "The early morning sky of Honolulu was filled with the furious buzzing of Jap Zero planes for nearly three hours, raining death and destruction on the airfields below. . . . A warship anchored beyond the Harbor was sunk. . . ."  12

We were switched to the White House. The fierce clack of teletype machines and the babble of voices surging in and out from the background almost drowned out the speaker's terse announcements.  13

With every fiber of my being I resented this war. I felt as if I were on fire. "Mama, they should never have done it," I cried. "Why did they do it? Why? Why?"  14

Mother's face turned paper white. "What do you know about it? Right or wrong, the Japanese have been chafing with resentment for years. It was bound to happen, one time or another. You're young, Ka-chan, you know very little about the ways of nations. It's not as simple as you think, but this is hardly the time to be quarreling about it, is it?"  15

"No, it's too late, too late!" and I let the tears pour down my face.  16

Father rushed home from the hotel. He was deceptively calm as he joined us in the living room. Father was a born skeptic, and he believed nothing unless he could see, feel and smell it. He regarded all newspapers and radio news with  17 deep suspicion. He shook his head doubtfully. "It must be propaganda. With the way things are going now between America and Japan, we should expect the most fantastic rumors, and this is one of the wildest I've heard yet." But we noticed that he was firmly glued to the radio. It seemed as if the regular Sunday programs, sounding off relentlessly hour after hour on schedule, were trying to blunt the catastrophe of the morning.

18    The telephone pealed nervously all day as people searched for comfort from each other. Chris called, and I told her how miserable and confused I felt about the war. Understanding as always, Chris said, "You know how I feel about you and your family, Kaz. Don't, for heaven's sake, feel the war is going to make any difference in our relationship. It's not your fault, nor mine! I wish to God it could have been prevented." Minnie called off her Sunday date with Henry. Her family was upset and they thought she should stay close to home instead of wandering downtown.

19    Late that night Father got a shortwave broadcast from Japan. Static sputtered, then we caught a faint voice, speaking rapidly in Japanese. Father sat unmoving as a rock, his head cocked. The man was talking about the war between Japan and America. Father bit his lips and Mother whispered to him anxiously, "It's true, then, isn't it, Papa? It's true?"

20    Father was muttering to himself, "So they really did it!" Now having heard the news in their native tongue, the war had become a reality to Father and Mother.

21    "I suppose from now on, we'll hear about nothing but the humiliating defeats of Japan in the papers here," Mother said, resignedly.

22    Henry and I glared indignantly at Mother, then Henry shrugged his shoulders and decided to say nothing. Discussion of politics, especially Japan versus America, had become taboo in our family for it sent tempers skyrocketing. Henry and I used to criticize Japan's aggressions in China and Manchuria while Father and Mother condemned Great Britain and America's superior attitude toward Asiatics and their interference with Japan's economic growth. During these arguments, we had eyed each other like strangers, parents against children. They left us with a hollow feeling at the pit of the stomach.

23    Just then the shrill peel of the telephone cut off the possibility of a family argument. When I answered, a young girl's voice fluttered through breathily, "Hello, this is Taeko Tanabe. Is my mother there?"

24    "No, she isn't, Taeko."

25    "Thank you," and Taeko hung up before I could say another word. Her voice sounded strange. Mrs. Tanabe was one of Mother's poet friends. Taeko called three more times, and each time before I could ask her if anything was wrong, she quickly hung up. The next day we learned that Taeko was trying desperately to locate her mother because FBI agents had swept into their home and arrested Mr. Tanabe, a newspaper editor. The FBI had permitted Taeko to try to locate her mother before they took Mr. Tanabe away while they searched

the house for contraband and subversive material, but she was not to let anyone else know what was happening.

Next morning the newspapers fairly exploded in our faces with stories about the Japanese raids on the chain of Pacific islands. We were shocked to read Attorney General Biddle's announcement that 736 Japanese had been picked up in the United States and Hawaii. Then Mrs. Tanabe called Mother about her husband's arrest, and she said at least a hundred others had been taken from our community. Messrs. Okayama, Higashi, Sughiri, Mori, Okada—we knew them all.

"But why were they arrested, Papa? They weren't spies, were they?"

Father replied almost curtly, "Of course not! They were probably taken for questioning."

The pressure of war moved in on our little community. The Chinese consul announced that all the Chinese would carry identification cards and wear "China" badges to distinguish them from the Japanese. Then I really felt left standing out in the cold. The government ordered the bank funds of all Japanese nationals frozen. Father could no longer handle financial transactions through his bank accounts, but Henry, fortunately, was of legal age so that business could be negotiated in his name.

In the afternoon President Roosevelt's formal declaration of war against Japan was broadcast throughout the nation. In grave, measured words, he described the attack on Pearl Harbor as shameful, infamous. I writhed involuntarily. I could no more have escaped the stab of self-consciousness than I could have changed my Oriental features.

Monday night a complete blackout was ordered against a possible Japanese air raid on the Puget Sound area. Mother assembled black cloths to cover the windows and set up candles in every room. All radio stations were silenced from seven in the evening till morning, but we gathered around the dead radio anyway, out of sheer habit. We whiled away the evening reading instructions in the newspapers on how to put out incendiary bombs and learning about the best hiding places during bombardments. When the city pulled its switches at blackout hour and plunged us into an ominous dark silence, we went to bed shivering and wondering what tomorrow would bring. All of a sudden there was a wild screech of brakes, followed by the resounding crash of metal slamming into metal. We rushed out on the balcony. In the street below we saw dim shapes of cars piled grotesquely on top of each other, their soft blue headlights staring helplessly up into the sky. Angry men's voices floated up to the house. The men were wearing uniforms and their metal buttons gleamed in the blue lights. Apparently two police cars had collided in the blackout.

Clutching at our bathrobes we lingered there. The damp winter night hung heavy and inert like a wet black veil, and at the bottom of Beacon Hill, we could barely make out the undulating length of Rainier Valley, lying quietly in the somber, brooding silence like a hunted python. A few pinpoints of light pricked the darkness here and there like winking bits of diamonds, betraying the uneasy vigil of a tense city.

33   It made me positively hivey the way the FBI agents continued their raids into Japanese homes and business places and marched the Issei men away into the old red brick immigration building, systematically and efficiently, as if they were stocking a cellarfull of choice bottles of wine. At first we noted that the men arrested were those who had been prominent in community affairs, like Mr. Kato, many times president of the Seattle Japanese Chamber of Commerce, and Mr. Ohashi, the principal of our Japanese language school, or individuals whose business was directly connected with firms in Japan; but as time went on, it became less and less apparent why the others were included in these raids.

34   We wondered when Father's time would come. We expected momentarily to hear strange footsteps on the porch and the sudden demanding ring of the front doorbell. Our ears became attuned like the sensitive antennas of moths, translating every soft swish of passing cars into the arrival of the FBI squad.

35   Once when our doorbell rang after curfew hour, I completely lost my Oriental stoicism which I had believed would serve me well under the most trying circumstances. No friend of ours paid visits at night anymore, and I was sure that Father's hour had come. As if hypnotized, I walked woodenly to the door. A mass of black figures stood before me, filling the doorway. I let out a magnificent shriek. Then pandemonium broke loose. The solid rank fell apart into a dozen separate figures which stumbled and leaped pell-mell away from the porch. Watching the mad scramble, I thought I had routed the FBI agents with my cry of distress. Father, Mother, Henry and Sumi rushed out to support my wilting body. When Henry snapped on the porch light, one lone figure crept out from behind the front hedge. It was a newsboy who, standing at a safe distance, called in a quavering voice, "I . . . I came to collect for . . . for the *Times.*"

36   Shaking with laughter, Henry paid him and gave him an extra large tip for the terrible fright he and his bodyguards had suffered at the hands of the Japanese. As he hurried down the walk, boys of all shapes and sizes crawled out from behind trees and bushes and scurried after him.

37   We heard all kinds of stories about the FBI, most of them from Mr. Yorita, the grocer, who now took twice as long to make his deliveries. The war seemed to have brought out his personality. At least he talked more, and he glowed, in a sinister way. Before the war Mr. Yorita had been uncommunicative. He used to stagger silently through the back door with a huge sack of rice over his shoulders, dump it on the kitchen floor and silently flow out of the door as if he were bored and disgusted with food and the people who ate it. But now Mr. Yorita swaggered in, sent a gallon jug of soy sauce spinning into a corner, and launched into a comprehensive report of the latest rumors he had picked up on his route, all in chronological order. Mr. Yorita looked like an Oriental Dracula, with his triangular eyes and yellow-fanged teeth. He had a mournfully long sallow face and in his excitement his gold-rimmed glasses constantly slipped to

the tip of his long nose. He would describe in detail how some man had been awakened in the dead of night, swiftly handcuffed, and dragged from out of his bed by a squad of brutal, tight-lipped men. Mr. Yorita bared his teeth menacingly in his most dramatic moments and we shrank from him instinctively. As he backed out of the kitchen door, he would shake his bony finger at us with a warning of dire things to come. When Mother said, "Yorita-san, you must worry about getting a call from the FBI, too," Mr. Yorita laughed modestly, pushing his glasses back up into place. "They wouldn't be interested in anyone as insignificant as myself!" he assured her.

But he was wrong. The following week a new delivery boy appeared at the back door with an airy explanation, "Yep, they got the old man, too, and don't ask me why! The way I see it, it's subversive to sell soy sauce now."

The Matsuis were visited, too. Shortly after Dick had gone to Japan, Mr. Matsui had died and Mrs. Matsui had sold her house. Now she and her daughter and youngest son lived in the back of their little dry goods store on Jackson Street. One day when Mrs. Matsui was busy with the family laundry, three men entered the shop, nearly ripping off the tiny bell hanging over the door. She hurried out, wiping sudsy, reddened hands on her apron. At best Mrs. Matsui's English was rudimentary, and when she became excited, it deteriorated into Japanese. She hovered on her toes, delighted to see new customers in her humble shop. "Yes, yes, something you want?"

"Where's Mr. Matsui?" a steely-eyed man snapped at her.

Startled, Mrs. Matsui jerked her thumb toward the rear of the store and said, "He not home."

"What? Oh, in there, eh? Come on!" The men tore the faded print curtain aside and rushed into the back room. "Don't see him. Must be hiding."

They jerked open bedroom doors, leaped into the tiny bathroom, flung windows open and peered down into the alley. Tiny birdlike Mrs. Matsui rushed around after them. "No, no! Whatsamalla, whatsamalla!"

"Where's your husband! Where is he?" one man demanded angrily, flinging clothes out of the closet.

"Why you mix 'em all up? He not home, not home." She clawed at the back of the burly men like an angry little sparrow, trying to stop the holocaust in her little home. One man brought his face down close to hers, shouting slowly and clearly, "WHERE IS YOUR HUSBAND? YOU SAID HE WAS IN HERE A MINUTE AGO!"

"Yes, yes, not here. *Mah, wakara nai hito da neh.* Such stupid men."

Mrs. Matsui dove under a table, dragged out a huge album and pointed at a large photograph. She jabbed her gnarled finger up toward the ceiling, saying, "Heben! Heben!"

The men gathered around and looked at a picture of Mr. Matsui's funeral. Mrs. Matsui and her two children were standing by a coffin, their eyes cast down, surrounded by all their friends, all of whom were looking down. The three men's lips formed an "Oh." One of them said, "We're sorry to have disturbed you. Thank you, Mrs. Matsui, and good-by." They departed quickly and quietly.

49    Having passed through this baptism, Mrs. Matsui became an expert on the FBI, and she stood by us, rallying and coaching us on how to deal with them. She said to Mother, "You must destroy everything and anything Japanese which may incriminate your husband. It doesn't matter what it is, if it's printed or made in Japan, destroy it because the FBI always carries off those items for evidence."

50    In fact all the women whose husbands had been spirited away said the same thing. Gradually we became uncomfortable with our Japanese books, magazines, wall scrolls and knickknacks. When Father's hotel friends, Messrs. Sakaguchi, Horiuchi, Nishibue and a few others vanished, and their wives called Mother weeping and warning her again about having too many Japanese objects around the house, we finally decided to get rid of some of ours. We knew it was impossible to destroy everything. The FBI would certainly think it strange if they found us sitting in a bare house, totally purged of things Japanese. But it was as if we could no longer stand the tension of waiting, and we just had to do something against the black day. We worked all night, feverishly combing through bookshelves, closets, drawers, and furtively creeping down to the basement furnace for the burning. I gathered together my well-worn Japanese language schoolbooks which I had been saving over a period of ten years with the thought that they might come in handy when I wanted to teach Japanese to my own children. I threw them into the fire and watched them flame and shrivel into black ashes. But when I came face to face with my Japanese doll which Grandmother Nagashima had sent me from Japan, I rebelled. It was a gorgeously costumed Miyazukai figure, typical of the lady in waiting who lived in the royal palace during the feudal era. The doll was gowned in an elegant purple silk kimono with the long, sweeping hemline of its period and sashed with rich-embroidered gold and silver brocade. With its black, shining coiffed head bent a little to one side, its delicate pink-tipped ivory hand holding a red lacquer message box, the doll had an appealing, almost human charm. I decided to ask Chris if she would keep it for me. Chris loved and appreciated beauty in every form and shape, and I knew that in her hands, the doll would be safe and enjoyed.

51    Henry pulled down from his bedroom wall the toy samurai sword he had brought from Japan and tossed it into the flames. Sumi's contributions to the furnace were books of fairy tales and magazines sent to her by her young cousins in Japan. We sorted out Japanese classic and popular music from a stack of records, shattered them over our knees and fed the pieces to the furnace. Father piled up his translated Japanese volumes of philosophy and religion and carted them reluctantly to the basement. Mother had the most to eliminate, with her scrapbooks of poems cut out from newspapers and magazines, and her private collection of old Japanese classic literature.

52    It was past midnight when we finally climbed upstairs to bed. Wearily we

closed our eyes, filled with an indescribable sense of guilt for having destroyed the things we loved. This night of ravage was to haunt us for years. As I lay struggling to fall asleep, I realized that we hadn't freed ourselves at all from fear. We still lay stiff in our beds, waiting.

Mrs. Matsui kept assuring us that the FBI would get around to us yet. It was just a matter of time and the least Mother could do for Father was to pack a suitcase for him. She said that the men captured who hadn't been prepared had grown long beards, lived and slept in the same clothes for days before they were permitted visits from their families. So Mother dutifully packed a suitcase for Father with toilet articles, warm flannel pajamas, and extra clothes, and placed it in the front hall by the door. It was a personal affront, the way it stood there so frank and unabashedly. Henry and I said that it was practically a confession that Papa was a spy. "So please help yourself to him, Mr. FBI, and God speed you."

Mother was equally loud and firm, "No, don't anyone move it! No one thought that Mr. Kato or the others would be taken, but they're gone now. Why should we think Papa's going to be an exception?"

Henry threw his hands up in the air and muttered about the odd ways of the Japanese.

Every day Mrs. Matsui called Mother to check Father in; then we caught the habit and started calling him at the hotel every hour on the hour until he finally exploded. "Stop this nonsense! I don't know which is more nerve-wracking, being watched by the FBI or by my family!"

When Father returned home from work, a solicitous family eased him into his favorite armchair, arranged pillows behind his back, and brought the evening paper and slippers to him. Mother cooked Father's favorite dishes frenziedly, night after night. It all made Father very uneasy.

We had a family conference to discuss the possibility of Father and Mother's internment. Henry was in graduate school and I was beginning my second year at the university. We agreed to drop out should they be taken and we would manage the hotel during our parents' absence. Every week end Henry and I accompanied Father to the hotel and learned how to keep the hotel books, how to open the office safe, and what kind of linen, paper towels, and soap to order.

Then a new menace appeared on the scene. Cries began to sound up and down the coast that everyone of Japanese ancestry should be taken into custody. For years the professional guardians of the Golden West had wanted to rid their land of the Yellow Peril, and the war provided an opportunity for them to push their program through. As the chain of Pacific islands fell to the Japanese, patriots shrieked for protection from us. A Californian sounded the alarm: "The Japanese are dangerous and they must leave. Remember the destruction and the sabotage perpetrated at Pearl Harbor. Notice how they have infiltrated into the harbor towns and taken our best land."

He and his kind refused to be comforted by Edgar Hoover's special report to the War Department stating that there had not been a single case of sabotage

53

54

55

56

57

58

59

60

committed by a Japanese living in Hawaii or on the Mainland during the Pearl Harbor attack or after. I began to feel acutely uncomfortable for living on Beacon Hill. The Marine Hospital rose tall and handsome on our hill, and if I stood on the west shoulder of the Hill, I could not help but get an easily photographed view of the Puget Sound Harbor with its ships snuggled against the docks. And Boeing airfield, a few miles south of us, which had never bothered me before, suddenly seemed to have moved right up into my back yard, daring me to take just one spying glance at it.

61    In February, Executive Order No. 9066 came out, authorizing the War Department to remove the Japanese from such military areas as it saw fit, aliens and citizens alike. Even if a person had a fraction of Japanese blood in him, he must leave on demand.

62    A pall of gloom settled upon our home. We couldn't believe that the government meant that the Japanese-Americans must go, too. We had heard the clamoring of superpatriots who insisted loudly, "Throw the whole kaboodle out. A Jap's a Jap, no matter how you slice him. You can't make an American out of little Jap Junior just by handing him an American birth certificate." But we had dismissed these remarks as just hot blasts of air from an overheated patriot. We were quite sure that our rights as American citizens would not be violated, and we would not be marched out of our homes on the same basis as enemy aliens.

63    In anger, Henry and I read and reread the Executive Order. Henry crumpled the newspaper in his hand and threw it against the wall. "Doesn't my citizenship mean a single blessed thing to anyone? Why doesn't somebody make up my mind for me? First they want me in the army. Now they're going to slap an alien 4-C on me because of my ancestry. What the hell!"

64    Once more I felt like a despised, pathetic two-headed freak, a Japanese and an American, neither of which seemed to be doing me any good. The Nisei leaders in the community rose above their personal feelings and stated that they would co-operate and comply with the decision of the government as their sacrifice in keeping with the country's war effort, thus proving themselves loyal American citizens. I was too jealous of my recently acquired voting privilege to be gracious about giving in, and felt most unco-operative. I noticed wryly that the feelings about the Japanese on the Hawaiian Islands were quite different from those on the West Coast. In Hawaii, a strategic military outpost, the Japanese were regarded as essential to the economy of the island and powerful economic forces fought against their removal. General Delos Emmons, in command of Hawaii at the time, lent his authoritative voice to calm the fears of the people on the island and to prevent chaos and upheaval. General Emmons established martial law, but he did not consider evacuation essential for the security of the island.

65    On the West Coast, General J. L. DeWitt of the Western Defense Command did not think martial law necessary, but he favored mass evacuation of the Japanese and Nisei. We suspected that pressures from economic and political

interests who would profit from such a wholesale evacuation influenced this decision.

Events moved rapidly. General DeWitt marked off Western Washington, Oregon, and all of California, and the southern half of Arizona as Military Area No. 1, hallowed ground from which we must remove ourselves as rapidly as possible. Unfortunately we could not simply vanish into thin air, and we had no place to go. We had no relatives in the east we could move in on. All our relatives were sitting with us in the forbidden area, themselves wondering where to go. The neighboring states in the line of exit for the Japanese protested violently at the prospect of any mass invasion. They said, very sensibly, that if the Coast didn't want the Japanese hanging around, they didn't either.

A few hardy families in the community liquidated their property, tied suitcases all around their cars, and sallied eastward. They were greeted by signs in front of store windows, "Open season for Japs!" and "We kill rats and Japs here." On state lines, highway troopers swarmed around the objectionable migrants and turned them back under governor's orders.

General DeWitt must have finally realized that if he insisted on voluntary mass evacuation, hundreds and thousands of us would have wandered back and forth, clogging the highways and pitching tents along the roadside, eating and sleeping in colossal disorder. He suddenly called a halt to voluntary movement, although most of the Japanese were not budging an inch. He issued a new order, stating that no Japanese could leave the city, under penalty of arrest. The command had hatched another plan, a better one. The army would move us out as only the army could do it, and march us in neat, orderly fashion into assembly centers. We would stay in these centers only until permanent camps were set up inland to isolate us.

The orders were simple:

> Dispose of your homes and property. Wind up your businesses. Register the family. One seabag of bedding, two suitcases of clothing allowed per person. People in District #1 must report at 8th and Lane Street, 8 p.m. on April 28.

I wanted no part of this new order. I had read in the papers that the Japanese from the state of Washington would be taken to a camp in Puyallup, on the state fairgrounds. The article apologetically assured the public that the camp would be temporary and that the Japanese would be removed from the fairgrounds and parking lots in time for the opening of the annual State Fair. It neglected to say where we might be at the time when those fine breeds of Holstein cattle and Yorkshire hogs would be proudly wearing their blue satin ribbons.

We were advised to pack warm, durable clothes. In my mind, I saw our permanent camp sprawled out somewhere deep in a snow-bound forest, an American Siberia. I saw myself plunging chest deep in the snow, hunting for small game to keep us alive. I decided that one of my suitcases was going to hold nothing but vitamins from A to Z. I thought of sewing fur-lined hoods and parkas for the family. I was certain this was going to be a case of sheer animal survival.

72      One evening Father told us that he would lose the management of the hotel unless he could find someone to operate it for the duration, someone intelligent and efficient enough to impress Bentley Agent and Company. Father said, "Sam, Joe, Peter, they all promised to stay on their jobs, but none of them can read or write well enough to manage the business. I've got to find a responsible party with experience in hotel management, but where?"

73      Sumi asked, "What happens if we can't find anyone?"

74      "I lose my business and my livelihood. I'll be saying good-by to a lifetime of labor and all the hopes and plans I had for the family."

75      We sagged. Father looked at us thoughtfully, "I've never talked much about the hotel business to you children, mainly because so much of it has been an uphill climb of work and waiting for better times. Only recently I was able to clear up the loans I took out years ago to expand the business. I was sure that in the next five or ten years I would be getting returns on my long-range investments, and I would have been able to do a lot of things eventually. . . . Send you through medical school," Father nodded to Henry, "and let Kazu and Sumi study anything they liked." Father laughed a bit self-consciously as he looked at Mother. "And when all the children had gone off on their own, I had planned to take Mama on her first real vacation, to Europe as well as Japan."

76      We listened to Father wide-eyed and wistful. It had been a wonderful, wonderful dream.

77      Mother suddenly hit upon a brilliant idea. She said maybe the Olsens, our old friends who had once managed the Camden Apartments, might be willing to run a hotel. The Olsens had sold the apartment and moved to Aberdeen. Mother thought that perhaps Marta's oldest brother, the bachelor of the family, might be available. If he refused, perhaps Marta and her husband might consider the offer. We rushed excitedly to the telephone to make a long-distance call to the Olsens. After four wrong Olsens, we finally reached Marta.

78      "Marta? Is this Marta?"

79      "Yes, this is Marta."

80      I nearly dove into the mouthpiece, I was so glad to hear her voice. Marta remembered us well and we exchanged news about our families. Marta and her husband had bought a small chicken farm and were doing well. Marta said, "I come from the farm ven I vas young and I like it fine. I feel more like home here. How's everybody over there?"

81      I told her that we and all the rest of the Japanese were leaving Seattle soon under government order on account of the war. Marta gasped, "Everybody? You mean the Saitos, the Fujinos, Watanabes, and all the rest who were living at the Camden Apartments, too?"

82      "Yes, they and everyone else on the West Coast."

83      Bewildered, Marta asked where we were going, what we were going to do,

would we ever return to Seattle, and what about Father's hotel. I told her about our business situation and that Father needed a hotel manager for the duration. Would she or any of her brothers be willing to accept such a job? There was a silence at the other end of the line and I said hastily, "This is a very sudden call, Marta. I'm sorry I had to surprise you like this, but we felt this was an emergency and . . ."

Marta was full of regrets. "Oh, I vish we could do someting to help you folks, but my husband and I can't leave the farm at all. We don't have anyone here to help. We do all the work ourselves. Magnus went to Alaska last year. He has a goot job up there, some kind of war work. My other two brothers have business in town and they have children so they can't help you much."   84

My heart sank like a broken elevator. When I said, "Oh . . ." I felt the family sitting behind me sink into a gloomy silence. Our last hope was gone. We finally said good-by, Marta distressed at not being able to help, and I apologized for trying to hoist our problem on them.   85

The next week end Marta and Karl paid us a surprise visit. We had not seen them for nearly two years. Marta explained shyly, "It was such a nice day and we don't go novair for a long time, so I tole Karl, 'Let's take a bus into Seattle and visit the Itois.'"   86

We spent a delightful Sunday afternoon taking about old times. Mother served our guests her best green tea and, as we relaxed, the irritating presence of war vanished. When it was time for them to return home, Marta's sparkling blue eyes suddenly filled. "Karl and I, we feel so bad about the whole ting, the war and everyting, we joost had to come out to see you and say 'good by.' God bless you. Maybe we vill see you again back home here. Anyvay, we pray for it."   87

Marta and Karl's warmth and sincerity restored a sense of peace into our home, an atmosphere which had disappeared ever since Pearl Harbor. They served to remind us that in spite of the bitterness war had brought into our lives, we were still bound to our home town. Bit by bit, I remembered our happy past, the fun we had growing up along the colorful brash waterfront, swimming through the white-laced waves of Puget Sound, and lolling luxuriously on the tender green carpet of grass around Lake Washington from where we could see the slick, blue-frosted shoulders of Mount Rainier. There was too much beauty surrounding us. Above all, we must keep friends like Marta and Karl, Christine, Sam, Peter and Joe, all sterling products of many years of associations. We could never turn our faces away and remain aloof forever from Seattle. ✤   88

---

## RESPONDING

1.  Have you ever felt that you had your rights taken away unfairly by a social institution, family, or a friend? Write a letter of protest to the individual or institution who you felt treated you unjustly.

2.  Working individually or in a group, outline the changes that took place in the lives of the Sone family from the bombing of Pearl Harbor to the evacuation of the Japanese Americans.

3.  In an essay, compare the attitudes and reactions of different members of the Sone family to the United States and Japan before and after Pearl Harbor or before and after the evacuation order. Does the older generation have a markedly different attitude from that of the younger generation?

4.  Sone states that the internment of her family violated their rights as American citizens. Using examples from her autobiography and other readings such as the Bill of Rights, write an essay agreeing or disagreeing with her statement.

# JOHN OKADA

*Born in Seattle, Washington, in 1923, John Okada served in the army during World War II. After earning a bachelor's degree from the University of Washington and a master's degree from Columbia University, he worked as a reference librarian and a technical writer. He died of a heart attack in 1971. Although Okada did not enjoy great fame during his lifetime, he is now considered by many to be one of the most important Japanese American writers.*

*The following excerpt from* No-no Boy, *first published in 1957, describes some of the conflicts within the Japanese community at the time of the war. In the passage, the main character begins to see how one's sense of loyalty is very often a function of one's position in society. He also discovers how people use both ideology and emotion to justify their decisions.*

# *From* NO-NO BOY

1   "ICHIRO."

2   He propped himself up on an elbow and looked at her. She had hardly changed. Surely, there must have been a time when she could smile and, yet, he could not remember.

3   "Yeah?"

4   "Lunch is on the table."

5   As he pushed himself off the bed and walked past her to the kitchen, she took broom and dustpan and swept up the mess he had made.

There were eggs, fried with soy sauce, sliced cold meat, boiled cabbage, and 6
tea and rice. They all ate in silence, not even disturbed once by the tinkling of
the bell. The father cleared the table after they had finished and dutifully retired
to watch the store. Ichiro had smoked three cigarettes before his mother ended
the silence.

"You must go back to school."                                                       7

He had almost forgotten that there had been a time before the war when            8
he had actually gone to college for two years and studiously applied himself to
courses in the engineering school. The statement staggered him. Was that all
there was to it? Did she mean to sit there and imply that the four intervening
years were to be casually forgotten and life resumed as if there had been no four
years and no war and no Eto who had spit on him because of the thing he had
done?

"I don't feel much like going to school."                                           9

"What will you do?"                                                                10

"I don't know."                                                                    11

"With an education, your opportunities in Japan will be unlimited. You             12
must go and complete your studies."

"Ma," he said slowly, "Ma, I'm not going to Japan. Nobody's going to Japan.        13
The war is over. Japan lost. Do you hear? Japan lost."

"You believe that?" It was said in the tone of an adult asking a child who         14
is no longer a child if he really believed that Santa Claus was real.

"Yes, I believe it. I know it. America is still here. Do you see the great         15
Japanese army walking down the streets? No. There is no Japanese army any
more."

"The boat is coming and we must be ready."                                         16

"The boat?"                                                                        17

"Yes." She reached into her pocket and drew out a worn envelope.                   18

The letter had been mailed from São Paulo, Brazil, and was addressed to a          19
name that he did not recognize. Inside the envelope was a single sheet of flimsy,
rice paper covered with intricate flourishes of Japanese characters.

"What does it say?"                                                                20

She did not bother to pick up the letter. "To you who are a loyal and             21
honorable Japanese, it is with humble and heartfelt joy that I relay this momen-
tous message. Word has been brought to us that the victorious Japanese government is presently making preparations to send ships which will return to
Japan those residents in foreign countries who have steadfastly maintained their
faith and loyalty to our Emperor. The Japanese government regrets that the
responsibilities arising from the victory compel them to delay in the sending of
the vessels. To be among the few who remain to receive this honor is a gratifying
tribute. Heed not the propaganda of the radio and newspapers which endeavor
to convince the people with lies about the allied victory. Especially, heed not
the lies of your traitorous countrymen who have turned their backs on the
country of their birth and who will suffer for their treasonous acts. The day of

glory is close at hand. The rewards will be beyond our greatest expectations. What we have done, we have done only as Japanese, but the government is grateful. Hold your heads high and make ready for the journey, for the ships are coming."

22 "Who wrote that?" he asked incredulously. It was like a weird nightmare. It was like finding out that an incurable strain of insanity pervaded the family, an intangible horror that swayed and taunted beyond the grasp of reaching fingers.

23 "A friend in South America. We are not alone."

24 "We *are* alone," he said vehemently. "This whole thing is crazy. You're crazy. I'm crazy. All right, so we made a mistake. Let's admit it."

25 "There has been no mistake. The letter confirms."

26 "Sure it does. It proves there's crazy people in the world besides us. If Japan won the war, what the hell are we doing here? What are you doing running a grocery store? It doesn't figure. It doesn't figure because we're all wrong. The minute we admit that, everything is fine. I've had a lot of time to think about all this. I've thought about it, and every time the answer comes out the same. You can't tell me different any more."

27 She sighed ever so slightly. "We will talk later when you are feeling better." Carefully folding the letter and placing it back in the envelope, she returned it to her pocket. "It is not I who tell you that the ship is coming. It is in the letter. If you have come to doubt your mother—and I'm sure you do not mean it even if you speak in weakness—it is to be regretted. Rest a few days. Think more deeply and your doubts will disappear. You are my son, Ichiro."

28 No, he said to himself as he watched her part the curtains and start into the store. There was a time when I was your son. There was a time that I no longer remember when you used to smile a mother's smile and tell me stories about gallant and fierce warriors who protected their lords with blades of shining steel and about the old woman who found a peach in the stream and took it home and when her husband split it in half, a husky little boy tumbled out to fill their hearts with boundless joy. I was that boy in the peach and you were the old woman and we were Japanese with Japanese feelings and Japanese pride and Japanese thoughts because it was all right then to be Japanese and feel and think all the things that Japanese do even if we lived in America. Then there came a time when I was only half Japanese because one is not born in America and raised in America and taught in America and one does not speak and swear and drink and smoke and play and fight and see and hear in America among Americans in American streets and houses without becoming American and loving it. But I did not love enough, for you were still half my mother and I was thereby still half Japanese and when the war came and they told me to fight for America, I was not strong enough to fight you and I was not strong enough to fight the bitterness which made the half of me which was you bigger than the half of me which was America and really the whole of me that I could not see or feel. Now that I know the truth when it is too late and the half of me

which was you is no longer there, I am only half of me and the half that remains is American by law because the government was wise and strong enough to know why it was that I could not fight for America and did not strip me of my birthright. But it is not enough to be American only in the eyes of the law and it is not enough to be only half an American and know that it is an empty half. I am not your son and I am not Japanese and I am not American. I can go someplace and tell people that I've got an inverted stomach and that I am an American, true and blue and Hail Columbia, but the army wouldn't have me because of the stomach. That's easy and I would do it, only I've got to convince myself first and that I cannot do. I wish with all my heart that I were Japanese or that I were American. I am neither and I blame you and I blame myself and I blame the world which is made up of many countries which fight with each other and kill and hate and destroy but not enough, so that they must kill and hate and destroy again and again and again. It is so easy and simple that I cannot understand it at all. And the reason I do not understand it is because I do not understand you who were the half of me that is no more and because I do not understand what it was about that half that made me destroy the half of me which was American and the half which might have become the whole of me if I had said yes I will go and fight in your army because that is what I believe and want and cherish and love . . .

Defeatedly, he crushed the stub of a cigarette into an ash tray filled with many other stubs and reached for the package to get another. It was empty and he did not want to go into the store for more because he did not feel much like seeing either his father or mother. He went into the bedroom and tossed and groaned and half slept. 29

Hours later, someone shook him awake. It was not his mother and it was not his father. The face that looked down at him in the gloomy darkness was his brother's. 30

"Taro," he said softly, for he had hardly thought of him. 31

"Yeah, it's me," said his brother with unmistakable embarrassment. "I see you got out." 32

"How've you been?" He studies his brother, who was as tall as he but skinnier. 33

"Okay. It's time to eat." He started to leave. 34

"Taro, wait." 35

His brother stood framed in the light of the doorway and faced him. 36

"How've you been?" he repeated. Then he added quickly for fear of losing him: "No, I said that before and I don't mean it the way it sounds. We've got things to talk about. Long time since we saw each other." 37

"Yeah, it's been a long time."

"How's school?" 38

"Okay." 39

"About through with high school?" 40

41

42 "Next June."

43 "What then? College?"

44 "No, army."

45 He wished he could see his face, the face of the brother who spoke to him as though they were strangers—because that's what they were.

46 "You could get in a year or two before the draft," he heard himself saying in an effort to destroy the wall that separated them. "I read where you can take an exam now and get a deferment if your showing is good enough. A fellow's got to have all the education he can get, Taro."

47 "I don't want a deferment. I want in."

48 "Ma know?"

49 "Who cares?"

50 "She won't like it."

51 "Doesn't matter."

52 "Why so strong about the army? Can't you wait? They'll come and get you soon enough."

53 "That isn't soon enough for me."

54 "What's your reason?"

55 He waited for an answer, knowing what it was and not wanting to hear it.

56 "Is it because of me? What I did?"

57 "I'm hungry," his brother said and turned into the kitchen.

58 His mother had already eaten and was watching the store. He sat opposite his brother, who wolfed down the food without looking back at him. It wasn't more than a few minutes before he rose, grabbed his jacket off a nail on the wall, and left the table. The bell tinkled and he was gone.

59 "Don't mind him," said the father apologetically. "Taro is young and restless. He's never home except to eat and sleep."

60 "When does he study?"

61 "He does not."

62 "Why don't you do something about it?"

63 "I tell him. Mama tells him. Makes no difference. It is the war that has made them that way. All the people say the same thing. The war and the camp life. Made them wild like cats and dogs. It is hard to understand."

64 "Sure," he said, but he told himself that he understood, that the reason why Taro was not a son and not a brother was because he was young and American and alien to his parents, who had lived in America for thirty-five years without becoming less Japanese and could speak only a few broken words of English and write it not at all, and because Taro hated that thing in his elder brother which had prevented him from thinking for himself. And in his hate for that thing, he hated his brother and also his parents because they had created the thing with their eyes and hands and minds which had seen and felt and thought as Japanese for thirty-five years in an America which they rejected as thoroughly as if they had never been a day away from Japan. That was the reason and it was difficult to believe, but it was true because he was the emptiness between

the one and the other and could see flashes of the truth that was true for his parents and the truth that was true for his brother.

"Pa," he said.                                                                    65

"Ya, Ichiro." He was swirling a dishcloth in a pan of hot water and working    66
up suds for the dishes.

"What made you and Ma come to America?"                                        67

"Everyone was coming to America."                                              68

"Did you have to come?"                                                        69

"No. We came to make money."                                                   70

"Is that all?"                                                                 71

"Ya, I think that was why we came."                                            72

"Why to make money?"                                                           73

"There was a man in my village who went to America and made a lot of          74
money and he came back and bought a big piece of land and he was very
comfortable. We came so we could make money and go back and buy a piece
of land and be comfortable too."

"Did you ever think about staying here and not going back?"                    75

"No."                                                                          76

He looked at his father, who was old and bald and washing dishes in a          77
kitchen that was behind a hole in the wall that was a grocery store. "How do
you feel about it now?"

"About what?"                                                                  78

"Going back."                                                                  79

"We are going."                                                                80

"When?"                                                                        81

"Oh, pretty soon."                                                             82

"How soon?"                                                                    83

"Pretty soon."                                                                 84

There didn't seem to be much point in pursuing the questioning. He went        85
out to the store and got a fresh pack of cigarettes. His mother was washing
down the vegetable stand, which stood alongside the entrance. Her thin arms
swabbed the green-painted wood with sweeping, vigorous strokes. There was a
power in the wiry, brown arms, a hard, blind, unreckoning force which coursed
through veins of tough bamboo. When she had done her work, she carried the
pail of water to the curb outside and poured it on the street. Then she came
back through the store and into the living quarters and emerged once more
dressed in her coat and hat.

"Come, Ichiro," she said, "we must go and see Kumasaka-san and Ashida-         86
san. They will wish to know that you are back."

The import of the suggested visits made him waver helplessly. He was too       87
stunned to voice his protest. The Kumasakas and the Ashidas were people from
the same village in Japan. The three families had been very close for as long as
he could recall. Further, it was customary among the Japanese to pay ceremo-
nious visits upon various occasions to families of close association. This was

particularly true when a member of one of the families either departed on an extended absence or returned from an unusually long separation. Yes, he had been gone a long time, but it was such a different thing. It wasn't as if he had gone to war and returned safe and sound or had been matriculating at some school in another city and come home with a sheepskin *summa cum laude*. He scrabbled at the confusion in his mind for the logic of the crazy business and found no satisfaction.

88     "Papa," his mother shouted without actually shouting.

89     His father hastened out from the kitchen and Ichiro stumbled in blind fury after the woman who was only a rock of hate and fanatic stubbornness and was, therefore, neither woman nor mother.

90     They walked through the night and the city, a mother and son thrown together for a while longer because the family group is a stubborn one and does not easily disintegrate. The woman walked ahead and the son followed and no word passed between them. They walked six blocks, then six more, and still another six before they turned in to a three-story frame building.

91     The Ashidas, parents and three daughters, occupied four rooms on the second floor.

92     "Mama," screamed the ten-year-old who answered the knock, "Mrs. Yamada."

93     A fat, cheerful-looking woman rushed toward them, then stopped, flushed and surprised. "Ichiro-san. You have come back."

94     He nodded his head and heard his mother say, with unmistakable exultation: "Today, Ashida-san. Just today he came home."

95     Urged by their hostess, they took seats in the sparsely furnished living room. Mrs. Ashida sat opposite them on a straight-backed kitchen chair and beamed.

96     "You have grown so much. It is good to be home, is it not, Ichiro-san?" She turned to the ten-year-old who gawked at him from behind her mother: "Tell Reiko to get tea and cookies."

97     "She's studying, Mama."

98     "You mustn't bother," said his mother.

99     "Go now, I know she is only listening to the radio." The little girl fled out of the room.

100     "It is good to see you again, Ichiro-san. You will find many of your young friends already here. All the people who said they would never come back to Seattle are coming back. It is almost like it was before the war. Akira-san—you went to school with him I think—he is just back from Italy, and Watanabe-san's boy came back from Japan last month. It is so good that the war is over and everything is getting to be like it was before."

101     "You saw the pictures?" his mother asked.

102     "What pictures?"

103     "You have not been to the Watanabes'?"

104     "Oh, yes, the pictures of Japan." She snickered. "He is such a serious boy. He showed me all the pictures he had taken in Japan. He had many of Hiroshima

and Nagasaki and I told him that he must be mistaken because Japan did not lose the war as he seems to believe and that he could not have been in Japan to take pictures because, if he were in Japan, he would not have been permitted to remain alive. He protested and yelled so that his mother had to tell him to be careful and then he tried to argue some more, but I asked him if he was ever in Japan before and could he prove that he was actually there and he said again to look at the pictures and I told him that what must really have happened was that the army only told him he was in Japan when he was someplace else, and that it was too bad he believed the propaganda. Then he got so mad his face went white and he said: 'How do you know you're you? Tell me how you know you're you!' If his mother had not made him leave the room, he might even have struck me. It is not enough that they must willingly take up arms against their uncles and cousins and even brothers and sisters, but they no longer have respect for the old ones. If I had a son and he had gone in the American army to fight Japan, I would have killed myself with shame."

"They know not what they do and it is not their fault. It is the fault of the 105 parents. I've always said that Mr. Watanabe was a stupid man. Gambling and drinking the way he does. I am almost ashamed to call them friends." Ichiro's mother looked at him with a look which said I am a Japanese and you are my son and have conducted yourself as a Japanese and I know no shame such as other parents do because their sons were not really their sons or they would not have fought against their own people.

He wanted to get up and dash out into the night. The madness of his mother 106 was in mutual company and he felt nothing but loathing for the gentle, kindly-looking Mrs. Ashida, who sat on a fifty-cent chair from Goodwill Industries while her husband worked the night shift at a hotel, grinning and bowing for dimes and quarters from rich Americans whom he detested, and couldn't afford to take his family on a bus ride to Tacoma but was waiting and praying and hoping for the ships from Japan.

Reiko brought in a tray holding little teacups and a bowl of thin, round 107 cookies. She was around seventeen with little bumps on her chest which the sweater didn't improve and her lips heavily lipsticked a deep red. She said "Hi" to him and did not have to say look at me, I was a kid when you saw me last but now I'm a woman with a woman's desires and a woman's eye for men like you. She set the tray on the table and gave him a smile before she left.

His mother took the envelope from São Paulo out of her dress pocket and 108 handed it to Mrs. Ashida.

"From South America." 109

The other woman snatched at the envelope and proceeded to read the 110 contents instantly. Her face glowed with pride. She read it eagerly, her lips moving all the time and frequently murmuring audibly. "Such wonderful news," she sighed breathlessly as if the reading of the letter had been a deep emotional experience. "Mrs. Okamoto will be eager to see this. Her husband, who goes out of the house whenever I am there, is threatening to leave her unless she gives up her nonsense about Japan. Nonsense, he calls it. He is no better than a Chinaman. This will show him. I feel so sorry for her."

111     "It is hard when so many no longer believe," replied his mother, "but they are not Japanese like us. They only call themselves such. It is the same with the Teradas. I no longer go to see them. The last time I was there Mr. Terada screamed at me and told me to get out. They just don't understand that Japan did not lose the war because Japan could not possibly lose. I try not to hate them but I have no course but to point them out to the authorities when the ships come."

112     "It's getting late, Ma." He stood up, sick in the stomach and wanting desperately to smash his way out of the dishonest, warped, and uncompromising world in which defeated people like his mother and the Ashidas walked their perilous tightropes and could not and would not look about them for having to keep their eyes fastened to the taut, thin support.

113     "Yes," his mother replied quickly, "forgive us for rushing, for you know that I enjoy nothing better than a visit with you, but we must drop in for a while on the Kumasakas."

114     "Of course. I wish you could stay longer, but I know that there will be plenty of opportunities again. You will come again, please, Ichiro-san?"

115     Mumbling thanks for the tea, he nodded evasively and hurried down the stairs. Outside, he lit a cigarette and paced restlessly until his mother came out.

116     "A fine woman," she said without stopping.

117     He followed, talking to the back of her head: "Ma, I don't want to see the Kumasakas tonight. I don't want to see anybody tonight. We'll go some other time."

118     "We won't stay long."

119     They walked a few blocks to a freshly painted frame house that was situated behind a neatly kept lawn.

120     "Nice house," he said.

121     "They bought it last month."

122     "Bought it?"

123     "Yes."

124     The Kumasakas had run a dry-cleaning shop before the war. Business was good and people spoke of their having money, but they lived in cramped quarters above the shop because, like most of the other Japanese, they planned someday to return to Japan and still felt transients even after thirty or forty years in America and the quarters above the shop seemed adequate and sensible since the arrangement was merely temporary. That, he thought to himself, was the reason why the Japanese were still Japanese. They rushed to America with the single purpose of making a fortune which would enable them to return to their own country and live adequately. It did not matter when they discovered that fortunes were not for the mere seeking or that their sojourns were spanning decades instead of years and it did not matter that growing families and growing

bills and misfortunes and illness and low wages and just plain hard luck were constant obstacles to the realization of their dreams. They continued to maintain their dreams by refusing to learn how to speak or write the language of America and by living only among their own kind and by zealously avoiding long-term commitments such as the purchase of a house. But now, the Kumasakas, it seemed, had bought this house, and he was impressed. It could only mean that the Kumasakas had exchanged hope for reality and, late as it was, were finally sinking roots into the land from which they had previously sought not nourishment but only gold.

Mrs. Kumasaka came to the door, a short, heavy woman who stood solidly on feet planted wide apart, like a man. She greeted them warmly but with a sadness that she would carry to the grave. When Ichiro had last seen her, her hair had been pitch black. Now it was completely white. 125

In the living room Mr. Kumasaka, a small man with a pleasant smile, was sunk deep in an upholstered chair, reading a Japanese newspaper. It was a comfortable room with rugs and soft furniture and lamps and end tables and pictures on recently papered walls. 126

"Ah, Ichiro, it is nice to see you looking well," Mr. Kumasaka struggled out of the chair and extended a friendly hand. "Please, sit down." 127

"You've got a nice place," he said, meaning it. 128

"Thank you," the little man said. "Mama and I, we finally decided that America is not so bad. We like it here." 129

Ichiro sat down on the sofa next to his mother and felt strange in this home which he envied because it was like millions of other homes in America and could never be his own. 130

Mrs. Kumasaka sat next to her husband on a large, round hassock and looked at Ichiro with lonely eyes, which made him uncomfortable. 131

"Ichiro came home this morning." It was his mother, and the sound of her voice, deliberately loud and almost arrogant, puzzled him. "He has suffered, but I make no apologies for him or for myself. If he had given his life for Japan, I could not be prouder." 132

"Ma," he said, wanting to object but not knowing why except that her comments seemed out of place. 133

Ignoring him, she continued, not looking at the man but at his wife, who now sat with head bowed, her eyes emptily regarding the floral pattern of the carpet. "A mother's lot is not an easy one. To sleep with a man and bear a son is nothing. To raise the child into a man one can be proud of is not play. Some of us succeed. Some, of course, must fail. It is too bad, but that is the way of life." 134

"Yes, yes, Yamada-san," said the man impatiently. Then, smiling, he turned to Ichiro: "I suppose you'll be going back to the university?" 135

"I'll have to think about it," he replied, wishing that his father was like this man who made him want to pour out the turbulence in his soul. 136

"He will go when the new term begins. I have impressed upon him the 137 importance of a good education. With a college education, one can go far in Japan." His mother smiled knowingly.

138     "Ah," said the man as if he had not heard her speak. "Bobbie wanted to go to the university and study medicine. He would have made a fine doctor. Always studying and reading, is that not so, Ichiro?"

139     He nodded, remembering the quiet son of the Kumasakas, who never played football with the rest of the kids on the street or appeared at dances, but could talk for hours on end about chemistry and zoology and physics and other courses which he hungered after in high school.

140     "Sure, Bob always was pretty studious." He knew, somehow, that it was not the right thing to say, but he added: "Where is Bob?"

141     His mother did not move. Mrs. Kumasaka uttered a despairing cry and bit her trembling lips.

142     The little man, his face a drawn mask of pity and sorrow, stammered: "Ichiro, you—no one has told you?"

143     "No. What? No one's told me anything."

144     "Your mother did not write you?"

145     "No. Write about what?" He knew what the answer was. It was in the whiteness of the hair of the sad woman who was the mother of the boy named Bob and it was in the engaging pleasantness of the father which was not really pleasantness but a deep understanding which had emerged from resignation to a loss which only a parent knows and suffers. And then he saw the picture on the mantel, a snapshot, enlarged many times over, of a grinning youth in uniform who had not thought to remember his parents with a formal portrait because he was not going to die and there would be worlds of time for pictures and books and other obligations of the living later on.

146     Mr. Kumasaka startled him by shouting toward the rear of the house: "Jun! Please come."

147     There was the sound of a door opening and presently there appeared a youth in khaki shirt and wool trousers, who was a stranger to Ichiro.

148     "I hope I haven't disturbed anything, Jun," said Mr. Kumasaka.

149     "No, it's all right. Just writing a letter."

150     "This is Mrs. Yamada and her son Ichiro. They are old family friends."

151     Jun nodded to his mother and reached over to shake Ichiro's hand.

152     The little man waited until Jun had seated himself on the end of the sofa. "Jun is from Los Angeles. He's on his way home from the army and was good enough to stop by and visit us for a few days. He and Bobbie were together. Buddies—is that what you say?"

153     "That's right," said Jun.

154     "Now, Jun."

155     "Yes?"

156     The little man looked at Ichiro and then at his mother, who stared stonily at no one in particular.

"Jun, as a favor to me, although I know it is not easy for you to speak of it, I want you to tell us about Bobbie." 157

Jun stood up quickly. "Gosh, I don't know." He looked with tender concern at Mrs. Kumasaka. 158

"It is all right, Jun. Please, just this once more." 159

"Well, okay." He sat down again, rubbing his hands thoughtfully over his knees. "The way it happened, Bobbie and I, we had just gotten back to the rest area. Everybody was feeling good because there was a lot of talk about the Germans' surrendering. All the fellows were cleaning their equipment. We'd been up in the lines for a long time and everything was pretty well messed up. When you're up there getting shot at, you don't worry much about how crummy your things get, but the minute you pull back, they got to have inspection. So, we were cleaning things up. Most of us were cleaning our rifles because that's something you learn to want to do no matter how anything else looks. Bobbie was sitting beside me and he was talking about how he going to medical school and become a doctor—" 160

A sob wrenched itself free from the breast of the mother whose son was once again dying, and the snow-white head bobbed wretchedly. 161

"Go on, Jun," said the father. 162

Jun looked away from the mother and at the picture on the mantel. "Bobbie was like that. Me and the other guys, all we talked about was drinking and girls and stuff like that because it's important to talk about those things when you make it back from the front on your own power, but Bobbie, all he thought about was going to school. I was nodding my head and saying yeah, yeah, and then there was this noise, kind of a pinging noise right close by. It scared me for a minute and I started to cuss and said, 'Gee, that was damn close,' and looked around at Bobbie. He was slumped over with his head between his knees. I reached out to hit him, thinking he was fooling around. Then, when I tapped him on the arm, he fell over and I saw the dark spot on the side of his head where the bullet had gone through. That was all. Ping, and he's dead. It doesn't figure, but it happened just the way I've said." 163

The mother was crying now, without shame and alone in her grief that knew no end. And in her bottomless grief that made no distinction as to what was wrong and what was right and who was Japanese and who was not, there was no awareness of the other mother with a living son who had come to say to her you are with shame and grief because you were not Japanese and thereby killed your son but mine is big and strong and full of life because I did not weaken and would not let my son destroy himself uselessly and treacherously. 164

Ichiro's mother rose and, without a word, for no words would ever pass between them again, went out of the house which was a part of America. 165

Mr. Kumasaka placed a hand on the rounded back of his wife, who was forever beyond consoling, and spoke gently to Ichiro: "You don't have to say anything. You are truly sorry and I am sorry for you." 166

167     "I didn't know," he said pleadingly.

168     "I want you to feel free to come and visit us whenever you wish. We can talk even if your mother's convictions are different."

169     "She's crazy. Mean and crazy. Goddamned Jap!" He felt the tears hot and stinging.

170     "Try to understand her."

171     Impulsively, he took the little man's hand in his own and held it briefly. Then he hurried out of the house which could never be his own.

172     His mother was not waiting for him. He saw her tiny figure strutting into the shadows away from the illumination of the street lights and did not attempt to catch her. ✤

---

## RESPONDING

1. Have you ever found yourself in serious conflict over a matter of conscience with a person whose opinion you valued such as a parent, teacher, religious leader, or special friend? Did the conflict produce inner turmoil? What was the outcome?

2. The story presents two contrasting attitudes toward Japan and America. Working individually or in a group, analyze the reasons for each point of view and present them to the class.

3. What is Ichiro's attitude toward his mother? Does it change in the course of the story? Write the dialogue that might have taken place between Ichiro and his mother on the way home from the Kumasakas' house.

4. Ichiro's statement "I wish with all my heart that I were Japanese or that I were American" (paragraph 28) expresses his inner conflict. In an essay, explain the divided loyalties that pull him in different directions.

---

# HISAYE YAMAMOTO

*Hisaye Yamamoto, who was born in Redondo Beach, California, in 1921, spent the war years interned with her family in Arizona. After the war she attended college and wrote for the* Los Angeles Tribune. *Since that time, Yamamoto has published short stories in such journals as* The Kenyon Review, Amerasia Journal, The Partisan Review, Arizona Quarterly, *and* Counterpoint. *Much of her writing was collected in the volume* Seventeen Syllables and Other Stories, *published in 1989.*

*"The Legend of Miss Sasagawara," from* Seventeen Syllables, *uses the concrete details of fiction to examine the effects of the internment camp's regimented life on one of its inmates; in a more general sense the story might be said to comment on the consequences of the Internment for many Japanese American young people who came of age during this period.*

⁜

# THE LEGEND OF MISS SASAGAWARA

EVEN IN THAT UNLIKELY PLACE OF WIND, sand, and heat, it was easy to imagine    1
Miss Sasagawara a decorative ingredient of some ballet. Her daily costume, brief and fitting closely to her trifling waist, generously billowing below, and bringing together arrestingly rich colors like mustard yellow and forest green, appeared to have been cut from a coarse-textured homespun; her shining hair was so long it wound twice about her head to form a coronet; her face was delicate and pale, with a fine nose, pouting bright mouth, and glittering eyes; and her measured walk said, "Look, I'm *walking*!" as though walking were not a common but a rather special thing to be doing. I first saw her so one evening after mess, as she was coming out of the women's latrine going toward her barracks, and after I thought I was out of hearing, I imitated the young men of the Block (No. 33), and gasped, "Wow! How much does *she* weigh?"

"Oh, haven't you heard?" said my friend Elsie Kubo, knowing very well I    2
had not. "That's Miss Sasagawara."

It turned out Elsie knew all about Miss Sasagawara, who with her father    3
was new to Block 33. Where had she accumulated all her items? Probably a morsel here and a morsel there, and, anyway, I forgot to ask her sources, because the picture she painted was so distracting: Miss Sasagawara's father was a Buddhist minister, and the two had gotten permission to come to this Japanese evacuation camp in Arizona from one further north, after the death there of Mrs. Sasagawara. They had come here to join the Rev. Sasagawara's brother's family, who lived in a neighboring Block, but there had been some trouble between them, and just this week the immigrant pair had gotten leave to move over to Block 33. They were occupying one end of the Block's lone empty barracks, which had not been chopped up yet into the customary four apartments. The other end had been taken over by a young couple, also newcomers to the Block, who had moved in the same day.

"And do you know what, Kiku?" Elsie continued. "Oooh, that gal is really    4
temperamental. I guess it's because she was a ballet dancer before she got stuck in camp, I hear people like that are temperamental. Anyway, the Sasakis, the new couple at the other end of the barracks, think she's crazy. The day they all moved in, the barracks was really dirty, all covered with dust from the dust storms and everything, so Mr. Sasaki was going to wash the whole barracks down with a hose, and he thought he'd be nice and do the Sasagawaras' side first. You

know, do them a favor. But do you know what? Mr. Sasaki got the hose attached to the faucet outside and started to go in the door, and he said all the Sasagawaras' suitcases and things were on top of the Army cots and Miss Sasagawara was trying to clean the place out with a pail of water and a broom. He said, 'Here let me flush the place out with a hose for you; it'll be faster.' And she turned right around and screamed at him, 'What are you trying to do? Spy on me? Get out of here or I'll throw this water on you!' He said he was so surprised he couldn't move for a minute, and before he knew it, Miss Sasagawara just up and threw that water at him, pail and all. Oh, he said he got out of that place fast, but fast. Madwoman, he called her."

5    But Elsie had already met Miss Sasagawara, too, over at the apartment of the Murakamis, where Miss Sasagawara was borrowing Mrs. Murakami's Singer, and had found her quite amiable. "She said she was thirty-nine years old—imagine, thirty-nine, she looks so young, more like twenty-five; but she said she wasn't sorry she never got married, because she's had her fun. She said she got to go all over the country a couple of times, dancing in the ballet."

6    And after we emerged from the latrine, Elsie and I, slapping mosquitoes in the warm, gathering dusk, sat on the stoop of her apartment and talked awhile, jealously of the scintillating life Miss Sasagawara had led until now and nostalgically of the few ballets we had seen in the world outside. (How faraway Los Angeles seemed!) But we ended up as we always did, agreeing that our mission in life, pushing twenty as we were, was first to finish college somewhere when and if the war ever ended and we were free again, and then to find good jobs and two nice, clean young men, preferably handsome, preferably rich, who would cherish us forever and a day.

7    My introduction, less spectacular, to the Rev. Sasagawara came later, as I noticed him, a slight and fragile-looking old man, in the Block mess hall (where I worked as a waitress, and Elsie, too) or in the laundry room or going to and from the latrine. Sometimes he would be farther out, perhaps going to the post office or canteen or to visit friends in another Block or on some business to the Administration buildings, but wherever he was headed, however doubtless his destination, he always seemed to be wandering lostly. This may have been because he walked so slowly, with such negligible steps, or because he wore perpetually an air of bemusement, never talking directly to a person, as though, being what he was, he could not stop for an instant his meditation on the higher life.

8    I noticed, too, that Miss Sasagawara never came to the mess hall herself. Her father ate at the tables reserved for the occupants, mostly elderly, of the end barracks known as the bachelors' dormitory. After each meal, he came up to the counter and carried away a plate of food, protected with one of the pinkish apple wrappers we waitresses made as wrinkleless as possible and put out for napkins, and a mug of tea or coffee. Sometimes Miss Sasagawara could be seen rinsing out her empties at the one double-tub in the laundry that was reserved for private dishwashing.

If any one in the Block or in the entire camp of 15,000 or so people had ⁹ talked at any length with Miss Sasagawara (everyone happening to speak of her called her that, although her first name, Mari, was simple enough and rather pretty) after her first and only visit to use Mrs. Murakami's sewing machine, I never heard of it. Nor did she ever willingly use the shower room, just off the latrine, when anyone else was there. Once, when I was up past midnight writing letters and went for my shower, I came upon her under the full needling force of a steamy spray, but she turned her back to me and did not answer my surprised hello. I hoped my body would be as smooth and spare and well-turned when I was thirty-nine. Another time Elsie and I passed in front of the Sasagawara apartment, which was really only a cubicle because the once-empty barracks had soon been partitioned off into six units for families of two, and we saw her there on the wooden steps, sitting with her wide, wide skirt spread splendidly about her. She was intent on peeling a grapefruit, which her father had probably brought to her from the mess hall that morning, and Elsie called out, "Hello there!" Miss Sasagawara looked up and stared, without recognition. We were almost out of earshot when I heard her call, "Do I know you?" and I could have almost sworn that she sounded hopeful, if not downright wistful, but Elsie, already miffed at having expended friendliness so unprofitably, seemed not to have heard, and that was that.

Well, if Miss Sasagawara was not one to speak to, she was certainly one to ¹⁰ speak of, and she came up quite often as topic for the endless conversations which helped along the monotonous days. My mother said she had met the late Mrs. Sasagawara once, many years before the war, and to hear her tell it, a sweeter, kindlier woman there never was. "I suppose," said my mother, "that I'll never meet anyone like her again; she was a lady in every sense of the word." Then she reminded me that I had seen the Rev. Sasagawara before. Didn't I remember him as one of the three bhikshus who had read the sutras at Grandfather's funeral?

I could not say that I did. I barely remembered Grandfather, my mother's ¹¹ father. The only thing that came back with clarity was my nausea at the wake and the funeral, the first and only ones I had ever had occasion to attend, because it had been reproduced several times since—each time, in fact, that I had crossed again the actual scent or suspicion of burning incense. Dimly I recalled the inside of the Buddhist temple in Los Angeles, an immense, murky auditorium whose high and huge platform had held, centered in the background, a great golden shrine touched with black and white. Below this platform, Grandfather, veiled by gauze, had slept in a long grey box which just fitted him. There had been flowers, oh, such flowers, everywhere. And right in front of Grandfather's box had been the incense stand, upon which squatted two small bowls, one with a cluster of straw-thin sticks sending up white tendrils of smoke, the other containing a heap of coarse, grey powder. Each mourner in turn had gone up to the stand, bowing once, his palms touching in prayer before he reached it; had bent in prayer over the stand; had taken then a pinch of incense from the bowl of crumbs and, bowing over it reverently, cast it into the other, the active bowl; had bowed, the hands praying again; had retreated a few steps and bowed one last time, the hands still joined, before returning to his seat. (I knew the ceremony well from having been severely coached in it on the evening of the wake.) There had been tears and tears and here and there a sudden sob.

12    And all this while, three men in black robes had been on the platform, one standing in front of the shining altar, the others sitting on either side, and the entire trio incessantly chanting a strange, melifluous language in unison. From time to time there had reverberated through the enormous room, above the singsong, above the weeping, above the fragrance, the sharp, startling whang of the gong.

13    So, one of those men had been Miss Sasagawara's father. . . . This information brought him closer to me, and I listened with interest later when it was told that he kept here in his apartment a small shrine, much more intricately constructed than that kept by the usual Buddhist household, before which, at regular hours of the day, he offered incense and chanted, tinkling (in lieu of the gong) a small bell. What did Miss Sasagawara do at these prayer periods, I wondered; did she participate, did she let it go in one ear and out the other, or did she abruptly go out on the steps, perhaps to eat a grapefruit?

14    Elsie and I tired one day of working in the mess hall. And this desire for greener fields came almost together with the Administration announcement that henceforth the wages of residents doing truly vital labor, such as in the hospital or on the garbage trucks that went from mess hall to mess hall, would be upped to nineteen dollars a month instead of the common sixteen.

15    "Oh, I've always wanted to be a nurse!" Elsie confided, as the Block manager sat down to his breakfast after reading out the day's bulletin in English and Japanese.

16    "What's stopped you?" I asked.

17    "Mom," Elsie said. "She thinks it's dirty work. And she's afraid I'll catch something. But I'll remind her of the extra three dollars."

18    "It's never appealed to me much, either," I confessed. "Why don't we go over to garbage? It's the same pay."

19    Elsie would not even consider it. "Very funny. Well, you don't have to be a nurse's aide, Kiku. The hospital's short all kinds of help. Dental assistants, receptionists. . . . Let's go apply after we finish this here."

20    So, willy-nilly, while Elsie plunged gleefully into the pleasure of wearing a trim blue-and-white striped seersucker, into the duties of taking temperatures and carrying bedpans, and into the fringe of medical jargon (she spoke very casually now of catheters, enemas, primiparas, multiparas), I became a relief receptionist at the hospital's front desk, taking my hours as they were assigned. And it was on one of my midnight-to-morning shifts that I spoke to Miss Sasagawara for the first time.

The cooler in the corridor window was still whirring away (for that desert     21
heat in summer had a way of lingering intact through the night to merge
with the warmth of the morning sun), but she entered bundled in an extraordinarily long black coat, her face made petulant, not unprettily, by lines of
pain.

"I think I've got appendicitis," she said breathlessly, without preliminary.     22

"May I have your name and address?" I asked, unscrewing my pen.     23

Annoyance seemed to outbalance agony for a moment, but she answered     24
soon enough, in a cold rush, "Mari Sasagawara, Thirty-three-seven C."

It was necessary also to learn her symptoms, and I wrote down that she had     25
chills and a dull aching at the back of her head, as well as these excruciating
flashes in her lower right abdomen.

"I'll have to go wake up the doctor. Here's a blanket, why don't you lie     26
down over there on the bench until he comes?" I suggested.

She did not answer, so I tossed the Army blanket on the bench, and when     27
I returned from the doctors' dormitory, after having tapped and tapped on the
door of young Dr. Moritomo, who was on night duty, she was still standing
where I had left her, immobile and holding onto the wooden railing shielding
the desk.

"Dr. Moritomo's coming right away," I said. "Why don't you sit down at     28
least?"

Miss Sasagawara said, "Yes," but did not move.     29

"Did you walk all the way?" I asked incredulously, for Block 33 was a good     30
mile off, across the canal.

She nodded, as if that were not important, also as if to thank me kindly to     31
mind my own business.

Dr. Moritomo (technically, the title was premature; evacuation had caught     32
him with a few months to go on his degree), wearing a maroon bathrobe,
shuffled in sleepily and asked her to come into the emergency room for an
examination. A short while later, he guided her past my desk into the laboratory,
saying he was going to take her blood count.

When they came out, she went over to the electric fountain for a drink of     33
water, and Dr. Moritomo said reflectively, "Her count's all right. Not appendicitis. We should keep her for observation, but the general ward is pretty full,
isn't it? Hm, well, I'll give her something to take. Will you tell one of the boys
to take her home?

This I did, but when I came back from arousing George, one of the     34
ambulance boys, Miss Sasagawara was gone, and Dr. Moritomo was coming out
of the laboratory where he had gone to push out the lights. "Here's George,
but that girl must have walked home," I reported helplessly.

"She's in no condition to do that. George, better catch up with her and take     35
her home," Dr. Moritomo ordered.

Shrugging, George strode down the hall; the doctor shuffled back to bed;     36 and soon there was the shattering sound of one of the old Army ambulances backing out of the hospital drive.

37    George returned in no time at all to say that Miss Sasagawara had refused to get on the ambulance.

38    "She wouldn't even listen to me. She just kept walking and I drove alongside and told her it was Dr. Moritomo's orders, but she wouldn't even listen to me."

39    "She wouldn't?"

40    "I hope Doc didn't expect me to drag her into the ambulance."

41    "Oh, well," I said. "I guess she'll get home all right. She walked all the way up here."

42    "Cripes, what a dame!" George complained, shaking his head as he started back to the ambulance room. "I never heard of such a thing. She wouldn't even listen to me."

43    Miss Sasagawara came back to the hospital about a month later. Elsie was the one who rushed up to the desk where I was on day duty to whisper, "Miss Sasagawara just tried to escape from the hospital!"

44    "Escape? What do you mean, escape?" I said.

45    "Well, she came in last night, and they didn't know what was wrong with her, so they kept her for observation. And this morning, just now, she ran out of the ward in just a hospital nightgown and the orderlies chased after her and caught her and brought her back. Oh, she was just fighting them. But once they got her back to bed, she calmed down right away, and Miss Morris asked her what was the big idea, you know, and do you know what she said? She said she didn't want any more of those doctors pawing her. *Pawing* her, imagine!"

46    After an instant's struggle with self-mockery, my curiosity led me down the entrance corridor after Elsie into the longer, wider corridor admitting to the general ward. The whole hospital staff appeared to have gathered in the room to get a look at Miss Sasagawara, and the other patients, or those of them that could, were sitting up attentively in their high, white, and narrow beds. Miss Sasagawara had the corner bed to the left as we entered and, covered only by a brief hospital apron, she was sitting on the edge with her legs dangling over the side. With her head slightly bent, she was staring at a certain place on the floor, and I knew she must be aware of that concentrated gaze, of trembling old Dr. Kawamoto (he had retired several years before the war, but he had been drafted here), of Miss Morris, the head nurse, of Miss Bowman, the nurse in charge of the general ward during the day, of the other patients, of the nurse's aides, of the orderlies, and of everyone else who tripped in and out abashedly on some pretext or other in order to pass by her bed. I knew this by her smile, for as she continued to look at that same piece of the floor, she continued, unexpectedly, to seem wryly amused with the entire proceedings. I peered at her wonderingly through the triangular peephole created by someone's hand on hip, while Dr. Kawamoto, Miss Morris, and Miss Bowman tried to persuade her to lie down

and relax. She was as smilingly immune to tactful suggestions as she was to tactless gawking.

There was no future to watching such a war of nerves as this; and besides, I was supposed to be at the front desk, so I hurried back in time to greet a frantic young mother and father, the latter carrying their small son who had had a hemorrhage this morning after a tonsillectomy yesterday in the out-patient clinic.

A couple of weeks later on the late shift I found George, the ambulance driver, in high spirits. This time he had been the one selected to drive a patient to Phoenix, where special cases were occasionally sent under escort, and he was looking forward to the moment when, for a few hours, the escort would permit him to go shopping around the city and perhaps take in a new movie. He showed me the list of things his friends had asked him to bring back for them, and we laughed together over the request of one plumpish nurse's aide for the biggest, richest chocolate cake he could find.

"You ought to have seen Mabel's eyes while she was describing the kind of cake she wanted," he said. "Man, she looked like she was eating it already!"

Just then one of the other drivers, Bobo Kunitomi, came up and nudged George, and they withdrew a few steps from my desk.

"Oh, I ain't particularly interested in that," I heard George saying.

There was some murmuring from Bobo, of which I caught the words, "Well, hell, you might as well, just as long as you're getting to go out there."

George shrugged, then nodded, and Bobo came over to the desk and asked for pencil and paper. "This is a good place. . . ." he said, handing George what he had written.

Was it my imagination, or did George emerge from his chat with Bobo a little ruddier than usual? "Well, I guess I better go get ready," he said, taking leave. "Oh, anything you want, Kiku? Just say the word."

"Thanks, not this time," I said. "Well, enjoy yourself."

"Don't worry," he said. "I will!"

He had started down the hall when I remembered to ask, "Who are you taking, anyway?"

George turned around. "Miss Sa-sa-ga-wa-ra," he said, accenting every syllable. "Remember that dame? The one who wouldn't let me take her home?"

"Yes," I said. "What's the matter with her?"

George, saying not a word, pointed at his head and made several circles in the air with his first finger.

"Really?" I asked.

Still mum, George nodded in emphasis and pity before he turned to go.

How long was she away? It must have been several months, and when, towards late autumn, she returned at last from the sanitarium in Phoenix, everyone in Block 33 was amazed at the change. She said hello and how are you as often and easily as the next person, although many of those she greeted were surprised and suspicious, remembering the earlier rebuffs. There were some who never did get used to Miss Sasagawara as a friendly being.

64     One evening when I was going toward the latrine for my shower, my youngest sister, ten-year-old Michi, almost collided with me and said excitedly, "You going for your shower now, Kiku?"

65     "You want to fight about it?" I said, making fists.

66     "Don't go now, don't go now! Miss Sasagawara's in there," she whispered wickedly.

67     "Well," I demanded. "What's wrong with that, honey?"

68     "She's scary. Us kids were in there and she came in and we finished, so we got out, and she said, 'Don't be afraid of me. I won't hurt you.' Gee, we weren't even afraid of her, but when she said that, gee!"

69     "Oh, go home and go to bed," I said.

70     Miss Sasagawara was indeed in the shower and she welcomed me with a smile. "Aren't you the girl who plays the violin?"

71     I giggled and explained. Elsie and I, after hearing Menuhin on the radio, had in a fit of madness sent to Sears and Roebuck for beginners' violins that cost five dollars each. We had received free instruction booklets, too, but unable to make heads or tails from them, we contented ourselves with occasionally taking the violins out of their paper bags and sawing every which way away.

72     Miss Sasagawara laughed aloud—a lovely sound. "Well, you're just about as good as I am. I sent for a Spanish guitar. I studied it about a year once, but that was so long ago I don't remember the first thing and I'm having to start all over again. We'd make a fine orchestra."

73     That was the only time we really exchanged words and some weeks later I understood she had organized a dancing class from among the younger girls in the Block. My sister Michi, becoming one of her pupils, got very attached to her and spoke of her frequently at home. So I knew that Miss Sasagawara and her father had decorated their apartment to look oh, so pretty, that Miss Sasagawara had a whole big suitcase full of dancing costumes, and that Miss Sasagawara had just lots and lots of books to read.

74     The fruits of Miss Sasagawara's patient labor were put on show at the Block Christmas party, the second such observance in camp. Again, it was a gay, if odd, celebration. The mess hall was hung with red and green crepe paper streamers and the greyish mistletoe that grew abundantly on the ancient mesquite surrounding the camp. There were even electric decorations on the token Christmas tree. The oldest occupant of the bachelors' dormitory gave a tremulous monologue in an exaggerated Hiroshima dialect; one of the young boys wore a bow-tie and whispered a popular song while the girls shrieked and pretended to be growing faint; my mother sang an old Japanese song; four of the girls wore similar blue dresses and harmonized on a sweet tune; a little girl in a grass skirt and a superfluous brassiere did a hula; and the chief cook came out with an ample saucepan and, assisted by the waitresses, performed the

familiar *dojo-sukui*, the comic dance about a man who is merely trying to scoop up a few loaches from an uncooperative lake. Then Miss Sasagawara shooed her eight little girls, including Michi, in front, and while they formed a stiff pattern and waited, self-conscious in the rustly crepe paper dresses they had made themselves, she set up a portable phonograph on the floor and vigorously turned the crank.

Something was past its prime, either the machine or the record or the 75 needle, for what came out was a feeble rasp but distantly related to the Mozart minuet it was supposed to be. After a bit I recognized the melody; I had learned it as a child to the words,

> When dames wore hoops and powdered hair,
> And very strict was e-ti-quette,
> When men were brave and ladies fair,
> They danced the min-u-et. . . .

And the little girls, who might have curtsied and stepped gracefully about under Miss Sasagawara's eyes alone, were all elbows and knees as they felt the Block's one-hundred-fifty or more pairs of eyes on them. Although there was sustained applause after their number, what we were benevolently approving was the great effort, for the achievement had been undeniably small. Then Santa came with a pillow for a stomach, his hands each dragging a bulging burlap bag. Church people outside had kindly sent these gifts, Santa announced, and every recipient must write and thank the person whose name he would find on an enclosed slip. So saying, he called by name each Block child under twelve and ceremoniously presented each eleemosynary package, and a couple of the youngest children screamed in fright at this new experience of a red and white man with a booming voice.

At the last, Santa called, "Miss Mari Sasagawara!" and when she came 76 forward in surprise, he explained to the gathering that she was being rewarded for her help with the Block's younger generation. Everyone clapped and Miss Sasagawara, smiling graciously, opened her package then and there. She held up her gift, a peach-colored bath towel, so that it could be fully seen, and everyone clapped again.

Suddenly I put this desert scene behind me. The notice I had long awaited, of 77 permission to relocate to Philadelphia to attend college, finally came, and there was a prodigious amount of packing to do, leave papers to sign, and goodbyes to say. And once the wearying, sooty train trip was over, I found myself in an intoxicating new world of daily classes, afternoon teas, and evening concerts, from which I dutifully emerged now and then to answer the letters from home. When the beautiful semester was over, I returned to Arizona, to that glowing heat, to the camp, to the family; for although the war was still on, it had been decided to close down the camps, and I had been asked to go back and spread the good word about higher education among the young people who might be dispersed in this way.

78 Elsie was still working in the hospital, although she had applied for entrance into the cadet nurse corps and was expecting acceptance any day, and the long conversations we held were mostly about the good old days, the good old days when we had worked in the mess hall together, the good old days when we had worked in the hospital together.

79 "What ever became of Miss Sasagawara?" I asked one day, seeing the Rev. Sasagawara go abstractedly by. "Did she relocate somewhere?"

80 "I didn't write you about her, did I?" Elsie said meaningfully. "Yes, she's relocated all right. Haven't seen her around, have you?"

81 "Where did she go?"

82 Elsie answered offhandedly. "California."

83 "California?" I exclaimed. "We can't go back to California. What's she doing in California?"

84 So Elsie told me: Miss Sasagawara had been sent back there to a state institution, oh, not so very long after I had left for school. She had begun slipping back into her aloof ways almost immediately after Christmas, giving up the dancing class and not speaking to people. Then Elsie had heard a couple of very strange, yes, very strange things about her. One thing had been told by young Mrs. Sasaki, that next-door neighbor of the Sasagawaras.

85 Mrs. Sasaki said she had once come upon Miss Sasagawara sitting, as was her habit, on the porch. Mrs. Sasaki had been shocked to the core to see that the face of this thirty-nine-year-old woman (or was she forty now?) wore a beatific expression as she watched the activity going on in the doorway of her neighbors across the way, the Yoshinagas. This activity had been the joking and loud laughter of Joe and Frank, the young Yoshinaga boys, and three or four of their friends. Mrs. Sasaki would have let the matter go, were it not for the fact that Miss Sasagawara was so absorbed a spectator of this horseplay that her head was bent to one side and she actually had one finger in her mouth as she gazed, in the manner of a shy child confronted with a marvel. "What's the matter with you, watching the boys like that?" Mrs. Sasaki had cried. "You're old enough to be their mother!" Startled, Miss Sasagawara had jumped up and dashed back into her apartment. And when Mrs. Sasaki had gone into hers, adjoining the Sasagawaras', she had been terrified to hear Miss Sasagawara begin to bang on the wooden walls with something heavy like a hammer. The banging, which sounded as though Miss Sasagawara were using all her strength on each blow, had continued wildly for at least five minutes. Then all had been still.

86 The other thing had been told by Joe Yoshinaga who lived across the way from Miss Sasagawara. Joe and his brother slept on two Army cots pushed together on one side of the room, while their parents had a similar arrangement on the other side. Joe had standing by his bed an apple crate for a shelf, and he was in the habit of reading his sports and western magazines in bed and throwing

them on top of the crate before he went to sleep. But one morning he had noticed his magazines all neatly stacked inside the crate, when he was sure he had carelessly thrown some on top the night before, as usual. This happened several times, and he finally asked his family whether one of them had been putting his magazines away after he fell asleep. They had said no and laughed, telling him he must be getting absent-minded. But the mystery had been solved late one night, when Joe gradually awoke in his cot with the feeling that he was being watched. Warily he had opened one eye slightly and had been thoroughly awakened and chilled in the bargain by what he saw. For what he saw was Miss Sasagawara sitting there on his apple crate, her long hair all undone and flowing about her. She was dressed in a white nightgown and her hands were clasped on her lap. And all she was doing was sitting there watching him, Joe Yoshinaga. He could not help it, he had sat up and screamed. His mother, a light sleeper, came running to see what had happened, just as Miss Sasagawara was running out the door, the door they had always left unlatched or even wide open in summer. In the morning Mrs. Yoshinaga had gone straight to the Rev. Sasagawara and asked him to do something about his daughter. The Rev. Sasagawara, sympathizing with her indignation in his benign but vague manner, had said he would have a talk with Mari.

And, concluded Elsie, Miss Sasagawara had gone away not long after. I was impressed, although Elsie's sources were not what I would ordinarily pay much attention to, Mrs. Sasaki, that plump and giggling young woman who always felt called upon to explain that she was childless by choice, and Joe Yoshinaga, who had a knack of blowing up, in his drawling voice, any incident in which he personally played even a small part (I could imagine the field day he had had with this one). Elsie puzzled aloud over the cause of Miss Sasagawara's derangement and I, who had so newly had some contact with the recorded explorations into the virgin territory of the human mind, sagely explained that Miss Sasagawara had no doubt looked upon Joe Yoshinaga as the image of either the lost lover or the lost son. But my words made me uneasy by their glibness, and I began to wonder seriously about Miss Sasagawara for the first time.

Then there was this last word from Miss Sasagawara herself, making her strange legend as complete as I, at any rate, would probably ever know it. This came some time after I had gone back to Philadelphia and the family had joined me there, when I was neck deep in research for my final paper. I happened one day to be looking through the last issue of a small poetry magazine that had suspended publication midway through the war. I felt a thrill of recognition at the name, Mari Sasagawara, signed to a long poem, introduced as ". . . the first published poem of a Japanese-American woman who is, at present, an evacuee from the West Coast making her home in a War Relocation center in Arizona."

It was a *tour de force*, erratically brilliant and, through the first readings, tantalizingly obscure. It appeared to be about a man whose lifelong aim had been to achieve Nirvana, that saintly state of moral purity and universal wisdom.

This man had in his way certain handicaps, all stemming from his having acquired, when young and unaware, a family for which he must provide. The day came at last, however, when his wife died and other circumstances made it unnecessary for him to earn a competitive living. These circumstances were considered by those about him as sheer imprisonment, but he had felt free for the first time in his long life. It became possible for him to extinguish within himself all unworthy desire and consequently all evil, to concentrate on that serene, eight-fold path of highest understanding, highest mindedness, highest speech, highest action, highest livelihood, highest recollectedness, highest endeavor, and highest meditation.

90    This man was certainly noble, the poet wrote, this man was beyond censure. The world was doubtless enriched by his presence. But say that someone else, someone sensitive, someone admiring, someone who had not achieved this sublime condition and who did not wish to, were somehow called to companion such a man. Was it not likely that the saint, blissfully bent on cleansing from his already radiant soul the last imperceptible blemishes (for, being perfect, would he not humbly suspect his own flawlessness?) would be deaf and blind to the human passions rising, subsiding, and again rising, perhaps in anguished silence, within the selfsame room? The poet could not speak for others, of course; she could only speak for herself. But she would describe this man's devotion as a sort of madness, the monstrous sort which, pure of itself, might possibly bring troublous, scented scenes to recur in the other's sleep. ✢

---

## RESPONDING

1.  In a journal entry, discuss the conditions of internment that you would have found most difficult. Would the rationale behind the Internment affect your response to the physical surroundings?

2.  Choose one of the characters in the story and write an informal essay explaining his or her reaction to the Internment. Working individually or in a group, share and classify the responses of the inmates.

3.  In an essay, argue that Miss Sasagawara's problems did or did not stem from the Internment. Use examples from the reading to support your argument.

4.  Write an essay analyzing Miss Sasagawara's poem as it is described in the story's next-to-last paragraph. What or who do you think the characters in the poem represent? Could they represent or symbolize more than one thing? You might research the eightfold path and its implications about reactions to imprisonment. Consider the title of the story. Why does the author call it a legend?

# Lawson Fusao Inada

*The poet and essayist Lawson Fusao Inada was born in 1938 in Fresno, California. He studied at the University of California at Berkeley, Fresno State College, and the University of Oregon, from which he earned his MFA in 1966. He has held teaching positions at several universities, including Southern Oregon State College in Ashland and the University of Hawaii. His writing has appeared in such journals as* Amerasia Journal, Bridge, *and* The Iowa Review. *His poems, which are widely anthologized, have been collected in three volumes,* Before the War: Poems as They Happened *(1971),* Legends from Camp: Poems *(1993), and* Drawing the Line *(1997). He also coedited several anthologies, including* Aiiieeeee: An Anthology of Asian-American Writers *(1974, 1982) and* The Big Aiiieeeee: An Anthology of Chinese American and Japanese American Literature *(1991).*

*In the poem that follows, the western landscape is presented as a constellation, each point of which marks the site of an internment camp. The poem is just one illustration of the way in which the camp image continues to be found in Japanese American literature, long after the closing of the camps.*

# CONCENTRATION CONSTELLATION

In this earthly configuration,
we have, not points of light,
but prominent barbs of dark.

It's all right there on the map.
It's all right there in the mind.          5
Find it. If you care to look.

Begin between the Golden State's
highest and lowest elevations
and name that location

*Manzanar.* Rattlesnake a line          10
southward to the zone
of Arizona, to the home
of natives on the reservation,
and call those *Gila, Poston.*

15    Then just take you time
      winding your way across
      the Southwest expanse, the Lone
      Star State of Texas, gathering
      up a mess of blues as you
20    meander around the banks
      of the humid Mississippi; yes,
      just make yourself at home
      in the swamps of Arkansas,
      for this is *Rohwer* and *Jerome.*

25    By now, you weary of the way.
      It's a big country, you say.
      It's a big history, hardly
      halfway through—with *Amache*
      looming in the Colorado desert,
30    *Heart Mountain* high in wide
      Wyoming, *Minidoka* on the moon
      of Idaho, then down to Utah's
      jewel of *Topaz* before finding
      yourself at northern California's
35    frozen shore of *Tule Lake* . . .

      Now regard what sort of shape
      this constellation takes.
      It sits there like a jagged scar,
      massive, on the massive landscape.
40    It lies there like the rusted wire
      of a twisted and remembered fence. ✠

---

## RESPONDING

1.  In a journal entry, tell about a place that has positive and negative associations for you.

2.  Working individually or in a group, plot the internment camps on a map of the United States. What do the locations of the camps suggest? Explain why you think those locations were chosen. Use information from the introduction to the chapter and the readings to support your explanation.

3.  In an essay, compare the image of a constellation of stars and the image of the constellation of camps. Why do you think the author chose to call the camps "concentration constellation"?

# GARRETT HONGO

*Garrett Hongo was born in 1951 in Volcano, Hawaii. After graduating from Pomona College in 1973, he pursued graduate study at the University of Michigan and the University of California, Irvine, from which he earned an MFA in 1980. He has taught at several universities, including the University of Oregon, Eugene; the University of California, Irvine; the University of Southern California; and the University of Missouri. His publications include* Yellow Light *(1982),* The River of Heaven *(1988), and* Volcano: A Memoir of Hawaii *(1995); he has also edited several volumes. His work has been awarded prizes from the National Endowment for the Arts and the Academy of American Poets, among others.*

*Hongo's essay "Kubota" recounts some of his grandfather's experiences during and after World War II and explores the ways in which his grandfather's story—and other such narratives—are both a burden for and a gift to the generations that follow.*

⚜

# KUBOTA

ON DECEMBER 8, 1941, the day after the Japanese attack on Pearl Harbor in Hawaii, my grandfather barricaded himself with his family—my grandmother, my teenage mother, her two sisters and two brothers—inside of his home in La'ie, a sugar plantation village on Oahu's North Shore. This was my maternal grandfather, a man most villagers called by his last name, Kubota. It could mean either "Wayside Field" or else "Broken Dreams," depending on which ideograms he used. Kubota ran La'ie's general store, and the previous night, after a long day of bad news on the radio, some locals had come by, pounded on the front door, and made threats. One was said to have brandished a machete. They were angry and shocked, as the whole nation was in the aftermath of the surprise attack. Kubota was one of the few Japanese Americans in the village and president of the local Japanese language school. He had become a target for their rage and suspicion. A wise man, he locked all his doors and windows and did not open his store the next day, but stayed closed and waited for news from some official.

He was a *kibei*, a Japanese American born in Hawaii (a U.S. territory then, so he was thus a citizen) but who was subsequently sent back by his father for formal education in Hiroshima, Japan, their home province. *Kibei* is written with two ideograms in Japanese: one is the word for "return" and the other is the word for "rice." Poetically, it means one who returns from America, known as the Land of Rice in Japanese (by contrast, Chinese immigrants called their new home Mountain of Gold).

3      Kubota was graduated from a Japanese high school and then came back to Hawaii as a teenager. He spoke English—and a Hawaiian creole version of it at that—with a Japanese accent. But he was well liked and good at numbers, scrupulous and hard working like so many immigrants and children of immigrants. Castle & Cook, a grower's company that ran the sugarcane business along the North Shore, hired him on first as a stock boy and then appointed him to run one of its company stores. He did well, had the trust of management and labor—not an easy accomplishment in any day—married, had children, and had begun to exert himself in community affairs and excel in his own recreations. He put together a Japanese community organization that backed a Japanese language school for children and sponsored teachers from Japan. Kubota boarded many of them, in succession, in his own home. This made dinners a silent affair for his talkative, Hawaiian-bred children, as their stern *sensei*, or teacher, was nearly always at table and their own abilities in the Japanese language were as delinquent as their attendance. While Kubota and the *sensei* rattled on about things Japanese, speaking Japanese, his children hurried through their suppers and tried to run off early to listen to the radio shows.

4      After dinner, while the *sensei* graded exams seated in a wicker chair in the spare room and his wife and children gathered around the radio in the front parlor, Kubota sat on the screened porch outside, reading the local Japanese newspapers. He finished reading about the same time as he finished the tea he drank for his digestion—a habit he'd learned in Japan—and then he'd get out his fishing gear and spread it out on the plank floors. The wraps on his rods needed to be redone, gears in his reels needed oil, and, once through with those tasks, he'd painstakingly wind on hundreds of yards of new line. Fishing was his hobby and his passion. He spent weekends camping along the North Shore beaches with his children, setting up umbrella tents, packing a rice pot and hibachi along for meals. And he caught fish. *Ulu'a* mostly, the huge surf-feeding fish known on the mainland as the jack crevalle, but he'd go after almost anything in its season. In Kawela, a plantation-owned bay nearby, he fished for mullat Hawaiian-style with a throw net, stalking the bottom-hugging, gray-backed schools as they gathered at the stream mouths and in the freshwater springs. In an outrigger out beyond the reef, he'd try for *aku*—the skipjack tuna prized for steaks and, sliced raw and mixed with fresh seaweed and cut onions, for *sashimi* salad. In Kahaluu and Ka'awa and on an offshore rock locals called Goat Island, he loved to go torching, stringing lanterns on bamboo poles stuck in the sand to attract *kumu'u*, the red goatfish, as they schooled at night just inside the reef. But in Lai'e on Laniloa Point near Kahuku, the northernmost tip of Oahu, he cast twelve- and fourteen-foot surf rods for the huge, varicolored, and fast-running *ulu'a* as they ran for schools of squid and baitfish just beyond the biggest breakers and past the low sand flats wadable from the shore

to nearly a half mile out. At sunset, against the western light, he looked as if he walked on water as he came back, fish and rods slung over his shoulders, stepping along the rock and coral path just inches under the surface of a running tide.

When it was torching season, in December or January, he'd drive out the afternoon before and stay with old friends, the Tanakas or Yoshikawas, shopkeepers like him who ran stores near the fishing grounds. They'd have been preparing for weeks, selecting and cutting their bamboo poles, cleaning the hurricane lanterns, tearing up burlap sacks for the cloths they'd soak with kerosene and tie onto sticks they'd poke into the soft sand of the shallows. Once lit, touched off with a Zippo lighter, these would be the torches they'd use as beacons to attract the schooling fish. In another time, they might have made up a dozen paper lanterns of the kind mostly used for decorating the summer folk dances outdoors on the grounds of the Buddhist church during O-Bon, the Festival for the Dead. But now, wealthy and modern and efficient killers of fish, Tanaka and Kubota used rag torches and Colemans and cast rods with tips made of Tonkin bamboo and butts of American-spun fiberglass. After just one good night, they might bring back a prize bounty of a dozen burlap bags filled with scores of bloody, rigid fish delicious to eat and even better to give away as gifts to friends, family, and special customers.

It was a Monday night, the day after Pearl Harbor, and there was a rattling knock at the front door. Two FBI agents presented themselves, showed identification, and took my grandfather in for questioning in Honolulu. He didn't return home for days. No one knew what had happened or what was wrong. But there was a roundup going on of all those in the Japanese-American community suspected of sympathizing with the enemy and worse. My grandfather was suspected of espionage, of communicating with offshore Japanese submarines launched from the attack fleet days before war began. Torpedo planes and escort fighters, decorated with the insignia of the Rising Sun, had taken an approach route from northwest of Oahu directly across Kahuku Point and on toward Pearl. They had strafed an auxiliary air station near the fishing grounds my grandfather loved and destroyed a small gun battery there, killing three men. Kubota was known to have sponsored and harbored Japanese nationals in his own home. He had a radio. He had wholesale access to firearms. Circumstances and an undertone of racial resentment had combined with wartime hysteria in the aftermath of the tragic naval battle to cast suspicion on the loyalties of my grandfather and all other Japanese Americans. The FBI reached out and pulled hundreds of them in for questioning in dragnets cast throughout the West Coast and Hawaii.

My grandfather was lucky; he'd somehow been let go after only a few days. Others were not as fortunate. Hundreds, from small communities in Washington, California, Oregon, and Hawaii, were rounded up and, after what appeared to be routine questioning, shipped off under Justice Department orders to holding centers in Leuppe on the Navaho reservation in Arizona, in Fort

Missoula in Montana, and on Sand Island in Honolulu Harbor. There were other special camps on Maui in Ha'iku and on Hawaii—the Big Island—in my own home village of Volcano.

8    Many of these men—it was exclusively the Japanese-American men suspected of ties to Japan who were initially rounded up—did not see their families again for more than four years. Under a suspension of due process that was only after the fact ruled as warranted by military necessity, they were, if only temporarily, "disappeared" in Justice Department prison camps scattered in particularly desolate areas of the United States designated as militarily "safe." These were grim forerunners of the assembly centers and concentration camps for the 120,000 Japanese-American evacuees that were to come later.

9    I am Kubota's eldest grandchild, and I remember him as a lonely, habitually silent old man who lived with us in our home near Los Angeles for most of my childhood and adolescence. It was the fifties, and my parents had emigrated from Hawaii to the mainland in the hope of a better life away from the old sugar plantation. After some success, they had sent back for my grandparents and taken them in. And it was my grandparents who did the work of the household while my mother and father worked their salaried city jobs. My grandmother cooked and sewed, washed our clothes, and knitted in the front room under the light of a huge lamp with a bright three-way bulb. Kubota raised a flower garden, read up on soils and grasses in gardening books, and planted a zoysia lawn in front and a dichondra one in back. He planted a small patch near the rear block wall with green onions, eggplant, white Japanese radishes, and cucumber. While he hoed and spaded the loamless, clayey earth of Los Angeles, he sang particularly plangent songs in Japanese about plum blossoms and bamboo groves.

10    Once, in the mid-sixties, after a dinner during which, as always, he had been silent while he worked away at a meal of fish and rice spiced with dabs of Chinese mustard and catsup thinned with soy sauce, Kubota took his own dishes to the kitchen sink and washed them up. He took a clean jelly jar out of the cupboard— the glass was thick and its shape squatty like an old-fashioned. He reached around to the hutch below where he kept his bourbon. He made himself a drink and retired to the living room where I was expected to join him for "talk story," the Hawaiian idiom for chewing the fat.

11    I was a teenager and, though I was bored listening to stories I'd heard often enough before at holiday dinners, I was dutiful. I took my spot on the couch next to Kubota and heard him out. Usually, he'd tell me about his schooling in Japan where he learned judo along with mathematics and literature. He'd learned the *soroban* there—the abacus, which was the original pocket calculator of the Far East—and that, along with his strong, judo-trained back, got him his first job in Hawaii. This was the moral. "Study *ha-ahd*," he'd say with pidgin emphasis. "Learn read good. Learn speak da kine *good* English." The message is the familiar one taught to any children of immigrants: succeed through education. And imitation. But this time, Kubota reached down into his past and

told me a different story. I was thirteen by then, and I suppose he thought me ready for it. He told me about Pearl Harbor, how the planes flew in wing after wing of formations over his old house in La'ie in Hawaii, and how, the next day, after Roosevelt had made his famous "Day of Infamy" speech about the treachery of the Japanese, the FBI agents had come to his door and taken him in, hauled him off to Honolulu for questioning, and held him without charge for several days. I thought he was lying. I thought he was making up a kind of horror story to shock me and give his moral that much more starch. But it was true. I asked around. I brought it up during history class in junior high school, and my teacher, after silencing me and stepping me off to the back of the room, told me that it was indeed so. I asked my mother and she said it was true. I asked my schoolmates, who laughed and ridiculed me for being so ignorant. We lived in a Japanese-American community, and the parents of most of my class-mates were the *nisei* who had been interned as teenagers all through the war. But there was a strange silence around all of this. There was a hush, as if one were invoking the ill powers of the dead when one brought it up. No one cared to speak about the evacuation and relocation for very long. It wasn't in our history books, though we were studying World War II at the time. It wasn't in the family albums of the people I knew and whom I'd visit staying over weekends with friends. And it wasn't anything that the family talked about or allowed me to keep bringing up either. I was given the facts, told sternly and pointedly that "it was war" and that "nothing could be done." "*Shikatta ga nai*" is the phrase in Japanese, a kind of resolute and determinist pronouncement on how to deal with inexplicable tragedy. I was to know it but not to dwell on it. Japanese Americans were busy trying to forget it ever happened and were having a hard enough time building their new lives after "camp." It was as if we had no history for four years and the relocation was something unspeakable.

But Kubota would not let it go. In session after session, for months it seemed, he pounded away at his story. He wanted to tell me the names of the FBI agents. He went over their questions and his responses again and again. He'd tell me how one would try to act friendly toward him, offering him cigarettes while the other, who hounded him with accusations and threats, left the interrogation room. Good cop, bad cop, I thought to myself, already superficially streetwise from stories black classmates told of the Watts riots and from my having watched too many episodes of *Dragnet* and *The Mod Squad*. But Kubota was not interested in my experiences. I was not made yet, and he was determined that his stories be part of my making. He spoke quietly at first, mildly, but once into his narrative and after his drink was down, his voice would rise and quaver with resentment and he'd make his accusations. He gave his testimony to me and I held it at first cautiously in my conscience like it was an heirloom too delicate to expose to strangers and anyone outside of the world Kubota made with his words. "I give you story now," he once said, "and you learn speak good, eh?" It was my job, as the disciple of his preaching I had then become, Ananda to his Buddha, to reassure him with a promise. "You learn speak good like the Dillingham," he'd say another time, referring to the wealthy scion of the grower family who had once run, unsuccessfully, for one of Hawaii's first senatorial seats. Or he'd then invoke a magical name, the name of one of his heroes, a man he thought particularly exemplary and righteous. "Learn speak dah good Ing-rish like *Mistah Inouye*," Kubota shouted. "He *lick* dah Dillingham even in debate. I saw on *terre-bision* myself." He was remembering the debates before the first senatorial election just before Hawaii was admitted to the Union as its fiftieth state. "You *tell* story," Kubota would end. And I had my injunction.

13     The town we settled in after the move from Hawaii is called Gardena, the independently incorporated city south of Los Angeles and north of San Pedro harbor. At its northern limit, it borders on Watts and Compton, black towns. To the southwest are Torrance and Redondo Beach, white towns. To the rest of L.A., Gardena is primarily famous for having legalized five-card draw poker after the war. On Vermont Boulevard, its eastern border, there is a dingy little Vegas-like strip of card clubs with huge parking lots and flickering neon signs that spell out "The Rainbow" and "The Horseshoe" in timed sequences of varicolored lights. The town is only secondarily famous as the largest community of Japanese Americans in the United States outside of Honolulu, Hawaii. When I was in high school there, it seemed to me that every *sansei* kid I knew wanted to be a doctor, an engineer, or a pharmacist. Our fathers were gardeners or electricians or nurserymen or ran small businesses catering to other Japanese Americans. Our mothers worked in civil service for the city or as cashiers for Thrifty Drug. What the kids wanted was a good job, good pay, a fine home, and no troubles. No one wanted to mess with the law—from either side—and no one wanted to mess with language or art. They all talked about getting into the right clubs so that they could go to the right schools. There was a certain kind of sameness, an intensely enforced system of conformity. Style was all. Boys wore moccasin-sewn shoes from Flagg Brothers, black A-1 slacks, and Kensington shirts with high collars. Girls wore their hair up in stiff bouffants solidified in hair-spray and knew all the latest dances from the slauson to the funky chicken. We did well in chemistry and in math, no one who was Japanese but me spoke in English class or in history unless called upon, and no one talked about World War II. The day after Robert Kennedy was assassinated, after winning the California Democratic primary, we worked on calculus and elected class coordinators for the prom, featuring the 5th Dimension. We avoided grief. We avoided government. We avoided strong feelings and dangers of any kind. Once punished, we tried to maintain a concerted emotional and social discipline and would not willingly seek to fall out of the narrow margin of protective favor again.

14     But when I was thirteen, in junior high, I'd not understood why it was so difficult for my classmates, those who were themselves Japanese American, to talk about the relocation. They had cringed, too, when I tried to bring it up during our discussions of World War II. I was Hawaiian-born. They were mainland-born. Their parents had been in camp, had been the ones to suffer

the complicated experience of having to distance themselves from their own history and all things Japanese in order to make their way back and into the American social and economic mainstream. It was out of this sense of shame and a fear of stigma I was only beginning to understand that the *nisei* had silenced themselves. And, for their children, among whom I grew up, they wanted no heritage, no culture, no contact with a defiled history. I recall the silence very well. The Japanese-American children around me were burdened in a way I was not. Their injunction was silence. Mine was to speak.

Away at college, in another protected world in its own way as magical to 15 me as the Hawaii of my childhood, I dreamed about my grandfather. Tired from studying languages, practicing German conjugations or scripting an army's worth of Chinese ideograms on a single sheet of paper, Kubota would come to me as I drifted off into sleep. Or I would walk across the newly mown ball field in back of my dormitory, cutting through a street-side phalanx of ancient eucalyptus trees on my way to visit friends off campus, and I would think of him, his anger, and his sadness.

I don't know myself what makes someone feel that kind of need to have a 16 story they've lived through be deposited somewhere, but I can guess. I think about *The Illiad*, *The Odyssey*, *The Peloponnesian Wars* of Thucydides, and a myriad of the works of literature I've studied. A character, almost a *topoi* he occurs so often, is frequently the witness who gives personal testimony about an event the rest of his community cannot even imagine. The sibyl is such a character. And Procne, the maid whose tongue is cut out so that she will not tell that she has been raped by her own brother-in-law, the king of Thebes. There are the dime novels, the epic blockbusters Hollywood makes into mini-series, and then there are the plain, relentless stories of witnesses who have suffered through horrors major and minor that have marked and changed their lives. I myself haven't talked to Holocaust victims. But I've read their survival stories and their stories of witness and been revolted and moved by them. My father-in-law, Al Thiessen, tells me his war stories again and again and I listen. A Mennonite who set aside the strictures of his own church in order to serve, he was a Marine codeman in the Pacific during World War II, in the Signal Corps on Guadalcanal, Morotai, and Bougainville. He was part of the island-hopping maneuver MacArthur had devised to win the war in the Pacific. He saw friends die from bombs which exploded not ten yards away. When he was with the 298th Signal Corps attached to the Thirteenth Air Force, he saw plane after plane come in and crash, just short of the runway, killing their crews, setting the jungle ablaze with oil and gas fires. Emergency wagons would scramble, bounding over newly bulldozed land men used just the afternoon before for a football game. Every time we go fishing together, whether it's in a McKenzie boat drifting for salmon in Tillamook Bay or taking a lunch break from wading the riffles of a stream in the Cascades, he tells me about what happened to him and the young men in his unit. One was a Jewish boy from Brooklyn. One was a foul-mouthed kid from Kansas. They died. And he *has* to tell me. And I *have* to listen. It's a ritual payment the young owe their elders who have survived. The evacuation and relocation is something like that.

17     Kubota, my grandfather, had been ill with Alzheimer's disease for some time before he died. At the house he'd built on Kamehameha Highway in Hau'ula, a seacoast village just down the road from La'ie where he had his store, he'd wander out from the garage or greenhouse where he'd set up a workbench, and trudge down to the beach or up toward the line of pines he'd planted while employed by the Work Projects Administration during the thirties. Kubota thought he was going fishing. Or he thought he was back at work for Roosevelt, planting pines as a windbreak or soilbreak on the windward flank of the Ko'olau Mountains, emerald monoliths rising out of sea and cane fields from Waialua to Kaneohe. When I visited, my grandmother would send me down to the beach to fetch him. Or I'd run down Kam Highway a quarter mile or so and find him hiding in the cane field by the roadside, counting stalks, measuring circumferences in the claw of his thumb and forefinger. The look on his face was confused or concentrated, I didn't know which. But I guessed he was going fishing again. I'd grab him and walk him back to his house on the highway. My grandmother would shut him in a room.

18     Within a few years, Kubota had a stroke and survived it, then he had another one and was completely debilitated. The family decided to put him in a nursing home in Kahuku, just set back from the highway, within a mile or so of Kahuku Point and the Tanaka Store where he had his first job as a stock boy. He lived there three years, and I visited him once with my aunt. He was like a potato that had been worn down by cooking. Everything on him—his eyes, his teeth, his legs and torso—seemed like it had been sloughed away. What he had been was mostly gone now and I was looking at the nub of a man. In a wheelchair, he grasped my hands and tugged on them—violently. His hands were still thick and, I believed, strong enough to lift me out of my own seat into his lap. He murmured something in Japanese—he'd long ago ceased to speak any English. My aunt and I cried a little, and we left him.

19     I remember walking out on the black asphalt of the parking lot of the nursing home. It was heat-cracked and eroded already, and grass had veined itself into the interstices. There were coconut trees around, a cane field I could see across the street, and the ocean I knew was pitching a surf just beyond it. The green Ko'olaus came up behind us. Somewhere nearby, alongside the beach, there was an abandoned airfield in the middle of the canes. As a child, I'd come upon it playing one day, and my friends and I kept returning to it, day after day, playing war or sprinting games or coming to fly kites. I recognize it even now when I see it on TV—it's used as a site for action scenes in the detective shows Hollywood always sets in the islands: a helicopter chasing the hero racing away in a Ferrari, or gun dealers making a clandestine rendezvous on the abandoned runway. It was the old airfield strafed by Japanese planes the day the major flight attacked Pearl Harbor. It was the airfield the FBI thought my grandfather had targeted in his night fishing and signaling with the long surf poles he'd stuck in the sandy bays near Kahuku Point.

Kubota died a short while after I visited him, but not, I thought, without  20
giving me a final message. I was on the mainland, in California studying for
Ph.D. exams, when my grandmother called me with the news. It was a relief.
He'd suffered from his debilitation a long time and I was grateful he'd gone. I
went home for the funeral and gave the eulogy. My grandmother and I took his
ashes home in a small, heavy metal box wrapped in a black *furoshiki*, a large silk
scarf. She showed me the name the priest had given to him on his death, scripted
with a calligraphy brush on a long, narrow talent of plain wood. Buddhist
commoners, at death, are given priestly names, received symbolically into the
clergy. The idea is that, in their next life, one of scholarship and leisure, they
might meditate and attain the enlightenment the religion is aimed at. "*Shaku
Shūchi*," the ideograms read. It was Kubota's Buddhist name, incorporating
characters from his family and given names. It meant "Shining Wisdom of the
Law." He died on Pearl Harbor Day, December 7, 1983.

After years, after I'd finally come back to live in Hawaii again, only once  21
did I dream of Kubota, my grandfather. It was the same night I'd heard HR 442,
the redress bill for Japanese Americans, had been signed into law. In my dream
that night Kubota was "torching," and he sang a Japanese song, a querulous and
wavery folk ballad, as he hung paper lanterns on bamboo poles stuck into the
sand in the shallow water of the lagoon behind the reef near Kahuku Point.
Then he was at a work table, smoking a hand-rolled cigarette, letting it dangle
from his lips Bogart-style as he drew, daintily and skillfully, with a narrow trim
brush, ideogram after ideogram on a score of paper lanterns he had hung in a
dark shed to dry. He had painted a talismanic mantra onto each lantern, the
ideogram for the word "red" in Japanese, a bit of art blended with some
superstition, a piece of sympathetic magic appealing to the magenta coloring on
the rough skins of the schooling, night-feeding fish he wanted to attract to his
baited hooks. He strung them from pole to pole in the dream then, hiking up
his khaki worker's pants so his white ankles showed and wading through the
shimmering black waters of the sand flats and then the reef. "The moon is
leaving, leaving," he sang in Japanese. "Take me deeper in the savage sea." He
turned and crouched like an ice racer then, leaning forward so that his unshaven
face almost touched the light film of water. I could see the light stubble of beard
like a fine, gray ash covering the lower half of his face. I could see his gold-
rimmed spectacles. He held a small wooden boat in his cupped hands and placed
it lightly on the sea and pushed it away. One of his lanterns was on it and,
written in small neat rows like a sutra scroll, it had been decorated with the
silvery names of all our dead. ✇

---

## RESPONDING

1. Imagine that you were Kubota. Write a journal entry about your reaction
   to being taken in for questioning by FBI agents the day after Pearl Harbor.

2. Working individually or in a group, retell historical events that were especially important to you or your family members. Were these events adequately covered in your history classes in elementary school, high school, college?

3. Hongo ends his essay by recounting a dream. Write your own essay explaining the significance of the dream and its message to the reader.

4. According to Hongo, what cultural factors resulted in the Japanese American silence about the Internment? In an essay, explore that silence and its effect on the young. What difference, if any, has breaking the silence made? Refer to the introduction to the chapter and outside knowledge if necessary.

# DICK THORNBURGH

*Dick Thornburgh was born in Pittsburgh in 1932. He earned his bachelor's degree from Yale University in 1954 and his bachelor of laws degree from the University of Pittsburgh in 1957. Thornburgh served as the governor of Pennsylvania from 1979 to 1987. From 1988 until 1991, he was U.S. attorney general in the administration of President Ronald Reagan. Since returning to public life he has authored studies in several areas related to politics, international relations, and the law, among them* Reform and Restructuring at the United Nations *(1993) and* Attorney-Client Privilege: Maintaining Business Privacy During Activist Litigation *(1993).*

*In the following address made after the U.S. Department of Justice agreed to separation payments totaling more than $1 billion, Mr. Thornburgh outlines the position the federal government assumed toward both the internment process and those Japanese Americans whose lives were affected by it.*

# MAKING AMENDS

1   YOUR STRUGGLE FOR REDRESS and the events that led to today are the finest examples of what our country is about and of what we have pledged to protect and defend. Your efforts have strengthened the nation's Constitution by reaffirming the inalienability of our civil rights.

2   We enjoy a precious system of government that is unsurpassed by any in the world. Even when that system failed you, you never lost your faith in it. On the contrary, you believed that through that system you could achieve the justice

which you had been denied. By finally admitting a wrong, a nation does not destroy its integrity but, rather, reinforces the sincerity of its commitment to the Constitution and hence to its people. In forcing us to re-examine our history, you have made us only stronger and more proud. For that, all Americans are indebted to you. I am not unmindful of the historic role this Department of Justice played in the internment. It is somehow entirely fitting that it is here we now celebrate redress. ✛

## RESPONDING

1. Imagine that you are one of the Japanese Americans who received a check from Attorney General Thornburgh. In a journal entry, respond to his statements.

2. Working individually or in a group, use the Internet and other sources to review the history of the struggle of interned Japanese Americans for reparations and an apology.

3. Write an essay agreeing or disagreeing that "By finally admitting a wrong, a nation does not destroy its integrity but, rather, reinforces the sincerity of its commitment to the Constitution and hence to its people" (paragraph 2). Should the United States apologize and pay reparation to other groups who have suffered injustices? For example, should African slaves, victims of race riots, and others receive some form of apology and reparation?

4. In an essay, discuss why it took so long for the U.S. government to apologize for its actions. How important is it for a government to acknowledge acts of injustice it perpetrates on its citizens?

# Bob Pool

*Bob Pool, who was born in Oceanfront, New Jersey, in 1945, earned a bachelor's degree in journalism from the California State University at Northridge in 1968. He worked as a reporter and photographer at several southern California newspapers before joining the* Los Angeles Times *in 1983, where he is currently a staff writer. He has won several awards for writing and photography.*

*In the piece that follows, Pool provides an update on the status of an extremely important set of papers from the Internment period.*

⁜

# UNCOVERING INTERNMENT PAPERS

1    SIXTEEN YEARS AFTER PROVING in a court of law that the World War II internment of 120,000 Japanese Americans was illegal, Fred T. Korematsu is turning to the court of public opinion.

2    The former welder, 80, doggedly fought to clear his name four decades after being convicted of violating wartime "evacuation orders." Now he has donated his history-making legal papers to UCLA's Asian American Studies Center.

3    Officials at the Westwood center plan to place them in a university research library and make them available to historians, legal scholars and others through the Internet.

4    Included among the documents are once-secret memos and reports that show how authorities lied to the U.S. Supreme Court to justify the unprecedented roundup and relocation of Japanese Americans in the early days of the war.

5    Korematsu was arrested and convicted in 1942 for refusing to leave his Northern California home and report to a detention camp.

6    He appealed his conviction. But in 1944 the Supreme Court upheld internment of Japanese Americans in the landmark case Korematsu vs. the United States.

7    Since then generations of law students have studied the case, learning that civil liberties were set aside in the dark days of war because the court believed there was an overriding military necessity to relocate Japanese Americans.

8    In 1983, Korematsu's conviction was overturned after a dozen lawyers and researchers helped him resurrect the case in U.S. District Court in San Francisco.

9    The case helped set the stage for the 1988 reparations paid by the U.S. government to surviving victims of the relocation roundups. But civil libertarians have been concerned that word of Korematsu's exoneration may have gotten lost.

10    Some students studying Korematsu vs. United States in constitutional law classes are still not being told of the 1983 reversal.

11    Just this week, a student seemed aware of only the earlier Korematsu case, said Lorraine Bannai, professor at Seattle University School of Law who was on the volunteer legal team in 1983. The student said the reversal was not in the case book he was studying. "I was disappointed; this is my school," Bannai said.

12    She is one of 10 team members who plan to be at UCLA on Sunday for a reunion with Korematsu and a ceremony marking his donation. The 1:30 p.m. event in the James West Alumni Center is open to the public.

13    Another scheduled to attend is Peter Irons, a UC San Diego political science professor. He broke the case by unearthing secret wartime memos showing that

government officials lied to the Supreme Court about the need for the internment.

Memos he found at the National Archives proved that authorities incarcerated Japanese Americans because of their race—but then falsely contended to the Supreme Court that the action was taken for military reasons. 14

"The factual underpinnings on which the [1944] Korematsu decision was based were knocked away," said Bay Area lawyer Donald K. Tamaki, who also helped Korematsu in the 1983 case. 15

Dale Minami, the attorney who headed the team, said every law student who studies the 1944 Korematsu case should also study the more recent one. 16

"When the fallibility of our systems is exposed, it teaches a lesson about our legal system and the fragility of civil rights," he said. 17

Files from the 1983 case were found scattered in the various lawyers' offices when the team decided to gather them. 18

Numerous institutions—including the Smithsonian, UC Berkeley and the National Archives—lobbied to get the 25-box collection after the paperwork was compiled, according to Don Nakanishi, a UCLA education professor who directs the Asian American Studies Center. 19

Korematsu said he is pleased that the papers will be accessible to the L.A. area's large Japanese American population. 20

"A lot of people are shocked when they hear what happened" in the internment, he said Thursday from his home in San Leandro. "We want to make them aware." 21

---

## RESPONDING

1. Should civil liberties in the United States be set aside when there is an overriding military necessity? In a journal entry, explain your opinion.

2. Working in a group, share your opinions and list and discuss the arguments for and against setting aside civil liberties.

3. According to Peter Irons, a University of California at San Diego political science professor, memorandums at the National Archives prove that authorities incarcerated Japanese Americans because of their race and then lied to the Supreme Court that the action had been taken for military reasons. These findings caused Korematsu's conviction for refusing to leave his northern California home and report to a detention camp to be overturned in 1988. Still, the casebooks law students study, and history books in general, do not yet reflect these developments. Imagine that you are an educator. How will you present this important information to your students?

# Ronald Takaki

*Ronald Takaki, who was born in 1939, is the grandson of Japanese immigrants who settled in Hawaii. He earned his bachelor's degree from the College of Wooster and his doctorate from the University of California at Berkeley, where he is currently a professor of ethnic studies. Takaki has written and edited several books on ethnic issues, including* A Pro-Slavery Crusade: The Agitation to Open the African Slave Trade *(1971),* Violence in the Black Imagination *(1972),* From Different Shores: Perspectives on Race and Ethnicity in America *(1987), and* A Different Mirror: A History of Multicultural America *(1993).*

*The excerpt that follows is from* Strangers from a Different Shore: A History of Asian Americans *(1989). In the passage, the author reflects on the Internment and its effects on the Japanese American community. Takaki calls on the people victimized by the Internment to "break the silence" in which they have lived for too long.*

✠

# ROOTS

1   TO CONFRONT THE CURRENT PROBLEMS OF RACISM, Asian Americans know they must remember the past and break the silence. This need was felt deeply by Japanese Americans during the hearings before the commission reviewing the issue of redress and reparations for Japanese Americans interned during World War II. Memories of the internment nightmare have haunted the older generation like ghosts. But the former prisoners have been unable to exorcise them by speaking out and ventilating their anger.

> When we were children,
> you spoke Japanese
> in lowered voices
> between yourselves.
>
> Once you uttered secrets
> which we should not know,
> were not to be heard by us.
> When you spoke
> of some dark secret,
> you would admonish us,
> "Don't tell it to anyone else."

It was a suffocated vow of silence.
What we have come to know
yet cannot tell
lingers like voiceless ghosts
wandering in our memory
as though memory is
desert bleached by
years of cruel exile.

It is the language
the silence within myself
I cannot fill with words,
the sound of mournful music
distantly heard.[1]

"Stigmatized," the ex-internees have been carrying the "burdens of shame"     [2]
for over forty painful years. "They felt like a rape victim," explained Congressman Norman Mineta, a former internee of the Heart Mountain internment camp. "They were accused of being disloyal. They were the victims but they were on trial and they did not want to talk about it." But Sansei, or third-generation Japanese Americans, want their elders to tell their story. Warren Furutani, for example, told the commissioners that young people like himself had been asking their parents to tell them about the concentration camps and to join them in pilgrimages to the internment camp at Manzanar. "Why? Why!" their parents would reply defensively. "Why would you want to know about it? It's not important, we don't need to talk about it." But, Furutani continued, they need to tell the world what happened during those years of infamy.[2]

Suddenly, during the commission hearings, scores of Issei and Nisei came     [3]
forward and told their stories. "For over thirty-five years I have been the stereotype Japanese American," Alice Tanabe Nehira told the commission. "I've kept quiet, hoping in due time we will be justly compensated and recognized for our years of patient effort. By my passive attitude, I can reflect on my past years to conclude that it doesn't pay to remain silent." The act of speaking out has enabled the Japanese-American community to unburden itself of years of

---

1. Richard Oyama, poem published in *Transfer 38* (San Francisco, 1979), p. 43, reprinted in Elaine Kim, *Asian American Literature: An Introduction to the Writings and Their Social Context* (Philadelphia, 1982), pp. 308–309.
2. Congressman Robert Matsui, speech in the House of Representatives on bill 442 for redress and reparations, September 17, 1987, *Congressional Record* (Washington, 1987), p. 7584; Congressman Norman Mineta, interview with author, March 26, 1988; Warren Furutani, testimony, reprinted in *Amerasia*, vol. 8, no. 2 (1981), p. 104.

anger and anguish. Sometimes their testimonies before the commission were long and the chair urged them to conclude. But they insisted the time was theirs. "Mr. Commissioner," protested poet Janice Mirikitani,

> So when you tell me my time is
> up I tell you this.
> Pride has kept my lips
> pinned by nails,
> my rage confined.
> But I exhume my past
> to claim this time.[3]

4    The former internees finally had spoken, and their voices compelled the nation to redress the injustice of internment. In August 1988, Congress passed a bill giving an apology and a payment of $20,000 to each of the survivors of the internment camps. When President Ronald Reagan signed the bill into law, he admitted that the United States had committed "a grave wrong," for during World War II, Japanese Americans had remained "utterly loyal" to this country. "Indeed, scores of Japanese Americans volunteered for our Armed Forces— many stepping forward in the internment camps themselves. The 442nd Regimental Combat Team, made up entirely of Japanese Americans, served with immense distinction to defend this nation, their nation. Yet, back at home, the soldiers' families were being denied the very freedom for which so many of the soldiers themselves were laying down their lives." Then the president recalled an incident that happened forty-three years ago. At a ceremony to award the Distinguished Service Cross to Kazuo Masuda, who had been killed in action and whose family had been interned, a young actor paid tribute to the slain Nisei soldier. "The name of that young actor," remarked the president, who had been having trouble saying the Japanese names, "—I hope I pronounce this right—was Ronald Reagan." The time had come, the president acknowledged, to end "a sad chapter in American history."[4]

5    Asian Americans have begun to claim their time not only before the commission on redress and reparations but elsewhere as well—in the novels of Maxine Hong Kingston and Milton Murayama, the plays of Frank Chin and Philip Gotanda, the scholarly writings of Sucheng Chan and Elaine Kim, the films of Steve Okazaki and Wayne Wang, and the music of Hiroshima and Fred

---

3. Alice Tanabe Nehira, testimony, reprinted in *Amerasia*, vol. 8, no. 2 (1981), p. 93; Janice Mirikitani, "Breaking Silences," reprinted ibid., p. 109.
4. "Text of Reagan's Remarks," reprinted in *Pacific Citizen*, August 19–26, 1988, p. 5; *San Francisco Chronicle*, August 5 and 11, 1988.

Houn. Others, too, have been breaking silences. Seventy-five-year-old Tomo Shoji, for example, had led a private life, but in 1981 she enrolled in an acting course because she wanted to try something frivolous and to take her mind off her husband's illness. In the beginning, Tomo was hesitant, awkward on the stage. "Be yourself," her teacher urged. Then suddenly she felt something surge through her, springing from deep within, and she began to tell funny and also sad stories about her life. Now Tomo tours the West Coast, a wonderful wordsmith giving one-woman shows to packed audiences of young Asian Americans. "Have we really told our children all we have gone through?" she asks. Telling one of her stories, Tomo recounts: "My parents came from Japan and I was born in a lumber camp. One day, at school, my class was going on a day trip to a show, and I was pulled aside and told I would have to stay behind. All the white kids went." Tomo shares stories about her husband: "When I first met him, I thought, 'wow.' Oh, he was so macho! And he wanted his wife to be a good submissive wife. But then he married me." Theirs had been at times a stormy marriage. "Culturally we were different because he was Issei and I was American, and we used to argue a lot. Well, one day in 1942 right after World War II started he came home and told me we had to go to an internment camp. 'I'm not going to camp because I'm an American citizen,' I said to him. 'You have to go to camp, but not me.' Well you know what, that was one time my husband was right!" Tomo remembers the camp: "We were housed in barracks, and we had no privacy. My husband and I had to share a room with another couple. So we hanged a blanket in the middle of the room as a partition. But you could hear everything from the other side. Well, one night, while we were in bed, my husband and I got into an argument, and I dumped him out of the bed. The other couple thought we were making violent love." As she stands on the stages and talks stories excitedly, Tomo cannot be contained: "We got such good, fantastic stories to tell. All our stories are different."[5]

Today, young Asian Americans want to listen to these stories—to shatter images of themselves and their ancestors as "strangers" and to understand who they are as Asian Americans. "What don't you know?" their elders ask. Their question seems to have a peculiar frame: it points to the blank areas of collective memory. And the young people reply that they want "to figure out how the invisible world the emigrants built around [their] childhoods fit in solid America." They wanted to know more about their "no name" Asian ancestors. They want to decipher the signs of the Asian presence here and there across the landscape of America—railroad tracks over high mountains, fields of cane virtually carpeting entire islands, and verdant agricultural lands.

6

---

5. Tomo Shoji, "Born Too Soon . . . It's Never Too Late: Growing Up Nisei in Early Washington," presentations at the University of California, Berkeley, September 19, 1987, and the Ohana Cultural Center, Oakland, California, March 4, 1988.

> Deserts to farmlands
> Japanese-American
> Page in history.[6]

7    They want to know what is their history and "what is the movies." They want to trace the origins of terms applied to them. "Why are we called 'Oriental'?" they question, resenting the appellation that has identified Asians as exotic, mysterious, strange, and foreign. "The word 'orient' simply means 'east.' So why are Europeans 'West' and why are Asians 'East'? Why did empire-minded Englishmen in the sixteenth century determine that Asia was 'east' of London? Who decided what names would be given to the different regions and peoples of the world? Why does 'American' usually mean 'white'?" Weary of Eurocentric history, young Asian Americans want their Asian ancestral lives in America chronicled, "given the name of a place." They have earned the right to belong to specific places like Washington, California, Hawaii, Punnene, Promontory Point, North Adams, Manzanar, Doyers Street. "And today, after 125 years of our life here," one of them insists, "I do not want just a home that time allowed me to have." Seeking to lay claim to America, they realize they can no longer be indifferent to what happened in history, no longer embarrassed by the hardships and humiliations experienced by their grandparents and parents.

> My heart, once bent and cracked, once
> ashamed of your China ways.
> Ma, hear me now, tell me your story
> again and again.[7] ✥

---

## RESPONDING

1.  Takaki writes that young Asians ask Americans, "Why are we called 'Oriental'?" (paragraph 7). Who gave them this name and what are its implications? Think about the connotations of names of groups. In a journal entry, explain the role of names in forming group images and individual identities. Consider the effect of derogatory names on children.

---

6. Kingston, *The Woman Warrior*, p. 6; poem in Kazuo Ito, *Issei: A History of Japanese Immigrants in North America* (Seattle, 1973), p. 493.

7. Kingston, *The Woman Warrior*, p. 6; Robert Kwan, "Asian v. Oriental: A Difference that Counts," *Pacific Citizen*, April 25, 1980; Sir James Augustus Henry Murry (ed.), *The Oxford English Dictionary* (Oxford, 1933); vol. 7, p. 200; Aminur Rahim, "Is Oriental an Occident?" in *The Asiandian*, vol. 5, no. 1, April 1983, p. 20; Shawn Wong, *Homebase* (New York, 1979), p. 111; Nellie Wong, "From a Heart of Rice Straw," in Nellie Wong, *Dreams in Harrison Railroad Park* (Berkeley, 1977), p. 41.

2. Working individually or in a group, discuss the role of being a witness to a historical event. Is it important to "testify"? Support your opinion with examples from the readings or your own knowledge.

3. Explain why Congressman Norman Mineta said that ex-internees have been "'stigmatized' . . . carrying the 'burdens of shame' for over forty painful years" (paragraph 2). What did the Japanese Americans feel ashamed about? Using information from the readings and your own knowledge of human nature, write an essay discussing the fact that though they were the victims of an injustice they felt shame rather than anger. Research Japanese culture to see if it helps explain this reaction or are feelings of shame and guilt typical reactions of victims?

4. In an essay, explain what caused Japanese Americans finally to break their silence about the Internment years. Discuss the role of their stories in helping the younger generation understand themselves and their heritage.

⁜

# CONNECTING

## *Critical Thinking and Writing*

1. Reread the Japanese Relocation Order. Why did the U.S. government think that the Japanese in America, including American citizens of Japanese descent, were a security risk? Did these reasons justify the government's actions? Many Japanese Americans as well as others have charged that the public's fears were based on racial prejudice. Write an essay supporting or refuting these charges.

2. Every individual represented in this chapter was influenced by the internment experience. Compare the varying responses to the Internment of two or more characters in these selections. Or write an essay classifying the range of responses to the Internment as exemplified in these readings.

3. For many of these authors, loyalty is an important issue. Reflect on the question of whom you owe loyalty to, your government, your parents, your friends? When loyalties conflict, which has first priority?

4. Language is often an important part of a person's identity. Compare the role of language in shaping and preserving the identity of at least two individuals in the readings in this and other chapters. For example, you might compare the significance in her life of Sone's native Japanese to the significance in her life of Elena's Spanish (see Mora, chapter 8).

5. Many of the readings in this chapter deal with the issue of trying to adapt to a new culture while retaining your own. Write an essay comparing the responses to this challenge of at least two individuals in the readings in this and other chapters.

6. Many of the readings in this text deal with the relationships between parents and children, old ways and new. Analyze the difficulties of communication that can develop between parents who were raised in one culture and children raised in another. For example, see Tan in chapter 4 and Cofer in chapter 6.

7. Write an essay agreeing or disagreeing with the statement that it is difficult to be a part of two cultures. Use the readings in this book and your own experiences and knowledge to support your argument.

8. Being pulled between two cultures is a theme that recurs throughout this book. Write an essay discussing what it means to be bicultural. Use examples from the text as well as your own experience.

9. Do your possessions define you? Describe the possessions that are most important to you and that reveal most about your personality and history. Is the Sone family defined by their possessions? What about the family being evicted in the excerpt from Ellison's *Invisible Man* in chapter 5?

10. Use the readings in this and other chapters to illustrate how personal ambitions can come into conflict with cultural expectations.

11. Write an essay discussing the role of the witness to history. Do different cultures have different interpretations of that role? Have those interpretations changed over time? What effect does the act of testifying to historical events have on the younger generation? Consider the reaction of Japanese Americans to the Internment, African Americans to slavery, Latin Americans to massacres in their native countries, or Jewish survivors to the Holocaust.

12. Using your school library or the Internet, research the history of the struggle of Japanese Americans to obtain justice for the wrongs done to them during the Internment period. Read the 1988 newspaper articles reporting the quest for an apology and reparations. What was the reaction of the Japanese American community when reparations were finally made? Were the reparations considered satisfactory?

### For Further Research

1. Research current laws protecting citizens' rights. Are there laws that would now prevent the internment of U.S. citizens? What organizations work to protect the rights of individuals and groups? Are there enough safeguards in our current system? What is your evaluation and what suggestions for changes would you make?

2. Though their families and friends were in internment camps, many Japanese Americans enlisted in the army and fought for the United States in Europe. Some units were cited for exceptional bravery. Examine the war record of one of those units.

3. The treatment of German Americans during World War II was quite different from the treatment of Japanese Americans. After studying the opinions of historians, sociologists, politicians, and victims about the reasons for the vastly different treatment each group received, write an essay trying to account for these differences.

## REFERENCES AND ADDITIONAL SOURCES

Broom, Leonard. *The Managed Casualty: The Japanese-American Family in World War II.* Berkeley: University of California Press, 1973.

Christgau, John. *Enemies: World War II Alien Internment.* Ames: Iowa State University Press, 1985.

Collins, Donald E. *Native American Aliens: Disloyalty and the Renunciation of Citizenship by Japanese Americans During World War II.* Westport, Conn.: Greenwood Press, 1985.

Daniels, Roger. *Concentration Camps: North America: Japanese in the United States & Canada During World War II.* Malabar, Fla.: R.E. Kreiger, 1981, 1989.

Fiset, Louis. *Imprisoned Apart: The World War II Correspondence of an Issei Couple.* Seattle: University of Washington Press, 1997.

Inada, Lawson. *Before the War: Poems as They Happened.* New York: Morrow, 1971.

Irons, Peter, ed. *Justice Delayed: The Record of the Japanese American Internment Cases.* Middleton, Conn.: Wesleyan University Press, 1989.

Kim, Elaine. *Asian American Literature: An Introduction to the Writings and Their Social Context.* Philadelphia: Temple University Press, 1982, 1984.

Masako, Herman. *The Japanese in America, 1843–1973: A Chronology and Fact Book.* Dobbs Ferry, N.Y.: Oceana, 1974.

Montero, Darrel. *Japanese Americans: Changing Patterns of Ethnic Affiliation over Three Generations.* Boulder, Col.: Westview Press, 1980.

Myer, Dillon S. *Uprooted Americans: The Japanese Americans and the War Relocation Authority During World War II.* Tucson: University of Arizona Press, 1971, 1972.

Nagata, Donna K. *Legacy of Injustice: Exploring the Cross-Generational Impact of the Japanese American Internment.* New York: Plenum Press, 1993.

Nishimoto, Richard S. *Inside an American Concentration Camp: Japanese American Resistance at Poston, Arizona,* Lane Ryo Hirabayashi, ed. Tucson: University of Arizona Press, 1995.

Okihiro, Gary Y. *Whispered Silences: Japanese Americans and World War II.* Photographs by Joan Myers. Seattle: University of Washington Press, 1996.

Takahashi, Jere. *Nisei/Sansei: Shifting Japanese American Identities and Politics.* Philadelphia: Temple University Press, 1997.

Takaki, Ronald. *Strangers from a Different Shore: A History of Asian Americans.* Boston: Little, Brown, 1989; New York: Penguin, 1993.

Taylor, Sandra C. *Jewel of the Desert: Japanese American Internment at Topaz.* Berkeley: University of California Press, 1993.

Uchida, Yoshiko. *Desert Exile: The Uprooting of a Japanese-American Family.* Seattle: University of Washington Press, 1982, 1991.

United States. Commission on Wartime Relocation and Internment of Civilians. *Personal Justice Denied: Report of the Commission on Wartime Relocation and Internment of Civilians.* Washington, D.C.: Civil Liberties Education Fund; Seattle: University of Washington Press, 1997.

Weglyn, Michi. *Years of Infamy: The Untold Story of America's Concentration Camps.* New York: Morrow, 1976.

Wilson, Robert A., and Bill Hosokawa. *East to America: A History of the Japanese in the United States*. New York: Morrow, 1980.

Yamamoto, Traise. *Masking Selves, Making Subjects: Japanese American Women, Identity, and the Body*. Berkeley: University of California Press, 1999.

# 8

## CHICANOS

### *Negotiating Political and Cultural Boundaries*

⚜

*Above:* César Chávez addressing United Farm Workers Union Members. *(© Victor Aleman/2 Mun-Dos Communications)*
*Opposite: Portrait of the Artist as the Virgin de Guadalupe,* by Yolanda M. Lopez.

# SETTING THE HISTORICAL AND CULTURAL CONTEXT

Iɴ ʜɪs ᴘᴏᴇᴍ "I Am Joaquín," Rodolfo "Corky" Gonzalez writes of the need to establish an identity within a collective experience:

> My fathers
>     have lost the economic battle
> and won
>     the struggle of cultural survival . . .
> And now I must choose
>     between the paradox
>     of the victory of the spirit
> [and] the sterilization of the soul
>  and a full stomach.

Gonzalez depicts a struggle with irreconcilable, opposing goals: to achieve economic success in the majority culture is to gain "a full stomach" but to lose one's soul. For the speaker, to maintain cultural identity, to survive as a culture, requires a process of retreat and separation:

> I withdraw to the safety
> within the circle of life
> MY OWN PEOPLE

Within the collective experience, Joaquín finds his own reason for being.

When it was first published in 1967, "I Am Joaquín" was considered to be a particularly important poem. Gonzalez led demonstrations for Chicano rights throughout the southwestern United States. In a larger sense, the poem helped to give voice to the Chicano Renaissance, a political and cultural movement in which many Chicanos were engaged during the late 1960s and early 1970s. Chicanos sought "the victory of the spirit" within the collective *raza*, the ideal of the homeland called Aztlán.

To search for Aztlán, the mythic homeland of the Aztec peoples, is to seek identity in the civilizations of the Mexican Indians that had shaped the Southwest and Mesoamerica centuries before the arrival of the Spanish conquistadors. These native peoples included the Mayans, the Pueblos, and the Aztecs. The Mayans of Yucatan and Central America had established a network of cities, a system of mathematics, and a calendar that predated the Gregorian calendar used in western Europe by one thousand years. The Pueblos of the Southwest, who emerged as a culture around A.D. 500, were known for their pottery and weaving. The Aztec civilization of central Mexico, which had many urban centers, was known for its use of astronomy, its system of

barter, and its military prowess. A polytheistic culture, the Aztecs relied on
human sacrifice to appease their deities. Although the classic Mayan culture
had dissolved by the time the conquistadors reached the continent in the
1500s, the Pueblo and Aztec civilizations still flourished.

Spanish explorers were attracted to the continent for several reasons. Explorers and adventurers such as Hernán Cortés and Francisco Vásquez de
Coronado sought natural resources and the promise of the Seven Cities of
Gold. When Cortés arrived in continental Yucatan in search of laborers, he
was treated well by the native people, whose legends taught them to be wary
of "bearded strangers." He was given Malinche, an Aztec noblewoman who
had been sold into slavery as a translator and mistress. Within two years,
Cortés had conquered Moctezuma's Aztec Empire and had claimed its territory and minerals for Spain. In Chicano culture, therefore, *la Malinche* has
come to signify a betrayal. In many Chicano works, *la Malinche* represents
one who sacrifices cultural affiliation for advancement within the larger society. Recently, Chicano and Chicana writers and artists have reconsidered
these views of Malinche, challenging them as prejudices of a traditional patriarchal culture.

The period of Spanish conquest and settlement was recorded in the journals and histories of Bernal Díaz del Castillo and Bartholomé de las Casas.
Explorers and missionaries had strategic, economic, and cultural motives for
settling the Southwest. Strategists sought a protective buttress for Mexican
territory farther south. Those seeking wealth, either for themselves or for the
Spanish crown, were drawn by the area's minerals and other natural resources. Missionaries who accompanied many expeditions wanted to convert
the native population to Catholicism.

The role of the Spanish explorers and missionaries in the economic and
cultural development of the American Southwest remains controversial.
Some credit the missionaries with educating native peoples about methods of
irrigation and planning, and ascribe to the intermarriage of explorers and
American Indians the formation of the *mestizo* (mixed) culture. Other historians view the Spanish expeditions as having primarily deleterious effects on
the native population. They point to the large numbers of American Indians
who perished after the arrival of the Spanish, both from diseases against
which they had no immunity and from the *encomienda* system of forced labor
sanctioned by the Roman Catholic Church. Despite the protests of the missionary Bartholomé de las Casas, who chronicled the abuse of the native
population in his letters to the Spanish government, the conditions persisted
for some time.

Spanish settlements extended throughout the area that now comprises
Texas, New Mexico, Arizona, and California. Despite the success of the *hacienda* system in California, the rest of the viceroyalty of Nueva España remained sparsely populated by Novohispanos. The Spanish, and later the
Mexican government, which had declared independence from Spain in 1821,
offered *norteamericanos* grants of property and livestock to establish settle-

ments in certain parts of the territory. After the discovery of mineral reserves and good fur-trapping areas, the population increased dramatically. In Austin Colony (now in Texas), for example, the population of *norteamericanos* increased during the 1820s from 300 families to more than 25,000 people.

Political factors also affected settlement of the territory. Many property owners in what is now Texas owned slaves, a violation of Mexican law; they wanted to secede from Mexico and have their territory admitted to the United States as a "slave state." Many other Americans subscribed to the doctrine of *manifest destiny*—the belief that it was the destiny of the United States to settle the entire American continent. (This term was first used to characterize the debate about the United States's annexation of Texas, as is further explained in the introduction to chapter 1.) Those people who were not Euro American, even those whose claims on the land predated those of the Euro Americans, were often viewed as obstacles to achieving this objective. Manifest destiny, coupled with the discovery of gold in California, helped to restructure the demographic patterns of the southwest territory.

During the mid-nineteenth century, Euro American settlers in both Texas and California revolted against Mexico. Texas declared its independence from Mexico and established itself as a republic in 1836; it immediately sought annexation by the United States. In California, Euro American settlers led by John Charles Frémont and others moved against Mexican authorities and established the Bear Flag Republic. These hostilities led to the United States-Mexican War in 1846 and, two years later, to the defeat of Mexican military forces. When it signed the Treaty of Guadalupe Hidalgo in 1848, Mexico surrendered all claims to Texas and ceded to the U.S. government, at a cost of $15 million, much of the land that now comprises Arizona, New Mexico, Utah, Nevada, and California. The treaty promised those living in the territory the option of remaining there as American citizens or leaving for Mexico. All citizens living in the area were guaranteed property rights and the freedom to choose their own language, religion, and culture. (As is shown in the chapter's first reading, Mexico and the United States ratified different versions of this treaty, with different guarantees.) For many Chicanos, the Treaty of Guadalupe Hidalgo represents a turning point in relations between Mexico and the United States. Because of the treaty, Mexico lost approximately half its territory to those to whom it had once granted generous settlement rights. For this reason, many Chicanos regard the border between Mexico and the United States as arbitrary and irrelevant.

Immigration laws notwithstanding, the migration of people across the border, which began long before the United States-Mexican War, continues to the present day. A great influx of immigrants, for example, occurred during the period between 1910 and 1920 as a result of the Mexican Revolution. Still, it might also be argued that the American economy, more than conditions in Mexico, has determined both the number of immigrants and their reception in the United States. During times of labor shortage, migrant workers are tolerated and even encouraged; indeed, many service industries in the Southwest depend on this cheap labor for their survival. Most of the time, when the U.S. economy weakens, however, and the demand for jobs by the white population increases, restrictions against Mexican migrant workers are more rigorously enforced. During the early years of the Great Depression, for example, more than 500,000 Mexicans or people of Mexican descent— one third of the Chicano population—were deported or repatriated to Mexico. Many of the deportees were U.S. citizens. In 1939 the United States established the so-called Bracero Program, which welcomed farm labor and renewed Mexican immigration into the United States. The program continued bringing migrant labor into the United States until 1964; it is estimated that 4 million people had been a part of it.

Migrant workers in the Southwest have also suffered from substandard working conditions. This group of workers, along with the Chinese and members of other immigrant groups, had contributed much of the labor needed to build railroads, work mines, and cultivate fields. Yet they have had few of the labor safeguards to which Euro American workers have grown accustomed. Mexicans have worked long hours without breaks, earning pay far below the national minimum wage. Frequently, they have had to house their families in shacks, without electricity or indoor plumbing, for months on end while they worked as seasonal laborers. The economic power of landowners, combined with the workers' frequent migrations and their marginal legal status, has discouraged the workers from unionizing and engaging in other collective bargaining activities.

During the 1960s and 1970s, César Chávez and his followers—the United Farm Workers Union—drew the nation's attention to the farmworkers' struggle by leading *huelgas*, or strikes, against the growers. The group also organized a nationwide boycott of California grapes, the largest such boycott in American history. These combined actions led to national recognition of the United Farm Workers Union and contracts for its members. Using boycotts, strikes, and hunger strikes, the group continues to work for the rights of farmworkers despite declining membership. Recently, the union has protested the exposure of farmworkers to potentially carcinogenic pesticides. The migrant workers in industry have fared worse; despite recent efforts at immigration reform, many people continue to work long hours in the modern equivalent of the nineteenth-century "sweat shop."

Several of the selections in this chapter either directly address or gain inspiration from the migrant worker. The second selection, written by César Chávez, provides a firsthand account of the struggle to organize the farmworkers. The situation of the migrant worker is presented from a different perspective in Tomás Rivera's story "La Noche Buena." Rivera, who was raised in a family of migrant workers that traveled from south Texas to the Midwest as farm laborers, considers the psychological effects of this lifestyle on the wife of a migrant worker.

The history of the Southwest since 1848 suggests that it is not only the migrant workers whose rights have been ignored. Despite the rights guaranteed by the Treaty of Guadalupe Hidalgo and the Constitution of the United States, Chicanos have suffered discrimination and sometimes violence at the hands of the dominant culture. The Texas Rangers, the state's principal law enforcement officers, became notorious for their cruel and arbitrary treatment of people of Mexican descent; indeed, some historians claim that there were more lynchings of Mexicans in the Southwest than of African Americans in the South. Despite guarantees of freedom of language, Chicano children in California were routinely segregated from white children during the nineteenth century; as recently as twenty years ago they were still subject to punishment for speaking Spanish.

Beginning in the 1950s and intensifying during the 1960s and 1970s, Chicanos more forcefully asserted their rights as citizens. Organizations such as the Mexican American Political Association and MEChA (*Movimiento Estudiantíl Chicano de Aztlán*) were founded to represent the interest of Chicano constituents. Student protestors in cities such as Los Angeles demanded that Chicanos be given more say in their education. Students and other activists organized the Chicano Moratorium of August 29, 1970, as a protest against the war in Vietnam. The historian Mario T. García has called the Chicano Moratorium "the largest demonstration ever organized in the United States by people of Mexican descent." The Mexican American Legal Defense and Education Fund was established to provide legal assistance for people who felt their civil rights were being violated.

Along with this political activism there emerged a heightened cultural awareness. Ruben Salazar, who was one of the first Chicano reporters for a major newspaper, wrote about the Chicano Moratorium. He was killed in 1970 while covering the story. Salazar's essay, "Who Is a Chicano?", illuminates some of the positions of the Chicano Moratorium period and the Chicano Renaissance that followed, as it explores the connotations of the term *Chicano*, which became popular with many during this time. As he suggests, the word embodied an attempt to move beyond the hyphenated appellation "Mexican-American" to a term that more strongly suggested ethnic pride: "A Chicano is a Mexican-American with a non-Anglo image of himself." The cultural production of the Chicano Renaissance provides many examples of the reassertion of cultural identity that Salazar describes.

Much of the writing of that cultural movement has addressed the issue of the border. As Héctor Calderón explains in "Reinventing the Border," an essay composed specifically for this anthology, "Whenever Chicanas and Chicanos write on behalf of their community, the border has always loomed in the background." Several of the readings in this chapter use the image of the border to examine issues of ownership, entitlement, and identity. Salazar's "A Mexican-American Hyphen," written in 1970, calls attention to the preconceptions that are held on each side of the border. In the chapter from Arturo Islas's *Migrant Souls*, the act of border crossing prompts the characters to address issues related to identity and affiliation. Calderón's essay explores the act of border crossing, in both personal and analytical terms. The essay acts out a kind of disciplinary and stylistic border crossing, as Calderón calls attention to "a centuries-old border culture with new social and economic realities . . . reasserting itself on the U.S. national scene" and invites his readers to consider the implications of that *mestizo* presence and its reassertion of self, in economic, political, and cultural terms. In Richard Rodriguez's essay, "Go North, Young Man," the border prompts other comparisons between Latin American and Euro American world views.

In Sandra Cisneros's story, "Woman Hollering Creek," the border image extends beyond legal and political constructs to embrace cultural and personal values as well. One of the key issues raised in her piece, as well as in several others in the chapter, concerns the borders of ethnicity, class, and gender. The construction of female identity is important in the fictional piece "La Noche Buena" by Tomás Rivera, one of the most significant writers of the Chicano Renaissance period; beyond the literal search described in the story, the wanderings of the main character can be interpreted as a kind of existential search for identity and affirmation. The excerpt from Graciela Limón's *The Memories of Ana Calderón* explores the effects of the migrant life on an adolescent female whose family has just moved from Mexico to Los Angeles in the 1930s. In contrast to the family's expectations that California would be a kind of paradisal garden, on arriving in Los Angeles the family finds itself living in a garage. Although Ana finds in the classroom the promise of a better life, she soon discovers that her ambitions conflict with the expectations of her father, specifically that she should leave school, begin work, and fashion for herself a life of obedience and service to the family. As Ana soon discovers, the life of the migrant is not easily abandoned; with the change in season, families habitually left whatever home they had established to follow the crops. In Cisneros's story, the main character Cleófilas, initially infatuated with the myth of the United States, learns to differentiate the legendary aspects from the lived experience and to exercise greater agency on behalf of her children; interestingly, it is the intervention of another female character that allows Cleófilas to resist the oppression she finds at home. Pat Mora's "Elena" reflects on the ways an individual fashions herself in response to or as a reaction against the ethnic and gender assumptions of others.

If the writings of early Euro Americans emphasized the Statue of Liberty and the "land of milk and honey," the writings of many Chicanos propose a kind of countermythology, with California, and the United States by extension, as a garden, a paradise. Their writings emphasize the importance both of education and of maintaining one's culture; they examine biculturalism as both a burden and a gift. Since the 1970s, members of the Chicano community have taken different stances on such issues as bilingual education, affirmative action, and the status of the undocumented worker. Yet in negotiating these borders in print and in public debate, there is reflected an assertion of heritage, pride, and identity. In the words of Joaquín, "The odds are great / but my spirit is strong . . . [and] I shall endure."

**BEGINNING: Pre-reading/Writing**

*Imagine that the place where you are living suddenly becomes part of another country and culture. What aspects of your life might change? How difficult do you think it will be to make those changes? In a journal entry, express your feelings about the situation and your plans for the future. Share your thoughts with the class.*

*The Treaty of Guadalupe Hidalgo, ratified in 1848, brought an end to the United States-Mexican War. As a part of the treaty, Mexico ceded to the United States much of the territory now referred to as the American Southwest, with the understanding that Mexican nationals living in the territory would be guaranteed their rights to property, religion, and liberty. The specific provisions guarding these rights, however, were never passed by the U.S. Congress. The excerpt below shows the treaty as passed by Congress, followed by the original version of Article IX and the excised Article X.*

# *From* THE TREATY OF GUADALUPE HIDALGO*

## *Articles 8–15*

## *Article VIII*

1   MEXICANS NOW ESTABLISHED IN TERRITORIES previously belonging to Mexico, and which remain for the future within the limits of the United States, as defined by the present treaty, shall be free to continue where they now reside, or to remove at any time to the Mexican Republic, retaining the property which they possess in the said territories, or disposing thereof, and removing the proceeds wherever they please, without their being subjected, on this account, to any contribution, tax or charge whatever.

2   Those who shall prefer to remain in the said territories, may either retain the title and rights of Mexican citizens, or acquire those of citizens of the United

*Reprinted from Hunter Miller, ed., *Treaties and Other International Acts of the United States of America*, Vol. 5 (Washington, D.C.: Government Printing Office, 1937).

States. But they shall be under the obligation to make their election within one year from the date of the exchange of ratifications of this treaty: and those who shall remain in the said territories, after the expiration of that year, without having declared their intention to retain the character of Mexicans, shall be considered to have elected to become citizens of the United States.

In the said territories, property of every kind, now belonging to Mexicans, not established there, shall be inviolably respected. The present owners, the heirs of these and all Mexicans who may hereafter acquire said property by contract, shall enjoy with respect to it, guarantees equally ample as if the same belonged to citizens of the United States.

## Article IX

The Mexicans who, in the territories aforesaid, shall not preserve the character of citizens of the Mexican Republic, conformably with what is stipulated in the preceding article, shall be incorporated into the Union of the United States and be admitted, at the proper time (to be judged of by the Congress of the United States) to the enjoyment of all the rights of citizens of the United States according to the principles of the Constitution; and in the mean time shall be maintained and protected in the free enjoyment of their liberty and property, and secured in the free exercise of their religion without restriction.

[*One of the amendments of the Senate struck out Article 10.*]

## Article XI

Considering that a great part of the territories which, by the present Treaty, are to be comprehended for the future within the limits of the United States, is now occupied by savage tribes, who will hereafter be under the exclusive control of the Government of the United States, and whose incursions within the territory of Mexico would be prejudicial in the extreme; it is solemnly agreed that all such incursions shall be forcibly restrained by the Government of the United States, whensoever this may be necessary; and that when they cannot be prevented, they shall be punished by the said Government, and satisfaction for the same shall be exacted; all in the same way, and with equal diligence and energy, as if the same incursions were meditated or committed within its own territory against its own citizens.

It shall not be lawful, under any pretext whatever, for any inhabitant of the United States, to purchase or acquire any Mexican or any foreigner residing in Mexico, who may have been captured by Indians inhabiting the territory of either of the two Republics, nor to purchase or acquiring horses, mules, cattle or property of any kind, stolen within Mexican territory by such Indians.

And, in the event of any person or persons, captured within Mexican Territory by Indians, being carried into the territory of the United States, the

Government of the latter engages and binds itself in the most solemn manner, so soon as it shall know of such captives being within its territory, and shall be able so to do, through the faithful exercise of its influence and power, to rescue them and return them to their country, or deliver them to the agent or representative of the Mexican Government. The Mexican Authorities will, as far as practicable, give to the Government of the United States notice of such captures; and its agent shall pay the expenses incurred in the maintenance and transmission of the rescued captives; who, in the mean time, shall be treated with the utmost hospitality by the American authorities at the place where they may be. But if the Government of the United States, before receiving such notice from Mexico, should obtain intelligence through any other channel, of the existence of Mexican captives within its territory, it will proceed forthwith to effect their release and delivery to the Mexican agent, as above stipulated.

9    For the purpose of giving to these stipulations the fullest possible efficacy, thereby affording the security and redress demanded by their true spirit and intent, the Government of the United States will now and hereafter pass, without unnecessary delay, and always vigilantly enforce, such laws as the nature of the subject may require. And finally, the sacredness of this obligation shall never be lost sight of by the said Government, when providing for the removal of the Indians from any portion of the said territories, or for its being settled by citizens of the United States; but on the contrary special care shall then be taken not to place its Indian occupants under the necessity of seeking new homes, by committing those invasions which the United States have solemnly obliged themselves to restrain.

## Article XII

10    In consideration of the extension acquired by the boundaries of the United States, as defined in the fifth Article of the present treaty, the Government of the United States engages to pay to that of the Mexican Republic the sum of fifteen Millions of Dollars.

11    Immediately after this treaty shall have been duly ratified by the Government of the Mexican Republic, the sum of three millions of dollars shall be paid to the said Government by that of the United States at the city of Mexico, in the gold or silver coin of Mexico. The remaining twelve millions of dollars shall be paid at the same place and in the same coin, in annual instalments of three millions of dollars each, together with interest on the same at the rate of six per centum per annum. This interest shall begin to run upon the whole sum of twelve millions, from the day of the ratification of the present treaty by the Mexican Government, and the first of the instalments shall be paid at the expiration of one year from the same day. Together with each annual instalment, as it falls due, the whole interest accruing on such instalment from the beginning shall also be paid.

## *Article XIII*

The United States engage moreover, to assume and pay to the claimants all amounts now due them, and those hereafter to become due, by reason of the claims already liquidated and decided against the Mexican Republic, under the conventions between the two Republics severally concluded on the eleventh day of April eighteen hundred and thirty-nine, and on the thirtieth day of January eighteen hundred and forty-three: so that the Mexican Republic shall be absolutely exempt for the future, from all expense whatever on account of the said claims.

## *Article XIV*

The United States do furthermore discharge the Mexican Republic from all claims of citizens of the United States, not heretofore decided against the Mexican Government, which may have arisen previously to the date of the signature of this treaty: which discharge shall be final and perpetual, whether the said claims be rejected or be allowed by the Board of Commissioners provided for in the following Article, and whatever shall be the total amount of those allowed.

## *Article XV*

The United States, exonerating Mexico from all demands on account of the claims of their citizens mentioned in the preceding Article, and considering them entirely and forever cancelled, whatever their amount may be, undertake to make satisfaction for the same, to an amount not exceeding three and one quarter millions of Dollars. To ascertain the validity and amount of those claims, a Board of Commissioners shall be established by the Government of the United States, whose awards shall be final and conclusive: provided that in deciding upon the validity of each claim, the board shall be guided and governed by the principles and rules of decision prescribed by the first and fifth Articles of the unratified convention, concluded at the City of Mexico on the twentieth day of November, one thousand eight hundred and forty-three; and in no case shall an award be made in favour of any claim not embraced by these principles and rules.

If, in the opinion of the said Board of Commissioners, or of the claimants, any books, records or documents in the possession or power of the Government of the Mexican Republic, shall be deemed necessary to the just decision of any claim, the Commissioners or the claimants, through them, shall, within such period as Congress may designate, make an application in writing for the same, addressed to the Mexican Minister for Foreign Affairs, to be transmitted by the Secretary of State of the United States; and the Mexican Government engages, at the earliest possible moment after the receipt of such demand, to cause any of the books, records or documents, so specified, which shall be in their possession or power (or authenticated Copies or extracts of the same) to be transmitted to the said Secretary of State, who shall immediately deliver them over to the said Board of Commissioners: provided that no such application shall be made, by, or at the instance of, any claimant, until the facts which it is expected to prove by such books, records or documents, shall have been stated under oath or affirmation.

## Articles 9 and 10 Before Senate Amendment

## Article IX

16   The Mexicans who, in the territories aforesaid, shall not preserve the character of citizens of the Mexican Republic, conformably with what is stipulated in the preceding Article, shall be incorporated into the Union of the United States, and admitted as soon as possible, according to the principles of the Federal Constitution, to the enjoyment of all the rights of citizens of the United States. In the mean time, they shall be maintained and protected in the enjoyment of their liberty, their property, and the civil rights now vested in them according to the Mexican laws. With respect to political rights, their condition shall be on an equality with that of the inhabitants of the other territories of the United States; and at least equally good as that of the inhabitants of Louisiana and the Floridas, when these provinces, by transfer from the French Republic and the Crown of Spain, became territories of the United States.

17   The same most ample guaranty shall be enjoyed by all ecclesiastics and religious corporations or communities, as well in the discharge of the offices of their ministry, as in the enjoyment of their property of every kind, whether individual or corporate. This guaranty shall embrace all temples, houses and edifices dedicated to the Roman Catholic worship; as well as all property destined to its support, or to that of schools, hospitals and other foundations for charitable or beneficent purposes. No property of this nature shall be considered as having become the property of the American Government, or as subject to be, by it, disposed of or diverted to other uses.

18   Finally, the relations and communication between the Catholics living in the territories aforesaid, and their respective ecclesiastical authorities shall be open, free and exempt from all hindrance whatever, even although such authorities should reside within the limits of the Mexican Republic, as defined by this treaty; and this freedom shall continue, so long as a new demarcation of ecclesiastical districts shall not have been made, conformably with the laws of the Roman Catholic Church.

## Article X

19   All grants of land made by the Mexican Government or by the competent authorities, in territories previously appertaining to Mexico, and remaining for

the future within the limits of the United States, shall be respected as valid, to the same extent that the same grants would be valid, if the said territories had remained within the limits of Mexico. But the grantees of lands in Texas, put in possession thereof, who, by reason of the circumstances of the country since the beginning of the troubles between Texas and the Mexican Government, may have been prevented from fulfilling all the conditions of their grants, shall be under the obligation to fulfill the said conditions within the periods limited in the same respectively; such periods to be now counted from the date of the exchange of ratifications of this treaty: in default of which the said grants shall not be obligatory upon the State of Texas, in virtue of the stipulations contained in this Article.

The foregoing stipulation in regard to grantees of land in Texas, is extended to all grantees of land in the territories aforesaid, elsewhere than in Texas, put in possession under such grants; and, in default of the fulfillment of the conditions of any such grant, within the new period, which, as is above stipulated, begins with the day of the exchange of ratifications of this treaty, the same shall be null and void.  20

The Mexican Government declares that no grant whatever of lands in Texas has been made since the second day of March one thousand eight hundred and thirty-six; and that no grant whatever of lands in any of the territories aforesaid has been made since the thirteenth day of May one thousand eight hundred and forty-six.  ✠  21

---

RESPONDING

1. In a journal entry, explain one of the effects of the treaty on people living in the region.

2. Working individually or in a group, identify on a map the parts of the United States that were originally settled by Mexico. Speculate on the reasons those particular areas would have been settled.

3. Write an essay explaining how regions of the United States that were originally settled by Mexico became American territory.

4. In an essay, discuss the effects of the Treaty of Guadalupe Hidalgo on Mexicans living in the disputed area. What rights were they guaranteed? What did they have to give up? In your opinion, was the treaty fair to Mexican citizens? To Americans? Support your answer with examples from the treaty and your own knowledge.

# CESAR CHAVEZ

*César Chávez (1927–1993) was best known as the founder of the United Farm Workers Union. Born in Yuma, Arizona, to a family of migrant workers, he experienced firsthand the deplorable working conditions of seasonal laborers. During the mid-1960s and early 1970s his union organized boycotts of California table grapes and nonunion lettuce. During the 1980s the union focused attention on the use of dangerous pesticides in the fields, documenting and publicizing the extraordinary number of miscarriages and cancerous tumors occurring among farmworkers exposed to these chemicals.*

*In the essay that follows, which was first published in* Ramparts *magazine in 1966, Chávez talks about his early involvement in the farmworkers' cause. In describing the attempt to obtain support from various community groups, the essay suggests the special demands that leadership makes on an individual.*

# THE ORGANIZER'S TALE

1   IT REALLY STARTED FOR ME 16 years ago in San Jose, California, when I was working on an apricot farm. We figured he was just another social worker doing a study of farm conditions, and I kept refusing to meet with him. But he was persistent. Finally, I got together some of the rough element in San Jose. We were going to have a little reception for him to teach the *gringo* a little bit of how we felt. There were about 30 of us in the house, young guys mostly. I was supposed to give them a signal—change my cigarette from my right hand to my left, and then we were going to give him a lot of hell. But he started talking and the more he talked, the more wide-eyed I became and the less inclined I was to give the signal. A couple of guys who were pretty drunk at this time still wanted to give the *gringo* the business, but we got rid of them. This fellow was making a lot of sense, and I wanted to hear what he had to say.

2   His name was Fred Ross, and he was an organizer for the Community Service Organization (CSO) which was working with Mexican-Americans in the cities. I became immediately really involved. Before long I was heading a voter registration drive. All the time I was observing the things Fred did, secretly, because I wanted to learn how to organize, to see how it was done. I was impressed with his patience and understanding of people. I thought this was a tool, one of the greatest things he had.

It was pretty rough for me at first. I was changing and had to take a lot of ridicule from the kids my age, the rough characters I worked with in the fields. They would say, "Hey, big shot. Now that you're a *politico*, why are you working here for 65 cents an hour?" I might add that our neighborhood had the highest percentage of San Quentin graduates. It was a game among the *pachucos* in the sense that we defended ourselves from outsiders, although inside the neighborhood there was not a lot of fighting.

After six months of working every night in San Jose, Fred assigned me to take over the CSO chapter in Decoto. It was a tough spot to fill. I would suggest something, and people would say, "No, let's wait till Fred gets back," or "Fred wouldn't do it that way." This is pretty much a pattern with people, I discovered, whether I was put in Fred's position, or later, when someone else was put in my position. After the Decoto assignment I was sent to start a new chapter in Oakland. Before I left, Fred came to a place in San Jose called the Hole-in-the-Wall and we talked for half an hour over coffee. He was in a rush to leave, but I wanted to keep him talking; I was scared of my assignment.

There were hard times in Oakland. First of all, it was a big city and I'd get lost every time I went anywhere. Then I arranged a series of house meetings. I would get to the meeting early and drive back and forth past the house, too nervous to go in and face the people. Finally I would force myself to go inside and sit in a corner. I was quite thin then, and young, and most of the people were middle-aged. Someone would say, "Where's the organizer?" And I would pipe up, "Here I am." Then they would say in Spanish—these were very poor people and we hardly spoke anything but Spanish—"Ha! This *kid*?" Most of them said they were interested, but the hardest part was to get them to start pushing themselves, on their own initiative.

The idea was to set up a meeting and then get each attending person to call his own house meeting, inviting new people—a sort of chain letter effect. After a house meeting, I would lie awake going over the whole thing, playing the tape back, trying to see why people laughed at one point, or why they were for one thing and against another. I was also learning to read and write, those late evenings. I had left school in the 7th grade after attending 67 different schools, and my reading wasn't the best.

At our first organizing meeting we had 368 people: I'll never forget it because it was very important to me. You eat your heart out; the meeting is called for 7 o'clock and you start to worry about 4. You wait. Will they show up? Then the first one arrives. By 7 there are only 20 people, you have everything in order, you have to look calm. But little by little they filter in and at a certain point you know it will be a success.

After four months in Oakland, I was transferred. The chapter was beginning to move on its own, so Fred assigned me to organize the San Joaquin Valley.

Over the months I developed what I used to call schemes or tricks—now I call them techniques—of making initial contacts. The main thing in convincing someone is to spend time with him. It doesn't matter if he can read, write or even speak well. What is important is that he is a man and second, that he has shown some initial interest. One good way to develop leadership is to take a man with you in your car. And it works a lot better if you're doing the driving; that way you are in charge. You drive, he sits there, and you talk. These little things were very important to me; I was caught in a big game by then, figuring out what makes people work. I found that if you work hard enough you can usually shake people into working too, those who are concerned. You work harder and they work harder still, up to a point and then they pass you. Then, of course, they're on their own.

9    I also learned to keep away from the established groups and so-called leaders, and to guard against philosophizing. Working with low-income people is very different from working with the professionals, who like to sit around talking about how to play politics. When you're trying to recruit a farmworker, you have to paint a little picture, and then you have to color the picture in. We found out that the harder a guy is to convince, the better leader or member he becomes. When you exert yourself to convince him, you have his confidence and he has good motivation. A lot of people who say OK right away wind up hanging around the office, taking up the workers' time.

10    During the McCarthy era in one Valley town, I was subjected to a lot of redbaiting. We had been recruiting people for citizenship classes at the high school when we got into a quarrel with the naturalization examiner. He was rejecting people on the grounds that they were just parroting what they learned in citizenship class. One day we had a meeting about it in Fresno, and I took along some of the leaders of our local chapter. Some redbaiting official gave us a hard time, and the people got scared and took his side. They did it because it seemed easy at the moment, even though they knew that sticking with me was the right thing to do. It was disgusting. When we left the building they walked by themselves ahead of me as if I had some kind of communicable disease. I had been working with these people for three months and I was very sad to see that. It taught me a great lesson.

11    That night I learned that the chapter officers were holding a meeting to review my letters and printed materials to see if I really was a Communist. So I drove out there and walked right in on their meeting. I said, "I hear you've been discussing me, and I thought it would be nice if I was here to defend myself. Not that it matters that much to you or even to me, because as far as I'm concerned you are a bunch of cowards." At that they began to apologize. "Let's forget it," they said. "You're a nice guy." But I didn't want apologies. I wanted a full discussion. I told them I didn't give a damn, but that they had to learn to distinguish fact from what appeared to be a fact because of fear. I kept

them there till two in the morning. Some of the women cried. I don't know if they investigated me any further, but I stayed on another few months and things worked out.

This was not an isolated case. Often when we'd leave people to themselves they would get frightened and draw back into their shells where they had been all the years. And I learned quickly that there is no real appreciation. Whatever you do, and no matter what reasons you may give to others, you do it because you want to see it done, or maybe because you want power: And there shouldn't be any appreciation, understandably. I know good organizers who were destroyed, washed out, because they expected people to appreciate what they'd done. Anyone who comes in with the idea that farmworkers are free of sin and that the growers are all bastards, either has never dealt with the situation or is an idealist of the first order. Things don't work that way. 12

For more than 10 years I worked for the CSO. As the organization grew, we found ourselves meeting in fancier and fancier motels and holding expensive conventions. Doctors, lawyers and politicians began joining. They would get elected to some office in the organization and then, for all practical purposes, leave. Intent on using the CSO for their own prestige purposes, these "leaders," many of them, lacked the urgency we had to have. When I became general director I began to press for a program to organize farmworkers into a union, an idea most of the leadership opposed. So I started a revolt within the CSO. I refused to sit at the head table at meetings, refused to wear a suit and tie, and finally I even refused to shave and cut my hair. It used to embarrass some of the professionals. At every meeting I got up and gave my standard speech: we shouldn't meet in fancy motels, we were getting away from the people, farmworkers had to be organized. But nothing happened. In March of '62 I resigned and came to Delano to begin organizing the Valley on my own. 13

By hand I drew a map of all the towns between Arvin and Stockton—86 of them, including farming camps—and decided to hit them all to get a small nucleus of people working in each. For six months, I traveled around, planting an idea. We had a simple questionnaire, a little card with space for name, address and how much the worker thought he ought to be paid. My wife, Helen, mimeographed them, and we took our kids for two or three day jaunts to these towns, distributing the cards door-to-door and to camps and groceries. 14

Some 80,000 cards were sent back from eight Valley counties. I got a lot of contacts that way, but I was shocked at the wages the people were asking. The growers were paying $1 and $1.15, and maybe 95 per cent of the people thought they should be getting only $1.25. Sometimes people scribbled messages on the cards: "I hope to God we win" or "Do you think we can win?" or "I'd like to know more." So I separated the cards with the pencilled notes, got in my car and went to those people. 15

We didn't have any money at all in those days, none for gas and hardly any 16 for food. So I went to people and started asking for food. It turned out to be about the best thing I could have done, although at first it's hard on your pride. Some of our best members came in that way. If people give you their food, they'll give you their hearts. Several months and many meetings later we had a working organization, and this time the leaders were the people.

17 None of the farmworkers had collective bargaining contracts, and I thought it would take ten years before we got that first contract. I wanted desperately to get some color into the movement, to give people something they could identify with, like a flag. I was reading some books about how various leaders discovered what colors contrasted and stood out the best. The Egyptians had found that a red field with a white circle and a black emblem in the center crashed into your eyes like nothing else. I wanted to use the Aztec eagle in the center, as on the Mexican flag. So I told my cousin Manuel, "Draw an Aztec eagle." Manuel had a little trouble with it, so we modified the eagle to make it easier for people to draw.

18 The first big meeting of what we decided to call the National Farm Workers Association was held in September 1962, at Fresno, with 287 people. We had our huge red flag on the wall, with paper tacked over it. When the time came, Manuel pulled a cord ripping the paper off the flag and all of a sudden it hit the people. Some of them wondered if it was a Communist flag, and I said it probably looked more like a neo-Nazi emblem than anything else. But they wanted an explanation. So Manuel got up and said, "When that damn eagle flies—that's when the farmworkers' problems are going to be solved."

19 One of the first things I decided was that outside money wasn't going to organize people, at least not in the beginning. I even turned down a grant from a private group—$50,000 to go directly to organize farmworkers—for just this reason. Even when there are no strings attached, you are still compromised because you feel you have to produce immediate results. This is bad, because it takes a long time to build a movement, and your organization suffers if you get too far ahead of the people it belongs to. We set the dues at $42 a year per family, really a meaningful dues, but of the 212 we got to pay, only 12 remained by June of '63. We were discouraged at that, but not enough to make us quit.

20 Money was always a problem. Once we were facing a $180 gas bill on a credit card I'd got a long time ago and was about to lose. And we *had* to keep that credit card. One day my wife and I were picking cotton, pulling bolls, to make a little money to live on. Helen said to me, "Do you put all this in the bag, or just the cotton?" I thought she was kidding and told her to throw the whole boll in so that she had nothing but a sack of bolls at the weighing. The man said, "Whose sack is this?" I said, well, my wife's, and he told us we were fired. "Look at all that crap you brought in," he said. Helen and I started laughing. We were going anyway. We took the $4 we had earned and spent it

at a grocery store where they were giving away a $100 prize. Each time you shopped they'd give you one of the letters of M-O-N-E-Y or a flag: you had to have M-O-N-E-Y plus the flag to win. Helen had already collected the letters and just needed the flag. Anyway, they gave her the ticket. She screamed, "A flag? I don't believe it," ran in and got the $100. She said "Now we're going to eat steak." But I said no, we're going to pay the gas bill. I don't know if she cried, but I think she did.

It was rough in those early years. Helen was having babies and I was not there when she was at the hospital. But if you haven't got your wife behind you, you can't do many things. There's got to be peace at home. So I did, I think, a fairly good job of organizing her. When we were kids, she lived in Delano and I came to town as a migrant. Once on a date we had a bad experience about segregation at a movie theater, and I put up a fight. We were together then, and still are. I think I'm more of a pacifist than she is. Her father, Fabela, was a colonel with Pancho Villa in the Mexican Revolution. Sometimes she gets angry and tells me, "These scabs—you should deal with them sternly," and I kid her, "It must be too much of that Fabela blood in you."

The movement really caught on in '64. By August we had a thousand members. We'd had a beautiful 90-day drive in Corcoran, where they had the Battle of the Corcoran Farm Camp 30 years ago, and by November we had assets of $25,000 in our credit union, which helped to stabilize the membership. I had gone without pay the whole of 1963. The next year the members voted me a $40 a week salary, after Helen had to quit working in the fields to manage the credit union.

Our first strike was in May of '65, a small one but it prepared us for the big one. A farmworker from McFarland named Epifanio Camacho came to see me. He said he was sick and tired of how people working the roses were being treated, and he was willing to "go the limit." I assigned Manuel and Gilbert Padilla to hold meetings at Camacho's house. The people wanted union recognition, but the real issue, as in most cases when you begin, was wages. They were promised $9 a thousand, but they were actually getting $6.50 and $7 for grafting roses. Most of them signed cards giving us the right to bargain for them. We chose the biggest company, with about 85 employees, not counting the irrigators and supervisors, and we held a series of meetings to prepare the strike and call the vote. There would be no picket line; everyone pledged on their honor not to break the strike.

Early on the first morning of the strike, we sent out 10 cars to check the people's homes. We found lights in five or six homes and knocked on the doors. The men were getting up and we'd say, "Where are you going?" They would dodge, "Oh, uh . . . I was just getting up, you know." We'd say, "Well, you're not going to work, are you?" And they'd say no. Dolores Huerta, who was driving the green panel truck, saw a light in one house where four rose-workers lived. They told her they were going to work, even after she reminded them of their pledge. So she moved the truck so it blocked their driveway, turned off the key, put it in her purse and sat there alone.

25 That morning the company foreman was madder than hell and refused to talk to us. None of the grafters had shown up for work. At 10:30 we started to go to the company office, but it occurred to us that maybe a woman would have a better chance. So Dolores knocked on the office door, saying, "I'm Dolores Huerta from the National Farm Workers Association." "Get out!" the man said, "you Communist. Get out!" I guess they were expecting us, because as Dolores stood arguing with him the cops came and told her to leave. She left.

26 For two days the fields were idle. On Wednesday they recruited a group of Filipinos from out of town who knew nothing of the strike, maybe 35 of them. They drove through escorted by three sheriff's patrol cars, one in front, one in the middle and one at the rear with a dog. We didn't have a picket line, but we parked across the street and just watched them go through, not saying a word. All but seven stopped working after half an hour, and the rest had quit by mid-afternoon.

27 The company made an offer the evening of the fourth day, a package deal that amounted to a 120 per cent wage increase, but no contract. We wanted to hold out for a contract and more benefits, but a majority of the rose-workers wanted to accept the offer and go back. We are a democratic union so we had to support what they wanted to do. They had a meeting and voted to settle. Then we had a problem with a few militants who wanted to hold out. We had to convince them to go back to work, as a united front, because otherwise they would be canned. So we worked—Tony Orendain and I, Dolores and Gilbert, Jim Drake and all the organizers—knocking on doors till two in the morning, telling people, "You have to go back or you'll lose your job." And they did. They worked.

28 Our second strike, and our last before the big one at Delano, was in the grapes at Martin's Ranch last summer. The people were getting a raw deal there, being pushed around pretty badly. Gilbert went out to the field, climbed on top of a car and took a strike vote. They voted unanimously to go out. Right away they started bringing in strikebreakers, so we launched a tough attack on the labor contractors, distributed leaflets portraying them as really low characters. We attacked one—Luis Campos—so badly that he just gave up the job, and he took 27 of his men out with him. All he asked was that we distribute another leaflet reinstating him in the community. And we did. What was unusual was that the grower would talk to us. The grower kept saying, "I can't pay. I just haven't got the money." I guess he must have found the money somewhere, because we were asking $1.40 and we got it.

We had just finished the Martin strike when the Agricultural Workers 29
Organizing Committee (AFL-CIO) started a strike against the grape growers,
DiGiorgio, Schenley liquors and small growers, asking $1.40 an hour and 25
cents a box. There was a lot of pressure from our members for us to join the
strike, but we had some misgivings. We didn't feel ready for a big strike like
this one, one that was sure to last a long time. Having no money—just $87 in
the strike fund—meant we'd have to depend on God knows who.

Eight days after the strike started—it takes time to get 1,200 people together 30
from all over the Valley—we held a meeting in Delano and voted to go out. I
asked the membership to release us from the pledge not to accept outside money,
because we'd need it now, a lot of it. The help came. It started because of the
close, and I would say even beautiful relationship that we've had with the
Migrant Ministry for some years. They were the first to come to our rescue,
financially and in every other way, and they spread the word to other bene-
factors.

We had planned, before, to start a labor school in November. It never 31
happened, but we have the best labor school we could ever have, in the strike.
The strike is only a temporary condition, however. We have over 3,000 members
spread out over a wide area, and we have to service them when they have
problems. We get letters from New Mexico, Colorado, Texas, California, from
farmworkers saying, "We're getting together and we need an organizer." It kills
you when you haven't got the personnel and resources. You feel badly about
not sending an organizer because you look back and remember all the difficulty
you had in getting two or three people together, and here *they're* together. Of
course, we're training organizers, many of them younger than I was when I
started in CSO. They can work 20 hours a day, sleep four, and be ready to hit
it again; when you get to 39 it's a different story.

The people who took part in the strike and the march have something more 32
than their material interest going for them. If it were only material, they
wouldn't have stayed on the strike long enough to win. It is difficult to explain.
But it flows out in the ordinary things they say. For instance, some of the
younger guys are saying, "Where do you think's going to be the next strike?"
I say, "Well, we have to win in Delano." They say, "We'll win, but where do
we go next?" I say, "Maybe most of us will be working in the fields." They say,
"No, I don't want to go and work in the fields. I want to organize. There are
a lot of people that need our help." So I say, "you're going to be pretty poor
then, because when you strike you don't have much money." They say they
don't care about that.

And others are saying, "I have friends who are working in Texas. If we could 33
only help them." It is bigger, certainly, than just a strike. And if this spirit grows
within the farm labor movement, one day we can use the force that we have to

help correct a lot of things that are wrong in this society. But that is for the future. Before you can run, you have to learn to walk.

34     There are vivid memories from my childhood—what we had to go through because of low wages and the conditions, basically because there was no union. I suppose if I wanted to be fair I could say that I'm trying to settle a personal score. I could dramatize it by saying that I want to bring social justice to farmworkers. But the truth is that I went through a lot of hell, and a lot of people did. If we can even the score a little for the workers then we are doing something. Besides, I don't know any other work I like to do better than this. I really don't, you know. ✠

---

## RESPONDING

1.   In a journal entry, identify the techniques Chávez learned that helped him become a labor organizer.

2.   Working individually or in a group, pool information about the McCarthy era. Explain what Chávez means when he says he was "subjected to a lot of redbaiting" (paragraph 10).

3.   Chávez says, "Whatever you do, and no matter what reasons you may give to others, you do it because you want to see it done, or maybe because you want power" (paragraph 12). In an essay, agree or disagree with this statement. Use examples from the essay to support your argument.

4.   Review the philosophy, focus, and methods of the organization Chávez founded. Write an essay that discusses the advantages and disadvantages of his method of going directly to the people.

# TOMAS RIVERA

*Tomás Rivera was born in Crystal City, Texas, in 1935, the child of migrant workers who had emigrated from Mexico. He spent his childhood working on farms from Texas to the Midwest. Rivera earned a bachelor's degree from Southwest Texas State University in 1964, a master's degree in educational administration from the same school in 1964, and a doctorate in Romance languages and literature from the University of Oklahoma in 1969.*

*From 1957 until his death, Rivera held several university teaching and administrative positions in Texas and California. In 1980 he was named chancellor of the University of California at Riverside; he was the youngest person and the first member of a minority group to earn this position. Rivera died in 1984 at the age of forty-eight.*

*Rivera's most famous work,* Y no se lo tragó la tierra (. . . And the Earth Did Not Part, *1969), examines the experience of a migrant family. While most of the book's chapters focus on the thoughts of a young boy, the excerpted chapter centers on the reactions of the family's mother. As it describes the townspeople's treatment of this woman, the passage asks us to consider the ways in which economic and political issues can affect both families and individual lives.*

⊹

# LA NOCHE BUENA

1　LA NOCHE BUENA SE APROXIMABA y la radio igualmente que la comioneta de la bocina que anunciaba las películas del Teatro Ideal parecían empujarla con canción, negocio y bendición. Faltaban tres días para la noche buena cuando doña María se decidió comprarles algo a sus niños. Esta sería la primera vez que les compraría juguetes. Cada añoy se proponía a hacerlo pero siempre terminaba diciéndose que no, que no podían. Su esposo de todas maneras les traía dulces y nueces a cado uno así que racionalizaba que en realidad no les faltaba nada. Sin embargo cada navidad preguntaban los niños por sus juguetes. Ella siempre los apaciguaba con lo de siempre. Les decía que se esperaran hasta el seis de enero, el día de los reyes magos y así para cuando se llegaba ese día ya hasta se les había olvidado todo a los niños. También había notado que sus hijos apreciaban menos y menos la venida de don Chon la noche de navidad cuando venía con el costal de naranjas y nueces.

　　—Pero, ¿por qué a nosotros no nos trae nada Santo Clos?
　　—¿Cómo que no? ¿Luego cuando viene y les trae naranjas y nueces?
　　—No, pero ése es don Chon.
　　—No, yo digo lo que siempre aparece debajo de la máquina de coser.
　　—Ah, eso lo trae papá, apoco cree que no sabemos. ¿Es que no somos buenos como los demás?
　　—Sí, sí son buenos, pero . . . pues espérense hasta el día de los reyes magos. Ese es el día en que de veras vienen los juguetes y los regalos. Allá en México no viene Santo Clos sino los reyes magos. Y no vienen hasta el seis de enero. Así que ése sí es el mero día.
　　—Pero, lo que pasa es que se les olvida. Porque a nosotros nunca nos han dado nada ni en la noche buena ni en el día de los reyes magos.
　　—Bueno, pero a lo mejor esta ves sí.
　　—Pos sí, ojalá.

2　Por eso se decidió comprarles algo. Pero no tenían dinero para gastar en juguetes. Su esposo trabajaba casi las diez y ocho horas lavando platos y haciendo de comer en un restaurante. No tenía tiempo de ir al centro para comprar juguetes. Además tenían que alzar cada semana para poder pagar para la ida al norte. Ya les cobraban por los niños aunque fueran parados todo el camino hasta Iowa. Así que les costaba bastante para hacer el viaje. De todas maneras le propuso a su esposa esa noche, cuando llegó bien cansado del trabajo, que les compraran algo.

# CHRISTMAS EVE

CHRISTMAS EVE WAS APPROACHING. The radio as well as the loudspeaker on the    1
pickup truck that advertised the movies for the Teatro Ideal seemed to draw it
closer with songs, business, and prayers. It was three days before Christmas
when doña María decided to buy something for her children. This would be
the first time that she had bought toys for them. She planned to do it every
year, but she always wound up convincing herself that they could not afford it.
Her husband brought candies and nuts for each one of them, so she rationalized
that they weren't missing anything. Still, every Christmas day the children would
ask for their toys. She always placated them with the same story. She would tell
them to wait until the sixth of January, the day of the Reyes Magos. By the time
the day arrived the children had completely forgotten about toys. She had also
noticed that her children appreciated less and less each year the visit by don
Chon with his sack of oranges and nuts.

"But why doesn't Santa Claus bring us anything?"

"What do you mean? What about the oranges and nuts that he brings you?"

"No, that's don Chon who brings them."

"No, I mean what is always left under the sewing machine."

"Oh, father brings that, don't think we don't know. Aren't we as good as
the other children?"

"Yes, of course you are, but why don't you wait until the day of the Reyes
Magos. That's really the day when toys and other gifts should be given. In
Mexico it isn't Santa Claus who brings toys, but the Reyes Magos. And they
don't come until the sixth of January. So, you see, that is the real day."

"But what happens is that you forget all about it. We've never received
anything either on Christmas Eve or on the day of the Reyes Magos."

"Well, maybe this time you will."

"Yes, I really hope so."

She decided to buy something for them. But she didn't have any money to    2
spend on toys. Her husband worked almost eighteen hours washing dishes and
cooking in a restaurant. He didn't have time to go downtown to buy toys.
Furthermore, every week they had to save some money to pay for the trip north.
They had to pay the children's fare even if they had to stand up all the way to
Iowa. It was very expensive for them to make the trip. In spite of all this, that
night when her husband arrived tired from work she suggested that they buy
something for them.

—Fíjate, viejo, que los niños quieren algo para crismes.

—¿Y luego las naranjas y las nueces que les traigo?

—Pos, sí, pero ellos quieren juguetes. Ya no se conforman con comida. Es que están más grandes y ven más.

—No necesitan nada.

—¿A poco tú no tenías juguetes cuando eras niño?

—Sabes que yo mismo los hacía de barro—caballitos, soldaditos. . . .

—Pos sí, pero aquí es distinto, como ven muchas cosas . . . ándale vamos a comprarles algo . . . yo misma voy al Kres.

—¿Tú?

—Sí, yo.

—¿No tienes miedo ir al centro? ¿Te acuerdas allá en Wilmar, Minesóra, cómo te perdiste en el centro? ¿'Tas segura que no tienes miedo?

—Sí, sí me acuerdo pero me doy ánimo. Yo voy. Ya me estuve dando ánimo todo el día y estoy segura que no me pierdo aquí. Mira, salgo a la calle. De aquí se ve la hielería. Son cuatro cuadras nomás, según me dijo doña Regina. Luego cuando llegue a la hielería volteo a la derecha y dos cuadras más y estoy en el centro. Allí está el Kres. Luego salgo del Kres, voy hacia la hielería y volteo para esta calle y aquí me tienes.

—De veras que no estaría difícil. Pos sí. Bueno, te voy a dejar dinero sobre la mesa cuando me vaya por la mañana. Pero tienes cuidado, vieja, en estos días hay mucha gente en el centro.

3    Era que doña María nunca salía de casa sola. La única vez que salía era cuando iba a visitar a su papá y a su hermana quienes vivían en la siguiente cuadra. Sólo iba a la iglesia cuando había difuntito y a veces cuando había boda. Pero iba siempre con su esposo así que nunca se fijaba por donde iba. También su esposo le traía siempre todo. El era el que compraba la comida y la ropa. En realidad no conocía el centro aun estando solamente a seis cuadras de su casa. El camposanto quedaba por el lado opuesto al centro, la iglesia también quedaba por ese rumbo. Pasaban por el centro sólo cuando iban de pasada para San Antonio o cuando iban o venían del norte. Casi siempre era de madrugada o de noche. Pero ese día traía ánimo y se preparó para ir al centro.

4    El siguiente día se levantó, como lo hacía siempre, muy temprano y ya cuando había despachado a su esposo y a los niños recogió el dinero de sobre la mesa y empezó a prepararse para ir al centro. No le llevó mucho tiempo.

—Yo no sé por qué soy tan miedosa yo, Dios mío. Si el centro está solamente a seis cuadras de aquí. Nomás me voy derechito y luego volteo a la derecha al pasar los traques. Luego, dos cuadras, y allí está el Kres. De allá para acá ando

"Look, viejo, the children would like something for Christmas."

"What about the oranges and nuts that I bring them?"

"Well, yes, but they want toys. They won't settle for food. They're older now, and they are aware of more things."

"They're not in need of anything."

"Don't tell me you didn't have any toys when you were a child."

"You know, I used to make them myself, out of clay. I'd make little horses, little soldiers. . . ."

"Well, yes, but it's different here since they see many things . . . come on, let's go buy something for them . . . I'll go to Kress myself."

"You?"

"Yes, me."

"Aren't you afraid to go downtown? Don't you remember what happened in Wilmar, Minnesota, when you got lost downtown? Are you sure you're not afraid?"

"Yes, yes, I remember, but I'll try to get up my courage. I'll go. I've been building up courage all day and I'm sure that I won't get lost. Look, all I have to do is go out to the street. I can see the ice plant from here. It's only four blocks away, according to doña Regina. When I get to the ice plant I'll turn right and two blocks more I'll be downtown. Kress is right there. Then I leave Kress, head toward the ice plant, turn into this street and here I am."

"It really won't be difficult at all. Alright, I'll leave you some money on the table when I leave in the morning. But be careful, vieja, there are a lot of people in town these days."

The fact was that doña María never went out of the house by herself. The only time she left the house was when she visited her father and her sister who lived a block away. She went to church only when someone passed away or sometimes when there was a wedding. But she always went with her husband, so she never noticed where she was going. Also, her husband always brought everything to her. He was the one who brought food and clothing. In reality she had never been downtown even though it was just six blocks away from her house. The cemetery was in the opposite direction from the downtown area, as was the church. They crossed the downtown area only when they were on their way to San Antonio or when they were on their way back from up north. Somehow it was always at dawn or during the night. But that day she had built up her courage and she got ready to go downtown.

The following day she got up very early, as she always did, and after she had sent off her husband and the children she picked up the money from the table and started to ready herself to go downtown. It didn't take her very long.

las dos cuadras, y luego volteo a la izquierda y luego hasta que llegue aquí otra vez. Dios quiera y no me vaya a salir algún perro. Al pasar los traques que no vaya a venir un tren y me pesque en medio . . . Ojalá y no me salga un perro . . . Ojalá y no venga un tren por los traques.

5     La distancia de su casa al ferrocarril la anduvo rapidamente. Se fue en medio de la calle todo el trecho. Tenía miedo andar por la banqueta. Se le hacía que la mordían los perros o que alguien la cogia. En realidad solamente había un perro en todo el trecho y la mayor parte de la gente ni se dio cuenta de que iba al centro. Ella, sin embargo, seguía andando por en medio de la calle y tuvo suerte de que no pasara un solo mueble si no no hubiera sabido que hacer. Al llegar al ferrocarril le entró el miedo. Oía el movimiento y el pitido de los trenes y esto la desconcertaba. No se animaba a cruzar los rieles. Parecía que cada vez que se animaba se oía el pitido de un tren y se volvía a su lugar. Por fin venció el miedo, cerró los ojos y pasó sobre los rieles. Al pasar se le fue quitando el miedo. Volteó a la derecha.

6     Las aceras estaban repletas de gente y se le empezaron a llenar los oídos de ruido, un ruido que después de entrar no quería salir. No reconocía a nadie en la banqueta. Le entraron ganas de regresarse pero alguien la empujó hacia el centro y los oídos se le llenaban más y más de ruido. Sentía miedo y más y más se le olvidaba la razón por la cual estaba allí entre el gentío. En medio de dos tiendas donde había una callejuela se detuvo para recuperar el ánimo un poco y se quedó viendo un rato a la gente que pasaba.

—Dios mío, ¿qué me pasa? Ya me empiezo a sentir como me sentí en Wilmar. Ojalá y no me vaya a sentir mal. A ver. Para allá queda la hielería. No, para allá. No, Dios mío, ¿qué me pasa? A ver. Venía andando de allá para acá. Así que queda para allá. Mejor me hubiera quedado en casa. Oiga, perdone usted, ¿dónde está el Kres, por favor? . . . Gracias.

7     Se fue andando hasta donde le habían indicado y entró. El ruido y la apretura de la gente era peor. Le entró más miedo y ya lo único que quería era salirse de la tienda pero ya no veía la puerta. Sólo veía cosas sobre cosas, gente sobre gente. Hasta oía hablar a las cosas. Se quedó parada un rato viendo vacíamente a lo que estaba enfrente de ella. Era que ya no sabía los nombres de las cosas. Unas personas se le quedaban viendo unos segundos otras solamente la empujaban para un lado. Permaneció así por un rato y luego empezó a andar de nuevo. Reconoció unos juguetes y los echó en su bolsa, luego vio una cartera y también la echó a la bolsa. De pronto ya no oía el ruido de la gente aunque sí veía todos los movimientos de sus piernas, de sus brazos, de la boca, de sus

"I don't know why I'm so timid, my God. Downtown is only six blocks away. I just go straight and I turn right when I cross the tracks. Then two blocks and there is Kress. On the way back I walk two blocks and then I turn left and then straight home. God willing I won't meet any dogs on the way. I'll be careful when I cross the tracks, or a train might come along and catch me in the middle of the tracks . . . I hope I don't meet any dogs . . . I hope there is no train."

Rapidly she walked the distance from her house to the railroad tracks. The entire distance she walked along the middle of the street. She was afraid to walk on the sidewalk. She was afraid of being bitten by dogs or of being accosted by someone. Actually there was only one dog along the entire route, and most of the people didn't even notice that she was going downtown. However, she kept on walking in the middle of the street, lucky that not a single car came along, otherwise she would not have known what to do. As she approached the railroad track she became afraid. She could hear movements and the whistles of the trains, and this unsettled her. She didn't dare cross the tracks. It seemed as though every time she built up enough courage to do so she heard a train whistle and she retreated. Finally she overcame her fear, closed her eyes and crossed the tracks. Her fear left her as she crossed the tracks. She turned to her right.

The streets were full of people and her ears became crowded with noise that once inside refused to leave. She didn't recognize anyone on the sidewalk. She felt the urge to go home, but someone pushed her toward downtown as more and more noises crowded into her ears. She was afraid. More and more she was forgetting the reason for being there among so many people. To regain her courage she stopped in an alley that separated two stores and for a while she looked at the people who passed by.

"My God, what's wrong with me? I'm beginning to feel the same way I felt in Wilmar. I hope I don't get sick. Let's see. The ice plant is in that direction. No, it's this other way. No, my God, what's happening to me? Let's see. I came from that direction toward here, so, it's in that direction. I should have stayed at home. Excuse me, can you tell me where Kress is, please? . . . Thank you."

She walked to the place that was pointed out to her and she went in. The noise was worse and the crowd was thicker. She became even more afraid and the only thing she wanted to do was to leave the store but she couldn't find the door. She only saw things piled on top of things, people piled on top of people. She could even hear the different things speak. She stood there for a while, emptily looking at what was in front of her. She could no longer remember the names of things. A few people stared at her for a second or so, others shoved her aside. She remained fixed in that position for a while and then started to walk again. She was able to make out some toys and she put them in her

ojos. Pero no oía nada. Por fin preguntó que dónde quedaba la puerta, la salida. Le indicaron y empezó a andar hacia aquel rumbo. Empujó y empujó gente hasta que llegó a empujar la puerta y salió.

8     Apenas había estado unos segundos en la acera tratando de reconocer dónde estaba, cuando sintió que alguien la cogió fuerte del brazo. Hasta la hicieron que diera un gemido.

—Here she is . . . these damn people, always stealing something, stealing. I've been watching you all along. Let's have that bag.

—¿Pero . . .?

9     Y ya no oyó nada por mucho tiempo. Sólo vio que el cemento de la acera se vino a sus ojos y que una piedrita se le metió en el ojo y le calaba mucho. Sentía que la estiraban de los brazos y aun cuando la voltearon boca arriba veía a todos muy retirados. Se veía a sí misma. Se sentía hablar pero ni ella sabía lo que decía pero sí se veía mover la boca. También veía puras caras desconocidas. Luego vio al empleado con la pistola en la cartuchera y le entró un miedo terrible. Fue cuando se volvió a acordar de sus hijos. Le empezaron a salir las lágrimas y lloró. Luego ya no supo nada. Sólo se sentía andar en un mar de gente. Los brazos la rozaban como si fueran olas.

—De a buena suerte que mi compadre andaba por allí. El fue el que me fue a avisar al restaurante. ¿Cómo te sientes?

—Yo creo que estoy loca, viejo.

—Por eso te pregunté que si no te irías a sentir mal como en Wilmar.

—¿Qué va a ser de mis hijos con una mamá loca? Con una loca que ni siquiera sabe hablar ni ir el centro.

—De todos modos, fui a traer al notario público. Y él fue el que fue conmigo a la cárcel. El le explicó todo al empleado. Que se te había volado la cabeza. Y que te daban ataques de nervios cuando andabas entre mucha gente.

—¿Y si me mandan a un manicomio? Yo no quiero dejar a mis hijos. Por favor, viejo, no vayas a dejar que me manden, que no me lleven. Mejor no hubiera ido al centro.

—Pos nomás quédate aquí dentro de la casa y no te salgas del solar. Que al cabo no hay necesidad. Yo te traigo todo lo que necesites. Mira, ya no llores, ya no llores. No, mejor llora, para que te desahogues. Les voy a decir a los muchachos que ya no te anden fregando con Santo Clos. Les voy a decir que no hay para que no te molesten con eso ya.

shopping bag; then she saw a wallet and put that in her shopping bag, too. Suddenly the noise of the crowd stopped, even though she could still see all the movements of their legs, their arms, their mouths and their eyes. But she couldn't hear anything. She finally asked where the door was, the way out. They pointed it out to her and she began to walk in that direction. She pushed and pushed people aside until finally she was pushing on the door and went out.

She had been outside only for a few seconds, on the sidewalk, trying to get 8 her bearings when she felt someone grab her strongly by the arm. The force with which she was seized forced a moan out of her.

"Here she is . . . these damn people, always stealing something, always stealing. I've been watching you all along. Let's have that bag."

"But . . .?"

And she didn't hear anything else for a long time. She only saw the sidewalk 9 cement rush to her eyes and a small pebble lodge in her eye and felt its irritation. She felt someone pull her arms, and when she was turned face up the people appeared elongated in shape. She looked at herself. She was aware that she was speaking but not even she understood what she was saying, even though she could see her lips move. Also, all the faces that she saw were unfamiliar to her. She then saw the store guard with a gun in his holster and she became terrified. It was then that she remembered her children. Tears rolled out and she cried. Then everything went blank. She was only aware of walking in a sea of people. Their arms touched her like ocean waves.

"It was a good thing my compadre was around. He was the one who rushed over to the restaurant with the news. How do you feel?"

"I think I'm insane, viejo."

"That's why I asked if you thought you might get sick as you did in Wilmar."

"What will become of my children with an insane mother like me? With an insane woman who can't even express herself nor go downtown?"

"I brought along the notary public just in case. He was the one who went with me to the jailhouse. He explained everything to the guard, that your thoughts became confused. And that you became very nervous when you were in a crowd."

"What if they send me to the insane asylum? I don't want to leave my children alone. Please, viejo, don't let them send me; don't let them take me. I shouldn't have gone downtown."

"Well, just stay here in the house and don't leave the yard. There is no need for you to go out anyway. I'll bring everything you need. Look, don't cry, don't cry. Well, maybe you should cry, it will ease your pain. I'm going to tell

—No, viejo, no seas malo. Díles que si no les trae nada en noche buena que es porque les van a traer algo los reyes magos.

—Pero . . . Bueno, como tú quieras. Yo creo que siempre lo mejor es tener esperanzas.

10    Los niños que estaban escondidos detrás de la puerta oyeron todo pero no comprendieron muy bien. Y esperaron el día de los reyes magos como todos los años. Cuando llegó y pasó aquel día sin regalos no preguntaron nada. ✢

the boys not to bother you anymore about Santa Claus. I'll tell them there is no Santa Claus so they won't bother you with that anymore."

"No, viejo, don't be mean. Tell them that if they didn't get anything for Christmas it's because the Reyes Magos will bring them something."

"But . . . well, whatever you say. I guess it's always best to have hope."

The children, who had been hiding behind the door, heard everything even  10
though they didn't understand too well. And they waited the coming of the Reyes Magos just as they did every year. When that day arrived and there were no gifts they didn't question anything.  ✣

## RESPONDING

1.  Have you ever been afraid to do something or tried to do something that was very frightening and failed in the attempt? Write a journal entry about this experience and compare it to doña María's experience. How did you feel about yourself? Did you try again? How does doña María feel about her attempt to go to the store? Do you think she will try again?

2.  Working individually or in a group, describe the attitude of the person who stopped doña María outside the store. What do the comments of this person reveal about attitudes toward the migrant community?

3.  In an essay, discuss Rivera's attitude toward doña María. Is he sympathetic or unsympathetic? How does he try to get the reader to share his viewpoint? Use examples from the text to support your opinion.

4.  Imagine that you are one of the following people in the crowd around doña María: a local banker, the store owner, the guard, a friend of doña María's, a migrant worker, one of doña María's children, a local newsman, a newsman from a large metropolitan area, a civil rights worker. Write a letter to a friend or a letter to the editor of the local paper about the incident.

# Pat Mora

*Although Pat Mora now lives in the Midwest, she incorporates much of the heritage of her native Southwest in her writing. Born in El Paso, Texas, she earned her master's degree from the University of Texas at El Paso in 1967. Since the late 1960s she has worked in the academic and cross-cultural fields, first by teaching English and later by working in university administration. In 1986 she was awarded a Kellogg National Fellowship to study cultural conservation issues; in 1994 she was awarded a fellowship from the National Endowment for the Arts. In addition to contributing poetry to numerous journals and anthologies, Mora has published many volumes including* Chants *(1984) and* Borders *(1986), which have received several awards;* Communion *(1991),* Agua Santa/Holy Water *(1995), and* Aunt Carmen's Book of Practical Saints *(1997); as well as more than a dozen books for children. Her works also include an essay collection* Nepantla: Essays from the Land in the Middle *(1993), and a memoir entitled* House of Houses *(1997), among others.*

*The following poem, from* Chants, *explores the effects of cultural boundaries on both the speaker and the audience.*

# ELENA

My Spanish isn't enough.
I remember how I'd smile
listening to my little ones,
understanding every word they'd say,
5  their jokes, their songs, their plots.
    *Vamos a pedirle dulces a mamá. Vamos.*
But that was in Mexico.
Now my children go to American high schools.
They speak English. At night they sit around
10  the kitchen table, laugh with one another.
I stand by the stove and feel dumb, alone.
I bought a book to learn English.
My husband frowned, drank more beer.
My oldest said, "*Mamá*, he doesn't want you
15  to be smarter than he is." I'm forty,
embarrassed at mispronouncing words,

embarrassed at the laughter of my children,
the grocer, the mailman. Sometimes I take
my English book and lock myself in the bathroom,
say the thick words softly,                                    20
for if I stop trying, I will be deaf
when my children need my help. ✢

---

## RESPONDING

1. In a journal entry, tell about a time when you or someone you know felt
   inadequate or out of touch with a situation.

2. Working individually or in a group, identify Elena's problem and suggest
   solutions. Share these with the class.

3. The poem suggests a conflict that arises between Elena's husband and
   herself. Write a scene in which this conflict unfolds.

4. Write an essay discussing the difficulties of moving to a new country and
   learning a new language. Use information from the poem, other readings,
   or your own experience.

---

# ARTURO ISLAS

*Arturo Islas was born in El Paso, Texas, in 1938. He earned his bachelor's,
master's, and doctoral degrees from Stanford University, where he served on
the faculty as a professor of English. In addition to contributing several essays,
short stories, poems, and reviews to literary journals, Islas published two novels,*
The Rain God *(1984) and* Migrant Souls *(1988). He was awarded the
Woodrow Wilson Fellowship (1963–1964), the Carnegie Mellon Faculty
Award (1974), and the Dinkelspiel Award for Outstanding Service to Undergraduate Education (1976), among others. Islas died of AIDS in 1991.*

*The following excerpt from* Migrant Souls *uses the backdrop of the
Thanksgiving holiday celebration to examine issues of heritage and cultural
tradition.*

⊞

# *From* **MIGRANT SOULS**

1   AFTER THE WAR, their mother took to raising chickens and pigeons in order to save money. Josie saw their neighbors enjoying life and thought that her mother had gone crazy. Eduviges had even bought a live duck from God knows where and kept it until the Garcias next door began complaining about all the racket it made at night. Josie and Serena had become attached to it, so much so that when it appeared piecemeal in a *mole poblano*, both of them refused to eat it.

2   "It's too greasy," Josie said, holding back her tears and criticizing her mother's cooking instead.

3   "Then let your sisters have your portion. Eat the beans," Sancho said from behind the hunting magazine that was his bible.

4   "I don't want it," Serena said, her tears falling unchecked. "Poor don Pato. He didn't make that much noise. The Garcias are louder than he ever was."

5   Ofelia was dutifully, even happily, chewing away. "I think he's delicious," she said.

6   Josie glared at her and held her hands tightly under the table and away from the knife next to her plate. In her mind, she was dumping its contents into Ofelia's lap.

7   Eduviges stared at her husband until the silence made him glance up from his magazine. "Well," she said, "if your little darlings won't eat what I raise, slaughter, and cook with my own hands, let them live on beans. I know Josie likes chicken well enough. And pigeon stew. From now on, she can do the killing before she eats them. Let's see how she likes it."

8   And then speaking to Josie directly, she added, "This is not a restaurant, young lady. You have to eat what I serve you. And that's that." She said nothing to Serena, who was blowing her nose loudly into a paper napkin and now glaring at her in an accusing way.

9   "Leave her alone," Sancho said, meaning Josie. "The child liked that dumb duck, that's all. She doesn't have to eat him if she doesn't want to." These words caused Josie to leave the table in tears, followed by Serena, now struck by another fit of weeping. Ofelia kept eating and asked that her sisters' portions be passed to her.

10   "Of course, darling," Eduviges said. Sancho returned to his magazine.

11   In their bedroom, Josie and Serena held each other until they stopped crying. "I'll never forgive her for killing him," Josie said.

12   "Oh, Josie, don't say that. I was crying because of the way you were looking at Ofelia and Mother. We can always get another duck."

13   After don Pato's transformation, their mother stuck to chickens and pigeons. Atoning for her harshness toward Josie, she cooked omelets and looked the other way whenever Serena slipped Josie a piece of chicken. But for Thanksgiving in 1947, Eduviges, in a fit of guilt, decided to bake a turkey with all the trimmings.

She had memorized the recipes in the glossy American magazines while waiting her turn at the Safeway checkout counter.

Because the girls were in public school and learning about North American holidays and customs, Eduviges thought her plan would please them. It did and even Josie allowed her mother to embrace her in that quick, embarrassed way she had of touching them. As usual, Sancho had no idea why she was going to such lengths preparing for a ritual that meant nothing to him. 14

"I don't see why we can't have the enchiladas you always make," he said. "I don't even like turkey. Why don't you let me bring you a nice, fat pheasant from the Chihuahua mountains? At least it'll taste like something. Eating turkey is going to turn my girls into little *gringos*. Is that what you want?" 15

"Oh, Daddy, please! Everybody else is going to have turkey." The girls, wearing colored paper headdresses they had made in art class, were acting out the Pocahontas story and reciting from "Hiawatha" in a hodgepodge of Indian sentiment that forced Sancho to agree in order to keep them quiet. 16

"All right, all right," he said, "Just stop all the racket, please. And Serena, *querida*, don't wear that stuff outside the house or they'll pick you up and send you to a reservation. That would be okay with me, but your mother wouldn't like it." 17

Serena and Josie gave each other knowing glances. "They" were the *migra*, who drove around in their green vans, sneaked up on innocent dark-skinned people, and deported them. Their neighbor down the block—Benito Cruz, who was lighter-skinned than Serena and did not look at all like an Indian—had been picked up three times already, detained at the border for hours, and then released with the warning that he was to carry his identification papers at all times. That he was an American citizen did not seem to matter to the immigration officers. 18

The Angel children were brought up on as many deportation stories as fairy tales and family legends. The latest border incident had been the discovery of twenty-one young Mexican males who had been left to asphyxiate in an airtight boxcar on their way to pick cotton in the lower Rio Grande Valley. 19

When they read the newspaper articles about how the men died, both Josie and Serena thought of the fluttering noises made by the pigeons their mother first strangled and then put under a heavy cardboard box for minutes that seemed eternal to the girls. They covered their ears to protect their souls from the thumping and scratching noises of the doomed birds. 20

Even their mother had shown sympathy for the Mexican youths, especially when it was learned that they were not from the poorest class. "I feel very bad for their families," she said, "Their mothers must be in agony." 21

What about their fathers? Josie felt like asking but did not. Because of the horror she imagined they went through, Josie did not want to turn her own feelings for the young men into yet another argument with her mother about "wetbacks" or about who did and did not "deserve" to be in the United States. 22

In the first semester of seventh grade, Josie had begun to wonder why being make-believe North American Indians seemed to be all right with their mother. 23

"Maybe it was because those Indians spoke English," Josie said to Serena. Mexican Indians were too close to home and the truth, and the way Eduviges looked at Serena in her art class getup convinced Josie she was on the right track.

24      That year on the Saturday before Thanksgiving, their mother and father took them across the river in search of the perfect turkey. Sancho borrowed his friend Tacho Morales' pickup and they drove down the valley to the Zaragoza crossing. It was closer to the ranch where Eduviges had been told the turkeys were raised and sold for practically nothing. Josie and Serena sat in the front seat of the pickup with their father. Eduviges and Ofelia followed them in the Chevy in case anything went wrong.

25      Sancho was a slower, more patient driver than their mother, who turned into a speed demon with a sharp tongue behind the wheel. More refined than her younger sisters, Ofelia was scandalized by every phrase that came out of Eduviges' mouth when some sorry driver from Chihuahua or New Mexico got in her way.

26      "Why don't they teach those imbecile cretins how to drive?" she said loudly in Spanish, window down and honking. Or, "May all your teeth fall out but one and may that ache until the day you die" to the man who pulled out in front of her without a signal.

27      Grateful that her mother was being good for once and following slowly and at a safe distance behind the pickup, Ofelia dozed, barely aware of the clear day so warm for November. Only the bright yellow leaves of the cottonwood trees reminded her that it was autumn. They clung to the branches and vibrated in the breeze, which smelled of burning mesquite and Mexican alders. As they followed her father away from the mountains and into the valley, Ofelia began to dream they were inside one of Mama Chona's Mexican blue clay bowls, suspended in midair while the sky revolved around them.

28      To Josie and Serena, it seemed their father was taking forever to get to where they were going. "Are we there yet?" they asked him until he told them that if they asked again, he would leave them in the middle of nowhere and not let their mother rescue them. The threat only made them laugh more and they started asking him where the middle of nowhere was until he, too, laughed with them.

29      "The middle of nowhere, smart alecks, is at the bottom of the sea and so deep not even the fish go there," Sancho said, getting serious about it.

30      "No, no," Serena said, "It's in the space between two stars and no planets around."

31      "I already said the middle of nowhere is in Del Sapo, Texas," Josie said, not wanting to get serious.

32      "I know, I know. It's in the Sahara Desert where not even the tumbleweeds will grow," their father said.

33      "No, Daddy. It's at the top of Mount Everest." Serena was proud of the B

she had gotten for her report on the highest mountain in the world. They fell silent and waited for Josie to take her turn.

"It's here," Josie said quietly and pointed to her heart. 34

"Oh, for heaven's sake, Josie, don't be so dramatic. You don't even know 35 what you are saying," Serena said. Their father changed the subject.

When they arrived at the ranch, he told Eduviges and the girls that the 36 worst that could happen on their return was that the turkey would be taken away from them. But the girls, especially, must do and say exactly as he instructed them.

Their mother was not satisfied with Sancho's simple directions and once 37 again told them about the humiliating body search her friend from New Mexico, *la señora* Moulton, had been subjected to at the Santa Fe Street bridge. She had just treated her daughter Ethel and her granddaughters, Amy and Mary Ann, to lunch at the old Central Cafe in Juarez. When *la señora* had been asked her citizenship, she had replied in a jovial way, "Well, what do I look like, sir?"

They made her get out of the car, led her to a special examining cell, ordered 38 her to undress, and made her suffer unspeakable mortifications while her relatives waited at least four hours in terror, wondering if they would ever see her again or be allowed to return to the country of their birth. Then, right on cue, Josie and Serena said along with Eduviges, "And they were Anglos and blond!"

While their parents were bargaining for the bird, the girls looked with awe 39 upon the hundreds of adult turkeys kept inside four large corrals. As they walked by each enclosure, one of the birds gobbled and the rest echoed its call until the racket was unbearable. Serena was struck by an attack of giggles.

"They sure are stupid," Josie said in Spanish to their Mexican guide. 40

"They really are," he said with a smile. "When it rains, we have to cover 41 the coops of the younger ones so they won't drown." He was a dark red color and very shy. Josie liked him instantly.

"How can they drown?" Serena asked him. "The river is nowhere near here. 42 Does it flood?"

"No," the young man said, looking away from them. "Not from the Rio 43 Bravo. From the rain itself. They stretch their necks, open their beaks wide and let it pour in until they drown. They keel over all bloated. That's how stupid they are." He bent his head back and showed them as they walked by an enclosure. "Gobble, gobble," the guide called and the turkeys answered hysterically.

Josie and Serena laughed all the way back to the pickup. Ofelia had not 44 been allowed to join them because of the way their mother thought the guide was looking at her. She was dreaming away in the backseat of the Chevy while their father struggled to get the newly bought and nervous turkey into a slatted crate. Eduviges was criticizing every move he made. At last, the creature was in the box and eerily silent.

"Now remember, girls," Sancho said, wiping his face, "I'll do all the talking 45 at the bridge. You just say 'American' when the time comes. Not another word, you hear? Think about Mrs. Moulton, Josie," He gave her a wink.

46    The turkey remained frozen inside the crate. Sancho lifted it onto the pickup, covered it with a yellow plastic tablecloth they used on picnics, and told Serena to sit on top of it with her back against the rear window.

47    "Serena," he said, "I'd hate to lose you because of this stupid bird, but if you open your mouth except to say 'American,' I won't be responsible for what happens. Okay?" He kissed her on the cheek as if in farewell forever, Josie thought, looking at them from the front seat. She was beginning to wish they had not begged so successfully for a traditional North American ceremony. Nothing would happen to Ofelia, of course. She was protected in their mother's car and nowhere near the turkey. Josie felt that Serena was in great peril and made up her mind to do anything to keep her from harm.

48    On the way to the bridge, Josie made the mistake of asking her father if they were aliens. Sancho put his foot on the brake so hard that Eduviges almost rear-ended the truck. He looked at Josie very hard and said, "I do not ever want to hear you use that word in my presence again. About anybody. We are not aliens. We are American citizens of Mexican heritage. We are proud of both countries and have never and will never be that word you just said to me."

49    "Well," Josie said. Sancho knew she was not afraid of him. He pulled the truck away from the shoulder and signaled for his wife to continue following them. "That's what they call Mexican people in all the newspapers. And Kathy Jarvis at school told me real snotty at recess yesterday that we were nothing but a bunch of resident aliens."

50    After making sure Eduviges was right behind them, Sancho said in a calmer, serious tone, "Josie, I'm warning you. I do not want to hear those words again. Do you understand me?"

51    "I'm only telling you what Kathy told me. What did she mean? Is she right?"

52    "Kathy Jarvis is an ignorant little brat. The next time she tells you that, you tell her that Mexican and Indian people were in this part of the country long before any *gringos*, Europeans (he said 'Yurrup-beans') or anyone else decided it was theirs. That should shut her up. If it doesn't, tell her those words are used by people who think Mexicans are not human beings. That goes for the newspapers, too. They don't think anyone is human." She watched him look straight ahead, then in the rearview mirror, then at her as he spoke.

53    "Don't you see, Josie? When people call Mexicans those words, it makes it easier for them to deport or kill them. Aliens come from outer space." He paused. "Sort of like your mother's family, the blessed Angels, who think they come from heaven. Don't tell her I said that."

54    Before he made that last comment, Josie was impressed by her father's tone. Sancho seldom became that passionate in their presence about any issue. He laughed at the serious and the pompous and especially at religious fanatics.

55    During their aunt Jesus Maria's visits, the girls and their cousins were sent out of the house in the summer or to the farthest room away from the kitchen

in the winter so that they would not be able to hear her and Sancho arguing about God and the Church. Unnoticed, the children sneaked around the house and crouched in the honeysuckle under the kitchen window, wide open to the heat of July. In horror and amusement, they listened to Jesus Maria tell Sancho that he would burn in hell for all eternity because he did not believe in an afterlife and dared to criticize the infallibility of the Pope.

"It's because they're afraid of dying that people make up an afterlife to believe in," Sancho said. 56

"That's not true. God created Heaven, Hell, and Purgatory before He created man. And you are going to end up in Hell if you don't start believing what the Church teaches us." Jesus Maria was in her glory defending the teachings of Roman Catholicism purged by the fires of the Spanish Inquisition. 57

"Oh, Jessie—" he began. 58

"Don't call me that. My name is Jesus Maria and I am proud of it." She knew the children were listening. 59

"Excuse me, Jesus Maria," he said with a flourish. "I just want to point out to you that it's hotter here in Del Sapo right now than in hell." He saw her bristle but went on anyway. "Haven't you figured it out yet? This is hell and heaven and purgatory right here. How much worse, better, or boring can the afterlife be?" Sancho was laughing at his own insight. 60

"If you are going to start joking about life-and-death matters, I simply won't talk about anything serious with you again," their aunt said. They knew she meant it. "I, like the Pope, am fighting for your everlasting soul, Sancho. If I did not love you because you are my sister's husband, I would not be telling you these things." 61

"Thank you, Jessie. I appreciate your efforts and love. But the Pope is only a man. He is not Christ. Don't you read history? All most popes have cared about is money and keeping the poor in rags so that they can mince about in gold lamé dresses." 62

"Apostate!" their aunt cried. 63

"What's that?" Serena whispered to Josie. 64

"I don't know but it sounds terrible. We'll look it up in the dictionary as soon as they stop." They knew the arguing was almost over when their aunt began calling their father names. Overwhelmed by the smell of the honeysuckle, the children ran off to play kick the can. Later, when Josie looked up the word "apostate," she kept its meaning to herself because she knew that Serena believed in an afterlife and would be afraid for her father. 65

That one word affected her father more than another was a mystery to Josie. She loved words and believed them to be more real than whatever they described. In her mind, she, too, suspected that she was an apostate but, like her father, she did not want to be an alien. 66

"All right, Daddy, I promise I won't say that word again. And I won't tell Mother what you said about the Angels." 67

They were now driving through the main streets of Juarez, and Sancho was 68 fighting to stay in his lane. "God, these Mexicans drive like your mother," he said with affection.

69     At every intersection, young Indian women with babies at their breast stretched out their hands. Josie was filled with dread and pity. One of the women knocked on her window while they waited for the light to change. She held up her baby and said, "*Señorita, por favor. Dinero para el niño.*" Her hair was black and shiny and her eyes as dark as Josie's. The words came through the glass in a muted, dreamlike way. Silent and unblinking, the infant stared at Josie. She had a quarter in her pocket.

70     "Don't roll down the window or your mother will have a fit," Sancho said. He turned the corner and headed toward the river. The woman and child disappeared. Behind them, Eduviges kept honking almost all the way to the bridge.

71     "I think it was blind," Josie said. Her father did not answer and looked straight ahead.

72     The traffic leading to the declaration points was backed up several blocks, and the stop-and-go movement as they inched their way to the American side was more than Josie could bear. She kept looking back at Serena, who sat like a *Virgen de Guadalupe* statue on her yellow plastic-covered throne.

73     Knowing her sister, Josie was certain that Serena was going to free the turkey, jump out of the truck with it, gather up the beggarly women and children, and disappear forever into the sidestreets and alleys of Juarez. They drove past an old Indian woman, her long braids silver gray in the sun, begging in front of Curley's Club. And that is how Josie imagined Serena years from that day—an ancient and withered creature, bare feet crusted with clay, too old to recognize her little sister. The vision made her believe that the middle of nowhere was exactly where she felt it was. She covered her chest with her arms.

74     "What's the matter? Don't tell me you're going to be sick," her father said.

75     "No. I'm fine. Can't you hurry?"

76     Seeing the fear in her face, Sancho told her gently that he had not yet figured out how to drive through cars without banging them up. Josie smiled and kept her hands over her heart.

77     When they approached the border patrolman's station, the turkey began gobbling away. "Oh, no," Josie cried and shut her eyes in terror for her sister.

78     "Oh, shit," her father said. "I hate this god-damned bridge." At that moment, the officer stuck his head into the pickup and asked for their citizenship.

79     "American," said Sancho.

80     "American," said Josie.

81     "Anything to declare? Any liquor or food?" he asked in an accusing way. While Sancho was assuring him that there was nothing to declare, the turkey gobbled again in a long stream of high-pitched gurgles that sent shivers up and down Josie's spine. She vowed to go into the cell with Serena when the search was ordered.

"What's that noise?" the patrolman wanted to know. Sancho shrugged and  82
gave Josie and then the officer a look filled with the ignorance of the world.

Behind them, Serena began gobbling along with the bird and it was hard  83
for them to tell one gobble from the another. Their mother pressed down on
the horn of the Chevy and made it stick. Eduviges was ready to jump out of the
car and save her daughter from a fate worse than death. In the middle of the
racket, the officer's frown was turning into anger and he started yelling at
Serena.

"American!" she yelled back and gobbled.  84

"What have you got there?" The officer pointed to the plastic-covered crate.  85

"It's a turkey," Serena shouted. "It's American, too." She kept gobbling  86
along with the noise of the horn. Other drivers had begun honking with
impatience.

The patrolman looked at her and yelled, "Sure it is! Don't move," he  87
shouted toward Sancho.

Eduviges had opened the hood and was pretending not to know what to  88
do. Rushing toward the officer, she grabbed him by the sleeve and pulled him
away from the pickup. Confused by the din, he made gestures that Sancho took
as permission to drive away. "Relax, *señora*. Please let go of my arm."

In the truck, Sancho was laughing like a maniac and wiping the tears and  89
his nose on his sleeve. "Look at that, Josie. The guy is twice as big as your
mother."

She was too scared to laugh and did not want to look. Several blocks into  90
South Del Sapo, she was still trembling. Serena kept on gobbling in case they
were being followed by the *migra* in unmarked cars.

Fifteen minutes later, Eduviges and Ofelia caught up with them on Alameda  91
Street. Sancho signaled his wife to follow him into the vacant lot next to Don
Luis Leal's Famous Tex-Mex Diner. They left the turkey unattended and silent
once more.

"Dumb bird," Sancho said. With great ceremony, he treated them to *menudo*  92
and *gorditas* washed down with as much Coca-Cola as they could drink. ✛

---

## RESPONDING

1. "The Angel children were brought up on as many deportation stories as
   fairy tales and family legends" (paragraph 19). In a journal entry, discuss the
   possible psychological effects of such stories on young children.

2. Working individually or in a group, list examples of the bicultural aspects
   of the Angel family's lifestyle. Discuss the advantages and disadvantages of
   being bicultural.

3. Taking the turkey over the border could be viewed as humorous, serious, or even frightening depending on your point of view. Imagine you are one of the characters in the story such as Sancho, Eduviges, Serena, the patrolman, or an onlooker and write a letter reporting the incident to a friend.

4. Explain Sancho's reaction to the term "aliens" (paragraph 53). How does he define the term, and why is it so offensive to him? Write an essay explaining why his reaction is or is not excessive.

# Sandra Cisneros

*Born in Chicago in 1954, the poet and short-story writer Sandra Cisneros earned her bachelor's degree from Loyola University of Chicago in 1976 and her master's degree from the University of Iowa Writers Workshop in 1978. While teaching at the Latino Youth Alternative High School and working as a counselor in the Educational Opportunities Program at Loyola University of Chicago during the early 1980s, she served as an artist-in-residence for the Illinois Arts Council. Cisneros has also held teaching and administrative positions in Texas, teaching creative writing at the Austin Women's Peace House, serving as an artist-in-the-schools, and directing the Guadalupe Cultural Arts Center in San Antonio. Since 1988 she has been a guest writer-in-residence at the University of California at Berkeley, the University of California at Irvine, and the University of Michigan.*

*Her published works include the poetry volumes* Bad Boys *(1980),* My Wicked, Wicked Ways *(1987), and* Loose Woman *(1994); the young adult novel* The House on Mango Street *(1983); and the short-story collection* Woman Hollering Creek and Other Stories *(1992). Her writing has earned her numerous fellowships and awards, among them the Roberta Holloway lectureship at the University of California at Berkeley (1988), two National Endowment for the Arts Creative Writing fellowships (1982 and 1988), the Before Columbus Foundation American Book Award (1985), and a MacArthur Fellowship (1995).*

*"Woman Hollering Creek" explores the way in which one character looks for strength in other people and in herself when she needs to make changes in her life.*

✛

# WOMAN HOLLERING CREEK

THE DAY DON SERAFÍN gave Juan Pedro Martínez Sánchez permission to take   1
Cleófilas Enriqueta DeLeón Hernández as his bride, across her father's threshold, over several miles of dirt road and several miles of paved, over one border
and beyond to a town four hours from the Rio Grande in the E.E.U.U., did he
divine already the morning his daughter would raise her hand over her eyes,
look south, and dream of returning to the chores that never ended, six good-
for-nothing brothers, and one old man's complaints.

He had said, after all, in the hubbubb of parting: I am your father, I will   2
never abandon you. He *had* said that, hadn't he, when he hugged and then let
her go. But at the moment Cleófilas was busy looking for Chela, her maid of
honor, to fulfill their bouquet conspiracy. She would not remember her father's
parting words until three years had passed since holding that ragged face in her
hands. I am your father, I will never abandon you.

Only now that she was a mother, now when she and Juan Pedrito sat by   3
the creek's edge, did she remember. When a man and a woman love each other,
how sometimes that love sours. But a parent's love for a child, a child's for its
parents, was another thing entirely.

This is what Cleófilas thought evenings when Juan Pedro did not come   4
home, and she lay on her side of the bed listening to the hollow roar of the
interstate, a distant dog barking, the pecan trees rustling like ladies in stiff
petticoats—shh-shh-shh, shh-shh-shh, soothing her to sleep.

In the town where she grew up, there isn't very much to do except accompany   5
the aunts and godmothers to the house of one or the other to play cards. Or
walk to the cinema to see this week's film again speckled and with one hair
quivering annoyingly on the screen. Or to the center of town to order a
milkshake that will appear in a day and a half as a pimple on her backside. Or
to the girlfriend's house to watch the latest telenovela episode and try to copy
the way the women comb their hair, wear their make-up.

But what Cleófilas has been waiting for, has been whispering and sighing   6
and giggling for, has been anticipating since she was old enough to lean against
the window displays of gauze and butterflies and lace, is passion. Not the kind
on the cover of the ¡Alarma! magazines, mind you, where the lover is photographed with the bloody fork she used to salvage her good name. But passion
in its purest crystalline essence. The kind the books and songs and telenovelas
describe when one finds, finally, the great love of one's life, and does whatever
one can, must do, at whatever the cost. Tú o Nadie. You or No One. The title
of the current favorite telenovela. The beautiful Lucía Méndez having to put
up with all kinds of hardships of the heart, separation and betrayal, and loving,
always loving no matter what, because *that* is the most important thing, and

did you see Lucía Méndez on the Bayer aspirin commercials, wasn't she lovely? Does she dye her hair do you think? Cleófilas is going to go to the farmacia and buy a hair rinse because her girlfriend Chela will apply it, it's not that difficult at all. Because you didn't watch last night's episode when Lucía confessed she loved him more than anyone in her life. In her life! And she sings the song "You or No One" in the beginning and end of the show. Tú o Nadie. Somehow one ought to live one's life like that, don't you think? You or no one. Because to suffer for love is good. The pain all sweet somehow, in the end.

7      Seguin. She had liked the sound of it. Far away and lovely. Not like Monclova, Coahuila. Ugly.

8      Seguín, Tejas. A nice sterling ring to it. The tinkle of money. She would get to wear outfits like the women on the tele, like Lucía Méndez. And have a lovely house, and wouldn't Chela be jealous.

9      And yes, they will drive all the way to Laredo to get her wedding dress. That's what they say. Because Juan Pedro wants to get married right away, without a long engagement since he can't take off too much time from work. He has a very important position in Seguin with, with . . . a beer company I think. Or was it tires? Yes, he has to be back. So they will get married in the spring when he can take off work, and then they will drive off in his new pickup—did you see it?—to their new home in Seguin. Well, not exactly new, but they're going to repaint the house. You know newlyweds. New paint and new furniture. Why not? He can afford it. And later on add maybe a room or two for the children. May they be blessed with many. Well, you'll see. Cleófilas has always been so good with her sewing machine. A little whirr, whirr, whirr of the machine and ¡zas! Miracles. She's always been so clever that girl. Poor thing. And without even a mama to advise her on things like her wedding night. Well, may God help her. What with a father with a head like a burro, and those six clumsy brothers. Well, what do you think. Yes, I'm going to the wedding. Of course! The dress I want to wear just needs to be altered a teensy bit to bring it up to date. See, I saw a new style last night that I thought would suit me. Did you watch last night's episode of "And the Rich Also Cry"? Well, did you notice the dress the mother was wearing.

10    La mujer gritando. Such a funny name for such a lovely arroyo. Though no one could say whether the woman had hollered from anger or pain. The natives only knew the arroyo one crossed on the way to San Antonio, and then once again on the way back, was called Woman Hollering, a name no one from these parts questioned, little less understood. Pues, allá de los Indios, quien sabe—who knows, the townspeople shrugged, because it was of no concern to their lives how this trickle of water received its curious name.

11    What do you want to know for? Trini the laundromat attendant asked in the same gruff Spanish she always used whenever she gave Cleófilas change or yelled at her for something. First for putting too much soap in the machines.

Later, for sitting on a washer. And still later, after Juan Pedrito was born, for not understanding that in this country you cannot let your baby walk around with no diaper and his pee-pee hanging out, it wasn't nice, entiendes? Pues.

How could Cleófilas explain to a woman like this why the name Woman 12 Hollering fascinated her. Well, there was no sense talking to Trini.

On the other hand there were the neighbor ladies, one on either side of the 13 house they rented near the arroyo. The woman Soledad on the left, the woman Dolores on the right.

The neighbor lady Soledad liked to call herself a widow though how she 14 came to be one was a mystery. Her husband had either died, or run away with an ice house floozie, or simply had gone out for cigarettes one afternoon and never come back. It was hard to say which since Soledad, as a rule, didn't mention him.

In the other house lives la señora Dolores, kind and very sweet, but her 15 house smelled too much of incense and candles from the altars that burned continuously in memory of two sons who had died in the last war and one husband who had died shortly after from grief. The neighbor lady Dolores divided her time between the memory of these men and her garden, famous for its sunflowers—so tall they had to be supported with broom handles and old boards; red red cockscombs, fringed and bleeding a thick menstrual color; and, especially, roses whose sad scent reminded Cleófilas of the dead. Each Sunday la señora Dolores clipped the most beautiful of these flowers and arranged them on three modest headstones at the Seguin cemetery.

The neighbor ladies, Soledad, Dolores, they might've known once the name 16 of the arroyo before it turned English but they did not know now. They were too busy remembering the men who had left either through choice or circumstance and would never come back.

Pain or rage, Cleófilas wondered when she drove over the bridge the first 17 time as a newlywed and Juan Pedro had pointed it out. La mujer gritando, he had said, and she had laughed. Such a funny name for a creek so pretty and full of happily ever after.

The first time she had been so surprised she didn't cry out nor try to defend 18 herself. She had always said she would strike back if a man, any man, were to touch her.

But when the moment came, and he slapped her once, and then again, and 19 again, until the lip split and bled an orchid of blood, she didn't fight back, she didn't break into tears, she didn't run away as she imagined she might when she saw such things in the telenovelas.

In her own home her parents had never raised a hand to each other nor to 20 their children. Although she admitted she may have been brought up a little leniently as an only daughter—la consentida, the princess—there were some things she would never tolerate. Ever.

Instead, when it happened the first time, when they were barely man and 21 wife, she had been so stunned, it left her speechless, motionless, numb. She had done nothing but reach up to the heat on her mouth and stare at the blood on her hand as if even then she didn't understand.

22    She could think of nothing to say, said nothing. Just stroked the dark curls of the man who wept and would weep like a child, his tears of repentance and shame, this time and each.

23    The men at the ice house. From what she can tell, from the times during her first year when still a newlywed she is invited and accompanies her husband, sits mute beside their conversation, waits and sips a beer until it grows warm, twists a paper napkin into a knot, then another into a fan, one into a rose, nods her head, smiles, yawns, politely grins, laughs at the appropriate moments, leans against her husband's sleeve, tugs at his elbow, and finally becomes good at predicting where the talk will lead.

24    From this Cleófilas concludes each is nightly trying to find the truth lying at the bottom of the glass like a gold doubloon on the sea bottom. They want to tell each other what they want to tell themselves. But what is bumping like a helium balloon at the ceiling of the brain never finds its way out. It bubbles and rises, it gurgles in the throat, it rolls across the surface of the tongue, and erupts from the lips—a belch.

25    If they are lucky, there are tears at the end of the long night. At any given moment, the fists try to speak. They are dogs chasing their own tail before lying down to sleep, trying to find a way, a route, an out, and—finally—get some peace.

26    In the morning sometimes before he opens his eyes. Or after they have finished loving. Or at times when he is simply across from her at the table putting pieces of food into his mouth and chewing. Cleófilas thinks, this is the man I have waited my whole life for.

27    Not that he isn't a good man. She has to remind herself why she loves him when she changes the baby's Pampers, or when she mops the bathroom floor, or tries to make the curtains for the doorways without doors, or whiten the linen. Or wonder a little when he kicks the refrigerator and says he hates this shitty house and is going out where he won't be bothered with the baby's howling and her suspicious questions, and her requests to fix this and this and this because if she had any brains in her head she'd realize he's been up before the rooster earning his living to pay for the food in her belly and the roof over her head and would have to wake up again early the next day so why can't you just leave me in peace, woman.

28    He is not very tall, no, and he doesn't look like the men on the telenovelas. His face still scarred from acne. And he has a bit of a belly from all the beer he drinks. Well, he's always been husky.

29    This man who farts and belches and snores as well as laughs and kisses and holds her. Somehow this husband whose whiskers she finds each morning in the

sink, whose shoes she must air each evening on the porch, this husband who cuts his fingernails in public, laughs loudly, curses like a man, and demands each course of dinner be served on a separate plate like at his mother's, as soon as he gets home, on time or late, and who doesn't care at all for music or telenovelas or romance or roses or the moon floating pearly over the arroyo, or through the bedroom window for that matter, shut the blinds and go back to sleep, this man, this father, this rival, this keeper, this lord, this master, this husband till kingdom come.

Slender like a hair. A washed cup set back on the shelf wrong side up. Her lip-  30
stick, and body talc, and hair brush all arranged in the bathroom a different way.

No. Her imagination. The house the same as always. Nothing.  31

Coming home from the hospital with her new son, her husband. Something  32
comforting in discovering her house slippers beneath the bed, the faded house-
coat where she left it on the bathroom hook. Her pillow. Their bed.

Sweet sweet homecoming. Sweet as the scent of face powder in the air,  33
jasmine, sticky liquor.

Smudged fingerprint on the door. Crushed cigarette in a glass. Wrinkle in  34
the brain crumpling to a crease.

Sometimes she thinks of her father's house. But how could she go back there?  35
What a disgrace. What would the neighbors say? Coming home like that with
one baby on her hip and one in the oven. Where's your husband?

The town of gossips. The town of dust and despair. Which she has traded  36
for this town of gossips. This town of dust, despair. Houses further apart
perhaps, though no more privacy because of it. No leafy zocalo in the center of
the town, though the murmur of talk is clear enough all the same. No huddled
whispering on the church steps each Sunday. Because here the whispering begins
at sunset at the ice house instead.

This town with its silly pride for a bronze pecan the size of a baby carriage  37
in front of the city hall. T.V. repair shop, drug store, hardware, dry cleaners,
chiropractor's, liquor store, bail bonds, empty storefront and nothing, nothing,
nothing of interest. Nowhere one could walk to any rate. Because the towns
here are built so that you have to depend on husbands. Or you stay home. Or
you drive. If you're rich enough to own, allowed to drive, your own car.

There is no place to go. Unless one counts the neighbor ladies. Soledad on  38
one side, Dolores on the other. Or the creek.

Don't go out there after dark, mi'jita. Stay near the house. No es bueno  39
para la salud. Mala suerte. Bad luck. Mal aire. You'll get sick and the baby too.
You'll catch a fright wandering about in the dark, and then you'll see how right
we were.

The stream sometimes only a muddy puddle in the summer, though now  40
in the springtime, because of the rains, a good-size alive thing, a thing with a
voice all its own, all day and all night calling in its high, silver voice. Is it La

Llorona, the weeping woman? La Llorona who drowned her own children. Perhaps La Llorona is the one they named the creek after, she thinks, remembering all the stories she learned as a child.

41     La Llorona calling to her. She is sure of it. Cleófilas sets the baby's Donald Duck blanket on the grass. Listens. The day sky turning to night. The baby pulling up fistfuls of grass and laughing. La Llorona. Wonders if something as quiet as this drives a woman to the darkness under the trees.

42     What she needs is . . . and made a gesture as if to yank a woman's buttocks to his groin. Maximiliano the foul-smelling fool from across the road said this and set the men laughing, but Cleófilas just muttered *grosero* and went on washing dishes.

43     She knew he said it not because it was true, but more because it was he who needed to sleep with a woman, instead of drinking each night at the ice house and stumbling home alone.

44     Maximiliano who was said to have killed his wife in an ice house brawl when she came at him with a mop. I had to shoot, he had said, she was armed.

45     Their laughter outside the kitchen window. Her husband's, his friends'. Manolo, Beto, Efrain, el Perico. Maximiliano.

46     Was Cleófilas just exaggerating as her husband always said? It seemed the newspapers were full of such stories. This woman found on the side of the interstate. This one pushed from a moving car. This one's cadaver, this one unconscious, this one beaten blue. Her ex-husband, her husband, her lover, her father, her brother, her uncle, her friend, her co-worker. Always. The same grisly news in the pages of the daily. She dunked a glass under the soapy water for a moment—shivered.

47     He had thrown a book. Hers. From across the room. A hot welt across the cheek. She could forgive that. But what stung more was the fact it was *her* book, a love story by Corin Tellado, what she loved most now that she lived in the U.S., without a television set, without the telenovelas.

48     Except now and again when her husband was away and she could manage it, the few episodes glimpsed at the neighbor lady Soledad's house because Dolores didn't care for that sort of thing, though Soledad was often kind enough to retell what had happened on what episode of "Maria de Nadie," the poor Argentine county girl who had the ill fortune of falling in love with the beautiful son of the Arrocha family, the very family she worked for, whose roof she slept under and whose floors she vacuumed, while in that same house, with the dustbrooms and floor cleaners as witnesses, the square-jawed Juan Carlos Arrocha had uttered words of love, I love you, Maria, listen to me, mi querida, but it was she who had to say no, no, we are not of the same class, and remind him it was not in his place nor hers to fall in love, while all the while her heart was breaking, can you imagine.

49     Cleófilas thought her life would have to be like that, like a telenovela, only

now the episodes got sadder and sadder. And there were no commercials in between for comic relief. And no happy ending in sight. She thought this when she sat with the baby out by the creek behind the house. Cleófilas de . . .? But somehow she would have to change her name to Topazio, or Yesenia, Cristal, Adriana, Stefania, Andrea, something more poetic than Cleófilas. Everything happened to women with names like jewels. But what happened to Cleófilas? Nothing. But a crack in the face.

Because the doctor has said so. She has to go. To make sure the new baby is alright, so there won't be any problems when he's born, and the appointment card says next Tuesday. Could he please take her. And that's all.  50

No, she won't mention it. She promises. If the doctor asks she can say she fell down the front steps or slipped when she was out in the back yard, slipped out back, she could tell him that. She has to go back next Tuesday, Juan Pedro, please, for the new baby. For their child.  51

She could write to her father and ask maybe for money, just a loan, for the new baby's medical expenses. Well then if he'd rather she didn't. All right, she won't. Please don't anymore. Please don't. She knows it's difficult saving money with all the bills they have, but how else are they going to get out of debt with the truck payments. And after the rent and the food and the electricity and the gas and the water and the who-knows-what, well, there's hardly anything left. But please, at least for the doctor visit. She won't ask for anything else. She has to. Why is she so anxious? Because.  52

Because she is going to make sure the baby is not turned around backwards this time to split her down the center. Yes. Next Tuesday at 5:30. I'll have Juan Pedrito dressed and ready. But those are the only shoes he has. I'll polish them, and we'll be ready. As soon as you come from work. We won't make you ashamed.  53

Felice? It's me, Graciela.  54

No, I can't talk louder. I'm at work.  55

Look, I need kind of a favor. There's a patient, a lady here who's got a problem.  56

Well, wait a minute. Are you listening to me or what?  57

I can't talk real loud 'cause her husband's in the next room.  58

Well, would you just listen.  59

I was going to do this sonogram on her—she's pregnant, right?—and she just starts crying on me. Hijole, Felice! This poor lady's got black-and-blue marks all over. I'm not kidding.  60

From her husband. Who else? Another one of those brides from across the border. And her family's all in Mexico.  61

Shit. You think they're going to help her? Give me a break. This lady doesn't even speak English. She hasn't been allowed to call home or write or nothing. That's why I'm calling you.  62

63    She needs a ride.

64    Not to Mexico, you goof. Just to the Greyhound. In San Anto.

65    No, just a ride. She's got her own money. All you'd have to do is drop her off in San Antonio on your way home. Come on, Felice. Please? If we don't help her, who will? I'd drive her myself, but she needs to be on that bus before her husband gets home from work. What do you say?

66    I don't know. Wait.

67    Right away she says. Tomorrow even.

68    Well, if tomorrow's no good for you . . .

69    It's a date, Felice. Thursday. At the Cash N Carry off I-80. Noon. She'll be ready.

70    Oh, and her name's Cleófilas.

71    I don't know. One of those Mexican saints I guess. A martyr or something.

72    Cleófilas. C-L-E-O-F-I-L-A-S. Cle. O. Fi. Las. Write it down.

73    Thanks, Felice, When her kid's born she'll name her after us, right?

74    Yeah, you got it. A regular soap opera sometimes. Que vida, comadre. Bueno bye.

75    All morning that flutter of half fear, half doubt. At any moment Juan Pedro might appear in the doorway. On the street. At the Cash N Carry. Like in the dreams she dreamed.

76    There was that to think about, yes, until the woman in the pickup drove up. Then there wasn't time to think about anything but the pickup pointed towards San Antonio. Put your bags in the back and get in.

77    But when they drove across the arroyo, the driver opened her mouth and let out a yell as loud as any mariachi. Which startled not only Cleófilas, but Juan Pedrito as well.

78    Pues, look how cute. I scared you two, right? Sorry. Should've warned you. Every time I cross that bridge I do that. Because of the name, you know. Woman Hollering. Pues, I holler. She said this in a Spanish pocked with English and laughed. Did you ever notice, Felice continued, how nothing around here is named after a woman. Really. Unless she's the Virgin. I guess you're only famous if you're a virgin. She was laughing again.

79    That's why I like the name of that arroyo. Makes you want to holler like Tarzan, right?

80    Everything about this woman, this Felice, amazed Cleófilas. The fact that she drove a pickup. A pickup mind you, but when Cleófilas asked if it was her husband's, she said she didn't have a husband. The pickup was hers. She herself had chosen it. She herself was paying for it.

I used to have a Pontiac Sunbird. But those cars are for viejas. Pussy cars.  81
Now this here is a *real* car.

What kind of talk was that coming from a woman, Cleófilas thought. But  82
then again, Felice was like no woman she'd ever met. Can you imagine. When
we crossed the arroyo she just started yelling like a crazy, she would say later
to her father and brothers. Just like that. Who would've thought.

Who would've? Pain or rage perhaps but not a hoot like the one Felice had  83
just let go. Makes you want to holler like Tarzan, Felice had said.

Then Felice began laughing again, but it wasn't Felice laughing. It was  84
gurgling out of her own throat, a long ribbon of laughter, like water.  ✛

---

## RESPONDING

1. Cleófilas acts to remove herself and her child from a dangerous situation.
   Write about a time when you or someone you know or have read about
   took a risk to make a bad situation better.

2. Working individually or in a group, discuss the pros and cons of the options
   available to Cleófilas. Which option would you have chosen if you were in
   her situation?

3. Why does Cleófilas think that "Felice was like no woman she'd ever met"
   (paragraph 82)? Is that observation a compliment or a criticism? Explain
   Cleófilas's attitude toward Felice in an essay.

4. Analyze the appeal of the telenovelas for Cleófilas. If her story appeared on
   a soap opera, how might the ending differ? Write an alternate ending for
   the story. Discuss the new possible endings with the class. In an essay,
   explain which ending you like best and why.

# GRACIELA LIMON

*Graciela Limón earned a bachelor's and master's degree in Spanish literature from Marymount College, Los Angeles (1965), and the University of the Americas at Mexico City (1969), respectively, followed by a doctorate in Latin American literature from the University of California, Los Angeles (1975). She is currently chair of the Department of Chicana and Chicano Studies and a professor of U.S. Hispanic literature at Loyola Marymount University in Los Angeles. Limón has written and published reviews and critical work on Mexican, Latin American, and Caribbean literature. Her fictional works include* In Search of Bernabé *(1993), which won the Before Columbus Foundation American Book Award (1994), the* Memories of Ana Calderón *(1994),* Song of the Hummingbird *(1996), and* The Day of the Moon *(1999).*

*The following selection from* The Memories of Ana Calderón *examines the ways in which gender expectations can determine the role one is expected to play in the family.*

✣

# *From* The Memories of Ana Calderón

1  *My* FIRST MEMORY *of the fringes of Los Angeles is of long tracks of flowers on the left side of the road as we headed for Reyes' house, and to the right of us were sloping hills that looked soft and golden in the declining sun. With the desert of the Yaqui River Valley still in our mind, the sight of those strips that alternated in red, white, lavender, amber, and then red again filled us with excitement. There were so many flowers that none of us could see where they ended. Jasmín came back into my mind because I remembered that 'Amá once told me that she had named my sister after a flower because she was born at dawn, when the sky was the color of lilacs and lilies.*

2  *As the truck slid alongside the flowers, I stretched my neck over to the driver's side of the cab and shouted to Reyes, "Is this where we're going to live?"*

3  *"No," he yelled back. "It all belongs to Chapos. They're the people who grow flowers and sell them at the main market in town."*

4  *I told myself that I would like to work with those people, even though at that time I didn't know what a Japanese person looked like.*

5  *When Reyes saw how excited we all were because of the flowers, he stopped the truck and stuck his head out the window. "This road is called Floral Drive because of all the flowers."*

6  *Soon after, we went down a steep hill to where the truck made a turn on Humphrys Avenue, and there Reyes stopped. He jumped out and announced, "We have arrived!" He shouted out his wife's name, and in a minute a very pretty woman came out of the front door. She was followed by several children, girls and boys, and they all looked just like Reyes.*

"It's only a garage, Rudy, but you and the kids can stay here until we find you a job. Tomorrow I'll take you over to some of the junk yards. I think something will turn up." 7

"'Apá, where are we going to eat?" Zulma blurted out what everyone was thinking, but her father ignored the question. 8

Rodolfo, with the children huddled behind him, stood in the middle of a rickety garage with a dirt floor. "Gracias, Reyes. I'm grateful. As soon as I can work, maybe we can find a house." 9

"Yeah." Reyes looked at Zulma and said, "You can eat in the kitchen with my kids. We got a lot of rice and beans." Then turning to Rodolfo, "In the meantime, my wife told me that the older kids better start off in school right away." 10

"'Apá! . . ." Several voices shouted out in protest. 11

"We don't know how to talk the way they do here. How can we go to school?" Alejandra confronted Rodolfo. "Why don't we work with you? That way we can get a house right away." 12

Rodolfo and Reyes looked at one another and then at the children. "No, Aleja, you need just a little bit of school. After that, you can start working." 13

It was late September when the Calderón children joined the rest of the barrio kids who walked to Hammel Street School. Ana and Octavio were placed in the sixth grade and Alejandra in the third, and their fear of not knowing how to speak English disappeared once they saw that most of the children were just like them. 14

Ana felt older than the other children in her class, but she liked school. It was difficult for her to forget the tomato fields and the women who had worked by her side. Her mind, however, was captivated from the beginning with learning the new language, and she concentrated on how her teacher used pictures and the blackboard to teach new words. 15

At the end of the first day in school, as Señora Soto was serving them dinner, the Calderón and Soto children jabbered about their experiences. When the noise got so loud, the woman was forced to shush them into silence. After a few minutes, the talking began all over again. 16

Ana looked at Octavio and said, "I learned to say some words in English. How about you?" 17

Octavio smiled at her, exposing the contents of his stuffed mouth, but he didn't answer her question. Alejandra made a face of disgust as she said, "I hated it. I don't want to be by myself with a bunch of kids I don't know. I wish we could go back home. I liked it better there." 18

"Ana and me were put with the older kids because we're smarter than you." Octavio laughed, showing her that he liked being in the same classroom with Ana. But Alejandra resented it when he bragged about himself and Ana. She felt insulted and could only glare at him as she mumbled, *"Burro!"* 19

20    Ana thought of the cove back home, the palm trees, and how she, her sister, and Octavio spent most of their time playing by the water. She looked down at the plate in front of her and wondered why she felt so different now. Not much time had passed, she told herself, and yet she didn't want to play with either Octavio or Alejandra any more. She spoke up again. "I liked the teacher a lot." Looking at Alejandra, she explained, "Her name is Miss Nugent, and she told me that if I try, I can learn right away."

21    "Liar! How could she tell you that if she doesn't know how to speak like us?" Alejandra challenged her sister's remark.

22    Ana stopped, fork in mid-air, wondering how it had happened. "No. I'm not a liar, and even if I don't know how she told me, still, I understood her."

23    Alejandra jumped out of her chair with the pretext of putting her plate in the sink, but once she was behind Ana, she put horns over her head, making everyone laugh.

24    The days that followed turned into weeks and months. Ana became fond of school. She learned new words every day until she began to put them together, and by the end of the term, she was able to stay after school to talk with Miss Nugent while helping to clean the blackboard and dust off the erasers.

25    Octavio, on the other hand, was not interested in learning anything, and from the first day, instead of concentrating on what the teacher was showing them, decided to become the class clown. He had a winning way about him, so much that he even became the teacher's preferred student almost immediately, despite his disinterest in her lessons.

26    He noticed his impact on girls, and when he realized that there was something about him that made them like him, he fooled around, intentionally making them blush and giggle. He liked that very much, and he soon understood that he had a special personality, one which made him admired even by the boys.

27    He was taller than most of them, and his features were already striking. His skin had a rich, dark mahogany tone and his hair, also dark brown, was wavy and shiny. His eyes were slanted and large, like those of a cat. His brow was medium-sized and his nose tended to be long and slender. His mouth was sensitive, and it appeared to be developing a sensuousness that would intensify as he grew older.

28    The months passed and by the time the first year of school ended for the Calderón children, Rodolfo was able to rent a small house across the street from the Reyes place. He needed help, however, and when most of the families of the barrio migrated up to Fresno and Salinas for the summer harvesting, he told Ana, Octavio, and Alejandra that they had to join the others and go to work.

29    "'Apá, let me stay here to look after the kids." Ana didn't want to return to the fields, to the outhouses, to the drunken Saturday nights. When her father

turned his face away from her, she pressed him with more intensity. "I can cook for you and the kids, really I can. Please let me stay and . . ."

"No! You have to earn your keep. Don't think you're fooling me; I know that the only reason you want to stay is to read more books. You're a lazy girl, Ana, but you don't fool your father. When you return in September, I expect you to bring money enough to pay for your food during the year." 30

"But 'Apá . . ." 31

"*Silencio!*" 32

Ana did as her father ordered, and she did this each summer until she ended the tenth grade in school. During the school year, however, she was able to read and keep in contact with her grammar-school teacher, Miss Nugent. But the more she learned, the more separated Ana felt from Octavio and Alejandra. And, she felt her father's resentment growing with each year. ✠ 33

## RESPONDING

1. Imagine that you are a migrant farmworker. Write a letter to one of the farm owners discussing the working conditions and explaining any complaints you may have.

2. Working individually or in a group, list everything you know about the history of migrant workers. Share your knowledge and construct a portrait of a migrant worker's life.

3. In an essay, compare Ana's wishes for herself with her family's plans for her. Explain the conflicts between the need for children to go to school and the need for them to work to help the family. How do expectations for sons and daughters differ?

4. English language fluency and formal education often help immigrants advance in society. In an essay, discuss the factors that might prevent a migrant worker's advancement.

# RUBEN SALAZAR

*Columnist Ruben Salazar was born in Ciudad Juarez, Mexico, in 1928; his family immigrated to the United States the same year. He became a natural-ized citizen, serving in the U.S. Army from 1950 to 1952. When he graduated from Texas Western College (later called the University of Texas at El Paso), he was one of the first Mexican Americans to earn a bachelor's degree in the state of Texas. After working for the* El Paso Post Herald, *he was hired as a journalist by the* Los Angeles Times *in 1959. In addition to covering local stories, he was assigned to* Times *bureaus in the Dominican Republic, Mexico, and Vietnam. In 1970, while covering the Chicano Mora-torium for the* Los Angeles Times, *he was killed by a tear gas projectile launched by Los Angeles County sheriffs during the unrest that occurred after the demonstration. The inquest into his death resulted in no convictions. Salazar's writing has recently been edited by Mario T. García in the volume* Border Correspondent: Selected Writings of Ruben Salazar, 1955–1970 *(1995).*

*In the selections that follow, Salazar reflects on the political and ideological contexts that surround the terms "Chicano" and "the border".*

# *From* BORDER CORRESPONDENT

## *Who Is a Chicano? And What Is It the Chicanos Want?*

### *February 6, 1970*

1    A CHICANO is a Mexican-American with a non-Anglo image of himself.

2    He resents being told Columbus "discovered" America when the Chicano's ancestors, the Mayans and the Aztecs, founded highly sophisticated civilizations centuries before Spain financed the Italian explorer's trip to the "New World."

3    Chicanos resent also Anglo pronouncements that Chicanos are "culturally deprived" or that the fact that they speak Spanish is a "problem."

4    Chicanos will tell you that their culture predates that of the Pilgrims and that Spanish was spoken in America before English and so the "problem" is not theirs but the Anglos' who don't speak Spanish.

5    Having told you that, the Chicano will then contend that Anglos are Spanish-oriented at the expense of Mexicans.

They will complain that when the governor dressed up as a Spanish noble-  6
man for the Santa Barbara Fiesta he's insulting Mexicans because the Spanish
conquered and exploited the Mexicans.

It's as if the governor dressed like an English Redcoat for a Fourth of July  7
parade, Chicanos say.

When you think you know what Chicanos are getting at, a Mexican-Ameri-  8
can will tell you that Chicano is an insulting term and may even quote the
Spanish Academy to prove that Chicano derives from chicanery.

A Chicano will scoff at this and say that such Mexican-Americans have been  9
brainwashed by Anglos and that they're Tio Tacos (Uncle Toms). This type of
Mexican-American, Chicanos will argue, don't like the word Chicano because
it's abrasive to their Anglo-oriented minds.

These poor people are brown Anglos, Chicanos will smirk.  10

What, then, is a Chicano? Chicanos say that if you have to ask you'll never  11
understand, much less become, a Chicano.

Actually, the word Chicano is as difficult to define as "soul."  12

For those who like simplistic answers, Chicano can be defined as short for  13
Mexicano. For those who prefer complicated answers, it has been suggested that
Chicano may have come from the word Chihuahua—the name of a Mexican
state bordering on the United States. Getting trickier, this version then contends
that Mexicans who migrated to Texas call themselves Chicanos because having
crossed into the United States from Chihuahua they adopted the first three
letters of that state, Chi, and then added cano, for the latter part of Texano.

Such explanations, however, tend to miss the whole point as to why Mexi-  14
can-American activists call themselves Chicanos.

Mexican-Americans, the second largest minority in the country and the  15
largest in the Southwestern states (California, Texas, Arizona, New Mexico and
Colorado), have always had difficulty making up their minds what to call
themselves.

In New Mexico, they call themselves Spanish-Americans. In other parts of  16
the Southwest they call themselves Americans of Mexican descent, people with
Spanish surnames or Hispanos.

Why, ask some Mexican-Americans, can't we just call ourselves Americans?  17

Chicanos are trying to explain why not. Mexican-Americans, though indige-  18
nous to the Southwest, are on the lowest rung scholastically, economically,
socially and politically. Chicanos feel cheated. They want to effect change. Now.

Mexican-Americans average eight years of schooling compared to the Ne-  19
groes' 10 years. Farm workers, most of whom are Mexican-American in the
Southwest, are excluded from the National Labor Relations Act, unlike other
workers. Also, Mexican-Americans often have to compete for low-paying jobs
with their Mexican brothers from across the border who are willing to work for
even less. Mexican-Americans have to live with the stinging fact that the word
Mexican is the synonym for inferior in many parts of the Southwest.

20    That is why Mexican-American activists flaunt the barrio word Chicano—as an act of defiance and a badge of honor. Mexican-Americans, though large in numbers, are so politically impotent that in Los Angeles, where the country's largest single concentration of Spanish-speaking live, they have no one of their own on the City Council. This, in a city politically sophisticated enough to have three Negro councilmen.

21    Chicanos, then, are merely fighting to become "Americans." Yes, but with a Chicano outlook.

### A Mexican-American Hyphen

#### February 13, 1970

22  The U.S.–Mexican border, or la frontera, is an 1,800-mile-long, virtually imaginary line of barbed wire fencing, an undergrowth of mesquite or chaparral and an easily forded river.

23    Orators, both American and Mexican, like to describe the border separating their countries as one of the two only such unfortified frontiers in the world, the other being the U.S.–Canadian border.

24    To many Americans living in the Southwest and to many Mexicans living in northern Mexico, however, the border is symbolic of the negative differences between the two nations.

25    Americans who know only the shady aspects of the border towns think of Mexico as a place where they can enjoy doing what is not allowed at home—but would be shocked, the morning after, if such goings on were allowed in "America."

26    Mexicans not lucky enough to be among the Latin affluent think of the American border towns as gold mines where nuggets can be picked off the streets. And when they discover this is not true, they blast the Americans as exploiters, unmindful that they had created their own false image of the United States.

27    These superficial and inaccurate concepts of both countries help only to widen the understanding gap between two peoples who are so close geographically and in many other ways so far apart.

28    That may help explain why Mexican-Americans can feel a deep and agonizing ambivalence about themselves.

29    They can love the United States for reasons Mexicans cannot understand, while loving Mexico for reasons Americans can understand.

30    Being a Mexican-American, a wag once said, can leave you with only the hyphen.

31    On the United States' other border there are no such esoteric considerations.

32    Canadians may conceivably feel bitter about the fact that the British Empire lost the 13 colonies but this chauvinism is tempered by knowing that, after all,

Canadians and Americans communicate easily and enjoy more or less the same material goods.

Chauvinistic Mexicans, however, are very cognizant of the fact that Mexico  33
lost what is now the American Southwest to the United States in the Mexican-American War which even Gen. Ulysses S. Grant called "unfair."

Mexicans like to argue that if the United States had not "stolen" half of  34
Mexico's territory, Mexico would be as rich as the United States is now. This historical controversy, now for the most part taken lightly, might have disappeared altogether by now, it is said, if Mexicans and Americans spoke the same language on both sides of the border and so understood each other better.

Yet, many Mexican-Americans in the Southwest, who speak both languages  35
and admire both countries, feel strangely foreign in their own land.

Members of other minorities—Italians, Irish, Poles, etc.—often wonder why  36
Mexican-Americans have not been able to assimilate as well as they have.

They tend to forget that Italy, Ireland, Poland, etc., are oceans away from  37
the United States while Mexico is very much in evidence to the Southwest's eight million or so Mexican-Americans.

This makes it difficult for the Mexican-Americans to think of Mexico in the  38
abstract as, for instance, Irish-Americans might think of Ireland.

The problems of Mexico are and will remain relevant to the Mexican-  39
American. Relations between Mexico and the United States can affect the Mexican-American in the Southwest materially and emotionally.

In the border areas, for instance, the large number of Mexicans crossing the  40
international line everyday to work in the United States can directly affect the economic lives of Mexican-Americans, who must compete with this cheap labor.

Projects such as Operation Intercept, a crackdown on dope smuggling across  41
the Mexican border, hurt the pride of southwest Mexican-Americans who feel the United States is trying to blame Mexicans for a problem which is to a large extent uniquely "Anglo."

The border may indeed be unfortified, but it separates two people who  42
created the Mexican-American—a person many times tormented by the pull of two distinct cultures.

### *Chicanos Would Find Identity Before Coalition with Blacks*

#### *February 20, 1970*

Mexicans and Negroes are learning that they must know each other better if  43
their differences are not to help those who would like to kill the civil rights movement.

This necessary lesson is not easy to come by.  44

Blacks, scarred by the bitter and sometimes bloody struggle for equality,  45 consider Mexican-Americans or Chicanos as Johnnies-come-lately who should follow black leadership until the Chicanos earn their spurs.

46 Chicanos, not untouched by bigotry and wary of the more sophisticated black leadership, insist on going their own way because, as they put it, "our problems are different from those of the Negroes."

47 Despite the loud mouthings of radicals, most blacks and Chicanos want the same thing: a fair chance to enter the mainstream of American society without abandoning their culture and uniqueness.

48 Much has been made of late of the growing rift between Negroes and Mexican-Americans. Chicanos complain that blacks get most of the government help in the fight against racism, while Negroes scoff that Mexican-Americans have not carried their share of the burden in the civil rights movement.

49 Leaders of both communities throw up their arms in despair, saying that the blacks and browns are fighting over peanuts and that political coalitions must be formed to make a real impact on the establishment.

50 Blacks and browns have always been cast together by the forces of history and the needs of these two peoples.

51 Los Angeles, for instance, was founded not by Spanish caballeros, as romantics would have it, but by blacks and browns.

52 Historian H. Bancroft points out that Los Angeles was founded on Sept. 4, 1781, with 12 settlers and their families, 46 persons in all, "whose blood was a strange mixture of Indian (Mexican) and Negro with here and there a trace of Spanish."

53 C. D. Willard, another historian, adds that "cataloguing this extraordinary collection of adults by nationality or color, we have two Spaniards, one mestizo, two Negroes, eight mulattoes and nine [Mexican] Indians."

54 The children of the settlers, continues Willard, were even more mixed, as follows: Spanish-Indian, four; Spanish-Negro, five; Negro-Indian, eight; Spanish-Negro-Indian, eight; Spanish-Negro-Indian, three; Indian, two.

55 Since then, Mexicans and Negroes have more or less followed their own separate destinies, due partly to their cultural and language differences but also because of the racist strain in American society.

56 Mexican-Americans have a saying about Negroes that goes, "Juntos pero no revueltos"—together but not mixed. Negroes, on the other hand, tend to think of Mexican-Americans—as do many Anglos—as "quaint and foreign."

57 One hundred and eighty years after the small group of black and brown people settled in what became Los Angeles, however, six Mexican-American children and six Negro children are involved in a Superior Court ruling in which Judge Alfred Gitelson ordered the Los Angeles school district desegregated.

58 When the Los Angeles school district is finally integrated, history will again have thrown the blacks and the browns together again.

59 To understand why Mexicans and Negroes are having their differences now, one must look at it in the light of the black revolution.

The revolution exploded partly from a condition which had been known all along but which became the basis for a black-white confrontation: the color of one's skin is all too important in America. White is good, Black is bad. 60

Faced with an identity crisis, many Mexican-Americans—especially the young who were excited by black militancy—decided they had been misled by the Mexican establishment into apathetic confusion. 61

It came as a shock at first: Mexican-Americans felt caught between the white and the black. Though counted as "white" by the Bureau of Census, Mexican-Americans were never really thought of as such. 62

The ambivalence felt vaguely and in silence for so long seemed to crystallize in the wake of the black revolution. A Mexican-American was neither white nor black. 63

One of the reasons for the growing distrust between Mexicans and Negroes is that the Chicano is still searching for his identity. 64

As yet, most Mexican-Americans seem not to identify with any one single overriding problem as Americans. Though they know they're somehow different, many still cling to the idea that Mexican-Americans are Caucasian, thus white, thus "one of the boys." 65

Many prove it: By looking and living like white Americans, by obtaining and keeping good jobs and by intermarrying with Anglos who never think of it as a "mixed marriage." 66

Many others, however, feel they have for too long been cheated by tacitly agreeing to be Caucasian in name only. These Mexican-Americans, especially the young Chicanos, feel that the coalition with the Anglos has failed. 67

And they're not about ready to form a new coalition—this time with the blacks—until they, the Chicanos, find their own identity in their own way. 68

### Mexican-American's Dilemma: He's Unfit in Either Language

#### February 27, 1970

". . . A Los Angeles Police Department officer was beating a Spanish-speaking motorist, calling him a dirty Mexican. Occupants in the motorist's car yelled out to the police officer that the person he was beating was not a Mexican, but that he was a Nicaraguan." 69

"At that moment the officer stopped beating him and obtained medical help for him." 70

So testified a psychiatric social worker at a hearing before the U.S. Commission on Civil Rights in December of 1968. 71

The testimony gives some insight into the complicated subject of the differences among the Spanish-speaking people in the United States. 72

Mexican-Americans, about 8 million of the 10 million Spanish-speaking 73 people in the country, are, ironically, among the most abused of this minority simply because they're Americans. This holds true for Puerto Ricans who are also Americans.

74    Non-American Spanish-speaking people, like Nicaraguans, Argentineans and Colombians, are as the police officer knew instantly, treated with more respect.

75    The reason may be that Americans, originally immigrants to this country, show more consideration for other immigrants than they do for indigenous people like Mexican-Americans and Indians.

76    Because of the civil rights movement, there has been an intense search for Spanish-speaking teachers, journalists, social workers, salesmen, etc.

77    Invariably, when found, these specialists turn out to be non-American Spanish-speaking people—Cubans, Central Americans, South Americans and native Mexicans.

78    The reason is simple. Non-American Spanish-speaking people have a better education—and so speak good Spanish—and assimilate well into Anglo society because they came here expressly to do this.

79    The Mexican-American, meanwhile, many of whom speak neither good Spanish nor good English, are victims of an educational system which purports to "Americanize" them while downgrading their ethnic background.

80    For instance, the first truly bilingual education program in this country was set up not for Mexican-Americans but for Cubans in the wake of the Cuban crisis. Bilingual education was made available to Cuban refugees at Florida's Dade County schools in 1963.

81    Yet, as late as December 1966, educators testified before the U.S. Commission on Civil Rights that Mexican-American children were being punished for speaking Spanish on school grounds in other parts of the country.

82    Cubans today, then, have a better chance of obtaining jobs requiring bilingual people—now that Spanish has been discovered as an asset instead of a liability—than do Mexican-Americans.

83    Belated bilingual education programs for Mexican-Americans are geared toward using the Spanish language as a tool only until the Chicano kid has learned enough English to overcome the "problem" of speaking Spanish. These are not truly bilingual programs, which should be the teaching of both languages on an equal basis.

84    The truth of the matter is that despite our talk in the Southwest about "our great Spanish heritage" and the naming of our towns and streets in Spanish, the Spanish language has never been taken seriously by American educators even in areas where both languages could be learned together and correctly.

85    Too often the difference between a Mexican-American and a non-American Spanish-speaking person is that the non-American can speak better Spanish than the Mexican-American—and so is more qualified for the emerging bilingual job.

86    And the difference between the Mexican-American and the Anglo-

American is that the Anglo speaks better English than the Mexican-American and so is better equipped for the more conventional jobs.

The pattern could change when the American educational system is as [87] considerate of Mexican-Americans as it was of Cubans in 1963.

## *Chicanos vs. Traditionalists*

### *March 6, 1970*

Last Saturday's Chicano Moratorium and the activities of the Catolicos por La [88] Raza dramatize the gulf which exists between the traditional-minded Mexican-Americans and the young activists.

Unless this is understood, observers can fall easily into the simplistic con- [89] clusions that the traditionalists are Tio Tacos (Uncle Toms) or that the activists are irresponsible punks.

Either conclusion misses the essence of the present Mexican-American [90] condition.

Traditional-minded Mexican-Americans blush at the mention of the word [91] Chicano. They blanch at the thought of being called brown people. The reason for this, outside of personal views, is the psychological makeup of the Mexican in general.

Octavio Paz, the Mexican poet-essayist-diplomat, has tried to explain it this [92] way: "The Mexican, whether young or old, white or brown, general or lawyer, seems to me to be a person who shuts himself away to protect himself. . . . He is jealous of his own privacy and that of others. . . . He passes through life like a man who has been flayed; everything can hurt him, including words and the very suspicion of words. . . ."

The Mexican, says Paz, "builds a wall of indifference and remoteness [93] between reality and himself, a wall that is no less impenetrable for being invisible. The Mexican is always remote, from the world and from other people. And also from himself."

Is it any wonder, then, that the more conservative Mexican-Americans—and [94] there are many of them—are embarrassed and angered at Chicanos (suspicious word) who say they don't want to fight the war in Vietnam and Catolicos who are questioning the church and the world about them?

The Mexican, says Paz, wears his face as a mask and believes "that opening [95] oneself up is a weakness or a betrayal."

The Chicano activists are trying to rid themselves of their masks and to [96] open themselves to themselves and to others. It is significant that in doing this they should pick as a means the Vietnam war and the Catholic Church.

That more than 3,000 people braved torrential rains last Saturday to par- [97] ticipate in the Chicano Moratorium is important not because so many people showed a distaste for the war—Anglos have done this in a bigger way—but because it was Mexican-Americans who did it.

98     Mexican-Americans, who include a disproportionate number of Medal of Honor winners and who, like the blacks, are suffering a disproportionate number of deaths in Vietnam, had up to now fought our wars without question.

99     It was part of the "machismo" traditions. When called to war, Mexican-Americans showed everyone how "macho" or manly they were and never questioned the justification for the war.

100     Mexicans, says Paz, judge manliness according to their "invulnerability to enemy arms or the impacts of the outside world. Stoicism is the most exalted of (Mexicans') military and political attributes."

101     The Chicano Moratorium strove to end this stoicism, which is hardly a democratic attribute.

102     "We weren't shedding our machismo," said a young marcher. "We were proving our machismo by asking the establishment the tough question: 'Why are we dying overseas when the real struggle is at home?'"

103     When the Catolicos por La Raza demonstrated during a midnight Christmas mass last year, they were also breaking with tradition and asking tough questions at the cost of going through the ordeal of being tried for disturbing the peace.

104     A San Antonio teacher, testifying before the U.S. Commission on Civil Rights last year, said he has noted that the difference between Anglo and Mexican-American students is that when "some situation befalls the Mexican-Americans," the Mexican-American tends to leave things up to God while the Anglo tries to solve it on his own.

105     Catolicos por La Raza, who greatly embarrassed the traditional-minded Mexican-Americans by their questioning of the Catholic Church's relevance to present society, were breaking with this concept.

106     Chicanos and traditional-minded Mexican-Americans are suffering from the ever-present communications gap. Traditionalists, more concerned with the, to them, chafing terms like Chicano, are not really listening to what the activists are saying. And the activists forget that tradition is hard to kill. ✢

---

## RESPONDING

1. In a journal entry, identify and label your own ethnic origin. Explain how and why you classify yourself as you do.

2. Working individually or in a group, discuss the period when these articles were written. Use the Internet or other sources to find out what was happening in the United States and in the world at that time. Have things changed for Chicanos since then? Does the term *Chicano* still signify an activist?

3.  In an essay, paraphrase and elaborate on Salazar's definition of *Chicano*. What does he mean when he says, "A Chicano is a Mexican-American with a non-Anglo image of himself" (paragraph 1)?

4.  Salazar talks about the pull of two distinct cultures on the Mexican-American. Write an essay analyzing that conflict and the problems as well as the benefits of being bicultural. What role does "the border" play in separating and/or connecting the two cultures? You may use examples from other readings, and your own experience, as well as from this essay.

# HECTOR CALDERON

*Héctor Calderón was born in the California border town of Calexico in 1945. He earned undergraduate degrees from UCLA (1968) and California State University of Los Angeles (1972), a master's degree from the University of California at Irvine (1975), and a doctorate in Latin American literature and comparative literature from Yale University (1981). He has taught at Stanford, Yale, and Scripps College, and is currently professor of Spanish American and Chicano literature at UCLA. Calderón has published numerous articles in his field including* Conciencia y lenguaje en el "Quijote" y "El obsceno pájaro de la noche" *(1987), and he is coeditor of* Criticism in the Borderlands: Studies in Chicano Literature, Culture, and Ideology *(1991).*

*The following essay was written specifically for the first edition of* American Mosaic *in 1990. Here Calderón uses his childhood experiences of growing up in a California border town as a backdrop for exploring Chicano heritage.*

# REINVENTING THE BORDER

*I*

*The creators of borders . . . are . . . great pretenders. They post their projects in the world with the sturdiest available signs and hope that conventions (or, in the instance of California, a language law) will keep them in place. But even as the first stakes are driven, the earth itself, in all its intractable shiftiness, moves toward displacement.*[1]

1. Houston A. Baker, Jr., "LimIts of the Border" (unpublished).

1　For the first eighteen years of my life the border, the line or *la línea*, was a daily presence. From the north end of the Imperial Valley in Brawley, Highway 86 winds down past agricultural fields and several cities—Imperial, El Centro, and Heber—to arrive eventually (as Highway 111) at the very limits of the American Southwest at the border, at Calexico, California. I, who grew up on Highway 111, also Imperial Avenue, four blocks from *la línea*, would rather think of the border not as a limit but as both a cultural and historical crossroads; for Calexico, like no other border town I know, has a mirror held up to it in Mexicali, Baja California. Both cities have been historical and cultural reflections of each other; both the same, yet quite different.

2　Calexico began in the 1890s as an encampment for laborers in a water diversion project that was to transform an area of the Sonora desert into one of the most productive agricultural regions of both the United States and Mexico. Mexicali, which had been an early extension of Calexico, rapidly outgrew its sister city. By the 1950s, and throughout my childhood, Calexico remained a dusty border town of eleven thousand, while Mexicali, the capital of Baja California del Norte, was a thriving (as only Mexican cities can thrive), tumultuous city of one hundred thousand. Nowadays, Calexico boasts a population of twenty-two thousand; I would wager that the population of Mexicali and its surrounding valleys is close to one million, with both its economy and its population boosted by assembly plants, *maquiladoras*, built since 1968 by U.S. companies on the Mexican side under the Border Industrial Program.

3　Both cities, ingeniously named around 1900 by a Mr. L. M. Holt, are, in fact, a single economic entity separated by a fence constructed in this century. Commercial traffic has flowed more or less freely across the border. Many Mexican families from Calexico, including mine, would "cross the line" into Mexicali three or four days of the week, whether to visit relatives, to shop or dine, or to seek any number of professional or medical services. The Mexicali upper crust would frequent our Calexico stores, while the lower class would compete with us for jobs as clerks, domestics, and, most important of all, agricultural workers. At 4:00 A.M. the sleeping border town would awaken, and the Calexico downtown, the four blocks on Second Street, would be busier than at any other time of the day with both foot and auto traffic on the way to "The Hole," *el hoyo*. At El Hoyo, labor contractors and their hawkers awaited men, women, and children, in summer taking them as far north as Indio to harvest Thompson seedless grapes and in winter as near as the outskirts of Holtville or El Centro to pick carrots or lettuce. The Imperial Valley, you see, has a year-around growing season; it is where the "sun spends the winter"; it is also where migrant worker families would return from northern California, from as far as Napa and California's central valley, to work on winter crops.

4　During the 1940s and '50s in this poor, working-class town, we were reminded of both what we were and what we were not. To the Euro-American minority of ranchers, shopkeepers, clerks, teachers, and government officials, we were not real Americans: we were foreigners, Mexicans. To our brothers and sisters on the other side of the line, we were *pochos:* inauthentic, Americanized

Mexicans, identifiable by our mutilated pachuco Spanish and our dress, "con lisas y tramados y calcos siempre bien shiniados."[2] I grew up *mestizo* and *rascuachi*, impure and lower class, in Calecia (Calexico) and Chikis (Mexicali), listening with my family to Spanish-language radio on XECL, enjoying the African rhythms of the mambo and the chachachá; the great big bands of Luis Alcaraz and Pérez Prado; the German-influenced Banda de Sinaloa; the border *corridos* and *norteña* polkas sung by the Alegres de Terán; the national idols of mariachi music, Jorge Negrete, Pedro Infante, Lola Beltrán, José Alfredo Jiménez, Amalia Mendoza; the romantic ballads composed by Augustín Lara interpreted by the Trío Los Panchos, Pedro Vargas, or Toña la Negra. Fridays were reserved for the Aztec Theatre, where we both laughed and cried to Mexican films by the exiled Spanish director Luis Buñuel or starring the Mexican national hero Cantinflas.

Many of our daily and seasonal activities were still dictated by Mexican oral and cultural traditions handed down to our family by our grandmother. Before we acquired a television set, our grandmother would narrate tales every night. However, our world was rapidly changing. The alternative to the Mexican radio station, XECL, was the appropriately named KROP of Brawley, on which we listened to R&B and rockabilly as they become rock 'n roll. We danced to James Brown, Little Richard, Chuck Berry, Laverne Baker, Buddy Holly and Ritchie Valens, the Platters, doo-wop, and Elvis and the Everlys—even Hank Williams and Patsy Cline on the "West Side of Your Hit Parade." We really hit the big time when the Ike and Tina Turner Revue came to the El Centro National Guard Armory and Little Richard played at the Mexicali Gimnasio. And yes, the Cisco Kid was a friend of mine.

This multicultural lens through which we viewed our world certainly made us "Mexicans" different from Euro-American Calexicans. However, in school we were told, assured, that we were white, Spanish, descendants of the conquistadors. Many years later, as I read my birth certificate, I think about how much our world has changed, for my race in 1945 was identified as white. But despite this, and even though we were legal citizens and should have been treated equally, we attended school in segregated classrooms. We were still, after all, foreigners, the children of Mexicans who had arrived in large numbers in the first decades of this century to play a significant role as agricultural laborers in a region that was undergoing a major economic transformation. My parents arrived shortly after the Mexican Revolution.[3] My mother belonged to a migrant worker family that traveled up and down California's central valley; my father, like all the males in his family, worked for the Southern Pacific Railroad.

These ethnic and class contradictions come back to me as I recall our most important annual festive occasion: the parade and pageant known as the Calexico

2. With *lisas* and *tramados* and always well-shined shoes. *Lisas* are a special type of loose fitting, long sleeve shirt worn buttoned to the neck. *Tramados* are baggy khaki pants.
3. Mexican Revolution of 1910.

Desert Cavalcade. Begun in the Depression years to boost the morale of the border community, the pageant was the invention of a Mrs. Keller, who had the support of the editor of the Calexico *Chronicle*, the local newspaper, and of the president of the Chamber of Commerce and representatives of the city's service clubs. This reenactment of California's past began, in the words of the organizing committee, "with the stout-hearted pioneers who brought God and civilization to the Southwest." My fourth-grade experience is especially memorable: dressed like all my classmates as a Plains Indian in feathers and buckskin, I fell in behind the gallant Juan Bautista de Anza and kindly, black-robed padres as we paraded past our two important side-by-side architectural landmarks, the neo-Spanish Hotel de Anza and the mission-like Our Lady of Guadalupe Catholic Church, on our way to Monterrey in Alta California. That de Anza did not establish a Mexican settlement in the area in 1775 was not important to some Calexicans. Actually, de Anza had the more important task of establishing an overland route from what is now southern Arizona to Alta California, a task made easier by existing Native American trails. It also did not matter to the Cavalcade organizers that their activities made no sense given the cultural, historical, and economic realities of this overwhelmingly Mexican town. The Cavalcade probably made no sense either to Mrs. Yokum, Pete Emmett, or Lucille, our African American neighbors, or to Mar Chan, our corner grocer.

8    We in the Southwest were never so different from our friends and relatives across the border in Mexico as when we asserted this, our Spanish heritage. Though biologically and culturally we were indistinct from one another—we were all Mexican *mestizos*—we had different national cultural heritages and ideologies imposed from above by educators, civic leaders, and government officials. Just a short distance across the border, buildings and monuments bore the names of Mexican revolutionary leaders like Obregón and Cárdenas. Not Spanish, but Native American culture had been purified into their norm of the classic after the Mexican Revolution of 1910. From José Vasconcelos's *La raza cósmica (The Cosmic Race)* of 1926 to Octavio Paz's *El laberinto de la soledad (The Labyrinth of Solitude)* of 1949, Native American culture was not only Mexico's historical base, but also its possibility for the future. In the idealized Mexican historical drama, Cuauhtémoc, Fallen Eagle, the last Aztec emperor, became the nation's hero, and Cortés, Spanish conqueror, became the archvillain. These different popular and intellectual traditions reveal why, until the Chicano movement of the 1960s, one side of the border was "Spanish" and the other "Mexican," although we shared the same Mexican-*mestizo* culture.

## *II*

9    Perhaps the single most influential agent of Euro-American cultural domination was Charles F. Lummis, whose lifelong activities and writings changed the image of a region, Mexican America, that had been acquired through military conquest some thirty-six years prior to his arrival in Santa Fe, New Mexico, in 1884. In

1925, three years before his death, Lummis boasted in *Mesa, Cañon and Pueblo*, that he had been the first to apply the generic name "Southwest," or more specifically, "Spanish Southwest," to the million square miles that include New Mexico, Arizona, southern California, and parts of Colorado, Utah, and Texas. In a span of nine years, from 1891 to 1899, Lummis published eleven books, changing what was a physical and cultural desert into a land internationally known for its seductive natural and cultural attractions. Though in truth an amateur inclined toward self-promotion and melodramatic and hyperbolic writing, Lummis became the founder of the "Southwest genre," recognized by both professionals and the popular media as the undisputed authority on the history, anthropology, and folklore of the Southwest.

In the West, Lummis discovered for his readers a culture much like that of the fictional characters and settings of romantic literature. Unlike the East, the West had an authentic folk culture of simple and picturesque, yet dignified, souls still existing in a pastoral or agricultural mode of production undisturbed by the modern world. So taken was Lummis by the alien culture he encountered that he adopted it as his own; he learned Spanish, took on the name of Don Carlos, and was fond of posing for photographs in Spanish, Western, Apache, and Navajo attire. He was a promoter of "Spanish" architecture and established the Landmarks Club to revive the California missions. He founded the Southwest Museum in Los Angeles to house his collections of Native American artifacts. *10*

Like other foreigners who make native culture their own, however, Lummis also had a conservative and patronizing side. He was intent on writing only about the most folkloric and romantic elements of Native American and *mestizo* culture. Thus in his first books, *A New Mexico David* (1891) and *The Land of Poco Tiempo* (1893), Lummis reveals his attraction to courtly dons, beautiful, dark-eyed Spanish señoritas, innocent Indian children, kind Mexican peons, witches, liturgical feast days, medieval-style penitents, haciendas, burros, carretas, and sunshine. Charmed by his "child-hearted" Spanish, Lummis became an apologist for the Spanish conquest of the Americas. His early book, *The Spanish Pioneers* (1893), is a history of the heroic padres and gallant Spaniards who brought God and civilization to the Americas. *11*

Of course, the past was not just a romance, and the present was more than Mexicans resting against adobe. This strategy of glorifying the past ignored the historical fact that the land upon which Lummis set foot in 1884 was conquered Mexican territory. For Lummis, it was as if Spain had become the United States without centuries of racial and cultural mixture. Yet Lummis's view of the conquest and colonization of Arizona, California, New Mexico, and Texas as the golden age of Hispanic culture in the Southwest became a standard interpretation of Euro-American and Hispanic academic scholarship early in the twentieth century, and it continues to flourish in the popular imagination in literature, mass media images and Hollywood films and in the celebrations of Spanish fiesta days throughout the Southwest. *12*

## *III*

13    But what about the cultural changes during the viceroyalty of New Spain and the young Mexican nation? These changes created new American cultural traditions throughout the years from the conquest of Mexico in 1521 to the establishment of Santa Fe in 1610 and down to the growth of Arizona, California, New Mexico, and Texas in the twentieth century. On these issues virtually nothing was written in the United States until the reinvention of the border from a Chicano perspective. I am referring to Américo Paredes's groundbreaking study in 1958, *"With His Pistol in His Hand": A Border Ballad and Its Hero.* As the title indicates, the book is a study of folk balladry along the Texas lower Rio Grande border, from the two Laredos in the north to Brownsville and Matamoros on the Gulf of Mexico. As a work of scholarship—it was Paredes's doctoral dissertation, presented in 1956 to the English department at the University of Texas at Austin—it did not differ from traditional studies. The author established a theory of genesis for border balladry, tracing its development from its origins in the Spanish *romance* to the Texas-Mexican *corrido.* But the book was more than this; it was a highly conscious, imaginative act of resistance that established for Chicanos a definition for the border, which is to say, not as a line but as Greater Mexico, a historically determined geopolitical zone of military, cultural, and linguistic conflict. For me, when I came upon Paredes's book by accident as a student at UCLA in 1965, it was the answer to the silencing of our voices, the stereotyping of our culture, and the reification of our history that resulted from the Southwest genre.

14    It is difficult to describe the complexity of Paredes's study. It is a hybrid form, blurring the boundaries between genres and disciplines; it is part history, anthropology, folklore, and fiction. It is a reconstruction of the history of the lower Río Grande Valley from Spanish colonization in 1749 to the displacement of a Mexican ranching culture by large-scale farming in the 1930s and '40s to the migrant worker culture of the post–World War II era. A graduate student at Austin faced up to the myth of the Texas Rangers and the white supremacist attitudes of Texas scholar Walter Prescott Webb, who had written in *The Texas Rangers* (1936) that Mexican blood "was no better than ditch water." Paredes dared to utter the unspeakable: that the development of a Texas-Mexican pastoral mode of production, a ranching culture, that had emerged from the mixture of Spanish and Native American elements and was beginning to extend up from the Rio Grande to the Nueces River, was cut short in 1836 and 1848 by a "restless and acquisitive people, exercising the rights of conquest."

15    "With His Pistol in His Hand" is also a theory of culture by a native anthropologist who understood that culture is not necessarily consensual but conflictual. Given the current temper of anthropological studies, in which the question of the objective gaze of the observer is being displaced by the acknowledgement of the institutional and political situation of the discipline, Paredes was ahead of his time. He turned his scholarly attention to the voices of his people, to the *corridos,* the ballads, that he had heard as a child, and chose to

study the "Corrido de Gregorio Cortez," the ballad of a Texas-Mexican vaquero who in 1901 had been wrongly accused of killing an Anglo sheriff. Unlike earlier scholars, Paredes studied the oral tradition in its context, to understand how it had developed. According to Paredes, after 1836 the Spanish *romance* developed into the *corrido* as a result of the border conflicts that became its dominant theme: the protagonist of the *corrido* defends his rights with his pistol in his hand. Other border heroes preceded and followed Cortez: Juan Nepomuceno Cortina, from Brownsville, who led a rebellion in 1859; Catarino Garza, of Brownsville-Matamoros, who was probably the first to rise up against the Mexican dictator Porfirio Diaz in 1890; and Aniceto Pizaña, who led a 1915 rebellion against the state of Texas.

While most critics of Chicano literature have focused their attention on  16 Gregorio Cortez as the complete and legitimate Texas-Mexican persona whose life of struggle was worthy of being told, I would rather think of Paredes as the writer who made the Chicano genre possible. After poking fun at the biased scholarship of his "objective" colleagues at the University of Texas in Chapter I, "The Country," the Texas-Mexican trickster Paredes disappears in Chapter II, "The Legend of Gregorio Cortez," giving way to a third-person plural narrative, told in the anonymous voices of the elders of the tribe who gather at night to tell the legend. Paredes transcribes and translates a group storytelling performance, so that, through his individual talents and inventive energy as a writer, the interests of the community are represented. As the elders relive the exploits of Gregorio Cortez, in a retelling spiced with humor and linguistic jokes, the hero becomes the embodiment of the cultural values that developed during a history of conflict and resistance. In Chapter IV, "The Hero's Progress," Paredes returns to this storytelling situation, explaining that the legend as it appears in Chapter II is his own creation; he put together those parts that seemed to him furthest removed from fact and the most revealing of folk attitudes. This narrative stance, with its folkloric, anthropological, and historical elements, seems to me the inner form of much of Chicano literature, from Tomás Rivera's *y no se lo tragó la tierra/And the Earth Did Not Part* (1971) and Rolando Hinojosa's *Klail City Death Trip Series* (1973–1989) to Sandra Cisneros's *The House on Mango Street* and Gloria Anzaldúa's *Borderlands/La Frontera: The New Mestiza* (1987).

## IV

Whenever Chicanas or Chicanos write on behalf of their community, the border  17 has always loomed in the background. This is true whether it is a real historical or cultural crossing back and forth between the United States and Mexico or a crossing of more symbolic barriers, as in confronting issues of racism and language, gender, sexual, and class differences. These issues found their way to paper in the early work of Jovita González (1930), Américo Paredes (1958), and Ernesto Galarza (1964), and also appear in the work of the writers of the Chicano movement selected for this volume.

18    Given these scholarly and creative traditions and the national and international preoccupation with the question of the border, it is not surprising that the Chicana lesbian activist Gloria Anzaldúa in her *Borderlands/La Frontera: The New Mestiza* (1987) should combine an autobiographical account with a reconceptualization of the border. Hers is a new historical and metaphorical version. For her, borders are established to protect what is "ours" from danger, from the "alien," because they are also places inhabited by what is forbidden. For those in power, border zones are inhabited by Chicanos, African Americans, Native Americans, Asian Americans, mulattos, *mestizos*, gays, lesbians, "wetbacks," illegals—in short, all those who are judged to be illegitimate. To sum up in another way, borders are those spaces, both geographical and conceptual, where the contradictions of power and repression, resistance and rebellion, are painfully visible.

19    To really know border zones, one has to overcome barriers, to be *atravesada*, a border crosser. Anzaldúa is a border writer who lives her contradictions at various levels. She is no longer a quiet woman. She speaks out and confronts her own Texas-Mexican patriarchal and heterosexist culture. She writes in both English and Spanish to find her own voice and rejects any linguistic inferiority imposed by nationalists from both sides of the border. As she explains, Chicano language was invented to communicate realities and values belonging to a border zone.

20    Like Paredes before her, Anzaldúa retells the history of Anglo-Texan domination of the Río Grande border; however, she bears witness to land fraud and usurpation suffered by both of her grandmothers. As she matured through the decade of the fifties, she saw her borderlands parcelled out for the benefit of U.S. companies. Like other Texas-Mexican families displaced from their ancestral homeland, the Anzaldúas became sharecroppers. The transformation of the Río Grande Valley did not stop at *la línea*. Nowadays, observes Anzaldúa, U.S. companies (RCA, Fairchild, Litton, Zenith, Motorola, among others) control the border economy through their assembly plants, the *maquiladoras*, whose workforces are mostly women. These new industrial forces have displaced older rural social and cultural structures.

## V

21    Anzaldúa's account should be inserted within a new historical problematic along the border: The dividing lines between north and south, First and Third World, are being effaced even as I write. We are witnessing dramatic demographic changes in the West and Southwest, and in northern Mexico, that will play a decisive role in the development of Chicano-Latino culture. Since the 1950s the population of major Mexican border towns, from Tijuana, on the Pacific Ocean, to Matamoros, on the Gulf of Mexico, has more than quadrupled, because women, men, and children from Mexico, Central America, and the Caribbean are flocking to these cities as points of entry into the United States, to work in U.S. assembly plants on the Mexican side, or to take advantage of a growing

international business and tourist trade. As if in a García Márquez tale, one of the largest flea markets in the Southwest has sprung up in an empty field on the outskirts of Calexico. The promise of inexpensive U.S. products offered by Asian entrepreneurs from Los Angeles draws Mexican nationals from isolated areas, who must travel days to reach Calexico. I heard from a touring Japanese family that some street vendors in Tijuana now speak Japanese. I imagine similar border crossings occur in Texas, New Mexico, and Arizona.

This multicultural world will have its effect on Mexico. Because of U.S. cultural and economic influence (U.S. assembly plants are now being constructed in the interior of Mexico), we hear from a frank Mexican historian that every Mexican national is a potential Chicano. Similar phenomena are occurring on the northern side of the border. California, we are told, is fast becoming a Third World state; soon after the year 2000, the Euro-American population will reach minority status. In the late 1970s, I taught as a substitute teacher in a Hollywood elementary school whose administrators had to deal with fifteen different languages. I have even heard that there exists in Los Angeles a community of Mexicans who speak their native *quiché* Maya. A recent concert of Filipino popular music in a white suburb of Los Angeles drew 10,000. It is therefore not surprising to read reports that if current population trends and birthrates continue, California will experience a complete reversal from its 1945 ratio of whites to nonwhites. Thus, a centuries-old border culture with new social and economic realities, extending from San Francisco in the West and Chicago in the Midwest to Mexico, Central America, and the Caribbean, is reasserting itself on the U.S. national scene.  22

However, we should not be totally celebratory of a multicultural United States. To understand the economic realities of the expanding border zone, we should also be aware that the gap between privileged and underprivileged along the border and in this country—including Chicanos and millions of Mexicans and other Latino and Third World groups—has never been greater. There exists the real possibility that some regions of this country, especially California, like the Third World countries in Latin America and, indeed, South Africa, will be composed of a ruling minority and an underprivileged majority. Although these political and economic problems will not be solved in the very near future, it is true at this moment that we can no longer ignore the centuries old Mexican-*mestizo* presence in the Southwest. ✠  23

---

## RESPONDING

1. Calderón reports that many of his daily and seasonal activities as a child were "dictated by Mexican oral and written traditions handed down to our family by our grandmother" (paragraph 5). In a journal entry, write about the influence of cultural or family traditions on your childhood.

2. Working individually or in a group, define *border*. Compare your definition with Calderón's. Are there many different kinds of borders?

3. Write an essay explaining what Calderón means when he says "we were reminded of both what we were and what we were not" (paragraph 4). Support your explanation with evidence from the essay.

4. In an essay, discuss the way in which Lummis romanticized the Southwest. Compare his version of history with the presentations in the other readings in this chapter.

---

# Richard Rodriguez

*The essayist and cultural critic Richard Rodriguez, who was born in 1944, earned a bachelor's degree at Stanford University (1967) and a master's degree at Columbia University (1969). He pursued graduate studies at the University of California, Berkeley (1969–1972), and at the Warburg Institute in London (1972–1973). His first book,* Hunger of Memory *(1983), established Rodriguez's reputation as a writer; it also discloses his ideological positions, which often challenge those of the Chicano mainstream. His second book,* Days of Obligation *(1993), explores more personal issues, including sexual orientation. Currently working as an editor at the Pacific News Service and as a contributor to the* Newshour *on PBS, Rodriguez has also published work in a variety of journals.*

*The following essay reflects on the nature of the border as a metaphor for other divisions between North American and Latino American ideologies.*

# GO NORTH, YOUNG MAN

1   WE ALL SPEAK of North America. But has anyone ever actually met a North American? I know one.

2   Traditionally, America has been an east-west country. We have read our history, right to left across the page. We were oblivious of Canada. We barely noticed Mexico, except when Mexico got in the way of our westward migration, which we interpreted as the will of God, "manifest destiny."

3   In a Protestant country that believed in rebirth (the Easter promise), land became our metaphor for possibility. As long as there was land ahead of us—Ohio, Illinois, Nebraska—we could believe in change; we could abandon our in-laws, leave disappointments behind, to start anew further west. California

symbolized ultimate possibility, future-time, the end of the line, where loonies and prophets lived, where America's fads necessarily began.

Nineteenth-century real estate developers and 20th-century Hollywood moguls may have advertised the futuristic myth of California to the rest of America. But the myth was one Americans were predisposed to believe. The idea of California was invented by Americans many miles away.

Only a few early voices from California ever warned against optimism. Two decades after California became American territory, the conservationist John Muir stood at the edge of California and realized that America is a finite idea: We need to preserve the land, if the dream of America is to survive. Word of Muir's discovery slowly traveled backward in time, from the barely populated West (the future) to the crowded brick cities of the East Coast (the past).

I grew up in California of the 1950s, when the state was filling with people from New York and Oklahoma. Everyone was busy losing weight and changing hair color and becoming someone new. There was, then, still plenty of cheap land for tract houses, under the cloudless sky.

The 1950s, the 1960s—those years were our golden age. Edmund G. "Pat" Brown was governor of optimism. He created the University of California system, a decade before the children of the suburbs rebelled, portraying themselves as the "counterculture." Brown constructed freeways that permitted Californians to move farther and farther away from anything resembling an urban center. He even made the water run up the side of a mountain.

By the 1970s, optimism was running out of space. Los Angeles needed to reinvent itself as Orange County. Then Orange County got too crowded and had to reinvent itself as North County San Diego. Then Californians started moving into the foothills or out to the desert, complaining all the while of the traffic and of the soiled air. And the immigrants!

Suddenly, foreign immigrants were everywhere—Iranians were buying into Beverly Hills; the Vietnamese were moving into San Jose; the Chinese were taking all the spaces in the biochemistry courses at UCLA. And Mexicans, poor Mexicans, were making hotel beds, picking peaches in the Central Valley, changing diapers, even impersonating Italian chefs at Santa Monica restaurants.

The Mexicans and the Chinese had long inhabited California. But they never resided within the golden myth of the state. Nineteenth-century California restricted the Chinese to Chinatowns or to a city's outskirts. Mexicans were neither here nor there. They were imported by California to perform cheap labor, then deported in bad economic times.

The East Coast had incorporated Ellis Island in its myth. The West Coast regarded the non-European immigrant as doubly foreign. Though Spaniards may have colonized the place and though Mexico briefly claimed it, California took its meaning from "internal immigrants"—Americans from Minnesota or Brooklyn who came West to remake their parents' version of America.

But sometime in the 1970s, it became clear to many Californians that the famous blond myth of the state was in jeopardy. ("We are sorry to intrude, senor, we are only looking for work.") Was L.A. "becoming" Mexican?

13     Latin Americans arrived, describing California as "el norte." The "West Coast" was a finite idea; el norte in the Latin American lexicon means wide-open. Whose compass was right?

14     Meanwhile, with the lifting of anti-Asian immigration restrictions, jumbo jets were arriving at LAX from Bangkok and Seoul. People getting off the planes said about California, "This is where the United States begins." Californians objected, "No, no. California is where the United States comes to an end—we don't have enough room for you." Whose compass was truer?

15     It has taken two more decades for the East Coast to get the point. Magazines and television stories from New York today describe the golden state as "tarnished." The more interesting possibility is that California has become the intersection between comedy and tragedy. Foreign immigrants are replanting optimism on California soil; the native-born know the wisdom of finitude. Each side has a knowledge to give the other.

16     Already, everywhere in California, there is evidence of miscegenation—Keanu Reeves, sushi tacos, blond Buddhists, Salvadoran Pentecostals. But the forces that could lead to marriage also create gridlock on the Santa Monica freeway. The native-born Californian sits disgruntled in traffic going nowhere. The flatbed truck in front of him is filled with Mexicans; in the Mercedes next to him is a Japanese businessman using a car phone.

17     There are signs of backlash. Pete Wilson has become the last east-west governor of California. In a state founded by people seeking a softer winter and famous internationally for being "laid back," Californians vote for Proposition 187, hoping that illegal immigrants will stay away if there are no welfare dollars.

18     But immigrants are most disconcerting to California because they are everywhere working, transforming the ethos of the state from leisure to labor. Los Angeles is becoming a vast working city, on the order of Hong Kong or Mexico City. Chinese kids are raising the admission standards to the University of California. Mexican immigrant kids are undercutting union wages, raising rents in once-black neighborhoods.

19     Californians used to resist any metaphor drawn from their state's perennial earthquakes and floods and fires. Now Californians take their meaning from natural calamity. People turn away from the sea, imagine the future as existing backward in time.

20     "I'm leaving California, I'm going to Colorado."

21     "I'm headed for Arizona."

22     After hitting the coastline like flies against glass, we look in new directions. Did Southern California's urban sprawl invent NAFTA? For the first time, Californians now talk of the North and the South—new points on our national compass.

23     "I've just bought a condo in Baja."

24     "I'm leaving California for Seattle."

25     "I'm moving to Vancouver. I want someplace cleaner."

*"Go North, young man."*    26

Puerto Ricans, Mexicans: Early in this century we were immigrants. Or not    27
immigrants exactly. Puerto Ricans had awakened one day to discover that they
suddenly lived on U.S. territory. Mexicans had seen Mexico's northern territory
annexed and renamed the southwestern United States.

We were people from the South in an east-west country. We were people    28
of mixed blood in a black and white nation. We were Catholics in a Protestant
land. Many millions of us were Indians in an east-west country that imagined
the Indian to be dead.

Today, Los Angeles is the largest Indian city in the United States, though    29
Hollywood filmmakers persist in making movies about the dead Indian. (For
seven bucks, you can see cowboys slaughter Indians in the Kevin Costner
movie—and regret it from your comfortable chair.) On any day along Sunset
Boulevard you can see Toltecs and Aztecs and Mayans.

Puerto Ricans, Mexicans—we are the earliest Latin American immigrants    30
to the United States. We have turned into fools. We argue among ourselves,
criticize one another for becoming too much the gringo or maybe not gringo
enough. We criticize each other for speaking too much Spanish or not enough
Spanish. We demand that politicians provide us with bilingual voting ballots,
but we do not trouble to vote.

Octavio Paz, the Mexican writer, has observed that the Mexican-American    31
is caught between cultures, thus a victim of history—unwilling to become a
Mexican again, unable to belong to the United States. Michael Novak, the
United States writer, has observed that what unites people throughout the
Americas is that we all have said goodbye to our motherland. To Europe. To
Africa. To Asia. Farewell!

The only trouble is: Adios was never part of the Mexican-American or    32
Puerto Rican vocabulary. There was no need to turn one's back on the past.
Many have traveled back and forth, between rivals, between past and future,
commuters between the Third World and First. After a few months in New
York or Los Angeles, it would be time to head "home." After a few months
back in Mexico or Puerto Rico, it would be time to head "home" to the United
States.

We were nothing like the famous Ellis Island immigrants who arrived in    33
America with no expectation of return to the "old country." In a nation that
believed in the future, we were a puzzle.

We were also a scandal to Puerto Rico and Mexico. Our Spanish turned    34
bad. Our values were changing—though no one could say why or how exactly.
"Abuelita" (grandmother) complained that we were growing more guarded.
Alone.

There is a name that Mexico uses for children who have forgotten their    35
true address: "pocho." The pocho is the child who wanders away, ends up in
the United States, among the gringos, where he forgets his true home.

The Americas began with a confusion about maps and a joke about our    36 father's mistake. Columbus imagined himself in a part of the world where there were Indians.

37 We smile because our 15th-century "papi" thought he was in India. I'm not certain, however, that even today we know where in the world we live. We are only beginning to look at the map. We are only beginning to wonder what the map of the hemisphere might mean.

38 Latin Americans have long complained that the gringo, with characteristic arrogance, hijacked the word "American" and gave it all to himself—"the way he stole the land." I remember, years ago, my aunt in Mexico City scolding me when I told her I came from "America." Pocho! Didn't I realize that the entire hemisphere is America? "Listen," my Mexican aunt told me, "people who live in the United States are norteamericanos."

39 Well, I think to myself—my aunt is now dead, God rest her soul—I wonder what she would have thought a couple of years ago when the great leaders—the president of Mexico, the president of the United States, the Canadian prime minister—gathered to sign the North American Free Trade Agreement. Mexico signed a document acknowledging that she is a North American.

40 I predict that Mexico will suffer a nervous breakdown in the next 10 years. She will have to check into the Betty Ford Clinic for a long rest. She will need to determine just what exactly it means that she is, with the dread gringo, a norteamericana.

41 Canada, meanwhile, worries about the impact of the Nashville music channel on its cable TV; Pat Buchanan imagines a vast wall along our southern flank; and Mexican nationalists fear a Clinton bailout of the lowly peso.

42 We all speak of North America. But has anyone ever actually met a North American? Oh, there are Mexicans. And there are Canadians. And there are so-called Americans. But a North American?

43 I know one.

44 Let me tell you about him—this North American. He is a Mixteco Indian who comes from the Mexican state of Oaxaca. He is trilingual. His primary language is the language of his tribe. His second language is Spanish, the language of Cortes. Also, he has a working knowledge of U.S. English, because, for several months of the year, he works near Stockton, California.

45 He commutes over thousands of miles of dirt roads and freeways, knows several centuries, two currencies, two sets of hypocrisy. He is a criminal in one country and an embarrassment to the other. He is pursued as an "illegal" by the U.S. border patrol. He is preyed upon by Mexican officers who want to shake him down because he has hidden U.S. dollars in his shoes.

46 In Oaxaca, he lives in a 16th-century village, where his wife watches blond Venezuelan soap operas. A picture of la Virgen de Guadalupe rests over his bed. In Stockton, there is no Virgin Mary, only the other Madonna—the material girl.

47 He is the first North American.

48 A journalist once asked Chou En-lai, the Chinese premier under Mao

Zedong, what he thought of the French Revolution. Chou En-lai gave a wonderful Chinese reply. "It's too early to tell."

I think it may even be too early to tell what the story of Columbus means. 49
The latest chapter of the Columbus saga may be taking place right now, as Latin American teenagers with Indian faces violate the U.S. border. The Mexican kids standing on the line tonight between Tijuana and San Diego—if you ask them why they are coming to the United States of America, they will not say anything about Thomas Jefferson or The Federalist Papers. They have only heard that there is a job in a Glendale dry cleaner's or that some farmer is hiring near Fresno.

They insist: They will be returning to Mexico in a few months. They are 50
only going to the United States for the dollars. They certainly don't intend to become gringos. They don't want anything to do with the United States, except the dollars.

But the months will pass, and the teenagers will be changed in the United 51
States. When they go back to their Mexican village, they will no longer be easy. They will expect an independence and an authority that the village cannot give them. Much to their surprise, they will have been Americanized by the job in Glendale.

For work in the United States is our primary source of identity. There is 52
no more telling question we Americans ask one another than "What do you do?" We do not ask about family or village or religion. We ask about work.

The Mexican teenagers will return to Glendale. 53

Mexicans, Puerto Ricans—most of us end up in the United States, living in 54
the city. Peasants end up in the middle of a vast modern metropolis, having known only the village, with its three blocks of familiar facades.

The arriving generation is always the bravest. New immigrants often change 55
religion with their move to the city. They need to make their peace with isolation, so far from relatives. They learn subway and bus routes that take them far from home every day. Long before they can read English, they learn how to recognize danger and opportunity. Their lives are defined by change.

Their children or their grandchildren become, often, very different. The 56
best and the brightest, perhaps, will go off to college—become the first in their family—but they talk about "keeping" their culture. They start speaking Spanish, as a way of not changing; they eat in the cafeteria only with others who look like themselves. They talk incessantly about "culture" as though it were some little thing that can be preserved and kept in a box.

The unluckiest children of immigrants drop out of high school. They speak 57
neither good English nor Spanish. Some end up in gangs—family, man—"blood." They shoot other kids who look exactly like themselves. If they try to leave their gang, the gang will come after them for their act of betrayal. If they venture to some other part of the city, they might get shot or they might merely be unable to decipher the freeway exits that speed by.

58    They retreat to their "turf"—three blocks, just like in their grandmother's village, where the journey began.

59    One of the things that Mexico had never acknowledged about my father—I insist that you at least entertain the idea—is the possibility that my father and others like him were the great revolutionaries of Mexico. Pocho pioneers. They, not Pancho Villa, not Zapata, were heralds of the modern age in Mexico. They left for the United States and then they came back to Mexico. And they changed Mexico forever.

60    A childhood friend of my father's—he worked in Chicago in the 1920s, then returned one night to his village in Michoacan with appliances for mamasita and crisp dollars. The village gathered round him—this is a true story—and asked, "What is it like up there in Chicago?"

61    The man said, "It's OK."

62    That rumor of "OK" spread across Michoacan, down to Jalisco, all the way down to Oaxaca, from village to village to village.

63    Futurists and diplomats talk about a "new moment in the Americas." The Latin American elite have condos in Miami and send their children to Ivy League schools. U.S. and Canadian businessmen project the future on a north-south graph. But for many decades before any of this, Latin American peasants have been traveling back and forth, north and south.

64    Today, there are remote villages in Latin America that are among the most international places on earth. Tiny Peruvian villages know when farmers are picking pears in the Yakima valley in Washington state.

65    I am the son of a prophet. I am a fool. I am a victim of history. I am confused. I do not know whether I am coming or going. I speak bad Spanish. And yet I tell Latin America this: Because I grew up Hispanic in California, I know more Guatemalans than I would if I had grown up in Mexico, more Brazilians than if I lived in Peru. Because I live in California, it is routine for me to know Nicaraguans and Salvadorans and Cubans. As routine as knowing Chinese or Vietnamese.

66    My fellow Californians complain loudly about the uncouth southern invasion. I say this to California: Immigration is always illegal. It is a rude act, the leaving of home. Immigration begins as a violation of custom, a youthful act of defiance, an insult to the village. I know a man from El Salvador who has not spoken to his father since the day he left his father's village. Immigrants horrify the grandmothers they leave behind.

67    Illegal immigrants trouble U.S. environmentalists and Mexican nationalists. Illegal immigrants must trouble anyone, on either side of the line, who imagines that the poor are under control.

68    But they have also been our civilization's prophets. They, long before the rest of us, saw the hemisphere whole. ❖

RESPONDING

1. In a journal entry, write about an event in your life that changed you. It might be when you began high school or college, or when you moved to another place. What was the effect of the change?

2. Working individually or in a group, use the Internet to trace the history of the relationship of the United States with Mexico.

3. In an essay explain what Rodriguez means when he says,

   > Illegal immigrants must trouble anyone, on either side of the line, who imagines that the poor are under control.
   >     But they have also been our civilization's prophets. They, long before the rest of us, saw the hemisphere whole. (paragraphs 67–68)

4. Write an essay discussing the problems immigrants have adapting to their new culture. If they successfully adapt, what effect does this have on them when they visit or return to their native land?

# AL MARTINEZ

*Columnist Al Martinez, who was born in 1949, attended San Francisco State College (1947–1950) and the University of California, Berkeley (1952–1953), before entering the field of journalism. After writing for the* Oakland Tribune *from 1955 to 1972, he joined the* Los Angeles Times, *where he has worked as a feature writer. In addition to publishing two books,* Rising Voices *(1974) and* Jigsaw *(1975), he has written for television and film.*

*In the following column, Martinez explores the prejudices with which people confront each other.*

# IT'S A MAD, MAD, MAD, MAD WORLD

IT DOESN'T TAKE A LOT OF ENERGY to hate. When you stop to think about it, it's a lot easier than loving or laughing. Hatred doesn't require a high IQ and, in fact, is defeated by too much smart.

All you've got to do is sit there and let the heat wash over you like the cozy warmth of an approaching brush fire. Well, yes, eventually the fire's going to get you, but meanwhile it feels *sooo* good.

3    Even acting out hatred is fairly easy. How much work can it be to write a letter, burn a cross, paint a swastika, carry a sign . . . or pull a trigger?

4    Beating someone requires a bit more sweat, but if you do it in a group it spreads out the energy requirements, right? That's why war works.

5    I'm thinking about this because I'm sort of wrapping things up before going on vacation. We're heading for China and hatred is on my mind.

6    It seems like only yesterday during the Korean War that we were supposed to be hating the Chinese. I never did hate anybody, but you couldn't avoid the propaganda. Now I'm going over there to say, you know, no hard feelings.

7    You shot at me and I shot at you and, thank God, we both missed.

8    That's the way the world works. One minute we're supposed to be despising someone like the Germans or the Japanese or the Chinese or the Russians, and the next minute we're drinking and singing together. Go figure.

9    Hatred seems to come in waves. I'm suddenly receiving mail, both electronically and otherwise, in which the letter-writers find it necessary to take on what they refer to as "your people."

10   They figure that My People are coming across the border in such numbers and gaining such power that pretty soon all the rest of you are going to either be driven into the sea or forced to live on refried beans the rest of your wretched lives.

11   I'll try smuggling in some onion bagels now and again, but I'm not promising anything.

12   Then there's the filth. My People, one man e-mailed me, are trashing America. He's particularly upset at finding soiled diapers stuffed into the shelves of supermarkets behind the macaroni and cheese.

13   I don't think he's saying the stores are selling used diapers. He means My People are putting them there after changing the baby because they're too damned ignorant to know what to do with them.

14   The man says he knows it's My People doing it because he saw the same thing in Mexico City. What he doesn't understand is that it's a cultural tradition. I haven't changed a baby's diaper in a long time, but when I did, I always looked for a supermarket to dispose of the dirty ones.

15   I preferred Ralphs, but Lucky was OK too.

16   One writer proclaimed that the reason My People always get the lousy jobs is because we are mentally impaired. Well, actually, "impeared" is the way he spelled it. He is, of course, correct.

17   I didn't do all that good in school because I was always dreaming of things like senoritas and mama's homemade tortillas, and look how I ended up. If only I'd have concentrated more, I could've had a nice job delivering mail and shooting up a post office somewhere.

But, hey, it wasn't my intention today to dwell on hatreds. I'm too busy  18
trying to find clothes that'll dry overnight to worry about angry gringos. Cinelli,
my wife, is trying to get me to pack light for our China trip, but I'm not taking
anything flimsy.

"That's woman's wear," I said when she held up a pair of silk undershorts  19
at Robinsons-May.

"But they're *soooo* sexy," she whispered. Her hot breath tickled my ear. So  20
I got 200 pair.

Her assumption is that the Chinese are tired of their Rickshaw Reputation  21
and we're probably going to have to carry our own luggage. Silk shorts and
nylon shirts lighten the load.

I don't blame them. My People are already becoming weary of cleaning  22
houses and shlepping burgers. They're reaching up. They're contributing.
They're keeping dirty diapers off the supermarket shelves.

The world is changing. New hatreds emerge along with new accommoda-  23
tions. Loving, because it requires patience and understanding, is more difficult
than hating. But we're getting there.

I'll do my part in Beijing. Everybody drink up. This round's on me.  24
*Salud!* ✠

## RESPONDING

1. In a journal entry, write a letter to the editor responding to Martinez's
   newspaper column.

2. Working individually or in a group, define the term *satire*. Discuss whether
   this column fits the definition and if it does, which parts are satirical.

3. In an essay, agree or disagree that satire or humor is an effective way to
   argue a point or to explain a position on an issue. Use examples from the
   reading to show why satire or humor is or is not effective in changing a
   reader's mind. You may want to use your own response to this column as
   support for your argument.

4. Write your own satirical or humorous column on a topic that arouses strong
   emotion in you.

⁜

# CONNECTING

### Critical Thinking and Writing

1.   Analyze the role economic realities play in the lives of the characters in this chapter. How do the financial situations limit or restrict their choices?

2.   A variety of women characters appear in this chapter. Choose two and compare their ways of coping with life's challenges. Or classify the women according to the way they respond to difficult situations. What elements might account for these different responses? Consider the women's personalities, characters, social circumstances, education, and economic situations.

3.   Compare the images of the traditional roles of men and women that emerge from the readings in this chapter. Which characters conform and which rebel against these roles?

4.   Eduviges in Arturo Islas's *Migrant Souls* has very different attitudes toward American Indians and Mexican Indians. Compare these attitudes and explain why someone might find her statements ironic. Do you think her views are widespread in American society?

5.   Working in a group, generate a list of essay questions based on issues raised in this chapter. Share your list with the class. Choose one question and answer it in an essay.

6.   Many of the older generation portrayed in these stories are bewildered by the changes taking place around them, though some accept change more easily than others. Compare the different ways the older people in the readings in this text deal with adjusting to life in America.

7.   Examine the role economic realities play in the lives of the early immigrants, American Indians, or any other group and compare their circumstances with those of Chicanos in the 1940s and 1950s.

8.   Using information from the readings, identify gender roles in two particular cultures during a specific period such as the Chicanos in the 1940s and 1950s, Jews in the late 1800s, or Chinese in the 1930s and 1940s and compare them to each other. Or identify gender roles for one group during a specific period and compare them to gender roles for that group in the present.

9.   Compare barriers that Chicanos faced in the 1950s with the problems faced

by other groups such as early immigrants, Japanese Americans during World War II, or African Americans before desegregation. What barriers still exist today that might prevent people from getting an education despite their desire to do so? Write an essay presenting the problems and suggesting solutions.

10. Adjusting to a new country means adjusting to a new culture and often a new language. For older people such an adjustment is often difficult, while younger people frequently adapt more quickly. This can cause conflict between the new values the children hold and the traditional values parents retain. Write an essay illustrating the difficulties that arise within families when children begin to move away from the beliefs of their parents. Use examples from this chapter and others in the text.

11. Choose one situation from the readings in this chapter, for example, the plight of Cleófilas in "Woman Hollering Creek" or of doña María in "La Noche Buena," and write a column about it in the style of Al Martinez.

### For Further Research

1. Use the Internet to research the current situation of migrant workers. Who are they? What are their working conditions? What organizations support them? What is their legal status?

2. Research the Chicano Moratorium Movement.

3. Explore the concept of *la raza* and its implication for various Chicano communities.

## REFERENCES AND ADDITIONAL SOURCES

Arce, Carlos H. "A Reconsideration of Chicano Culture and Identity." *Daedalus*, Spring 1981: 177–92.

*Aztlán: Essay on the Chicano Homeland*, Rudolfo A. Anaya and Francisco Lomeli, eds. Albuquerque: University of New Mexico Press, 1989.

Bruce-Novoa, Juan D. *Chicano Authors: Inquiry by Interview*. Austin: University of Texas Press, 1980.

————. *Chicano Poetry: A Response to Chaos*. Austin: University of Texas Press, 1982.

————. *RetroSpace: Collected Essays on Chicano Literature, Theory, and History*. Houston: Arte Publico Press, 1990.

Calderón, Héctor. "At the Crossroads of History, On the Borders of Change: Chicano Literary Studies Past, Present and Future," in *Left Politics and the Literary Profession*,

M. Bella Mirabella and Lennard J. Davis, eds. New York: Columbia University Press, 1990.

Castro, Tony. *Chicano Power: The Emergence of Mexican America.* New York: Saturday Review, 1974.

Durán, Livie Isauro, and J. Russell Bernard. *Introduction to Chicano Studies: A Reader.* New York: Macmillan, 1973.

Estrada, Leobardo F., et al. "Chicanos in the United States: A History of Exploitation and Resistance." *Daedalus,* Spring 1981: 103–32.

García, Mario T. "Introduction" to *Border Correspondent,* by Ruben Salazar. Berkeley: University of California Press, 1995.

Garlaza, Ernesto. *Merchants of Labor: The Mexican Bracero Story: An Account of the Managed Migration of the Mexican Farm Workers in California, 1942–1960.* Charlotte and Santa Barbara, Calif.: McNally and Loftin, 1964; McNally and Loftin, West, 1978.

Gonzales, Manuel G. *Mexicanos: A History of Mexicans in the United States.* Bloomington: Indiana University Press, 1999.

Gutierrez, David G., ed. *Between Two Worlds: Mexican Immigrants in the United States.* Wilmington, Del.: Scholarly Resources, Inc., 1996.

———. *Walls and Mirrors: Mexican Americans, Mexican Immigrants, and the Politics of Ethnicity.* Berkeley: University of California Press, 1995.

Hernández, Guillermo. *Chicano Satire: A Study in Literary Culture.* Austin: University of Texas Press, 1991.

Herrera-Sobek, Maria. *Northward Bound: The Mexican Immigrant Experience in Ballad and Song.* Bloomington: Indiana University Press, 1993.

Herrera-Sobek, Maria, and Helena Maria Viramontes, eds. *Chicana Creativity and Criticism: Charting New Frontiers in American Literature.* Houston: Arte Publico Press, 1993.

Limón, Graciela. *In Search of Bernabé.* Houston: Arte Publico Press, 1993.

López, Tiffany Ana, ed. *Growing Up Chicano: An Anthology.* New York: Morrow, 1993.

McKenna, Teresa. *Migrant Song: Politics and Process in Contemporary Chicano Literature.* Austin: University of Texas Press, 1997.

McWilliams, Carey. *North from Mexico: The Spanish Speaking People of the United States.* Philadelphia: JB Lippincott Co., 1949; Westport, Conn.: Greenwood Press, 1968, 1990.

Meier, Matt S., and Feliciano Rivera. *The Chicanos: A History of Mexican Americans.* New York: Hill and Wang, 1972.

Moquin, Wayne, and Charles Van Doren, eds. *A Documentary History of the Mexican Americans.* New York: Praeger, 1971; New York: Bantam, 1972.

Paredes, Raymúnd. "The Evolution of Chicano Literature," in *Three American Literatures:*

*Essays in Chicano, Native American, and Asian-American Literature for Teachers of American Literature*, Houston A. Baker, Jr., ed. New York: Modern Language Association of America, 1982.

Rebolledo, Tey Diana. *Women Singing in the Snow: A Cultural Analysis of Chicana Literature*. Tucson: University of Arizona Press, 1995.

Rendon, Armando. *Chicano Manifesto*. New York: Macmillan, 1971; New York: Collier, 1972.

Saldívar, Ramon. *Chicano Narrative: The Dialects of Difference*. Madison: University of Wisconsin Press, 1990.

Servin, Manuel P. *An Awkward Minority: The Mexican Americans*, 2nd ed. New York: Macmillan, 1974; Beverly Hills, Calif.: Glencoe Press, 1974.

Soto, Gary, ed. *Pieces of the Heart: New Chicano Fiction*. San Francisco: Chronicle Books, 1993.

Tantum, Charles M. *Chicano Literature*. Boston: Twayne, 1982.

# 9

## THE NEW IMMIGRANTS

*Reviving, Challenging, and Refashioning the American Dream*

*Above: Anywhere in Europe 1933–45,* Gertrude Jacobson. Acrylic and steel barbed wire on board, 34 x 44 x 4 inches. A memorial to Holocaust victims. *(Courtesy of the Yad Vashem Art Museum, Jerusalem, Israel)*

*Opposite:* Kosevar-Albanian refugees. *(Vincent DeWitt / Stock, Boston)*

# SETTING THE HISTORICAL AND CULTURAL CONTEXT

THE NOTION OF THE AMERICAN DREAM has been rediscovered, revived, and refashioned in the works of newer immigrants. In the excerpt from his novel *Our House in the Lost World*, Oscar Hijuelos describes a recent immigrant's reaction to the abundance of material goods that he finds in his relative's Americanized kitchen:

> There was so much of everything! Milk and wine and beer, steaks and rice and chicken and sausages and ham and plantains and ice cream and black bean soup and Pepsi Cola and Hershey chocolate bars and almond nougat, and popcorn, and Wise potato chips and Jiffy peanut butter, and rum and whiskey, marshmallows, spaghetti, flan and pasteles and chocolate cake and pie, more than enough to make them delirious. And even though the walls were cracked and it was dark, there was a television set and a radio and light-bulbs and toilet paper and pictures of the family and crucifixes and tooth-paste and soap and more.

The exhaustive list is both a celebration and a mocking of the limitless consumer opportunities the immigrant discovers in the United States. The profusion of material goods, the seemingly unlimited choices sharply contrast with the shortages and rationing of the old country.

But with new economic opportunity often comes a new kind of confusion, as Hijuelos suggests: "It was 'Thank God for freedom and bless my family' from Luisa's mouth, but her daughters were more cautious. . . . In the food-filled kitchen Alejo told them how happy he was to have them in his house, and they were happy because the old misery was over, but they were still without a home and in a strange world. Uncertainty showed in their faces." Such disorientation is reflected in several of the other selections in this chapter, among them Carlos Bulosan's "My Education," which traces the speaker's personal transition from what he terms "rootlessness" to a feeling of "growing and becoming a living part of America."

Since World War II, persons of many nationalities have sought refuge in the United States. Among these were individuals displaced by the war, including many survivors of the Holocaust. Refugees from oppressive regimes in China, the Soviet Union, eastern Europe, and Greece sought political asylum in the late 1940s and early 1950s. During the 1960s Cubans took *vuelos de libertad* (freedom flights) to escape the regime of Fidel Castro; the Mariél Boat Lift of the late 1970s allowed other Cubans to leave their homeland. The fall of Saigon in 1975 led many Vietnamese to emigrate. During the late 1970s and 1980s Central Americans fled oppressive regimes and death squads. Since the massacre at Tiananmen Square in 1989, many Chinese nationals, already in the nation on student visas, have sought to extend their stays on the grounds of political asylum. The collapse of the Berlin Wall, the disintegration of the Soviet Union, and the ethnic cleansing wars that have been taking place throughout eastern Europe have led still others to seek entry.

During the past fifty years, the U.S. government has responded to these demands in various ways. Indeed, the nation has seemed more welcoming at some times than at others. The federal government has passed legislation to increase immigration quotas for some groups and to provide asylum for others. During the 1940s, for example, President Roosevelt ordered that immigration quotas be increased for persons fleeing political persecution. After World War II, the Truman administration granted new immigration privileges to so-called displaced persons. The Refugee Relief Act of 1953, passed during the Eisenhower administration, allowed for the admission of those fleeing communist regimes. This process continued in the 1970s, with the admission of the Vietnamese "boat people," and the Mariél refugees from Cuba. After the Tiananmen Square massacre, President Bush signed an executive order allowing some of the student refugees from China to remain in the United States after the time designated on their visas.

The United States has offered amnesty to persons seeking refuge from political persecution. Those who have entered the country illegally, but who feel that they are victims of political persecution, have sometimes been given refuge as well. The Immigration and Nationality Act of 1980, for example, outlines a procedure whereby those persons who fear for their lives can seek amnesty from deportation. Nonetheless, because of legislation dating back to the Cold War, immigrants are still subject to deportation even after they have become American citizens. Many immigration policy experts contend that the enforcement and administration of immigration laws—with their continued focus on foreign policy toward the country of origin, rather than on the applicant's own situation—are often arbitrary and unfair. The essay by Peter H. Schuck, which concludes this chapter, explores some of the elements of the controversial issue of "national origin."

Earlier chapters of this book have shown the promise of America often threatened by periods of exclusionary legislation and anti-immigrant sentiment. During periods of austerity, for example, unions have regarded an influx of immigrant labor to be a threat to job security. Those associating refugees and immigrants with the potential for subversive activity have lobbied to keep out of the country anyone who would question the government or participate in "un-American activities." Exclusionists have traditionally cited isolated events as proof of an imminent threat from "foreigners." Some of the more famous of these events include the Haymarket Riots of 1886, in which mostly German-speaking immigrants involved in a Chicago labor protest were blamed for instigating a violent uprising that claimed several lives; the Sacco and Vanzetti case of 1920, in which two Italian immigrants were executed for a murder that they might not have committed (indeed, they were exonerated of the crimes by then-governor Michael Dukakis, in 1977, fifty years after they had been put to death); and the World Trade Center explosion of 1992, which has been cited by many who would endorse stricter enforcement of immigration laws.

In the late 1980s and early 1990s, exclusionary legislation increased. In 1986, Congress passed the Immigration Reform and Control Act, which required that anyone employed in the United States be able to prove his or her legal status; the act also offered amnesty to those undocumented workers who had crossed the border before 1982. Although an immigration act passed in 1990 had raised the number of immigrants allowed entry to the United States to 700,000, that number was reduced by 25,000 five years later. In 1993, Congress considered several bills that sought to lengthen the sponsorship period required for new immigrants. Many of the selections in this chapter can be read in the context of the often conflicting social values presented by the U.S. government and its people.

Several readings discuss the motivations for immigration to the United States. Carlos Bulosan's essay mentions the colonialist system of absentee land ownership, which "had shattered the life and future of [his] generation" during the first decades of the twentieth century, and Oscar Hijuelos's fiction depicts a family's disillusionment with communism. The poetry of José Alejandro Romero describes one of the atrocities believed to have been committed by the right-wing totalitarian regime that ruled El Salvador during the late 1970s and 1980s.

Other readings explore the consequences of immigration, on both economic and psychological levels. Van B. Luu's essay discusses the difficulties that refugees from Vietnam sometimes experience in adjusting to life in a new country, among them separation from their family and a form of "survivor's guilt." In addition to exploring the newcomer's disorientation, Bulosan makes use of personal narrative to reflect on the kinship he developed with other artists, intellectuals, and "disinherited persons." Bharati Mukherjee explores some of the consequences of this change in orientation and alteration in the pace of life, suggesting as well the ways in which one's habits, protocols, and rules of conduct may become modified in a new country. Indeed, the tension in her story derives from a misinterpretation of those protocols.

In several readings, the issue is not so much a choice between one option and another, but a negotiation among alternatives. Many of the works in this chapter, including those by Cathy Song and Naomi Shihab Nye, stress a kind of communal experience, a ritual act that helps to provide a sense of memory and continuity and escape. Language can also allow one to come to terms with what Nye has called "the burden and the gift" that is one's culture.

The act of writing is itself an act of exchange and transformation. The immigrant writer and the reader from the dominant culture exchange positions of centrality and marginality. At the same time there is another kind of transformation, a new kind of fusing. As Mukherjee says in the preface to her collection, "I see my 'immigrant story' replicated in a dozen American cities, and instead of seeing my Indianness as a fragile entity to be preserved . . . I see it now as a set of fluid identities to be celebrated. I see myself as in the tradition of other immigrant writers [telling] stories of broken identities and discarded languages, and the will to bond oneself to a new community, against the ever present fear of failure and betrayal." In this way the new immigrant participates in the continual reshaping of the multiethnic culture of the United States.

---

## BEGINNING: Pre-reading/Writing

*Throughout its history, the United States has often been a haven for citizens of other countries who are seeking improved political and economic conditions. Working individually or in a group, speculate about recent political and economic situations in specific countries that might prompt their citizens to emigrate. Discuss why they might choose to come to the United States, the possible problems of immigrating here, and the difficulties they would face once they arrive.*

---

*Some people immigrate to the United States for political and religious reasons. In fleeing their repressive governments, they fear for their lives if they are denied entry to our country and are forced to return to their homelands. This section of the Immigration and Nationality Act (1980) outlines the procedures whereby individuals can apply for political asylum. If asylum is denied, the applicant may appeal the decision, first to the Immigration Court and then to the Board of Immigration Appeals. In rare cases, the appeal process has been taken as far as the Supreme Court.*

# From **IMMIGRATION AND NATIONALITY ACT OF 1980**

## *Asylum Procedure*

SEC. 208. [8 U.S.C. 1158] (a) The Attorney General shall establish a procedure for an alien physically present in the United States or at a land border or port of entry, irrespective of such alien's status, to apply for asylum, and the alien may be granted asylum in the discretion of the Attorney General if the Attorney General determines that such alien is a refugee within the meaning of section 101(a)(42)(A).

2     (b) Asylum granted under subsection (a) may be terminated if the Attorney General, pursuant to such regulations as the Attorney General may prescribe, determines that the alien is no longer a refugee within the meaning of section 101(a)(42)(A) owing to a change in circumstances in the alien's country of nationality or, in the case of an alien having no nationality, in the country in which the alien last habitually resided.

3     (c) A spouse or child (as defined in section 101(b)(1)(A), (B), (C), (D), or (E)) of an alien who is granted asylum under subsection (a) may, if not otherwise eligible for asylum under such subsections, be granted the same status as the alien if accompanying, or following to join, such alien.

### Adjustment of Status of Refugees

4     SEC. 209. [8 U.S.C. 1159] (a)(1) Any alien who has been admitted to the United States under section 207—

5     (A) whose admission has not been terminated by the Attorney General pursuant to such regulations as the Attorney General may prescribe,

6     (B) who has been physically present in the United States for at least one year, and

7     (C) who has not acquired permanent resident status, shall, at the end of such year period, return or be returned to the custody of the Service for inspection and examination for admission to the United States as an immigrant in accordance with the provisions of sections 235, 236, and 237.

8     (2) Any alien who is found upon inspection and examination by an immigration officer pursuant to paragraph (1) or after a hearing before a special inquiry officer to be admissible (except as otherwise provided under subsection (c)) as an immigrant under this Act at the time of the alien's inspection and examination shall, notwithstanding any numerical limitation specified in this Act, be regarded as lawfully admitted to the United States for permanent residence as of the date of such alien's arrival into the United States. ✢

---

## RESPONDING

1.  In a journal entry, explain the provisions of the asylum regulations in your own words. If you were writing the law, how would you define *refugee*?

2.  Working individually or in a group, discuss the reasons why your family members came to the United States. Was it difficult for them to enter the country? What were immigration policies during that period? If you don't know the answers to these questions, consider *why* you don't know. Were your relatives unwilling to talk about their experiences? Why might that be?

3. Write about the experience of someone you know or have read, studied, or heard about who has had to seek asylum in the United States. What circumstances caused this person to leave his or her country? How do you think the circumstances of immigration affected his or her adjustment?

4. What do you think the U.S. policy should be regarding immigration? Who should be granted asylum? Choose a historical event such as the massacre in Rwanda and discuss whether we should give asylum to participants in that event.

# Carlos Bulosan

*Novelist and essayist Carlos Bulosan was born in the Philippines in 1903. After immigrating to the United States in 1930, he wrote several books, including* Letter from America *(1942) and* America Is in the Heart *(1946), which enjoyed substantial popularity during the 1940s. In addition to writing, he worked to support the Filipino labor movement, particularly on the West Coast. Bulosan died in 1956. His work has recently been reissued and edited by E. San Juan Jr.*

*In the following essay, Bulosan not only reflects on his process of self-education, but also describes how changes in the American political climate have affected his perceptions of his environment and of himself.*

⁜

# MY EDUCATION

I CAME TO AMERICA sixteen years ago from the village where I was born in the Philippines. In reality it was only the beginning of a tortuous search for roots in a new world. I hated absentee-landlordism, not only because it had driven my family from our home and scattered us, but also because it had shattered the life and future of my generation. This system had originated in Spanish times when most of the arable lands and navigable waters were controlled by the church and powerful men in the government. It came down [through] our history and threatened the security of the peasantry till it became a blight in our national life.

But now that I was in America I felt a vague desire to see what I had not seen in my country. I did not know how I would approach America. I only knew that there must be a common denominator which every immigrant or native

American should look for in order to understand her and be of service to her people. I felt like Columbus embarking upon a long and treacherous voyage. I felt like Icarus escaping from prison to freedom. I did not know that I was coming closer to American *reality.*

3      I worked for three months in an apple orchard in Sunnyside, in the state of Washington. The labor movement was under persecution and the minorities became the natural scapegoat. Toward the end I was disappointed. I had worked on a farm all my life in the Philippines, and now I was working on a farm again. I could not compromise my picture of America with the filthy bunkhouses in which we lived and the falling wooden houses in which the natives lived. This was not the America I wanted to see, but it was the first great lesson in my life.

4      I moved to another town and found work on a farm again. Then again I moved to another farm town. I followed the crops and the seasons, from Washington to Oregon to California, until I had worked in every town on the Pacific Coast. In the end I was sick with despair. Wherever I went I found the same horror, the same anguish and fear.

5      I began to ask if this was the real America—and if it was, why did I come? I was sad and confused. But I believed in the other men before me who had come and stayed to discover America. I knew they came because there was something in America which needed them and which they needed. Yet slowly I began to doubt the *promise* that was America.

6      If it took me almost a decade to dispel this doubt, it was because it took me that long to catch a glimpse of the *real* America. The nebulous and dynamic qualities of the dream took hold of me immensely. It became the periscope of my search for roots in America. I was driven back to history. But going back to history was actually a return to the early beginnings of America.

7      I had picked hops with some Indians under the towering shadow of Mt. Rainier. I had pruned apples with the dispossessed Americans in the rich deltas of the Columbia River. I had cut and packed asparagus in California. I had weeded peas with Japanese in Arizona. I had picked tomatoes with Negroes in Utah. Yet I felt that I did not belong in America. My departure from the Philippines was actually the breaking of my ground, the tearing up of my roots. As I stayed longer and searched farther, this feeling of not belonging became more acute, until it distorted my early vision of America. I did not know what part of America was mine, and my awareness of not belonging made me desperate and terribly lonely.

8      The next two years were like a nightmare. There were sixteen million unemployed. I joined these disinherited Americans. Again I saw the rich fields and wide flat lands. I saw them from the top of a passing freight train. Sometimes I saw them from the back of a truck. I became more confused and rootless.

9      I was sick with despair. I was paralyzed with fear. Everywhere I went I saw the shadow of this country falling. I saw it in the anguish of girls who cried at night. I saw it in the abstract stares of unemployed workers. I saw it in the

hollow eyes of children. I saw it in the abuses suffered by immigrants. I saw it in the persecution of the minorities. *I heard some men say that this was America—the dream betrayed. They told me that America was done for—dead. I fought against believing them. Yet, when I was socially strangled, I almost believed what they said about America—that she was dead.*

I do not recall how I actually started to identify myself with America. The   10
men and women around me were just as rootless as I was in those years. I spent the next two years reading in public libraries. How well I remember those long cold nights of winter and the months of unemployment. Perhaps the gambling houses that opened only at night with one free meal for everybody—perhaps reading at the libraries in the daytime and waiting for the dark to hide my dirty clothes in the streets—perhaps all these terrible humiliations gave me the courage to fight through it all, until the months passed into years of hope and the *will* to proceed became obdurate and illumined with a sincere affinity for America. Finally, I realized that the great men who contributed something positive to the growth of America also suffered and were lonely.

I read more books, and became convinced that it was the duty of the artist   11
to trace the origins of the disease that was festering American life. I was beginning to be aware of the dynamic social ideas that were disturbing the minds of leading artists and writers in America. I felt angry with those who fled from her. I hated the expatriates in Paris and Madrid. I studied Whitman with naive anticipations, hoping to find in him an affirmation of my growing faith in America. For a while I was inclined to believe that Whitman was the key to my search for roots. And I found that he also was terribly lonely, and he wrote of an America that would be.

I began to wonder about those who stayed in America and suffered the   12
narrowness of the society in which they lived. I read Melville and Poe, who chose to live and work in a narrow world. I became intimate with their humiliations and defeats, their hopes and high moments of success. Then I began to hate the crass materialism of our age and the powerful chains and combines that strangled human life and made the world a horrible place to live in. Slowly, I was beginning to feel that I had found a place in America. The fight to hold onto this feeling convinced me that I was becoming a growing part of living America.

It was now toward the end of 1935, and the trade union movement was in   13
turmoil. The old American Federation of Labor was losing power and a new union was being born. I started to write my own impressions of America. Now I was beginning to give meaning to my life. It was a discovery of America and myself. Being able to write, now, was a personal triumph and a definite identification with a living tradition. I began to recognize the forces that had driven many Americans to other countries and had made those who stayed at home homeless. *Those who went away never escaped from themselves; those who stayed at home never found themselves.*

I [was] determined to find out why the artist took flight or revolted against   14 his heritage. Then, [while] doing organization work among agricultural workers, I fell sick with a disease caused by the years of hunger and congested living. I was forced to lie in a hospital for more than two years. Now, all that I had won seemed irrelevant to my life. Here I was dying—six years after my arrival in America. What was wrong? Was America so dislocated that she had no more place for the immigrant?

15    I could not believe that the resources of this country were exhausted. I almost died in the hospital. I survived death because I was determined to convince those who had lost faith in America. I knew in convincing them I would be convincing myself that America was not dead.

16    The Civil War in Spain was going on: it was another factor that gave coherence to the turmoil and confusion in my life. The ruthless bombings of churches and hospitals by German and Italian planes clarified some of my beliefs. I believe that this intellectual and spiritual participation in the Spanish conflict fired in me a new vision of life.

17    It was at this period that the Congress of Industrial Organizations came to power in industry. At last its militant stand in labor disputes re-invigorated me. Some of my democratic beliefs were confirmed. I felt that I had found the mainsprings of American democracy. In this feeling I found some coherence and direction and the impulse to create became more ardent and necessary.

18    America's most articulate artists were stirring. They refused to follow the example of those who went into voluntary exile and those who stayed at home and were angry with America. They knew that they could truly work if they stayed near their roots and walked proudly in familiar streets. They no longer created alone. They framed a program broad enough to cover the different aspects of their needs and abilities. It was not a *vow* to write for art's sake.

19    I found a new release. I reacted to it as a sensitive artist of my generation without losing my firm belief that America was happy and alive if her artists were happy and alive. But Spain was lost and a grand dream was lost with her. The equilibrium of the world was dislocated, and the writers were greatly affected by the setback of democratic forces.

20    I tried in the next two years to work with the progressive forces. But some of the organizations dribbled into personal quarrels and selfish motives. There were individuals who were saturated with the false values of capitalism and the insidiousness of their bourgeois prejudices poisoned their whole thinking. I became convinced that they could not liberate America from decay. And I became doubly convinced, as Hitler seized one country after another, that their prejudices must be challenged by a stronger faith in America.

21    We were now moving toward the end of another decade. Writing was not sufficient. Labor demanded the active collaboration of writers. In the course of eight years I had relived the whole course of American history. I drew inspiration from my active participation in the workers' movement. The most decisive move that the writer could make was to take his stand with the workers.

22    I had a preliminary knowledge of American history to guide me. What could

I do? I had read *Gone With the Wind,* and saw the extent of the lie that corrupted the American dream. I read Dreiser, Anderson, Lewis, and their younger contemporaries: Faulkner, Hemingway, Caldwell, Steinbeck. I had hoped to find in these writers a weapon strong enough to blast the walls that imprisoned the American soul. But they were merely describing the disease—they did not reveal any evidence that they knew how to eradicate it.

Hemingway was too preoccupied with himself, and consequently he wrote 23 of himself and his frustrations. I was also disappointed with Faulkner. Why did he give form to decay? And Caldwell, Steinbeck—why did they write in costume? And Odets, why *only* middle-class disintegration? Am I not an immigrant like Louis Adamic? Perhaps I could not understand America like Richard Wright, but I felt that I would be ineffectual if I did not return to my own people. I believed that my work would be more vital and useful if I dedicated it to the cause of my own people.

It was now almost ten years since I had landed in America. But as we moved 24 rapidly toward the war with Japan, I realized how foolish it was to believe then that I could define roots in terms of places and persons. I knew, then, that I would be as rootless in the Philippines as I was in America, because roots are not physical things, but the quality of faith deeply [ingrained] and clearly understood and integrated in one's life. The roots I was looking for were not physical but intellectual and spiritual things. In fact, I was looking for a common faith to believe in and of which I could be a growing part.

Now I knew that I was living in the collective era. Where was I to begin? 25 I read Marxist literature. Russia was then much in the minds of my contemporaries. In the Soviet system we seemed to have found a workable system and a common belief which bound races and peoples together for a creative purpose. I studied Russian history as I had studied American history. I tried to explain the incoherence of my life on the grounds that I was living in a decaying capitalist society.

Then we felt that something was bound to happen in America. Socialist 26 thinking was spreading among the workers, professionals, and intellectuals. Labor demanded immediate political action. For the first time a collective faith seemed to have appeared. To most of us it was a revelation—and a new morning in America. Here was a collective faith dynamic enough to release the creative spirit that was long thwarted in America. My personal predicaments seemed to vanish and for the first time I could feel myself growing and becoming a living part of America.

It was now the middle of 1941. The dark clouds of war were approaching 27 our shores. Then December 7 came to awaken a decadent world. Japan offered us a powerful collective faith which was pervasive enough to sweep away our fears and doubts of America. Suddenly I began to see the dark forces that had uprooted me from my native land and had driven me to a narrow corner of life in America. . . . At last the full significance of my search for roots came to me, because the war against Japan and Fascism revealed the whole meaning of the fears that had driven me as a young writer into hunger and disease and despair.

28    I wrote in my diary: "It is well that we in America take nourishment from a common spring. The Four Freedoms may not be realized in our times but if the war against Fascism ends, we may be sure that we have been motivated by a native force dynamic enough to give form to the creative spirit in America. Now I believe that all of us in America must be bound together by a common faith and work toward one goal. . . ." ✛

## RESPONDING

1.  In a journal entry, explain why Bulosan was disappointed in what he found in America.

2.  Working individually or in a group, describe conditions in America during the Great Depression of the 1930s.

3.  Bulosan, at the height of his despair, says that the anguish of the workers made many feel that "this was America—the dream betrayed. . . . America was done for—dead" (paragraph 9). In an essay, compare what Bulosan believed he would find in America with what he found. How was his faith in America restored?

4.  For Bulosan, reading and writing played an important role in his development as an American. In an essay, explain how he describes the changing role of the artist as social conditions in America changed.

# Oscar Hijuelos

*Oscar Hijuelos was born in New York City in 1951 of Cuban parentage. After earning his bachelor's and master's degrees from the City College of the City University of New York in 1975 and 1976, he worked in advertising, finally devoting himself to writing full time in 1984. His writing, which includes the novels* Our House in the Lost World *(1983),* The Mambo Kings Play Songs of Love *(1989),* The Fourteen Sisters of Emilio Montez O'Brien *(1993),* Mr. Ives' Christmas *(1995), and* Empress of the Splendid Season *(1999), as well as several short stories, has earned him several awards, among them a National Endowment for the Arts Creative Writing Fellowship (1985), an American Academy in Rome Fellowship in Literature (1985), and the Pulitzer Prize for Fiction (1990).*

*"Visitors, 1965," from* Our House in the Lost World, *reflects the experiences of some Cuban émigrés living in the United States. In this chapter the narrator explains the community's reactions to news of Fidel Castro's victory. The text's references to the overthrow of Batista, the Bay of Pigs invasion, and the rationing system help to provide the novel with a sense of historical context. At the same time, the narrative explores the ways in which such events are connected to each person's sense of personal and collective identity.*

⊕

# VISITORS, 1965

## *1*

DOWN IN THE COOL BASEMENT of the hotel restaurant, Alejo Santinio looked over a yellowed newspaper clipping dating back to 1961. He had not looked at it recently, although in the past had always been proud to show it to visitors. And why? Because it was a brief moment of glory. In the newspaper picture Alejo and his friend Diego were in their best dress whites standing before a glittering cart of desserts. Beside them was a fat, cheery beaming face, the Soviet premier Nikita Khrushchev, who was attending a luncheon in his honor at the hotel.

Alejo always told the story: The governor and mayor were there with the premier, who had "great big ears and a bright red nose." The premier had dined on a five-course meal. The waiters and cooks, all nervous wrecks, had fumbled around in the kitchen getting things into order. But outside they managed an orderly composed appearance. After the meal had been served, the cooks drew lots to see who would wheel out the dessert tray. Diego and Alejo won.

Alejo put on his best white uniform and apron and waited in the foyer, chainsmoking nervously, while, outside, news reporters fired off their cameras and bodyguards stood against the walls, watching. Alejo and Diego did not say anything. Alejo was bewildered by the situation: Only in America could a worker get so close to a fat little guy with enormous power. These were the days of the new technology: mushroom-cloud bombs and satellites and missiles. And there he was, a hick from a small town in Cuba, slicked up by America, thinking, "If only my old compañeros could see me now! and my sisters and Mercedes."

When the time came, they went to the freezer, filled up shiny bowls with ice cream, brought out the sauces and hot fudge, and loaded them all onto a dessert cart. Alejo was in charge of cherries. They went out behind the maître d' and stood before the premier's table. They humbly waited as the smiling premier looked over the different cakes, tarts, pies, fruits, sauces, and ice creams. Through a translator the premier asked for a bowl of chocolate and apricot ice cream topped with hot fudge, cocoanut, and a high swirl of fresh whipped cream. This being served, Alejo picked out the plumpest cherry from a bowl and nimbly placed it atop the dessert.

5    Delighted, the premier whispered to the translator, who said, "The premier wishes to thank you for this masterpiece."

6    As Diego and Alejo bowed, lightbulbs and cameras flashed all around them. They were ready to wheel the cart back when the premier rose from the table to shake Diego's and Alejo's hands. Then through the translator he asked a few questions. To Alejo: "And where do you come from?"

7    "Cuba," Alejo answered in a soft voice.

8    "Oh yes, Cuba," the premier said in halting English. "I would like to go there one day, Cuba." And he smiled and patted Alejo's back and then rejoined the table. A pianist, a violinist, and a cellist played a Viennese waltz.

9    Afterward reporters came back into the kitchen to interview the two cooks, and the next morning the *Daily News* carried a picture of Alejo, Diego, and Khrushchev with a caption that read: DESSERT CHEFS CALL RUSKY PREMIER HEAP BIG EATER! It made them into celebrities for a few weeks. People recognized Alejo on the street and stopped to talk with him. He even went on a radio show in the Bronx. The hotel gave him a five-dollar weekly raise, and for a while Alejo felt important, and then it played itself out and became the yellowed clipping, stained by grease on the basement kitchen wall.

10    In Alejo's locker Khrushchev turned up again, on the cover of a *Life* magazine. He was posed, cheek against cheek, with the bearded Cuban premier Fidel Castro. "What was going to happen in Cuba?" Alejo wondered. He shook his head. "How could Cuba have gone 'red'?" It had been more than six years since the fall of Batista on New Year's Eve, 1958, the year of getting rid of the evil in Cuba, and now Alejo and Mercedes were going to sponsor the arrival of Aunt Luisa, her daughters, and a son-in-law, Pedro. They were coming to the United States via *un vuelo de la libertad,* or freedom flight, as the U.S. military airplane trips from Havana to Miami were called. Khrushchev was going to eat up Cuba like an ice cream sundae. Things had gotten out of hand, bad enough for Luisa, who had loved her life in Holguín, to leave. Gone were the days of the happy-go-lucky Cubans who went on jaunts to Miami and New York to have a high time ballroom hopping; gone were the days when Cubans came to the States to make money and see more of the world. Now Cubans were leaving because of Khrushchev's new pal, Fidel Castro, the Shit, as some Cubans called him.

## 2

11    Alejo had supported Castro during the days of the revolution. He had raised money for the pro-Castro Cubans in Miami by hawking copies of the *Sierra Maestra* magazine to pals on the street. This magazine was printed in Miami by pro-Castro Cubans and was filled with pictures of tortured heroes left on the

streets or lying in the lightless mortuary rooms with their throats cut and their heads blood-splattered. They were victims of the crooked Batista regime, and now it was time for Batista and his henchmen to go! Alejo was not a political creature, but he supported the cause, of course, to end the injustices of Batista's rule. When someone brought him a box of Cuban magazines to sell, Alejo went down on Amsterdam Avenue and sold them to friends. Alejo always carried one of those magazines in his pocket, and he was persuasive, selling them. In his soft calm voice he would say, "Come on, it's only a dollar and for the cause of your countrymen's freedom!" And soon he would find himself inviting all the buyers back to his apartment, where they sat in the kitchen drinking and talking about what would save the world: "An honest man with a good heart, out of greed's reach," was the usual consensus. Political talk about Cuba always led to nostalgic talk, and soon Alejo's friends would soften up and bend like orchid vines, glorying in the lost joys of childhood. Their loves and regrets thickened in the room in waves, until they began singing along with their drinking and falling down. With their arms around each other and glasses raised, they toasted Fidel as "the hope for the future."

Alejo and Mercedes had been happy with the success of the revolution. The day Castro entered Havana they threw a party with so much food and drink that the next morning people had to cross into the street to get around the stacks of garbage bags piled on the sidewalk in front of the building. Inside, people were sprawled around everywhere. There were sleepers in the kitchen and in the hall, sleepers in the closet. There was a *dudduhduh* of a skipping needle over a phonograph record. A cat that had come in through the window from the alley was going around eating leftover scraps of food. **12**

Soon the papers printed that famous picture of Castro entering Havana with his cowboy-looking friend, Camilio Cienfuegos, on a tank. They were like Jesus and John the Baptist in a Roman epic movie. The *Sierra Maestra* magazine would later feature a centerfold of Castro as Jesus Christ with his hair long and golden brown, almost fiery in a halo of light. And for the longest time Cubans, Alejo and Mercedes among them, referred to Castro with great reverence and love, as if he were a saint. **13**

In a few years, however, kids in the street started to write slogans like *Castro eats big bananas!* The New York press ran stories about the Castro visit to New York. Alejo and Hector stood on the corner one afternoon, watching his motorcade speed uptown to a Harlem hotel. There, the press said, Castro's men killed their own chickens and ate them raw. Castro even came to give a talk at the university. Alejo and Hector were among a crowd of admirers that clustered around him to get a look. Castro was very tall for a Cuban, six-feet-two. He was wearing a long raincoat and took sips from a bottle of Pepsi-Cola. He listened to questions intently, liked to smile, and kept reaching out to shake hands. He also signed an occasional autograph. He was, the newspapers said, unyielding in his support of the principles of freedom. **14**

In time Castro announced the revolutionary program. Alejo read the *El* **15**

*Diario* accounts intently while Mercedes wandered around the apartment asking, "What's going to happen to my sisters?" By 1962, after the Bay of Pigs invasion and the beginning of the Cuban ration-card programs, an answer to her question came in the form of letters. Standing by the window Mercedes would read the same letter over and over again, sighing and saying out loud, "Oh my Lord! They are so unhappy!"

16      "Ma, what's going on?" Hector would ask her.

17      "Things are very bad. The Communists are very bad people. Your aunts have nothing to eat, no clothes to wear, no medicine. The Communists go around taking things away from people! And if you say anything they put you in jail!"

18      Mercedes's stories about the new life in Cuba made Hector think of a house of horrors. In his sleep he pictured faceless, cowled abductors roaming the streets of Holguín in search of victims to send to brainwashing camps. He pictured the ransacking of old mansions, the burning of churches, deaths by firing squads. He remembered back many years and saw the door of Aunt Luisa's house on Arachoa Street, and then he imagined guards smashing that door open to search Luisa's home.

19      All the news that came into the house in those letters fed such visions: "Ai, Hector, do you remember your cousin Paco? He has been sent to prison for a year, and all he did was get caught with a pound of sugar under his shirt!" A year later: "Oh your poor cousin Paco! He just came out of prison and now my sister can hardly recognize him. Listen to what Luisa says: 'He has lost most of his hair and is as thin as a skeleton with yellowed, jaundiced skin. He has aged twenty years in one.'" Another letter: "Dear sister, the headaches continue. Everything is upside down. You can't even go to church these days without someone asking, 'Where are you going?' Everyone in the barrio watches where you go. No one has any privacy. If you are not in the Party then you're no good. Many of them are Negroes, and now that they have the power, they are very bad to us. I don't know how long we can endure these humiliations. We hope for Castro's fall." Another letter: "Dear sister, last week your niece Maria was kicked out of dental school, and do you know what for? Because she wouldn't recite 'Hail Lenin!' in the mornings with the other students. I went to argue with the headmaster of the school, but there was nothing I could do. On top of that, poor Rina's roof was hit by lightning but she can't get the materials to fix it. When it rains the floors are flooded—all because she is not in the Party. . . . As usual I ask for your prayers and to send us whatever you can by way of clothing, food and medicine. Aspirins and penicillin are almost impossible to find these days, as are most other things. I know I'm complaining to you, but if you were here, you would understand. With much love, Luisa."

20      To help her sisters, Mercedes went from apartment to apartment asking neighbors for any clothing they might not need. These clothes were packed into boxes and sent down to Cuba at a cost of fifty dollars each. Mercedes paid for this out of her own pocket. She had been working at night cleaning in a nursery

school since the days of Alejo's illness. Alejo too contributed. He came home with boxes of canned goods and soap and toothpaste from the hotel and he bought such items as rubbing alcohol, aspirins, mercurochrome, iodine, Tampax, Q-Tips, cotton, and toilet paper to send to Cuba.

"The world is going to the devil," Mercedes would say to Alejo as she  21 packed one of the boxes. "Imagine having to use old newspapers for toilet paper! The Russians are the new masters, they have everything, but what do Luisa and Rina have? Nothing!"

Of the family, Mercedes was the most outspoken about the revolution. Alejo  22 was very quiet in his views. He didn't like Castro, or, for that matter, Khrushchev. But he would never argue with a friend about politics. He was always more concerned about keeping his friendships cordial. To please two different sets of neighbors he subscribed to both the *Daily Worker* and the *Republican Eagle*. He read neither of them, but still would nod emphatically whenever he came upon these neighbors in the hallway and they bombarded him with their philosophies. "Certainly," Alejo would say to them, "why don't you come inside and have a drink with me?" When there was a gathering of visitors with different points of view, Alejo used liquor to keep the wagging tongues in line. Get them drunk and make them happy, was his motto.

But Mercedes didn't want to hear about Fidel Castro from anyone, not even  23 from Señor Lopez, a union organizer and good friend of the family who lived in the building. He would come to the apartment to recount the declines in illiteracy, prostitution, and malnutrition in Cuba. "No more of this!" he would declare, showing Mercedes and Alejo and Hector a picture from *La Bohemia* of a decrepit old Negro man dying in bed, with bloated stomach, festering sores on his limbs, and a long gray worm literally oozing out of his navel. "You won't see this anymore now that Castro is in power!"

"And what about the decent people who supported Castro in the first place,  24 and who now have nothing but troubles?" she would ask.

"Mercita, the revolution is the will of the majority of the Cuban people!"  25

"You mean the people who were the good-for-nothings?"  26

"No, the people who had nothing because they were allowed nothing."  27

"Oh yes? And what about my family?"  28

"Mercita, use your brains. I don't like to put it this way, but as the saying  29 goes, 'To make an omelet you have to break a few eggs.'"

"My family are not eggs! If you like eggs so much, why don't you go down  30 to Cuba and live there? Chickens have more to eat than what you would get. Go there and see what freedom is like!"

By 1965 it was becoming clear that Castro was not going to fall from power.  31 Cubans who had been hoping for a counterrevolution were now growing desperate to leave. Luisa and her family were among them. One evening an errand boy from the corner drugstore knocked at the door. There was a call from Cuba. Mercedes and Hector hurried down the hill. The caller was Aunt Luisa. Her sad voice was so far away, interrupted by sonic hums and clicking static echoes. It sounded like the voices of hens reciting numbers in Spanish. With the jukebox going, it was a wonder that Luisa's voice could be heard over mountains and rivers and across the ocean.

32    "How is it over there now?" Mercedes asked.

33    "It's getting worse here. There are too many headaches. We want to leave. Pedro, Virginia's husband, lost his mechanic's shop. There is no point in our staying."

34    "Who wants to come?"

35    "Me, Pedro, Virginia, and Maria."

36    "And what about Rina?"

37    "She is going to stay for the time being with Delores and her husband." Delores was Rina's daughter. She had a doctorate in pedagogy that made her a valuable commodity in those days of literacy programs. "Delores has been appointed to a government post and she is too afraid to refuse the Party, for fear they will do something to Rina or to her husband. But we will come. I have the address of the place where you must write for the sponsorship papers. We've already put our name on the government waiting list. When our name reaches the top of the list we'll be able to go."

38    The only other way was to fly either to Mexico or Spain, but at a cost of two thousand dollars per person to Mexico, three thousand dollars per person to Spain. The family did not have that kind of money.

39    Mercedes then gave Hector the telephone. He listened to his aunt's soft voice, saying, "We will be with you soon, and you will know your family again. Pray for us so that we will be safe," Her voice sounded weak. There was clicking, like a plug being pulled. Perhaps someone was listening in the courthouse, where the call was being made.

40    Luisa spoke with Mercedes for another minute, and then their time was up and Mercedes and Hector returned home.

41    Alejo took care of the paperwork. He wrote to immigration authorities in Miami for their visas and for the special forms that would be mailed out by him, approved by the U.S. Immigration Department, and sent to Cuba.

42    In February 1966 Luisa and her daughters and son-in-law left Cuba. First they waited in front of the house on Arachoa Street in Holguín, where they had all been living, for the army bus that would take them on the ten-hour journey west to Havana. When they arrived at the José Martí Airport, they waited in a wire-fenced compound. A Cuban official went over their papers and had them stand in line for hours before they boarded the military transport jet to America.

43    On the day that Alejo looked at the clipping of Khrushchev again, they received word that Luisa and her daughters and a son-in-law were coming, and a sort of shock wave of apprehension and hope passed through them.

*3*

44    For Hector the prospect of Aunt Luisa's arrival stirred up memories. He began to make a conscious effort to be "Cuban," and yet the very idea of *Cubanness*

inspired fear in him as if he would grow ill from it, as if micróbios would be transmitted by the very mention of the word *Cuba*. He was a little perplexed because he also loved the notion of Cuba to an extreme. In Cuba there were so many pleasant fragrances, like the smell of Luisa's hair and the damp clay ground of the early morning. Cuba was where Mercedes had once lived a life of style and dignity and happiness. And it was the land of happy courtship with Alejo and the land where men did not fall down. Hector was tired of seeing Mercedes cry and yell. He was tired of her moroseness and wanted the sadness to go away. He wanted the apartment to be filled with beams of sunlight, like in the dream house of Cuba.

He was sick at heart for being so Americanized, which he equated with   45 being fearful and lonely. His Spanish was unpracticed, practically nonexistent. He had a stutter, and saying a Spanish word made him think of drunkenness. A Spanish sentence wrapped around his face, threatened to peel off his skin and send him falling to the floor like Alejo. He avoided Spanish even though that was all he heard at home. He read it, understood it, but he grew paralyzed by the prospect of the slightest conversation.

"Hablame en espanol!" Alejo's drunken friends would challenge him. But   46 Hector always refused and got lost in his bedroom, read *Flash* comic books. And when he was around the street Ricans, they didn't want to talk Spanish with Whitey anyway, especially since he was not getting high with them, just getting drunk now and then, and did not look like a hood but more like a goody-goody, round-faced mama's boy: a dark dude, as they used to say in those days.

Even Horacio had contempt for Hector. Knowing that Hector was nervous   47 in the company of visitors, he would instigate long conversations in Spanish. When visiting men would sit in the kitchen speaking about politics, family, and Cuba, Horacio would play the patrón and join them, relegating Hector to the side, with the women. He had disdain for his brother and for the ignorance Hector represented. He was now interested in "culture." He had returned from England a complete European who listened to Mozart instead of diddy-bop music. His hair was styled as carefully as Beau Brummell's. His wardrobe consisted of English tweed jackets and fine Spanish shoes; his jewelry, his watches, his cologne, everything was very European and very far from the gutter and the insecurity he had left behind. As he put it, "I'm never going to be fuckin' poor again."

He went around criticizing the way Mercedes kept house and cooked, the   48 way Alejo managed his money (buying everything with cash and never on credit) and the amounts of booze Alejo drank. But mostly he criticized Hector. The day he arrived home from the Air Force and saw Hector for the first time in years, his face turned red. He could not believe his eyes. Hector was so fat that his clothes were bursting at the seams, and when Hector embraced him, Horacio shook his head and said, "Man, I can't believe this is my brother."

And now the real Cubans, Luisa and her daughters and son-in-law, were   49 coming to find out what a false life Hector led. Hector could not sleep at night, thinking of it. He tried to remember his Spanish, but instead of sentences, pictures of Cuba entered into his mind. But he did not fight this. He fantasized about Cuba. He wanted the pictures to enter him, as if memory and imagination would make him more of a man, a Cuban man.

50    The day before Luisa arrived he suddenly remembered his trip to Cuba with Mercedes and Horacio in 1954. He remembered looking out the window of the plane and seeing fire spewing from the engines on the wing. To Cuba. To Cuba. Mercedes was telling him a story when the plane abruptly plunged down through some clouds and came out into the night air again. Looking out the window he saw pearls in the ocean and the reflection of the moon in the water. For a moment he saw a line of three ships, caravels with big white sails like Columbus's ships, and he tugged at Mercedes's arm. She looked but did not see them. And when he looked again, they were gone.

51    Hector tried again for a genuine memory. Now he saw Luisa's house on Arachoa Street, the sun a haze bursting through the trees.

52    "Do you remember a cat with one eye in Cuba?" he asked Horacio, who was across the room reading *Playboy* magazine.

53    "What?" he said with annoyance.

54    "In Cuba, wasn't there a little cat who used to go in and out of the shadows and bump into things? You know, into the steps and into the walls, because it only had one eye. And then Luisa would come out and feed it bits of meat?"

55    "You can't remember anything. Don't fool yourself," he replied.

56    But Hector could not stop himself. He remembered bulldozers tearing up the street and that sunlight again, filtering through the flower heads, and flamingos of light on the walls of the house. He remembered the dog with the pathetic red dick running across the yard. Then he remembered holding an enormous, trembling white sunhat. His grandmother, Doña Maria, was sitting nearby in a blue-and-white dotted dress, and he took the sunhat to show her. But it wasn't a sunhat. It was an immense white butterfly. "¡Ai, que linda!" Doña Maria said. "It's so pretty, but maybe we should let the poor thing go." And so Hector released the butterfly and watched it rise over the house and float silently away.

57    Then he saw Doña Maria, now dead, framed by a wreath of orchids in the yard, kissing him—so many kisses, squirming kisses—and giving advice. She never got over leaving Spain for Cuba and would always remain a proud Spaniard. "Remember," she had told Hector. "You're Spanish first and then Cuban."

58    He remembered sitting on the cool steps to Luisa's kitchen and watching the road where the bulldozers worked. A turtle was crawling across the yard, and iguanas were licking up the sticky juice on the kitchen steps. Then he heard Luisa's voice: "Come along, child," she called. "I have something for you." And he could see her face again through the screen door, long and wistful.

59    Inside, she had patted Hector's head and poured him a glass of milk. Cuban milk alone was sour on the tongues of children, but with the Cuban magic potion, which she added, it was the most delicious drink Hector ever tasted.

With deep chocolate and nut flavors and traces of orange and mango, the bitter with the sweet, the liquid went down his throat, so delicious. "No child, drink that milk," Luisa said. "Don't forget your *tia*. She loves you."

Then a bam! bam! came from the television and Hector could hear voices 60 of neighbors out in the hallway. No, he wasn't used to hearing Luisa's niceties anymore, and he couldn't remember what was in the milk, except that it was Cuban, and then he wondered what he would say to his aunt and cousins, whether he would smile and nod his head or hide as much as possible, like a turtle on a hot day.

## 4

It was late night when a van pulled up to the building and its four exhausted 61 passengers stepped onto the sidewalk. Seeing the arrival from the window, Mercedes was in a trance for a moment and then removed her apron and ran out, almost falling down the front steps, waving her arms and calling, "Aaaaiiii, aaaaiiii, aaaaiiii! Oh my God! My God! My God," and giving many kisses. Alejo followed and hugged Pedro. The female cousins waited humbly, and then they began kissing Mercedes and Alejo and Hector and Horacio, their hats coming off and teeth chattering and hair getting all snarled like ivy on an old church . . . kisses, kisses, kisses . . . into the warm lobby with its deep, endless mirrors and the mailbox marked *Delgado/Santinio*. The female cousins, like china dolls, were incredibly beautiful, but struck dumb by the snow and the new world, silent because there was something dreary about the surroundings. They were thinking Alejo had been in this country for twenty years, and yet what did he have? But no one said this. They just put hands on hands and gave many kisses and said, "I can't believe I'm seeing you here." They were all so skinny and exhausted-looking, Luisa, Virginia, Maria, and Pedro. They came holding cloth bags with all their worldly possessions: a few crucifixes, a change of clothing, aspirins given to them at the airport, an album of old photographs, prayer medals, a Bible, a few Cuban coins from the old days, and a throat-lozenge tin filled with some soil from Holguín, Oriente province, Cuba.

After kissing and hugging them Alejo took them into the kitchen where 62 they almost died: There was so much of everything! Milk and wine and beer, steaks and rice and chicken and sausages and ham and plantains and ice cream and black bean soup and Pepsi Cola and Hershey chocolate bars and almond nougat, and popcorn and Wise potato chips and Jiffy peanut butter, and rum and whiskey, marshmallows, spaghetti, flan and pasteles and chocolate cake and pie, more than enough to make them delirious. And even though the walls were cracked and it was dark, there was a television set and a radio and lightbulbs and toilet paper and pictures of the family and crucifixes and toothpaste and soap and more.

It was "Thank God for freedom and bless my family" from Luisa's mouth, 63 but her daughters were more cautious. Distrusting the world, they approached everything timidly. In the food-filled kitchen Alejo told them how happy he was to have them in his house, and they were happy because the old misery was over, but they were still without a home and in a strange world. Uncertainty showed in their faces.

64     Pedro, Virginia's husband, managed to be the most cheerful. He smoked and talked up a storm about the conditions in Cuba and the few choices the Castro government had left to them. Smoking thick, black cigars, Horacio and Alejo nodded and agreed, and the conversation went back and forth and always ended with "What are you going to do?"

65     "Work until I have something," was Pedro's simple answer.

66     It was such a strong thing to say that Hector, watching from the doorway, wanted to be like Pedro. And from time to time, Pedro would look over and wink and flash his Victor Mature teeth.

67     Pedro was about thirty years old and had been through very bad times, including the struggle in 1957 and 1958 to get Castro into power. But wanting to impress Hector with his cheeriness, Pedro kept saying things in English to Hector like, "I remember Elvis Presley records. Do you know *You're My Angel Baby*?" And Hector would not even answer that. But Pedro would speak on, about the brave Cubans who got out of Cuba in the strangest ways. His buddy back in Holguín stole a small airplane with a few friends and flew west to Mexico, where they crash-landed their plane on a dirt road in the Yucatán. He ended up in Mexico City, where he found work in the construction business. He was due in America soon and would one day marry Maria, who wanted a brave man. These stories only made Hector more and more silent.

68     As for his female cousins, all they said to him was: "Do you want to eat?" or "Why are you so quiet?" And sometimes Horacio answered for him, saying: "He's just dumb when it comes to being Cuban."

69     Aunt Luisa, with her good heart, really didn't care what Hector said or didn't say. Each time she encountered him in the morning or the afternoons, she would take his face between her hands and say, "Give me a kiss and say 'Tia, I love you.'" And not in the way Alejo used to, falling off a chair and with his eyes desperate, but sweetly. Hector liked to be near Luisa with her sweet angelic face.

70     He felt comfortable enough around Aunt Luisa to begin speaking to her. He wasn't afraid because she overflowed with warmth. One day while Aunt Luisa was washing dishes, Hector started to think of her kitchen in Cuba. He remembered the magic Cuban drink.

71     "Auntie," he asked her. "Do you remember a drink that you used to make for me in the afternoons in Cuba? What was it? It was the most delicious chocolate but with Cuban spices."

72     She thought about it. "Chocolate drink in the afternoon? Let me see . . ." She wiped a plate clean in the sink. She seemed perplexed and asked, "And it was chocolate?"

73     "It was Cuban chocolate. What was it?"

She thought on it again and her eyes grew big and she laughed, slapping     74
her knee. "Ai, bobo. It was Hershey syrup and milk!"

After that he didn't ask her any more questions. He just sat in the living     75
room listening to her tell Mercedes about her impressions of the United States.
For example, after she had sat out on the stoop or gazed out the window for a
time, she would make a blunt declaration: "There are a lot of airplanes in the
sky." But usually when Mercedes and Luisa got to talking, they drifted toward
the subject of spirits and ghosts. When they were little girls spiritualism was
very popular in Cuba. All the little girls were half mediums, in those days. And
remembering this with great laughter, Luisa would say, "If only we could have
seen what would happen to Papa! Or that Castro would turn out to be so bad!"

"Yes, Papa, that would have been something," Mercedes answered with wide     76
hopeful eyes. "But Castro is something else. What could a few people do about
him?"

"Imagine if you're dead in Cuba," said Luisa, "and you wake up to that     77
mess. What would you do?"

"I would go to Miami, or somewhere like that."     78

"Yes, and you would go on angel wings."     79

It was Luisa's ambition to ignore America and the reality of her situation     80
completely. So she kept taking Mercedes back to the old days: "You were such
a prankster, so mischievous! You couldn't sit down for a moment without being
up to something. Poor Papa! What he had to do with you!" And then, turning
to Hector, she would add, "Look at your Mama. This innocent over here was
the fright of us all. She was always imagining things. Iguanas, even little baby
iguanas, were dragons. A rustle in the bushes was ghosts of fierce Indians looking
for their bones!" She laughed. "There are ghosts, but not as many as she saw.
She was always in trouble with Papa. He was very good to her but also strict.
But his punishments never stopped your mother. My, but she was a fresh girl!"

When she wasn't talking to Mercedes, Luisa watched the Spanish channel     81
on the television, or ate, or prayed. Pedro went out with Alejo and Horacio,
looking for work. Maria and Virginia helped with the housecleaning and the
cooking, and then they studied their books. They were very quiet, like felines,
moving from one spot to another without a sound. Sometimes everyone went
out to the movies; Alejo paid for it. Or they all went downtown to the department stores to buy clothing and other things they needed. Again, Alejo paid for
everything, angering Mercedes, for whom he bought nothing.

"I know you're trying to be nice to my family, but remember we don't have     82
money."

Still, he was generous with them, as if desperate to keep Luisa and her     83
daughters in the apartment. Their company made him as calm and happy as a
mouse. Nothing pleased Alejo more than sitting at the head of the dinner table,
relishing the obvious affection that Luisa and her daughters and son-in-law felt
for him. At meals Alejo would make toast after toast to their good health and
long life, drink down his glass of rum or whiskey quickly, and then fill another

and drink that and more. Mercedes always sat quietly wondering, "What does my sister really think of me for marrying him?" while Hector waited for Alejo suddenly to fall off his chair, finally showing his aunt and cousins just who the Santinios really were.

84     One night Alejo fell against the table and knocked down a big stack of plates. The plates smashed all around Alejo, who was on the floor. Hector scrambled to correct everything before Virginia and Maria and Pedro came to look. He scrambled to get Alejo up before they saw him. He pulled with all his strength, the way he and Horacio used to, but Alejo weighed nearly three hundred pounds. As the cousins watched in silence, Hector wished he could walk through the walls and fly away. He thought that now they would know one of his secrets, that the son is like the father. He tried again to pull Alejo up and had nearly succeeded when Pedro appeared and, with amazing strength, wrapped his arms around Alejo's torso and heaved him onto a chair with one pull.

85     Hector hadn't wanted them to see this, because then they might want to leave and the apartment would be empty of Pedro and Luisa and her daughters. those fabulous beings. He didn't want them to see the dingy furniture and the cracking walls and the cheap decorative art, plaster statues, and mass-produced paintings. He didn't want them to see that he was an element in this world, only as good as the things around him. He wanted to be somewhere else, be someone else, a Cuban . . . And he didn't want the family perceived as the poor relations with the drunk father. So he tried to laugh about Alejo and eventually went to bed, leaving Luisa and Pedro and his cousins still standing in the hall. Eventually, they did move away. Virginia and Maria found work in a factory in Jersey City, and Pedro came home one evening with the news that he had landed a freight dispatcher's job in an airport. Just like that. He had brought home a big box of pastries, sweet cakes with super-sweet cream, chocolate eclairs, honey-drenched cookies with maraschino cherries in their centers.

86     As Alejo devoured some of these, he said to Pedro, "Well, that's good. You're lucky to have such good friends here. Does it pay you well?"

87     Pedro nodded slightly and said, "I don't know, it starts out at seven thousand dollars a year, but it will get better."

88     Alejo also nodded, but he was sick because after twenty years in the same job he did not make that much, and this brought down his head and made him yawn. He got up and went to his bedroom where he fell asleep.

89     A few months later, they were ready to rent a house in a nice neighborhood in Jersey. The government had helped them out with some emergency funds. ("We never asked the government for even a penny," Mercedes kept saying to Alejo.) Everyone but Luisa was bringing home money. They used that money to buy furniture and to send Virginia to night computer school taught by Spanish instructors. Instead of being cramped up in someone else's apartment with rattling pipes and damp plaster walls that seemed ready to fall in, they had a three-story house with a little yard and lived near many Cubans who kept the

sidewalks clean and worked hard, so their sick hearts would have an easier time of it.

Hector was bereft at their leaving, but more than that he was astounded by how easily they established themselves. One day Pedro said, "I just bought a car." On another, "I just got a color TV." In time they would be able to buy an even larger house. The house would be filled with possessions: a dishwasher, a washing machine, radios, a big stereo console, plastic-covered velour couches and chairs, electric clocks, fans, air conditioners, hair dryers, statues, crucifixes, lamps and electric-candle chandeliers, and more. One day they would have enough money to move again, to sell the house at a huge profit and travel down to Miami to buy another house there. They would work like dogs, raise children, prosper. They did not allow the old world, the past, to hinder them. They did not cry but walked straight ahead. They drank but did not fall down. Pedro even started a candy and cigarette business to keep him busy in the evenings, earning enough money to buy himself a truck.

"Qué bueno," Alejo would say.

"This country's wonderful to new Cubans," Mercedes kept repeating. But then she added, "They're going to have everything, and we . . . what will we have?" And she would go about sweeping the floor or preparing chicken for dinner. She would say to Alejo, "Doesn't it hurt you inside?"

Alejo shrugged. "No, because they have suffered in Cuba."

He never backed off from that position and always remained generous to them, even after their visits became less frequent, even when they came only once a year. And when Pedro tried to repay the loans, Alejo always waved the money away. By this time Virginia was pregnant, so Alejo said, "Keep it for the baby."

"You don't want the money?"

"Only when you don't need it. It's important for you to have certain things now."

But Mercedes stalked around the apartment, screaming, "What about the pennies I saved? What about us?" ✚

---

## RESPONDING

1. In a journal entry, explain Horacio's definition of *culture* (paragraph 47). Compare his definition with other definitions of *culture*.

2. Compare Alejo and Mercedes's attitudes toward the Cuban revolution before and after Castro came to power. Working in pairs, write a dialogue between Alejo or Mercedes and a supporter of the revolution, their neighbor, Señor Lopez.

3. Hector is "sick at heart for being so Americanized, which he equated with being fearful and lonely" (paragraph 45). Using examples from the reading, write an essay explaining the ways in which Hector is Americanized. Compare his feelings about America with his feelings about Cuba. What does Cuba seem to represent to him?

4. Why is Mercedes angry at the end of the story? Compare the situation for the new immigrants arriving in 1965 with that of immigrants arriving twenty years earlier. Why do you think Pedro and his family become prosperous while Alejo and his family remain poor? Using information from the reading, your own knowledge, and any relevant news coverage you have seen or reading you have done, speculate about each family's reception in the new country.

# Van B. Luu

*Van B. Luu left Vietnam at the age of twelve. She holds a bachelor's degree from the University of California, Berkeley. Her work has appeared in* Making Waves: An Anthology of Writings by and About Asian American Women.

*In the essay that follows, Luu makes use of traditional academic resources— books, journal articles, doctoral dissertations, and government documents. She also includes information obtained through interviews she conducted in Vietnamese with some of the refugees themselves. In this way, her essay provides a unique perspective on the issues faced by one group of immigrant women.*

# THE HARDSHIPS OF ESCAPE FOR VIETNAMESE WOMEN

1  AT PRESENT ONLY A LIMITED AMOUNT of research is being done on Vietnamese refugee women. In writing this essay, which is based on personal interviews and research, I hope to contribute some knowledge and understanding to the study of these women's lives and experiences in America. In addition to their stressful escape, they are also facing new challenges during their resettlement. What makes these experiences significant is that they have a great impact on the women's mental health. In this essay, I will focus on the external causes of mental

health problems rather than their psychological manifestations. Understanding the evacuation and resettlement of Vietnamese women is a necessary prerequisite to understanding their needs and problems. Thus, I will examine the problem from the period of the women's escape to their present situation. And since the majority of problems are experienced by the women who have come to America in recent years, I will concentrate on them in this discussion.

Ever since the Communists took over South Vietnam in 1975, thousands of Vietnamese refugees have left their country in search of freedom. Despite the increasing risks and dangers such as piracy, a majority of people, 575,000 in total, have fled by sea.[1] After arriving at an asylum camp in Hong Kong, Malaysia, the Philippines, or Thailand, they hope they will be able to resettle in new countries—Japan, France, Canada, and especially the United States, the nation most willing to accept refugees. By the end of 1981, over 450,000 refugees had resettled in the United States; approximately 45 percent of these people are women.[2] Only recently have the women been recognized as a vulnerable group that needs special programs and attention. In addition to their poor mental health resulting from the traumatic experiences during their escapes, many Vietnamese women also suffer emotional problems during their adjustment in the United States.

## *Leaving Their Homes*

Vietnamese women—both those who work in the home and those outside the home—experience a great deal of grief and loss.[3] The separation from family, in many ways, causes depression among the Vietnamese women. Because of the high cost of leaving the country—approximately two thousand dollars per person is charged by boat owners—usually only wealthy families can afford to raise enough money to transport the entire family. Other families must decide which member has the most potential in their future endeavors and transport him or her out of the country, leaving the less promising relatives at home. This has created a dilemma because Vietnamese families are traditionally close-knit: name, status, and personal as well as financial support all come from the family.[4] As in other Asian cultures, children are expected to take care of their aged parents to "compensate the gift of birth and upbringing."[5] It is very common to find several generations living together under one roof.

After settling in America, the Vietnamese women, as well as the men, often

---

1. U.S. Committee for Refugees, *Vietnamese Boat People: Pirates' Vulnerable Prey* (Washington, D.C., February 1984), I. [Author's note]
2. Lani Davidson, "Women Refugees: Special Needs and Programs," *Journal of Refugee Resettlement* I (1981): 17. [Author's note]
3. Kasumi Hirayama, "Effects of the Employment of Vietnamese Refugee Wives on Their Family Roles and Mental Health" (Ph.D. diss., University of Pennsylvania, 1980), 156.
4. Lynelle Burmark-Parasurman, *Interfacing Two Cultures: Vietnamese and Americans* (California: Alameda County, 1982), 58.
5. Burmark-Parasurman, *Interfacing Two Cultures*, 58.

feel guilty about leaving their relatives behind. According to Dr. Le Tai Rieu, director of Indo-Chinese Mental Health Projects in San Francisco, the Vietnamese refugees are plagued by "survivor's guilt"—they feel that they have run away while their relatives are still suffering.[6] Some women save money from work and often send gifts through the black market such as medicine and, if possible, currency, so their relatives can pay for the passage of the remaining family members. However, many times their dreams of reuniting with their relatives are very difficult to fulfill because the passage to the asylum camp is unsafe. Consequently, the Vietnamese women feel helpless and continue to bear depression and guilt as the years go by in the new land.

5     The ability to finance an escape to foreign countries does not guarantee admission into asylum camps. Hong Kong, Malaysia, the Philippines, and Thailand were chosen by the refugees as sites for the camps because of their proximity to the escape points, which are located mostly along the southern coast of Vietnam. (Some refugees have also found ways of leaving the country by land route, walking through Laos and Cambodia with paid guides who speak several languages and lead them to safety in Thailand.) In recent years many countries that experienced an early influx of refugees have begun to deny admissions. In 1979 Malaysia refused entry to 55,000 refugees, and Indonesia deployed a twenty-four vessel force to prevent refugees from reaching its soil.[7] Apparently these governments are afraid of the economic problems in feeding and housing the refugees, as well as the interethnic conflict resulting from longstanding tension among these countries' peoples. However, their efforts to stem the migration have not been successful due to the refugees' desperation to find shelter after their long struggle for survival during their exodus.

### Robbery and Violence at Sea

6     The interval between deciding to leave their homes and arriving in a safe camp can be long and very harrowing. The boats in which the refugees escape are small and in poor condition; they can easily be sunk en route to the asylum camps. Sometimes sinking boats have been saved in time by passing vessels; sometimes not. This tragedy resulted in 150,000 refugee deaths in the ocean from May 1975 to mid-1979.[8] The fortunate refugees who survive the exodus still must face the possibility of witnessing the deaths of their family members or other passengers. In one case, Tran Hue Hue, a sixteen-year-old girl, was the only survivor out of fifty people during the escape in 1980. She suffered the

6. Bill Soiffer, "Viet Mental Health Project in a Bind," *San Francisco Chronicle*, 14 January 1980, 7.
7. Scott Stone and John McGowan, *Wrapped in the Wind Shawl: Refugees of Southeast Asia and the Western World* (San Rafael: Presidio Press, 1980), 39.
8. Bruce Grant, *The Boat People: An Age Investigation of Bruce Grant* (New York: Penguin Books, 1979), 80.

traumatic experiences of watching both her brother and aunt pass away and being stranded on a tiny atoll before her rescue. Despite the long years spent resettling in her new country, Tran Hue Hue still suffers from the grief of her lost relatives.

Since 1978 one of the main hindrances to safe passage has been piracy. Many people believe that refugees carry fortunes in gold, jewelry, and U.S. dollars, and that "collectively the wealth could be substantial, especially when in 1978 the boats became larger and started carrying not a few score but as many as 600 to 700 people."[9] With the lure of their potential wealth, these refugees on the rickety boats are brutally attacked by the pirates in the waters joining Vietnam's Mekong Delta, the coasts of southern Thailand, and northeast Malaysia. Some pirates rob but provide food and water in return. However, in recent years the incidence of violent attacks has increased dramatically, with the pirates using a variety of weapons—including guns, daggers, knives, and even hammers—to attack the defenseless refugees. U.S. refugee officials interviewing the victims often write the initials "RPM" in their case histories. "RPM" stands for "rape, pillage, and murder," a summary of the dreadful experiences of these new-comers.[10]

Female Vietnamese refugees are in a particularly vulnerable situation, one that began back in their old country where they were oppressed in the traditional caste system. There these women held an inferior status and had fewer privileges than men. Usually the males were encouraged to get a good education while the females were expected to take care of the household and later become good wives and mothers. In addition, the importance of *noi doi tong duaon*, that is, carrying the family name from one generation to the next through the male heir, led to the increasing practice of bigamy until just recently. Pressure from the society as well as from the family often made women share their husbands with others; it was not surprising to see men with three or four wives living under one roof. Many women had a hard time getting out of this unwanted situation because when a woman married, she became part of the husband's family. To leave their husbands, even in instances of bad marriages, was a great risk because they feared slander, which was very difficult to withstand in the caste society of Vietnam. At present the women are found to be less oppressed than in the past, but problems still exist.

Even after leaving their country, the ordeal of Vietnamese women may continue because they are subjected to risks of sexual abuse. They suffer not only from the terrible journey to the asylum camps, but also from rape and violence at the hands of Thai fishermen, otherwise known as "sea pirates." Nhat Tien, a famous Vietnamese writer and an expert on the Vietnamese refugee issue, says that "these women deserve very special consideration and assistance,

9. Ibid., 63–64.
10. Ibid., 65.

much different from that prescribed for ordinary boat people, special materials as well as psychological and emotional support necessary to enable them to stand secure and build a fine new life in the U.S."[11]

10    In a personal interview[12] Mrs. L., a thirty-three-year-old nurse, described her painful experiences during her escape in 1983:

> Staying on the boat was very uncomfortable, because sixty-six people had been crammed together in a small boat. There was neither food, drinks, nor shelter. We had to wait until the rain came to get fresh water. One day, the boat suddenly stopped moving and a storm arrived. The men teamed up to work on the engine and at the same time they tried to scoop the water out of the boat. No other women helped out, except me. As I was scooping out the water, I had a sudden impulse to smear my face with black oil from the engine. I looked filthy and disgusting. Up until now, I do not know why I did that, but it surely saved me from the pirates who later attacked our boat.

11    About twenty pirates from two boats set upon the refugees' vessel. Armed with guns, hammers, and large metal bars, they demanded gold, money, and other valuables. They carefully searched both the boats and the people to make sure Mrs. L. and her fellow escapees had not hidden anything from them. Then the pirates, satisfied with their booty, turned their attention to the women on board.

> Everyone felt so helpless since we were unarmed. After searching, the pirates started the rape and abuse of the women. They took all of them, except me, to the back of the boat and raped them. I was so lucky because I looked so ugly and filthy. I fainted and couldn't see anything. . . . I closed my eyes really tight to stop myself from witnessing the horrible scene, but I could not help hearing the moans and groans, and especially the beggings for mercy by those poor women. There were thirteen or fourteen women altogether, whose ages ranged from fifteen to early forties. I really felt sorry for a young girl: she was about fifteen. She was raped continuously by four or five pirates. The whole ordeal lasted for two hours.

12    The pirates eventually left, but stripped the engine and motor from the boat, and left the refugees stranded in the middle of the ocean. Mrs. L. remembers thinking that "death seemed to approach closer and closer daily," even though the men tried to get the boat moving by using whatever means they could devise. After about seven days and nights adrift at sea, the refugees

11. Nhat Tien, Thuy Vu, and Duong Phuc, "Report on the Kro-Kra Trial" (Unpublished report compiled by the Boat People S.O.S. Committee, San Diego, 1980).
12. This and subsequent interviews were conducted in Vietnamese by the author in 1985.

managed to land on the Malaysian shore where they were finally taken in by the authorities.

One of the most notorious incidents that shocked the Vietnamese community in America took place on Kro-Kra Island, located in southern Thailand, where many Vietnamese refugees were captured in 1980. Due to the isolated location of the island, the Vietnamese refugees could not find ways to escape, and almost every female was raped.

According to a United Nation High Commissioner of Refugees report, a woman was severely burned when pirates set fire to the hillside where she was hiding in an attempt to force her to come out. Another had stayed for days in a cave, waist-deep in water despite the attack of crabs on her legs.[13] One victim who later settled in America explained, "Thai pirates used steel bars to strike any Vietnamese man who struggled against the attacks on the women."[14] Fortunately, some of these women were lucky enough to return to their families. Others were not. And most women were reluctant to press charges against the barbaric pirates in Thailand, because they were afraid that any legal action might delay or jeopardize their departure for resettlement in the new country.

Other problems can plague the women. Some, for instance, suffer from rape-related medical difficulties, such as vaginal disorders, which often interfere with their daily lives. Aside from the physical problems, these women experience long-lasting psychological and emotional problems, including depression and anxiety over unwanted pregnancies and possible reduced chances for a happy marriage.[15]

Most of the Vietnamese women do not want to talk about their experiences with anybody, even their close friends and relatives; they remain silent even after settling in America. Vinh, a rape victim from the Kro-Kra Island incident, says that most people can never understand that what she went through is painful and cannot be described in words.[16] The women are afraid of rejection by their relatives if their experiences became known. But because they are silent about the rapes, no specific report or information is available on the mental health of this group of Vietnamese women. Nevertheless, it is clear to many people that these women do suffer, both physically and mentally, from their trauma. "Perhaps those who suffered silently were more affected by the rape experience than those who spoke more openly," said Eve Burton, a prominent writer on Vietnamese women refugee issues who in recent years sponsored the entry of four Vietnamese rape victims.[17]

---

13. Barry Wain, *The Refused: the Agony of the Indochina Refugees* (New York: Simon and Schuster, 1981), 71.

14. Eve Burton, "Surviving the Flight of Horror: The Story of Refugee Women," *Indochina Issue* (February 1982), I.

15. U.S. Committee for Refugees, *Vietnamese Boat People*, 6.

16. Burton, "Flight of Horror," 2.

17. Ibid., I.

### *Economic Adjustment*

17    Vietnamese women coming to America have experienced fatigue, humiliation, and anger, and continue to face new obstacles here. "Their main problem is feeling helpless and ineffective in coping with reality in this country. They are overwhelmed with the needs of adjustment, especially with their roles in the family," said Dr. Ton That Toai, a psychologist of Prince William County Public School in Virginia, during a personal interview. Thirty percent of his clients are Vietnamese women having psychological problems who have been referred to him by American social workers.

18    The employment of the Vietnamese wives places these women in a highly stressful situation because the traditional Vietnamese culture is deeply influenced by Confucian doctrine: authority of parent over children, husbands over wives, older children over younger ones. Confucianism also stresses that women have to be submissive: first to their fathers, then later to their husbands.[18] In Vietnam, the women are expected to take care of the household, raise the children, and obey their husbands. Although most women in the past were primarily restricted to the home, some had to take outside jobs due to the continuing war in Vietnam. They had to make a living while their husbands were on the battlefields. "Even though my husband was an officer in the navy, his salary was not enough to support the family. Luckily, I was employed before our marriage so I just continued being a nurse," said Mrs. L., one of the more fortunate women who had skills and a good job. Women with a lower level of education had difficulties in becoming self-sufficient or helping out their families. Even though many became shopkeepers, others were trapped in prostitution.

19    When Vietnamese women come to America, more of them drift from their traditional roles in order to help the family financially. This has caused additional cultural stress. The employment of women brings out in the open the conflict between the traditional Vietnamese role of wife and mother, and the role of women in modern American society.[19] Now able to contribute money to the family, the women feel they should have more power in the family than before. Moreover, they want to be treated as equals with their husbands. "The women should have an equal partnership in the marriage. This is America, not Vietnam," said Lan Nguyen during an interview with the author. Lan was a Vietnamese housewife who was able to obtain a technical position in a high-tech company after receiving special training.

20    These drastic changes in the roles of Vietnamese women have disturbed many men. They cannot cope well with the changes in the deeply-rooted Vietnamese customs and traditions; they cannot easily accept their loss of dominance within the family, their declining role as patriarch of the family. "Despite the recent importation of Western-style ways of life and the current

18. Hirayama, "Effects of Employment," 4.
19. Ibid., 13.

feminist movements including the Women's Liberation Movement in the United States, the Vietnamese man in his country is still the boss, [even] if not the big boss anymore," comments Dr. Gia Thuy Vuong, a language and culture specialist.[20] The loss of their home in Vietnam appears to mean also the loss of men's authoritarian role within the family.

The husbands have not found it easy to use their working skills in America and consequently have to accept any available job. Approximately 65 percent of the Vietnamese refugees formerly working in white-collar professions have had to enter blue-collar professions in the United States, and then can no longer support their families as they did in Vietnam. Ironically, whereas many men experience downward mobility, many wives experience upward mobility in their work because they are exposed to more occupational opportunities here than in Vietnam. For instance, many electronics companies have been hiring Vietnamese women for electro-mechanical positions. With this type of job, the women do not need to speak English well, have a high level of education, or do heavy physical work. Other refugee women enter service jobs, such as beauticians, and some open little shops and restaurants to serve the local Vietnamese community.

### *Marital Status*

The man's loss of status and power, coupled with his downward mobility, has placed severe pressure on the traditional marriage relationship. An increase in spousal abuse, which is accepted to some degree in Vietnam, is a direct result of the stress marriage faces in the transition to a new, modern culture.[21] According to Dr. Ton, violence does exist in the homes of the Vietnamese, but it rarely gets reported. Though women are physically abused by their spouses, they do not want to discuss the experience. Therefore, counselors cannot pursue the matter even though they are aware of it.

In a 1979 survey, marital conflict was found to be one of the top four problems of Vietnamese refugees in America.[22] The divorce rate among Vietnamese couples is increasing markedly. "Women in Vietnam are very dependent," says Thang Cao, a young man who is disturbed by the changes he sees in Vietnamese women.[23] "You can be sure your wife will stay with you forever. Husbands feel safe," he adds. However, in the United States where divorce is more common and acceptable, Vietnamese women are able to end their marriages without suffering as much from gossip or humiliation in the community.

Some divorced husbands have blamed their wives' new roles and new freedom for the break-up of their marriages. During a personal interview,

20. Gia Thuy Vuong, *Getting to Know the Vietnamese and Their Culture* (New York: Frederick Ungar Publishing Co., 1976), 23.
21. Daniel Dinh Phuoc Le, "Vietnamese Refugees' Perceptions and Methods for Coping with Mental Illness" (Ph.D. diss., United States International University, 1979), 41.
22. Davidson, "Women Refugees," 17.
23. John Hubner and Carol Rafferty, "After the Storm," *San Jose Mercury News*, 17 October 1982.

Mr. H., recently divorced after ten years of marriage, gave his reaction to the difficulties associated with the changing roles of women:

> Back in the country, my role was only to bring home money from work, and my wife would take care of the household. Now everything has changed. My wife had to work as hard as I did to support the family. Soon after, she demanded more power at home. In other words, she wanted equal partnership. I am so disappointed! I realized that things are different now, but I could not help feeling the way I do. It is hard to get rid of or change my principles and beliefs which are deeply rooted in me.

### *Language and Cultural Differences*

25   In addition to problems within the family, Vietnamese women also face adjustment to the outside community. Women may suffer more than men during the resettlement period because most of the responsibility of survival has traditionally fallen on them: they are expected to take care of the children and do all the same household chores they performed in Vietnam. Unfortunately in the new environment and culture, unfamiliar situations prevent women from doing all these tasks as easily as they once did.

26   Most of the older women are not literate because they were never encouraged to go to school in Vietnam. This fact combined with an inability to communicate in English presents a major problem. Because they often do not know how to read the labels on merchandise, everyday chores are difficult or even risky when women mistakenly use cleaning fluids in cooking. Their lack of formal education and their limited exposure to Western ways make adjustment in the United States both hard and frustrating. "I can imagine life would be difficult without my husband's help since I cannot speak English well. I feel frustrated when I cannot express myself to Americans. Therefore, at home I always try my best to learn the new language through books or television," said Mrs. L. when she was interviewed for this essay.

27   Inevitably, the women also come face to face with cultural differences. Vietnamese mothers lack familiarity with the new customs and are often misunderstood by the American public. Social workers often conclude inaccurately that these women do not know how to take care of their children properly, because, for example, some women let their children attend school wearing pajamas.[24] The mothers in this case think the attire is quite appropriate, however, because wearing pajamas as street clothes in Vietnam is a common and socially acceptable practice.

28   Confusion about American values and customs contributes to the mental health problems suffered by Vietnamese immigrant women. This confusion can

---

24. Davidson, "Women Refugees," 18.

lead to feelings of rejection and then depression. As Mrs. L. said, "I know that there are cultural differences, so I am very careful when I go out. I try to dress properly because I do not want to be looked down upon by the Americans as they occasionally did with the other Vietnamese women down the block." Mental health problems are most frequent among refugees who have limited experience in Western culture and have little formal education or knowledge of English. And it is clear that the majority of Vietnamese immigrant women fall into this category.

## *Conclusion*

Past harrowing experiences and present difficulties combine to make resettle-    29
ment a very strenuous process for Vietnamese women. They face a dichotomy between tradition and modernity. The emotional problems caused by the exodus may not have an immediate effect. After settling in, however, the old problems merge with new ones. "The women have been emotionally distressed constantly because their roles change so drastically. In addition, male expectations have not changed. At home, [Vietnamese women] are required to be totally submissive to their husbands, while at work they are respected by co-workers and friends," commented Dr. Ton in our interview. "Many also have problems outside the home in adjusting to the new environment. They are in need of psychological help, but they would not come to see me if they are not constantly pushed by the American social workers," he added. Without help, they usually remain silent and pretend to be fine when they see other Vietnamese.

The Vietnamese culture favors repression of negative or aggressive feel-    30
ings.[25] Emotional problems are considered a personal matter to be resolved by oneself or within the family. It is very hard to find out exactly how much impact changing roles has on these women's mental health, especially because they are reluctant to reveal their emotional problems. Though the limited studies on Vietnamese women do not emphasize their mental health problems, the phenomenon still remains an issue within the Vietnamese American community, especially among the women.

What can be done to help them? The past cannot be undone, but with    31
appropriate and well-conceived programs, the mental health of these women can be improved. They need encouragement to open up and talk about their problems so they can receive help and support in overcoming their difficulties. A small program with specially trained counselors can be a source of relief and information for the women. The program must be promoted so the Vietnamese people can become acquainted with the service. In time a successful program will have the old members coming back to help the new members overcome their hardships. To alleviate the difficulty of adjusting to a new culture and

25. Hirayama, "Effects of Employment," 144.

environment, the program could be expanded to teach Vietnamese women about the American way of life and Vietnamese men about the need to be more understanding and compassionate.

32        Vietnamese women hope to be more productive and contribute to their new society, and to enjoy their lives after the long struggle for freedom and happiness. And overall there is a positive outlook for the Vietnamese woman. As Lan Nguyen said, "I would not exchange anything for the life that I have now. A woman now has a chance to lead a happy and meaningful life for herself, instead of devoting it only to her husband and family." ✢

RESPONDING

1.    In a journal entry, discuss the way you handle stress. Do you feel comfortable talking to others, or do you prefer to keep silent? How does your response to stress compare to the way Luu says Vietnamese women are expected to respond to stressful situations? How much of your and their behavior is a result of acculturation?

2.    Working individually or in a group, discuss the hardships faced by Vietnamese women during their evacuation and resettlement. In your opinion, which problems are the most difficult to cope with: those connected with leaving a familiar culture, those connected with entering an unfamiliar one, or other problems? Share your conclusions with the class.

3.    According to Luu, one of the major upheavals in Vietnamese family life in the United States has been the changing role of women. Write an essay that explores this change and analyzes the factors in American society that have resulted in changing roles for both men and women.

4.    Conduct your own interview of a recent immigrant to the United States, your state, or your city. Write a report for the class investigating the difficulties of moving to a new place and adapting to a new culture.

# JOSE ALEJANDRO ROMERO

*José Alejandro Romero, a Salvadorean émigré, has witnessed and attempted to protest against the repression and barbarism of El Salvador's right-wing dictatorship. Some of his poetry reflects on the suffering of that country. It is within this context of repression that Romero places the incident at Sumpul, where six hundred men, women, and children were massacred—while a few nursing mothers watched horrified from the shore. As the author explains, "Sumpul is a river dividing El Salvador and Honduras. On May 14, 1980, peasants fleeing to Honduras were pursued by the Salvadoran army for many days. Reaching Sumpul and what they believed would be safety, they faced on the other side the hostile Honduran army. While most of the people were in the middle of the river, which was at that point about 100 meters wide, the two armies opened fire, shooting until everyone in the water was dead. No sign of life remained, only the water mixed with the blood of the dead."*

*In the poem that follows, the river Sumpul becomes a mirror, for it reflects the pain of those who were helpless witnesses to the massacre, and those whose bodies have found no other grave.*

✛

# SUMPUL

The afternoon has fallen into black dust,
and from the dust emerges death.
In the red river we swam, desperate to live.
We splashed in its waters and then,
bruised, we were floated by them.                                    5
From the river the massacred body arose.
Sumpul drowned in blood,
Sumpul deafened by the shots,
river turned red,
river swollen with anguish,                                          10
witnessing river, your hidden heart
containing the anonymous screams of martyrs—
of children, tender shoots,
of mothers, fruiting trees
and old ones ancient oaks.                                           15

Facing you is Yankee torture,
murderous sounds and the growl of the dog,
splattering this universe with shrapnel,
splitting open pregnant stars,
20    slashing the face of the peasant.
Beast, take note:
the worker's face will carry this scar.

River,
We seek your water made holy by force,
25    and with it anoint our arms,
with reddened eyes.
In a single, slaughtered droplet we watch
the sun, its hopeful yellow;
in its yellow is a future,
30    a victory, a triumph, a people.
In your winding current
We seek the wide and war-injured reflection of the people
confronting a vast machine;
their last words cursing despotism
35    their words like weapons, their body a shield,
their ideals, pure light.

I want to respond to the screams of the people,
to fixed eyes shooting off hatred,
to hoist your spirit in the fighting flag of guns.
40    I salute you with each shot aimed at the enemy
I swear to remember you in our future land,
and in the sky brimming with stars,
and in the first maize field of winter,
and in the waters of every river where I live.  ✠

---

## RESPONDING

1. In a journal entry, respond to what the river has witnessed. Were you aware
   of the historical event presented here? Did prior knowledge or lack of
   knowledge influence your reaction to the poem? You may want to describe
   your feelings as you read.

2. Working individually or in a group, describe the speaker in the poem. What is the speaker's situation? Be sure to use specific lines or phrases from the poem to support your interpretation.

3. The author uses poetry to express his feelings about an important event in his country's history. Write a poem about a place or event that is particularly meaningful to you.

---

# BHARATI MUKHERJEE

*Born in Calcutta, India, in 1940, Bharati Mukherjee has lived since the 1960s in the United States and Canada. After earning her master's degree from the University of Baroda in 1961 and her doctorate from the University of Iowa in 1969, she has taught English at McGill University in Montreal, Quebec, Skidmore College in New York, and the University of California, Berkeley. In addition to contributing stories and essays to journals, Mukherjee has published several novels, including* The Tiger's Daughter *(1972),* Wife *(1975),* Jasmine *(1989),* Leave It to Me *(1992), and* The Holder of the World *(1993); the short-story collections* Darkness *(1985) and* The Middleman and Other Stories *(1988); as well as several nonfiction works. Her writing has won awards from many sources, including the Canadian government, the Canadian Arts Council, the Guggenheim Foundation, the National Endowment for the Arts, and the National Book Critics.*

*"Visitors" explores how a person's cultural background helps determine how one behaves and how one can interpret or misinterpret the behavior of others.*

⊞

# VISITORS

WHEN VINITA LIVED IN CALCUTTA, she had many admirers. Every morning at ten minutes after nine o'clock when she left home for Loreto College where she majored in French literature, young men with surreptitious hands slipped love notes through the half-open windows of her father's car and were sternly rebuked by the chauffeur. The notes were almost always anonymous; when she read them in class, tucked between the pages of Rimbaud and Baudelaire, the ferocity of passion never failed to thrill and alarm her.

2    For a time after college she worked as a receptionist in the fancy downtown Chowringhee office of a multinational corporation. She had style, she had charm, and everyone genuinely liked her. Especially two junior executives from the fifth floor which was occupied by a company that exported iron manhole covers. If it hadn't been for Vinita's tact, and her ability to make each of the suitors feel that he was the one who made her happier, the two men might have become embittered rivals. She was quietly convivial and on weekdays went, usually in a group of six or eight, for Chinese lunches to the Calcutta Club. Even the club waiters brightened up when they saw Vinita, though she had never actually been heard to say anything more personal to them than, "A lime soda, please, no ice," or "I'll have the Chou En Lai carp."

3    She had known all along that after marriage she would have to leave Calcutta. Her parents wanted to marry her off to a doctor or engineer of the right caste and class but resident abroad, preferably in America. The groom they finally selected for her was a thirty-five-year-old accountant, Sailen Kumar, a well-mannered and amiable-looking man, a St. Stephen's graduate who had gone on to London University and Harvard and who now worked for a respectable investment house in Manhattan and lived in a two-bedroom condominium with access to gym, pool and sauna across the river. He was successful—and well off, Vinita's parents decided—by anyone's standards. Six days after the wedding, Vinita took an Air India flight to citizenship in the New World.

4    Marriage suits Vinita. In the months she has been a wife in Guttenberg, New Jersey, she has become even prettier. Her long black hair has a gloss that owes as much to a new sense of well-being as to the new shampoos she tries out and that leave her head smelling of herbs, fruits and flowers. Her surroundings—the sleek Bloomingdale's furniture Sailen had bought just before flying out to find a bride in India, the coordinated linen for bed and bath, and the wide, gleaming appliances in the kitchenette—please her. She finds it hard to believe that she has been gifted the life of grace and ease that she and her Loreto College friends had coveted from reading old copies of *Better Homes and Gardens* in Calcutta. This life of grace and ease has less to do with modern conveniences such as the microwave oven built into a narrow wall which is covered with designer wallpaper, and more to do with moods and traits she recognizes as new in herself. Happiness, expressiveness, bad temper: all these states seem valuable and exciting to her. But she is not sure she deserves this life. She has done nothing exceptional. She has made no brave choices. The decision to start over on a new continent where hard work is more often than not rewarded with comfort has been her parents', not hers. If her father had brought her a proposal and photograph from an upright hydraulics engineer living in a government project site in the wilds of Durgapur or from a rich radiologist with a clinic on a quiet boulevard in South Calcutta, she would have accepted the proposal with the same cheerfulness she has shown Sailen Kumar. She's a little taken aback by the

idea of just desserts. Back home good fortune had been exactly that: a matter of luck and fortune, a deity's decision to humor and indulge. She remembered the fables she read as a child in which a silly peasant might find a pitcher of gold *mohurs* on his way to the village tank for his bath. But in America, at least in New Jersey, everyone Vinita meets seems to acknowledge a connection between merit and reward. Everyone looks busy, distraught from overwork. Even the building's doorman; she worries about Castro, the doorman. Such faith in causality can only lead to betrayal.

Vinita expected married life, especially married life in a new country and with no relatives around, to change her. Overnight she would become mature, complex, fascinating: a wife, instead of a daughter. Thoughts of change did not frighten her. Discreet, dutiful, comfortable with her upper-class status, she had been trained by her mother to stay flexible, to roll with whatever punches the Communist government of Calcutta might deliver. In Vinita's childhood, the city had convulsed through at least two small revolutions. Some nights in Guttenberg, New Jersey, even with her eyes closed, she can see a fresh, male corpse in a monsoon muddy gutter. Her parents still talk of the two boys who had invaded their lawn one heady afternoon of class struggle and pointed pipe-guns at the trembling gardener. Sometimes the designer wallpaper seems to ripple like leaves in a breeze, and she feels herself being watched.

But it's not the corpse, not the undernourished child-rebels, who feed her nightmares. It's nothing specific. She considers fear of newness a self-indulgence, quite unworthy of someone who has wanted all along to exchange her native world for an alien one. The slightest possibility of disruption pleases her. But if change has come into her life as Mrs. Sailen Kumar, it has seeped in so gradually that she can't fix it with one admiring stare when she Windexes toothpaste flecks off the bathroom mirror.

This afternoon Vinita has three visitors. Two of them are women, Mrs. Leela Mehra and Mrs. Kamila Thapar, wives of civil engineers. They stay just long enough to have spiced tea with onion pakoras and to advise her on which Indian grocers carry the freshest tropical products in the "Little India" block on Lexington. Vinita is convinced the real reason they have come to visit is to check out what changes she, the bride, has made to Sailen's condominium. They have known her husband for almost ten years. Mr. Thapar and Sailen roomed together when both were new to America (she has trouble visualizing the dark-suited, discreetly groomed men as callow foreign students forty pounds lighter with little money and too much ambition). Sailen, while sketching in his bachelor life—all those years when she had not known that the man of her dreams would have only nine fingers—had told her how the Thapars and the Mehras made themselves his substitute family in the new world, how they fed him curries most weekends, made him sleep on their lumpy front room sofas instead of letting him take a late-night bus back to Manhattan, and how the two women hummed bits of old Hindi film songs to tease him into nostalgia. Otherwise, they said, he'd become bad-tempered and self-centered, too American. In Mrs. Mehra's and Mrs. Thapar's presence, Vinita is the intruder.

8      After they leave, Vinita takes out a rubber-banded roll of aerogrammes from a desk built into the wall system. She makes a list of the people she must write today:

1.   her parents (a short but vivacious note)
2.   her closest Loreto College friend who now works for Air India
3.   her married sister in Bombay (it can wait till the weekend)
4.   Mother Stella, the Mauritian nun who'd taught her French.

9      Writing letters on the pale blue aerogramme paper makes her feel cheerful and just a little noble. Writing to Mother Stella puts her in a special mood, a world tinged slightly with poetic, even rhapsodic passion. Even lines of Rimbaud's deemed unsuitable for maidenly Calcutta teenagers were somehow tamed by Mother Stella's exquisite elocution. How preposterous was a passion—*le dos de ces Mains est la place qu'en baisa tout Révolté fier!*—parsed by a half-Indian, French-speaking, Mauritian nun.

10     She writes her mother, converting each small episode—buying half a dozen cheese Danishes, spraying herself with expensive fragrances from tester atomizers—into grand adventures. When she licks and seals each envelope, she is grateful Sailen agreed to her father's proposal of marriage and that she is now cut off from her moorings. Her letters are intended to please and comfort. She knows that when the postman rings his bicycle bell and keels into the driveway twice a day, the servants, her mother, her sister, her friend and even the nun who has taught her all she knows about literature and good manners run to the front door hoping for a new installment of her idylls in America. But before Vinita can decide what vivacious clichés to end her last letter with, a third visitor arrives at the door and holds out a bright, amateurish poster announcing an Odissi dance recital on the Columbia campus.

11     "Mrs. Kumar, I thought you would be interested in dance performances," the visitor says. He smiles, but does not step into the tiny hall which is crowded with a pair of Vishnupuri clay horses and a tall, cylindrical Chinese vase that holds umbrellas. "I was afraid that you and Mr. Kumar might not have heard about Rooma Devi coming to Columbia."

12     "Odissi style?" She knows it is up to her to invite him in or send him away. She has met him, yes, she has talked to him at three, maybe four, cultural evenings organized by one of the Indian Associations in Manhattan. He is a graduate student in history at Columbia.

13     "Mrs. Kumar, if you don't mind my saying so, the first time I saw you I could tell that you yourself were a dancer. Right?"

14     She glances at him shyly, and steps back, her slippers grazing the rough clay foot of one of the giant horses. Still she doesn't ask him in. Let him make that

decision. In India, she would feel uncomfortable—she knows she would!—if she found herself in an apartment alone with a man not related to her, but the rules are different in Guttenberg. Here one has to size up the situation and make up one's own rules. Or is it, here, that one has to seize the situation?

"You have the grace of a *danseuse*," he says. 15

Vinita has not heard anyone use the word *danseuse*. She likes the word; it 16 makes her feel elegant and lissom. "I'll have to confess I am. I've danced a bit. But not in years."

She blushes, hoping to pass off for modesty the guilt she feels at having 17 lied. She is not a dancer, not a real dancer. She has studied Rabindra-style dancing for about six years. Her mother, who regarded dancing as necessary a feminine accomplishment as singing and gourmet cooking, had forced the two sisters to take weekly lessons at a fine arts academy in Ballygunge. She looks down at the floor, at his two-tone New Balance running shoes. The shoes deepen her blush. She is in a new country with no rules. No grown man in India she knows wears gym shoes except for cricket or squash. But there's mud on his New Balances, a half-moon of mud around each toe part. He has taken the bus to Guttenberg, New Jersey, just to make sure that she'll know about the recital. Because he has guessed—he had divined—that she is a *danseuse*.

She takes two hesitant steps back, her left hand entwined with the elongated 18 clay neck of the larger horse. Here, as in India, friends stop by without calling, and she is foolish to worry over why the graduate student in his running shoes has come with a poster in the early afternoon. ("All that formality of may-I-come? or hope-we're-not-disturbing-you is for Westerners," the immigrants joke among themselves. She has heard it once already this afternoon from Mrs. Thapar. "We may have minted a bit of money in this country, but that doesn't mean we've let ourselves become Americans. You can see we've remained one hundred percent simple and *deshi* in our customs.") Vinita wants to remain *deshi* too, but being *deshi* and letting in this good-looking young man (a line darts across an imaginary page, enunciated in rotund Mauritian French and Vinita almost giggles: *Le jeune homme dont l'oeil est brillant, la peau brune, Le beau corps de vingt ans qui devrait aller nu* . . . and Vinita blushes again, more deeply), a young man who told her the first time they met, after a movie, that he'd been born in Calcutta but immigrated with his parents when he was just a toddler—letting him in might lead to disproportionate disaster.

"It is very kind of you, Mr. Khanna, to bring over Rooma Devi's poster," 19 she says miserably. She has never heard of Rooma Devi. Rooma Devi cannot possibly be a ranking Odissi dancer. Yet Rooma Devi has succeeded in pounding thin whatever tranquility the promise of letter-writing had produced in Vinita.

"You remember my name, Mrs. Kumar?" It is not so much a question as 20 an ecstatic exhalation. "But please call me Rajiv. Unless you want to call me Billoo, which was my pet name in India. Just don't call me Bill."

She is relieved that Rajiv Khanna is inside the condominium and that the 21 period of indecision is over. He has somehow shut the front door behind him and has suspended his baseball cap on the smaller horse's ear.

22    "Would you like some authentic India-style tea?" she asks. It is the correct thing for an Indian hostess to do, even in New Jersey; to offer the guest something to drink, even if it's just a glass of water. "I am making it exactly like the *chai wallahs*. I am boiling tea leaves in a mixture of milk, water and sugar, and throwing in pinches of cardamom, cloves, cinnamon, etcetera."

23    "I don't want you stuck in the kitchen," he laughs. "I want you to tell me stories about Calcutta. I was only three when Baba took the post-doctoral fellowship at Madison but I still remember what our alley smelled like in July and August." He laughs again, hyper and nervous. "Let's use teabags. You must take advantage of American shortcuts."

24    Rajiv Khanna stalks her into the living room, forcing her to take quicker steps than usual so his New Balances won't catch the thin, stiff leather edges of her Sholapuri slippers. She begins to see Sailen's Bloomingdale decor—the pastel conversation pit made up of modular sofas, the patio-atrium corner defined by white wicker—the way a hard-up graduate student might, as opulent, tasteful. When Rajiv compliments her artistic touch, she swings back to smile at him, bashful but flattered.

25    An issue of *Technology Review* on an obviously new coffee table catches his eye, and he lingers in the conversation pit, one knee resting deeply on an ottoman. In that pose, he reminds her of marsh birds she had seen on vacations in rural Bengal. The image automatically makes her pitch her voice low. Her gestures now softly wary, so the bird will not fly off.

26    She slips off to the kitchenette to make tea. The work counter of butcher's block is a barrier against the unseemly jokes that fate might decide to try out on her. In fact, in the bluish-white fluorescent light that threatens to never burn out, her earlier fears now seem absurd.

27    "I miss the cultural events of Calcutta," she says chattily. "It's such a lively city. Always some theatrical program, some crafts exhibit, something that touches the heart." From the asylum of the kitchenette, she watches him flip through the pages of Sailen's magazine without actually reading. There's an archness to her posture, she knows. She can feel her body tauten the way it often had in college while Mother Stella sanitized the occasional salacious verse. *On n'est pas sérieux, quand on a dix-sept ans*, Rimbaud said, but now she thinks twenty-five is not a matronly age. Mrs. Mehra and Mrs. Thapar are at least ten years older than her. Sailen had specified to his parents that he wanted a youngish bride, one who could speak fluent English and who could—once he felt he could afford it—bear him two or three children. He has spoken to her of his dream of having a son play in Little League games. Hearing him dream aloud, she assumed that it wasn't so much a son that he wanted as to assimilate, to be a *pukka* American.

28    Rajiv Khanna ignores her comment. He sits astride the new coffee table (she's distracted with worry that if the glass top breaks, it cannot be replaced; or more accurately, that if the table falls apart she'll have to confess, but confess

seductive, charming and inviolable. They alternate between being deferential and being flirtatious. They plague her with questions about local politics in India. They tease her about being a spoiled, rich girl and therefore, a novice cook who makes pakors and samosas. They beg her to sing them a Tagore song (but my harmonium hasn't arrived yet!) because it's already gotten around (from that nice Khanna boy who studies at Columbia, a bright boy, says Sailen) that she must be a talented singer. She is ecstatic; she serves the men and manipulates them with her youth and her beauty and her unmistakable charm. She has no idea that she is on the verge of hysteria. She has no idea.

53 That night in bed, for the first time since she has left Calcutta, she is bothered by insomnia. Within reach, but not touching her, Sailen sleeps on his stomach. He is breathing through his mouth. She imagines his fleshy lips; they flap like rubber tires. He is a good man, and one day he will be a millionaire. He has never, not once, by gesture or word, made her feel that she is anything but the queen of his heart.

54 Why then is she moved by an irresistible force to steal out of his bed in the haven of his expensive condominium, and run off into the alien American night where only shame and disaster can await her? ✤

## RESPONDING

1. Imagine that Vinita had waited to write her letters until after Rajiv Khanna's visit. Consider how her letters might change, and write the letter she might have written to her parents, her closest college friend, her married sister, or Mother Stella. In whom might she confide?

2. Working individually or in a group, list the behavior expected from a traditional Indian woman. How traditional is Vinita? Compare what is required of her by her family and society with what you believe to be required of American women.

[Continue] the story or write an essay that explains how the story might [c]ontinue. Will Vinita stay with her husband or strike out on her own? Do [sh]ame and disaster await her if she leaves her husband? If she remains, how [wil]l she feel? Consider what might influence her decision and the gains and [loss]es of either position.

[the]re a stereotype of a new immigrant? If so, does Vinita fit that stereo-[type?] Explain your answers in an essay that presents the characteristics of [the st]ereotype and compares Vinita with it. If you believe there is no [stereoty]pe, compare Vinita with another new immigrant you have read [or] know personally.

to what?) and drums his thighs with his fingertips. The fingers are long, the fingers of a poet. No wonder he has not been absorbed by Sailen's *Technology Review*. She waits for him to make small talk, to keep up his part as charming guest.

29 "I can't believe I went through with it!" It's an outburst, and it confuses her. She busies herself with cups and saucers.

30 "I can't believe I had the courage!"

31 She steals a look at him, thankful for the cumulous clouds of steam from the boiling water. Courage for what? Instinctively, she smooths down the hair on her crown which she knows from experience turns frizzy in hot, humid weather. Girls should make the best of their looks. She's been taught this by the nuns at school and by her relatives for so long that prettying herself has become a habit, not a vanity. Rajiv approaches her, his gait uneven, nervous; he is a potential invader of her kitchenette-fortress.

32 "I knew you were special the very first time I saw you. At the India Republic Day celebrations at the Khoranas'. I told myself this is it, this is the goddess of my dreams. I couldn't get you out of my mind."

33 Vinita finishes steeping two Twining teabags in a teapot before responding to the young visitor's outburst. She is not as shocked as she had expected to be. Yes, she has rehearsed moments like this; she has put herself on the television screen, in the roles of afternoon wives taken in passion. Not as shocked as she *should* have been, she worries. A warmth (from Rajiv's compliment? from anxiety? the kettle's steam?) swirls just under her glycerine-and-rose-watered skin. She concentrates on making tea; the brew must be just the right amber color. But tea-making in New Jersey is no challenge. She plucks and dunks each bag repeatedly by its frail string. You give up a little taste, but you grab a little convenience cleaning up. The new world forces you to know what you really want.

34 He barks again. "You haven't discouraged me."

35 She shrinks behind the counter. He shakes an accusatory index finger. She draws the loose end of her sari over her right shoulder so that her arms, her silk-bloused breasts and bare midriff are swathed. But the sari was bought at the Sari Palace on Lexington, and her breasts seem to her to loom and soar, through the Japanese chiffon. The young man has turned her into a siren.

36 "I don't know what you mean." She wants to sound stuffy, but it comes out, she knows, innocent, simpering.

37 "You should have thrown me out minutes ago. You could have refused to let me in. I know you Indian girls. You could have taken the poster and slammed the door in my face. But you didn't!"

38 He is a madman. It's true; he *is* a madman, but she is no siren. She repeats this to herself, a litany against calamity. Because of his windbreaker and his running shoes she has assumed he was just another American, no one to convert her into a crazy emblem. She had assumed that he was the looter of American culture, not hers, and she had envied the looting. Her own transition was slow and wheezing.

39 "You offered to make tea instead." He sounds triumphant.

40 "It was the least I could offer a guest," she retorts. "I haven't lost all my manners because I've moved to a new country. I know some Americans won't even give you a glass of water when you drop in."

41 He is not listening. He blabs, high-pitched angry words undulating from his fleshy lips. Love, it would appear, torments Rajiv. The face, which she had initially considered symmetrical, now devastates her from across the butcher's block counter, the features harsh, moody. His New Balance shoes are anachronistic; he is a lover from the turn-of-the-century novels of Sarat Chandra, the poems of Rimbaud—*Oh! quel Rêve les a saisies . . . un rêve inouï des Asies, Des Khenghavars ou des Sions?*—unmoored by passion. One long-lashed furtive glance from the woman next door, the servant girl, the movie star, and the hero's calamitous fate is sealed. But this is America, she insists. There is no place for feelings here! We are both a new breed, testing new feelings in new battle-grounds. We must give in to the old world's curb.

42 "Let's be civilized," she pleads, by which she means, let's be modern and Indian. "Take your cup, and let's sit in the patio. My husband will be here any minute and he'd be so disappointed if you left without seeing him. He thinks you're a brilliant boy." She's pleased at her own diplomacy. She has nipped passion before it can come to full fury, she has flattered his intelligence and she has elevated herself to the role of older sister or youngish aunt.

43 "Confess!" he demands. "I must mean something special to you. Otherwise you wouldn't have tolerated me this long. You'd have called Mr. Kumar or the police."

44 "I think you are unwell," she ventures. She hates him for considering her lascivious. She hates herself for not having thought of calling her husband. But what could she have said over the phone to a dark-suited man in an office cubicle concentrating hard on a computer terminal? Please come home and protect me from that Khanna boy who fancies he's in love with me?

45 He lunges at her. Suddenly the kitchenette counter seems a frail barrier. Tea spurts into a pretty saucer and stains the butcher's block. She has no time to tear off squares of paper towel and wipe up the spill. His right arm snakes toward her, reaches up through the chiffon sari; the snake's jaws, closing on a breast, scratch her hand instead.

46 "Madman!" she screams. Her side, her breast, her hand, all burn with shame. The snake's jaws have found the breast. She is paralyzed.

47 "You have no right to play with my feelings, Vinita! Confess at once!"

48 The situation is absolutely preposterous. She has been taught by Mother Stella and by her parents how to deal with revolutions. She can disarm an emaciated Communist pointing a pipe-gun at her pet chihuahua. She can drive her father's new Hindustan Ambassador and she's beginning to drive on weekends to local shopping malls. But banal calamities, the mad passions of a maladjusted failed American make her shudder.

49 Rajiv lets go. He picks up his cup and saucer and flounces off to the patio.

She watches him curl up on the wicker love seat, his New Balance shoes polluting the new cushions with street germs. He admires Sailen's careful grouping of rare orchids with all the confidence of an invited guest. All but one of the orchids are in their prime this afternoon, and their thick petals glow in the odd New Jersey light. Her breast tingles. It feels warm; it feels recently caressed. She leans her forehead against the fake Ionic column that marks off the alcove for the refrigerator, and wonders if the torment that the madman in her atrium feels is the same torment she too would have suffered if she had the courage to fall in love.

50 At seven-twenty, Sailen comes home. Tonight he has brought Vinod Mehra and Kailash Kapoor with him. They go to the same fitness club after work. Rajiv Khanna left soon after finishing his cup of tea, so Vinita has had time to bathe at five-thirty as usual (she maintains the Indian habit of bathing twice a day), to put on a purple silk sari she knows looks quite seductive on her, dress her long hair elaborately with silver pins and cook dinner. The dinner includes six courses, not counting the bottled pickles and the store-bought pie for dessert. Cooking a fancy meal has been her self-acknowledged expiation, though in h heart she is sure (why shouldn't she be sure?) that she has committed transgression. Now seeing the unexpected guests, she is relieved that thei coincides with the night of her extra effort. What if she had made noth *dal*, rice and a vegetable curry? Rumors about Sailen Kumar's brid Sailen Kumar would have startled to swirl through highrises in Br Rego Park.

The men congregate in the atrium. It is quite obviously Sai joy; therefore, by extension, it is Vinita's pride and joy, too. S show off his newest acquisitions in plants and flowers. In gardener and his grandson had taken care of such things. blossoms only in terms of interior decoration, how the ground of new pink silk drapes, for instance. Now differently, as though selecting them at the florist's, winter in overheated rooms and pruning them to self-expression. In fact, she has heard Sailen ju condominium in New Jersey instead of across pointing at the atrium. You couldn't afford t you were a millionaire. Of course, she k millionaire, as do his close friends, especi Indian community knows that Vinod M he is fifty. He plays the stock marke Everybody respects him for being a

She reminds her husband to fi about shaking cocktails and pour infectious laugh—and runs between and deep-fried tidbits like vegetable paku

# CATHY SONG

*Cathy Song was born in Honolulu, Hawaii, in 1955. She attended the University of Hawaii, graduated from Wellesley College in 1977, and received a master's degree in creative writing from Boston University in 1981. Her poems have appeared in many journals, among them* Amerasia Journal, The American Poetry Review, Poetry, *and* The Seneca Review. *Her publications include* Picture Bride *(1982),* Frameless Windows, Squares of Light *(1988), and* School Figures *(1994). She was selected as the winner of the Yale Series of Younger Poets Competition in 1982, which praised her poems for "remind[ing] a loud, indifferent, hard world of what truly matters to the human spirit."*

*Song's poem "Easter: Wahiawa, 1959," which appears in* Picture Bride, *explores the special significance of simple objects as parts of both a family ritual and a personal exchange between a young person and her grandfather.*

❖

## *EASTER: WAHIAWA, 1959*

### *1*

The rain stopped for one afternoon.
Father brought out
his movie camera and for a few hours
we were all together
under a thin film                                          5
that separated the rain showers
from that part of the earth
like a hammock
held loosely by clothespins.

Grandmother took the opportunity                          10
to hang the laundry
and Mother and my aunts
filed out of the house
in pedal pushers and poodle cuts,
carrying the blue washed eggs.                            15

Grandfather kept the children
penned in on the porch,
clucking at us in his broken English
whenever we tried to peek
20     around him. There were bread crumbs
stuck to his blue gray whiskers.

I looked from him to the sky,
a membrane of egg whites
straining under the weight
25     of the storm that threatened
to break.

We burst loose from Grandfather
when the mothers returned
from planting the eggs
30     around the soggy yard.
He followed us,
walking with stiff but sturdy legs.
We dashed and disappeared
into bushes,
35     searching for the treasures;
the hard-boiled eggs
which Grandmother had been simmering
in vinegar and blue color all morning.

**2**

When Grandfather was a young boy
40     in Korea,
it was a long walk
to the riverbank,
where, if he were lucky,
a quail egg or two
45     would gleam from the mud
like gigantic pearls.
He could never eat enough
of them.

It was another long walk
through the sugarcane fields                                    50
of Hawaii,
where he worked for eighteen years,
cutting the sweet stalks
with a machete. His right arm
grew disproportionately large                                   55
to the rest of his body.
He could hold three
grandchildren in that arm.

I want to think
that each stalk that fell                                       60
brought him closer
to a clearing,
to that palpable field
where from the porch
to the gardenia hedge                                           65
that day he was enclosed
by his grandchildren,
scrambling around him,
for whom he could at last buy
cratefuls of oranges,                                           70
basketfuls of sky blue eggs.

I found three that afternoon.
By evening, it was raining hard.
Grandfather and I skipped supper.
Instead, we sat on the porch                                    75
and I ate what he peeled
and cleaned for me.
The scattering of the delicate
marine-colored shells across his lap
was something like what the ocean gives                         80
the beach after a rain. ✛

## RESPONDING

1. Write a poem or a short story about a favorite relative.

2. Working in groups, read the poem aloud. Pay special attention to the way things look, sound, feel, and smell, and try to relay these perceptions using as much specific detail as you can. Listen to the language of the poem, observing rhythms and recurring sounds. Where do these occur and what is their effect?

3. Discuss the time, the setting, and the activities presented in the poem in an essay. Why do you think Song chose to write about an Easter egg hunt?

4. The author gives the reader hints about the history of the family in the poem. Write a prose version that fills in the family history. Use clues in the poem to tell you who they are, where they originally came from, and what their lives are like. The poet speaks in the first person, but are these her family members and is this a real memory?

# NAOMI SHIHAB NYE

*The poet Naomi Shihab Nye was born in 1952 of an American mother and a Palestinian father in St. Louis, Missouri. She graduated from Trinity University in 1974 and now lives in San Antonio, Texas, where she plays an instrumental role in the state poetry-in-the-schools program. Her works include* Different Ways to Pray *(1980),* On the Edge of the Sky *(1981),* Hugging the Jukebox *(1982),* This Same Sky: A Collection of Poems from Around the World *(1993),* Connected *(1994),* The Words Under the Words: Selected Poems *(1995), and* Fuel: Poems *(1998). Her awards include the Pushcart Prize, the Texas Institute of Letters Poetry Prize, the Charity Fandall Prize for Spoken Poetry from the International Poetry Forum, and the I. B. Lavan Award from the Academy of American Poets.*

*The three prose poems that follow reflect on the importance of grandparents, a sense of place, and saved objects in helping the writer fashion an identity.*

✣

# WHITE COALS

SCARCELY ANYTHING BIGGER THAN THE QUESTIONS I didn't ask. What happened    1
to my mouth? I traveled all the way across the ocean with my mouth and couldn't
get the questions out. A stiff-haired cat perched on the high stone wall between
leafless brambles staring down at me. The cat with his elegant command of two
silences. It was *cold.* My grandmother had *bare feet.* She held her feet by a crooked
brazier of whitened coals. She turned her hands over and over. In the six years
since our last meeting a tiredness had gathered itself, stonelike, in the corners
of her eyes. She could say anything she wanted but she didn't want much.
Holding her gaze to the floor, she wouldn't look up for pictures. I wanted to
describe the silent women on Maunakea Street in Honolulu who sit all day
poking needles through the hearts of flowers. The tight purple orchid, its silken
lips. I wanted to ask advice: What should we tell our child about his living? But
my mouth went heavy, my mouth wouldn't say. It said, Would you like these
socks? My grandmother who will never wear a lei, I string you with questions,
from a great distance each one flies to your shoulders, pulsing, a bird turned
into a flower, folding its wings.

# BROKEN CLOCK

WHAT DOES TIME LOOK LIKE from your chair? Once you cowered in a ditch as    1
Turkish soldiers on horseback roared past. Your family remembers this when
they try to calculate your age. You don't throw anything away. You've saved bits
of a smashed blue plate, a broken clock. Recently my father heard of a blind
woman in the next village with a documented age of 106 who had known you
all her life. Take me there, he said. He stood in the outer room while the
woman's son addressed her loudly. "You remember your friend Khadra Shihab's
youngest son Aziz?" The woman shouted back immediately. "You mean that
terrible awful boy who broke his mother's heart by going to America? Of course
I remember him! How could I forget?"

My father, in the next room, shrinking to the size of a button. Ushered into    2
the woman's presence with a stuck jaw. A peep. "How old is my mother?" She
said without hesitating, 104. They always had two years between them. You
know if someone else is a little younger than you are, but not much. You know.
She remembered, in fact, when Khadra was born, in those other houses, that
other world. When they were very young, even then, two years. "And what will
you do now?" she asked him. "After so much being away, how does it feel to
return? Does anything know you now? Do the trees know you? Does the prayer
know you? And where do you go when you leave here? Does this place really
let you leave?"

# SPEAKING ARABIC

1    "Why, if i'm part arab, can't I speak Arabic?" My son, age five, wanting to answer his cousin who calls him to follow her into the kitchen, she shows how she turns the pot of rice and eggplant over onto the silver tray. How the food slips out to stand up like a building. The sizzled pine nuts, poured over the top in a fine fragrant flourish. Then she carries it all on her head into the room where we sit, and we eat with forks from the same giant platter, which I have never gotten used to. The cousins and neighbors file in to say, "Keef ha-lik?"— the door opening into a thousand rooms.

2    For months in America our son will be placing plates on his head. "This is how Janan would do it."

3    Why, if we're part anything, does it matter? I had to live in a mostly Mexican-American city to feel what it meant to be part-Arab. It meant Gift. It meant Take the Ribbon and Unwind it Slowly.

4    Why can't I forget the earnest eyes of the man who said to me in Jordan, "Until you speak Arabic, you will not understand pain"? Ridiculous! I thought. He went on, something to do with the back of the head, an Arab carrying sorrow in the back of the head that only language cracks. A few words couldn't do it. A general passive understanding wasn't enough. At a neighborhood fair in Texas, somewhere between the German Oom-pah Sausage Stand and the Mexican Gorditas booth, I overheard a young man say to his friend, "I wish *I* had a heritage. Sometimes I feel—so lonely for one." And the tall American trees were dangling their thick branches right down over his head.  ✣

---

RESPONDING

1.   In a journal entry, write about a time you visited family you hadn't seen for a long time or a place where you once lived. How did you feel? Had things changed? Were there adjustments to make?

2.   Working individually or in a group, discuss the selections. Are they prose or poetry? Support your opinion with evidence from the readings. Then focus on the individual selections. Fill in the information the reader must supply in order to fully understand each piece. For example, who is speaking? What is taking place? Why did the author expect the reader to fill in many of the narrative details?

3.  In "Speaking Arabic," Nye quotes a young American, "'I wish *I* had a heritage. Sometimes I feel—so lonely for one.' And the tall American trees were dangling their thick branches right down over his head" (paragraph 4). In an essay, define and discuss the American heritage. Why do you think the young American feels the way he does?

4.  One of the implications of the selection "Speaking Arabic" is that language is an important part of a culture and that until you know the language, you're not really a part of that culture. Do you agree or disagree? Support your argument with evidence from the reading, other sources, and your own observations.

# PETER H. SCHUCK

*Peter H. Schuck, who earned a bachelor's degree from Cornell University and a law degree from Harvard University, is currently Simeon E. Baldwin Professor at the Yale Law School. He has held several positions in public and private sectors, including Director of the District Office of the Consumers' Union, and Deputy Assistant Secretary for Planning and Evaluation at the U.S. Department of Health, Education, and Welfare. A visiting scholar at the American Enterprise Institute in 1979, he has been a member of the Yale Law School faculty since 1981. The author of several studies, including two studies of immigration law, he has also received a Guggenheim Fellowship.*

*In the essay that follows, Schuck outlines some of the difficulties with current immigration law and its enforcement.*

⁜

# BORDER CROSSING

AMERICA IS A NATION OF IMMIGRANTS. This is a cliché, of course, but it also raises an arresting, paradoxical question: Can we be a nation when we are so diverse? 1

A century ago, the confident, affirmative answer to this question was expressed in another cliché: the melting pot. Today, however, many Americans prefer other images—a stew, a salad, a mosaic—in which the many parts do not fully merge into the whole but instead retain their distinctive identities. To some Americans, this metaphorical shift calls for celebration; to others it is a source of profound anxiety. Although the jury is still out, I believe that the ultimate verdict will vindicate the optimists. 2

3    Immigration law has always mirrored the tensions among these competing images. In the beginning, there wasn't much law. Local communities actively recruited immigrants to work in their high-growth economies or else to join them as coreligionists. The few legal restrictions newcomers faced were imposed by states and localities concerned with revenue, public health, and the control of indigents. (Slaves, of course, were not voluntary immigrants and were intricately regulated.) Federal immigration restrictions, which would largely supplant state regulation, were not adopted until 1875 and did not significantly limit entry (except by Asians) until the 1920s.

4    Until recently, the constitutional law of immigration was remarkably simple and straightforward. The "plenary power doctrine" left Congress free to treat aliens pretty much as it liked, both procedurally and substantively. The Supreme Court in a 1953 case defined aliens' due process rights as whatever process Congress chose to provide. Congress delegated enormous administrative discretion to the Immigration and Naturalization Service (INS), and although aliens could challenge their deportation orders, the scope of review was usually narrow.

5    Even during the 1960s and 1970s, when the courts expanded constitutional rights and often overturned agency decisions in environmental, consumer, and other regulatory cases, immigration law remained anomalous, resisting the dominant rights-oriented trends in public law. While the courts occasionally read statutes creatively to protect aliens, the more typical pattern was one of abject judicial deference, producing a strikingly simple rule of decision: Unless the INS erred egregiously, the government won. Immigration law practice remained something of a backwater.

6    The first persistent signs of change occurred in the early 1980s, when political and doctrinal developments began to propel immigration law into the mainstream. An unprecedented surge of illegal migration to the United States, along with the new asylum process established under the Refugee Act of 1980, provided even undocumented aliens who were bound to lose on the merits with a fragile procedural foothold in the country. As a result of the new law, even a weak asylum claim could delay their removal for months or years. Not surprisingly, hundreds of thousands of undocumented aliens invoked the new process.

7    The courts now faced a host of new and difficult legal issues. They had to define the legal standards—substantive, procedural, and evidentiary—governing asylum claims, standards derived from both domestic and international law. Moreover, many hard constitutional issues were raised by the government's efforts to interdict aliens on the high seas or at the border, discourage them from applying for asylum, deny them social services and work permits, and detain (i.e., imprison) them pending completion of their proceedings (or indefinitely, if their countries refused to repatriate them).

8    An increasingly sophisticated, resourceful, and well-organized immigration bar litigated these complex issues. In addition to private firms, enterprising,

imaginative young public interest lawyers funded by foundation grants, public subsidies, and statutory fee awards, and sometimes allied with pro bono private practitioners and law school clinics, won many important cases against an overburdened, often outlawyered INS. To be sure, most of these victories were won in the lower federal courts, while the U.S. Supreme Court continued to defer to Congress and the INS, citing the old plenary power chestnuts. But even the Court renovated immigration law during the 1980s, liberally interpreting the procedural rights of returning resident aliens, the statutory rights of asylum claimants under the Refugee Act, and the constitutional rights of undocumented alien children to attend public schools at taxpayers' expense.

Meanwhile, legal immigration was steadily rising to near-record levels. Many immigration lawyers prospered by serving corporate clients, which routinely sought green cards, nonimmigrant (i.e., temporary) visas, status adjustments, and other immigration benefits needed for their existing and future employees. Family-based immigration practice, often overlapping with the business side, also grew. By 1990 business immigration law was a recognized boutique specialty in many large, diversified, full-service private firms. And as labor shortages developed during the mid- and late 1990s, this area of practice boomed. (Indeed, Congress recently authorized employers in the computer industry to import still more skilled workers.) Immigration law and practice had finally come of age.

Ironically, even the rise of illegal immigration has fueled business immigration practice. Congress's enactment of employer sanctions in 1986, although aimed at illegal aliens, has given immigration lawyers new corporate counseling and litigation opportunities. Moreover, almost half of the illegal aliens entered the U.S. legally but overstayed or otherwise violated their visa conditions. Their employers must often hire lawyers to prevent the INS from removing them.

While many of the recent changes target immigration lawyers' domestic and foreign business clients, other reforms primarily affect individual immigrants and their families. In 1996 Congress passed three statutes—the Antiterrorism and Effective Death Penalty Act (AEDPA), the Illegal Immigration Reform and Immigrant Responsibility Act (IIRIRA), and the so-called welfare reform law—that profoundly altered the balance that Congress and the courts had previously struck between law enforcement interests and immigrant rights.

AEDPA and IIRIRA impose harsh restrictions on the procedures available for determining aliens' legal status. IIRIRA created a process to summarily exclude aliens who arrive at the U.S. border without documents or with papers deemed fraudulent by INS inspectors, an error-prone process that may impede legitimate asylum claims. It also severely limits judicial review of INS decisions. And both the new laws impose particularly tough sanctions on aliens who committed crimes even long ago, requiring the INS to detain and remove them swiftly. At the same time, Congress also eliminated most of the INS's traditional discretion to waive exclusion, deportation, and detention for humanitarian, administrative, or other compelling reasons.

13    Many of the new provisions, such as one barring out-of-status aliens from receiving a legal visa for many years, target illegal aliens. Some, however, restrict even law-abiding, long-term legal immigrants. For example, IIRIRA makes it harder for low-income families to bring their relatives to the U.S., and the welfare reform law, even after recent liberalizing amendments, leaves many legal immigrants ineligible for most federally funded and state funded benefits, including SSI, AFDC, and food stamps. The 1996 laws together constitute the most radical reform of immigration law in decades—or perhaps ever. They responded to some genuinely difficult law enforcement problems. Congress, for example, was properly concerned about the endless procedural delays that many immigration lawyers and their clients have used to prolong their stays while they work and try to remain permanently through marriage, employment, amnesty, the visa lottery, or going underground if necessary. Congress was also concerned about the soaring criminal alien population. In 1980 fewer than 1,000 federal inmates were foreign-born, 3.6 percent of the total. By 1996 the number had grown to almost 31,000, or 29 percent of the total. Much the same was true of state prisons; the foreign-born accounted for an estimated 21 percent of California's prisoners and 13 percent of New York's. Nationwide, 300,000 or more deportable criminal aliens were in custody or under other legal supervision—almost ten times as many as in 1980—at an estimated cost of $6 billion per year. Yet despite a high-priority INS effort to deport these criminals, the agency managed to remove only 55,000 of them in 1998. (And even that low number represented a major improvement for the agency.)

14    Still, some of the new provisions are so extreme, misguided, or perverse that even the INS leadership considers them arbitrary, unfair, and unadministrable. Precluding the INS from granting aliens discretionary relief from deportation in hardship cases prevents the agency from making the humane, prudent adjustments that are often needed. Discretionary relief can also enable the agency to use its scarce enforcement resources more effectively and avoid public censure and embarrassment when its absurdly and cruelly inflexible decisions are brought to light, as they frequently are. The law's summary removal procedure for undocumented asylum claimants gives even the lowest-level inspector practically final say over such life-and-death issues as whether the individual will face persecution if returned to his country of origin. And the new restrictions on judicial review may well be unconstitutional if interpreted to preclude access to habeas corpus.

15    There is much to criticize in these measures, and Congress should revise them accordingly. Many immigrant advocates view these provisions as proof of a racist, xenophobic public backlash against recent immigrants, most of whom now come from underdeveloped countries in Latin America and Asia, not

Europe. These advocates also point to California voters' approval of ballot propositions in 1994 and 1998; the former (enjoined by a federal court) would bar illegal aliens from access to many public services, and the latter limits bilingual education programs.

Public attitudes toward immigration, however, are far more complicated— and interesting. Consider the following facts. First, challenges to the historically high levels of legal immigration set by the 1990 law have consistently failed. Congress has shown little interest even in the restrictions recommended by its own blue-ribbon Commission on Immigration Reform. Second, even illegal aliens have fared well in Congress, which not only legalized 2.7 million of them, mostly Mexicans, in the late 1980s but also within the last year enacted a new amnesty for some 400,000 more from elsewhere in Central America. In the wake of Hurricane Mitch, even more may receive "temporary" amnesty. Congress also grandfathered in other illegal aliens under a now-lapsed provision allowing them to gain permanent residence simply by paying a $1,000 fee and filing their green cards in the U.S., thus relieving them even of the inconvenience of going home to apply for U.S. admission. Third, Congress and the states have now restored many of the SSI and food stamp benefits for low-income immigrants that Congress eliminated only two years ago, although many remain ineligible. Finally, the kind of xenophobic violence and politics that have become so chillingly common in Europe and Asia are relatively rare here. Many Republican Party leaders strongly support immigration, seeing that the social conservatism, upward mobility, and entrepreneurial spirit of many newcomers could attract them to a more immigrant-friendly GOP, a point underscored by the influential role of Hispanic voters in the recent congressional elections, particularly in the key states of California, Texas, and Florida.

These recent gains for immigrants, moreover, have occurred in the face of politically inauspicious conditions. Illegal immigration continues at very high levels, and even new legal immigrants are less white, English-speaking, and Protestant than their predecessors. Nor is California the only state where bilingual education has become a major curricular and fiscal battleground as evidence mounts that many costly programs retard English fluency. About half the states have now established English as their official language. The ever more politicized debate over ethnicity and language, coupled with attacks by some immigrant advocates on the traditional assimilative ideal, have aggravated long-standing anxieties about what Arthur Schlesinger calls the "disuniting of America." Indeed, the affirmative action debate has been sharpened by the anomaly that newcomers who never suffered discrimination in the U.S. compete for preferences with the already beleaguered descendants of enslaved African-Americans. Even citizenship has come under a cloud. Federal indictments allege that over 13,000 naturalization exams were falsified, and growing numbers of new Americans hold dual nationality and may be able to vote in their old countries.

18    Despite these challenges, public support for legal, ethnically diverse immigration remains strong, most legal immigrants appear to be assimilating as quickly as their predecessors did, and the strength of the American polity and economy remains the envy of the world. More than ever, we are the nation of immigrants that our political myths and rhetoric proclaim us to be. Although diversity poses an unprecedented test of our national unity, the evidence so far suggests that we are passing it with flying colors. ✤

---

## RESPONDING

1.  Imagine that you are a new immigrant to the United States. In a journal entry, discuss your feelings about becoming part of this new culture. If you are anxious to assimilate, how will you go about it? If you want to remain part of your former culture, how will you ensure that you still maintain your native language and cultural practices?

2.  Working individually or in a group, outline the changes in immigration laws that have taken place since they were first adopted in 1875. Use the article or other sources, such as the Internet, for information.

3.  Schuck states that immigration law has always mirrored the tensions among the competing images of America as a stew, a salad, or a mosaic. In an essay, use his examples or others with which you are familiar to explain how the immigration laws reflect these images and public opinion during the period of the laws' passage.

4.  Schuck is very optimistic about America's response to the challenges a diverse population presents. In an essay, agree or disagree with Schuck that "although diversity poses an unprecedented test of our national unity, the evidence so far suggests that we are passing it with flying colors" (paragraph 18).

⁘

# CONNECTING

## *Critical Thinking and Writing*

1.   Most of the readings in this chapter focus on the experiences of immigrants to America. Some of these people left their homelands for better economic opportunities; others were forced to leave because of political conditions. Write an essay classifying the immigrants in this chapter according to their reasons for emigrating.

2.   Immigrating to a new country can mean new opportunities or a traumatic change. Using examples from the readings and from your own experience, write an essay discussing the difficulties of adapting to a new country and a new culture.

3.   Cultural expectations can facilitate or inhibit successful adaptation to a new country. Discuss the problems some groups face because of the dramatic differences between their native culture and American culture.

4.   Some of the writers in this chapter, for example, Nye and Bulosan, explore their personal heritages. In what ways do they use their personal experiences as inspiration for and the content of their professional writing? Are they able to give their personal experiences wider application and appeal?

5.   Using examples from the readings in this chapter or from your own or a friend's experience, discuss how race, gender, and/or social class help determine the circumstances of a person's life.

6.   Working with the class, generate a series of essay questions about the issues dealt with in this chapter. Choose one question and answer it in an essay.

7.   Compare the reasons that people immigrated to the United States in the 1970s and 1980s with the reasons that immigrants came in the 1870s and 1880s. You might compare the reasons of a single group, such as the Chinese, or you might compare the reasons of different groups, such as the eastern Europeans in the 1800s and recent Latin American immigrants. Consider any changes in conditions that the immigrants encountered after they arrived in the United States.

8. Luu and Mukherjee write about tradition and its influence on individuals. Compare the role of tradition in the lives of the women they present with the women in works by Ole Edvart Rölvaag (chapter 3), Connie Young Yu (chapter 4), or Piri Thomas (chapter 6).

9. Many new immigrants see the United States as a promised land where they can fulfill the American dream. What do you think the American dream means to these people? How does this dream differ from that of the founders of the country? How is it similar?

### For Further Research

1. Choose one of the groups represented in this chapter, and use the Internet to investigate the history of their immigration and their current situation in the United States. You might consider, for example, the reasons for and difficulties of immigration, economic and social opportunities in the United States, and settlement patterns.

2. Research current U.S. immigration laws and policies. How does someone immigrate to this country? Who is allowed to enter? What procedures must they follow?

## REFERENCES AND ADDITIONAL SOURCES

Anzaldúa, Gloria. *Borderlands: The New Mestiza-La Frontera*. San Francisco: Spinsters/Aunt Lute Book Co., 1987.

Archdeacon, Thomas J. *Becoming America: An Ethnic History*. New York: The Free Press, 1983.

Barkan, Elliott Robert, ed. *A Nation of Peoples: A Sourcebook on America's Multicultural Heritage*. Westport, Conn.: Greenwood Press, 1999.

Boelhower, William. *Immigrant Autobiography in the United States*. Verona: Essedue Edizioni, 1982.

Brodsky, Joseph. *Less Than One: Selected Essays*. New York: Farrar, Straus & Giroux, 1986.

Bulosan, Carlos. *America Is in the Heart: A Personal History*. Seattle: University of Washington Press, 1943.

Chan, Jeffrey Paul, et al., eds. *The Big Aiiieeeee!: An Anthology of Chinese American and Japanese American Literature*. New York: Meridian, 1991.

Cheung, King-Kok. *Articulate Silences: Hisaye Yamamoto, Maxine Hong Kingston, Joy Kogawa*. Ithaca, N.Y.: Cornell University Press, 1993.

Cheung, King-Kok, ed. *An Interethnic Companion to Asian American Literature*. Cambridge, England, and New York: Cambridge University Press, 1997.

Chin, Frank, et al., eds. *Aiiieeeee!: An Anthology of Asian American Writers*. Washington: Howard University Press, 1974.

Colombo, Gary, Robert J. Cullen, and Bonnie Lisle, eds. *Rereading America*. New York: St. Martin's Press, 1989.

Delgado, Asunción Horno. *Breaking Boundaries: Latin Writing and Critical Readings*. Amherst: University of Massachusetts Press, 1989.

De Vos, George, and Lola Romanucci-Ross, eds. *Ethnic Identity: Cultural Continuities and Change*. Palo Alto, Calif.: Mayfield, 1975; Chicago: University of Chicago Press, 1982, with a new introduction by the authors.

Espada, Martín, ed. *El Coro: A Chorus of Latino and Latina Poetry*. Amherst: University of Massachusetts Press, 1997.

Fanon, Fantz. *The Wretched of the Earth*. New York: Grove Press, 1963.

Fisher, Dexter, ed. *The Third Woman: Minority Women Writers of the United States*. Boston: Houghton Mifflin, 1980.

Gage, Nicholas. *A Place for Us: Eleni's Family in America*. Boston: Houghton Mifflin, 1989.

Herrera-Sobek, Maria. *Northward Bound: The Mexican Immigrant Experience in Ballad and Song*. Bloomington: Indiana University Press, 1993.

Hwang, David Henry. *Family Devotions, Broken Promises: Four Chinese American Plays*. New York: Avon, 1983.

Iglesias, José. *The Goodbye Land*. New York: Pantheon, 1967.

Karim, Persis M., and Mohammad Mehdi Khorrami, eds. *A World Between: Poems, Short Stories, and Essays by Iranian Americans*. New York: George Braziller, 1999.

Kim, Richard E. *Lost Names: Scenes from a Korean Boyhood*. New York: Praeger, 1970.

Kincaid, Jamaica. *A Small Place*. New York: Farrar, Straus & Giroux, 1988.

Knippling, Alpana Sharma, ed. *New Immigrant Literatures in the United States: A Sourcebook to Our Multicultural Literary Heritage*. Westport, Conn.: Greenwood Press, 1996.

Luis, William. *Dance Between Two Cultures: Latino Caribbean Literature Written in the United States*. Nashville, Tenn.: Vanderbilt University Press, 1997.

Marchetti, Gina. *Romance and the "Yellow Peril:" Race, Sex, and Discursive Strategies in Hollywood Fiction*. Berkeley: University of California Press, 1993.

McCarus, Ernest, ed. *The Development of Arab-American Identity*. Ann Arbor: University of Michigan Press, 1994.

Mehta, Ved. *Face to Face: An Autobiography*. Boston: Little, Brown, 1957.

Milosz, Czeslaw. *Native Realm: A Search for Self-Definition*. Translated by Catherine S. Leach. Garden City, N.Y.: Doubleday, 1968.

———. *Visions from San Francisco Bay*. Translated by Richard Lourie. New York: Farrar, Straus & Giroux, 1975.

Mirikitani, Janice, ed. *Time to Greez! Incantations from the Third World*. San Francisco: Glide Publications, 1975.

Mukherjee, Bharati. *The Middleman and Other Stories*. New York: Grove Press, 1988.

Muller, Gilbert H. *New Strangers in Paradise: The Immigrant Experience and Contemporary American Fiction*. Lexington: University Press of Kentucky, 1999.

Oboler, Suzanne. *Ethnic Labels, Latino Lives: Identity and the Politics of (Re)presentation in the United States*. Minneapolis: University of Minnesota Press, 1995.

Orfalea, Gregory, ed. *Wrapping the Grape Leaves: A Sheaf of Contemporary Arab-American Poets*. Washington, D.C.: American-Arab Anti-Discrimination Committee, 1982.

Reed, Ishmael. *Yardbird Lives!* New York: Grove Press, 1978.

Rischin, Moses, ed. *Immigration and the American Tradition*. Indianapolis, Ind.: Bobbs-Merril, 1976.

Rose, Peter I., Stanley Rochman, and William Julius Wilson, eds. *Through Different Eyes: Black and White Perspectives on American Race Relations*. New York: Oxford University Press, 1973.

Rustomji-Kerns, Roshni, ed. *Living in America: Poetry and Fiction by South Asian American Writers*. Boulder, Colo.: Westview Press, 1995.

Said, Edward, ed. *Literature and Society*. Baltimore: Johns Hopkins University Press, 1980.

Simonson, Rick, and Scott Walker, eds. *Multicultural Literacy*. Greywold Annual Five Series. St. Paul, Minn.: Greywolf, 1988.

Smith, Derek. "A Refugee by Any Other Name: An Examination of the Board of Immigration Appeals' Actions in Asylum Cases." *Virginia Law Review* 75 (1989): 681–721.

Sunoo, Brenda. *Korean American Writing: Selected Material from "Insight," a Korean American Bimonthly*. 1975.

Takaki, Ronald. *A Different Mirror: A History of Multicultural America*. Boston: Little, Brown, 1993.

———, ed. *From Different Shores: Perspectives on Race and Ethnicity in America*. New York: Oxford University Press, 1987.

Todorov, Tzvetan. *The Conquest of America: The Question of the Other.* Translated by Richard Howard. New York: Harper & Row, 1984.

TuSmith, Bonnie. *All My Relatives: Community in Contemporary Ethnic American Literatures.* Ann Arbor: University of Michigan Press, 1993.

Ungar, Sanford J. *Fresh Blood: The New American Immigrants.* New York: Simon and Schuster, 1995.

# PERMISSIONS ACKNOWLEDGMENTS

# INDEX

## DATE DUE

| | | | |
|---|---|---|---|
| | | | |
| | | | |
| | | | |
| | | | |
| | | | |
| | | | |
| | | | |
| | | | |
| | | | |
| | | | |
| | | | |
| | | | |
| | | | |
| | | | |
| | | | |
| | | | |
| GAYLORD | | | PRINTED IN U.S.A. |

AUG '05